General Paper II Casebook

16th edition

Part I Equity and Trusts edited by Andrew J Cutler
LLB, Solicitor (England and Wales and Hong Kong)

Part II The Law of Contract edited by P A Read
LLB, DPA, Barrister

HLT Publications

HLT PUBLICATIONS
200 Greyhound Road, London W14 9RY

First published 1979
16th edition 1996

© The HLT Group Ltd 1996

All HLT publications enjoy copyright protection and the copyright belongs to The HLT Group Ltd.

All rights reserved. No part of this publication may be reproduced or transmitted in any form or by any means, electronic, mechanical, photocopying, recording or otherwise, or stored in any retrieval system of any nature without either the written permission of the copyright holder, application for which should be made to The HLT Group Ltd, or a licence permitting restricted copying in the United Kingdom issued by the Copyright Licensing Agency.

Any person who infringes the above in relation to this publication may be liable to criminal prosecution and civil claims for damages.

ISBN 0 7510 0678 5

British Library Cataloguing-in-Publication.
A CIP Catalogue record for this book is available from the British Library.

Acknowledgement
The publishers and author would like to thank the Incorporated Council of Law Reporting for England and Wales for kind permission to reproduce extracts from the Weekly Law Reports, and Butterworths for their kind permission to reproduce extracts from the All England Law Reports.

Printed and bound in Great Britain

Contents

Preface *v*

Table of Main Cases *vii*

   Equity and Trusts *vii*

   The Law of Contract *xvii*

Equity and Trusts

1 The Three Certainties *3*

2 Formal Requirements for Creating a Trust *21*

3 Completely and Incompletely Constituted Trusts *25*

4 Secret Trusts *48*

5 Implied and Resulting Trusts *66*

6 Constructive Trusts *88*

7 Trusts of Imperfect Obligation *127*

8 Charitable Trusts *140*

9 The Cy-près Doctrine *193*

10 Appointment, Retirement and Removal of Trustees *202*

11 Trustees' Fiduciary Duties *204*

12 Investment of Trust Funds *218*

13 Conversion and Apportionment *228*

14 Duty to Distribute *233*

15 Miscellaneous Duties of Trustees *235*

16 Powers of Trustees *240*

17 Breach of Trust I: Personal Remedies *254*

18 Breach of Trust II: Tracing *271*

The Law of Contract

19 Contents of Contracts *283*

20 Misrepresentation *319*

21 Exclusion Clauses *341*
22 Undue Influence and Restraint of Trade *368*
23 Frustration *394*
24 Discharge of the Contract *408*
25 Remedies for Breach of Contract – Damages *423*
26 Remedies for Breach of Contract – Equitable Remedies *473*

Preface

HLT Casebooks have been produced as companion volumes to the textbooks for certain Bar and LLB subjects. Their aim is to supplement and enhance a student's understanding and interpretation of a particular area of the law, and provide essential background reading.

In addition to the regular updating, this year the *General Paper II Casebook* has been revised to better reflect the contents of the textbook.

As usual, 1995 has produced a number of Equity and Trusts cases of note, often in related areas. Included amongst these were a spate of first instance cases relating to charities and also the presumption of advancement, of the latter the most interesting being the decision of the Court of Appeal in *McGrath v Wallis*. However, the year's leading case is that of the Privy Council's decision in *Royal Brunei Airline Sdn v Tan* [1995] 3 All ER 97 (PC) which established a new four-part test for determining whether a stranger to a trust could be held liable as a constructive trustee through knowing assistance. That test, which replaces the earlier laid down in the *Baden Delvaux* case, removes the need for dishonesty on the part of the trustee and places that criterion on the shoulders of the stranger.

In the Equity and Trusts part, the law is as stated at 1 January 1996.

Of the considerable number of new cases included in Contract part all but a few were decided at Court of Appeal level or higher. The topics covered by these cases include form of contract; conditions and warranties; exclusion clauses; mistake; frustration; anticipatory breach; no fewer than three cases on hitherto unconsidered aspects of quantification of damages; several cases on agency; and cases on sale of goods and supply of goods and services.

Additionally the book has been thoroughly revised, with a view to clarifying and streamlining the whole casebook.

Contract cases reported up to mid-February 1996 have been taken into consideration.

Table of Main Cases: Equity and Trusts

Adams and the Kensington Vestry, Re (1884) 27 Ch D 394   *3, 48*
Agip (Africa) Ltd *v* Jackson [1991] Ch 547; [1989] 3 WLR 1367   *88, 271*
Allen-Meyrick's WT, Re [1966] 1 WLR 499   *233*
Allhusen *v* Whittell (1867) LR 4 Eq 295   *228*
Ames' Settlement, Re [1946] Ch 217   *66*
Armstrong, Re (1969) 7 DLR (3d) 36   *48*
Astor's Settlement, Re [1952] Ch 534   *4, 127*
Atkinson, Re [1978] 1 WLR 586   *140*
Att-Gen *v* Mayor of Dartmouth (1883) 48 LT 933   *191*
Att-Gen *v* Ockover (1736) 1 Ves Sen 536   *191*
Att-Gen *v* Ross [1986] 1 WLR 252   *140*
Att-Gen for Hong Kong *v* Charles Warwick Reid and Others [1993] 3 WLR 1143   *88*
Att-Gen of the Bahamas *v* Royal Trust Co [1986] 1 WLR 1001   *142*

Baden, Delvaux and Lecuit *v* Société Générale pour Favouriser le Devéloppement de commerce et de l'Industrie en France SA [1993] 1 WLR 509   *89*
Baden's Deed Trusts (No 1), Re *see* McPhail *v* Doulton
Baden's Deed Trusts (No 2), Re [1973] Ch 9   *4*
Bahin *v* Hughes (1886) 31 Ch D 390   *254*
Baker *v* Baker (1993) The Times 23 February   *90*
Bannister *v* Bannister [1948] 2 All ER 133   *90*
Barclays Bank *v* Quistclose Investments Ltd [1970] AC 567   *66*
Barker, Re (1909) 25 TLR 753   *192*
Barlow's WT, Re [1979] 1 WLR 278   *5*
Barnes *v* Addy (1874) 9 Ch App 244   *91*
Bartlett *v* Barclays Bank Trust Co (No 1) [1980] Ch 515   *218, 228, 240, 254*
Basham (deceased), Re [1987] 1 All ER 405   *91*
Beaumont, Re [1902] 1 Ch 889   *25*
Beaumont *v* Oliveira (1869) 4 Ch 309   *191*
Belchier, ex parte (1754) Amb 218   *240*
Bell's Indenture, Re [1980] 1 WLR 1217   *254*
Belmont Finance Corporation Ltd *v* Williams Furniture Ltd [1979] 1 Ch 250   *92*
Benjamin, Re [1902] 1 Ch 723   *6, 233*
Bennet *v* Bennet (1879) 10 Ch D 474   *67*
Bernard *v* Josephs [1982] Ch 391   *67*
Berry *v* Green [1938] AC 575   *240*
Binions *v* Evans [1972] Ch 359   *94*
Birch *v* Treasury Solicitor [1951] Ch 298   *25*
Biscoe *v* Jackson (1887) 35 Ch D 460   *193*
Bishopsgate Investment Management Ltd (In Liquidation) *v* Maxwell (No 2) [1994] 1 All ER 261   *235*

Bishopsgate Investment Management Ltd (In Liquidation) v Homan and Others [1994] 3 WLR 1270 *273*
Biss, Re [1903] 2 Ch 40   *204*
Blair v Duncan [1902] AC 37   *142*
Boardman v Phipps [1967] 2 AC 46   *95, 205, 273*
Bonar Law Memorial Trust v IRC (1933) 49 TLR 220   *191*
Bourne v Keane [1919] AC 815   *127*
Bowden, Re [1936] Ch 71   *26*
Boyce v Boyce (1849) 16 Sim 476   *6*
Boyes, Re (1884) 26 Ch D 531   *48*
Brandt's (William) Sons & Co v Dunlop Rubber Co [1905] AC 454   *26*
British Museum v White (1826) 2 S & S 594   *191*
British Museum (Trustees of) v Att-Gen [1984] 1 All ER 337   *219*
British School of Egyptian Archaeology, Re [1954] 1 WLR 546   *143*
Brockbank, Re [1948] Ch 206   *241*
Budgett v Budgett [1895] 1 Ch 202   *205*
Bull v Bull [1955] 1 QB 234   *68*
Bunn v Markham (1816) 7 Taunt 244   *27*
Burns v Burns [1984] Ch 317   *69*
Bushnell, Re [1975] 1 WLR 1596   *143*

Caffoor Trustees v Commissioner of Income Tax, Colombo [1961] AC 584   *143*
Cain v Moon [1896] 2 QB 283   *27*
Cannon v Hartley [1949] Ch 213   *28*
Carl Zeiss Stiftung v Smith (Herbert) & Co (No 2) [1969] 2 Ch 276   *99*
Carreras Rothmans Ltd v Freeman Matthews Treasure Ltd [1985] 3 WLR 1016   *72*
Caus, Re [1934] Ch 162   *127*
Cavendish-Brown's ST, Re [1916] WN 341   *28*
Chapman v Browne [1902] 1 Ch 785   *220*
Chapman v Chapman [1954] AC 429   *241*
Chapple, Re (1884) 27 Ch D 584   *205*
Chesterfield's (Earl of) Trusts, Re (1883) 24 Ch D 643   *228*
Chichester Diocesan Fund and Board of Finance Inc v Simpson [1944] AC 341   *144*
Chillingworth v Chambers [1896] 1 Ch 685   *255*
Christchurch Enclosure Act, Re (1888) 36 Ch D 520   *192*
Clarke, Re [1923] 2 Ch 407   *145*
Clayton's Case, Devaynes v Noble (1816) 1 Mer 529   *274*
Clergy Society, Re (1856) 2 K & J 65   *192*
Clout & Frewers Contract, Re [1924] Ch 230   *202*
Cochrane's ST, Re [1955] Ch 309   *73*
Cole, Re [1964] Ch 175   *29*
Combe, Re [1925] Ch 210   *6*
Comiskey v Bowring-Hanbury [1905] AC 84   *7*
Commissioner of Stamp Duties (Queensland) v Livingston [1965] AC 694   *21, 274*
Compton, Re [1945] Ch 123   *145*
Conservative Central Office v Burrell [1982] 2 All ER 1   *127*
Consul Development Pty Ltd v DPC Estates Pty Ltd (1975) 132 CLR 373   *99*
Cook v Deeks [1916] 1 AC 554   *99*

Cook's ST, Re [1965] Ch 902   *29*
Cooke v Head [1972] 1 WLR 518   *99*
Cooper (Colin), Re [1939] Ch 811   *49*
Corsellis, Re (1887) 34 Ch D 675   *205*
Cottam, Re [1955] 1 WLR 1299   *192*
Cowan v Scargill [1985] 3 WLR 501   *235*
Cowcher v Cowcher [1972] 1 WLR 425   *73*
Coxen, Re [1948] Ch 747   *145*
Crabb v Arun District Council [1976] Ch 179   *100*
Cradock v Piper (1850) 1 Mac & G 664   *206*
Cranstoun's WT, Re [1949] Ch 523   *192*
Crippen, In The Estate of [1911] P 108   *101*
Cunnack v Edwards [1896] 2 Ch 679   *74*

Dale (deceased), Re, Proctor v Dale [1993] 3 WLR 652   *102*
Dalziel, Re [1943] Ch 277   *128*
Davitt v Titcumb [1990] Ch 110   *102*
Dean, Re (1889) 41 Ch D 552   *128*
Delamere's ST, Re [1984] 1 All ER 588   *242*
Delius, Re [1957] Ch 299   *145*
Denley's Trust Deed, Re [1969] 1 Ch 373   *129*
Devaynes v Noble *see* Clayton's Case
Dillwyn v Llewellyn (1862) 4 De GF & J 517   *30, 102*
Dingle v Turner [1972] AC 601   *146*
Diplock, Re [1948] Ch 465   *103, 257, 274*
Docker v Somes (1834) 2 My & K 655   *263*
Dominion Students' Hall Trusts, Re [1947] 1 Ch 183   *193*
Dorman (deceased), Re, Smith v National Children's Home and Orphanage Registered [1994] 1 WLR 282   *7*
Dougan v McPherson [1902] AC 197   *207*
Dover Coalfield Extension Ltd, Re [1908] 1 Ch 65   *207*
Dowse v Gorton [1891] AC 190   *207*
Drummond, Re [1914] 2 Ch 90   *147*
Dudman, Re [1925] Ch 553   *31*
Dunne v Byrne [1912] AC 407   *148*
Dyer v Dyer (1788) 2 Cox Eq 92   *74*

Eagle Trust plc v SBC Securities Ltd [1992] 4 All ER 488   *103*
Eastes, Re [1948] Ch 257   *148*
Eaves v Hickson (1861) 30 Beav 136   *233*
Ebrand v Dancer (1680) 2 Ch Ca 26   *74*
El Ajou v Dollar Land Holdings plc and Another [1994] 2 All ER 685   *104*
Emery's Investment Trusts, Re [1959] Ch 410   *75*
England's ST, Re [1918] 1 Ch 24   *208*
English v Dedham Vale Properties Ltd [1978] 1 WLR 93   *104*
Erlanger v New Sombrero Phosphate Co (1878) 3 App Cas 1218   *105*
Eves v Eves [1975] 1 WLR 1338   *75*
Eykyn's Trusts, Re (1877) 6 Ch D 115   *75*

Faraker, Re [1912] 2 Ch 488   *193*
Farley v Westminster Bank Ltd [1939] AC 430   *149*
Fawcett, Re [1940] Ch 402   *229*
Finger's WT, Re [1972] Ch 286   *194*
Fletcher v Collis [1905] 2 Ch 24   *264*
Fletcher v Fletcher (1844) 4 Hare 67   *32*
Fowkes v Pascoe (1875) 10 Ch App 343   *76*
Freeland, Re [1952] Ch 110   *32*
Fry, Re [1946] Ch 312   *33*
Fry v Tapson (1884) 28 Ch D 268   *243*

Gardner (No 2), Re [1923] 2 Ch 230   *51*
Gardom, Re [1914] 1 Ch 662   *192*
Gartside v IRC [1968] AC 553   *7*
Gestetner, Re [1953] Ch 672   *8*
Giles, Re [1972] Ch 544   *105*
Gillingham Bus Disaster Fund, Re [1958] Ch 300   *76*
Gilmour v Coates [1949] AC 426   *129*
Golay, Re [1965] 1 WLR 1969   *8*
Gonin, Re [1979] Ch 16   *33*
Good, Re [1905] 2 Ch 60   *149*
Goodman v Gallant [1986] Fam 106; [1986] 2 WLR 236   *77*
Goodman v Saltash Corporation (1882) 7 App Cas 633   *150*
Grant v Edwards [1986] Ch 638   *77*
Grant's WT, Re [1980] 1 WLR 360   *131*
Gray, Re [1925] Ch 362   *150*
Greasley v Cooke [1980] 1 WLR 1306   *106*
Grey v IRC [1960] AC 1   *21*
Grove-Grady, Re [1929] 1 Ch 557   *150*
Guild (Executor Nominate of the late James Young Russell) v IRC [1992] 2 WLR 397   *151*
Gwyon, Re, Public Trustee v Att-Gen [1930] 1 Ch 255   *151*

Hagger, Re [1930] 2 Ch 190   *106*
Hallett's Estate, Re (1880) 13 Ch D 696   *107, 274*
Hamilton, Re [1895] 2 Ch 370   *8*
Harari's ST, Re [1949] 1 All ER 430   *220*
Hardoon v Belilios [1901] AC 118   *208*
Harries and Others v Church Commissioners for England and Another [1992] 1 WLR 1241   *237*
Harrison v Southampton Corporation (1854) 2 Sm & G 387   *191*
Harwood, Re [1936] Ch 285   *195*
Harwood v Harwood [1991] Fam Law 418   *79*
Head v Gould [1898] 2 Ch 250   *264*
Hetherington, Gibbs v McDonnell, Re [1989] 2 All ER 129   *131, 152*
Hill v Langley (1988) The Times 28 January   *209*
Hoare v Osborne (1866) LR 1 Eq 585   *191*
Hodgson v Marks [1971] Ch 892   *80*
Holder v Holder [1968] Ch 353   *209*
Holding and Management Ltd v Property Holding and Investment Trust plc and Others [1989] 1 WLR 1313   *210*

Hooley v Hatton; *see* Ridges v Morrison
Hooper, Re [1932] 1 Ch 38   *131*
Hopkins' WT, Re [1965] Ch 669   *153*
Houston v Burns [1918] AC 337   *191*
Howe v Dartmouth (Earl of) (1802) 7 Ves 137   *229*
Hummeltenberg, Re, Beatty v London Spiritualistic Alliance [1923] 1 Ch 237   *155*
Hunter v Moss [1994] 1 WLR 452   *9*
Hunter's Executors, Petitioners (1992) The Scotsman 17 June   *107*
Hussey v Palmer [1972] 1 WLR 1286   *80, 107*

Income Tax Special Purposes Commissioners v Pemsel [1891] AC 531   *155*
Incorporated Council of Law Reporting for England and Wales v Att-Gen [1972] Ch 73   *156*
Industrial Development Consultants Ltd v Cooley [1972] 1 WLR 443   *107*
International Sales and Agencies Ltd v Marcus [1982] 3 All ER 551   *108*
Inwards v Baker [1965] 2 QB 29   *108*
IRC v Baddeley [1955] AC 572   *159*
IRC v Broadway Cottages Trust [1955] Ch 20   *9*
IRC v City of Glasgow Police Athletic Association [1953] AC 380   *161*
IRC v Educational Grants Association Ltd [1967] Ch 123   *161*
IRC v McMullen [1981] AC 1   *162*
IRC v Yorkshire Agricultural Society [1928] 1 KB 611   *192*
Irvine v Sullivan (1869) LR 8 Eq 673   *51*

James, Re [1935] Ch 449   *34*
Jefferys v Jefferys (1841) Cr & Ph 138   *34*
Jenkins' WT, Re [1966] Ch 249   *196*
Johnson v Ball (1851) 5 De G & Sm 85   *52*
Jones v Jones (1989) The Independent 27 January   *10, 243*
Jones v Lock (1865) 1 Ch App 25   *22*
Jones (AE) v Jones (FW) [1977] 1 WLR 438   *109*

Karak Rubber Co Ltd v Burden (No 2) [1972] 1 WLR 602   *110*
Kay's Settlement, Re [1939] Ch 329   *35*
Kayford Ltd, Re [1975] 1 WLR 279   *10, 22*
Keen, Re [1937] Ch 236   *53*
Khoo Tek Keong v Ching Joo Tuan Neoh [1934] AC 529   *221*
King, Re [1923] 1 Ch 243   *164*
Kingscroft Insurance Co Ltd v HS Weavers (Underwriting) Agencies Ltd (1992) The Times 21 August   *81*
Knight v Knight (1840) 3 Beav 148   *11*
Knott v Cottee (1852) 16 Beav 77   *265*
Koeppler's WT, Re [1985] 2 All ER 869   *165*
Koettgen's WT, Re [1954] Ch 252   *165*
Kolb's WT, Re [1962] 3 WLR 1034   *222*

Lambe v Eames (1871) 6 Ch App 597   *12*
Leahy v Att-Gen for New South Wales [1959] AC 457   *132*
Learoyd v Whiteley (1887) 12 App Cas 727   *222*
Lee v Sankey (1872) LR 15 Eq 204   *110*

Table of Main Cases: Equity and Trusts

Lepton's Charity, Re [1972] 1 Ch 276   *196*
Letterstedt v Broers (1884) 9 App Cas 371   *202*
Lewis, Re [1955] Ch 104   *192*
Lillingston, Re [1952] 2 All ER 184   *35*
Lipinski's WT, Re [1976] Ch 235   *133*
Lipkin Gorman v Karpnale Ltd [1987] 1 WLR 987; [1989] 1 WLR 1340; [1991] 3 WLR 10   *110*
Liverpool City Council v Att-Gen (1992) The Times 1 May   *192*
Lloyds Bank plc v Rosset [1990] 2 WLR 867   *81, 111*
London Hospital Medical College v IRC [1976] 1 WLR 613   *166*
Londonderry's Settlement, Re [1965] Ch 918   *237*
Lowther v Bentinck (1874) LR 19 Eq 166   *244*
Lucas, Re [1922] 2 Ch 52   *167*
Lucking's WT, Re [1968] 1 WLR 866   *223*
Lysaght v Edwards (1876) 2 Ch D 499   *22, 112*
Lyus v Prowsa Developments [1982] 1 WLR 104   *113*

Macadam, Re [1946] Ch 73   *211*
Macardle, Re [1951] Ch 699   *35*
Macaulay's Estate, Re, Macaulay v O'Donnell [1943] Ch 435   *135*
McCormick v Grogan (1869) LR 4 HL 82   *56*
Macduff, Re [1896] 2 Ch 451   *192*
McGeorge, Re [1963] Ch 544   *244*
McGovern v Att-Gen [1982] Ch 321   *167*
McGrath v Wallis (1995) The Times 13 April   *81*
McPhail v Doulton [1971] AC 424   *12*
Maddock, Re [1902] 2 Ch 220   *56*
Manisty's Settlement, Re [1974] Ch 17   *16*
Manser, Re [1905] 1 Ch 68   *192*
Mara v Browne [1896] 1 Ch 199   *114, 266*
Mariette, Re [1915] 2 Ch 284   *170*
Marley and Others v Mutal Security Bank and Trust Co Ltd [1991] 3 All ER 198   *246*
Marshall, Re [1914] 1 Ch 192   *234, 247*
Mascall v Mascall (1984) LS Gaz 2218   *36*
Mason v Fairbrother [1983] 2 All ER 1078   *224*
Mead's Trust Deed, Re [1961] 1 WLR 1244   *170*
Mercier v Mercier [1903] 2 Ch 98   *82*
Mettoy Pension Trustees Ltd v Evans and Others [1990] 1 WLR 1587   *17*
Milligan v Mitchell (1833) 1 My & K 446   *266*
Mills v Farmer (1815) 1 Mer 55   *170*
Ministry of Health v Simpson [1951] AC 251   *275*
Montagu's ST, Re [1987] 2 WLR 1192   *115*
Morice v Bishop of Durham (1805) 10 Ves 522   *17, 135*
Moss, Re [1949] 1 All ER 495   *171*
Moss v Cooper (1861) 1 J & H 352   *57*

National Anti-Vivisection Society v IRC [1948] AC 31   *171*
National Trustees Executors and Agency Co of Australasia Ltd v General Finance etc Co of Australia Ltd [1905] AC 373   *266*
Neville Estates Ltd v Madden [1962] Ch 832   *135*

Niyazi's WT, Re [1978] 1 WLR 910   *171*
Norfolk's (Duke of) ST, Re [1981] 3 WLR 455   *212*

Oatway, Re [1903] 2 Ch 356   *276*
Oldham Borough Council v Att-Gen (1992) The Times 5 August   *196*
Oppenheim v Tobacco Securities Trust Co Ltd [1951] AC 297   *173*
O'Sullivan v Management Agency [1985] 3 All ER 351   *118*
Ottaway v Norman [1972] Ch 698   *58*
Oughtred v IRC [1960] AC 206   *22*

Palmer v Simmonds (1854) 2 Drew 221   *18*
Parry, Re, Brown v Parry [1947] Ch 23   *230*
Pascoe v Turner [1979] 1 WLR 431   *36*
Paul v Constance [1977] 1 WLR 527   *37*
Paul v Paul (1882) 20 Ch D 742   *37*
Pauling's ST, Re (No 1) [1964] Ch 303   *247*
Peggs v Lamb [1994] 2 WLR 1   *177*
Perrins v Bellamy [1899] 1 Ch 797   *267*
Peso Silver Mines Ltd v Cropper (1966) 58 DLR (2d) 11   *120*
Peters v Chief Adjudication Officer [1989] Fam Law 318   *248*
Pettitt v Pettitt [1970] AC 777   *82*
Pilkington v IRC [1964] AC 612   *248*
Pinion, Re [1965] Ch 85   *178*
Pirbright v Sawley [1896] WN 86   *136*
Pleasants, Re (1923) 39 TLR 675   *192*
Plumptre's Marriage Settlement, Re [1910] 1 Ch 609   *38*
Power's WT, Re [1947] Ch 572   *224*
Protheroe v Protheroe [1968] 1 WLR 519   *213*
Pryce, Re [1917] 1 Ch 234   *38*
Pugh's WT, Re [1967] 1 WLR 1262   *59*
Pullan v Koe [1913] 1 Ch 9   *39*

Queensland Mines Ltd v Hudson (1978) 18 ALR 1   *213*

Raine, Re [1929] 1 Ch 716   *40, 249*
Ralli's WT, Re [1964] Ch 288   *40*
Recher's WT, Re [1972] Ch 526   *136*
Reddel v Dobree (1839) 10 Sim 244   *41*
Rees, Re [1950] Ch 204   *60*
Regal (Hastings) Ltd v Gulliver [1942] 1 All ER 378   *120*
Resch's WT, Re [1969] 1 AC 514   *179*
Risch v McFee (1990) The Times 6 July   *120*
Roberts, Re [1963] 1 WLR 406   *197*
Roscoe (James) (Bolton) Ltd v Winder [1915] 1 Ch 62   *277*
Rose, Re [1952] Ch 499   *41*
Rowntree Housing Assoc v Att-Gen [1983] Ch 159   *180*
Royal Brunei Airlines Sdn Bhd v Philip Tan Kok Ming [1995] 3 All ER 97   *121*
Royal Choral Society v IRC [1943] 2 All ER 101   *183*
Russell v Jackson (1852) 10 Hare 204   *61*

Rymer, Re [1895] 1 Ch 19   *197*

Sargeant and Another v National Westminster Bank plc and Another (1990) The Times 10 May   *214*
Satterthwaite's WT, Re [1966] 1 WLR 277   *198*
Saunders v Vautier (1841) 4 Beav 115   *18, 234, 250*
Sayer's Trust, Re [1957] Ch 423   *19*
Scarisbrick's WT, Re [1951] Ch 622   *183*
Scottish Burial Reform and Cremation Society Ltd v Glasgow Corporation [1968] AC 138   *184*
Sekhon v Alissa [1989] FLR 94   *83*
Selangor United Rubber Estates Ltd v Cradock (No 3) [1968] 1 WLR 1555   *122*
Sen v Headley [1991] Ch 425   *42*
Shakespeare Memorial Trust, Re [1923] 2 Ch 398   *186*
Shaw, Re [1957] 1 WLR 729   *137*
Shaw v Cates [1909] 1 Ch 389   *225, 268*
Shaw's WT, Re [1952] Ch 163   *186*
Shephard v Cartwright [1955] AC 431   *83*
Sick and Funeral Society of St John's Sunday School, Golcar, Re [1973] Ch 51   *83*
Sinclair v Brougham [1914] AC 398   *278*
Slevin, Re [1891] 2 Ch 236   *198*
Smith, Re, Public Trustee v Aspinall [1928] Ch 915   *250*
Snowden (deceased), Re [1979] Ch 528   *61*
Somerset, Re [1894] 1 Ch 231   *268*
South Place Ethical Society, Re, Barralet v Att-Gen [1980] 1 WLR 1565   *186*
Speight v Gaunt (1883) 9 App Cas 1   *250*
Spence's WT, Re [1979] Ch 483   *199*
Spencer's Will, Re (1887) 3 TLR 822   *63*
Sprange v Barnard (1789) 2 Bro CC 585   *19*
Spurling's WT, Re [1966] 1 All ER 745   *215*
Stafford (Earl of), Re [1980] Ch 28   *251*
Stead, Re [1900] 1 Ch 237   *63*
Steele's WT, Re [1948] Ch 603   *19*
Stemson's WT, Re [1970] Ch 16   *200*
Stewart, Re [1908] 2 Ch 251   *43*
Stokes v Anderson (1991) The Independent 10 January   *123*
Strahan, Re (1856) 8 De GM & G 291   *269*
Strong v Bird (1874) LR 18 Eq 315   *43*
Stuart, Re, Smith v Stuart [1897] 2 Ch 583   *226*
Sutton, Re, Stone v Att-Gen (1885) 28 Ch D 464   *188*

Target Holdings Ltd v Redferm (a firm) and Another [1995] 3 All ER   *269*
Tee v Ferris (1856) 2 K & J 357   *64*
Tempest, Re (1866) Ch App 485   *203*
Tempest v Lord Camoys (1882) 21 Ch D 571   *238*
Thomas v Howell (1874) LR 18 Eq 198   *192*
Thompson's Settlement, Re [1985] 2 All ER 720   *215*
Thomson, Re [1930] 1 Ch 203   *124, 216*
Tilley's WT, Re [1967] Ch 1179   *278*
Tinker v Tinker [1970] P 136   *84*
Tito v Waddell (No 2) [1977] Ch 106   *217*

Tollemache, Re [1903] 1 Ch 955   *226*
Tuck's ST, Re [1978] Ch 49   *20*
Tyler, Re [1891] 3 Ch 252   *138*

Ulverston & District New Hospital Building Fund, Re [1956] Ch 622   *200*
Ungarian v Lesnoff [1988] 3 WLR 840   *84*
United Grand Lodge of Ancient Free and Accepted Masons of England v Holborn Borough Council [1957] 1 WLR 1080   *189*

Vagliano, Re [1905] WN 179   *192*
Vandervell v IRC [1967] AC 291   *23*
Vaughan, Re (1886) 33 Ch D 187   *138*
Vaughan v Barlow Clowes International Ltd (1992) The Times 6 March   *279*
Verge v Somerville [1924] AC 496   *189*
Vernon's WT, Re [1972] Ch 300n   *201*
Verrall, Re [1916] 1 Ch 100   *192*
Vickery, Re [1931] 1 Ch 572   *252*
Vinogradoff, Re [1935] WN 68   *85*
Voyce v Voyce (1991) 62 P & CR 290   *45*

Wakeman, Re [1945] Ch 177   *227*
Wale, Re [1956] 1 WLR 1346   *45*
Walker, Re, Walker v Walker (1890) 59 LJ Ch 386   *227*
Warren v Gurney [1944] 2 All ER 472   *85*
Webb v O'Doherty and Others (1991) The Times 11 February   *190*
Wedgwood, Re [1915] 1 Ch 113   *139, 190*
West Sussex Constabulary's Widows, Children and Benevolent (1930) Fund Trusts, Re [1971] Ch 1   *85*
Westerton, Re [1919] 2 Ch 104   *46*
Wilkes v Allington [1931] 2 Ch 104   *47*
Williams v Barton [1927] 2 Ch 9   *124, 217*
Williams v Kershaw (1835) 5 Cl & F 111n   *190*
Williams v Williams (1881) 17 Ch D 437   *125*
Williams' Trustees v IRC [1947] AC 447   *191*
Williams-Ashman v Price & Williams [1942] Ch 219   *125*
Willmott v Barber (1880) 15 Ch D 96   *125*
Windeler v Whitehall (1990) 154 JP 29   *126*
Wokingham Fire Brigade Trusts, Re [1951] Ch 373   *192*
Woodward v Woodward [1991] Fam Law 470   *47*
Wragg, Re [1919] 2 Ch 58   *227*

Young (deceased), Re [1951] Ch 344   *64*

Table of Main Cases: The Law of Contract

Addis v Gramophone Co Ltd [1909] AC 488   *423*
Afovos Shipping Co SA v Pagnan, The Afovos [1983] 1 All ER 449   *408*
Ailsa Craig Fishing Co Ltd v Malvern Fishing Co Ltd [1983] 1 WLR 964   *341*
Alev, The *see* Vantage Navigation Corp v Suhail and Bahwan Building Materials LLC
Alghussein Establishment v Eton College [1988] 1 WLR 587   *473*
Allcard v Skinner (1887) 36 Ch D 145   *368*
American Cyanamid Co v Ethicon Ltd [1975] AC 396; [1975] 2 WLR 316   *473*
Amoco Australia Pty Ltd v Rocca Bros Engineering Pty Ltd [1975] AC 561; [1975] 2 WLR 779   *369*
Anglia Television Ltd v Reed [1972] 1 QB 60; [1971] 3 WLR 528   *424*
Armstrong v Jackson [1917] 2 KB 822   *319*
Ateni Maritime Corporation v Great Marine (1991) Financial Times 13 February   *409*
Atlantic Baron, The *see* North Ocean Shipping v Hyundai Construction
Attwood v Lamont [1920] 3 KB 571   *370*
Avery v Bowden (1855) 5 E & B 714   *409*

Backhouse v Backhouse [1978] 1 WLR 243   *371*
Bank of Baroda v Shah [1988] 3 All ER 24   *371*
Bank of Credit and Commerce International SA v Aboody [1989] 2 WLR 759   *372*
Barclays Bank plc v O'Brien [1993] 3 WLR 786   *374*
Bell v Lever Bros Ltd [1932] AC 161   *319*
Bentley (Dick) Productions Ltd v Harold Smith (Motors) Ltd [1965] 1 WLR 623   *283*
Beoco Ltd v Alfa Laval Co Ltd (1994) The Times 12 January   *425*
Bettini v Gye (1876) 1 QBD 183   *284*
Bissett v Wilkinson [1927] AC 177   *320*
Blackburn Bobbin Co Ltd v TW Allen & Sons Ltd [1918] 2 KB 467   *394*
Bliss v South East Thames Regional Health Authority [1985] IRLR 308   *425*
Brace v Calder [1895] 2 QB 253   *426*
Bradburn v Great Western Railway (1874) LR 10 Ex 1   *426*
Briggs v Oates [1991] 1 All ER 407   *374*
Brikom Investments Ltd v Seaford Estates Ltd [1981] 1 WLR 863   *321*
British and Commonwealth Holdings plc v Quadrex Holdings Inc [1989] 3 WLR 723   *410*
British Crane Hire Corporation Ltd v Ipswich Plant Hire Ltd [1975] QB 303; [1974] 2 WLR 856   *284, 341*
British Westinghouse Electric and Manufacturing Company Limited v Underground Electric Railways Company of London Limited [1912] AC 673   *427*
Brown v Raphael [1958] Ch 636   *322*
Bunge Corp v Tradax SA [1981] 1 WLR 711   *285*

C & P Haulage v Middleton [1983] 1 WLR 1461   *429*
CCC Films (London) Ltd v Impact Quadrant Films Ltd [1984] 3 WLR 245   *430*
CIBC Mortgages plc v Pitt [1993] 3 WLR 802   *375*

Cehave NV v Bremer Handelsgesellschaft mbH, The Hansa Nord [1976] QB 44; [1975] 3 WLR 447 *286*
Cellulose Acetate Silk Company Limited v Widnes Foundry (1925) Limited [1933] AC 20 *430*
Chaplin v Hicks [1911] 2 KB 786 *431*
Chelsea Football & Athletic Co Ltd v SB Property Co Ltd [1992] TLR 175 *289*
Choko Star, The *see* Industrie Chimiche Italia Centrale & Cerealfin SA v Alexander G Tsavliris & Sons, etc
Clarke v Dickson (1858) EB & B 148 *325*
Clarke v Newland [1991] 1 All ER 397 *375*
Clayton (Herbert) and Jack Waller Ltd v Oliver [1930] AC 209 *432*
Cleveland Petroleum Co Ltd v Dartstone Ltd [1969] 1 WLR 116 *376*
Clydebank Engineering and Shipbuilding Co v Castaneda [1905] AC 6 *433*
Computer and Systems Engineering plc v John Lelliott Ltd (1991) The Times 21 February *342*
Constantine (Joseph) Steamship Line Ltd v Imperial Smelting Corporation Ltd [1942] AC 154 *394*
Cornish v Midland Bank plc [1985] 3 All ER 513 *377*
Cresswell v Potter [1978] 1 WLR 255n *378*
Curtis v Chemical Cleaning & Dyeing Co [1951] 1 KB 805 *342*
Cutter v Powell (1795) 6 Term Rep 320 *411*

Dakin (H) & Co Ltd v Lee [1916] 1 KB 566 *411*
Davis Contractors Ltd v Fareham Urban District Council [1956] AC 696 *395*
Decro-Wall International SA v Practitioners in Marketing Ltd [1971] 1 WLR 361 *412, 475*
De Lassalle v Guildford [1901] 2 KB 215 *290*
Derry v Peek (1889) 14 App Cas 337 *324*
Dillon v Baltic Shipping Co, The Mikhail Lermontov [1991] 2 Lloyd's Rep 155 *343*
Doyle v Olby (Ironmongers) Ltd [1969] 2 QB 158; [1969] 2 WLR 673 *324, 434*
Dunk v George Waller & Sons Ltd [1970] 2 QB 163; [1970] 2 WLR 1241 *435*
Dunlop Pneumatic Tyre Co Ltd v New Garage and Motor Co Ltd [1915] AC 79 *436*

East v Maurer [1991] 2 All ER 733 *325*
Edgington v Fitzmaurice (1885) 29 Ch D 459 *326*
Edwards v Society of Graphical and Allied Trades [1971] Ch 354; [1970] 3 WLR 713 *437*
Erlanger v New Sombrero Phosphate Co (1878) 3 App Cas 1218 *326*
Ertel Bieber & Co v Rio Tinto Co Ltd [1918] AC 260 *396*
Esso Petroleum Co Ltd v Harper's Garage (Stourport) Ltd [1968] AC 269; [1967] 2 WLR 871 *378*
Esso Petroleum Co Ltd v Mardon [1976] QB 801; [1976] 2 WLR 583 *290, 327*
Eurymedon, The *see* New Zealand Shipping Co Ltd v AM Satterthwaite & Co Ltd
Evans (J) & Son (Portsmouth) Ltd v Andrea Merzario Ltd [1976] 1 WLR 1078 *292*
Evening Standard Co Ltd v Henderson [1987] IRLR 64 *475*
Evia Luck, The *see* Dimskal Shipping Co SA v International Transport Workers' Federation
Eyre v Measday [1986] 1 All ER 488 *292*
Export Credits Guarantee Department v Universal Oil Products Co [1983] 1 WLR 399 *438*

Federal Commerce and Navigation Ltd v Molena Alpha Inc, The Nanfri, The Benfri, The Lorfri, [1979] AC 757; [1978] 3 WLR 991 *293, 413*
Fercometal SARL v Mediterranean Shipping Co SA, The Simona [1988] 3 WLR 200 *413*
Ferguson v John Dawson and Partners (Contractors) Ltd [1976] 1 WLR 1213 *294*
Fibrosa Spolka Akcyjna v Fairburn Lawson Combe Barbour Ltd [1943] AC 32 *397*
Fitch v Dewes [1921] 2 AC 158 *380*

Flamar Interocean Ltd *v* Denmac Ltd, The Flamar Pride and The Flamar Progress [1990] 1 Lloyd's Rep 434   *343*
Forsikringsaktieselskapet Vesta *v* Butcher [1988] 3 WLR 565   *439*
Frost *v* Knight (1872) LR 7 Ex 111   *414*
Fry *v* Lane (1888) 40 Ch D 312   *381*

GA Estates *v* Caviapen Trustees Ltd (1991) The Times 22 October   *295*
Galoo *v* Bright Grahame Murray [1994] 1 WLR 1360   *440*
Gamerco SA *v* ICM/Fair Warning Agency Ltd [1995] 1 WLR 1226   *397*
Gebrüder Metalmann GmbH & Co KG *v* NBR (London) Ltd [1984] 1 Lloyd's Rep 614   *441*
George Mitchell (Chesterhall) Ltd *v* Finney Lock Seeds Ltd [1983] 2 AC 803; [1983] QB 284; [1983] 3 WLR 163   *344*
Golden Bay Realty Ltd *v* Orchard Twelve Instruments Ltd [1991] 1 WLR 981   *442*
Goldsoll *v* Goldman [1915] 1 Ch 292   *382*
Graham *v* Pitkin [1992] 1 WLR 403   *295*
Gran Gelato Ltd *v* Richcliff (Group) Ltd [1992] 1 All ER 865   *327*

Hadley *v* Baxendale (1854) 9 Exch 341   *442*
Hannah Blumenthal, The *see* Paal Wilson & Co A/S *v* Partenreederei Hannah Blumenthal
Hansa Nord, The *see* Cehave NV *v* Bremer Handelsgesellschaft mbH
Harris *v* Wyre Forest District Council *see* Smith *v* Eric S Bush
Harrods Ltd *v* Schwarz-Sackin & Co Ltd [1991] FSR 209   *415*
Hayes *v* James & Charles Dodd [1990] 2 All ER 815   *444*
Heilbut, Symons & Co *v* Buckleton [1913] AC 30   *296*
Heron II, The *see* Koufos *v* Czarnikow Ltd
Hill *v* CA Parsons & Co Ltd [1972] Ch 305; [1971] 3 WLR 995   *476*
Hochster *v* De La Tour (1853) 2 E & B 678   *415*
Hollier *v* Rambler Motors (AMC) Ltd [1972] 2 QB 71; [1972] 2 WLR 401   *344*
Home Counties Dairies Ltd *v* Skilton [1970] 1 WLR 526   *383*
Hong Kong Fir Shipping Co Ltd *v* Kawasaki Kisan Kaisha Ltd [1962] 2 QB 26; [1962] 2 WLR 474   *298*
Howard Marine and Dredging Co Ltd *v* A Ogden & Sons (Excavations) Ltd [1978] QB 574; [1978] 2 WLR 515   *328*
Hussey *v* Eels [1990] 2 WLR 234   *445*

Ingram *v* Little [1961] 1 QB 31; [1960] 3 WLR 504   *178*
Iron Trade Mutual Insurance Co Ltd *v* JK Buckenham Ltd [1989] 2 Lloyd's Rep 89   *445*

Jackson *v* Horizon Holidays Ltd [1975] 3 WLR 1468   *446*
Jackson *v* Union Marine Insurance Co Ltd (1873) LR 10 CP 125   *399*
Jarvis *v* Swan Tours Ltd [1973] 2 QB 233; [1972] 3 WLR 954   *447*
Jobson *v* Johnson [1989] 1 WLR 1026   *447*
Johnson *v* Agnew [1980] AC 367; [1979] 2 WLR 487; [1979] 1 All ER 883   *476*

Kaines (UK) Ltd *v* Osterreichische Warrenhandelgesellschaft Austrowaren Gesellschaft mbH [1993] 2 Lloyd's Rep 1   *448*
Kingsnorth Trust *v* Bell [1986] 1 WLR 119   *383*
Koufos *v* C Czarnikow Ltd, The Heron II [1969] 1 AC 350; [1967] 3 WLR 1491   *449*
Krell *v* Henry [1903] 2 KB 740   *399*

Laurence v Lexcourt Holdings Ltd [1978] 1 WLR 1128; [1978] 2 All ER 810   *329*
Lavarack v Woods of Colchester Ltd [1967] 1 QB 278; [1966] 3 WLR 706   *453*
Leaf v International Galleries [1950] 2 KB 86   *330*
Leeds Industrial Co-Operative Society Ltd v Slack [1924] AC 851   *477*
L'Estrange v Graucob (F) Ltd [1934] 2 KB 394   *345*
Levison v Patent Steam Carpet Cleaning Co Ltd [1978] QB 69; [1977] 3 WLR 90   *345, 384*
Liverpool City Council v Irwin [1977] AC 236; [1976] 2 WLR 562   *300*
Lloyds Bank Ltd v Bundy [1975] QB 326; [1974] 3 WLR 501   *384*
Lombard North Central plc v Butterworth [1987] 2 WLR 7   *301, 454*
London Export Corporation Ltd v Jubilee Coffee Roasting Co Ltd [1958] 1 WLR 661   *301*
Long v Lloyd [1958] 1 WLR 753   *331*
Lumley v Wagner (1852) 1 De GM & G 604   *478*
Luxor (Eastbourne) Ltd v Cooper [1941] AC 108   *301*

McAlpine, Humberoak Ltd v McDermott International Inc (1992) Financial Times 13 March   *400*
McCutcheon v David MacBrayne Ltd [1964] 1 WLR 125   *346*
Malcolm v Chancellor, Masters and Scholars of the University of Oxford (1990) The Times 23 March   *302*
Maple Flock Co Ltd v Universal Furniture Products (Wembley) Ltd [1934] 1 KB 148   *416*
Maredelanto Compania Naviera SA v Bergbau-Handel GmbH, The Mihalis Angelos [1970] 1 QB 164; [1970] 3 WLR 601   *303*
Mareva Compania Naviera SA v International Bulk Carriers SA, The Mareva [1980] 1 All ER 213   *478*
Maria D, The *see* Elpis Maritime Co Ltd v Marti Chartering Co Inc
Maritime National Fish Ltd v Ocean Trawlers Ltd [1935] AC 524   *400*
Mason v Provident Clothing and Supply Co Ltd [1913] AC 724   *385*
Melrose v Davidson 1993 SLT 611   *347*
Metropolitan Water Board v Dick, Kerr & Co Ltd [1918] AC 119   *401*
Micklefield v SAC Technology Ltd [1990] 1 WLR 1002   *348*
Midland Bank plc v Shephard [1988] 3 All ER 17   *386*
Mihalis Angelos, The *see* Maredelanto Compania Naviera SA v Bergbau-Handel GmbH
Mikhail Lermontov, The *see* Dillon v Baltic Shipping Co
Millers Wharf Partnership Ltd v Corinthian Column Ltd (1990) 61 P & CR 461   *416*
Monarch Steamship Co Ltd v A/B Karlshamns Oljefabriker [1949] AC 196   *456*
Moorcock, The (1889) 14 PD 64   *304*
Museprime Properties Ltd v Adhill Properties Ltd (1990) 36 EG 114   *332*

National Carriers Ltd v Panalpina (Northern) Ltd [1981] AC 675; [1981] 2 WLR 45   *402*
National Westminster Bank plc v Morgan [1985] 2 WLR 588   *388*
Naughton v O'Callaghan [1990] 3 All ER 191   *456*
Neilson v Stewart 1991 SLT 523   *305*
Nema, The *see* Pioneer Shipping Ltd v BTP Tioxide Ltd
New York Star, The *see* Port Jackson Stevedoring Pty Ltd v Salmon & Spraggon Pty (Australia) Ltd
Nordenfelt v Maxim Nordenfelt Guns and Ammunition Co Ltd [1894] AC 535   *389*

O'Laoire v Jackel International Ltd (1991) The Times 12 February   *458*
Olley v Marlborough Court Ltd [1949] 1 KB 532   *349*
Oscar Chess Ltd v Williams [1957] 1 WLR 370; [1957] 1 All ER 325   *305*

Paal Wilson & Co A/S *v* Partenreederei Hannah Blumenthal, The Hannah Blumenthal [1983] AC 854; [1982] 3 WLR 1149   *403*
Page One Records Ltd *v* Britton [1968] 1 WLR 157   *479*
Parker *v* South Eastern Railway Co (1877) 2 CPD 416   *349*
Parsons (H) (Livestock) Ltd *v* Uttley, Ingham & Co Ltd [1978] QB 791; [1977] 3 WLR 990   *458*
Patel *v* Ali [1984] Ch 283; [1984] 2 WLR 960   *480*
Payzu Ltd *v* Saunders [1919] 2 KB 581   *460*
Peyman *v* Lanjani [1985] Ch 457; [1985] 2 WLR 154   *332*
Philips Hong Kong Ltd *v* Attorney-General of Hong Kong (1993) The Times 15 February   *460*
Phillips *v* Brooks Ltd [1919] 2 KB 243   *333*
Phillips Products *v* Hyland *see* Thompson *v* T Lohan (Plant Hire Ltd)
Photo Production Ltd *v* Securicor Transport Ltd [1980] AC 827; [1980] 2 WLR 283   *351, 417*
Pilkington *v* Wood [1953] Ch 770; [1953] 2 All ER 810   *461*
Pioneer Shipping Ltd *v* BTP Tioxide Ltd, The Nema [1982] AC 724; [1981] 3 WLR 292   *404*
Posner *v* Scott-Lewis [1986] 3 WLR 531   *481*
Post Chaser, The *see* Société Italo-Belge *v* Palm and Vegetable Oils
Prenn *v* Simmonds [1971] 1 WLR 1381   *308*
Price *v* Strange [1978] Ch 337; [1977] 3 WLR 943   *482*
Public Works Commissioners *v* Hills [1906] AC 368   *463*

Quadrant Visual Communications Ltd *v* Hutchinson Telephone (UK) Ltd (1991) The Times 4 December   *483*

R & B Customs Brokers Ltd *v* United Dominions Trust Ltd [1988] 1 All ER 847; [1987] 1 WLR 659n   *354*
Reardon Smith Line *v* Yngvar Hansen-Tangen [1976] 1 WLR 989   *309, 417*
Redgrave *v* Hurd (1881) 20 Ch D 1   *334*
Reigate *v* Union Manufacturing Co (Ramsbottom) Ltd [1918] 1 KB 592   *310*
Richco International Ltd *v* Bunge and Co Ltd [1991] 2 Lloyd's Rep 93   *311*
Royscott Trust *v* Rogerson [1991] 3 WLR 57   *334, 464*
Rutter *v* Palmer [1922] 2 KB 87   *355*
Ruxley Electronics & Construction Ltd *v* Forsyth; Laddingford Enclosures Ltd *v* Same [1995] 3 WLR 118   *464*
Ryan *v* Mutual Tontine Westminster Chambers Association [1893] 1 Ch 116   *484*

St Albans City and District Council *v* International Computers Ltd (1994) The Times 11 November   *356*
St Marylebone Property Co Ltd *v* Payne (1994) 45 EG 156   *335*
Sagar *v* H Ridehalgh & Son Ltd [1931] 1 Ch 310   *311*
Schawel *v* Reade [1913] 2 Ir Rep 81   *312*
Schroeder (A) Music Publishing Co Ltd *v* Macaulay [1974] 1 WLR 1308   *390*
Schuler (L) AG *v* Wickman Machine Tool Sales Ltd [1974] AC 235; [1973] 2 WLR 683   *313*
Seven Seas Properties Ltd *v* Al-Essa [1993] 3 All ER 577   *466*
Sharneyford Supplies Ltd *v* Edge [1987] 2 WLR 363; [1985] 1 All ER 976   *335, 467*
Shell (UK) Ltd *v* Lostock Garage Ltd [1976] 1 WLR 1187   *314, 484*
Shepherd (FC) & Co Ltd *v* Jerrom [1986] 3 WLR 801   *405*
Siboen, The; Sibotre, The *see* Occidental Worldwide Investment Corp *v* Skibs A/S Avanti
Simona, The *see* Fercometal SARL *v* Mediterranean Shipping Co SA
Skopas, The [1983] 1 WLR 857; [1983] 2 All ER 1   *334, 337*

Table of Main Cases: The Law of Contract

Sky Petroleum Ltd v VIP Petroleum Ltd [1974] 1 WLR 576   *484*
Smith v Eric S Bush [1989] 2 WLR 790   *356*
Smith v Hughes (1871) LR 6 QB 597   *338*
Smith v South Wales Switchgear Ltd [1978] 1 WLR 165   *358*
Smith New Court Securities Ltd v Scrimgeour Vickers (Asset Management) Ltd and Another [1994] 4 All ER 225   *338*
Southern Foundries (1926) Ltd v Shirlaw [1940] AC 701   *316*
Southway Group Ltd v Wolff (1991) The Independent 30 August   *417*
Spurling (J) Ltd v Bradshaw [1956] 1 WLR 461   *361*
Staffordshire Area Health Authority v South Staffordshire Waterworks Co [1978] 1 WLR 1387   *467*
Stour Valley Builders v Stuart (1993) The Times 9 February   *417*
Suisse Atlantique Société d'Armament Maritime SA v NV Rotterdamsche Kolen Centrale [1967] 1 AC 361; [1966] 2 WLR 944   *362*
Sumpter v Hedges [1898] 1 QB 673   *418*
Surrey CC v Bredero Homes Ltd [1992] 3 All ER 302   *468*
Sutton v Sutton [1984] 2 WLR 146   *485*
Sybron Corp v Rochem Ltd [1983] 3 WLR 713   *339*

Taylor v Caldwell (1863) 3 B & S 826   *406*
Texaco Melbourne, The (1991) Financial Times 7 August   *469*
Thake v Maurice [1986] 2 WLR 337   *317*
Thompson v T Lohan (Plant Hire) Ltd [1987] 1 WLR 649   *365*
Thornton v Abbey National plc (1993) The Times 4 March   *418*
Toepfer (Alfred C) International GmbH v Itex Itagrani Export SA [1993] 1 Lloyd's Rep 360   *419*
Tsakiroglou & Co Ltd v Noblee Thorl GmbH [1962] AC 93; [1961] 2 WLR 633   *407*
Tudor Grange Holdings Ltd v Citibank NA [1991] 4 All ER 1; [1991] TLR 217   *367*

United Dominions Corporation (Jamaica) Ltd v Shoucair [1969] 1 AC 340; [1968] 3 WLR 893   *419*
Universe Sentinel, The *see* Universe Tankships Inc of Monrovia v International Transport Workers Federation

Victoria Laundry (Windsor) Ltd v Newman Industries Ltd [1949] 2 KB 528   *469*
Vitol SA v Norelf Ltd [1995] 3 WLR 549   *420*

Warner Bros Pictures Inc v Nelson [1937] 1 KB 209   *486*
Watson v Prager [1991] 1 WLR 726   *391*
Watts v Morrow [1991] 1 WLR 1421   *470*
Weld-Blundell v Stephens [1920] AC 956   *470*
Wells (Merstham) Ltd v Buckland Sand and Silica Co Ltd [1965] 2 QB 170; [1964] 2 WLR 453   *318*
White and Carter (Councils) Ltd v McGregor [1962] AC 413; [1962] 2 WLR 17   *421*
White Arrow Express Ltd v Lamey's Distribution Ltd [1995] TLR 430   *471*
With v O'Flanagan [1936] Ch 575   *340*
Woodstead Finance v Petrou (1986) 136 NLJ 188   *392*
Wroth v Tyler [1974] Ch 30; [1973] 2 WLR 405   *472*

EQUITY AND TRUSTS

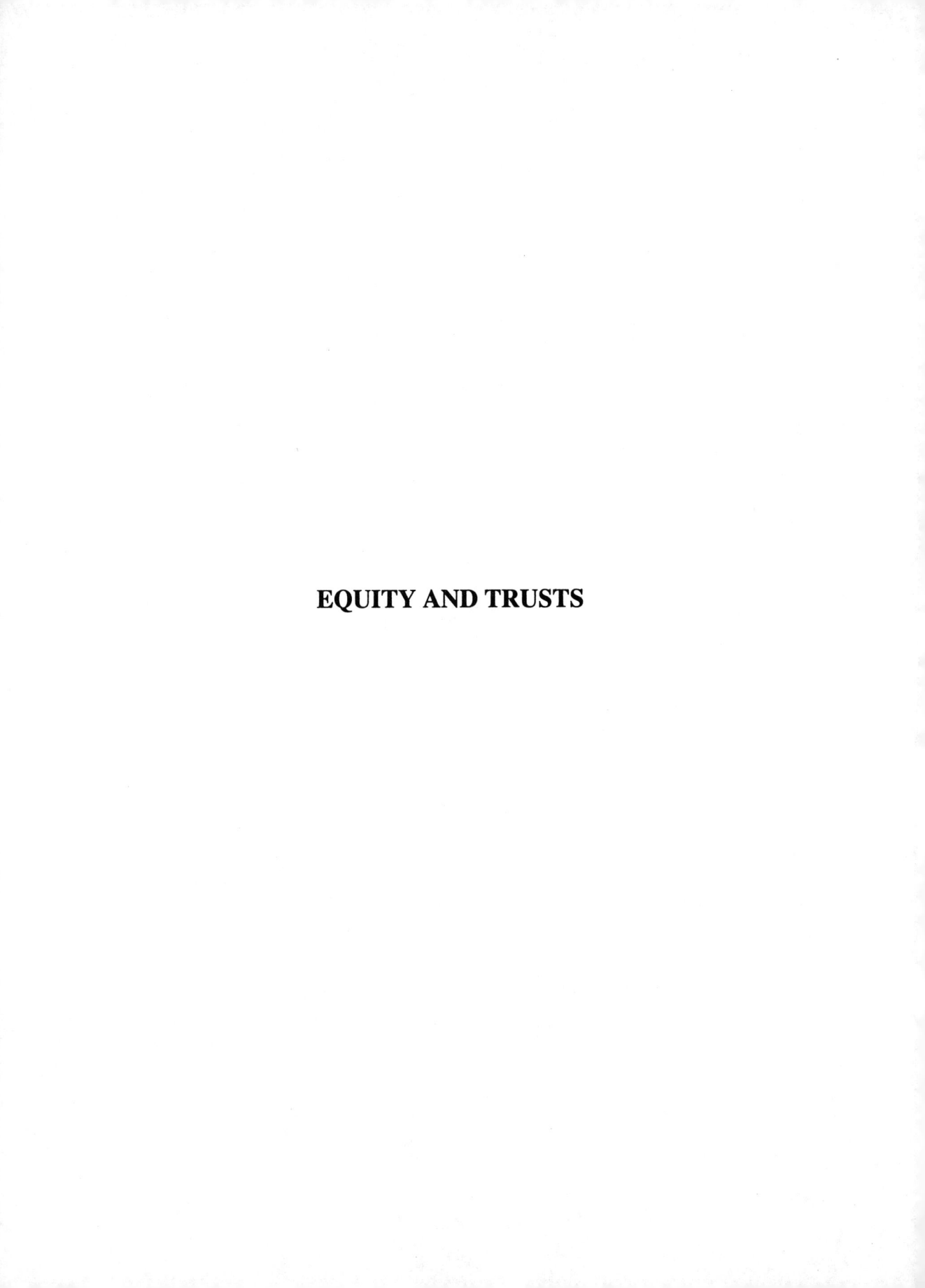

1 The Three Certainties

Adams and the Kensington Vestry, Re (1884) 27 Ch D 394 Court of Appeal (Baggallay, Cotton and Lindley LJJ)

Certainty of words: precatory words

Facts
A testator left his property 'unto and to the absolute use of my wife ... in full confidence that she will do what is right as to the disposal thereof between my children, either in her lifetime or by will after her decease.'

Held
These words were not imperative; they did not create a trust so the wife took the property absolutely.

Cotton LJ:

'I am of the same opinion. The question before us is whether, upon the true construction of the will of George Smith, he imposed upon his wife Harriet a trust. Now just let us look at it, in the first instance, alone, and see what we can spell out of it, and see what was expressed by the will. Reading that will, and I will not repeat it, because it has been already read, it seems to me perfectly clear what the testator intended. He leaves his wife, his property absolutely, but what was in his mind was this: "I am the head of the family, and it is laid upon me to provide properly for the members of my family – my children: my widow will succeed me when I die, and I wish to put her in the position I occupied as the person who is to provide for my children." Not that he entails upon her any trust so as to bind her, but he simply says, in giving her this, I express to her, and call to her attention, the moral obligation which I myself had and which I feel that she is going to discharge. The motive of the gift is, in my opinion, not a trust imposed upon her by the gift in the will. He leaves the property to her; he knows that she will do what is right, and carry out the moral obligation which he thought lay on him, and on her if she survived him, to provide for the children. But it is said that the testator would be very much astonished if he found that he had given his wife power to leave the property away. That is a proposition which I should express in a different way. He would be much surprised if the wife to whom he had left his property absolutely should so act as not to provide for the children, that is to say, not to do what is right. That is a very different thing. He would have said: "I expected that she would do what was right, and therefore I left it to her absolutely. I find she has not done what I think is right, but I cannot help it, I am very sorry that she has done so." That would be the surprise, I think, that he would express, and feel, if he could do either, if the wife did what was unreasonable as regards the children ...

... I have no hesitation in saying myself, that I think some of the older authorities went a great deal too far in holding that some particular words appearing in a will were sufficient to create a trust. Undoubtedly, confidence, if the rest of the context shows that a trust is intended, may make a trust, but what we have to look at is the whole of the will which we have to construe, and if the confidence is that she will do what is right as regards the disposal of the property, I cannot say that that is, on the true construction of the will, a trust imposed upon her. Having regard to the later decisions, we must not extend the old cases in any way, or rely upon the mere use of any particular words, but, considering all the words which are used, we have to see what is their true effect, and what was the intention of the testator as expressed in his will. In my opinion here he has expressed his will in such a way as not to shew an intention of imposing a trust on the wife but on the contrary in my opinion, he has shewn an intention to leave the property, as he says he does, to her absolutely ...'

Astor's Settlement, Re [1952] Ch 534 Chancery Division (Roxburgh J)

Certainty of objects: purpose trust: unenforceable

Facts
In 1945 Lord Astor made an inter vivos settlement for a number of non-charitable objects including (1) 'The maintenance ... of good understanding, sympathy and co-operation between nations, (2) The preservation of the independence and integrity of newspapers ... (3) The protection of newspapers ... from being absorbed or controlled by combines.'

Held
The trusts failed. The objects of the trust were void for uncertainty and further, they were not for the benefit of individuals and were, therefore, purpose trusts which failed.

Roxburgh J:

> "Let me then sum up the position so far. On the one side there are Lord Parker's two propositions with which I began. These were not new, but merely re-echoed what Sir William Grant had said as Master of the Rolls in *Morice* v *The Bishop of Durham* (1805) 10 Ves 522 as long ago as 1804: "There must be somebody, in whose favour the court can decree performance." The position was recently restated by Harman J in *Re Wood* [1949] Ch 498: "A gift on trust must have a cestui que trust", and this seems to be in accord with principle. On the other side is a group of cases relating to horses and dogs, graves and monuments – matters arising under wills and intimately connected with the deceased – in which the courts have found means of escape from these general propositions and also *Re Thompson* [1934] Ch 324 and *Re Price* [1943] Ch 422, which I have endeavoured to explain. *Re Price* belongs to another field. The rest may, I think, properly be regarded as anomalous and exceptional and in no way destructive of the proposition which traces descent from or through Sir William Grant through Lord Parker to Harman J. Perhaps the late Sir Arthur Underhill was right in suggesting that they may be concessions to human weaknesses or sentiment (see Law of Trusts, 8th Ed p79). They cannot, in my judgment, of themselves (and no other justification has been suggested to me) justify the conclusion that a Court of Equity will recognise as an equitable obligation affecting the income of large funds in the hands of trustees a direction to apply it in furtherance of enumerated non-charitable purposes in a manner which no court or department can control or enforce. I hold that the trusts here in question are void on the first of the grounds submitted by Mr Jennings and Mr Buckley.'

Baden's Deed Trusts (No 2), Re [1973] Ch 9 Court of Appeal (Sachs, Megaw and Stamp LJJ)

Certainty of objects

Facts
McPhail v *Doulton* (supra) was remitted to the lower courts by the House of Lords for the lower courts to determine whether the trust was valid or void for uncertainty. Under the name *Re Baden* the case came back to the Court of Appeal.

Held
The trust was valid, but different approaches were taken by members of the Court.

Sachs LJ thought it was necessary to distinguish between conceptual uncertainty and evidential difficulty and said the test laid down by the House of Lords only affected conceptual uncertainty and not evidential uncertainty. The court would not be defeated by evidential uncertainty. He observed: 'Once the class of persons to be benefited is conceptually certain, it becomes a question of fact whether any postulant has on enquiry been proved to be within it. That position remains the same whether the class to be benefited happens to be small (such as "first cousins") or large (such as the members of the X Trade Union, or 'those who have served in the Royal Navy').'

The idea of conceptual certainty is concerned with whether the definition of the class is 'certain' – first cousins would be but something like 'friends' would not.

On evidential uncertainty, Sachs LJ said: 'The suggestion that such trusts could be invalid because it might be impossible to prove of a given individual that he was not in the relevant class is wholly fallacious ...' This is really a part of the test in *McPhail* v *Doulton*.

Megaw LJ took the view that a trust for selection would not fail because the whole range of objects could not be ascertained. He observed: 'To my mind, the test is satisfied if, as regards at least a substantial number of objects, it can be said with certainty that they fall within the trust; even though, as regards a substantial number of other persons, if they ever for some fanciful reason fell to be considered, the answer would have to be, not "they are outside the trusts" but "it is not proven whether they are in or out"...'

The application of these tests in *Re Baden* concerned the word 'relatives' used in the trust deed.

Sachs LJ concluded that the fact it might be impossible to prove that a person was not a relative of any employee or ex-employee did not make the expression too uncertain.

Megaw LJ concluded that the word relative did not cause uncertainty and did so by construing relative to mean 'next-of-kin' or 'nearest blood relations'. He was, however, of the opinion that if 'relative' was construed as meaning descendants of a common ancestor there would be uncertainty.

Barlow's Will Trusts, Re [1979] 1 WLR 278 Chancery Division (Browne-Wilkinson J)

Certainty of objects

Facts
T died leaving a valuable collection of paintings. After specific bequests she directed that the remainder of the paintings be sold, but that 'any members of my family and any friends of mine who wish to do so' be allowed to purchase any of the paintings at the price shown in a catalogue compiled in 1970 or at probate value, whichever was the lower.

Held
1. The direction to allow 'friends' to purchase the paintings did not require all the members of the class to be ascertained because any uncertainty as to some of the beneficiaries did not affect the quantum of the gift to those who qualified.
2. In the absence of issue, the prima facie meaning of 'family' means 'relations', ie those related by blood to the testatrix.

Browne-Wilkinson J:

'In my judgment, it is clear that Lord Upjohn in *Re Gulbenkian* [1970] AC 508 was considering only cases where it was necessary to establish all the members of the class. He made it clear that the reason for the rule is that in a gift which requires one to establish all the members of the class, (eg "a gift to all my friends in equal shares") you cannot hold the gift good in part, since the quantum of each friend's share depends on how many friends there are. So all persons intended to benefit by the donor must be ascertained if any effect is to be given to the gift. In my judgment, the adoption of Lord Upjohn's test by the House of Lords in *McPhail* v *Doulton* [1971] AC 424 is based on the same reasoning, even though in that case the House of Lords held that it was only necessary to be able to survey the class of objects of a power of appointment and not to establish who all the members were. But such reasoning has no application to a case where there is a condition or description attached to one or more individual gifts; in such cases, uncertainty as to some other persons who may have been intended to take does not in any way affect the quantum of the gift to persons who undoubtedly possess the qualification.

The effect ... is to confer on friends of the testatrix a series of options to purchase. Although it is obviously desirable as a practical matter that steps should be taken to inform those entitled to the options of their rights, it is common ground that there is no legal necessity to do so. Therefore, each person coming forward to exercise the option has to prove that he is a friend; it is not legally necessary, in my judgment, to discover who all the friends are. In order to decide whether an individual is entitled to purchase, all that is required is that the executors should be able to say of that individual whether he has proved that he is a friend. The word "friend", therefore, is a description or qualification of the option holder.'

Benjamin, Re [1902] 1 Ch 723

See Chapter 14.

Boyce v *Boyce* (1849) 16 Sim 476 Vice-Chancellor's Court (Kindersley V-C)

Certainty of subject matter

Facts
A testator devised houses to trustees on trust for his wife for life, and on her death, in trust to convey any one house to his daughter, D1, the house to be chosen by her, and to convey the other houses to another daughter, D2. D1 died before the testator without having made a choice.

Held
The trust in favour of D2 was void; there was uncertainty as to the property which it was to comprise.

Combe, Re [1925] Ch 210 Chancery Division (Tomlin J)

Mere powers and trust powers

Facts
The testator left life interests to his wife and son and then his trustees were to hold 'in trust for such person or persons as my ... son shall by will appoint, but I direct that such appointment must be confined to any relation or relations of mine of the whole blood'.

Held
A mere power not a trust power was created by the testator, as on construction of the words there was no general intention in favour of the class as a whole.

Comiskey* v *Bowring-Hanbury [1905] AC 84 House of Lords (Lord Halsbury LC, Lord Davey, Lord James, Lord Robertson, Lord Macnaghten; Lord Lindley dissenting)

Precatory words: the modern practice

Facts
The testator gave all his property to his wife 'absolutely in full confidence that she will make such use of it as I would have made myself and that at her death she will devise it to such one or more of my nieces as she may think fit'.

Held
On a true construction of the whole will, the words 'in full confidence' created a trust, despite the word 'absolutely'.

Dorman (deceased), Re, Smith* v *National Children's Home and Orphanage Registered [1994] 1 WLR 282 Chancery Division (David Neuberger QC)

Specific legacies – trustee unknowingly transfers monies before testator's death

Facts
D executed a will bequeathing monies in a specified account in favour of a trust fund administered by AD. AD was also the donee of an enduring power of attorney on behalf of D. However, unknown to D, prior to D's death AD transferred the monies from the specified account (being unaware of the provisions in D's will) into another account earning a higher rate of interest. D then died leaving his residue estate in favour of various charities. The charities claimed the monies.

Held
There was, practically, no difference between the specified account and the new higher interest rate account. D had, arguably, not known of the transfer and his intentions had not changed. The funds would be construed as being in favour of the trust fund.

Gartside* v *IRC [1968] AC 553 House of Lords (Lord Reid, Lord Morris, Lord Guest, Lord Hodson and Lord Wilberforce)

Discretionary trust: nature of beneficiary's interest

Facts
A beneficiary under a discretionary trust died, and the trustees refused to pay death duty on his share on the ground that he did not have a sufficient interest to be liable to it.

Held
The trustees were correct and he did not have sufficient interest to pay tax. Lord Reid reviewed what rights a beneficiary in these circumstances did acquire, and held that they included (1) a right to prevent misappropriation of the capital; (2) a right to require the trustees to act *bona fide* in exercising their discretion over distribution; (3) a right to take whatever part of the income the trustees chose to give him.

Gestetner, Re [1953] Ch 672 Chancery Division (Harman J)

Certainty of objects in powers and trusts

Facts

Capital was held on trust for trustees to appoint at their discretion among: certain named individuals; any person living or thereafter born who was a descendant of the settlor's father or uncle; any spouse, widow or widower of such person; five named charities; any former employee of the settlor or his wife, or widow or widower of such employee; any director or employee of a named company.

Held

The trustees were not under a duty to distribute and therefore not obliged to 'survey the world from China to Peru' to establish all the possible recipients. It was necessary only to say of any given possible recipient that he did or did not fall within the class designated. Accordingly the instrument created a discretionary power not a discretionary trust, and as the eligibility of any given candidate could be determined with certainty, it was valid.

Golay, Re [1965] 1 WLR 1969 Chancery Division (Ungoed-Thomas J)

Certainty of subject matter

Facts

The testator, by his will dated October 1957, directed his executors to let his daughter to enjoy one of his flats during her lifetime 'and to receive a reasonable income from my other properties...' The question arose whether the direction to let the daughter receive a reasonable income was void for uncertainty.

Held

That the words 'reasonable income' provided an effective determinant which the court could apply to give effect to the testator's intention. Therefore, the bequest was not defeated by uncertainty.

Ungoed-Thomas J:

> '... the yardstick indicated by the testator is not what he or any other specified person subjectively considers to be reasonable but what he identifies objectively as "reasonable income". The court is constantly involved in making such objective assessments of what is reasonable and it is not to be deterred from doing so because subjective influences can never by wholly excluded. In my view, the testator intended by "reasonable income" the yardstick which the court could and would apply in quantifying the amount so that the direction in the will is not in my view defeated by uncertainty.'

Hamilton, Re [1895] 2 Ch 370 Court of Appeal (Lindley, Lopes and Kay LJJ)

Certainty of words: precatory words.

Facts

A testator left legacies to her two nieces stating 'I wish them to bequeath the same equally between the families of O and P in such mode as they shall consider right.'

Held

The words showed no intention to create a trust and the two nieces took them absolutely.

Lopes LJ:

> '... it seems to me perfectly clear that the current of decisions with regard to precatory trusts is now changed, and that the result of the change is this, that the Court will not allow a precatory trust to be raised unless on the consideration of all the words employed it comes to the conclusion that it was the intention of the testator to create a trust.'

Hunter v *Moss* [1994] 1 WLR 452 Court of Appeal (Dillon, Mann and Hirst LJJ)

Oral declaration of trust – shares – certainty of subject matter – unascertained property

Facts
M was the registered shareholder of 950 out of 1,000 shares in a company. At trial the deputy judge ruled that M had made a valid oral declaration of trust of five per cent of the company's shares which applied to 50 of the 950 shares held by M. M appealed, applying for the judgment to be set aside by arguing that the judge had not considered M's alternative, further, argument that the trust failed for want of certainty of subject matter.

Held
Dismissing M's appeal, by motion. There was sufficient certainty of subject matter if immediately after a valid, even if oral, declaration of trust the Court could order the trust's execution. Further, so long as there was property available which could fulfil the trust, even if that property was intangible, the requirement of certainty did not entail appropriation or segregation of specific property to fulfil the trust. In this instance M had sufficient shares to fulfil the declaration in respect of 5 per cent of the company's shares and it was unnecessary for any particular 50 shares to have been identified.

IRC v *Broadway Cottages Trust* [1955] Ch 20 Court of Appeal (Jenkins, Hodson and Singleton LJJ)

Certainty of objects

Facts
The trustees held funds on trust to apply the income for the benefit of all or any of a class (relations or members of the family) as they thought fit.

Held
The words created a trust which was void for uncertainty of objects; a power, which in those terms would have been valid, could not be created out of what the settlor had clearly intended as a trust.

Jenkins LJ:

> 'Lord Tomlin's view [in *Re Ogden* [1933] Ch 678], which we take to be that a trust for such members of a given class of objects as the trustees shall select is void for uncertainty unless the whole range of objects eligible for selection is ascertained or capable of ascertainment, seems to us to be based on sound reasoning, and we accept it accordingly ... We do not think a valid power is to be spelt out of an invalid trust.'

Jones v *Jones* (1989) The Independent 27 January Court of Appeal (judges not named)

The beneficiaries' interests under a discretionary trust

Facts
A mother died and by will left property to trustees on a discretionary trust for her children with power to the trustees to advance capital and income during their minority, the fund to become theirs absolutely on their majority. The maternal grandmother had custody, and applied for maintenance from the children's father. He argued that their interest from the trust should be taken into account to reduce his liabilities.

Held
It was correct to take the fund into account, but not to assume that the whole income must necessarily be available. The trustees must not be put under pressure in exercising their discretion, and the father, while he should not be asked to pay more than he could reasonably afford, should not at the same time be able to regard the trust as a windfall for him, when it was intended for the children's benefit throughout their lives.

Commentary
For the position of a non-discretionary trust and Social Security entitlements, see *Peters* v *Chief Adjudication Officer* in Chapter 16.

Kayford Ltd, Re [1975] 1 WLR 279 Chancery Division (Megarry J)

Certainty of intention

Facts
A mail order company which was in financial difficulties took professional advice as to how it could protect customers' moneys sent to purchase goods in case it became insolvent. Following the advice given, the company designated a separate bank account called Customers' Trust Deposit Account in which all moneys received from customers were paid pending delivery of the goods, so that if the company went into liquidation the money could be returned to the customers. Subsequently, the company went into liquidation and the question arose whether the moneys in the account were held on trust for the customers or formed part of the general assets of the company.

Held
A trust for the customers had been created. All the requirements for a valid trust of personalty were present and the company had shown a clear intention to create a trust in its efforts to ensure that the moneys sent remained in the beneficial ownership of those who sent them.

Megarry J:

> 'The property concerned is pure personalty, and writing, though desirable, is not an essential. There is no doubt about the so-called three certainties of a trust. The subject-matter to be held on trust is clear and so are the beneficial interests therein, as well as the beneficiaries. As for the requisite certainty of words, it is well settled that a trust can be created without using the words "trust" or "confidence" or the like: the question is whether in substance a sufficient intention to create a trust has been manifested.'

Knight v *Knight* (1840) 3 Beav 148 Rolls Court (Lord Langdale MR)

The three certainties

Facts
A who died in 1824 left all his estates real and personal to his brother, Thomas Andrew Knight, and failing him to his nephew, Thomas Andrew Knight the younger. The will stated: 'I do hereby constitute and appoint the person who shall inherit my said estates under this my will my sole executor and trustee, to carry the same and everything contained therein duly into execution; confiding in the approved honour and integrity of my family, to take no advantage of any technical inaccuracies, but to admit all the comparatively small reservations which I make out of so large a property ...'

The will stated that the testator's intention was that the estates should be settled on the next descendant in the direct male line of the testator's grandfather, Richard Knight of Downton. On the testator's death Thomas Andrew Knight, the testator's brother, succeeded to the estates. In 1827 Thomas Andrew Knight the younger died childless, intestate, and the testator's brother immediately settled the estates upon persons who were not the next descendants in the direct male line of Richard Knight of Downton. The question arose whether the testator had imposed a binding trust on his brother.

Held
The words which the testator had used in his will were not sufficiently imperative to create a trust which was binding.

Lord Langdale MR:

'... it is not every wish or expectation a testator may express nor every act which he may wish his successors to do, that can or ought to be executed or enforced as a trust in this Court; and in the infinite variety of expressions which are employed, and of the cases which thereupon arise, there is often the greatest difficulty in determining whether the act desired or recommended is an act which the testator intended to be executed as a trust, or which this Court ought to deem fit to be, or capable of being enforced as such ...

As a general rule, it has been laid down, that when property is given absolutely to any person, and the same person is, by the giver who has power to command, recommended or entreated, or wished, to dispose of that property in favour of another, the recommendation, entreaty, or wish shall be held to create a trust.

First, if the words were so used, that upon the whole, they ought to be construed as imperative;

Secondly, if the subject of the recommendation or wish be certain; and

Thirdly, if the objects or persons intended to have the benefit of the recommendation or wish be also certain.

In simple cases there is no difficulty in the application of the rule thus stated.

If a testator gives £1,000 to AB, desiring, wishing or recommending or hoping that AB will, at his death, give the same sum or any certain part of it to CD, it is considered that CD is an object of the testator's bounty, and AB is a trustee for him. No question arises upon the intention of the testator, upon the sum or subject intended to be given, or upon the person or object of the wish.

So, if a testator gives the residue of his estate, after certain purposes are answered, to AB, recommending AB, after his death, to give it to his own relations, or such of his own relations as he shall think most deserving, or as he shall choose, it has been considered that the residue of the property, though a subject to be ascertained, and that the relations to be selected, though persons or objects to be ascertained, are nevertheless so clearly and certainly ascertainable – so capable of being made certain – that the rule is applicable to such cases.

On the other hand, if the giver accompanies his expression of wish, or request by other words, from which it is to be collected, that he did not intend the wish to be imperative: or if it appears from the context that the first taker was intended to have a discretionary power to withdraw any part of the subject from the object of the wish or request; or if the objects are not such as may be ascertained with sufficient certainty, it has been held that no trust is created.'

Lambe v *Eames* (1871) 6 Ch App 597 Court of Appeal in Chancery (James and Mellish LJJ)

Precatory words

Facts
The testator left his estate to his widow 'to be at her disposal in any way she may think best, for the benefit of herself and her family'.

Held
The words did not create a precatory trust. The will made an absolute gift of the estate to the widow. Older cases which strove to create trusts were deprecated by Lord Justice James:

> 'In hearing case after case cited, I could not help feeling that the officious kindness of the Court of Chancery in interposing trusts where in many cases the father of the family never meant to create trusts, must have been a very cruel kindness indeed.'

McPhail v *Doulton* [1971] AC 424 House of Lords (Viscount Dilhorne, Lord Reid, Lord Hodson, Lord Guest and Lord Wilberforce)

Certainty of objects: discretionary trusts and powers

Facts
Under a trust deed dated 17 July 1941, Bertram Baden established a fund for the benefit of the staff of Matthew Hall & Co Ltd. In 1960 he died and the executors of his estate claimed that the trust deed was invalid for uncertainty of objects. Clause 9(a) of the trust deed stated:

> 9(a) 'The Trustees shall apply the net income of the Fund in making at their absolute discretion grants to or for the benefit of any of the officers and employees or ex-officers or ex-employees of the company or to any relatives or dependents of any such persons in such amounts at such times and on such conditions (if any) as they think fit and any such grant may at their discretion be made by payment to the beneficiary or to any institution or person to be applied for his or her benefit and in the latter case, the Trustees shall be under no obligation to see to the application of the money.'

It was contended by the executors of the estate that clause 9(a) constituted a trust and not a power and that following the Court of Appeal decision in *IRC* v *Broadway Cottages Trust* [1955] Ch 20, the trust was not valid because it was not possible to draw up a complete list of all the possible beneficiaries, as that decision required. The trustees of the fund argued that *IRC* v *Broadway Cottages Trust* ought to be overruled and a new test of certainty of objects laid down.

Held
1. Clause 9(a) was a trust power and accordingly took effect as a trust. The language used in the deed was mandatory; the word 'shall' combined with a power of selection created a trust for the distribution of income.
2. The test of certainty of objects to be applied was similar to that in powers. If it can be said with certainty whether any given individual is or is not a member of the class, then the trust will not fail merely because it is impossible to ascertain every member of the class.

Lord Wilberforce:

'... Before dealing with these two questions some general observations, or reflections, may be permissible. It is striking how narrow and in a sense artificial is the distinction, in cases such as the present, between trusts or as the particular type of trust is called, trust powers, and powers. It is only necessary to read the learned judgments in the Court of Appeal to see that what to one mind may appear as a power of distribution coupled with a trust to dispose of the undistributed surplus, by accumulation or otherwise, may to another appear as a trust for distribution coupled with a power to withhold a portion and accumulate or otherwise dispose of it. A layman, and I suspect also a logician, would find it hard to understand what difference there is.

It does not seem satisfactory that the entire validity of a disposition should depend on such delicate shading. And if one considers how in practice reasonable and competent trustees would act, and ought to act, in the two cases, surely a matter very relevant to the question of validity, the distinction appears even less significant. To say that there is no obligation to exercise a mere power and that no court will intervene to compel it, whereas a trust is mandatory and its execution may be compelled, may be legally correct enough but the proposition does not contain an exhaustive comparison of the duties of persons who are trustees in the two cases. A trustee of an employees' benefit fund, whether given a power or a trust power, is still a trustee and he would surely consider in either case that he has a fiduciary duty; he is most likely to have been selected as a suitable person to administer it from his knowledge and experience, and would consider he has a responsibility to do so according to its purpose. It would be a complete misdescription of his position to say that, if what he has is a power unaccompanied by an imperative trust to distribute, he cannot be controlled by the court unless he exercised it capriciously, or outside the field permitted by the trust (cf. *Farwell on Powers*, 3rd ed p524). Any trustee would surely make it his duty to know what is the permissible area of selection and then consider responsibly, in individual cases, whether a contemplated beneficiary was within the power and whether, in relation to other possible claimants, a particular grant was appropriate.

Correspondingly a trustee with a duty to distribute, particularly among a potentially very large class, would surely never require the preparation of a complete list of names, which anyhow would tell him little that he needs to know. He would examine the field, by class and category; might indeed make diligent and careful inquiries, depending on how much money he had to give away and the means at his disposal, as to the composition and needs of particular categories and of individuals within them; decide upon certain priorities or proportions, and then select individuals according to their needs or qualifications. If he acts in this manner, can it really be said that he is not carrying out the trust?

Differences there certainly are between trust (trust powers) and powers, but as regards validity, should they be so great as that in one case complete, or practically complete, ascertainment is needed, but not in the other? Such distinction as there is would seem to lie in the extent of the survey which the trustee is required to carry out: if he has to distribute the whole of a fund's income, he must necessarily make a wider and more systematic survey than if his duty is expressed in terms of a power to make grants. But just as, in the case of a power, it is possible to underestimate the fiduciary obligation of the trustee to whom it is given, so, in the case of a trust (trust power), the danger lies in overstating what the trustee requires to know or to inquire into before he can properly execute his trust. The difference may be one of degree rather than of principle: in the well-known words of Sir George Farwell, *Farwell on Powers*, 3rd ed (1916) p10, trusts and powers are often blended, and the mixture may vary in its ingredients.

With this background I now consider whether the provisions of clause 9(a) constitute a trust or a power. I do so briefly because this is not a matter on which I or, I understand, any of your Lordships have any doubt. Indeed, a reading of the judgments of Goff J and of the majority in the Court of Appeal leave the strong impression that, if it had not been for their leaning in favour of possible validity and the state of the authorities, these learned judges would have found in favour of a trust. Naturally read, the intention of the deed seems to me clear: clause 9(a), whose language is mandatory ("shall"), creates, together with a power of selection, a trust for distribution of the income, the strictness of which is qualified by clause 9(b), which allows the income of any one year to be held up and (under clause 6(a) either placed, for the time, with a bank, or, if thought fit, invested … I therefore agree with Russell LJ and would to that extent allow the appeal, declare that the provisions of clause 9(a) constitute a trust and remit the case to the Chancery Division for determination whether on this basis clause 9 is (subject to the effects of section 164 of the Law of Property Act, 1925) valid or void for uncertainty.

This makes it necessary to consider whether, in so doing, the court should proceed on the basis that the relevant test is that laid down in *Inland Revenue Commissioners* v *Broadway Cottages Trust* or some other test.

That decision gave the authority of the Court of Appeal to the distinction between cases where trustees are given a power of selection and those where they are bound by a trust for selection. In the former case the position, as decided by this House, is that the power is valid if it can be said with certainty whether any given individual is or is not a member of the class and does not fail simply because it is impossible to ascertain every member of the class (*In re Gulbenkian's Settlements*) [1970] AC 58. But in the latter case it is said to be necessary, for the trust to be valid, that the whole range of objects (I use the language of the Court of Appeal) should be ascertained or capable of ascertainment.

The respondents invited your Lordships to assimilate the validity test for trusts to that which applies to powers. Alternatively they contended that in any event the test laid down in the *Broadway Cottages* case was too rigid, and that a trust should be upheld if there is sufficient practical certainty in its definition for it to be carried out, if necessary with the administrative assistance of the court, according to the expressed intention of the settlor. I would agree with this, but this does not dispense from examination of the wider argument. The basis for the *Broadway Cottages* principle is stated to be that a trust cannot be valid unless, if need be, it can be executed by the court, and (though it is not quite clear from the judgment where argument ends and decision begins) that the court can only execute it by ordering an equal distribution in which every beneficiary shares. So it is necessary to examine the authority and reason for this supposed rule as to the execution of trusts by the court.

Assuming, as I am prepared to do for present purposes, that the test of validity is whether the trust can be executed by the court, it does not follow that execution is impossible unless there can be equal division.

As a matter of reason, to hold that a principle of equal division applies to trusts such as the present is certainly paradoxical. Equal division is surely the last thing the settlor ever intended: equal division among all may, probably would, produce a result beneficial to none. Why suppose that the court would lend itself to a whimsical execution? And as regards authority, I do not find that the nature of the trust, and of the court's powers over trusts, calls for any such rigid rule. Equal division may be sensible and has been decreed, in cases of family trusts, for a limited class; here there is life in the maxim 'equality is equity,' but the cases provide numerous examples where this has not been so, and a different type of execution has been ordered, appropriate to the circumstances.'

His Lordship examined several of the early authorities and continued:

'I now consider the modern English authorities, particularly those relied on to show that complete ascertainment of the class must be possible before it can be said that a discretionary trust is valid.

In *Re HJ Ogden* [1933] Ch 678 is not a case which I find of great assistance. The argument seems to have turned mainly on the question whether the trust was a purpose trust or a trust for ascertained objects. The latter was held to be the case and the court then held that all the objects of the discretionary gift could be ascertained. It is weak authority for the requirement of complete ascertainment.

The modern shape of the rule derives from *In re Gestetner's Settlement* [1953] Ch 672 where the judgment of Harman J, to his later regret, established the distinction between discretionary powers and discretionary trusts. The focus of this case was upon powers. The judgment first establishes a distinction between, on the one hand, a power collateral, or appurtenant, or other powers "which do not impose a trust on the conscience of the donee" (at p684), and on the other hand a trust imposing a duty to distribute. As to the first, the learned judge said (ibid): "I do not think it can be the law that it is necessary to know of all the objects in order to appoint to one of them." As to the latter he uses these words (at p685): "it seems to me there is much to be said for the view that he must be able to review the whole field in order to exercise his judgment properly." He then considers authority on the validity of powers, the main stumbling-block in the way of his own view being some words used by Fry J in *Blight* v *Hartnoll* (1881) 19 Ch D 294, which had been adversely commented on in *Farwell on Powers* (3rd ed at pp168, 169), and I think it worth while quoting the words of his conclusion. He says:

> "The settlor had good reason, I have no doubt, to trust the persons whom he appointed trustees; but I cannot see here that there is such a duty as makes it essential for these trustees, before parting with any income or capital, to survey the whole field, and to consider whether A is more deserving to bounty than B. That is a task which was and which must have been known to the settlor to be impossible, having regard to the ramification of the persons who might become members of this class.
>
> If, therefore, there be no duty to distribute, but only a duty to consider, it does not seem to me that there is any authority binding on me to say that this whole trust is bad. In fact, there is no difficulty, as has been admitted, in ascertaining whether any given postulant is a member of the specified class. Of course, if that could not be ascertained the matter would be quite different, but of John Doe or Richard Roe it can be postulated easily enough whether he is or is not eligible to receive the settlor's bounty. There being no uncertainty in that sense, I am reluctant to introduce a notion of uncertainty in the other sense, by saying that the trustees must worry their heads to survey the world from China to Peru, when there are perfectly good objects of the class in England."

Subject to one point which was cleared up in this House in *In re Gulbenkian's Settlements* all of this, if I may say so, seems impeccably good sense, and I do not understand the learned judge to have later repented of it. If the judgment was in any way the cause of future difficulties, it was in the indication given – not by way of decision, for the point did not arise – that there was a distinction between the kind of certainty required for powers and that required for trust. There is a difference perhaps but the difference is a narrow one, and if one is looking to reality one could hardly find better words than those I have just quoted to describe what trustees, in either case, ought to know. A second look at this case, while fully justifying the decision, suggests to me that it does not discourage the application of a similar test for the validity of trusts.

So I come to *Inland Revenue Commissioners* v *Broadway Cottages Trust*. This was certainly a case of trust, and it proceeded on the basis of an admission, in the words of the judgment, "that the class of 'beneficiaries' is incapable of ascertainment". In addition to the discretionary trust of income, there was a trust of capital for all the beneficiaries living or existing at the terminal date. This necessarily involved equal division and it seems to have been accepted that it was void for uncertainty since there cannot be equal division among a class unless all the members of the class are known. The Court of Appeal applied this proposition to the discretionary trust of income, on the basis that execution by the court was only possible on the same basis of equal division. They rejected the argument that the trust could be executed by changing the trusteeship, and found the relations cases of no assistance as being in a class by themselves. The court could not create an arbitrarily restricted trust to take effect in default of distribution by the trustees. Finally they rejected the submission that the trust could take effect as a power: a valid power could not be spelt out of an invalid trust.

My Lords, it will have become apparent that there is much in this which I find out of line with principle and authority but before I come to a conclusion on it, I must examine the decision of this House in *In re Gulbenkian's Settlements* on which the appellants placed much reliance as amounting to an endorsement of the *Broadway Cottages* case. But is this really so? That case was concerned with a power of appointment coupled with a gift over in default of appointment. The possible objects of the power were numerous and were defined in such wide terms that it could certainly be said that the class was unascertainable. The decision of this House was that the power was valid if it could be said with certainty whether any given individual was or was not a member of the class, and did not fail simply because it was impossible to ascertain every member of the class. In so deciding, their Lordships rejected an alternative submission, to which countenance had been given in the Court of Appeal, that it was enough that one person should certainly be within the class. So as a matter of decision, the question now before us did not arise or nearly arise. However, the opinions given were relied on, and strongly, as amounting to an endorsement of the "complete ascertainment" test as laid down in the *Broadway Cottages* case ...'

His Lordship reviewed the *Re Gulbenkian* decision and the discussion therein of the *Broadway Cottages* case and continued:

'... So I think that we are free to review the *Broadway Cottages* case. The conclusion which I would reach, implicit in the previous discussion, is that the wide distinction between the validity test for powers and that for trust powers is unfortunate and wrong, that the rule recently fastened upon the courts by *Inland Revenue Commissioners* v *Broadway Cottages Trust* ought to be discarded, and that the test for the validity of trust powers ought to be similar to that accepted by this House in *In re Gulbenkian's Settlements* for powers, namely, that the trust is valid if it can be said with certainty that any given individual is or is not a member of the class ...

... Assimilation of the validity test does not involve the complete assimilation of trust powers with powers. As to powers, I agree with my noble and learned friend Lord Upjohn in *In re Gulbenkian's Settlements* that although the trustees may, and normally will, be under a fiduciary duty to consider whether or in what way they should exercise their power, the court will not normally compel its exercise. It will intervene if the trustees exceed their powers, and possibly if they are proved to have exercised it capriciously. But in the case of a trust power, if the trustees do not exercise it, the court will; I respectfully adopt as to this the statement in Lord Upjohn's opinion. I would venture to amplify this by saying that the court, if called upon to execute the trust power, will do so in the manner best calculated to give effect to the settlor's or testator's intentions. It may do so by appointing new trustees, or by authorising or directing representative persons of the classes of beneficiaries to prepare a scheme of distribution, or even, should the proper basis for distribution appear by itself, directing the trustees so to distribute. The books give many instances where this has been done, and I see no reason in principle why they should not do so in the modern field of discretionary trusts (see *Brunsden* v *Woolredge* (1765) Amb 507, *Supple* v *Lowson* (1773) Amb 729, *Liley* v *Hey* (1842) I Hare 580 and *Lewin on Trusts*, 16th ed (1964) p630). Then, as to the trustees' duty of inquiry or ascertainment, in each case the trustees ought to make such a survey of the range of objects or possible beneficiaries as will enable them to carry out their fiduciary duty (cf *Liley* v *Hey*). A wider and more comprehensive range of inquiry is called for in the case of trust powers than in the case of powers.

Two final points: first, as to the question of certainty. I desire to emphasise the distinction clearly made and explained by Lord Upjohn between linguistic or semantic uncertainty which, if unresolved by the court, renders the gift void, and the difficulty of ascertaining the existence or whereabouts of members of the class, a matter with which the court can appropriately deal on an application for directions. There may be a third case where the meaning of the words used is clear but the definition of beneficiaries is so hopelessly wide as not to form "anything like a class" so that the trust is administratively unworkable or in Lord Eldon's words one that cannot be executed (*Morice* v *Bishop of Durham* (1805) 10 Ves 522). I hesitate to give examples for they may prejudice future cases, but perhaps "all the residents of Greater London" will serve. I do not think that a discretionary trust for "relatives" even of a living person falls within this category.

I would allow the appeal.'

Commentary
See also *Re Baden's Deed Trusts (No 2)* (above).

Manisty's Settlement, Re [1974] Ch 17 Chancery Division (Templeman J)
Certainty of objects

Facts
The trustees were given a power to include any person, corporation or charity in the class of beneficiaries

under the settlement other than members of an 'excepted class'. The trustees purported to add the mother of the settlor and any widow he might leave.

Held
This power was valid, observing: 'The mere width of a power cannot make it impossible for the trustees to perform their duty or prevent the court from determining whether the trustees are in breach ...'

Mettoy Pension Trustees Ltd v *Evans and Others* [1990] 1 WLR 1587 Chancery Division (Warner J)

Exercise of fiduciary powers: the court's role

Facts
A company pension scheme conferred benefit on company pensioners at the absolute discretion of company (the employer). A surplus existed on the company being wound up.
    The trustee issued a summons requesting directions for the distribution of the surplus.

Held
The discretion conferred on the company was a 'fiduciary power'. It was not a company asset and therefore did not rest in the company liquidator. Because the company (trustee) no longer existed, the court would step in to decide on an appropriate exercise of discretion.

Warner J:

> 'A power in this category cannot be released; the donee of it owes a duty to the objects of the power to consider it, as and when may be appropriate, whether and if so, how he ought to exercise it ...'

Morice v *Bishop of Durham* (1805) 10 Ves 522 Lord Chancellor's Court (Lord Eldon LC)

Certainty of objects

Facts
It concerned a gift upon trust for 'such objects of benevolence and liberality as the Bishop of Durham shall most approve of'.

Held
The trust failed because there were no ascertainable beneficiaries.

Lord Eldon LC:

> 'As it is a maxim, that the execution of a trust shall be under the control of the court; it must be of such a nature, that it can be under such control; so that the administration of it can be reviewed by the court; or, if the trustee dies, the court itself can execute the trust: a trust therefore, which in case of maladministration could be reformed; and a due administration directed; and then, unless the subject and the objects can be ascertained, upon principles, familiar in other cases, it must be decided, that the court can neither reform maladministration, nor direct a due administration.'

Palmer v *Simmonds* (1854) 2 Drew 221 Vice-Chancellor's Court (Kindersley V-C)

Certainty of subject matter

Facts

A testatrix left her residuary estate to A 'for his own use and benefit, as I have full confidence in him that if he should die without lawful issue he will, after providing for his widow during her life, leave the bulk of my said residuary estate units …' to certain named beneficiaries equally. One of the questions which arose after A's death whether there was a good trust in favour of the named beneficiaries who took after A's death.

Held

As the subject-matter of the trust was not clearly designated no trust had been created and A took the property absolutely.

Kindersley V-C:

'… But when we come to the clause in question, we find her using this language: she expresses her confidence that Harrison will give "the bulk of my said residuary estate". Now what she there meant could not be her residuary estate, which she had already in clear terms given; but the bulk of it. Then it is said that word is to be construed by the clause for providing for the widow; and that what is intended is to give a power to make provision for the widow, and then the bulk means what remains; or else that it means a provision for the widow for life out of the income, and then the word bulk means the corpus of the estate. But the answer is that, as to either of these constructions, the term bulk is not appropriate. No such term is used by the testatrix when giving capital as distinguished from income; nor is the term appropriate to express what remains after Harrison shall have exhausted some of the capital. What is the meaning then of bulk? The appropriate meaning, according to its derivation, is something which bulges out, etc. (His Lordship referred to Todd's Johnson and Richardson's Dictionary for the different meanings and etymology of the word.) Its popular meaning we all know. When a person is said to have given the bulk of his property, what is meant is not the whole but the greater part, and that is in fact consistent with its classical meaning. When, therefore, the testatrix uses that term, can I say she has used a term expressing a definite, clear, certain part of her estate, or the whole of her estate? I am bound to say she has not designated the subject as to which she expresses her confidence; and I am therefore of opinion that there is no trust created; that Harrison took absolutely, and those claiming under him now take.'

Saunders v *Vautier* (1841) 4 Beav 115 Rolls Court (Lord Langdale MR)

Nature of the beneficiary's interest: transfer to beneficiary

Facts

The testator left stock on trust to accumulate the income until a sole beneficiary should reach the age of 25, and then transfer to him the stock and accumulated income. When the beneficiary was 21 he claimed to have the fund transferred to him.

Held

The beneficiary was entitled to have the fund transferred to him.

Lord Langdale MR:

'I think that principle has been repeatedly acted upon; and where a legacy is directed to accumulate for a certain period, or where the payment is postponed, the legatee, if he has an absolute indefeasible interest in the legacy, is not bound to wait until the expiration of that period, but may require payment the moment he is competent to give a valid discharge.'

Sayer's Trust, Re [1957] Ch 423 Chancery Division (Upjohn J)

Discretionary powers and trusts

Facts
Trustees were given power to distribute among employees, ex-employees, their widows, children and dependants.

Held
Applying the test in *Re Gestetner* (supra) the eligibility of any given candidate could be ascertained (ie by establishing a 'list') and therefore this was a valid power.

Sprange v *Barnard* (1789) 2 Bro CC 585 Rolls Court (Sir R P Arden MR)

Certainty of subject matter

Facts
A testatrix left her husband £300 for his sole use 'and, at his death, the remaining part of what is left, and he does not want for his own wants and use, to be divided between my brother John Crapps, my sister Wickenden and my sister Banden, to be equally divided between them'.

Held
No trust was created because there could be no certainty as to what would be left at the husband's death and therefore he took the £300 absolutely.

Sir R P Arden MR:

> 'It is contended, for the persons to whom it is given, in remainder, that he shall only have it for his life, and that the words are strictly mandatory on him to dispose of it in a certain way; but is only to dispose of what he has no occasion for: therefore the question is whether he may not call for the whole; and it seems to be perfectly clear on all the authorities that he may. I agree with the doctrine in *Pierson* v *Garnet* (1787) 2 Bro CC 226, following the cases of *Harland* v *Trigg* (1782) 1 Bro CC 142 and *Wynne* v *Hawkins* (1782) 1 Bro CC 179, that the property and the person to whom it is to be given, must be certain in order to raise a trust. Now here the property is wasting, as it is only what shall remain at his death.'

Steele's Will Trust, Re [1948] Ch 603 Chancery Division (Wynn-Parry J)

Precatory words

Facts
The testator had used exactly the same formulation which had in a former case been held to create a precatory trust.

Held
Despite the generally accepted modern rule that each instrument would be construed according to its

apparent intention, where a form of words was used which had been upheld as a trust in an earlier case, they would continue to be so held.

Tuck's Settlement Trusts, Re [1978] Ch 49 Court of Appeal (Lord Denning MR, Killowen and Eveleigh LJJ)

Condition precedent and certainty of objects

Facts
Trustees were given discretionary power to make gifts to members of the settlor's family, provided each married a woman of Jewish blood and faith.

Held
These were valid individual gifts subject to a condition precedent.

2 Formal Requirements for Creating a Trust

Commissioner of Stamp Duties (Queensland) v *Livingston* [1965] AC 694 Privy Council (Viscount Radcliffe, Lord Evershed, Lord Pearce, Lord Reid and Lord Upjohn)

Time of commencement of beneficial interest

Facts
A testator, domiciled in New South Wales, bequeathed his real and personal property to his executors and trustees, with one third of his estate to be held on trust for his widow absolutely. The widow subsequently died before the testator's estate had been administered. The Commissioner of Stamp Duties then sought to levy succession duty on the widow's beneficial interest, under the testators trust, against the widow's own administrator, alternatively her next-of-kin entitled to the trust property.

Held
Until the testator's estate is fully administered the residuary legatee or next of kin are not beneficial owners of the unadministered assets in the hands of the personal representatives. Therefore no succession duty could be levied.

Grey v *Inland Revenue Commissioners* [1960] AC 1 House of Lords (Viscount Simonds, Lord Radcliffe, Lord Cohen, Lord Keith and Lord Reid)

Formal requirements

Facts
The Stamp Act 1891, s54, imposes stamp duty on instruments 'whereby any property, or any estate or interest in any property, upon the sale thereof is transferred to or vested in a purchaser, or any other person on his behalf or by his direction'. Thus, stamp duty is imposed on the instrument and not the transfer made thereunder and the amount of duty payable is related to the value of the beneficial interest transferred. In order to avoid paying stamp duty, settlors often made transfers of beneficial interests without using an instrument. In this case, a settlor had transferred property to trusts on trust for his grandchildren in 1949. In 1955 he transferred 18,000 £1 shares to the same trustees to hold as nominees for himself on six bare settlements he had previously created. Subsequently, he orally directed the trustees to hold the shares in the six settlements for his grandchildren thus having avoided stamp duty.

The trustees, at a later date, executed deeds declaring that they held the property on trust for the grandchildren and the settlor also executed them to confirm his oral instructions. The Revenue challenged this procedure and claimed stamp duty was payable on the deeds of declaration because LPA s53(1)(c) required the disposition of an equitable interest to be in writing and there had been no effective disposition of the settlor's interest in the shares until the deeds had been executed.

Held

The settlor's oral instructions to the trustees were a 'disposition' of his equitable interest in the shares to the trustees. However, since they were not in writing they were ineffective. This defect had been rectified by the subsequent deed and stamp duty was therefore payable. 'Disposition' in s53(1)(c) should be given a wide definition to cover every method by which a beneficial interest in a settlor was transferred.

Jones v *Lock* (1865) 1 Ch App 25 Court of Appeal in Chancery (Lord Cranworth LC)

Formal requirements: incompletely constituted trust

Facts

Mr Jones on returning home from a business trip to Birmingham, was scolded for not having brought back anything for his baby son. He went upstairs and came down with a cheque made out in his own name for £900 and said, in the presence of his wife and nurse: 'Look you here, I give this to baby', and he then placed the cheque in baby's hand. It was obvious that he was intending to make a gift of the cheque to the baby but such gift was not effective because it was in his name and had not been endorsed over to the baby. Other evidence showed that he went to see his solicitor, Mr Lock, to make provision for the baby boy, but he died before he could do so. It was argued that the existence of a trust could be inferred from Mr Jones' conduct.

Held

No valid declaration of trust could be inferred from Mr Jones' actions or words.

Lord Cranworth LC:

> '... The case turns on a very short question whether Jones intended to make a declaration that he held the property in trust for the child; and I cannot come to any other conclusion than that he did not. I think it would be of very dangerous example if loose conversations of this sort, in important transactions of this kind, should have the effect of declarations of trust ...'

Kayford, Re

See Chapter 1.

Lysaght v *Edwards*

See Chapter 6.

Oughtred v *Inland Revenue Commissioners* [1960] AC 206 House of Lords (Viscount Radcliffe, Lord Cohen, Lord Keith, Lord Denning and Lord Jenkins)

Formal requirements

Facts

A mother owned 72,700 shares in a company absolutely, and, was also tenant for life of another 200,000 shares in the same company under a settlement with her son entitled in remainder. In 1956, in order to save estate duty on the mother's death, the mother and son agreed orally that the son should transfer his remainder interest to the mother in exchange for her 72,700 shares. A deed of release was executed, between the mother, the son and the trustees of the settlement which stated that the 200,000 shares were to be held on trust for the mother. Deeds were also executed: (i) by the trustees transferring the 200,000 shares to the mother; and (ii) by the mother transferring the 72,700 shares to the son. The Revenue claimed that these transfers were 'a conveyance or transfer on sale of any property' under the Stamp Act 1891 and so attracted ad valorem stamp duty on the value of the consideration. As a test case, they challenged the transfer to the mother. It was argued that there was no conveyance or transfer because the mother was already the owner of the shares in equity from the date of the oral agreement to transfer by virtue of her right to enforce that agreement and that the deed was only a formal transfer of a bare legal estate. The Revenue met this argument by reference to s53(1)(c) saying that as the agreement was oral, there was no effective disposition of the son's equitable interest in the shares at the time it was made; this remained in the son until he executed the deed of transfer.

Held
The position was similar to a contract for the purchase of land and the deed was merely completion of the oral contract and stamp duty was chargeable.

Lord Jenkins:

'This interest under the contract is no doubt a proprietary interest of a sort, which arises, so to speak, in anticipation of the execution of the transfer for which the purchaser is entitled to call. But its existence has never (so far as I know) been held to prevent a subsequent transfer, in performance of the contract, of the property contracted to be sold from constituting for stamp duty purposes a transfer on sale of the property in question. Take the simple case of a contract for the sale of land. In such a case, a constructive trust in favour of the purchaser arises on the conclusion of the contract for sale but (so far as I know) it has never been held on this account that a conveyance subsequently executed in performance of the contract is not stampable ad valorem as a transfer on sale.'

It was also argued on behalf of the mother that there was a constructive trust in her favour after Peter (the son) orally agreed to transfer the shares to her, thus making the trust exempt from s53(1)(c) by virtue of s53(1)(c). Lord Denning said: 'I do not think the oral agreement was effective to transfer Peter's reversionary interest to his mother. I should have thought that the wording of s53(1)(c) clearly made writing necessary to effect a transfer and s53(2) does not do away with that necessity.' The other two law lords, Lords Jenkins and Keith, found it unnecessary to decide this point.

Vandervell v *Inland Revenue Commissioners* [1967] AC 291 House of Lords (Lord Reid, Lord Pearce, Lord Upjohn, Lord Donovan and Lord Wilberforce)

Formal requirements

Facts
Vandervell directed trustees who held some shares on trust for him to transfer them to the Royal College of Surgeons to found a chair of pharmacology. As part of this arrangement, he also gave a family trust an option to purchase the shares from the College for £5,000 in five years time. The family trust exercised the option to purchase. The question arose as to whether Vandervell had divested himself of all his interest in the shares as this was material in deciding if he was liable to pay surtax on the income of the shares. One argument put forward by the Revenue was that the trustees had only conveyed the legal interest in the shares to the College and that the equitable interest was still vested in Vandervell because there was no writing, as required under s53(1)(c), disposing of the equitable interest.

Held
Section 53(1)(c) did not apply. The equitable interest had passed with the legal interest, for the transfer

of the greater includes the less; where it is the intention that the legal estate should carry the beneficial ownership of the property, there is no need for any further documents.

Lord Upjohn:

'... The object of the section, as was the object of the old Statute of Frauds, is to prevent hidden oral transactions in equitable interests in fraud of those truly entitled, and making it difficult, if not impossible, for the trustees to ascertain who are in truth the beneficiaries. When the beneficial owner, however, owns the whole beneficial estate and is in a position to give directions to his bare trustee with regard to the legal as well as the equitable estate there can be no possible ground for invoking the section where the beneficial owner wants to deal with the legal estate as well as the equitable estate.

I cannot agree with Diplock LJ that prima facie a transfer of the legal estate carries with it the absolute beneficial interest in the property transferred; this plainly is not so, eg the transfer may be on a change of trustee; it is a matter of intention in each case. If, however, the intention of the beneficial owner in directing the trustee to transfer the legal estate to X is that X should be the beneficial owner, I can see no reason for any further document or further words in the document assigning the legal estate also expressly transferring the beneficial interest; the greater includes the less. X may be wise to secure some evidence that the beneficial owner intended him to take the beneficial interest in case his beneficial title is challenged at a later date but it certainly cannot, in my opinion, be a statutory requirement that to effect its passing there must be some writing under s53(1)(c) ...

Counsel for the Crown admitted that where the legal and beneficial estate was vested in the legal owner and he desired to transfer the whole legal and beneficial estate to another he did not have to do more than transfer the legal estates and he did not have to comply with s53(1)(c); and I can see no difference between that case and this ...

As I have said, that section is, in my opinion, directed to cases where dealings with the equitable estate are divorced from the legal estate and I do not think any of their Lordships in *Grey* v *IRC* [1960] AC 1 and *Oughtred* v *IRC* [1960] AC 206 had in mind the case before your Lordships.

To hold the contrary would make assignments unnecessarily complicated; if there had to be assignments in express terms of both legal and equitable interests that would make the section more productive of injustice than the supposed evils it is intended to prevent.'

Lord Donovan:

'If owning the entire estate, legal and beneficial, in a piece of property, and desiring to transfer that entire estate to another, I do so by means of a disposition which ex facie deals only with the legal estate, it would be ridiculous to argue that s53(1)(c) has not been complied with, and that therefore the legal estate alone had passed. The present case, it is true, is different in its facts in that the legal and equitable estates in the shares were in separate ownership; but when the taxpayer, being competent to do so, instructed the bank to transfer the shares to the College, and made it abundantly clear that he wanted to pass, by means of that transfer, his own beneficial or equitable interest, plus the bank's legal interest, he achieved the same result as if there had been no separation of interests. The transfer thus made pursuant to his intentions and instructions was a disposition, not of the equitable interest alone, but of the entire estate in the shares. In such a case, I see no room for the operation of s53(1)(c).'

3 Completely and Incompletely Constituted Trusts

Beaumont, Re [1902] 1 Ch 889 Chancery Division (Buckley J)

What may be the subject of a donatio mortis causa

Facts
Beaumont was terminally ill and drew a cheque for £300 in favour of E. E then presented it at B's bank who refused to honour it as B's bank account was overdrawn. However (as held by the Court), the bank's main concern was concerning the signature on the cheque which the bank questioned the genuine nature of. E re-presented the cheque to the bank some days later but after B had died.

Held
Under the rule in *Veal* v *Veal* (1859) 27 Beav 303 (relied on in *Re Dillon* (1890) 44 Ch D 76), promissory notes and cheques drawn on a third party's bank account are capable of passing as donatio mortis causa, but this does not apply to a cheque drawn by the donor on his own bank account, because it does not constitute property in itself but is merely an instruction to the donor's bank which is revoked on his death.

Commentary
Note, however, that this does not apply if the donee receives payment or negotiates the cheque in the donor' lifetime, see *Re While* [1928] WN 182.

Birch v *Treasury Solicitor* [1951] Ch 298 Chancery Division (Wynn-Parry J)

Donatio mortis causa: what can pass title

Facts
A donor who was dying gave the plaintiffs: (i) a Post Office Savings Book; (ii) a London Trustee Savings Bank Book; (iii) a Barclays Bank deposit pass book; and (iv) a Westminster Bank deposit account book saying, 'I want you to take them home and keep them and if anything happens to me I want you and Frank to have the money in the banks.'

The donor died shortly afterwards. The question arose whether there was a valid donatio mortis causa of the bank books other than the Post Office Savings Book (that having been decided in the affirmative in *Re Weston* [1902] 1 Ch 680.

Held
The books were evidence or indicia of title and a gift of them was a donatio mortis causa of the money in the banks. This was because there could be a donatio mortis causa of property other than such as was capable only of manual delivery. The test in cases of property not capable of manual delivery is whether

the delivery of the document giving title to the property expresses terms on which the subject-matter is held or the terms under which it came into existence.

Bowden, Re [1936] Ch 71 Chancery Division (Bennett J)

Completely constituted trust: transfer of property

Facts

The settlor became a nun and purported to transfer to trustees any property to be left to her on her father's death. The property was duly and properly settled. Many years later she asked the trustees to transfer the property back to her as sole beneficial owner, as the settlement was voluntary.

Held

Declaration in favour of the trustees.

Bennett J:

> 'Counsel for the settlor submitted ... that the property the subject of the trusts of the settlement should be transferred to her. He based his argument on the authority of *Meek* v *Kettlewell* (1842) Hare 464 and *Re Ellenborough* [1903] 1 Ch 697 and contended that the settlement, being a voluntary settlement, was void and altogether unenforceable. Neither of these authorities supports his propositions. All that was decided in *Meek* v *Kettlewell* (1) was that where the assistance of the Court of Equity is needed to enable the trustees of a voluntary settlement to obtain possession of property subjected to the trusts of a voluntary settlement, the property not having been vested in the trustees, a Court of Equity will render no assistance to the plaintiff.
>
> But here nobody is seeking the assistance of the Court of Equity to enforce the voluntary settlement. Under a valid authority, unrevoked, the persons appointed trustees under the settlement received the settlor's interest under her father's will, and, immediately after it had been received by them, as a result of her own act and her own declaration, contained in the voluntary settlement, it became impressed with the trusts contained in the settlement.
>
> No assistance is required from a Court of Equity to put the property into the hands of the trustees.'

Brandt's (William) Sons & Co v *Dunlop Rubber Co* [1905] AC 454 House of Lords (Lord Halsbury LC, Lord James, Lord Lindley and Lord Macnaghten)

Transfer of property: written notice

Facts

Kramrisch and Co, merchants, were financed by Brandt's Bank, and arranged that goods which they sold should be paid for by remittance direct from the purchasers to the Bank. When Kramrisch's sold goods the Bank sent written notice to the purchasers that the merchants had made the right to receive the purchase money over to the Bank, and requested them to pay the Bank. In an action to recover the amount Walton J at first instance found for the Bank but was reversed in the Court of Appeal.

Held

In the House of Lords, judgment for the Bank, on the evidence the documents were notice.

Lord Macnaghten:

> 'Why that which would have been a good equitable assignment before the statute should now be invalid and inoperative because it fails to come up to the requirements of the statute I confess I do not understand.

The statute does not forbid or destroy equitable assignments or impair their efficacy in the slightest degree. When the rules of equity and the rules of common law conflict, the rules of equity are to prevail. Before the statute there was a conflict as regards assignments of debts and other choses in action. At law it was considered necessary that the debtor should enter into some engagement with the assignee. That was never the rule in equity ... In certain cases the Judicature Act places the assignee in a better position than he was before. Whether the present case falls within the favoured class may perhaps be doubted.

... "But", says the Lord Chief Justice, "the document does not on the face of it purport to be an assignment nor use the language of an assignment." An equitable assignment does not always take that form. It may be addressed to the debtor. It may be couched in the language of command. It may be a courteous request. It may assume the form of mere permission. The language is immaterial if the meaning is plain. All that is necessary is that the debtor should be given to understand that the debt has been made over by the creditor to some third person. If the debtor ignores such a notice, he does so at his peril. If the assignment be for valuable consideration and communicated to the third person, it cannot be revoked by the creditor or safely disregarded by the debtor. I think that the documents which passed between Brandt's and the company would of themselves and apart from Kramrisch & Co's undertaking and engagements given to Brandt's, have constituted a good equitable assignment. But the real question is, were they notice to the company that Brandt's were interested in the money?'

Bunn v *Markham* (1816) 7 Taunt 224 Exchequer Chamber (Gibbs CJ, Dallas Park and Burrough JJ)

Delivery necessary for donatio mortis causa

Facts
The deceased directed the property claimed as donatio mortis causa to be sealed in three parcels with the names of the donees written on them. The parcels were placed in a chest to which the deceased retained a key, saying that the parcels were to be given to the donees after his death.

Held
No sufficient parting with dominion had taken place and therefore the donatio mortis causa was not proved.

Cain v *Moon* [1896] 2 QB 283 Court of Appeal (Lord Russell CJ, Wills J)

Conditions for donatio mortis causa

Facts
Cain, administrator for his deceased wife, claimed recovery of £50 from Moon. In short Moon had been given a credit note for £50, deposited by the deceased wife in a bank account, and told that the money was hers for past services. At that time the wife was ill but subsequently recovered. However, the wife subsequently fell ill again and, expecting to die, repeated to Moon that she was to have the money (during this time Moon had retained possession of the bank's credit note) for past services. On his wife's death Cain denied that there had been a valid inter vivos gift or alternatively a valid gift by donatio mortis causa and claimed the money back from Moon.

Held (on appeal by Cain)
Lord Russell CJ:

A valid gift by donatio mortis causa required:

a) The gift must have been made in contemplation of death.
b) The subject-matter of the gift must have been delivered to the donee.
c) The gift is made in circumstances which show that the property is to revert to the donor if he recovers.

Here there was no inter vivos gift of the money, however, there was a valid gift by donatio mortis causa.

Cannon v Hartley [1949] Ch 213 Chancery Division (Romer J)

Covenant to settle: covenantee a volunteer party

Facts
A deed of separation was executed between a husband and wife to which their daughter was a party. The husband covenanted to settle his after-acquired property on certain trusts under which the daughter was the ultimate beneficiary. The husband failed to settle his property according to the terms of the covenant and the daughter sued him for damages for breach of covenant.

Held
The daughter, though a volunteer, could sue in her own name as a direct covenantor and claim damages. Since the contract was made under seal, the daughter's failure to provide consideration was immaterial. However, specific performance would not be granted to her in equity, for settlement of the actual property specified in the covenant, because she was a volunteer.

Romer J:

> '... In the present case, the plaintiff, although a volunteer, is not only a party to the deed of separation but is also a direct covenantee under the very covenant upon which she is suing. She does not require the assistance of the court to enforce the covenant for she has a legal right to enforce it. She is not asking for equitable relief but for damages at common law for breach of covenant.
>
> For my part, I am quite unable to regard *In re Pryce* (1), which was a different case dealing with totally different circumstances, or anything which Eve J said therein, as amounting to an authority negativing the plaintiff's right to sue in the present case. I think that what Eve J was pointing out *In re Pryce* [1917] 1 Ch 234 was that the next-of-kin who were seeking to get an indirect benefit had no right to come to a court of equity because they were not parties to the deed and were not within the consideration of the deed and, similarly, they would have no right to proceed at common law by an action for damages, as the court of common law would not entertain a suit at the instance of volunteers who were not parties to the deed which was sought to be enforced, any more than the court of equity would entertain such a suit.'

Cavendish-Brown's Settlement Trust, Re [1916] WN 341 Chancery Division (Younger J)

Completely and incompletely constituted trusts: promise to settle

Facts
By a voluntary settlement a settlor covenanted with the trustees that she would transfer all the property both real and personal to which she became entitled under the wills of certain people. The settlor died without having satisfied the covenant by transferring property she received under the wills. The trustees sought a declaration whether their part of the property the settlor had received under the wills ought to be paid to the trustees by way of damages for breach of covenant.

Held
The trustees were entitled to recover substantial damages for breach of covenant, the measure of damages being the value of the property which would have come to the hands of the trustees had the covenant been duly performed.

Cole, Re [1964] Ch 175 Court of Appeal (Harman and Pearson LJJ and Pennycuick J)

Incompletely constituted trust: imperfect gift

Facts
A husband bought a house in London in 1945 and furnished it for his family who lived elsewhere at the time. The wife came up to London and the husband showed her the house and said: "It's all yours". When the husband was declared bankrupt in 1962 the wife claimed as against his trustee in bankruptcy that the house and its contents belonged to her.

Held
A gift of chattels cannot be perfected merely by showing them to the donee and speaking words of gift. The donee must prove some unequivocal act of delivery or change in possession.

Pearson LJ:

'... an act to constitute delivery must be one which in itself shows an intention of the donor to transfer the chattel to the donee. If the act in itself is equivocal – consistent equally with an intention of the husband to transfer the chattels to his wife or with an intention on his part to retain possession but give to her the use and enjoyment of the chattels as his wife – the act does not constitute delivery.

In the present case the intended gift was from husband to wife. Be it assumed that he spoke words of gift – words expressing an intention of transferring the chattels to her, and not merely an intention to give her the use and enjoyment of them as his wife – and that in the circumstances the chattels intended to be given were sufficiently identified by the words of gift. There was no pre-existing possession of the donee in this case. The husband was the owner of the chattels and therefore considered in law to be in possession of them. No act of delivery has been proved, because the acts relied upon are in themselves equivocal – consistent equally with an intention of the husband to transfer the chattels to his wife or with an intention on his part to retain possession but give to her the use and enjoyment of them as his wife.

Mr Megarry's main proposition was that there is a perfect gift where the intending donor shows the chattel to the donee and utters words of present gift in the presence of the donee and the chattel. He also relied upon several special features of this case as adding strength to his main proposition. The special features mentioned were (a) that the husband brought the wife to the chattels; (b) that some of the chattels were bulky, so that handing over would not be a natural mode of transfer; (c) that the chattels were in a place where they would be under the wife's physical control, and she could touch and move them; and (d) the wife handled some of the chattels in the husband's presence.

The argument was clearly and cogently presented, but in the end the answer to it is simply that it fails to show any delivery of the chattels...'

Cook's Settlement Trusts, Re [1965] Ch 902 Chancery Division (Buckley J)

Covenant to settle: consideration

Facts
In 1934 a settlement of family property was made between Sir Herbert Cook, his son Sir Francis, and the trustees of the settlement. Certain paintings became the son's absolutely but the son covenanted for

valuable consideration that should any of the paintings be sold during his lifetime, the proceeds of sale should be paid to the trustees of the settlement for the benefit of the son's children. The son gave his wife a Rembrandt picture in 1962. The wife desired to sell it. The question arose whether on the sale of the Rembrandt the trustees would be obliged to enforce the covenant.

Held

As the covenant was not made in consideration of marriage, the children could not have it enforced by this means. Therefore, the children were mere volunteers and the court would make a declaration that trustees ought not to enforce the covenant against the settlor.

Buckley J:

> 'Mr Goff, appearing for Sir Francis, has submitted first that, as a matter of law, the covenant contained in clause 6 of the settlement is not enforceable against him by the trustees of the settlement ... (He) submits that the covenant was a voluntary and executory contract to make a settlement in a future event and was not a settlement of a covenant to pay a sum of money to the trustees. He further submits that as regards the covenant, all the beneficiaries under the settlement are volunteers, with the consequence that not only should the court not direct the trustees to take proceedings on the covenant but it should positively direct them not to take proceedings. He relies upon *Re Pryce* [1917] 1 Ch 234 and *Re Kay's Settlement* [1939] Ch 329. Counsel for the second and third defendants have contended that on the true view of the facts there was an immediate settlement of the obligation created by the covenant, and not merely a covenant to settle something in the future. It was said, as Mr Monckton put it, that by the agreement, Sir Herbert bought the rights arising under the covenant for the benefit of the cestui que trust under the settlement and that, the covenant being made in favour of the trustees, these rights became assets of the trust. He relied on *Fletcher* v *Fletcher* (1844) 4 Hare 67, *Williamson* v *Codrington* (1750) 1 Ves Sen 511 and *Re Cavendish Browne's Settlement Trusts* [1916] WN 341. I am not able to accept that argument. The covenant with which I am concerned did not, in my opinion, create a debt enforceable at law, that is to say, a property right, which, although to bear fruit only in the future and upon a contingency, was capable of being made the subject of an immediate trust, as was held in the case of *Fletcher* v *Fletcher* (3). Nor is this covenant associated with property which was the subject of an immediate trust as in *Williamson* v *Codrington*. Nor did the covenant relate to property which then belonged to the covenantor, as in *Re Cavendish Browne's Settlement Trusts*. In contrast to all these cases, this covenant upon its true construction is, in my opinion, an executory contract to settle a particular fund or particular funds of money which at the date of the covenant did not exist and which might never come into existence. It is analogous to a covenant to settle an expectation or to settle after-acquired property. The case in my judgment, involves the law of contract, not the law of trusts.'

Dillwyn v *Llewellyn* (1862) 4 De GF & J 517 Lord Chancellor's Court (Lord Westbury LC)

Imperfect gift: estoppel

Facts

A father placed one of his sons in possession of land belonging to the father, and at the same time signed a memorandum that he had presented the land to the son so that the latter could build a dwelling house on it. The son with the assent and approval of the father, built at his own expense a house on the land and resided there. On the father's death the son sought a declaration that he was entitled to call for a conveyance of the fee simple. The Master of the Rolls decreed that he was only entitled to a life interest.

Held
This was not a mere incomplete gift of a life interest but it was clear the memorandum was to vest in the son the absolute ownership of the estate. As the son had been put into possession and incurred expenditure on the land, with the approbation of the father, equity would intervene and perfect the imperfect gift.

Lord Westbury LC:

'About the rules of the court there can be no controversy. A voluntary agreement will not be completed or assisted by a Court of Equity, in cases of mere gift. If anything be wanting to complete the title of the donee, a Court of equity will not assist him in obtaining it; for a mere donee can have no right to claim more than he has received. But the subsequent acts of the donor may give the donee the right or ground of claim which he did not acquire from the original gift. Thus, if A gives a house to B, but makes no formal conveyance, and the house is afterwards, on the marriage of B, included, with the knowledge of A, in the marriage settlement of B, A would be bound to complete the title of the parties claiming under that settlement. So if A puts B in possession of a piece of land, and tells him, "I give it to you that you may build a house on it", and B on the strength of that promise, with the knowledge of A, expends a large sum of money in building a house accordingly, I cannot doubt that the donee acquires a right from the subsequent transaction to call on the donor to perform that contract and complete the imperfect donation which was made. The case is somewhat analogous to that of verbal agreement not binding originally for the want of the memorandum in writing signed by the party to be charged, but which becomes binding by virtue of the subsequent part performance. The early case of *Foxcroft* v *Lester*, decided by the House of Lords, is an example nearly approaching to the terms of the present case.

The Master of the Rolls, however, seems to have thought that a question might still remain as to the extent of the estate taken by the donee, and that in this particular case the extent of the donee's interest depended on the terms of the memorandum. I am not of that opinion. The equity of the donee and the estate to be claimed by virtue of it depend on the transaction, that is, on the acts done, and not on the language of the memorandum, except as that shows the purpose and intent of the gift. The estate was given as the site of a dwelling house to be erected by the son. The ownership of the dwelling house and the ownership of the estate must be considered as intended to be co-extensive and co-equal. No one builds a house for his own life only, and it is absurd to suppose that it was intended by either party that the house, at the death of the son, should become the property of the father. If, therefore, I am right in the conclusion of law that the subsequent expenditure by the son, with the approbation of the father, supplied a valuable consideration originally wanting, the memorandum signed by the father and son must be thenceforth regarded as an agreement for the soil extending to the fee-simple of the land. In a contract for sale of an estate no words of limitation are necessary to include the fee-simple; but further, upon the construction of the memorandum itself, taken apart from the subsequent acts, I should be of opinion that it was the plain intention of the testator to vest in the son the absolute ownership of the estate. The only inquiry therefore, is, whether the son's expenditure on the faith of the memorandum supplied a valuable consideration and created a binding obligation. On this I have no doubt; and it therefore follows that the intention to give the fee-simple must be performed, and that the decree ought to declare the son the absolute owner of the estate comprised in the memorandum.'

Dudman, Re [1925] Ch 553 Chancery Division (Russell J)
Held
A gift made in contemplation of suicide cannot be a donatio mortis causa

Commentary
Sed quaere since the Suicide Act 1961, which rendered suicide no longer a crime. Part of the ratio seems to have been that the donor was contemplating a crime.

Fletcher v *Fletcher* (1844) 4 Hare 67 Vice-Chancellor's Court (Wigram V-C)

Completely and incompletely constituted trusts: trust of a promise

Facts
Ellis Fletcher covenanted with five trustees, for himself, his heirs, executors and administrators, to pay the trustees £60,000 within twelve months of his death to be held on trust for his sons John and Jacob. If both sons were alive at his death and attained the age of twenty-one, the money was to be held for them in equal shares as tenants-in-common; if only one of them satisfied the above conditions, then he was to have the whole fund. Both sons survived the testator but John died without attaining the age of 21. Jacob claimed that as he had attained 21, he had become solely entitled to the £60,000. Jacob asked that his father's executors might be ordered to pay him the £60,000. However, the trustees did not wish to accept the trust or receive the money and they declined to take proceedings to recover it or to permit their names to be used to recover it unless ordered to do so by the court.

Held
Jacob could claim the £60,000 from the executors. The trust was already perfect, the covenantor had subjected himself to liability at law because the covenant would be enforced at law without consideration. The interposition of a trustee of the covenant did not make any difference and consequently equity would allow Jacob to use the names of the trustees to sue at law, or to recover in his own name in equity.

Wigram V-C (at the close of argument):

> 'In trying the equitable question I shall assume the validity of the instrument at law. If there was any doubt of that, it would be reasonable to allow the plaintiff to try the right by suing in the name of the surviving trustee.
>
> Or, in the case of new trustees being appointed (perhaps by the plaintiff himself, there being a power to appoint new trustees), supposing his own nominees to be willing to sue, the other trustees might refuse to sue. I think the answer to these and like questions must be in the negative. the testator has bound himself absolutely. There is a debt created and existing. I give no assistance against the testator. I only deal with him as he was dealt by himself, and, if in such a case the trustee will not sue without the sanction of the court, I think it is right to allow the cestui que trust to sue for himself, in the name of the trustee, either at law, or in this court, as the case may require. The rights of the parties cannot depend upon mere accident and caprice. Having come to this conclusion upon abstract reasoning, it was satisfactory to me to find that this view of the case is not only consistent with, but is supported by the cases of *Clough* v *Lambert* (1839) 10 Sim 174 and *Williamson* v *Codrington* (1750) 1 Ves Sen 511. If the case, therefore, depended simply upon the covenant being voluntary my opinion is that the plaintiff would be entitled to use the name of the trustee at law, or to recover the money in this court, if it were unnecessary to have the right decided at law, and, where the legal right is clear, to have the use of the deed, if that use is material.'

Freeland, Re [1952] Ch 110 Court of Appeal (Sir Raymond Evershed MR, Jenkins and Morris LJJ)

Imperfect future gift not perfected under *Strong* v *Bird*

Facts
The plaintiff alleged that the testatrix had given her her Hillman motor car which the testatrix kept immobilised in a garage. Shortly after the alleged gift the plaintiff claimed that the car had been fixed and lent to the defendant, whose car had broken down, by the testatrix with the plaintiff's consent. The defendant was in possession of the car at the testatrix's death and he refused to part with it. Both the

plaintiff and the defendant were appointed executors of the testatrix's will. The plaintiff claimed a declaration that the car was hers under the rule in *Strong* v *Bird* (1874) LR 18 Eq 315.

Held
There was no continuing intention to make the gift of the car to the plaintiff up until the testatrix's death. It was not possible to apply the rule in cases where the donee had an intention to make a gift but first desired to apply the subject-matter of the gift to some other purpose. Such a state of affairs showed an intention to make a future gift and necessarily excluded the principle in *Strong* v *Bird*.

Sir Raymond Evershed MR:

> '… the words "an intention to give" may mean either one of two things: they may mean an intention of giving, that is to say, an intention to do that which at the time of doing it was meant to be a gift out and out; or they may mean an intention to make a gift in the future, which is in effect a promise, not enforceable in the eyes of the law, to make a gift thereafter.
>
> I am quite satisfied that the doctrine enunciated in *Strong* v *Bird* does not apply to the latter of the two types of case. There must, for the application of the doctrine, be an intention of giving, as distinct from an intention to give …'

Fry, Re [1946] Ch 312 Chancery Division (Romer J)

Imperfect gift: incomplete transfer

Facts
The donor of shares, who was domiciled in the USA, executed a transfer of those shares by way of gift but the company was unable to register his transfer since the consent of the Treasury as required under the Defence (Finance) Regulations 1939 had not yet been obtained. The donor had signed the necessary forms for obtaining consent but died before it was given.

Held
The gift was imperfect because even after the consent had been given, it was necessary for the donor to effect confirmatory transfers.

Gonin, Re [1979] Ch 16 Chancery Division (Walton J)

Imperfect gift not perfected under *Strong* v *Bird:* no continuing intention

Facts
The plaintiff was born out of wedlock but her parents subsequently married. In 1944 the plaintiff's parents asked her to give up her job at the Air Ministry to return home to look after them. This the plaintiff agreed to do and in return the parents promised to give her the house and its contents. The plaintiff's father died in 1957 and the plaintiff's mother died intestate in 1968. Prior to her death, the mother believed that she could not make a valid will in favour of the plaintiff because the latter was illegitimate. However, the mother sold off several building plots from the grounds of the house and offered the plaintiff the money she received which the plaintiff refused to take. In addition, the mother made gifts of several items of furniture to the plaintiff. As administrator of her mother's estate, the plaintiff claimed that the house and its contents should be vested in her as beneficial owner under the rule in *Strong* v *Bird* (1874) 18 Eq 315.

Held

The rule in *Strong* v *Bird* did not apply to the house because there was no continuing intention on the part of the mother to make a gift of it. The manner in which she had sold off plots of land and offered the plaintiff the proceeds of sale, not as owner but as recompense for her hard work without remuneration, pointed against any continuing intention. So far as the furniture and contents were concerned, there was a continuing intention and the subsequent gifts of items of furniture by the mother to the plaintiff were merely affirmation of her intention.

Walton J criticised the decision in *Re James* [1935] Ch 499 where Farwell J held that *Strong* v *Bird* applied to cases where the gift was perfected through the donee being appointed an administrator. He said:

'I start from the simple proposition that if the defendant in *Strong v Bird* itself had been an administrator instead of an executor the case would have been decided the other way, since it distinctly proceeded on the basis that at law the appointment of the person as an executor effected a release of any debt due from the executor to the testator, a doctrine which was never applied to an administrator: see *Nedham's Case, Wankford* v *Wankford, Seagram* v *Knight*.

One can see why this should be so: by appointing the executor the testator has by his own act made it impossible for the debtor to sue himself. And, indeed, so far has the rule been taken, that although it will no longer apply if the person appointed executor has renounced probate, yet it will still apply if power to prove has been reserved to him. *Re Applebee, Leveson* v *Beales*.

The appointment of an administrator, on the other hand, is not the act of the deceased but of the law. It is often a matter of pure chance which of many persons equally entitled to a grant of letters of administration finally takes them out. Why, then should any special tenderness be shown to a person so selected by law and not the will of the testator, and often indifferently selected among many with an equal claim?

It would seem an astonishing doctrine of equity that if the person who wishes to take the benefit of the rule in *Strong* v *Bird* manages to be the person to obtain a grant then he will be able to do so, but if a person equally entitled manages to obtain a prior grant, then he will not be able to do so. This appears to me to treat what ought to be a simple rule of equity, namely, that if the legal title to a gift is perfected by the appointment by the intending donor of the intended donee as his executor ... as something in the nature of a lottery.'

James, Re [1935] Ch 449 Chancery Division (Farwell J)

Perfecting an imperfect gift

Held

The rule in *Strong* v *Bird* applies to an administrator who acquires the title to property thus perfecting a gift.

Jeffreys v *Jeffreys* (1841) Cr & Ph 138 Lord Chancellor's Court (Lord Cottenham LC)

Incompletely constituted trusts and volunteers: covenant to settle

Facts

A father voluntarily conveyed freeholds, and covenanted to surrender copyholds, to trustees on trust for his daughters. He never surrendered the copyholds, and by will devised some of the same estates to his wife, who was admitted to some of the copyholds.

Held
As to the freeholds, the trust was completely constituted and the daughters could enforce them. But the trust of the copyholds was incompletely constituted and would not be enforced as the daughters were volunteers.

Kay's Settlement, Re [1939] Ch 329 Chancery Division (Simonds J)

Covenant to settle: refusal

Facts
By a voluntary settlement, a young spinster covenanted to settle all her after-acquired property inter alia for any children she should have. Some years later she married and eventually she had three children. Subsequently, she became entitled to a legacy and a share of residue under her mother's will which fell within the terms of the covenant. The trustees asked her to settle this property but she refused to do so.

Held
As the settlement was not made in consideration of marriage, the children were mere volunteers and had no right to enforce it. The trustees would, therefore, be directed not to take any proceedings to enforce the covenant.

Lillingston, Re [1952] 2 All ER 184 Chancery Division (Wynn-Parry J)

Delivery in donatio mortis causa

Facts
L expected to die shortly and told P that she could have her jewellery, kept in a safe deposit box at Harrods. L then gave P the keys to a trunk in L's room which contained the key to the deposit box.

Held
Donatio mortis causa will not operate where the donor hands over a locked box but retains the only key himself. This does not amount to a sufficient delivery, however, in this instance L had effectively given P possession of the key by giving her the only keys to the trunk in which it was kept. For donatio mortis causa the gift must be revocable in the donor's lifetime and only become absolute on his death, but must not remain under the donor's control so that no effective delivery of the gift has taken place.

Macardle, Re [1951] Ch 669 Court of Appeal (Sir Raymond Evershed, Jenkins and Hodson LJJ)

Voluntary assignment of an equitable interest

Facts
M and his brothers and sisters were beneficially interested in their father's estate, part of which comprised a house in which M and his wife lived. Mr and Mrs M carried out various works on the house to improve it and, subsequently, M and his brothers and sisters signed a document voluntarily agreeing to repay to Mrs M, out of their interest in their father's estate, the cost of those works. Quaere: was past consideration sufficient to enforce the assignment; alternatively, could an equitable assignment which contemplated future action be valid?

Held
The equitable assignment was valid.

Sir Raymond Evershed MR:

> 'The mode or form of the assignment is absolutely immaterial provided the intention is clear.'

Per contra, Jenkins LJ:

> 'A voluntary equitable assignment, to be valid, must be in all respects complete and perfect so that the assignee is entitled to demand payment from the trustee or holder of the fund, and the trustee is bound to make payment to the assignee, with no further act on the part of the assignor remaining to be done to perfect the assignee's title.'

Mascall v *Mascall* (1984) 81 LS Gaz 2218 Court of Appeal (Lawton and Browne-Wilkinson LJJ and Sir Denys Buckley)

Completely constituted trusts: compliance with formalities

Facts
The father agreed to sell his house to his son for £9,000. The documents were executed and sent to the Land Registry for stamping and registration. The father retrieved the documents before completion.

The son was in action to force the father to return the documents.

Held
Transfer had been duly effected and therefore binding on the father. This was despite the fact that the documents had not been completely executed at the Registry. The court also disregarded provisions of s18 LPA 1925 which required the vendor to arrange for registration. The practice of the purchaser arranging the registration had superceded this technicality.

Pascoe v *Turner* [1979] 1 WLR 431 Court of Appeal (Orr, Lawton and Cumming-Bruce LJJ)

Imperfect gift: estoppel

Facts
P, a well-to-do business man, and D, a widow, met in the early 1960's and D moved into P's house as his housekeeper. Subsequently they lived as man and wife and moved into another house owned by P. In 1973 P met another woman with whom he went to live but told D he would never see her without a roof over her head and told her, 'The house is yours and everything in it'. P also said he would have a conveyance drawn up in D's favour but never got round to it. D stayed in the house and in reliance on P's declarations that he had given her the house she spent money on it in redecorations, improvements and repairs. In 1976 P and D quarrelled and P determined to throw D out of the house if he could and accordingly sought an order for possession. In defence and counterclaim D sought a declaration that the house and its contents were hers and that P was estopped from denying that he held them on trust for her or that he had given her a licence to occupy the house for her lifetime. In the county court the judge found a constructive trust in favour of D and granted her a declaration that P held the house and contents on trust for her. P appealed.

Held
There was nothing on the facts from which a constructive trust could be inferred. The case was one of

estoppel arising from the encouragement or acquiescence of P between 1973 and 1976 when, in reliance on his declaration that he was giving and, later he had given the house to her, she spent a substantial part of her capital on repairs and improvements.

The proper remedy to satisfy D's equity was a choice between (a) a licence to D to occupy the hose for her lifetime or, (b) a transfer to her of the fee simple. In the circumstances, the proper remedy was the transfer of the fee simple. What D required was security of tenure quiet enjoyment and freedom of action to do repairs and improvements without interference from P. As P had determined to throw D out of the house if he could, a licence would be insufficient as it could not be regarded as a land charge and would therefore have no bearing on the rights of any bona fide purchaser to whom P might sell the property.

Paul v *Constance* [1977] 1 WLR 527 Court of Appeal (Cairns, Scarman and Bridge LJJ)

Completely constituted trust: declaration of self as trustee

Facts
Shortly after C separated from his wife, he took up with Mrs Paul and cohabited with her. C and Mrs Paul had a joint bank account into which C put £950 initially which he had received as damages for personal injuries. Both C and Mrs Paul drew on the account and on many occasions both prior to the money being deposited and subsequently C told Mrs Paul that the money was as much hers as his. From time to time, further sums of money were withdrawn and shared between C and Mrs Paul. C died intestate in March 1974 and his wife took out letters of administration to his estate. At C's death the original £950 was still in the bank account; his wife closed the account. Mrs Paul claimed the money saying that C had declared a trust for himself and her.

Held
The words used by C on many occasions that the money was as much Mrs Paul's as his were sufficient to constitute a declaration of trust. There was a clear intention to create a trust; Mrs Paul was entitled to the £950 accordingly.

Scarman LJ:

> 'In this court the issue becomes: was there sufficient evidence to justify the judge reaching that conclusion of fact? (that there was a declaration of trust). In submitting that there was, counsel for the plaintiff draws attention first and foremost to the words used. When one bears in mind the unsophisticated character of Mr Constance and his relationship with the plaintiff during the last few years of his life, counsel for the plaintiff submits that the words that he did use on more than one occasion namely "This money is as much yours as mine" convey clearly a present declaration that the existing fund was as much the plaintiff's as his own. The judge accepted that conclusion. I think he was well justified in doing so and, indeed, I think he was right to do so.'

Paul v *Paul* (1882) 20 Ch D 742 Court of Appeal (Jessel MR, Brett and Cotton LJJ)

Marriage settlement: completely constituted trust

Facts
By the terms of a marriage settlement, property was settled on the husband and wife for life with remainder to the children of the marriage. If there were no children of the marriage and the wife survived the husband, she was to take absolutely, but, if the husband survived the wife, the property was to pass on

such trusts as the wife appointed by her will and in default to the next-of-kin. The trust was completely constituted. There were no children of the marriage so the husband and wife sought to have the fund paid to them on the ground that the next-of-kin, who would take on default of appointment by the wife, were mere volunteers.

Held
That as the funds were settled there was a trust in favour of the next-of-kin and even if they were volunteers the trustees could not part with the funds without their consent.

Plumptre's Marriage Settlement, Re [1910] 1 Ch 609 Chancery Division (Eve J)

Marriage settlement: constitution of the trust: covenant to settle

Facts
In 1878 a husband and wife covenanted on their marriage with trustees of the marriage settlement to settle the wife's after-acquired property on trust for the husband and wife successively for life, then for the issue of the marriage, with an ultimate trust for the next-of-kin. In 1884, the husband bought stock in his wife's name. The wife sold this and purchased other stock subsequently. On the wife's death in 1909, the stock was worth £1,125. There were no children of the marriage. The husband was administrator of the wife's estate. The next-of-kin sought to enforce the covenant against the husband.

Held
The next-of-kin were mere volunteers and strangers to the marriage consideration. They could not enforce the covenant against the husband. Further, the trustees could not sue for damages for breach of contract since the claim was statute-barred by lapse of time.

Pryce, Re [1917] 1 Ch 234 Chancery Division (Eve J)

Covenant to settle: refusal

Facts
A marriage settlement made in 1887 contained a covenant to settle the wife's after-acquired property. In 1904 the husband made a gift by deed of certain reversionary interests, to which he would be entitled on his mother's death to the wife. The husband died in 1907 and his mother in 1916. At the latter date the reversionary interests remained outstanding in another settlement. By the terms of the marriage settlement, the wife was to have a life interest in the trust fund if she survived the husband with remainder to the children and ultimate remainders to the next-of-kin. There were no children of the marriage. The trustees sought a declaration whether the reversionary interests were caught by the marriage settlement and whether they were entitled to enforce them.

Held
Although the reversionary interests were caught by the covenant of the wife, the trustees ought not to take any steps to recover them. The next-of-kin, who were ultimately entitled, were volunteers who could neither maintain an action to enforce the covenant nor for damages for breach of it, the court would not give them by indirect means what they could not obtain by direct procedure.

Eve J:

> 'The position of the wife's fund is somewhat different, in that her next-of-kin would be entitled to it on her death; but they are volunteers, and although the Court would probably compel fulfilment of the contract to settle at the instance of any persons within the marriage consideration – see per Cotton LJ in *In re D'Angibau* (1880) 15 Ch D 228 – and in their favour will treat the outstanding property as subjected to an enforceable trust – *Pullan* v *Koe* [1913] 1 Ch 9 – volunteers have no right whatever to obtain specific performance of a mere covenant which has remained as a covenant and has never been performed; see per James LJ in *In re D'Angibau*. Nor could damages be awarded either in this Court, or, I apprehend, at law, where, since the Judicature Act 1873, the same defences would be available to the defendant as would be raised in an action brought in this Court for specific performance or damages. In these circumstances, seeing that the next-of-kin could neither maintain an action to enforce the covenant nor for damages for breach of it, and that the settlement is not a declaration of trust constituting the relationship of trustee and cestui que trust between the defendant and the next-of-kin, in which case effect could be given to the trusts even in favour of volunteers, but is a mere voluntary contract to create a trust, ought the Court now for the sole benefit of these volunteers to direct the trustees to take proceedings to enforce the defendant's covenant? I think it ought not; to do so would be to give the next-of-kin by indirect means relief they cannot obtain by any direct procedure, and would in effect be enforcing the settlement as against the defendant's legal right to payment and transfer from the trustees of the parents' marriage settlement.'

Pullan v *Koe* [1913] 1 Ch 9 Chancery Division (Swinfen Eady J)

Marriage settlement: constitution of the trust: covenant to settle

Facts
By a marriage settlement made in 1859, a wife covenanted to settle after-acquired property of £100 and over. In 1879 she received a gift of £285 from her mother. The money was paid into her husband's bank account on which she had power to draw and later invested in securities which remained at the bank. On the husband's death in 1909 the trustees of the marriage settlement claimed the securities from the husband's executor. The executor pleaded the Statute of Limitations in defence.

Held
The property was not part of the husband's estate. When received by the wife it was immediately bound by the covenant and subject to the trusts in favour of the children as persons within the marriage consideration. The trustees' claim at law for damages arising in 1879 for breach of contract was statute barred by lapse of time but a claim in equity for the property itself, still unsettled, was maintainable.

Swinfen Eady J:

> 'It was contended that the bonds never in fact became trust property as both the wife and husband were only liable in damages for breach of covenant, and, that the case was different from cases where property which has once admittedly become subject to the trusts of an instrument has been improperly dealt with, and is sought to be recovered. In my opinion as soon as the £285 was paid to the wife it became in equity bound by and subject to the trusts of the settlement. The trustees could have claimed that particular sum, could have obtained at once the appointment of a receiver of it, if they could have shown a case of jeopardy, and, if it had been invested and the investment could be traced, could have followed the money and claimed the investment.
>
> This point was dealt with by Jessel MR in *Smith* v *Lucas* (1881) Ch D 531 where he said: "What is the effect of such a covenant in equity? It has been said that the effect in equity of the covenant of the wife, as far as she is concerned, is that it does not affect her personally, but that it binds the property: that is to say, it binds the property under the doctrine of equity that that is to be considered as done which ought to

be done. That is in the nature of specific performance of the contract no doubt. If, therefore, this is a covenant to settle the future-acquired property of the wife, and nothing more is done by her, the covenant will bind the property."

Again in *Collyer* v *Isaacs* (1881) 19 Ch D 342 Jessel MR said: "A man can contract to assign property which is to come into existence in the future, and when it has come into existence, equity, treating as done that which ought to be done, fastens upon that property, and the contract to assign thus becomes a complete assignment. If a person contract for value, eg in his marriage settlement, to settle all such real estate as his father shall leave him by will, or purports actually to convey by the deed all such real estate, the effect is the same. It is a contract for value which will bind the property if the father leaves any property to his son."

The property being thus bound, these bonds became trust property, and can be followed by the trustees and claimed from a volunteer.

Again trustees are entitled to come into a Court of Equity to enforce a contract to create a trust, contained in a marriage settlement, for the benefit of the wife and the issue of the marriage, all of whom are within the marriage consideration. The husband covenanted that he and his heirs, executors, and administrators should, as soon as circumstances would admit, convey, assign, and surrender to the trustees the real or personal property to which his wife should become beneficially entitled. The trustees are entitled to have that covenant specifically enforced by a Court of Equity. In *In re D'Angibau* (1880) 15 Ch D 228 and in *In re Plumptre's Marriage Settlement* [1910] 1 Ch 609 it was held that the Court would not interfere in favour of volunteers, not within the marriage consideration, but here the plaintiffs are the contracting parties and the object of the proceeding is to benefit the wife and issue of the marriage.'

Ralli's Will Trusts, Re [1964] Ch 288 Chancery Division (Buckley J)
Covenant to settle perfected under Strong v Bird (1)

Facts
By his will of 1892 a testator left the residue of his estate on trust for his wife for life with remainder to his two daughters, Helen and Irene, absolutely. By her marriage settlement of 1924, Helen covenanted to settle all her existing and after-acquired property on certain trusts which failed and ultimately for the children of Irene. Irene's husband was appointed a trustee of the marriage settlement and in 1946 he was also appointed a trustee of the testator's will of 1892. Helen died in 1956 and the testator widow died in 1961. At the latter date Irene's husband held the residue of the testator's estate as trustee of the will. The question arose as to whether he could, as trustee of the will and the marriage settlement, hold the residue on the trusts of the marriage settlement having received it as trustee of the will. The case was defended by the personal representatives of Helen who claimed her half-share of the residue.

Held
The covenant to settle after-acquired property had been satisfied, the rule in *Strong* v *Bird* (1874) LR 18 Eq 315 applied and it was irrelevant how the trustee had become the legal owner.

Buckley J:

'In my judgment, the circumstance that the plaintiff holds the fund because he was appointed a trustee of the will is irrelevant. He is, at law, the owner of the fund, and the means by which he became so have no effect upon the quality of his legal ownership. The question is: For whom, if anyone, does he hold the fund in equity? In other words, who can successfully assert an equity against him disentitling him to stand upon his legal right? It seems to me to be indisputable that Helen, if she were alive, could not do so, for she has solemnly covenanted under seal to assign the fund to the plaintiff, and the defendants can stand in no better position ... It is also true that, if it were necessary to enforce the performance of the covenant, equity would not assist the beneficiaries under the settlement, because they are mere volunteers ... As matters stand, however, there is no occasion to invoke the assistance of equity to enforce the performance of the covenant.

It is for the defendants to invoke the assistance of equity to make good their claim to the fund. To do so, they must show that the plaintiff cannot conscientiously withhold it from them. When they seek to do this, he can point to the covenant which, in my judgment, relieves him from any fiduciary obligation he would otherwise owe to the defendants as Helen's representatives. In doing so, the plaintiff is not seeking to enforce an equitable remedy against the defendants on behalf of persons who could not enforce such a remedy themselves: he is relying upon the combined effect of his legal ownership of the fund and his rights under the covenant …'

Reddel v *Dobree* (1839) 10 Simm 244 Chancery (Sir L Shadwell V-C)

Donatio mortis causa; no gift where other conditions are attached

Facts
A cash box was handed to the donee with the condition that it be returned to the donor every three months so that he could check its contents.

Held
No donatio mortis causa because there was a condition attached other than that it should be returned if the donor survived.

Rose, Re [1952] Ch 499 Court of Appeal (Sir Raymond Evershed MR, Jenkins and Morris LJJ)

Completely and incompletely constituted trusts: transfer to trustees

Facts
The settlor transferred two blocks of shares in a property company to trustees to be held on certain trusts in March 1943. The transfer was made in a form which corresponded exactly with the requirements of the company's regulations. The transfer was registered in June 1943 by the company. The settlor died more than five years after he had made the transfer of the shares but less than five years after the transfer had been registered with the company. Under the Finance Act 1894, a voluntary disposition of property made more than five years before a person's death was exempt from estate duty. The question therefore arose as to whether the shares were exempt and this turned on which date the transfer should be regarded as having taken place on.

Held
The settlor had done all in his power to transfer the shares to the trustees and the transfer was accordingly completed in March 1943. There was no duty payable.

Sir Raymond Evershed MR:

'… but if a document is apt and proper to transfer the property – is, in truth the appropriate way in which the property must be transferred – then it does not seem to me to follow from the statement of Turner LJ that, as a result, either during some limited period or otherwise, a trust may not arise, for the purpose of giving effect to the transfer. The simplest case will, perhaps, provide an illustration. If a man executes a document transferring all his equitable interest, say, in shares, that document, operating and intended to operate as a transfer, will give rise to and take effect as a trust, for the assignor will then be a trustee of the legal estate in the shares for the person in whose favour he has made an assignment of his beneficial interest. As for my part, I do not think that *Milroy* v *Lord* (1862) 4 De GF & J 264 is an authority which compels this court to hold that in this case, where, in terms of Turner LJ's judgment, the settlor did everything which, according to the nature of the property comprised in the settlement, was necessary to be done by him in order to transfer the property, the result necessarily negatives the conclusion that, pending registration, the settlor was a trustee of the legal interest for the transferee.

The view of the limitations of *Milroy* v *Lord* which I have tried to express was much better expressed by Jenkins J in the recent case which also bears the name of *Re Rose* [1949] Ch 78 (though that is a coincidence). It is true that the main point, the essential question to be determined, was whether there had been a transfer eo nomine of certain shares within the meaning of a will. The testator in that case, Rose, by his will had given a number of shares to one Hook, but the gift was subject to this qualification: "If such ... shares have not been transferred to him previously to my death." The question was: Had the shares been transferred to him in these circumstances? He had executed (as had this Mr Rose) a transfer in appropriate form, and handed the transfer and the certificate to Hook, but, at the time of his death, the transfer had not been registered. It was said, therefore, that there had been no transfer, and (following the argument of counsel for the Crown) there had been no passing to Hook of any interest, legal or beneficial, whatever, by the time the testator died. If that view were right, then, of course, Hook would be entitled to the shares under the will. But Jenkins J went a little more closely into the matter because it was obvious that on one view of it, if it were held that there was a "transfer" within the terms of the will, though the transfer was inoperative in the eye of the law and not capable of being completed after the death, then Mr Hook suffered the misfortune of getting the shares neither by gift inter vivos nor by testamentary benefaction. Therefore, Jenkins J considered *Milroy* v *Lord* and in regard to it he used this language: "I was referred on that to the well-known case of *Milroy* v *Lord* and also to the recent case of *Re Fry* [1946] Ch 312. Those cases, as I understand them, turn on the fact that the deceased donor had not done all in his power, according to the nature of the property given, to vest the legal interest in the property in the donee. In such circumstances, it is, of course, well settled that there is no equity to complete the gift at the date of the donor's death; the court will not compel his personal representatives to do that act and the gift remains incomplete and fails. In *Milroy* v *Lord* the imperfection was due to the fact that the wrong form of transfer was used for the purpose of transferring certain bank shares. The document was not the appropriate document to pass any interest in the property at all." Then he referred to *Re Fry* which is another illustration, and continued: "In this case, as I understand it, the testator had done everything in his power to divest himself of the shares in question to Mr Hook. He had executed a transfer. It is not suggested that the transfer was not in accordance with the company's regulations. He had handed that transfer together with the certificate to Mr Hook. There was nothing else the testator could do." I venture respectfully to adopt the whole of the passage I have read which, in my judgment, is a correct statement of the law. If that be so, then it seems to me that it cannot be asserted on the authority of *Milroy* v *Lord*, and I venture to think it also cannot be asserted as a matter of logic and good sense or principle, that because, by the regulations of the company, there had to be a gap before Mrs Rose could, as between herself and the company claim the rights which the shares gave her vis-a-vis the company. Mr Rose was not in the meantime a trustee for her of all his rights and benefits under the shares. That he intended to pass all those rights, as I have said, seems to me too plain for argument.'

Sen v *Headley* [1991] Ch 425 Court of Appeal (Purchas, Nourse and Leggatt LJJ)

Whether land can be the subject matter of a donatio mortis causa

Facts
The deceased gave a friend the key to a steel box in which, he told her, the deeds to his house were to be found, and he indicated that, knowing that he was dying, he wished her to have the house on his death. He died intestate, and the friend claimed a valid donatio mortis causa in respect of the house.

This claim was dismissed at first instance by Mummery J and the friend then appealed to the Court of Appeal.

Held

A valid donatio mortis causa had been constituted in this situation and the appeal would be allowed. As Nourse LJ stated delivering the judgment of the Court of Appeal, for a valid donatio mortis causa to arise, three general requirements must be satisfied. 'First, the gift had to be made in contemplation, although not necessarily in expectation, of impending death. Second, the gift had to be made upon the condition that it was to be absolute and perfected only on the donor's death, being revocable until that event and ineffective otherwise. Third, there had to be a delivery of the subject matter of the gift, or the essential *indicia* of title thereto, which amounted to a parting with dominion and not mere physical possession over the subject matter.' At first instance, Mummery J, while accepting that the first two of these requirements had been fulfilled, took the view that the deceased had not effectively parted with dominion over the house in that he retained until his death the whole of the legal and equitable interest in it.

In the Court of Appeal, Nourse LJ while accepting the need for a parting of dominion took the view that this condition had been fulfilled by parting with dominion over 'the essential *indicia* of title' – ie the title deeds to the house. Although the view expressed obiter by Lord Eldon in *Duffield* v *Elwes* (1827) 1 Bli (NS) 497 to the effect that land cannot be the subject matter of a donatio mortis causa had hitherto generally been accepted (see, eg Snell's Principles of Equity), the point was never, in fact, actually decided by the House of Lords. Accordingly, as Nourse LJ stated, the Court of Appeal '... could not decide a case in 1991 as the House of Lords would have decided it, but did not decide it, in 1827'. As Nourse LJ observed earlier in his judgment: 'It was agreed that the doctrine was anomalous. Anomalies did not justify anomalous exceptions.'

Stewart, Re [1908] 2 Ch 251 Chancery Division (Neville J)

Imperfect gift perfected under *Strong* v *Bird*

Facts

A testator had given his wife certain bonds and other securities and these securities had been enumerated in a document at the foot of which the testator had written in pencil, 'Coming in next year £1,000', and on the evidence this was construed as an intention to give a further £1,000 to his wife the next year. In reinvesting his bonds the next year, the testator made a profit which he used to buy three further bonds. He took the contract note for those three further bonds to his wife and handed it to her in an envelope and said, 'I have bought these for you'. Nothing more was done and the testator died subsequently, having appointed his wife executrix.

Held

There was a present intention to give when the testator gave the wife the contract note and that the gift was imperfect because he had not handed the bonds over to his wife. However, the principle of *Strong* v *Bird* (1874) LR 18 Eq 315 was applicable, there having been an attempted gift, imperfect though it might have been. The subsequent appointment of the wife as executrix perfected the gift by vesting in her the legal interest in the bonds.

Strong v *Bird* (1874) LR 18 Eq 315 Court of Chancery (Sir George Jessel MR)

Incomplete gift: perfected

Facts

Bird borrowed £1,100 from his stepmother who lived in his house paying £212.10s per quarter for board. It was agreed that the debt should be paid off by the stepmother deducting £100 from each quarterly payment when it fell due. This was done for two quarters but on the third quarter the stepmother refused to make any further deductions and paid the full £212.10s. This she did until her death four years later. Bird was appointed sole executor of his stepmother's estate. The next-of-kin claimed that Bird owed the estate £900.

Held

The debt had gone; the appointment of Bird as executor released the debt at law as he could not sue himself. Further, she had shown a clear intention to forgive him the debt and this intention continued up until her death.

Sir George Jessel MR:

'There are, however, two modes in which, as it appears to me, the validity of this transaction can be supported. First of all, we must consider what the law requires. The law requires nothing more than this, that in a case where the thing which is the subject of donation is transferable or releasable at law, the legal transfer or release shall take place. The gift is not perfect until what has been generally called a change of the property at law has taken place. Allowing this rule to operate to its full extent, what occurred was this. The donor, or the alleged donor, had made her will, and by that will had appointed Mr Bird, the alleged donee, executor. After her death he proved the will, and the legal effect of that was to release the debt in law, and therefore the condition which is required, namely, that the release shall be perfect at law, was complied with by the testatrix making him executor. It is not necessary that the legal change shall knowingly be made by the donor with a view to carry out the gift. It may be made for another purpose; but if the gift is clear, and there is to be no recall of the gift, and no intention to recall it, so that the person who executes the legal instrument does not intend to invest the person taking upon himself the legal ownership with any other character, there is no reason why the legal instrument should not have its legal effect.

For instance, suppose this occurred that the person made a memorandum on the title-deeds of an estate to this effect: "I give Blackacre to AB", and afterwards conveyed that estate to AB by a general description, not intending in any way to change the previous gift, would there be any equity to make the person who had so obtained the legal estate a trustee for the donor? The answer would be that there is no resulting trust: this is rebutted by shewing that the person who conveyed did not intend the person taking the conveyance to be a trustee, and although the person conveying actually thought that that was not one of the estates conveyed, because that person thought that he had not given the estate before, still the estate would pass at law, notwithstanding that idea, and there being no intention to revoke the gift, surely it would get rid of any resulting trust. On the same principle, when a testator makes his debtor executor, and thereby releases the debt at law, he is no longer liable at law. It is said that he would be liable in this Court: and so he would, unless he could shew some reason for not being made liable. Then what does he shew here? Why, he proves to the satisfaction of the Court a continuing intention to give; and it appears to me that there being the continuing intention to give, and there being a legal act which transferred the ownership or released the obligation – for it is the same thing – the transaction is perfected, and he does not want the aid of a Court of Equity to carry it out, or to make it complete, because it is complete already, and there is no equity against him to take the property away from him.

On that ground I shall hold that this gentleman had a perfect title to the £900; but there is another ground which I think is equally clear, namely, the testatrix living for more than nine quarters after the period when she forgave the debt, and paying the full amount for board, without any deduction.

Now, what were her legal rights? By the bargain that was made her legal right was to retain £100 every quarter out of the quarterly amount payable for board. It was not a question of set-off, but it was a legal debt. She, therefore, when the quarter expired, owed this gentleman £112.10s and no more, and if he had brought an action for more, she could, by paying the £112.10s into Court, without any plea of set-off, have succeeded in the action. His legal right was to obtain from her at the end of each quarter £112.10s. At the end of each quarter she pays him another £100 which she does not owe him, and when she has made nine of these payments she has paid him £900. It is not any question of intended gift; it is a complete payment by her paying the £900 by instalments of £100 each, which she intended to give him, and which she has given him at each period as they became due by actual payments, and I think that that would enable him to say, "Having been paid, I have a right to retain, because the testatrix intended me to retain", and the gift is perfectly established in that way also.

On both grounds, therefore, I think that this gentleman is entitled to succeed, and I shall allow the summons accordingly.'

Voyce v *Voyce* (1991) 62 P & CR 290 Court of Appeal (Dillon, Nicholls and Russell LJJ)

Acquisition of property by estoppel of other party

Facts
A mother allowed her son (the defendant) to live in a cottage which she owned, together with some adjoining land. This was a gift to the defendant provided he did work on the cottage to the mother's reasonable satisfaction. The defendant incurred considerable expense in carrying out the work but no deed of gift was executed in his favour. However, the mother subsequently executed a deed of gift in respect of the cottage in favour of the defendant's brother (the plaintiff). The mother then died but shortly afterwards the defendant began an extension of the cottage. The plaintiff, who claimed ownership of the cottage, applied to the court to prevent the defendant continuing with the new work and also seeking to compel the defendant to vacate the land apart from the cottage. It was held at first instance that the plaintiff must transfer the freehold of the cottage to the defendant. The plaintiff appealed to the Court of Appeal.

Held
The appeal must be dismissed. The plaintiff, as a volunteer, was in the same position as his mother would have been. Since the defendant had incurred considerable expenditure in reliance on his mother's promise she would have been estopped from asserting her title to the cottage – so also would be the plaintiff. It would be inequitable for the plaintiff to claim continuing ownership in these circumstances.

Wale, Re [1956] 1 WLR 1346 Chancery Division (Upjohn J)

Completely and incompletely constituted trusts: assignment of chose in action

Facts
A settlor made a voluntary settlement of shares in 1939 to trustees on trust for her daughter. The shares consisted of some 'A' investments of which the settlor was the absolute owner and some 'B' investments to which the settlor was entitled under her late husband's will and registered in the names of her late husband's executors. After the settlor made the settlement, she forgot about it and did not make any effort to transfer the shares to it. At her death the settlor left a will leaving all her property to her two sons. The question arose as to who was entitled to the shares, the daughter under the settlement or the sons under the will.

Held
As to the 'A' investments, the settlor held the legal title to these and as she had failed to transfer it to the

trustees the trust was incompletely constituted as regards them. The court would not assist the daughter here because she was a volunteer so the shares passed under the will to the sons.'

As to the 'B' investments, the settlor had only an equitable interest in these (the legal title being in her husband's executors). The settlement operated as a valid assignment of these shares because the settlor only had an equitable interest in them and as an equitable chose in action no formalities or consideration was needed to transfer them other than writing under s53(1)(c) LPA 1925: the daughter was therefore entitled to them.

Upjohn J:

'... another familiar principle is that an assignment of an equitable estate need not be in any particular form. As Lord Macnaghten said in *Brandt's (William) Sons & Co Ltd v Dunlop Rubber Co Ltd* [1905] AC 454: "The language is immaterial if the meaning is plain". That, in my judgment, applies as much to a voluntary assignment as to one for valuable consideration as in that case. (See also *Lambe v Orton* (1860) 1 Drew & Sm 125). An equitable assignment may take many forms. It may in terms purport to operate as an assignment, or it may take the form of a direction to the trustees in whom the legal estate is outstanding to hold the property on trust for the donee or on new trusts.

That last method is a perfectly good equitable assignment. As Sargant J said in *In re Chrimes* [1917] 1 Ch 30: "Now it is well established that in the case of an equitable interest outstanding in trustees or other holders a voluntary direction by the owner to the trustees or holders to hold the whole or part of that interest upon trust for a third person operates as a complete and effectual transfer of the interest to which the direction extends ..." .'

Westerton, Re [1919] 2 Ch 104 Chancery Division (Sargant J)

Written assignment of a chose in action: consideration and notice

Facts

The testator gave his landlady an envelope containing a deposit receipt for £500 from a bank, and a letter saying 'I ... [give] you the amount of £500 now on deposit as per receipt enclosed.' He said 'I will keep it for you', and after showing it to her, put it in his safe where it was found after his death. He had left a will in which he left all his estate elsewhere. There was no consideration and no notice had been given to the Bank.

Held

The landlady had good title.

Sargant J:

' ... No notice of the assignment was given to the Bank at the time; but ... mere omission to give notice at the time was of no consequence so long as notice was given before action brought. The omission in no way affected the efficacy of the assignment as between the donor and the donee, though if the bank, having had no notice of the assignment, had paid the money to the testator, the payment would have been a good payment as against the donee ... It seems to me that apart from the Judicature Act 1873 s25(6) [now s136 LPA] the want of consideration would have been fatal. Prior to the Judicature Act 1873 a legal chose in action such as this debt could not have been transferred at law, and equity would not have granted ... relief unless the assignment had been for valuable consideration. But ... the effect of ... [the section] has been to improve the position of an assignee of a chose in action who satisfies the words of the sub-section, that is to say, an assignee under an absolute assignment by writing under the hand of the assignor not purporting to be by way of charge only ... The result ... is that an assignee who takes under such an absolute assignment ... can now sue at law in his own name.'

Wilkes v *Allington* [1931] 2 Ch 104 Chancery Division (Lord Tomlin sitting as a Chancery judge)

Donatio mortis causa reason for donor's belief

Facts
The donor made a donatio in the belief that he was dying of cancer. In fact he was not, but he caught a chill and died of pneumonia.

Held
The donatio was good, as the other conditions were fulfilled, and the donor genuinely expected to die. The fact that he did so from a cause other than the one he expected was immaterial.

Woodard v *Woodard* [1991] Fam Law 470 Court of Appeal (Dillon and Nicholls LJJ and Sir John Megaw)

Donatio mortis causa

Facts
This case was concerned with a dispute between a mother (plaintiff) and her son (defendant) with regard to a car which had belonged to the deceased – ie the plaintiff's late husband and the defendant's father. When the husband/father was admitted to hospital for a serious illness he had told a friend that he had given his car to the son. However, on leaving hospital he had resumed use of the car for his own purposes. Later on he was re-admitted to hospital and eventually died there. A few days before his impending death the father told the son, in the mother's presence, that he could keep the car keys since he would not need the car any more. The son then sold the car and spent the proceeds.

The mother, who was the deceased's sole beneficiary and sole personal representative, claimed the proceeds of sale for the estate. At first instance it was held that the car had been an immediate gift to the son in the father's lifetime. It was common ground that at all relevant times the son had had use and possession of the car, with one set of keys. The plaintiff appealed. By a late amendment, which was allowed, the defendant pleaded, as an alternative, that the car had constituted a donatio mortis causa in his favour.

Held
The appeal should be dismissed. The son was, however, held to be the recipient of a valid donatio mortis causa, rather than an immediate gift. Dillon LJ indicated that delivery of a car's documentation did not always constitute transfer of dominion – there had to be sufficient evidence of intention. Where, as here, the object of the gift was already in possession of the relevant property as bailee, the words of gift operated to change the nature of that possession to that of donee. The defendant was thus entitled to the car as a donatio mortis causa.

4 Secret Trusts

Adams and the Kensington Vestry, Re
See Chapter 1.

Armstrong, Re (1969) 7 DLR (3d) 36 Canada
Half-secret trust: attestation by legatee

Facts
A half-secret trust appeared in a will which was, however, witnessed by the legatee who was to take subject to the trust.

Held
The trust was good as the legatee, though taking the legal estate, did not take beneficially.

Boyes, Re (1884) 26 Ch D 531 Chancery Division (Kay J)
Fully secret trust: communication to legatee

Facts
A testator had a will drawn up by his solicitor by which he left all his estate to the solicitor absolutely and appointed him executor. The testator told the solicitor prior to drawing up the will that he wished him to hold the property according to directions he would communicate by letter. No directions were ever given to the solicitor but after the testator's death an unattested document was found which was addressed to the solicitor and instructed him to hold the whole estate for a Miss Brown. The testator's next-of-kin sought a declaration that they were beneficially entitled to the estate. The solicitor argued that there was a binding fully secret trust.

Held
There was no fully secret trust. It was essential that the testator should have communicated the objects of the trust during his lifetime to the legatee. This he had failed to do and to allow the trust to stand would be contrary to the probate doctrine of incorporation by reference for the unattested document would have to be admitted.

Kay J:

'If it had been expressed on the face of the will that the defendant was a trustee, but the trusts were not thereby declared, it is quite clear that no trust afterwards declared by a paper not executed as a will could be binding: *Johnson* v *Ball* (1851) 5 De G & Sm 85; *Briggs* v *Penny* (1851) 3 Mac & G 546; *Singleton* v *Tomlinson* (1878) 3 App Cas 404. In such a case the legatee would be a trustee for the next-of-kin.

There is another well-known class of cases where no trust appears on the face of the will, but the testator has been induced to make the will, or, having made it, has been induced not to revoke it, by a promise on the part of the devisee or legatee to deal with the property, or some part of it, in a specified manner. In these cases the court has compelled discovery and performance of the promise, treating it as a trust binding the conscience of the donee, on the ground that otherwise a fraud would be committed, because it is to be presumed that if it had not been for such promise the testator would not have made or would have revoked the gift. The principle of these decisions is precisely the same as in the case of an heir who has induced a testator not to make a will devising the estate away from him by a promise that if the estate were allowed to descend he would make a certain provision out of it for a named person: *Stickland v Aldridge* (1804) 9 Ves 516; *Wallgrave v Tebbs* (1855) 2 K & J 313; *McCormick v Grogan* (1869) LR 4 HL 82. But no case has ever yet decided that a testator can, by imposing a trust upon his devisee or legatee, the objects of which he does not communicate to him, enable himself to evade the Statute of Wills by declaring those objects in an unattested paper found after his death.

The essence of all those decisions is that the devisee or legatee accepts a particular trust which thereupon becomes binding upon him, and which it would be a fraud in him not to carry into effect.

If the trust was not declared when the will was made, it is essential, in order to make it binding, that it should be communicated to the devisee or legatee in the testator's lifetime and that he should accept that particular trust. It may possibly be that he would be bound if the trust had been put in writing and placed in his hands in a sealed envelope, and he had engaged that he would hold the property given to him by the will upon the trust so declared, although he did not know the actual terms of the trust: *McCormick v Grogan*. But the reason is that it must be assumed that if he had not so accepted, the will would be revoked. Suppose the case of an engagement to hold the property not upon the terms of any paper communicated to the legatee or put into his hands, but of any paper that might be found after the testator's death.

The evidence in this case does not amount to that, but if it did the rule of law would intervene, which prevents a testator from declaring trusts in such a manner by a paper which was not executed as a will or codicil. The legatee might be a trustee, but the trust declared by such an unattested paper would not be good. For this purpose there is no difference whether the devisee or legatee is declared to be a trustee on the face of the will, or by an engagement with the testator not appearing on the will. The devisee or legatee cannot by accepting an indefinite trust enable the testator to make an unattested codicil.

I cannot help regretting that the testator's intention of bounty should fail by reason of an informality of this kind, but in my opinion it would be a serious innovation upon the law relating to testamentary instruments if this were to be established as a trust in her favour.

The defendant, however, having admitted that he is only a trustee, I must hold, on the authority of *Muckleston v Brown* (1801) 6 Ves 52, *Briggs v Penny* and *Johnson v Ball*, that he is a trustee of the property for the next-of-kin for the testator.'

Cooper (Colin), Re [1939] Ch 811 Court of Appeal (Sir Wilfrid Greene MR, Clauson and Goddard LJJ)

Fully secret trust: communication to legatee

Facts
By his will the testator gave a £5,000 legacy jointly to two persons to hold on a secret trust which he had communicated to them before executing the will. The testator executed another will at a later date which purported to cancel the earlier will except for certain bequests and stated: 'The sum of £5,000 bequeathed to my trustees in the will now cancelled is to be increased to £10,000, they knowing my wishes regarding that sum.' The increased bequest was never communicated to the legatees by the testator in his lifetime.

Held
There was a secret trust of the first £5,000 but not the second £5,000.

Sir Wilfrid Greene MR:

'In the present case there is no question that when the testator made his will of 10 February 1938, the legacy of £5,000 thereby bequeathed to the two named trustees was effectively given and the giving of it complied with the requirements of a secret trust; the terms had been communicated, the trustees had acquiesced and the testator made his will upon the faith of that acquiescence. But the only trust which was in the picture on that occasion was one which related to a defined and stated sum of £5,000. That was the legacy the intention to bequeath which was communicated to the trustees; that was the legacy in respect of which they gave their acceptance; that was the legacy which the testator, induced by that acceptance, in fact bequeathed. At a later date when, after an unfortunate sudden illness which proved fatal in South Africa, the testator made a will on 27 March 1938, he had no communication with those trustees with regard to the dispositions which he thereby made; there was no acquiescence by the trustees in the dispositions in question: he made that will not induced by any such acquiescence by the trustees although he made it quite clearly in the belief that what he was doing would be effective and that his trustees would carry it out; but none of the necessary elements to constitute a valid secret trust were present on the occasion of the making of that will. The actual form of that will was a cancellation of the will of February 1938, and the reinstatement of an earlier will. He then goes on to say: "The sum of £5,000 bequeathed to my trustees in the will now cancelled is to be increased to £10,000, they knowing my wishes regarding this sum." The learned judge construed the testamentary instructions of the testator by saying that the original gift of £5,000 was not revoked by this will and that in substance the effect of this will was to leave that gift in the earlier will unrevoked and to add to it a further £5,000. Speaking for myself, I do not think that any difference in principle emerges based on a distinction between the revocation of the original legacy and the bequest of a new legacy of larger amount, and the leaving of the original legacy unrevoked and the addition to it of a further sum. It does not seem to me possible to say that anything can turn on so fine a point. The substance of the matter is that, having imposed on the conscience of these two trustees the trust in relation to the legacy of £5,000 and having written that legacy into his will of February 1938, by this will he in effect is giving another legacy of the same amount to be held upon the same trusts. It seems to me that upon the facts of this case it is impossible to say that the acceptance by the trustees of the onus of trusteeship in relation to the first and earlier legacy is something which must be treated as having been repeated in reference to the second legacy or the increased legacy, whichever way one chooses to describe it.

In order that a secret trust might be made effective with regard to that added sum in my opinion precisely the same factors were necessary as were required to validate the original trusts, namely, communication, acceptance or acquiescence, and the making of the will on the faith of such acceptance or acquiescence. None of these elements, as I have said, were present. It is not possible, in my opinion, to treat the figure of £5,000 in relation to which the consent of the trustees was originally obtained as something of no essential importance. I cannot myself see that the arrangement between the testator and the trustees can be construed as though it had meant "£5,000 or whatever sum I may hereafter choose to bequeath". That is not what was said and it was not with regard to any sum other than the £5,000 that the consciences of the trustees (to use a technical phrase) were burdened. It must not be thought from what I have been saying that some trifling excess of the sum actually bequeathed over the figure mentioned in the first bequest to the trustees would necessarily not be caught. Such an addition might come within the rule of de minimis if the facts justified it. Similarly it must not be thought that, if a testator, having declared to his trustees trusts in relation to a specified sum, afterwards in his will inserts a lesser sum, that lesser sum would not be caught by the trusts. In such a case the greater would I apprehend be held to include the less. In the present case neither of these two possible methods of dealing with the difficulty is available, because here we have something to which the rule of de minimis could not possibly apply, for it is an increase and a very substantial increase of the legacy originally bequeathed. There is no ground, in my opinion, which would justify the Court in treating the reference to that specific sum which passed between the testator and the trustees as having a significance of so loose and indeterminate a character that it could be expanded at will.'

Gardner (No 2), Re [1923] 2 Ch 230 Chancery Division (Romer J)

Secret trusts operate outside the will

Facts
The testatrix by her will left her estate to her husband absolutely 'knowing that he will carry out my wishes'. The trusts were that the property was to be divided out at the husband's death between three named beneficiaries. The husband died five days after the testatrix and it was discovered that one of the three named beneficiaries had died before the wife. The issue was whether her share could be successfully claimed by his personal representatives.

Held
The personal representatives could take the beneficiaries' share. She received her share under the trust not the will, so it did not lapse.

Romer J:

> 'The question raised by his summons is whether persons claiming through the niece who predeceased the testatrix are entitled to a one-third share of the estate of the testatrix. The Court of Appeal in arriving at their decision were acting on a long established principle, that if the owner of property makes a gift of it on the faith of a promise by the donee that he will deal with the property in a particular way, an obligation so to deal with it is placed upon the donee and can be enforced in these Courts if the donee becomes entitled. Most of the cases where the principle has been applied are cases where the gift has been made by a will; but the principle operates whether the gift is made by settlement inter vivos, or by will, or where the owner of property refrains from making a will and so allows the property to pass to the donee as on an intestacy. That being the principle, I cannot see why a trust for the benefit of individuals engrafted upon property given to the donee by a will or by means of an intestacy should be treated as a gift made to those individuals by the will of the donor any more than it should be so treated where the property has been given to the donee by the donor in his lifetime. The principle has nothing to do with the fact that the gift has been made by one method rather than by another. Apart from authority I should, without hesitation, say that in the present case the husband held the corpus of the property upon trust for the two nieces and the nephew, notwithstanding the fact that the niece predeceased the testatrix. The rights of the parties appear to me to be exactly the same as though the husband, after the memorandum had been communicated to him by the testatrix in the year 1909, had executed a declaration of trust binding himself to hold any property that should come to him upon his wife's partial intestacy upon trust as specified in the memorandum.'

Commentary
The reference to the Court of Appeal at the beginning of Romer J's judgment is to the decision of that court in a previous action in this case.

Irvine v Sullivan (1869) LR 8 Eq 673 Chancery (James V-C)

Half-secret trust: trustee taking beneficially

Facts
The will gave property to the defendant 'trusting that she will carry out my wishes with regard to the same, with which she is fully acquainted'.

Held

Though in general the trustee under a half-secret trust would not be permitted to take beneficially, in this case on the true construction of the will the intention was that there should be a gift to the trustee on condition that she fulfilled the duties committed to her.

Johnson v Ball (1851) 5 De G & Sm 85 Court of Chancery (Parker V-C)

Half-secret trusts: communication

Facts

A testator gave a policy of assurance to two legatees 'to hold the same upon the uses appointed by letter signed by them and myself'. No such letter existed at the date of the will but the testator had previously asked the legatees to accept the bequest for the benefit of objects then named by him and they had agreed to do so. Long after the date of the will the testator wrote a letter to his executors stating that he had left the policy to the two legatees and asked them to deliver a sealed letter enclosed therewith to the legatees. This letter contained instructions to them. At the same time the testator executed a memorandum, declaring the trusts on which the legatees were to hold the policy. On the testator's death it was argued that the secret trust was invalid.

Held

The half-secret trust failed; a testator cannot reserve to himself a power to make future testamentary dispositions as this would be contrary to the Wills Act.

Parker V-C:

> 'The testator's language appears to point at some letter already signed by him and the trustees; but even supposing it to refer to a letter to be afterwards signed, it is impossible to give effect to any such letter as a declaration by the testator of the trusts on which he had bequeathed the policy to his trustees. To give them any such effect, would be to receive, as part of or as codicils to the will, papers subsequent in date to the will, which are unattested and which have not been and could not be admitted to probate. A testator cannot by his will prospectively create for himself a power to dispose of his property by an instrument not duly executed as a will or codicil. The decisions to this effect on devises of real estate under the Statute of Frauds are clearly applicable, and have been applied, under the existing law, to testamentary dispositions of any kind: *Countess De Zichy Ferraris v Marquis of Hertford* (1844) 4 Moo PC 339, *Briggs v Penny* (1851) 3 Mac & G 546.
>
> It was argued that the policy is bequeathed to the trustees; and that, as they admit a trust in favour of the plaintiff and her children, the Court will execute the trust so admitted. But the trustees have no interest in the policy which enables them to admit any such trust. The bequest is to them expressly upon trusts to be appointed by the testator; and, as the testator has made no effectual appointment, the trustees, if the bequest has not wholly failed, are trustees for the residuary legatees, and cannot, by their admission, create any other trust. Cases in which there is no trust appearing on the will, and where the Court establishes a trust on the confession of the legatee, have no application to the present; nor, as it appears to me, have those cases cited in the argument, in which the will refers to a trust created by the testator by communication with the legatee antecedently to or contemporaneously with the will.
>
> The testator's letters cannot operate as a gift or settlement by act inter vivos; because they do no more than refer to the bequest made by the will, and declare the purpose for which the policy was to be held by the trustees to whom it was left. The letters were merely in furtherance of the testamentary dispositions; and if the will had been revoked, the letters must have dropped with it.'

Keen, Re [1937] Ch 236 Court of Appeal (Lord Wright MR, Greene and Romer LJJ)

Half-secret trust: communication

Facts
By clause 5 of his will the testator gave £10,000 to his executors and trustees 'to be held on trust and disposed of by them among such person, persons or charities as may be notified by me to them or either of them during my lifetime ...' Before making his will the testator handed one of the executors a sealed envelope containing the name of the intended beneficiary and directed her not to open the envelope until after the testator's death. She was not informed of the contents. On the testator's death the executors sought a declaration as to whether there was a valid secret trust or whether the £10,000 fell into residue. At first instance Farwell J held that the £10,000 fell into residue because the secret trust was invalid. On appeal:

Held
As the sealed envelope was delivered before the date of the will it was not a communication consistent with the terms of the will. Consequently there was no effective communication of the terms of the secret trust. Further, on the true construction of the will, the testator had reserved the power to make a future unattested disposition contrary to s9 of the Wills Act 1837.

Lord Wright MR:

> 'The summons came before Farwell J, who decided adversely to the claims of the lady on the short ground that she could not prove that she was a person notified to the trustees by the testator during his lifetime within the words of clause 5. His opinion seems to be that the clause required the name and identity of the lady to be expressly disclosed to the trustees during the testator's lifetime so that it was not sufficient to place these particulars in the physical possession of the trustees or one of them in the form of a memorandum which they were not to read till the testator's death.
>
> I am unable to accept this conclusion, which appears to me to put too narrow a construction on the word "notified" as used in clause 5 in all the circumstances of the case. To take a parallel, a ship which sails under sealed orders, is sailing under orders though the exact terms are not ascertained by the captain till later. I note that the case of a trust put into writing which is placed in the trustees' hands in a sealed envelope, was hypothetically treated by Kay J as possibly constituting a communication in a case of this nature: *In re Boyes* (1884) 26 Ch D 531. This so far as it goes, seems to support my conclusion. the trustees had the means of knowledge available whenever it became necessary and proper to open the envelope. I think Mr Evershed was right in understanding that the giving of the sealed envelope was a notification within clause 5.
>
> This makes it necessary to examine the matter on a wider basis, and to consider the principles of law which were argued both before Farwell J and this Court, but which the judge found it merely necessary to mention. There are two main questions: first, how far parol evidence is admissible to define the trust under such a clause as this, and, secondly and in particular, how far such evidence if admissible at all would be excluded on the ground that it would be inconsistent with the true meaning of clause 5.
>
> It is first necessary to state what, in my opinion, is the true construction of the words of the clause.
>
> These words, in my opinion, can only be considered as referring to a definition of trusts which have not yet at the date of the will been established and which between that date and the testator's death may or may not be established. Mr Roxburgh has strenuously argued, basing himself in particular on the word "may", that the clause even though it covers future dispositions, also includes a disposition antecedent to or contemporaneous with the execution of the will. I do not think that even so wide a construction of the word '"may" would enable Mr Roxburgh's contention to succeed, but in any case I do not feel able to accept it. The words of the clause seem to me to refer only to something future and hypothetical, to something as to which the testator is reserving an option whether to do or not to do it.

It must then be considered whether the first paragraph of the clause can be held valid as a testamentary disposition. It is said on behalf of the residuary legatees, some of whom are infants, that it cannot, and that the only trust which takes effect is that which operates in their favour in the event of the provisions of the first part of the clause proving ineffective.

The principles of law or equity relevant in a question of this nature have now been authoritatively settled or discussed by the House of Lords in *Blackwell* v *Blackwell* [1929] AC 318. In 1869 in *McCormick* v *Grogan* (1869) LR 4 HL 82 the House of Lords had held that a secret trust, that is a trust created by an expression of the testator's wishes communicated to and accepted by the legatee, bound the conscience of the legatee, though in the terms of the will the bequest was absolute. Such a trust was held to be altogether outside the will; the will took effect according to its terms and the property passed absolutely to the legatee: but the Court, it was held, would compel the legatee to apply that property according to the undertaking he had assumed to carry out the wishes of the testator. It would be a fraud or breach of faith not to fulfil the undertaking which the legatee had given to carry out the purposes for which the bequest to him was made.

No complication was involved in such a case by reason of section 9 of the Wills Act 1837. The testamentary disposition, which had been duly attested, received full effect. But a different question had to be considered when in the will itself the property was left to the legatee in trust, but neither the nature of the trust nor its beneficiaries were defined in the will. That was the case decided in *Blackwell* v *Blackwell*. There was in that case a bequest to trustees to apply the income "for the purposes indicated by me and at any time to pay part of the corpus to such person or persons indicated by me as they think fit, the balance to fall into the residuary estate". The testator had by parol at or before the execution of the will indicated or defined the nature of the trust and the beneficiaries and the trustees had accepted the trust on those terms. It was held that parol evidence was admissible to explain the trusts and to prove that the trustees had accepted the legacy on the condition of fulfilling them. The trusts were accordingly, when thus established, proper to be enforced by the Court. There was, it was held, in such a case no conflict between the express terms of the will and the actual trusts intended, and the evidence was not admitted to add to or vary or contradict what the will said or to fill up blanks in it or to specify what was left vague. As Lord Sumner said: 'It is communication of the purpose to the legatee, coupled with acquiescence or promise on his part, that removes the matter from the provision of the Wills Act, and brings it within the law of trusts, as applied in this instance to trustees, who happen also to be legatees.' The conclusion thus was that just as much as in the case of a secret trust of the type discussed in *McCormick* v *Grogan* the conscience of the legatee was affected; it made no difference whether according to its terms the will left the property to the legatee absolutely or on a trust which the will did not specify. The essential conditions were that the trust had been disclosed to the legatee as the testator's object in leaving the property and had been accepted by him.

So it was held by the House of Lords following a series of decisions since 1688, first under the Statute of Frauds and later under the Statute of Wills, which was held to have made no change in the law in this respect. Doubts had been expressed by eminent lawyers as to the correctness of these earlier decisions, but they were thus disposed of by the House of Lords in *Blackwell* v *Blackwell*; the general equitable jurisdiction to prevent a breach of faith or the failure of a trust duly declared and accepted, was held to override the technical objections. Lord Sumner stated his conclusion, which agreed with that expressed in the speeches of Lord Buckmaster and Lord Warrington, in the following words: "Accordingly I think the conclusion is confirmed, which the frame of section 9 of the Wills Act seems to me to carry on its face, that the legislation did not purport to interfere with the exercise of a general equitable jurisdiction, even in connection with secret dispositions of a testator, except in so far as reinforcement of the formalities required for a valid will might indirectly limit it. the effect, therefore of a bequest being made in terms on trust, without any statement in the will to show that the trust is, remains to be decided by the law as laid down by the Courts before and since the Act and does not depend on the Act itself."

But he goes on to add qualifications which are essentially relevant for the determination of the present case. These are qualifications which flow from the circumstance that the will is not completely silent as to the trust, as is the case in wills of the type discussed in *McCormick* v *Grogan* but does in express terms indicate that there is a trust. The qualifications are thus stated by Lord Sumner: "The limits, beyond which the rules as to unspecified trusts must not be carried, have often been discussed. A testator cannot reserve to himself a power of making future unwitnessed dispositions by merely naming a trustee and leaving the purposes of the trust to be supplied afterwards, nor can a legatee give testamentary validity to a unexecuted codicil by accepting an indefinite trust, never communicated to him in the testator's lifetime: *Johnson* v *Ball* (1851) 5 De G & Sm 85; *In re Boyes*; *Riordan* v *Banon* Ir R 10 Eq 469; *In re Hetley* [1902] 2 Ch 866. To hold otherwise would indeed be to enable the testator to 'give the go-by' to the requirements of the Wills Act, because he did not choose to comply with them."

As in my judgment clause 5 should be considered as contemplating future dispositions and as reserving to the testator the power of making such dispositions without a duly attested codicil simply by notifying them during his lifetime, the principles laid down by Lord Sumner must be fatal to the appellant's claim. Indeed they would be equally fatal even on the construction for which Mr Roxburgh contended, that the clause covered both anterior or contemporaneous notifications as well as future notifications. The clause would be equally invalid, but, as already explained, I cannot accept that construction. In *Blackwell* v *Blackwell*; *In re Fleetwood* (1880) 15 Ch D 594 and *In re Huxtable* [1902] 2 Ch 793, the trusts had been specifically declared to some or all of the trustees at or before the execution of the will and the language of the will was consistent with that fact. There was in these cases no reservation of a future power to change the trusts, in whole or in part. Such a power would involve a power to change a testamentary disposition by an unexecuted codicil and would violate section 9 of the Wills Act. This was so held in *In re Hetley*; *Johnson* v *Ball* is again a somewhat different example of the rule against dispositions made subsequently to the date of the will in cases where the will in terms leaves the property on trust, and shows that the position may be different from the position where the will in terms leaves the gift absolutely. The trusts referred to but undefined in the will must be described in the will as established prior to or at least contemporaneously with its execution.

But there is still a further objection which in the present case renders the appellant's claim unenforceable; the trusts which it is sought to establish by parol evidence would be inconsistent with the express terms of the will. That such an objection is fatal appears from the cases already cited, such as *In re Huxtable*. In that case an undefined trust of money for charitable purposes was declared in the will as in respect of the whole corpus, and accordingly evidence was held inadmissible that the charitable trust was limited to the legatee's life so that he was free to dispose of the corpus after his death. Similarly in *Johnson* v *Ball* the testator by the will left the property to trustees upon the uses contained in a letter signed "by them and myself": it was held that evidence was not admissible to show that though no such letter was in existence at the date of the will, the testator had made a subsequent declaration of trust; the Court held that these trusts could not be enforced. Lord Buckmaster in *Blackwell*'s case described *Johnson* v *Ball* as an authority pointing to "a case where the actual trusts were left over after the date of the will to be subsequently determined by the testator." That in his opinion would be a contravention of the Wills Act. I know of no authority which would justify such a contravention. Lord Buckmaster also quotes the grounds on which Parker V-C based his decision as being both "that the letter referred to in the will had no existence at the time when the will was made and that supposing it referred to a letter afterwards signed it is impossible to give effect to it as a declaration of the trusts, since it would admit the document as part of the will and it was unattested".

In the present case, while clause 5 refers solely to a future definition or to future definitions of the trust subsequent to the date of the will, the sealed letter relied on as notifying the trust was communicated (as I find the facts) before the date of the will. That it was communicated to one trustee only and not to both would not, I think, be an objection (see Lord Warrington's observation in the *Blackwell* case). But the objection remains that the notification sought to be put in evidence was anterior to the will and hence not within the language of clause 5, and inadmissible simply on that ground as being inconsistent with what the will prescribes.

It is always with reluctance that a Court refuses to give effect to the proved intention of the testator. In the present case it may be said that the objection is merely a matter of drafting and that the decision in *Blackwell* v *Blackwell* would have been applicable if only clause 5 had been worded as applying to trusts previously indicated by the testator. The sealed letter would then have been admissible, subject to proof of the communication and acceptance of the trust. This may be true, but the Court must deal with the matter as in fact it is. It would be impossible to give effect to the appellant's contention without not merely extending the rule laid down in *Blackwell* v *Blackwell*, but actually contravening the limitations which have been placed on that rule as necessarily arising from the Wills Act and, in addition, from the fact that the conditions prescribed by the will cannot be contradicted.'

McCormick v *Grogan* (1869) LR 4 HL 82 House of Lords (Lord Hatherley LC, Lord Cairns, Lord Colonsay and Lord Westbury)

Basis of secret trusts

Facts

The testator made a will leaving all his property to Grogan. On his deathbed he sent for Grogan and said that there was a letter with the will, but did not ask Grogan to say that he would observe it. The letter named beneficiaries but also said 'I do not wish you to act strictly to the foregoing instructions, but leave it entirely in your good judgment to do as you think I would if living and as the parties are deserving'. In fact Grogan gave nothing to one of the people named, who brought an action claiming that there was a secret trust in his favour laid down in the letter.

Held

The testator had not intended a legally binding obligation and therefore there was no secret trust. In the Court of Appeal in Ireland, Christian LJ said: 'The real question is, what did he intend should be the sanction? Was it to be authority of a Court of Justice, or the conscience of the devisee? In my opinion, expressly and exclusively the latter.'

Lord Westbury:

'The jurisdiction which is invoked here is founded altogether on personal fraud. It is a jurisdiction by which a Court of Equity, proceeding on the ground of fraud, converts the party who has committed it into a trustee for the party who is injured by that fraud. Now, being a jurisdiction founded on personal fraud, it is incumbent on the Court to see that a fraud, a malus animus, is proved by the clearest and most indisputable evidence. You are obliged, therefore, to show most clearly and distinctly that the person you wish to convert into a trustee acted malo animo. You must show distinctly that he knew that the testator or intestate was beguiled or deceived by his conduct. If you are not in a condition to affirm that without any misgiving, or possibility of mistake, you are not warranted in affixing on the individual the delictum of fraud, which you must do before you convert him into a trustee.

... The Court of Equity has, from a very early period, decided that even an Act of Parliament shall not be used as an instrument of fraud; and if in the machinery of perpetrating a fraud an Act of Parliament intervenes, the Court of Equity, it is true, does not set aside the Act of Parliament, but it fastens on the individual, who gets a title under that Act, and imposes on him a personal obligation, because he applies the Act as an instrument for accomplishing a fraud. In this way the Court of Equity has dealt with the Statute of Frauds, and in this manner, also, it deals with the Statute of Wills.'

Maddock, Re [1902] 2 Ch 220 Court of Appeal (Collins MR, Stirling and Cozens-Hardy LJJ)

Secret trusts: basis

Facts
An order for administration of assets was sought in an estate where there were insufficient personal assets to pay the debts of the estate. The testatrix had executed a memorandum which it was held should be treated as a codicil. The memorandum contained certain trusts and the question was whether those who took subject to the memorandum were bound by it and the rights of those under it.

Held
As the memorandum was treated as though its contents were part of the will or a codicil the trust of the specified property stood in the position of the specific bequest of that part. The testatrix's debts were therefore to be borne first by that part not seized of the trust and any deficiency thereafter pro rata by the specified part of the residue and realty.

Cozens Hardy LJ:

'It is necessary to consider upon that principle the undoubted rule of the Court, that effect is to be given under certain circumstances to declarations in writing not properly attested is based. It is clear that no unattested document can be admitted to probate or treated as part of the will. It is established that a devisee or legatee, who is entitled absolutely upon the terms of the will, is in no way affected by the existence of a document shewing that he was not intended to enjoy beneficially, if he had no knowledge of the document until after the death of the testator. Such a memorandum may or may not influence him as a man of honour, but no legal effect can be given to it. If, however, the devisee or legatee is informed of the testator's intention, either before the will in his favour is made or at any time afterwards before the testator's death, different considerations arise. It is sometimes said that under such circumstances a trust is created in favour of the beneficiaries under the memorandum. At other times it has been said that the devisee or legatee under the will is bound by contract, express or implied, to give effect to the testator's wishes. Now, the so-called trust does not affect the property except by reason of a personal obligation binding the individual devisee or legatee. If he renounces and disclaims, or dies in the lifetime of the testator, the persons claiming under the memorandum can take nothing against the heir-at-law or next-of-kin or residuary devisee or legatee.'

Moss v *Cooper* (1861) 1 J & H 352 Vice-Chancellor's Court (Wood V-C)

Fully secret trust: communication to legatee

Facts
A testator wished to apply his residuary estate to charity and was advised that he must give it absolutely to the legatees followed by a memorandum setting out how the residue might be divided among the charities he wished to benefit. The testator left his residue equally between Gawthorn, Sedman and Owen. A memorandum was prepared by Gawthorn on the testator's instructions after the will was executed giving a detailed account of the residue and its disposal to charity. The statement and a copy of the will were communicated by Gawthorn to Sedman and Owen, and received by them without any express acceptance or refusal of the trust. Sedman afterwards told the testator that he would endeavour to carry out his wishes, Owen preserved silence on the subject to the last. Gawthorn died before the testator. The next-of-kin challenged the disposition saying it was an invalid secret trust.

Held
There was prima facie evidence that Gawthorn was authorised by the testator to make the communication and was known or believed by both Sedman and Owen to be so authorised; and therefore the legatees could not take for their own benefit. It did not matter either whether the promise to hold on a secret trust

was made before or after the date of the will; this question only required consideration where the promise had been made by one of several joint legatees (See *Re Stead*, infra), a matter which had not arisen here.

Wood V-C:

'Here it is said that the testator intended to give the legatees full and complete control over the property. On the face of the will he did; but the question is, whether, behind that intention, he had not a further desire to secure as far as possible their obedience to his wishes. Barber's (the testator's solicitor) advice did not go beyond this – that the gift must be absolute; and he did not warn the testator not to mention the subject to the legatees. If, immediately after making his will (for a bargain before the will is not at all essential), the testator had invited Gawthorn, Owen and Sedman to his house, and had said to them, 'Here is my will, made in this form, because I am told that the property must be put entirely at your disposal; but I want a promise from you to dispose of it in a particular way': and if they, by their silence, led him to believe that they would so apply it, I apprehend it is quite clear that a trust would be created, and that it is altogether immaterial whether the promise is made before or after the execution of the will, that being a revocable instrument...

... When you prove that the testator desired to create a trust, and that his desire was communicated to the legatee by one who had acted as the testator's agent in the preparation of the will, you have prima facie evidence that the communication was made by the testator's direction. It is not necessary, for the purpose of my decision, to consider what the Court might do in a case where the testator is proved to have had a particular wish, and that wish is proved to have been communicated to the legatee without the sanction or authority of the testator. That question does not, in my opinion, arise here and when it does arise it may require some consideration, what would be the result if the legatee, after receiving this unauthorised information, abstains from making any communication to the testator as to his acceptance or refusal of the trusts. That will be an entirely new case. But, here, there are sufficient grounds to infer that Gawthorn, in fact, and to the knowledge or belief of Owen, had authority to make the communication; and, in that case, Owen's silence is a sufficient acceptance of the trust to exclude him from any beneficial enjoyment of the property.'

Ottaway v *Norman* [1972] Ch 698 Chancery Division (Brightman J)

Fully secret trust: acceptance by legatee

Facts

By his will the testator devised his bungalow together with all the furniture, fixtures and fittings to his housekeeper, Mrs Hodges, apparently absolutely. He also gave her a legacy of £1,500 and half the residue. On the occasion of one of the testator's sons visits to the testator's home, the testator told his son, in the presence of Mrs Hodges, that it was his intention that Mrs Hodges should have the bungalow for the rest of her life but that she should leave it to him on her death. Mrs Hodges agreed to this. When the testator died, Mrs Hodges immediately made a will leaving the bungalow to the son. However, in 1967 she had a disagreement with the son and made a new will leaving the bungalow to someone else. On her death in 1968, the son sought a declaration that the bungalow was held on trust for him.

Held

There was a secret trust. Clear evidence showed that the testator had communicated the secret trust to Mrs Hodges and she had accepted it.

Brightman J:

'... It will be convenient to call the person on whom such a trust is imposed the "primary donee" and the beneficiary under the trust the "secondary donee". The essential elements which must be proved to exist are, (i) the intention of the testator to subject the primary donee to an obligation in favour of the secondary donee; (ii) communication of that intention to the primary donee; and (iii) the acceptance of that obligation by the primary donee either expressly or by acquiescence. It is immaterial whether these elements precede or succeed the will of the donor. I am informed that there is no recent reported case where the obligation imposed on a primary donee is an obligation to make a will in favour of the secondary donee as distinct from some form of inter vivos transfer. But, it does not seem to me that that can really be a distinction which can validly be drawn on behalf of the defendant in the present case. The basis of the doctrine of a secret trust is the obligation imposed on the conscience of the primary donee and it does not seem to me that there is any materiality in the machinery by which the donor intends that that obligation shall be carried out ...'

Pugh's Will Trusts, Re [1967] 1 WLR 1262 Chancery Division (Pennycuick J)

Half-secret trusts: disposition of residue

Facts

By his will the testator appointed his solicitor executor and trustee and after giving £1,500 legacies each to his two brothers, he left the residue to the solicitor 'to dispose of the same in accordance with any letters or memoranda I may leave with this my will and otherwise in such manner as he may in his absolute discretion think fit'. The testator died in 1964 without leaving any letters or memoranda with his will. The solicitor sought a declaration as to whether he was entitled to take the residue beneficially or whether he held it for the testator's next-of-kin.

Held

The direction to apply the residuary estate in accordance with letters and memoranda imposed a fiduciary obligation on the solicitor in the nature of a trust. As this trust had no defined objects it was void for uncertainty.

Pennycuick J:

'This direction clearly imposes upon the trustee, at any rate, some degree of fiduciary obligation, and it is impossible to construe the gift as a simple and absolute gift to the trustee. The nature of the fiduciary obligation is first to dispose of the residuary estate in accordance with any letters or memoranda which the testator may leave with the will and secondly otherwise – and that I think means subject to any such letter or memorandum – to dispose of the residuary estate in such manner as the trustee may in his absolute discretion think fit. I have so far referred to the duty imposed upon the trustee as a fiduciary obligation, but one may as well use the word 'trust' because that fiduciary obligation is in the nature of a trust. It is impossible to say that a direction to dispose of the estate in accordance with letters or memoranda does not constitute the trustee a trustee of the estate to the extent to which there are effective letters or memoranda left with the will. The construction of clause 6 then is, I think, quite free from doubt.

It remains then to consider what, as a matter of law, is the effect of a provision in those terms. At first sight the second limb of the direction looks like a general power, but there is a long train of authority which is, I think, conclusive to the contrary. The effect of the authorities, to which I will refer in a moment, is that where one finds a gift upon trust to apply the subject matter in such manner or for such purposes, or whatever the words may be, as the donee may think fit, then that represents a trust for undefined objects such as the court cannot execute, and the trust is void, always of course in the absence of any further indication of intention ...'

Rees, Re [1950] Ch 204 Court of Appeal (Sir Raymond Evershed MR, Cohen and Asquith LJJ)

Half-secret trust: residue

Facts

By his will the testator appointed a friend and his solicitor to be executors and trustees thereof and devised and bequeathed the whole of his property to 'my trustees absolutely they well knowing my wishes concerning the same'. The testator told the executors and trustees at the time of making the will that he wished them to make certain payments out of the estate and retain the remainder for their own use. After the payments were made there was a substantial surplus. The executors contended that they were entitled to keep the surplus in that there was no secret trust but a gift to them conditional on making certain payments.

Held

That part of the estate which was not required to give effect to the testator's wishes was undisposed of by his will and passed on intestacy. The executors and trustees could not claim it because a fiduciary obligation had been imposed upon them.

Sir Raymond Evershed MR:

'That makes it necessary to consider the second question. As I have already indicated, I agree with the judge that to admit evidence to the effect that the testator informed one of the executors – or, I will assume in Mr Milner Holland's favour, both of the executors – that he intended them to take beneficial interests and that his wishes included that intention, would be to conflict with the terms of the will as I have construed them; for the inevitable result of admitting that evidence and giving effect to it would be that the will would be regarded not as conferring a trust estate only upon the two trustees, but as giving them a conditional gift which on construction is the thing which, if I am right, it does not do. Mr Milner Holland's answer is that, once the "wishes concerning the same", so far as they relate to third parties, are admitted, then there is no inconsistency, since this, after all, is part of the wishes. According to the evidence, I think that not entirely clear, but I assume it in Mr Milner Holland's favour. Still, as I think, that does not get over the difficulty. The admission of this evidence would involve that the trustees took not a trust estate but a conditional gift. The point was thus put by my brother Cohen during the argument: suppose that the express wishes were contained in some document, and that the document stated that, subject to satisfaction of these various gifts, the residue should belong to the two named persons absolutely: what would be the situation then? My first answer would be that that does not happen to be the fact in this case; but if it were so and such a document were referred to in the will, then it seems to me that prima facie that document would have to be included in the probate, and the question then would have been one of the construction of the two documents, the will and the memorandum together ...

... The judge in the next sentence expressed some regret at having come to a conclusion which probably defeated the wishes of the testator. I also am not insensible to that. At the same time my own regrets are moderated to this extent: in the general public interest it is not to be forgotten that Parliament has laid it down that prima facie a will disposing of the property of a deceased person must follow certain strict forms. These courts have also been very insistent on the importance of the principle that those who assume the office of trustees should not, so far as they fairly can prevent it, allow themselves to be in a position in which their interests and their duties conflict. This is a case in which the will, as I have said, was drawn by a solicitor, or by a member of a solicitor's firm, and the claim is that that solicitor is entitled, either absolutely or jointly with another, to the whole beneficial interest. In the general public interest it seems to me desirable that if a testator wishes his property to go to his solicitor and the solicitor prepares the will, that intention on the part of the testator should appear plainly on the will and should not be arrived at by the more oblique method of what is sometimes called a secret trust ...'

Russell v *Jackson* (1852) 10 Hare 204 Chancery (Turner V-C)

Communication to joint tenants of secret trusts

Facts
The testator created a joint tenancy subject to a secret trust. Before making the will he communicated the trusts to some of the trustees who agreed to be bound by it.

Held
All the joint tenants were bound by the trust whether they had accepted it or not, since the testator had been induced to make his will by the promise of those to whom it was communicated that they would observe his wishes, and to allow others without knowledge to avoid the trust would be to allow them to take a benefit procured by fraud.

Commentary
Contrast *Moss* v *Cooper*, above.

Snowden (deceased), Re [1979] Ch 528 Chancery Division (Megarry V-C)

Fully secret trust: legal not moral obligation required: standard of proof

Facts
A testatrix who could not decide how to divide her residuary estate among her numerous nephews and nieces instructed her solicitor to draft a will leaving all her residue to her brother. She told the solicitor that her brother could then distribute the residue 'between her nephews and nieces equally' and that her brother 'could then see everybody and look after the division for her'. Other evidence showed that the testatrix wanted to be fair to 'everyone' and that her brother 'would know what to do'. The brother agreed to deal with everything for the testatrix. The testatrix died six days after making the will, and the brother died six days later, leaving all his estate to his only son. The question arose whether a secret trust was imposed on the brother.

Held
The standard of proof required to establish a secret trust was the ordinary civil standard required to establish an ordinary trust. The testatrix had clearly executed the will on the basis of some arrangement between herself and her brother. To see if this arrangement was a secret trust it was necessary to show that she intended the sanction of the court to enforce the arrangement if the brother did not carry it out. On the evidence there was no such intention, there was only a moral obligation on the brother and he accordingly took the residue free from any trust.

Megarry V-C:

'I cannot say that there is no evidence from which it could be informed that a secret trust was created. At the same time, that evidence is far from being overwhelming. One question that arises is thus whether the standard of proof required to establish a secret trust is merely the ordinary civil standard of proof, or whether it is a higher and more cogent standard. If it is the latter, I feel no doubt that the claim that there is a secret trust must fail. On this question, *Ottaway* v *Norman* [1972] Ch 698 was cited; it was, indeed, the only authority that was put before me. According to the headnote, the standard of proof "was not an exceptionally high one but was analogous to that required before the court would rectify a written instrument". When one turns to the judgment, one finds that what Brightman J said was that Lord

Westbury's words in *McCormick* v *Grogan* (1869) LR 4 HL 82, a case on secret trusts, did not mean that an exceptionally high standard of proof was needed, but meant more that that.

> "If a will contains a gift which is in terms absolute, clear evidence is needed before the court will assume that the testator did not mean what he said. It is perhaps analogous to the standard of proof which this court requires before it will rectify a written instrument, for there again, a party is saying that neither meant what they have written."

On this, I would make four comments. First, the headnote seems to me to be liable to mislead, since it omits the judge's precautionary word "perhaps" which preceded the "analogous" and so gives a firmness to the proposition which the judge avoided.

Second, the standard for rectification is indeed high, and certainly higher than ordinary standards ...

Third, I feel some doubt about how far rectification is a fair analogy to secret trusts in this respect. Many cases of rectification do of course involve a party in saying that neither meant what they have written, and requiring that what they have written should be altered. On the other hand, the whole basis of secret trusts, as I understand it, is that they operate outside the will, changing nothing that is written in it, and allowing it to operate according to its tenor, but then fastening a trust on to the property in the hands of the recipient ...

Fourth, I am not sure that it is right to assume that there is a single uniform standard of proof for all secret trusts. The proposition of Lord Westbury in *McCormick* v *Grogan* with which Brightman J was pressed in *Ottaway* v *Norman* was that the jurisdiction in cases of secret trusts was -

> "founded altogether on personal fraud. It is a jurisdiction by which a Court of Equity, proceeding on the ground of fraud, converts the party who has committed it into a trustee for the party who is injured by that fraud. Nor, being a jurisdiction founded on personal fraud, it is incumbent on the Court to see that a fraud, a malus animus, is proved by the clearest and most indisputable evidence."

Of that it is right to say that the law on the subject has not stood still since 1869, and that it is now clear that secret trusts may be established in cases where there is no possibility of fraud. *McCormick* v *Grogan* has to be read in the light of both earlier cases that were not cited, and also of subsequent cases, in particular, *Blackwell* v *Blackwell* [1972] Ch 698. It seems to me that fraud comes into the matter in two ways. First, it provides an historical explanation of the doctrine of secret trusts: the doctrine was evolved as a means of preventing fraud. That, however, does not mean that fraud is an essential ingredient for the application of the doctrine: the reason for the rule is not part of the rule itself. Second, there are some cases within the doctrine where fraud is indeed involved. There are cases where for the legatee to assert that he is a beneficial owner, free from any trust, would be a fraud on his part.

It is to this latter aspect of fraud that it seems to me that Lord Westbury's words are applicable. If a secret trust can be held to exist in a particular case only by holding the legatee guilty of fraud, then no secret trust should be found unless the standard of proof suffices for fraud. On the other hand, if there is no question of fraud, why should so high a standard apply? In such a case, I find it difficult to see why the mere fact that the historical origin of the doctrine lay in the prevention of fraud should impose the high standard of proof for fraud in a case in which no issue of fraud arises. In accordance with the general rule of evidence, the standard of proof should vary with the nature of the issue and its gravity: see *Hornal* v *Neuberger Products Ltd* [1957] 1 QB 247.

I therefore hold that in order to establish a secret trust where no question of fraud arises, the standard of proof is the ordinary civil standard of proof that is required to establish an ordinary trust ... I cannot therefore dispose of the case summarily on the footing that a high standard of proof has plainly not been achieved, but I must consider the evidence in some detail to see whether the ordinary standard of proof has been satisfied. The initial question, of course, is whether the brother was bound by a secret trust, or whether he was subject to no more than a moral obligation.

In considering this, I have found considerable assistance in two passages in the judgment of the Court of Appeal in Ireland in *McCormick* v *Grogan*, delivered by Christian LJ. Speaking of the testator in that case he said:

"... The real question is, what did he intend should be the *sanction*? Was it to be the authority of a Court of Justice, or the conscience of the devisee? In my opinion, expressly and exclusively the latter."

Then later he said that if we could look into the thoughts of the testator as they were when he was writing the will and the letter that he left with it -

"I am persuaded that what we should find there would be a purpose to this effect – to set up after his decease, not an executor or a trustee, but as it were a second self, whom, while he communicates to him confidentially his ideas as to the distribution of his property, he desires to invest with all his own irresponsibility in carrying them into effect."

On appeal, this latter passage was cited with approval by Lord Hatherley LC, and the latter part of it was cited with approval by Stirling LJ in *Re Pitt-Rivers* [1902] 1 Ch 403.'

Spencer's Will, Re (1887) 3 TLR 822 Court of Appeal (Cotton, Bowen and Fry LJJ)

Half-secret trust: evidence of communication

Facts
The will gave property to persons 'relying, but not by way of trust, upon their applying the sum in or towards the objects privately communicated to them' by the testator.

Held
Evidence would be admissible to show that the testator had in fact communicated and the legatees accepted a fully secret trust.

Stead, Re [1900] 1 Ch 237 Chancery Division (Farwell J)

Fully secret trust: communication to all trustees

Facts
The testatrix left her residuary estate to two of her three executors, Mrs Witham and Mrs Andrews, absolutely. After the death of the testatrix, Mrs Witham alleged that prior to the execution of her will, the testatrix told her that she wished her and Mrs Andrews to hold the residuary estate on a trust not declared on the face of the will and that £2,000 should be given to a Mr Collect and the remainder given to such charities mentioned in the will as they thought proper. Mrs Witham also alleged that the will was executed on the faith of a promise by her to accept and carry out the trust and in the confidence it would be carried out by Mrs Andrews. Mrs Andrews alleged that as there had been no communication of the trust to her in the testatrix's lifetime, that she was entitled beneficially to a moiety of the residuary estate.

Held
On the facts there was not sufficient evidence to show that the testatrix intended to create a secret trust but Farwell J then went on to set out the position on the authorities where there are two trustees of the secret trust.

Farwell J:

'The authorities establish the following propositions: If A induces B either to make or to abstain from revoking a will leaving him property by expressly promising or tacitly consenting to carry out B's wishes concerning it, the Court will hold this to be a trust and will compel A to execute it: see *McCormick* v *Grogan* (1869) LR 4 HL 82 where Lord Hatherley says:

"But this doctrine evidently requires to be carefully restricted within proper limits. It is in itself a doctrine which involves a wide departure from the policy which induced the Legislature to pass the Statute of Frauds, and it is only in clear cases of fraud that this doctrine has been applied – cases in which the Court has been persuaded that there has been a fraudulent inducement held out on the part of the apparent beneficiary in order to lead the testator to confide to him the duty which he so undertook to perform."

If A induces B either to make, or to leave unrevoked, a will leaving property to A and C as tenants in common, by expressly promising, or tacitly consenting, that he and C will carry out the testator's wishes, and C knows nothing of the matter until after A's death, A is bound, but C is not bound: *Tee* v *Ferris* (1856) 2 K & J 357; the reason stated being, that to hold otherwise would enable one beneficiary to deprive the rest of their benefits by setting up a secret trust. If, however, the gift were to A and C as joint tenants, the authorities have established a distinction between those cases in which the will is made on the faith of an antecedent promise by A and those in which the will is left unrevoked on the faith of a subsequent promise. In the former case, the trust binds both A and C: *Russell* v *Jackson* (1852) 10 Hare 204; *Jones* v *Badley* LR 3 Ch 362, the reason stated being that no person can claim an interest under a fraud committed by another; in the latter case A and not C is bound: *Burney* v *Macdonald* 15 Sim 6 and *Moss* v *Cooper* (1861) 1 J & H 532, the reason stated being that the gift is not tainted with any fraud in procuring the execution of the will. Personally I am unable to see any difference between a gift made on the faith of an antecedent promise and a gift left unrevoked on the faith of a subsequent promise to carry out the testator's wishes; but apparently a distinction has been made by the various judges who have had to consider the question. I am bound, therefore, to decide in accordance with these authorities, and accordingly I hold that the defendant Mrs Andrews is not bound by any trust.'

Tee v Ferris (1856) 2 K & J 357 Chancery (Wood V-C)

Communication of fully secret trust

Facts
The testator by his will gave his residue to Ferris and three other persons as tenants in common. By a memorandum of even date he expressed confidence that the four persons would appropriate the residue 'to charity objects'. Ferris alone was informed of this in the testator's lifetime.

Held
Ferris's one-fourth was affected by the memorandum but the other three-fourths were not so affected.

Young (deceased), Re [1951] Ch 344 Chancery Division (Danckwerts J)

Secret trusts operate outside the will

Facts
By his will, the testator made a bequest to his wife 'leaving such small legacies as she knows I wish to be paid ...' Before the execution of the will the testator told the wife that he wished her to give his chauffeur Thomas Cobb £2,000, the wife agreed to do this. The chauffeur was one of the witnesses to the will and the question arose at the testator's death whether he could take the £2,000 as s15 of the Wills Act 1837 prevented a witness taking any benefits under the will.

Held
The secret trust operated outside the Wills Act. Therefore the £2,000 to the chauffeur was not affected by it and he could retain it.

Danckwerts J:

'There is one other point, which is rather interesting, concerning the validity of one of these legacies. The widow has testified that the testator's intention, as communicated to her, was that the man who had been employed by the testator for many years as chauffeur and general factotum should receive a legacy of £2,000. The chauffeur was one of the two attesting witnesses to the will, and if he takes the legacy under the terms of the will the result of s15 of the Wills Act 1837, is to make his legacy ineffective. The question is whether he takes the legacy under the will. Mr Christie, on behalf of the next-of-kin, referred to *In re Fleetwood* (1880) 15 Ch D 594, a case of a secret trust, decided by Hall V-C, where it was held that, as a woman intended to be a beneficiary was one of the attesting witnesses to the fourth codicil, the trust for her failed as to her beneficial interest, as it would have done, Hall V-C said, had it been declared in the codicil. It appears that the point was not argued in that particular case, which was concerned with a number of other points; and it seems to me that that particular decision is contrary to principle. The whole theory of the formation of a secret trust is that the Wills Act has nothing to do with the matter because the forms required by the Wills Act are entirely disregarded, since the persons do not take by virtue of the gift in the will, but by virtue of the secret trusts imposed upon the beneficiary, who does in fact take under the will.

In the Irish case of *O'Brien v Condon* [1905] 1 IR 51, Sir Andrew Porter, MR, had to consider the matter with the decision of *In re Fleetwood* before him. He pointed out in a judgment which seems to me to be entirely in accordance with principle and common sense that *In re Fleetwood* was inconsistent with the principle of the matter, and inconsistent with certain other cases, one of which was a decision of the House of Lords on an Irish appeal, namely *Cullen v Attorney-General for Ireland* (1866) LR 1 HL 190. Sir Andrew Porter MR pointed out in *O'Brien v Condon* that the point was not argued before Hall V-C, *In re Fleetwood* and accordingly he decided to differ from the decision in *In re Fleetwood* and to apply what seems to me to be the proper statement of the principle.

I agree with the decision in *O'Brien v Condon* and I think it right to follow it in the circumstances of this case, because the particular point was not argued before Hall V-C, and I think that his judgment on it was given per incuriam.

It seems to me that according to *Cullen v Attorney-General for Ireland* and the later decision of *In re Gardner* [1923] 2 Ch 230, every consideration connected with this principle requires me to reach the conclusion that a beneficiary under a secret trust does not take under the will, and that he is not, therefore, affected by s15 of the Wills Act 1837.

Accordingly, the legacy intended for Thomas Cobb, though given in an indirect manner, is effective and he has not forfeited it. That being so, the whole of the estate is effectively disposed of, and there is no question of any intestacy.'

5 Implied and Resulting Trusts

Ames' Settlement, Re [1946] Ch 217 Chancery Division (Vaisey J)
Automatic resulting trust: failure of purpose

Facts
A father transferred £10,000 to be held on the trusts of a marriage settlement on the occasion of the marriage of his son in 1908. The marriage was annulled in 1926 and the father died in 1933. However, the son received the income of the marriage settlement up until his death in 1945. On his death the trustees sought directions as to whom the fund should be paid: (i) the father's estate; or (ii) the son's next-of-kin.

Held
As the marriage was void ab initio the consideration for the marriage settlement failed and the £10,000 was consequently held on a resulting trust for the father's estate.

Vaisey J:

'I regard the contest as merely this: The plaintiffs hold certain funds in their hands, and they ask to which of the alternative claimants they ought to make those funds over. I think it would not be incorrect to say that the problem is really which of those parties has the better equity. The persons who constitute the hypothetical next-of-kin say "Look at the deed of settlement. We are the persons there designated to take the fund, and there is no reason why we should not do so", and therefore claim to have the better equity. On the other hand it is said "But that trust, with the other trusts, were all based on the consideration and contemplation of a valid marriage, and now that it has been judicially decided that there never was a marriage that trust cannot possibly form the foundation of a good equitable right." The settlor's representatives say that theirs is the better equity because the money was only parted with by their testator on a consideration which was expressed but which in fact completely failed. It seems to me that the claim of the executors of the settlor in this case must succeed. I think that the case is, having regard to the wording of the settlement, a simple case of money paid on a consideration which failed.'

Barclays Bank v *Quistclose Investments Ltd* [1970] AC 567 House of Lords (Lord Reid, Lord Morris, Lord Guest, Lord Pearce and Lord Wilberforce)
Resulting trust on the failure of a purpose for which money was lent

Facts
During the closing stages of Rolls Razor Ltd's collapse, Quistclose lent money to the company expressly and solely for the purpose of paying a dividend on the company's shares. Before that could be done the company went into liquidation. The money had been paid into an account at the company's bank.

Held
The money having been lent for a particular purpose which had failed, it was then held on resulting

trust for the lender. The Bank had notice of the purpose and therefore was constructive trustee and could not use the money to reduce the company's overdraft.

Bennet v *Bennet* (1879) 10 Ch D 474 Chancery Division (Jessel MR)

Presumption of advancement

Facts
For various financial reasons the mother raised £3,000 in favour of her son (albeit secured by various life policies paid by her son until his death). On the son's death the mother claimed the £3,000 plus interest from the son's estate on the basis that this was advanced only as a loan and not a gift.

Held
The presumption of advancement does not arise as between mother and child, because the mother, unlike the father, is under no moral obligation to provide for the child. The son's estate was therefore liable to repay the money to the mother.

Bernard v *Josephs* [1982] Ch 391 Court of Appeal (Lord Denning MR, Kerr and Griffiths LJJ)

Property jointly owned by unmarried couples

Facts
A house was conveyed to an unmarried couple in their joint names but with no declaration of trust of the beneficial interest. They lived in the house together, but then separated; the man continued to live in the house and later married someone else and they occupied the house together. The former girlfriend sued for the sale of the property and an order that she should have one half of the proceeds of sale.

Held
The declaration as sought was given, subject to the provision that the sale need not take place if the man paid the woman £6000 within four months.

Griffiths LJ:

'... the nature of the relationship between the parties is a very important factor when considering what inferences should be drawn from the way they have conducted their affairs. There are many reasons why a man and a woman may decide to live together without marrying, and one of them is that each values his independence and does not wish to make the commitment of marriage; in such a case it will be misleading to make the same assumptions and to draw the same inferences from their behaviour as in the case of a married couple. The judge must look most carefully at the nature of the relationship, and only if satisfied that it was intended to involve the same degree of commitment as marriage will it be legitimate to regard them as no different from a married couple.

... In the absence of any special circumstances ... the time at which the beneficial interest crystallised is the time of the acquisition, but to ascertain this [the judge] must look at all the evidence including all the contributions made by the parties. As a general rule the only relevant contributions will be those up to the date of the separation but it does not necessarily follow that what happens after the separation will in every case be irrelevant. In my opinion the judge should examine all the evidence placed before him and not regard the date of separation as the cut-off point. The task imposed upon the judge is so difficult that every scrap of evidence may be of value, and should be available to him.'

Obiter, also Griffiths LJ, on the question of a house bought with a mortgage:

> 'The judge must look at the contributions of each to the "family" finances and determine as best he may what contribution each was making towards the purchase of the house. This is not to be carried out as a strictly mathematical exercise ... The contributions must be viewed broadly by the judge to guide him to the parties' unexpressed and probably unconsidered intentions as to the beneficial ownership. There is of course an air of unreality about the whole exercise, but the judge must do his best and only as a last resort abandon the attempt in favour of applying the presumption of equality.'

Bull v Bull [1955] 1 QB 234 Court of Appeal (Denning, Hodson and Parker LJJ)

Co-owners who have contributed unequal shares: tenancy in common and trust for sale

Facts

In 1949, the plaintiff and his mother, the defendant, together purchased a freehold house; the plaintiff contributing a larger part of the purchase price than the defendant and the conveyance was taken in his name alone. The money contributed by the defendant was not intended to be a gift from her to the plaintiff and the defendant accordingly became entitled to an equitable interest proportionate to her contribution – there was a resulting trust in favour of the defendant. They lived together in the house until April 1953, when the plaintiff married and it was arranged that the defendant should occupy two rooms and that the plaintiff and his wife should occupy the rest of the house. Differences arose between the parties and the plaintiff brought this action for possession of the rooms occupied by the defendant.

Held

The effect of the purchase of the house in 1949 was that the plaintiff and defendant became beneficial tenants in common of the proceeds of sale of the property which was subjected to a statutory trust for sale. The defendant had an equitable interest which entitled her to remain in the house as tenant in common with the plaintiff until the house was sold. If they disagreed, the house should be sold and the proceeds divided between them in the proper proportions. The plaintiff could not turn the defendant out at will and his action for possession failed.

Denning LJ:

> 'The son is, of course, the legal owner of the house, but the mother and son are, I think, equitable tenants in common. Each is entitled in equity to an undivided share in the house, the share of each being in proportion to his or her respective contribution ... Each of them is entitled to the possession of the land and to the use and enjoyment of it in a proper manner. Neither can turn out the other; but, if one of them should take more than his proper share, the injured party can bring an action for an account. If one of them should go so far as to oust the other, he is guilty of trespass ...
>
> ... I realise that since 1925 there has been no such thing as a legal tenancy in common. All tenancies in common now are equitable only and they take effect behind a trust for sale. (Settled Land Act 1925 s36(4)). Nevertheless, until a sale takes place, these equitable tenants in common have the same right to enjoy the land as legal tenants used to have ...
>
> My conclusion, therefore, is that when there are two equitable tenants in common, then, until the place is sold, each of them is entitled concurrently with the other to the possession of the land and to the use and enjoyment of it in a proper manner: and that neither of them is entitled to turn out the other.
>
> The question may be asked: What is to happen when the two fall out, as they have done here? The answer is that the house must then be sold and the proceeds divided between mother and son in the proper proportions. The son is the legal owner and he holds it on the statutory trust for sale. He cannot, at the present moment, sell the house because he cannot give a valid receipt for the proceeds. It needs two trustees to give a receipt. The son could get over this difficulty by appointing another trustee who

would agree with him to sell the house. The two trustees would no doubt have to consider the mother's wishes, but as the son appears to have made the greater contribution, he could in theory override her wishes about a sale. (Law of Property Act 1925 s26(3)). The difficulty of the two trustees would be a practical difficulty because so long as the mother is there, they could not sell with vacant possession.

... The mother here is in possession and in actual occupation as equitable co-owner and, by virtue of that interest, she could not be turned out by the trustees except with her consent. In this situation, if the trustees wished to sell with vacant possession, the only thing they could do would be to apply to the court under s30 of the Law of Property Act 1925 on the ground that the mother's consent could not be obtained. The court could then make such order as it thought fit and this would include, I think, an order to turn the mother out if it was right and proper for such an order to be made.'

Burns v *Burns* [1984] Ch 317 Court of Appeal (Waller, Fox and May LJJ)

Beneficial interests in property jointly acquired or occupied

Facts

P, who was known as Mrs Burns, left home in 1961 and started living with D when aged 20. She then had a job as a tailor earning £12 per week. This relationship lasted 19 years and P and D were never married. The parties initially lived in rented accommodation and P gave birth to a child in 1962. In 1963 the parties moved to a house which D purchased in his name with a mortgage of £4,900. P had another child in 1963. Up until 1975 P did not earn, as she had to stay at home to look after the children. When she did earn she made no distinction between her own earnings and the housekeeping money D gave her. She used this for fixtures and fittings for the house, decorations, electrical goods and furniture. When P was forced to leave the house in 1980 after her relationship with D broke down, she brought proceedings, claiming that she was entitled to a beneficial interest in the house by reason of her contributions to the household over the 19 year relationship. At first instance Dillon J held that P was not entitled to any beneficial interest in the house. On appeal:

Held

P's appeal would be dismissed. The powers conferred by the Matrimonial Causes Act 1973 in relation to the division of the property of married couples on divorce did not apply to unmarried couples so the court had no power to make an order on the basis of what was fair and reasonable. There was no evidence that P had made any contribution direct or indirect to the purchase of the house. Further, there was nothing to impute a common intention to the parties down to the date of separation that P should have a beneficial interest in the property, and the court would not infer such an intention from the fact that the relationship had lasted 19 years.

May LJ:

'... If a man and a woman marry, acquire a home, live in it together, bring up children, but sadly sooner or later separate and divorce, the courts have a wide discretion to adjust their subsequent respective financial situations under the provisions of the Matrimonial Causes Act 1973. In particular, the court has power to determine the spouses' respective rights to the matrimonial home, which is usually the family's main asset, and by virtue of s25(1) of the 1973 Act is given a wide discretion to exercise its powers to place the parties, so far as it is practicable and just to do so, in the financial position in which they would have been if the marriage had not broken down and each had properly discharged his or her financial obligations and responsibilities towards the other.

However, it is becoming increasingly frequent that couples live together without being married, but just as if they were so. They acquire a home for themselves and their children, whom they bring up in the same way as the family next door. Nevertheless, it also happens, just like their married friends, that differences do arise between the couple and they separate. In some cases the man and the woman can agree what is to happen in those circumstances, for instance to their erstwhile joint home. But if they do not agree, they come to the courts for the resolution of their dispute. In the case of an unmarried couple in these circumstances there is no statute which gives a court similar power to those which it has as between husband and wife. In these cases the question therefore arises: what principles is the court to apply?

For my part, I agree that the principles which the courts must apply are those laid down in *Pettitt* v *Pettitt* [1970] AC 777 and *Gissing* v *Gissing* [1971] AC 886. Those two cases concerned disputes between couples who had in fact been married, where the claims were made under s17 of the Married Women's Property Act 1882 and not under the matrimonial legislation. But it is quite clear that the House of Lords decided that s17 is merely a procedural section giving the courts no overriding general discretion in such circumstances, and that the principles to be applied are in general the same whether the couple have been married or not. I respectfully agree however with the warning expressed by Griffiths LJ in *Bernard* v *Josephs* [1982] Ch 391 where he said:

> "... but the nature of the relationship between the parties is a very important factor when considering what inferences should be drawn from the way they have conducted their affairs. There are many reasons why a man and a woman may decide to live together without marrying, and one of them is that each values his independence and does not wish to make the commitment of marriage; in such a case it will be misleading to make the same assumptions and to draw the same inferences from their behaviour as in the case of a married couple. The judge must look most carefully at the nature of the relationship, and only if satisfied that it was intended to involve the same degree of commitment as marriage, will it be legitimate to regard them as no different from a married couple."

Further, in this particular field, different people have very different views about the problems and relationships involved. In my view, as Parliament has not legislated for the unmarried couple as it has for those who have been married, the courts should be slow to attempt in effect to legislate themselves ...

... It follows that in these disputes between unmarried couples who have broken up, the courts do not have a general power to do what they think is fair and reasonable in all the circumstances, as they have under the appropriate provisions of the Matrimonial Causes Act 1973 ...

... The speeches in *Pettitt* v *Pettitt* and *Gissing* v *Gissing* also make it clear that there is no general concept in English law of "family property" or "family assets": see *Pettitt* v *Pettitt* per Lord Reid, Lord Hodson and Lord Upjohn and *Gissing* v *Gissing* per Viscount Dilhorne. Lord Diplock recognised in his speech in the latter case that the view which he had expressed to the contrary in *Pettitt* v *Pettitt* had been disapproved by the majority.

I think that one therefore reaches the position that the resolution of these disputes must depend on the ascertainment according to normal principles of the respective property rights between the man and the woman.

Further, two similar factors militate against and indeed prevent any application of general principles of contract law to the problem. First, it is seldom if ever that the man and the woman in these circumstances in fact come to any agreement between themselves about what should happen to the matrimonial home if they were to part ...

... Second, even if it be shown in any particular case that the parties had reached some agreement between themselves, there is I think real doubt whether this can be said to have been intended to create enforceable legal relations between them: cf *Balfour* v *Balfour* ...

... In the result, my opinion is that the correct and general approach to these cases should be that summed up in a passage from Lord Pearson's speech in *Gissing* v *Gissing* where he said:

> "I think it must often be artificial to search for an agreement made between husband and wife as to their respective ownership rights in property used by both of them while they are living together. In most cases they are unlikely to enter into negotiations or conclude contracts or even make agreements. The arrangements which they make are likely to be lacking in precision and finality which an agreement would be expected to have. On the other hand, an intention can be imputed; it can be inferred from the evidence of their conduct and the surrounding circumstances. The starting point, in a case where substantial

contributions are proved to have been made, is the presumption of a resulting trust, though it may be displaced by rebutting evidence. It may be said that the imputed intent does not differ very much from an implied agreement. Accepting that, I still think it is better to approach the question through the doctrine of resulting trusts rather than through contract law. Of course, if an agreement can be proved it is the best evidence of intention."

Where the legal estate to the family home had been taken in joint names, then generally the beneficial interests will depend on the respective contributions of the parties to the acquisition of the property: see *Crisp* v *Mullings* (1974) 233 EG 511 and the recent decision of this court in *Walker* v *Hall* [1983] LS Gaz R 2139.

Where the legal estate in the family home has, however, been taken in the name of one of the parties only, then prima facie it will carry with it the whole of the beneficial interest. But for the reasons to which I have briefly referred, a claim to a beneficial interest in land made by a person in whom the legal estate is not vested can in certain circumstances be made by resorting to the doctrine of resulting trusts. Where the legal estate to the family home is in one name only, which is usually the male member of the couple, and the parties to the acquisition of the house have not expressed their common intention that the beneficial interest should be shared between them, it may nevertheless be possible to infer that common intention from their conduct, and thus give rise to a resulting trust to which the courts will give effect. It may be demonstrably inequitable to permit the legal title holder to retain the whole of the beneficial interest in the property. The inference about the parties' common intention to which the court will give effect in this way is that which objectively a reasonable man would draw from their words and conduct at the relevant time.

At the hearing of this appeal our attention was drawn to a number of authorities, to some of which I shall briefly refer, and thereafter state what I think is the general approach adopted by the courts to these disputes which can be deduced from the two leading cases in 1970 and 1971 and those which have followed them...'

His Lordship then referred to *Falconer* v *Falconer* [1970] 1 WLR 1333; *Hazell* v *Hazell* [1972] 1 WLR 301; *Cooke* v *Head* [1972] 1 WLR 518; *Richards* v *Dove* [1974] 1 All ER 888; *Eves* v *Eves* [1975] 1 WLR 1338; *Hall* v *Hall* [1981] 3 FLR 379; and *Bernard* v *Josephs* [1982] Ch 391 and continued:

'... I think that the approach which the courts should follow, be the couples married or unmarried, is now clear. What is difficult however, is to apply it to the facts and circumstances of any given case. Where the family home is taken in the joint names, then unless the facts are very unusual, I think that both the man and the woman are entitled to a share in the beneficial interest. Where the house is bought outright and not on mortgage, then the extent of their respective shares will depend on a more or less arithmetical calculation of the extent of their contributions to the purchase price. Where, on the other hand, as is more usual nowadays, the house is bought with the aid of a mortgage, then the court has to assess each party's respective contributions in a broad sense; nevertheless, the court is only entitled to look at the financial contributions, or their real or substantial equivalent, to the acquisition of the house; that the husband may spend his weekends redecorating or laying a patio is neither here nor there, nor is the fact that the woman has spent so much of her time looking after the house, doing the cooking and bringing up the family.

The inquiry becomes even more difficult when the home is taken in only one of the two names. For present purposes I will assume that it is the man, although the same approach will be followed if it is taken in the name of the woman. Where a matrimonial or family home is bought in the man's name alone on mortgage by the mechanism of deposit and instalments, then if the woman pays or contributes to the initial deposit this points to a common intention that she should have some beneficial interest in the house. If thereafter she makes direct contributions to the instalments, then the case is a fortiori and her rightful share is likely to be greater. If the woman, having contributed to the deposit, but although not making direct contributions to the instalments, nevertheless uses her own money for other joint household expenses so as to enable the man the more easily to pay the mortgage instalments out of his money, then her position is the same. Where a woman has made no contribution to the initial deposit, but makes regular and substantial contributions to the mortgage instalments, it may still be reasonable to infer a common intention that she should share the beneficial interest from the outset, or infer a fresh agreement after the original conveyance that she should acquire such a share. It is only when there is no evidence on which a court can reasonably draw an inference about the extent of the share of the contributing woman that it should fall back on the maxim 'equity is equality'. Finally, when the house is taken in the man's name alone, if the woman makes no 'real' or 'substantial' financial contribution towards either the purchase price, deposit or mortgage instalments by means of which the family home was acquired, then she is not entitled to any share in the beneficial interest in that home even though over a very substantial number of years she may have worked just as hard as the man in maintaining the family, in the sense of keeping house, giving birth to and looking after and helping to bring up the children of the union.'

Carreras Rothmans Ltd v *Freeman Matthews Treasure Ltd* [1984] 3 WLR 1016
Chancery Division (Peter Gibson J)

Quistclose trust: resulting or constructive trust

Facts
Carreras Rothmans Ltd (CR), a cigarette manufacturer, used Freeman Matthews Treasure Ltd (FMT), an advertising agency, to do their advertising work. CR paid FMT on a monthly basis and the fee paid by CR to FMT was for FMT's services as well as the costs involved in placing advertisements in the media. In 1983 FMT got into financial difficulties and CR feared that the collapse of FMT could do considerable damage to its business. Consequently, CR made special arrangements with FMT for payment of FMT's monthly invoices. A special bank account was opened into which CR would pay a sum every month which FMT was to use solely for settling its fees due from CR and the monies owed to media creditors for CR advertising. On 26 July 1983 CR paid £597,128 into the special bank account but on 3 August 1983 FMT went into liquidation. The liquidator of FMT would not pay any money out of the special bank account. CR claimed that the money in the account was held on trust for the sole purpose of paying FMT's fees and monies owed to media creditors and sought a declaration accordingly.

Held
Applying *Barclays Bank Ltd* v *Quistclose Investments* [1970] AC 567 the money in the special bank account was held upon trust.

Peter Gibson J:

> '... Mr Millett contended that the language of the contract letter was apt to create a trust and that such trust was fully constituted as to the *moneys* in the special account when FMT agreed to the terms of the contract letter and received the moneys from CR. He relied on the line of cases of which *Barclays Bank Ltd* v *Quistclose Ltd* is the highest authority ...
>
> ... CR was concerned about the adverse effect on it if FMT, which CR knew to have financial problems, ceased trading and third party creditors of FMT were not paid at a time when FMT had been put in funds by CR ... For this purpose a special account was to be set up with a special designation. The moneys payable by CR were to be paid not to FMT beneficially but directly into that account so that FMT was never free to deal as it pleased with the moneys so paid. The moneys were to be used only for the specific purpose of paying the third parties and, as the cheque letter indicated, the amount paid matched the specific invoices presented by FMT to CR. The account was intended to be little more than a conduit pipe, but the intention was plain that whilst in the conduit pipe the moneys should be protected. There was even a provision covering the possibility that there might be a balance left after payment and in that event the balance was to be paid to CR and not kept by FMT. It was thus clearly intended that the moneys once paid would never become the property of FMT. That was the last thing CR wanted in view of its concern about FMT's financial position ...

'... There is, of course, ample authority that moneys paid by A to B for a specific purpose which has been made known to B are clothed with a trust. In the *Quistclose* case Lord Wilberforce referred to the recognition, in a series of cases over some 150 years, that arrangements for the payment of a person's creditors by a third person gives rise to 'a relationship of a fiduciary character or trust, in favour, as a primary trust, of the creditors, and secondarily, if the primary trust fails, of the third person'. Lord Wilberforce in describing the facts of the *Quistclose* case said a little earlier that the mutual intention of the provider of the moneys and the recipient of the moneys, and the essence of the bargain, was that the moneys should not become part of the assets of the recipient but should be used exclusively for payment of a particular class of its creditors. That description seems to me to be apt in relation to the facts of the present case too...'

Cochrane's Settlement Trusts, Re [1955] Ch 309 Chancery Division (Harman J)

Resulting trust where the settlement fails to cover the events which actually happen

Facts
The husband and wife both brought property into a post-nuptial settlement. The limitations were that the income was payable to the wife for life 'so long as she shall continue to reside with the husband'; after her death or 'the prior determination of the trust in her favour' to the husband for life, with a gift over of the capital after the death of the survivor. The wife ceased to live with the husband, but he died leaving her the survivor.

Held
The events which actually happened were not envisaged in the limitations; accordingly there were resulting trusts of the income from the parts respectively provided by the spouses, the husband's for his estate and the wife's for herself for life.

Cowcher v *Cowcher* [1972] 1 WLR 425 Chancery Division (Bagnall J)

Matrimonial cases: imposition of a trust

Facts
The wife had contributed one-third of the value of the house. The court was asked to make a division on the break-up of the marriage.

Held
The wife should be entitled by way of resulting trust to the third she had contributed and no more; it was difficult to infer from conduct some consensus other than the objective fact of contribution.

Bagnall J:

'In any individual case the application of (established principles of property law) may produce a result which appears unfair. So be it: in my view that is not an injustice. I am convinced that, in determining rights, particularly property rights, the only justice that can be attained by mortals, who are fallible and not omniscient, is justice according to law; the justice that flows from the application of sure and settled principles to proved or admitted facts. So in the field of equity the length of the Chancellor's foot has been measured or is capable of measurement. This does not mean that equity is past child-bearing; simply that its progeny must be legitimate – by precedent out of principle. It is as well that this should be so, otherwise "no lawyer could safely advise on title and every quarrel would lead to a law suit".'

Cunnack v *Edwards* [1896] 2 Ch 679 Court of Appeal (A L Smith and Rigby LJJ)

No resulting trust of money given on condition when it is fulfilled

Facts
A society was formed to raise subscriptions from members to provide for widows of deceased members. A surplus remained when the last widow died.

Held
It was held that the surplus went bona vacantia to the Crown as the contributors did not retain any interest in the money they gave but gave it out-and-out.

AL Smith LJ:

> 'As the member paid his money to the society, so he divested himself of all interest in this money for ever, with one reservation, that if the member left a widow, she was to be provided for during her widowhood. Except as to this he abandoned and gave up the money for ever.'

Dyer v *Dyer* (1788) 2 Cox Eq 92 Court of Chancery (Eyre CB)

Presumed resulting trust: purchase in the name of another

Facts
D purchased copyhold property and took a grant to himself, his wife and his younger son to take in succession for their lives, and to the survivor for life. A bill was taken out to determine whether the son was trustee for the father.

Held
On the facts of the case there was a presumption of advancement by the father of the son who therefore took as a gift but presumed resulting trusts were defined.

Eyre CB:

> 'The clear result of all the cases, without a single exception, is that the trust of a legal estate, whether freehold or copyhold, or leasehold; whether taken in the names of the purchasers or jointly, or in the name of others without that of the purchaser; whether in one name or in several; whether jointly or successive, results to the man who advances the purchase money. This is a general proposition supported by all the cases, and there is nothing to contradict it; and it goes on a strict analogy to the rule of the common law, that where a feeoffment is made without consideration, the use results to the feeoffer. It is the established doctrine of a court of equity that this resulting trust may be rebutted by circumstances in evidence ... The circumstance of ... the nominee being a child of the purchaser, is to operate by rebutting the resulting trust. ... In the ... case ... of a father purchasing in the name of his son ... this shows the father intended an advancement and therefore the resulting trust is rebutted.'

Ebrand v *Dancer* (1680) 2 Ch Ca 26 Chancery (Lord Nottingham LC)

Purchase in the name of another: presumption of advancement

Facts
A grandfather purchased in the name of his grandchild. The child's father was dead.

Held
The grandfather stood in loco parentis to the grandchild (the grandfather having looked after the grandchild following the father's death) so as to give rise to the presumption of advancement.

Emery's Investment Trusts, Re [1959] Ch 410 Chancery Division (Wynn Parry J)

Presumption of advancement

Facts
The husband purchased shares in the name of the wife to evade the revenue laws of a foreign country.

Held
The presumption of advancement would apply especially in view of the husband's inequitable intention which could not be set up in rebuttal.

Eves v *Eves* [1975] 1 WLR 1338 Court of Appeal (Lord Denning MR, Browne LJ, Brightman J)

Joint interests of an unmarried couple

Facts
A couple lived together intending to marry when free; they had two children by the time of the separation. At the time of the purchase of the joint home, the man told the woman the house would be their home but would have to be conveyed into his name alone as she was still under 21; in point of fact she was over 21 by the time of the conveyance. The man admitted the question of age had been used as an excuse to avoid using joint names. She made no financial contribution but did a great deal of heavy work 'much more than many wives would do' to the house and garden.

Held
The woman was to take a beneficial interest. The majority of the court held this on the grounds that there was an enforceable bargain between them that she should have such an interest because of the work she contributed. Lord Denning came to the same conclusion, but by way of a constructive trust imposed because the man's conduct meant it would be inequitable to deny her a share.

Eykyn's Trusts, Re (1877) 6 Ch D 115 Chancery Division (Malins V-C)

Presumption of advancement between husband and wife

Facts
Property was purchased by the husband in the name of himself and his wife, in the name of the wife, and in the name of another.

Held
Purchase in the name of a wife by a husband gives rise to the presumption of advancement; the fact that property was also purchased in the stranger's name at the same time is irrelevant.

Malins V-C:

> 'The law of the courts is perfectly settled that when a husband transfers money or other property into the name of his wife only, then the presumption is, that it is intended as a gift or advancement to the wife absolutely at once ... and if a husband invests money, stock or otherwise, in the name of himself and his wife, then also it is an advancement for the benefit of the wife absolutely if she survives her husband, but if he survives her then it reverts to him as joint tenant with his wife.'

Fowkes v *Pascoe* (1875) 10 Ch App 343 Court of Appeal (James and Mellish LJJ)

Purchase in the name of another

Facts
Mrs Baker had no nearer relatives than the son of her widowed daughter-in-law. He lived in her house and she provided for him. She held a large quantity of stock in her sole name, but purchased some further similar stock in the joint names of herself and the man. She died intestate as to the stock.

Held
The surviving joint tenant would normally hold on a resulting trust for Mrs Baker's estate, but in view of all the facts the court found she intended an advancement and he took absolutely. The resulting trust operated as to the income in her favour for her life, but in his favour after her death.

Mellish LJ:

> '... the presumption [of a trust] must, beyond all question, be of very different weight in different cases. In some cases it would be very strong indeed. If, for instance, a man invested a sum of stock in the name of himself and his solicitor, the inference would be very strong indeed that it was intended solely for the purpose of a trust, and the court would require very strong evidence on the part of the solicitor to prove that it was intended as a gift; and certainly his own evidence would not be sufficient. On the other hand a man may make an investment of stock in the name of himself and some other person, although not a child or a wife, yet in such a position to him as to make it extremely probable that the investment was intended as a gift. In such a case, though the rule of law, if there was no evidence at all, would compel the court to say that the presumption of trust must prevail, even if the court might not believe that the fact was in accordance with the presumption, yet, if there is evidence to rebut the presumption, then, in my opinion, the court must go into the actual facts.'

Gillingham Bus Disaster Fund, Re [1958] Ch 300 Chancery Division (Harman J)

Resulting trust purpose fulfilled

Facts
An appeal was made following a road accident in which 24 Royal Marine cadets were killed and several others severely injured. The appeal was not charitable and after the stated objective had been achieved there was a surplus. Nearly all the money was given by donations from both known and unknown contributors.

Held
As regards the unknown contributors, that there was a resulting trust for them and that the money should be paid into court pending their claiming it.

Goodman v Gallant [1986] 2 WLR 236 Court of Appeal (Slade, Purchas LJJ and Sir R Cumming-Bruce)

Resulting trusts and joint tenants

Facts
Mrs Goodman and Mr Gallant purchased a house which was conveyed into their names as joint tenants (ie in equal shares). Mrs Goodman served a notice severing the joint tenancy and claimed three quarters of the proceeds of sale as this was the amount she had contributed to the purchase price.

Held
The declaration was conclusive of the interests of the parties and the court could not go behind it except for fraud or mistake, neither of which were present.

Slade LJ:

> 'In a case where the legal estate in property is conveyed to two or more persons as joint tenants, but neither the conveyance or any other written document contains any express declaration of trust concerning the beneficial interests in the property (as would be required for an express declaration of this nature by virtue of s53(1)(b) of the LPA 1925) the way is open for persons claiming a beneficial interest in it or its proceeds of sale to rely on the doctrine of "resulting, implied or constructive trusts" ... If, however, the relevant conveyance contains an express declaration of trust which comprehensively declares the beneficial interest in the property or its proceeds of sale, there is no room for the application of the doctrine ... unless and until the conveyance is set aside or rectified; until that event the declaration contained in the document speaks for itself.'

Grant v Edwards [1986] 1 Ch 638 Court of Appeal (Sir Nicholas Browne-Wilkinson V-C, Mustill and Nourse LJJ)

Beneficial interests in jointly acquired property

Facts
The plaintiff who had split from her husband in 1967 commenced co-habiting with the defendant in 1969. Although the defendant intended to live permanently with the plaintiff he bought a house for this purpose in the joint names of himself and his brother and excluded the plaintiff from holding a legal interest in the property. The defendant explained to the plaintiff that it was not wise to include her name on the title deeds of the property as this might adversely affect the plaintiff's claim against her husband for matrimonial relief. Even although the plaintiff's name was not on the deeds she made a substantial contribution to the co-habitation expenses by paying housekeeping expenses out of her earnings. Indirectly her contribution assisted the defendant in paying the mortgage instalments on the property.

Held
The plaintiff had acted to her detriment in providing financial contributions towards the housekeeping in the belief that she would thereby acquire a beneficial interest in the property. Further the parties had a common intention that they would each hold a beneficial interest in the property and the defendant's reason for not including the plaintiff's name on the title deeds established this common intention. Accordingly a constructive trust arose in the plaintiff's favour whereby she acquired a 50 per cent beneficial interest in the house.

Nourse LJ:

'A number of authorities were cited by the judge. In holding that any of the instalments under the second mortgage which may have been paid by the plaintiff as part of the general expenses of the household would not have been substantial enough to give the plaintiff a beneficial interest in the house, he based himself primarily on a passage in the judgment of May LJ in *Burns* v *Burns* [1984] Ch 317.

In order to decide whether the plaintiff has a beneficial interest in 96 Hewitt Road we must climb again the familiar ground which slopes down from the twin peaks of *Pettitt* v *Pettitt* [1970] AC 777 and *Gissing* v *Gissing* [1971] AC 886. In a case such as the present, where there has been no written declaration or agreement, nor any direct provision by the plaintiff of part of the purchase price so as to give rise to a resulting trust in her favour, she must establish a common intention between her and the defendant, acted upon by her, that she should have a beneficial interest in the property. If she can do that, equity will not allow the defendant to deny that interest and will construct a trust to give effect to it.

In most of these cases the fundamental, and invariably the most difficult, question is to decide whether there was the necessary common intention, being something which can only be inferred from the conduct of the parties, almost always from the expenditure incurred by them respectively. In this regard the court has to look for expenditure which is referable to the acquisition of the house: see per Fox LJ in *Burns* v *Burns*. If it is found to have been incurred, such expenditure will perform the twofold function of establishing the common intention and showing that the claimant has acted upon it.

There is another and rarer class of case, of which the present may be one, where, although there has been no writing, the parties have orally declared themselves in such a way as to make their common intention plain. Here the court does not have to look for conduct from which the intention can be inferred, but only for conduct which amounts to an acting upon it by the claimant. And although that conduct can undoubtedly be the incurring of expenditure which is referable to the acquisition of the house, it need not necessarily be so.

The clearest example of this rarer class of case is *Eves* v *Eves* [1975] 1 WLR 1338. That was a case of an unmarried couple where the conveyance of the house was taken in the name of the man alone. At the time of the purchase he told the woman that if she had been 21 years of age, he would have put the house into their joint names, because it was to be their joint home. He admitted in evidence that that was an excuse for not putting the house into their joint names, and this court inferred that there was an understanding between them, or a common intention, that the woman was to have some sort of proprietary interest in it; otherwise no excuse would have been needed. After they had moved in, the woman did extensive decorative work to the downstairs rooms and generally cleaned the whole house. She painted the brickwork of the front of the house. She also broke up with a 14lb sledge hammer the concrete surface which covered the whole of the front garden and disposed of the rubble into a skip, worked in the back garden and, together with the man, demolished a shed there and put up a new shed. She also prepared the front garden for turfing. Pennycuick VC at first instance, being unable to find any link between the common intention and the woman's activities after the purchase, held that she had not acquired a beneficial interest in the house. On an appeal to this court the decision was unanimously reversed, by Lord Denning MR on a ground which I respectfully think was at variance with the principles stated in *Gissing* v *Gissing* and by Browne LJ and Brightman LJ on a ground which was stated by Brightman J:

> "The defendant clearly led the plaintiff to believe that she was to have some undefined interest in the property, and that her name was only omitted from the conveyance because of her age. This, of course, is not enough by itself to create a beneficial interest in her favour; there would at best be mere 'voluntary declaration of trust' which would be 'unenforceable for want of writing': per Lord Diplock in *Gissing* v *Gissing*. If, however, it was part of the bargain between the parties, expressed or to be implied, that the plaintiff should contribute her labour towards the reparation of a house in which she was to have some beneficial interest, then I think that the arrangement becomes one to which the law can give effect. This seems to be consistent with the reasoning of the speeches in *Gissing* v *Gissing*."

He added that he did not find much difficulty in inferring the link which Pennycuick VC had been unable to find, observing in the process that he found it difficult to suppose that the woman would have been wielding the 14lb sledge hammer and so forth except in pursuance of some expressed or implied arrangement and on the understanding that she was helping to improve a house in which she was to all practical intents and purposes promised that she had an interest. Browne LJ, at p1343, agreed with Brightman J about the basis for the court's decision in favour of the woman and was prepared to draw the inference that the link was there.

About that case the following observations may be made. First, as Brightman J himself observed, if the work had not been done the common intention would not have been enough. Secondly, if the common intention had not been orally made plain, the work would not have been conduct from which it could be inferred. That, I think, is the effect of the actual decision in *Pettitt* v *Pettitt*. Thirdly, and on the other hand, the work was conduct which amounted to an acting upon the common intention by the woman.

It seems therefore, on the authorities as they stand, that a distinction is to be made between conduct from which the common intention can be inferred on the one hand and conduct which amounts to an acting upon it on the other. There remains this difficult question: what is the quality of conduct required for the latter purpose? The difficulty is caused, I think because although the common intention has been made plain, everything else remains a matter of inference. Let me illustrate it in this way. It would be possible to take the view that the mere moving into the house by the woman amounted to an acting upon the common intention. But that was evidently not the view of the majority in *Eves* v *Eves*. And the reason for that may be that, in the absence of evidence, the law is not so cynical as to infer that a woman will only go to live with a man to whom she is not married if she understands that she is to have an interest in their home. So what sort of conduct is required? In my judgment it must be conduct on which the woman could not reasonably have been expected to embark unless she was to have an interest in the house. If she was not to have such an interest, she could reasonably be expected to go and live with her lover, but not, for example, to wield a 14lb sledge hammer in the front garden. In adopting the latter kind of conduct she is seen to act to her detriment on the faith of the common intention.

I should add that, although *Eves* v *Eves* was cited to the judge, I think it doubtful whether the significance of it was fully brought to his attention. He appears to have assumed that the plaintiff could only establish the necessary common intention if she could point to expenditure from which it could be inferred. I do not find it necessary to decide whether, if the common intention had not been orally made plain, the expenditure in the present case would have been sufficient for that purpose. That raises a difficult and still unresolved question of general importance which depends primarily on a close consideration of the speeches of their Lordships in *Gissing* v *Gissing* and the judgments of Fox and May LJJ in *Burns* v *Burns*. If it be objected that the views which I have expressed will expose the possibility of further fine distinctions on these intellectual steeps, I must answer that that is something which is inherent in the decision of the majority of this court in *Eves* v *Eves*. Be that as it may, I am in no doubt that that authority is a sure foundation for a just decision of the present case.'

Harwood v *Harwood* [1991] Fam Law 418 Court of Appeal (Slade and Butler-Sloss LJJ)

Beneficial interest of contributor towards purchase price

Facts
This case arose out of ancillary relief proceedings on marriage breakdown between H and W – only one aspect of this dispute being considered in the present case-note.

H had been a partner in a publishing partnership and this partnership had contributed to the funds needed for the purchase of a house which had been H and W's matrimonial home. The house was, in fact, conveyed into the joint names of H and W. The Court of Appeal was asked, inter alia, to rule on the beneficial interest of the partnership in regard to the house.

Held
Since there was no clear agreement or understanding between the parties that the partnership would have a beneficial interest in the house it was necessary for the court to consider the conduct of the parties from which to infer their common intention. From this it was clear that W was aware that the partnership had contributed two-sevenths of the purchase price. Citing *Dyer* v *Dyer* (1788) 2 Cox Eq Case 92, Slade LJ pointed out: 'Where property was conveyed into the names of persons who had not provided the whole of the purchase price, a presumption of law arose that it was the parties' intention that the third party should have (at least) an interest in the property proportionate to his contribution to the purchase price.' But in this case two-sevenths was the limit of the partnership's entitlement.

Hodgson v *Marks* [1971] Ch 892 Court of Appeal (Buckley, Cairns and Russell LJJ)

Resulting trust: transfer into the name of another

Facts
Mrs H owned a freehold house. In June 1960 she transferred the legal title to her lodger to prevent her son turning the lodger out. The lodger orally agreed with Mrs H that she would continue to be beneficial owner. The lodger sold the house to Marks who did not know of Mrs H's interest in the house.

Held
The absence of writing as required by s53(1)(b) LPA did not prevent Mrs H asserting her claim in equity. The house was registered land and Mrs H's interest was an overriding interest within s70(1)(g). There was, therefore, a resulting trust for her and she was equitable owner of the house.

Hussey v *Palmer* [1972] 1 WLR 1286 Court of Appeal (Lord Denning MR, Phillimore and Cairns LJJ)

Resulting and constructive trusts: overlap

Facts
The plaintiff, whose house had been condemned, was invited to come and live with her daughter and son-in-law. However, their house was rather small so the plaintiff put up some money to enable the son-in-law to build an extension to the house. Unfortunately, family dissensions arose and the plaintiff left. Shortly afterwards she became short of money and claimed repayment of the money expended in building the extension. In the lower courts there was some difference as to whether there was a loan or a resulting trust. On appeal:

Held (Cairns LJ dissenting)
The plaintiff was entitled to the money under a constructive trust which was imposed on the son-in-law as legal owner of the house.

Phillimore LJ was of the opinion that the trust to be imposed in this case was an implied or resulting trust rather than a constructive one.

Lord Denning MR:

> 'If there was no loan, was there a resulting trust? And, if so, what were the terms of the trust? Although the plaintiff alleged that there was a resulting trust, I should have thought that the trust in this case, if there was one, was more in the nature of a constructive trust: but that is more a matter of words than anything else. The two run together. By whatever name it is described, it is a trust imposed by law whenever justice

and good name and good conscience require it. It is a liberal process, founded upon large principles of equity, to be applied in cases where the legal owner cannot conscientiously keep the property for himself alone, but ought to allow another to have the property or the benefit of it or a share in it. The trust may arise at the outset when the property is acquired, or later on, as the circumstances may require. It is an equitable remedy by which the court can enable an aggrieved party to obtain restitution. It is comparable to the legal remedy of money had and received which, as Lord Mansfield said, is "very beneficial and therefore, much encouraged" (*Moses* v *MacFerlan* (1760) 2 Burr 1005). Thus we have repeatedly held that, when one person contributes towards the purchase price of a house, the owner holds it on a constructive trust for him, proportionate to his contribution, even though there is no agreement between them, and no declaration of trust to be found, and no evidence of any intention to create a trust. Instances are numerous where a wife has contributed money to the initial purchase of a house or property; or later on to the payment of mortgage instalments; or has helped in business: see *Falconer* v *Falconer* [1970] 1 WLR 1333, *Heseltine* v *Heseltine* [1971] 1 WLR 342 and *Re Cummins* [1972] Ch 62. Similarly, when a mistress has contributed money, or money's worth, to the building of a house: *Cooke* v *Head* [1972] 1 WLR 518. Very recently we held that a purchaser, who bought a cottage subject to the rights of an occupier, held in on trust for her benefit: *Binions* v *Evans* [1972] Ch 359 [see Chapter 6]. In all those cases it would have been quite inequitable for the legal owner to take the property for himself and exclude the other from it. So the law imputed or imposed a trust for his or her benefit.'

Kingscroft Insurance Co Ltd v *HS Weavers (Underwriting) Agencies Ltd* (1992) The Times 21 August Chancery Division (Harman J)

Agency agreement – deposits held for principal

Facts
K employed W to collect premiums as an underwriting agent. These premiums were to be kept as a 'working balance', although held on deposit for K. W was to be kept in funds by K to meet any of K's liabilities under the agreement. W claimed the relationship was akin to that of 'banker/customer', entitling him to claim an equitable charge over the deposited monies for sums due from K.

Held
W's claim was dismissed. There was no 'banker/customer' relationship. Further, the deposited funds did not form any part of monies due to W under the agreement. K was not a trustee, either implied or constructive, as no purpose had attached to the funds as claimed by W, nor had there been any bad faith on the part of K and relied on by W.

Lloyds Bank plc v *Rosset*

See Chapter 6.

McGrath v *Wallis* (1995) The Times 13 April Court of Appeal (Nourse and Hirst LJJ and Sir Ralph Gibson)

General doctrine of presumption of advancement – doctrine of last resort

Facts
In 1959 the father of the plaintiff and the defendant had acquired, in his sole name, a house in Luton. This remained the family home until 1986 when the father decided to sell the house. The plaintiff having married left the house some years earlier while the defendant remained living with the father. A new

property was purchased using the funds from the Luton house, supplemented by a mortgage. The father was no longer working and the mortgage was therefore in the name of the defendant, with the new property being conveyed solely to the defendant.

The father died intestate in 1990. The plaintiff claimed a share in the property. The defendant denied this and relied, inter alia, on the doctrine of presumption of advancement.

Held (on appeal)
The plaintiff's appeal from the first instance decision would be allowed. Where a house had been acquired with a view to joint occupation but was conveyed into the name of only one of the occupants the equitable presumption of advancement was to be considered as a judicial instrument of last resort. This applied not only in cases between husband and wife but also in those between father and child, with the presumption being rebuttable by comparatively slight evidence. In this instance there was sufficient evidence that it was not the father's intention to convey the property into the sole name of the defendant including, inter alia, a declaration of trust stating that the property should be held in 80 per cent and 20 per cent shares between the father and the defendant respectively, albeit that that declaration of trust had mistakenly never been signed by the father.

Commentary
Arguably, the case sounds the death knell for the doctrine of presumption of advancement explained by Jessel MR in *Bennet* v *Bennet* (1879) 10 Ch D 474, save in circumstances where there is absolutely no evidence to rebut the, apparently, otherwise weak presumption.

Mercier v *Mercier* [1903] 2 Ch 98 Court of Appeal (Vaughan-Williams, Romer and Cozens Hardy LJJ)

As between wife and husband purchase in the name of the other raises a resulting trust not a presumption of advancement

Facts
Husband and wife had a joint bank account composed almost entirely of the wife's income. Land was purchased out of the account, but conveyed into the husband's name.

Held
The husband held the property on resulting trust for the wife.

Pettitt v *Pettitt* [1970] AC 777 House of Lords (Lord Diplock, Lord Morris, Lord Reid, Lord Hodson and Lord Upjohn)

Contribution to joint property

Facts
The wife had purchased a cottage in her name with her own funds. The husband had made improvements to it, which he valued at £723, and he claimed that this improved the sale value of the house by £1,000.

Held
The husband had acquired no rights as a result of his work which consisted of leisure time jobs of a

kind which husbands normally did. The presumption of advancement had been much diminished in importance and strength in the modern world.

Sekhon v *Alissa* [1989] 2 FLR 94 Chancery Division (Hoffmann J)

Presumption of resulting trust unless evidence to rebut is adduced

Facts
The defendant contracted to buy a house in her sole name for £36,000 of which she paid £15,000 and her mother, the plaintiff, paid the balance. The mother claimed that the purchase was a joint commercial venture, but the daughter claimed it was a gift or an interest-free loan. The evidence was that the money amounted to the whole of the mother's life savings, that she believed a joint conveyance would incur capital gains tax, that she regarded the joint venture as an investment to give her a better return on her capital, that no member of the family thought it was a gift, that the daughter had accounted to the mother for some of the rents received, and had taken legal advice at one stage on the possibility of giving the mother some legal interest in the property.

Held
The law presumed a resulting trust in favour of the mother in the absence of evidence to rebut it. The evidence did not show that a gift or loan was intended, and the mother was therefore to have some interest in the property, the extent to be determined by the amount of her contribution.

Shephard v *Cartwright* [1955] AC 431 House of Lords (Viscount Simonds, Lord Morton, Lord Reid, Lord Tucker and Lord Somervell)

Presumption of advancement: evidence of rebuttal: admissibility

Facts
A father promoted several private companies and the shares he subscribed for were put into the name of his three children. There were a number of subsequent transactions, with the children signing the necessary documents at their father's request without understanding what they were doing. The shares were sold and the proceeds eventually spent by the father in a manner that was largely unexplained at the time of his death.

Held
The father, by registering the shares in the names of the children, had invoked the presumption of advancement. In supporting or rebutting this presumption acts and declarations of the parties before or at the time of the transaction were admissible for or against them. But, acts and declarations after the transaction were only admissible against them. The acts of the children subsequent to the transaction were admissible against them even though they showed that they were ignorant of precisely what was happening. In the circumstances, there was nothing to rebut the presumption so the children could recover repayment as against the executors of their father's estate.

Sick and Funeral Society of St John's Sunday School, Golcar, Re [1973] Ch 51 Chancery Division (Megarry J)

Unincorporated body: distribution of assets

Facts
The association had two classes of members when it was dissolved, those who paid full subscriptions and those who paid half subscriptions.

Held
Division would be ordered on the basis of a ratio of 2:1.

Tinker v *Tinker* [1970] P 136 Court of Appeal (Lord Denning MR, Cross and Salmon LJJ)

Presumption of advancement between husband and wife

Facts
Some time after the marriage the husband purchased the matrimonial home but had it conveyed into the wife's name in case his business should fail. She had made no contribution. The marriage later broke up.

Held
The husband had no claim to the house, the presumption of advancement being if anything strengthened by the husband's reason for purchasing in the wife's name, given that the intention was not fraudulent (which the court had found it was not).

Commentary
It is however possible since s24(1)(c) Matrimonial Causes Act 1973 the court would have power to award the husband some share as a postnuptial settlement within that section.

Ungarian v *Lesnoff* [1988] 3 WLR 840 Chancery (Vinelott J)

Settled Land Act protection and powers for a co-habitee

Facts
A house was bought in London under a complicated arrangement whereby the house was conveyed in the name of the male partner only, but with an intention to provide a home for life for the female partner.

Held
Following the majority opinion in *Binions* v *Evans* [1972] Ch 359 (see Chapter 6), a trust for life was construed which entitled the female partner to a vesting deed under the Settled Land Act. As tenant for life she would be entitled to exercise all the statutory powers including the right to sell and re-invest the proceeds. In basing his judgment on the majority opinion in the former case, the judge discussed Lord Denning's dissenting opinion.

Vinelott J:

> 'Although ... every opinion of Lord Denning is entitled to the greatest respect, I do not find the reasons he gives for the conclusion that the defendant in *Binions* v *Evans* ... was not a tenant for life persuasive. A person with a right to reside in an estate for his or her life, or for a period determinable on some earlier event, has a life or a determinable interest as the case may be. The estate is necessarily limited in trust for reasons by way of succession. That is so whether the trust is express or arises by operation of law. Of course, the power of sale given to the tenant for life by the SLA 1925 may override and defeat the

intentions of the settlor or of the parties to a transaction which gives rise to a constructive trust or settlement.'

Vinogradoff, Re [1935] WN 68 Chancery Division (Farwell J)

Presumed resulting trust: transfer into the name of another

Facts
Eight years before she died the testatrix transferred £800 stock from herself to herself and her four-year-old grandchild. Her executors took out a summons to decide whether the child held the stock beneficially or as trustee on a resulting trust. It was argued that s20 of the LPA 1925 renders all appointments of infants as trustees void, and therefore no presumption of resulting trust could arise, or if it did the presumption was rebutted by the presumed trustee's infancy.

Held
The argument that the section altered the presumption was taking its effects too far, as was the suggestion that the testatrix must be taken to have know the effect of the section so that she could not have intended to transfer the stock to the child as trustee. The section was not intended and did not operate to make any difference to the presumption of a resulting trust in these circumstances, so that the stock did not become the property of the grandchild but remained part of the estate of the testatrix.

Warren v *Gurney* [1944] 2 All ER 472 Court of Appeal (Lord Greene MR, Finlay and Morton LJJ)

Rebuttal of the presumption of advancement

Facts
The father purchased land in the son's name. However he retained the title deeds and was later known to have said that he did not intend a gift to the son.

Held
The subsequent conduct and declarations of the father were sufficient to rebut the presumption of advancement.

West Sussex Constabulary's Widows, Children and Benevolent (1930) Fund Trusts, Re [1971] Ch 1 Chancery Division (Goff J)

Automatic resulting trust: fulfilment of purpose

Facts
A fund was established to provide payments to widows and dependants of deceased members of the West Sussex Constabulary. Receipts to the fund came from members' subscriptions, the proceeds of entertainments, sweepstakes, raffles, collecting boxes and donations and legacies. The constabulary was amalgamated with other police forces on 1 January 1968 and there were no longer any persons able to receive these benefits. The question as to the distribution of the fund arose.

Held
The fund should be distributed on the following basis:

1. Where members of the constabulary had made contributions through subscriptions these had been made on the basis of £1 per member per month and existing members of the constabulary could not claim these because they had all they contracted for, either because their widows and dependants had received or were in receipt of prescribed benefits or because they did not have a widow or dependant. Past members of the constabulary could not claim either because they put their money up on a contractual basis and not on the basis of a trust. Accordingly, such contributions by way of subscription went bona vacantia to the Crown.
2. As to the proceeds of entertainments, raffles and sweepstakes, these went bona vacantia to the Crown being paid under a contract rather than a trust.
3. The proceeds of collecting boxes by unknown donors went to the Crown as bona vacantia on the assumption that they intended to part out and out absolutely with the money.
4. Donations, including legacies if any, were returnable by way of resulting trust.

Goff J:

'Then counsel divided the outside moneys into three categories, first, the proceeds of entertainments, raffles and sweepstakes; secondly, the proceeds of collecting boxes; and, thirdly, donations, including legacies if any, and he took particular objections to each.

I agree that there cannot be any resulting trust with respect to the first category. I am not certain whether Harman J in *Re Gillingham Bus Disaster Fund* [1958] Ch 300 meant to decide otherwise. In stating the facts at p304 he referred to "street collections and so forth". In the further argument at p309 there is mention of whist drives and concerts but the judge himself did not speak of anything other than gifts. If, however, he did, I must respectfully decline to follow his judgment in that regard, for whatever may be the true position with regard to collecting-boxes, it appears to me to be impossible to apply the doctrine of resulting trust to the proceeds of entertainments and sweepstakes and such-like money-raising operations for two reasons: first, the relationship is one of contract and not of trust; the purchaser of a ticket may have the motive of aiding the cause or he may not; he may purchase a ticket merely because he wishes to attend the particular entertainment or to try for the prize, but whichever it be, he pays his money as the price of what is offered and what he receives; secondly, there is in such cases no direct contribution to the fund at all; it is only the profit, if any, which is ultimately received and there may even be none.

In any event, the first category cannot be any more susceptible to the doctrine than the second to which I now turn. Here one starts with the well-known dictum of PO Lawrence J in *Re Welsh Hospital (Netley) Fund* [1921] 1 Ch 655 where he said:

"So far as regards the contributors to entertainments, street collections etc, I have no hesitation in holding that they must be taken to have parted with their money out-and-out. It is inconceivable that any person paying for a concert ticket or placing a coin in a collecting-box presented to him in the street should have intended that any part of the money so contributed should be returned to him when the immediate object for which the concert was given or the collection made had come to an end. To draw such an inference would be absurd on the face of it."

This was adopted by Upjohn J in *Re Hillier's Trusts* [1954] 1 WLR 700, where the point was actually decided ...

(The analysis of Upjohn J) was approved by Denning LJ in the Court of Appeal although it is true he went on to say that the law makes a presumption of charity. I quote from p714:

"Let me first state the law as I understand it in regard to money collected for a specific charity by means of a church collection, a flag day, a whist drive, a dance, or some such activity. When a man gives money on such an occasion, he gives it, I think, beyond recall. He parts with his money out-and-out."

In *Re Ulverston and District New Hospital Building Trusts* [1956] Ch 622 Jenkins LJ threw out a suggestion that there might be a distinction in the case of a person who could prove that he put a specified sum in a collecting box, and, in the *Gillingham* case Harman J after noting this, decided that there was a resulting trust with respect to the proceeds of collections. He said at p314 (quoting the last paragraph extracted p187 ante:)

"It will be observed that Harman J considered that *Re Welsh Hospital (Netley) Fund)*; *Re Hillier's Trusts* and *Re Ulverston and District New Hospital Building Trusts*, did not help him greatly because they were charity cases. It is true that they were, and, as will presently appear, that is in my view very significant in relation to the third category, but I do not think it was a valid objection with respect to the second, and for my part I cannot reconcile the decision of Upjohn J in *Re Hillier's Trust* with that of Harman J in the *Gillingham case*. As I see it, therefore, I have to choose between them. On the one hand it may be said that Harman J had the advantage, which Upjohn J had not, of considering the suggestion made by Jenkins LJ. On the other hand that suggestion, with all respect, seems to me somewhat fanciful and unreal. I agree that all who put their money into collecting-boxes should be taken to have the same intention, but why should they not all be regarded as intending to part with their money out-and-out absolutely in all circumstances? I observe that PO Lawrence J in *Re Welsh Hospital* used very strong words. He said any other view was inconceivable and absurd on the face of it. That commends itself to my humble judgment, and I therefore prefer and follow the judgment of Upjohn J in *Re Hillier's Trusts* ... " (His Lordship referred to *Re Hillier's Trusts* and continued): "Therefore, where, as in the present case, the object was neither equivocal nor charitable, I can see no justification for infecting the third category with the weaknesses of the first and second, and I cannot distinguish this part of the case from *Re Abbott Fund Trusts* [1990] 2 Ch 326."'

6 Constructive Trusts

Agip (Africa) Ltd* v *Jackson and Others [1991] Ch 547 Court of Appeal (Fox, Butler-Sloss and Beldam LJJ)

Requisites of 'knowing assistance' liability

Facts
In this case the plaintiffs claimed that the defendants were constructive trustees as a consequence of two of the defendants' alleged assistance in 'laundering' money belonging to the plaintiffs. This claim was upheld at first instance by Millett J – [1989] 3 WLR 1367. The judge's ruling was confirmed by the Court of Appeal.

Held
At first instance Millett J pointed out that to make a stranger to a trust liable for 'knowing assistance' constructive notice of someone else's fraud is not sufficient. His lordship thus stated that: 'Dishonest furtherance of the dishonest scheme of another is an understandable basis for liability; negligent but honest failure to appreciate that someone else's scheme is dishonest is not.' But his lordship also went on to indicate that if such a stranger to a trust 'did suspect wrongdoing yet failed to make inquiries because "he did not want to know" ...' or because he regarded it as "none of his business" ... then, 'such conduct is dishonest, and those who are guilty of it cannot complain if, for the purpose of civil liability, they are treated as if they had actual knowledge.'

The Court of Appeal confirmed that the judge had reached the correct conclusion.

With regard to the plaintiffs' further claim to trace certain property the Court of Appeal also confirmed the judge's finding to the effect that since there had been an initial breach of fiduciary duty (by the plaintiffs' chief accountant), *equitable* tracing was possible against anyone having possession of the plaintiffs' property other than a bona fide purchaser without notice. Thus the plaintiffs could trace *in equity* any of their money in the defendants' possession (and paid into court by them), even if 'mixing' had taken place. (For further details concerning this case at first instance see Chapter 18.)

Attorney-General for Hong Kong* v *Charles Warwick Reid and Others [1993] 3 WLR 1143 Privy Council (Lord Templeman, Lord Goff of Chieveley, Lord Lowry, Lord Lloyd of Berwick and Sir Thomas Eichelbaum)

Payment of bribe – debtor/creditor relationship or constructive trustee

Facts
Whilst a Crown servant in Hong Kong R allegedly received bribes in breach of his fiduciary duty. This money was used to purchase two properties in New Zealand (allegedly) conveyed to R and his wife and a third property conveyed to his solicitor. The Attorney-General for Hong Kong obtained caveats against the title for the three properties after R pleaded guilty to offences under the Prevention of Bribery Ordinance and was sentenced to eight years imprisonment and fined HK $12.4 million.

The Attorney-General appealed to the Privy Council after the First Instance and Court of Appeal of New Zealand refused an application by the Attorney-General to renew the caveats on the basis that the Crown had no equitable interest in the three properties.

Held
The Attorney-General's application was upheld.

Lord Templeman, giving the Privy Council's recommendation to Her Majesty:

> 'A bribe is a gift accepted by a fiduciary as an inducement to him to betray his trust. A secret benefit [or profit], which may or may not constitute a bribe, is a benefit which the fiduciary derives from trust property or obtains from knowledge which he acquires in the course of acting as a fiduciary. A fiduciary is not always accountable for a secret benefit but he is undoubtedly accountable for a secret benefit which consists of a bribe. ...
>
> Equity, however, acts in personam, insists that it is unconscionable for a fiduciary to obtain and retain a benefit in breach of duty ... The false fiduciary who received the bribe in breach of duty must pay and account for the bribe to the person to whom that duty was owed. ...
>
> ... it is said that if the fiduciary is in equity a debtor to the person injured, he cannot also be a trustee of the bribe. But there is no reason why equity should not provide two remedies, so long as they do not result in double recovery.'

After specifically discussing, then disapproving of, the long established and applied (but often criticised) decision in *Lister & Co v Stubbs* (1890) 45 Ch D 1 Lord Templeman stated that:

> 'The decision in *Lister & Co v Stubbs* is not consistent with the principles that a fiduciary must not be allowed to benefit from his own breach of duty, that the fiduciary should account for the bribe as soon as he receives it and that equity regards as done that which ought to be done. From these principles it would appear to follow that the bribe and the property from time to time representing the bribe are held on a constructive trust for the person injured. A fiduciary remains personally liable for the amount of the bribe [on a debtor-creditor basis] if, in the event, the value of the property then recovered by the injured person proved to be less than that amount.'

Baden, Delvaux and Lecuit v Société Générale pour Favoriser le Développement de commerce et de l'Industrie en France SA [1993] 1 WLR 509 (Peter Gibson J)

Definition of 'knowing assistance' so as to render a stranger constructive trustee though none of the property has come into his hands

Facts
The facts of this case are highly complex and add little to the basic principles applied as to whether strangers have 'knowingly assisted' so as to render themselves constructive trustees. However, suffice to say the case involved an action for recovery of some US$4 million from a bank which had transferred those monies to Panama (thereby putting the funds out of the reach of the plaintiffs).

Held
There must be four elements for a case of 'knowing assistance':
1. the existence of a trust;
2. the existence of a dishonest and fraudulent design on the part of the trustees;
3. the assistance of the stranger in that design;
4. the knowledge of the strangers.

On the facts the bank did not have sufficient knowledge to make themselves liable.

Baker v Baker (1993) The Times 23 February Court of Appeal (Dillon, Beldam and Roch LJJ)

Constructive trust: proprietory estoppel

Facts
The plaintiff was the tenant of a council house and enjoyed security of tenure. Having accumulated substantial savings he agreed with his son (the defendant), and his son's wife, to assist them in purchasing a house for their family. This involved his granting his son his savings (approximately £20,000) with the quid pro quo being the father having the right to live in the property rent free for the rest of his life. The house was purchased, and the family moved in. A subsequent falling out resulted in the father being forced out. The father brought an action for a beneficial interest based on his contribution to its purchase price.

Held
1. At first instance (Bristol District Registry, Judge Hywel Moseley QC) the plaintiff obtained a judgment in his favour that his original contribution be repaid (with interest) or, in default, charged against the property.
2. On appeal the court found that the Judge at First Instance had correctly found that the plaintiff did not have a direct interest in the property by virtue of his contribution. Rather the intention had been to benefit his son and family, whilst securing rent free accommodation for the rest of his life. However, the proper basis for calculating the father's loss was not to order repayment of his contribution; rather his loss was that of rent free accommodation for the rest of his life. The matter was re-submitted to the lower court for this to be determined.

Bannister v Bannister [1948] 2 All ER 133 Court of Appeal (Scott and Asquith LJJ and Jenkins J)

Fraud: constructive trust

Facts
The plaintiff and the defendant made an oral contract by which the plaintiff agreed to buy two cottages from the defendant. One of the terms of the contract was that the defendant should be allowed to live in one of the cottages as long as she liked rent-free. There was no mention of this undertaking in the conveyance and the purchase price was £250 when the value of the cottages was about £400. Afterwards, the plaintiff sought possession of the cottage from the defendant so that he could re-sell it with vacant possession. The county court judge found that there was a constructive trust imposed upon the plaintiff who appealed claiming that at most there was a tenancy-at-will in the absence of writing and the provisions of ss53 and 54 of the Law of Property Act 1925 and that as there was no actual fraud there could not be a constructive trust.

Held
There was a trust for the defendant to live in the cottage rent-free as long as she liked even if there was no written evidence of this for the purposes of s53.

Scott LJ:

> 'It is, we think, clearly a mistake to suppose that the equitable principle on which a constructive trust is raised against a person who insists on the absolute character of a conveyance to himself for the purpose

of defeating a beneficial interest, which according to the true bargain, was to belong to another, is confined to cases in which the conveyance itself was fraudulently obtained. The fraud which brings the principle into play arises as soon as the absolute character of the conveyance is set up for the purpose of defeating the beneficial interest, and that is the fraud to cover which the Statute of Frauds or the corresponding provisions of the Law of Property Act 1925 cannot be called in aid in cases in which no written evidence of the real bargain is available. Nor is it in our opinion, necessary that the bargain on which the absolute conveyance is made should include any express stipulation that the grantee is in so many words to hold as trustee. It is enough that the bargain should have included a stipulation under which some sufficiently defined beneficial interest in the property was to be taken by another.'

Barnes v *Addy* (1874) 9 Ch App 244 Court of Appeal in Chancery (Lord Selbourne LC, James and Mellish LJJ)

Strangers to the trust dealing honestly not constructive trustees

Facts
A settlor settled funds on trust as to one half for A's wife and children and as to one half for B's wife and children. A was the sole surviving trustee and in exercising a power of appointing new trustees he appointed B sole trustee of that half of the fund held on trust for B's wife and children. In making the appointment A acted on the advice of a solicitor, Duffield, who executed a deed of appointment and indemnity. B acted on the advice of another solicitor, Preston, who warned B's wife of the risk of a sole trustee being appointed. However, she consented to the appointment of B and the deed of indemnity in favour of A was sealed accordingly. B later misapplied the trust funds and was declared bankrupt. B's children sought to make A liable for a breach of trust in appointing B sole trustee on the ground it was a fraud on the power of appointing new trustees. They also sought to make both solicitors liable for the loss of the fund. A died two years before the action.

Held
The estate of A was liable to make good the loss but the solicitors were not liable for reasons which Lord Selborne LC expressed:

'... strangers are not to be made constructive trustees merely because they act as the agents of trustees in transactions within their legal powers, transactions, perhaps of which a Court of Equity may disapprove, unless those agents receive and become chargeable with some part of the trust property, or unless they assist with knowledge in a dishonest and fraudulent design on the part of the trustees. Those are the principles as it seems to me, which we must bear in mind in dealing with the facts of the case. If those principles were disregarded, I know not how anyone could, in transactions admitting of doubt, as to the view which a Court of Equity might take of them, safely discharge the office of solicitor, of banker, or of agent of any sort to trustees. But, on the other hand, if persons, dealing honestly as agents, are at liberty to rely on the legal power of the trustees, and are not to have the character of trustees constructively imposed upon them, then the transactions of mankind can safely be carried through; and I apprehend those who create trusts do expressly intend, in the absence of fraud and dishonesty, to exonerate such agents of all classes from the responsibilities which are expressly incumbent, by reason of the fiduciary relation upon the trustees.'

Basham (deceased), Re [1987] 1 All ER 405 Chancery Division (Edward Nugee QC sitting as a High Court judge)

Proprietary estoppel

Facts

The deceased died in 1985 intestate, and leaving an estate of £43,000 which included a cottage worth £21,000. In 1936 the deceased married the plaintiff's mother when the plaintiff was about 15. The plaintiff herself got married in 1941 and eventually had a family. For over 30 years, from 1936, the plaintiff worked for the deceased without payment helping him to run several public houses and a service station. During this time the plaintiff contemplated obtaining a regular job to supplement her husband's income and was persuaded to continue working for the deceased by promises such as 'You don't have to worry about money, you'll be alright'. The deceased never paid the plaintiff and her understanding was that when he died she would inherit his property. On several occasions the plaintiff and her husband considered moving away from where they lived so that the husband could get better employment. The deceased dissuaded them and again assured them that he would look after them. The deceased retired in 1966 and after that the plaintiff and her husband cared for both him and the plaintiff's mother and after the death of the plaintiff's mother in 1976 the plaintiff and her husband lived near the deceased and regularly cared for him. He assured them on many occasions that money they spent on his cottage would not be lost to them. Before his death from a stroke in 1985 the deceased indicated that he wished the plaintiff to have the cottage but died before he could make a will. The plaintiff sought a declaration that she was entitled to the cottage and its effects and the remainder of the deceased's estate.

Held

The plaintiff was entitled to the deceased's estate under proprietary estoppel as the deceased had encouraged her to act to her detriment on the faith of a belief that she would inherit his estate on his death.

Edward Nugee QC:

> 'The rights to which proprietary estoppel gives rise, and the machinery by which effect is given to them, are similar in many respects to those involved in cases of secret trusts, mutual wills and other comparable cases in which property is vested in B on the faith of an understanding that it will be dealt with in a particular manner ... In cases of proprietary estoppel the factor which gives rise to the equitable obligation is A's alteration of his position on the faith of the understanding ...'

The judge went on to indicate that if estoppel applied and an equity arose in favour of the party claiming under estoppel that equity was in the nature of a constructive trust and it was not necessary that that party should already have some interest in the property, it was sufficient if he believed that he would obtain an interest in the property in the future.

Belmont Finance Corporation Ltd v *Williams Furniture Ltd* [1979] 1 Ch 250 Court of Appeal (Buckley, Orr and Goff LJJ)

Constructive trusts: dishonest dealing: knowledge

Facts

This case was concerned with a breach of s54 of the Companies Act 1948 (now replaced by s42-44 CA 1981) which prohibited a company giving financial assistance in the acquisition by another of its shares. The reason for this prohibition lies in the fact that it could have serious repercussions on the financial standing of the company. A constructive trust will arise if such a breach occurs. The facts of this case are very complicated and no purpose is served, for trusts law, in studying them.

Held

On the issue of constructive trusts it was said by Buckley LJ:

> '.. I think two questions need to be considered. First, is it necessary when a person is sought to be charged as a constructive trustee that the design of which he is alleged to have had knowledge should be a

fraudulent and dishonest design? For this purpose I do not myself see that any distinction is to be drawn between the words "fraudulent" and "dishonest"; I think they mean the same thing, and to use the two of them together does not add to the extent of dishonesty required. The second question is: if this is necessary, does the statement of claim here allege dishonesty with sufficient particularity?

The plaintiff has contended that in every case the court should consider whether the conduct in question was so unsatisfactory, whether it can be strictly described as fraudulent or dishonest in law, as to make accountability on the footing of constructive trust equitably just. This, as I have said, is admitted to constitute an extension of the rule as formulated to Lord Selborne LC. That formation has stood for more than 100 years. To depart from it now would, I think, introduce an undesirable degree of uncertainty to the law, because if dishonesty is not to be the criterion, what degree of unethical conduct is to be sufficient? I think we should adhere to the formula used by Lord Selborne LC. So in my judgment the design must be shown to be a dishonest one, that is to say, a fraudulent one.

The knowledge of that design on the part of the parties sought to be made liable may be actual knowledge. If he wilfully shuts his eyes to dishonesty, or wilfully or recklessly fails to make such enquiries as an honest and reasonable man would make, he may be found to have involved himself in the fraudulent character of the design, or at any rate to be disentitled to rely on lack of actual knowledge of the design as a defence. But otherwise, as it seems to me, he should not be held to be affected by constructive notice. It is not strictly necessary, I think, for us to decide that point on this appeal; I express that opinion merely as my view at the present stage without intending to lay it down as a final decision ...'

Goff LJ:

'It seems to me, therefore, that there are three questions which we have to decide: first is it necessary to prove that the alleged breaches of trust by the directors were fraudulent or dishonest (and I agree with Buckley LJ that the two things really mean one and the same); secondly, if so, is that sufficiently pleaded; and thirdly, was it necessary to specify, either in the body of the statement of claim or in the prayer, the claim for relief on the footing of constructive trusteeship?

On the first point counsel for the plaintiff, to support his argument that it is permissible to extend the principle of *Barnes* v *Addy* (1874) 9 Ch App 244, relied on two passages in the *Selangor* case [1968] 1 WLR 1555 ... first ...where Ungoed-Thomas J said:

"It seems to me imperative to grasp and keep constantly in mind that the second category of constructive trusteeship (which is the only category with which we are concerned) is nothing more than a formula for equitable relief. The court of equity says that the defendant shall be liable in equity, as though he were a trustee. He is made liable in equity as a trustee by the imposition of construction of the court of equity. This is done because in accordance with equitable principles applied by the court of equity it is equitable that he should be held liable as though he were a trustee. Trusteeship and constructive trusteeship are equitable conceptions."

In the second passage, which was introduced by the judge saying, "I come to the third element, dishonest and fraudulent design on the part of the trustees" Ungoed-Thomas J said:

"It seems to me unnecessary and, indeed, undesirable to attempt to define 'dishonest and fraudulent design', since a definition in vacuo, without the advantage of all the circumstances that might occur in cases that might come before the court, might be to restrict their scope by definition without regard to, and in ignorance of, circumstances which would patently come within them. The words themselves are not terms of art and are not taken from a statute or other document demanding construction. They are used in a judgment as the expression and indication of an equitable principle and not in a document as constituting or demanding verbal application and, therefore, definition. They are to be understood 'according to the plain principles of a court of equity', to which Sir Richard Kindersley V-C referred (in *Bodenham* v *Hoskins* (1852) 21 LJ Ch 864), and these principles, in this context at any rate, are just plain, ordinary commonsense. I accept that 'dishonest and fraudulent', so understood, is certainly conduct which is morally reprehensible; but what is morally reprehensible is best left open to identification and not to be confined by definition."

If and so far as Ungoed-Thomas J intended, as I think he did, to say that it is not necessary that the breach of trust "in respect of which it is sought to make the defendant liable as a constructive trustee" should be fraudulent or dishonest, I respectfully cannot accept that view. I agree that it would be dangerous and wrong to depart from the safe path of the principle as stated by Lord Selborne LC to the uncharted sea of something not innocent (and counsel for the plaintiff conceded that mere innocence would not do) but still short of dishonesty ...'

Binions v *Evans* [1972] Ch 359 Court of Appeal (Lord Denning MR, Megaw and Stephenson LJJ)

Constructive trust as a method of protecting equitable interests in licencees

The court can enforce a licence by imposing a constructive trust on the licensor, which it can then enforce against a purchaser with notice.

Facts

The defendant's husband had worked for the landlords all his life. Until the husband's death, he and the defendant had lived in a cottage owned by the landlords. After his death, the landlords made a written agreement with the defendant by which, 'in order to provide a temporary home' for her, they agreed to permit her to reside in and occupy the cottage 'as Tenant at will of them free of rent for the remainder of her life or until determined as hereinafter provided'. The agreement provided that the defendant might determine the 'tenancy hereby created' by giving the landlords four weeks' notice in writing. It further provided that she should personally occupy and live in the cottage as a private residence and not assign or sublet it and 'upon ceasing personally to live there vacant possession shall forthwith be given to the Landlords'. The agreement contained obligations on the defendant to keep and maintain the cottage in a proper condition and on the landlords to pay all rates, taxes and outgoings and concluded ... 'the tenancy hereby created shall unless previously determined forthwith determine on the death of the defendant'. Two years later, the landlords sold their estate, which included the cottage, to the plaintiffs. In the contract of sale, they inserted a clause which stated that the property was sold subject to the defendant's tenancy of the cottage (with which the landlords had provided the plaintiffs a copy) and continued: 'The plaintiffs, having been supplied with a copy of the ... Tenancy Agreement ... shall purchase with full knowledge thereof and shall not be entitled to raise any requisitions or objections in respect of any matters contained therein or arising thereout.' By reason of that, the plaintiffs paid a reduced price for the property. Seven months after completion of the conveyance, the plaintiffs gave the defendant notice to quit and subsequently brought proceedings, claiming that the defendant was a tenant at will and that, her tenancy having been determined, she was a trespasser.

Held

The plaintiffs were not entitled to possession of the cottage for the following reasons:

1. Although the words 'tenant at will' were used in the agreement, the rest of the agreement contained terms which were quite inconsistent with a tenancy at will; thus, the defendant was to be permitted to stay for the remainder of her life and the landlords could not turn her out at will; the defendant was not, therefore, a tenant at will.
2. (Per Lord Denning MR) although the agreement did not constitute a tenancy, it did confer on the defendant a contractual licence to occupy the cottage for the rest of her life; where an owner sold land to a purchaser and at the same time stipulated that he should take it 'subject to' a contractual licence, the court would impose on the purchaser a constructive trust in favour of the licensee; accordingly, the defendant as a contractual licensee, had acquired an equitable interest in the cottage which the court would protect by granting an injunction to restrain the landlord from turning her out; when the

plaintiffs bought the cottage 'subject to' the defendant's rights under the agreement, they took it on a constructive trust to permit the defendant to reside there during her life or as long as she might desire.
3. (Per Megaw and Stephenson LJJ) the effect of the agreement was that the landlords held the cottage on trust to permit the defendant to occupy it so long as she might desire; she was, therefore, a tenant for life within the meaning of the Settled Land Act 1925; since the plaintiffs took with express notice of the agreement which gave rise to the trust, they could not turn her out of the cottage against her will.
4. Per Lord Denning MR: Even if a purchaser does not take expressly 'subject to' the rights of a licensee, he may do so impliedly, at any rate when the licensee is in actual occupation of the land. Whenever the purchaser takes the land impliedly subject to the rights of the contractual licensee, a court of equity will impose a constructive trust for the beneficiary.

Having first held that Mrs Evans was not a tenant at will, nor a lessee, nor a tenant for life under the Settled Land Act 1925, Lord Denning MR said:

'Seeing that the defendant has no legal estate or interest in the land, the question is what right has she? At any rate, she has a contractual right to reside in the house for the remainder of her life or as long as she pleases to stay. I know that in the agreement it is described as a tenancy, but that does not matter. The question is: What is it in reality? To my mind, it is a licence and no tenancy. It is a privilege which is personal to her ... it ranks as a contractual licence and not a tenancy.

What is the status of such a licence as this?... a right to occupy for life, arising by contract, gives to the occupier an equitable interest in the land ...

Suppose, however, that the defendant did not have an equitable interest at the outset, nevertheless it is quite plain that she obtained one afterwards when the Tredegar Estate sold the cottage. They stipulated with the plaintiffs that they were to take the house "subject to" the defendants' rights under the agreement. They supplied the plaintiffs with a copy of the contract; and the plaintiffs paid less because of her right to stay there. In these circumstances, this court will impose on the plaintiffs a constructive trust for her benefit: for the simple reason that it would be utterly inequitable for the plaintiffs to turn the defendant out contrary to the stipulation subject to which they took the premises.

Wherever the owner sells the land to a purchaser and at the same time stipulates that he shall take it "subject to" a contractual licence, I think it plain that a court of equity will impose on the purchaser a constructive trust in favour of the beneficiary. It is true that the stipulation (that the purchaser shall take it subject to the rights of the licensee) is a stipulation for the benefit of one who is not a party to the contract of sale, but ... that is just the very case in which equity will "come to the aid of the common law" per Lord Upjohn in *Beswick* v *Beswick* [1968] AC 58. It does so by imposing a constructive trust on the purchaser.

In my opinion, the defendant, by virtue of the agreement, had an equitable interest in the cottage which the court would protect by granting an injunction against the landlords by restraining them from turning her out. When the landlords sold the cottage to a purchaser "subject to" her rights under the agreement, the purchaser took the cottage on a constructive trust to permit the defendant to reside there during her life, or as long as she might desire. The courts will not allow the purchaser to go back on that trust.'

Boardman v *Phipps* [1967] 2 AC 46 House of Lords (Lord Cohen, Lord Hodson, Lord Guest; Viscount Dilhorne and Lord Upjohn)

Fiduciary as constructive trustee

Facts
The Phipps family trust owned 8,000 out of 30,000 shares in a private company. The plaintiff John Phipps was one of the beneficiaries under the trust and the defendants were Boardman who was a solicitor and Tom Phipps a beneficiary. Boardman acted as solicitor to the trust.

The defendants were dissatisfied with the way in which the private company was run so in 1956 they made enquiries about it on behalf of the trust and received much confidential information about its affairs. In particular they learned the value of the company's assets and the size of its profit and while the former were high the latter were low. The defendants realised it would be advantageous to sell some of the company's non-profit making assets. The defendants, with the trustees' consent, decided to purchase a controlling interest in the company and to implement a scheme to sell off non-profit making assets. The scheme was highly profitable and the trust gained in respect of its holding and the defendants gained in respect of the shares they had purchased themselves. The plaintiff called upon the defendants to account for the profits they had made. There was no question of any dishonesty by the defendants, they had offered the shares they purchased to the trustees first but being unable to find money for this purpose they refused.

Held (Viscount Dilhorne and Lord Upjohn dissenting)
The defendants were accountable as constructive trustees for the profits which they had made. The information that the shares were a good investment and the opportunity to bid for them came as a result of their position, they would not have received this as ordinary members of the public.

Lord Cohen:

'... Information is, of course, not property in the strict sense of that word and, as I have already stated, it does not necessarily follow that because an agent acquired information and opportunity while acting in a fiduciary capacity he is accountable to his principals for any profit that comes his way as the result of the use he makes of that information and opportunity. His liability to account must depend on the facts of the case. In the present case much of the information came the appellant's way when Mr Boardman was acting on behalf of the trustees on the instructions of Mr Fox and the opportunity of binding for the shares came because he purported for all purposes except for making the bind to be acting on behalf of the owners of the 8,000 shares in the company. In these circumstances it seems to me that the principle of the Regal case applies and that the courts below came to the right conclusion.

That is enough to dispose of the case but I would add that an agent is, in my opinion, liable to account for profits he makes out of trust property if there is a possibility of conflict between his interest and his duty to his principal. Mr Boardman and Tom Phipps were not general agents of the trustees but they were their agents for certain limited purposes. The information they had obtained and the opportunity to purchase the 21,986 shares afforded them by their relations with the directors of the company – an opportunity they got as the result of their introduction to the directors by Mr Fox – were not property in the strict sense but that information and that opportunity they owed to their representing themselves as agents for the holders of the 8,000 shares held by the trustees. In these circumstances they could not, I think, use that information and that opportunity to purchase the shares for themselves if there was any possibility that the trustees might wish to acquire them for the trust.'

Lord Upjohn:

'... Chapter 1 begins in December 1956, when Mr Fox, a practising chartered accountant and the active trustee, received the accounts of the company which he thought were very unsatisfactory. So he consulted the family solicitor, the appellant Boardman, who also advised the trustees from time to time. Mr Fox, who had already formed the impression that the directors were unfriendly to the Phipps family, wanted to see the majority holding in friendly hands and not in unfriendly hands.

It was decided that Mr Boardman and the appellant Tom Phipps (Tom), who was engaged in the textile industry, should go to the annual general meeting of the company on 28 December 1956, with the idea of getting Tom appointed a director and they were given proxies for that purpose. Mrs Noble, Tom's sister, another trustee, was kept in touch with events by Mr Boardman, her mother, the third trustee, being too old and ill to pay any attention to trust affairs. So Tom and Mr Boardman attended the meeting and Mr Boardman explained that the Phipps family were very dissatisfied with the accounts. There was a good deal of argument about the validity of certain proxy forms of the Harris family and a number of questions on the accounts put by Mr Boardman were answered by the chairman, Mr Smith, a solicitor. Mr Boardman proposed that Tom should be elected to the board, but the chairman after much discussion refused to accept the motion. So the meeting ended in the defeat of the Phipps representatives and they reported to Mr Fox that they had met with a very hostile reception.

Then there were discussions and Mr Boardman suggested that Tom should try to buy a controlling interest in the company, but the latter felt that the operation was too big for him and wanted Mr Boardman to come in with him and the latter agreed to do so. Mr Fox was most happy at this idea as he could see the company getting under far more efficient management than in the past. So they set about making a bid for the outside shares accordingly. It is of cardinal importance, and, in my view fundamental to the decision of this case, to appreciate that at this stage there was no question whatever of the trustees contemplating the possibility of a purchase of further shares in the company. Mr Fox (whose evidence was accepted by the judge) made it abundantly plain that he would not consider any such proposition. The reasons for this attitude are worth setting out in full: (a) The acquisition of further shares in the company would have been a breach of trust, for they were not shares authorised by the investment clause in the will; (b) although not developed in evidence it must have been obvious to those concerned that no court would sanction the purchase of further shares in a small company which the trustees considered to be badly managed. It would have been throwing good money after bad. It would also have been necessary to bring in proposals for installing a new management. Mr Fox, was a busy practising chartered accountant who obviously would not have considered it; no one from start to finish ever suggested that Tom, who was running the family concern of Phipps & Son Ltd, would be willing to undertake this arduous task on behalf of the trustees; (c) the trustees had no money available for the purchase of further shares ...

... In general, information is not property at all. It is normally open to all who have eyes to read and ears to hear. The true test is to determine in what circumstances the information has been acquired. If it has been acquired in such circumstances that it would be a breach of confidence to disclose it to another then courts of equity will restrain the recipient from communicating it to another. In such cases such confidential information is often and for many years has been described as the property of the donor, the books of authority are full of such references; knowledge of secret processes, "know-how", confidential information as to the prospects of a company or of someone's intention or the expected results of some horse race based on stable or other confidential information. But in the end the real truth is that it is not property in any normal sense but equity will restrain its transmission to another if in breach of some confidential relationship.

With all respect to the views of Russell LJ, I protest at the idea that information acquired by trustees in the course of their duties as such is necessarily part of the assets of the trust which cannot be used by the trustees except for benefit of the trust. Russell LJ referred to the fact that two out of three of the trustees could have no authority to turn over this aspect of trust property to the appellants except for the benefit of the trust; this I do not understand, for if such information is trust property not all the trustees acting together could do it for they cannot give away trust property.

We heard much argument upon the impact of the fact that the testator's widow was at all material times incapable of acting in the trust owing to disability. Of course trustees must act all of them and unanimously in matters affecting trust affairs, but in this case they never performed any relevant act on behalf of the trust at all; I quoted Mr Fox's answer earlier for this reason. At no time after going to the meeting in December 1956, did Mr Boardman or Tom rely on any express or implied authority or consent of the trustees in relation to trust property. They understood rightly that there was no question of the trustees acquiring any further trust property by purchasing further shares in the company, and it was only in the purchase of other shares that they were interested.

There is, in my view, and I know of no authority to the contrary, no general rule that information learnt by a trustee during the course of his duties is property of the trust and cannot be used by him. If that were to be the rule it would put the Public Trustee and other corporate trustees out of business and make it difficult for private trustees to be trustees of more than one trust. This would be the greatest possible pity for corporate trustees and others may have much information which they may initially acquire in connection with some particular trust but without prejudice to that trust can make it readily available to other trusts to the great advantage of those other trusts.

The real rule is, in my view, that knowledge learnt by a trustee in the course of his duties as such is not in the least property of the trust and in general may be used by him for his own benefit or for the benefit of other trusts unless it is confidential information which is given to him: (1) in circumstances which, regardless of his position as a trustee, would make it a breach of confidence for him to communicate to anyone for it has been given to him expressly or impliedly as confidential; or (2) in a fiduciary capacity, and its use would place him in a position where his duty and his interest might possibly conflict. Let me give one or two simple examples. A, as trustee of two settlements X and Y holding shares in the same small company, learns facts as trustee of X about the company which are encouraging. In the absence of special circumstances (such, for example, that X wants to buy more shares) I can see nothing whatever which would make it improper for him to tell his co-trustees of Y who feel inclined to sell that he has information that this would be a bad thing to do.

Another example: A as trustee of X learns facts that make him and his co-trustees want to sell. Clearly he could not communicate his knowledge to his co-trustees of Y until at all events the holdings of X have been sold for there would be a plain conflict, reflected in the prices that might or might possibly be obtained.

My Lords, I do not think for one moment that Lord Brougham in *Hamilton* v *Wright* (1842) 9 Cl & Fin 111, quoted in the speech of my noble and learned friend Lord Guest, was saying anything to the contrary; you have to look and see whether the knowledge acquired was capable of being used for his own benefit *to injure* the trust (my italics). That test can have no application to the present. There was no possibility of the information being used to injure the trust. The knowledge obtained was used not in connection with trust property but to enhance the value of the trust property by the purchase of other property in which the trustees were not interested.

With these general observations on the applicable principles of law let me apply them to the facts of this case.

Chapter 2. At this stage the appellants went to the meeting with the object of persuading the shareholders to appoint Tom a director; admittedly they were acting on behalf of the trustees at that meeting. It is the basis of the respondent's case that this placed the appellants in a fiduciary relationship which they never after lost or, as it was argued, it 'triggered off a chain of events' and gave them the opportunity of acquiring knowledge so that they thereafter became accountable to the trustees. From this it must logically follow that in acquiring the 2,925 shares they became constructive trustees for the trust.

My Lords, I must emphatically disagree. The appellants went to the meeting for a limited purpose (the election of Tom as a director) which failed. Then the appellants' agency came to an end. They had no further duties to perform. The discussions which followed showed conclusively that the trustees would not consider a purchase of further shares. So when Chapter 2, phase 1, opened I can see nothing to prevent the appellants from making an offer for shares for themselves, or for that matter, I cannot see that Mr Boardman would have been acting improperly in advising some other client to make an offer for shares (other than the 8,000) in the company.

In the circumstances, the appellants' duties having come to an end, they owed no duty and there was no conflict of interest and duty, they were in no way dealing in trust property. Further, of course, they had the blessing of two trustees in their conduct in trying to buy further shares.

So had phase 1 of Chapter 2 been successful I can see nothing to make them constructive trustees of the shares they purchased for the trust.

Consider a simple example. Blackacre is trust property and next to it is Whiteacre; but there is no question of the trustees being interested in a possible purchase of Whiteacre as being convenient to be held with Blackacre. Is a trustee to be precluded from purchasing Whiteacre for himself because he may have learnt something about Whiteacre while acting as a trustee of Blackacre? I can understand the owner of Whiteacre being annoyed but surely not the beneficial owners of Blackacre; they have no interest in Whiteacre and their trustees have no duties to perform in respect thereof ...'

Carl Zeiss Stiftung v *Herbert Smith & Co (No 2)* [1969] 2 Ch 276 Court of Appeal (Sachs and Edmund-Davies LJJ)

Strangers to the trust: knowledge

Facts
This case concerned a claim by an East German company against a West German company. Each company had been founded on division of the Zeiss foundation after the Second World War and each claimed the right to use the Zeiss trademark. In this action the East German company claimed that the solicitors who acted for the West German company in the main action held their legal fees on constructive trust for them because they claimed to own all the assets of the West German company.

Held
As the solicitors had no effective notice of such a claim there was no constructive trust imposed upon them.

Commentary
Sachs and Edmund-Davies LJJ reaffirmed the traditional approach to constructive trusts in reaching their conclusion, but see *Selangor United Rubber Estates* v *Craddock* (infra) for a different approach.

Consul Development Pty Ltd v *DPC Estates Pty Ltd* (1975) 132 CLR 373 Australian High Court (Gibbs J)

Knowledge required for a stranger to become constructive trustee

Held
As to the degree of knowledge of a breach of trust required to render a stranger a constructive trustee, Gibbs J said:

' ... it does not seem to me to be necessary to prove that the stranger who participated in a breach of trust and fiduciary duty with knowledge of all the circumstances did so actually knowing that what he was doing was improper. It would not be just that a person who had full knowledge of all the facts could escape liability because his own moral obtuseness prevented him from recognising an impropriety that would have been apparent to an ordinary man.'

Cook v *Deeks* [1916] 1 AC 554 Privy Council (Lord Buckmaster LC, Lord Sumner, Lord Parker and Viscount Haldane)

Self-dealing by directors

Held
Contracts negotiated by directors for the benefit of the company cannot be taken by the directors for their personal benefit.

Cooke v *Head* [1972] 1 WLR 518 Court of Appeal (Lord Denning MR, Karminski and Orr LJJ)

Constructive trusts: the Denning cases

Facts
A man and mistress acquired a property by their joint efforts. At first instance, Plowman J found that the mistress had contributed one-twelfth of the value of the property and awarded her one-twelfth on resulting trusts.

Held
Taking all circumstances into account, she would be awarded one-third.

Lord Denning MR:

> 'It is now held that, whenever two parties by their joint efforts acquire property to be used for their joint benefit, the courts may impose or impute a constructive or resulting trust. The legal owner is bound to hold the property on trust for them both. This trust ... applies to husband and wife, to engaged couples and to man and mistress, and maybe other relationships too.'

Crabb v *Arun District Council* [1976] Ch 179 Court of Appeal (Lord Denning MR, Lawton and Scarman LJJ)

Proprietary estoppel

Facts
The plaintiff and the defendant were adjoining landowners. The plaintiff claimed a right of way over the defendant's land onto the public highway as his land was in fact landlocked. For various reasons, the plaintiff had no right of way by necessity or by prescription but had by the conduct of the defendants wanted £3,000 for the grant of a right of way. The plaintiff claimed that by their conduct they were estopped from denying that he had a right of way.

Held
The plaintiff was entitled to the right of way as the defendants had, by their words and conduct, led him to believe that they would grant him such a right and in consequence he had acted to his detriment.

Scarman LJ:

> '... If the plaintiff has any right, it is an equity arising out of the conduct and relationship of the parties. In such a case, I think it is now well-settled law that the court having analysed and assessed the conduct and relationship of the parties, has to answer three questions. First, is there an equity established? Secondly, what is the extent of the equity, if one is established? And, thirdly, what is the relief appropriate to satisfy the equity?
>
> See *Duke of Beaufort* v *Patrick* (1853) 17 Beav 60; *Plimmer* v *Mayor of Willington* (1884) 9 App Cas 699, and *Inwards* v *Baker* [1965] 2 QB 29, a decision of this court, and particularly the observations of Lord Denning MR. Such, therefore, I believe to be the nature of the enquiry that the courts have to conduct in a case of this sort. In pursuit of that enquiry, I do not find helpful the distinction between promissory and proprietary estoppel. The distinction may indeed be valuable to those who have to reach or expound the law. But I do not think that in solving the particular problem raised by a particular case putting the law into categories is of the slightest assistance ...
>
> I come now to consider the first of the three questions which I think in a case such as this the court has to consider. What is needed to establish an equity? In the course of an interesting addition to his submission this morning, counsel for the defendants cited *Ramsden* v *Dyson* (1866) LR 1 HL 129 to support his proposition that in order to establish an equity by estoppel, there must be a belief by the plaintiff in the existence of a right created or encouraged by the words or actions of the defendant. With respect, I do not think that that is today a correct statement of law. I think the law has developed so that today it is to be considered as correctly stated by Lord Kingsdown in his dissenting speech in *Ramsden* v

Dyson. Like Lord Denning MR, I think that the point of dissent in *Ramsden* v *Dyson* was not on the law but on the facts. Lord Kingsdown's speech, in so far as it dealt with proposition of law, has been often considered and recently followed, by this court in *Inwards* v *Baker*. Lord Kingsdown said:

> "The rule of law applicable to the case appears to me to be this: If a man, under a verbal agreement with a landlord for a certain interest in land, or what amounts to the same thing, under an expectation, created or encouraged by the landlord, that he shall have a certain interest, takes possession of such land, with the consent of the landlord, and upon the faith of such promise or expectation, with the knowledge of the landlord, and without objection by him, lays out money upon the land, a Court of Equity will compel the landlord to give effect to such promise or expectation."

That statement of the law is put into the language of landlord and tenant because it was a landlord and tenant situation with which Lord Kingsdown was concerned: but it has been accepted as of general application. While *Ramsden* v *Dyson* may properly be considered as the modern starting point of the law of equitable estoppel, it was analysed and spelt out in a judgment of Fry J in *Willmott* v *Barber* (1880) 15 Ch D 96, a decision to which Pennycuick V-C referred in his judgment. I agree with Pennycuick V-C in thinking that the passage from Fry J's judgment is a valuable guide as to the matters of fact which have to be established in order that a plaintiff may establish this particular equity. Moreover, counsel for the defendants sought to make a submission in reliance on the judgment. Fry J said:

> "It has been said that the acquiescence which will deprive a man of his legal rights must amount to fraud, and in my view that is an abbreviated statement of a very true proposition. A man is not to be deprived of his legal rights unless he has acted in such a way as would make it fraudulent for him to set up those rights. What, then, are the elements or requisites necessary to constitute fraud of that description? In the first place the plaintiff must have made a mistake as to his legal rights. Secondly, the plaintiff must have expended some money or must have done some act (not necessarily upon the defendant's land) on the faith of his mistaken belief.
>
> Thirdly, the defendant, the possessor of the legal right, must know of the existence of his own right which is inconsistent with the right claimed by the plaintiff. If he does not know of it he is in the same position as the plaintiff, and the doctrine of acquiescence is founded upon conduct with a knowledge of your legal rights. Fourthly, the defendant, the possessor of the legal right, must know of the plaintiff's mistaken belief of his rights. If he does not, there is nothing which calls upon him to assert his own rights. Lastly, (if I may digress, this is the important element as far as this appeal is concerned), the defendant, the possessor of the legal right, must have encouraged the plaintiff in his expenditure of money or in the other acts which he has done, either directly or by abstaining from asserting his legal right.".'

Scarman LJ then said later in his judgment that as regards the first question: is there an equity established? 'In order to reach a conclusion on that matter, the court has to consider the history of the case under the five headings to which Fry J referred ...'

As to the other two questions: what is the extent of the equity? and, what is the relief appropriate to satisfy the equity?, it appears that these are decided with reference to all the circumstances of the case.

Commentary
The references to the judgment of Pennycuick V-C are references to the decisions at first instance in this case.

Crippen, In the Estate of [1911] P 108 Probate Division (Sir Samuel Evans President)

Serious crime: constructive trust for victim's estate

Facts
Crippen was hanged for the murder of his wife. He would have inherited her substantial estate on her intestacy, and this would have gone to his mistress by his will.

Held
No-one could be allowed to profit from serious crime, and a constructive trust would be imposed and the estate distributed without reference to what those claiming under Crippen would have had.

Commentary
The Forfeiture Act 1982 may have altered this situation.

Dale (deceased), Re, Procter v *Dale* [1993] 3 WLR 652 Chancery Division (Morritt J)

Mutual wills – husband and wife – whether doctrine required survivor to obtain personal financial benefit

Facts
Husband and wife executed mutual wills each bequeathing their individual estates to their son and daughter in equal shares or to the survivor. The husband died and the estate was distributed in accordance with the will, namely in equal shares to son and daughter. The wife then changed her will substantially in favour of the son. Following the wife's death the daughter commenced an action claiming that the mother (ie wife) was irrevocably bound to dispose of her estate in accordance with the terms of the original agreement.

Held
The doctrine of mutual wills was intended to prevent one party from fraudulently reneging on an agreement to enter into mutual wills and thereafter be bound by and not revoke them. This doctrine did not expressly require, nor was it limited to, the surviving testator to benefit financially under the terms of the mutual wills. The son was therefore deemed to hold the daughter's share of their mother's estate on trust for the daughter.

Davitt v *Titcumb* [1990] Ch 110 Chancery Division (Scott J)

Property obtained by crime

Facts
D and G formed an association and together purchased a freehold property. This was secured by an endowment policy on both lives, assigned to the mortgagee building society. The conveyance declared D and G as equitable tenants in common. D subsequently murdered G. The building society applied the endowment policy funds to pay off the mortgage and the property was then sold.

Held
Scott J found that D could not claim a share in the set proceeds of sale. Rather the entire proceeds were held in favour of G's estate as administered by her personal representatives.

Dillwyn v *Llewellyn*

See Chapter 3.

Diplock, Re
See Chapter 17.

Eagle Trust plc v *SBC Securities Ltd* [1992] 4 All ER 488 Chancery Division (Vinelott J)
Conditions for making a stranger liable as a constructive trustee

Facts
This was an application by the defendants for the striking out of the plaintiffs' claim that the defendants be held liable to account for money, after they had parted with it, which had been paid to them by another party in breach of trust.

Held
The defendants' application would be allowed and the plaintiffs' action would be struck out. In reaching this conclusion Vinelott J explained that '... the question was whether, if the plaintiffs were able to establish the truth of all the allegations, many of which were disputed, in its statement of claim, and if the defendants were to call no evidence, the plaintiffs could succeed'. His Lordship referred to the categories of knowledge set out by Peter Gibson J in the *Baden Delvaux* case [1993] 1 WLR 509: '(i) actual knowledge; (ii) wilfully shutting one's eyes to the obvious; (iii) wilfully and recklessly failing to make such enquiries as an honest and reasonable man would make; (iv) knowledge of circumstances which would indicate the facts to an honest and reasonable man; (v) knowledge of circumstances which would put an honest and reasonable man on enquiry.'

Although Peter Gibson J had accepted a concession made by counsel that all five of the above categories were relevant in respect of rendering a person a constructive trustee, Vinelott did not agree that this concession had been rightly made. (Millett J in *Agip (Africa) Ltd* v *Jackson and Others* [1989] 3 WLR 1367 also expressed disagreement with this concession.)

In the view of Vinelott J, knowledge within categories (i), (ii) or (iii) was essential to impose liability on a stranger to a trust although, as his Lordship also pointed out '... in the absence of any explanation by the defendant, that kind of knowledge could be inferred and would be, if the circumstances were such that an honest and reasonable man would have inferred from them that the money was probably trust money and was being misapplied.' However, the facts allowed no such inference to be made in the instant case and the action had thus to be struck out.

Commentary
This is another important case concerned with the mental state necessary to render a stranger to a trust liable as constructive trustee in respect of his involvement with trust property. It should be noted that, while rejecting the final two of Peter Gibson J's categories as a basis for such liability, Vinelott J indicated that there can be circumstances in which the knowledge requisite for such liability may be inferred; see above. Compare this with the dichotomy which Millett J pointed out in *Agip (Africa) Ltd* v *Jackson and Others*, between honesty and dishonesty, for the purpose of this type of liability.

Note also on this topic the dictum of May LJ in *Lipkin Gorman* v *Karpnale Ltd & Another* [1989] 1 WLR 1340, at p1355 (see, infra, this Chapter).

El Ajou v *Dollar Land Holdings plc and Another* [1994] 2 All ER 685 Court of Appeal (Nourse, Rose and Hoffmann LJJ)

Company – director – constructive trusts – constructive knowledge of company imputed from employee

Facts

The details of this case are somewhat complex and, in the main, not relevant for present purposes. However, suffice to say that the plaintiff owned substantial funds and securities in the control of an investment manager who had been bribed to invest those funds, without the plaintiff's authority, in fraudulent share schemes operated by three parties through the medium of two Dutch companies. The proceeds of that fraudulent trading had then been channelled back into a London property development project in conjunction with the first defendant who was unconnected with the fraud. However, Dollar Land Holdings' (DLH) chairman controlled a separate company which had, in turn, received part of the monies derived from the fraud and had himself misappropriated these funds. The plaintiff subsequently learnt of the fraud and sought to recover, inter alia, from DLH by way of tracing.

Held (on appeal)

The directing mind and will of the company was not necessarily that of the person or persons with actual general management and control, rather it was necessary to identify the person who had management and control in relation to the act or omission in issue. On the facts as, whilst not a director at the pertinent time, DLH's chairman had such management and control; as such his knowledge of the fraud would be imputed to DLH thereby permitting tracing.

Nourse LJ:

> 'It is important to emphasise that management and control is not something to be considered generally or in the round. It is necessary to identify the natural person or persons having management and control in relation to the act or omission in point.'

Commentary

Whilst unsurprising the case will, no doubt, form a useful test for future litigation in respect of the ever increasing number of constructive trust cases stemming from a series of spectacular corporate frauds which have dogged that late 1980s and early 1990s.

English v *Dedham Vale Properties* [1978] 1 WLR 93 Chancery Division (Slade J)

Constructive trusts: categories not closed

Facts

P owned a bungalow and four acres of land which had development potential, but no planning permission. D, a development company, offered to buy the property from P for £7,750, a value less than that P could have obtained if planning permission to develop the property had been granted. Before contracts were exchanged by the parties, D instructed one of their employees to submit an application for permission to develop a small strip at the front of the property by the erection of a house and garage. The application was made in P's name and signed by D's employee as 'agent' for P and requested the decision notice should be sent to the employee's address. P was not informed of the application at any stage, nor was her consent to it obtained and she did not receive notice of the final decision which granted planning permission. At the date of completion, P did not know planning permission had been granted and only learned of how it had been obtained some months afterwards. P contended D was liable to account to her for the profits accruing from the grant of planning permission as D had put themselves in the position of self-appointed agents of P in making the planning application and there was a fiduciary relationship which made D constructive trustees.

Held
Where during negotiations for a contract for the sale and purchase of property the proposed purchaser took some action with regard to the property in the name of and purportedly as agent of the vendor which, if disclosed to the vendor might influence him in deciding whether or not he should sign the contract, a fiduciary relationship arose between the two parties and imposed on the purchaser a duty to tell the vendor what he had done as the vendor's purported agent before he signed the contract. In the event of non-disclosure, the purchaser was liable to account to the vendor for any profit he made during the purported agency unless the vendor consented to his retaining the profit.

Slade J:
> '... I do not think that the categories of fiduciary relationships which give rise to constructive trusteeship should be regarded as falling into a limited number of strait-jackets or as being necessarily closed. They are, after all, no more than formulae for equitable relief ...'

Erlanger v *New Sombrero Phosphate Co* (1878) 3 App Cas 1218 House of Lords (Lord Cairns LC, Lord Penzance, Lord Hatherley, Lord Gordon, Lord Blackburn, Lord Selborne and Lord O'Hagan)

Fiduciary who sells his own property may become constructive trustee of the profits made

Facts
Erlanger had bought an island for £55,000. He formed a company and sold the island to it for £110,000. The facts were not revealed to those invited to subscribe for shares.

Held
Erlanger was in a fiduciary position to the company and was constructive trustee for it of the profit he had made on the sale.

Giles, Re [1972] Ch 544 Chancery Division (Pennycuick V-C)

Serious crimes: constructive trust for victim's estate

Facts
A woman was convicted and sentenced for the manslaughter of her husband by reason of diminished responsibility. She would have inherited his estate.

Held
A constructive trust would be imposed and his estate distributed without reference to her rights.

Commentary
The Forfeiture Act 1982 may have altered this situation.

Greasley v *Cooke* [1980] 1 WLR 1306 Court of Appeal (Lord Denning MR, Waller and Dunn LJJ)

Proprietary estoppel: burden of proof

Facts
The defendant pleaded estoppel as a defence.

Held
The burden of proving that the defendant did not act to his detriment rests with the plaintiff.

Lord Denning MR:

> 'The first point is on the burden of proof. Counsel for the defendant referred us to many cases, such as *Reynell* v *Sprye* (1852) 1 De GM & G 660, *Smith* v *Chadwick* (1882) 20 Ch D 27 and *Brikom Investments Ltd* v *Carr* [1979] QB 467 where I said that, when a person makes a representation intending that another should act on it:
>
>> "It is no answer for the maker to say: 'You would have gone on with the transaction anyway.' That must be mere speculation. No-one can be sure what he would, or would not, have done in a hypothetical state of affairs which never took place ... Once it it shown that a representation was calculated to influence the judgment of a reasonable man, the presumption is that he was so influenced."
>
> So here. These statements to the defendant were calculated to influence her, so as to put her mind at rest, so that she should not worry about being turned out. No-one can say what she would have done if Kenneth and Hedley had not made those statements. It is quite possible that she would have said to herself: "I am not married to Kenneth. I am on my own. What will happen to me if anything happens to him? I had better look out for another job now rather than stay here where I have no security." So, instead of looking for another job, she stayed on in the house looking after Kenneth and Clarice. There is a presumption that she did so relying on the assurances given to her by Kenneth and Hedley. The burden is not on her but on them to prove that she did not rely on their assurances. They did not prove it, nor did their representatives. So she is presumed to have relied on them. So on the burden of proof it seems to me that the judge was in error.
>
> The second point is about the need for some expenditure of money, some detriment, before a person can acquire any interest in a house or any right to stay in it as long as he wishes. It so happens that in many of these cases of proprietary estoppel there has been expenditure of money. But that is not a necessary element. I see that in *Snell on Equity* (27th Edn, 1973, p565) it is said that A must have incurred expenditure or otherwise have prejudiced himself. But I do not think that that is necessary. It is sufficient if the party, to whom the assurance is given, acts on the faith of it, in such circumstances that it would be unjust and inequitable for the party making the assurance to go back on it (see *Moorgate* v *Twitchings* [1976] 1 QB 225 and *Crabb* v *Arun District Council* [1976] Ch 179). Applying those principles here it can be seen that the assurances given by Kenneth and Hedley to the defendant, leading her to believe that she would be allowed to stay in the house as long as she wished, raised an equity in her favour. There was no need for her to prove that she acted on the faith of those assurances. It is to be presumed that she did so. There is no need for her to prove that she acted to her detriment or to her prejudice. Suffice it that she stayed on in the house, looking after Kenneth and Clarice, when otherwise she might have left and got a job elsewhere. The equity having thus been raised in her favour, it is for the courts of equity to decide in what way that equity should be satisfied. In this case it should be by allowing her to stay on in the house as long as she wishes.'

Hagger, Re [1930] 2 Ch 190 Chancery Division (Clauson J)

Mutual wills: constructive trust

Facts
A husband and wife executed a joint mutual will giving everything they possessed to the survivor for life with remainder to certain named beneficiaries. The wife died first and the husband received the income from her estate until his death. A beneficiary survived the wife but predeceased the husband. The question arose as to whether the beneficiary's estate was entitled to benefit under the mutual will.

Held
It was under the wife's will on her death that the beneficiaries took interests under the mutual will. From that time the husband held the property subject to his own life interest, on trust for those entitled in remainder under the mutual will. Therefore, there was no lapse of the gift to the beneficiary who predeceased the wife as he took an interest under a trust and not under a will.

Clauson J:

> 'To my mind *Dufour* v *Pereira* 1 Dick 413 decides that where there is a joint will such as this, on the death of the first testator the position as regards that part of the property which belongs to the survivor is that the survivor will be treated in this Court as holding the property on trust to apply it so as to carry out the effect of the joint will ...'

Hallett's Estate, Re

See Chapter 18.

Hunter's Executors, Petitioners (1992) The Scotsman 17 June Inner House

Forfeiture – intestacy – murder

Facts
H was found guilty of murdering his wife. Under the terms of her will H was to receive her residuary estate, and in default it was to be distributed according to additional provisions.

Held
H, as per established public policy, could not benefit from his crime. However, the deceased's estate was to be distributed as if she had died intestate, rather than pursuant to the default provisions in her will.

Hussey v *Palmer*

See Chapter 5.

Industrial Development Consultants Ltd v *Cooley* [1972] 1 WLR 443 Chancery Division (Roskill J)

Secret profits: directors as constructive trustees

Facts
Cooley had worked in the private sector and was appointed a director of IDC specifically to help the firm acquire new business of that type. Cooley was approached in a private capacity by a concern in the public sector, and it became clear to him that he could obtain a lucrative contract if he were not bound by his ties to IDC. He retired from IDC on feigned ill-health grounds, formed his own company and

performed the contract at a substantial profit. Although IDC would probably never have acquired the contract they sought to recover the profits from him as constructive trustee.

Held

He was liable to account because he was under a fiduciary duty to IDC to pass on to them information which would be of interest to them. The fact that IDC would not have had the contract was unimportant because, per Roskill J:

> 'When one looks at the way the cases have gone over the centuries it is plain that the question whether or not the benefit would have been obtained but for the breach of trust has always been treated as irrelevant.'

International Sales and Agencies Ltd v *Marcus* [1982] 3 All ER 551 Chancery Division (Lawson J)

Stranger with knowledge as constructive trustee

Facts

£30,000 from company funds was applied to paying the personal debts of one of the directors to the defendant.

Held

The defendant was held to know that the money received was company funds, and that they had been paid by way of an improper application; he was therefore held to be a constructive trustee of the money in favour of the company.

Inwards v *Baker* [1965] 2 QB 29 Court of Appeal (Lord Denning MR, Danckwerts and Salmon LJJ)

Proprietary estoppel: nature of relief

Facts

In 1931 a father suggested to his son, who was looking for a site for a bungalow, that he should build it on some land owned by the father. The father said: 'Why don't you build the bungalow on my land and make it a bit bigger?' Encouraged by this the son did not look further for a site and built a bungalow on the father's land by his own labour. The son went into occupation and was visited by the father on several occasions at the bungalow. The father died in 1951 and by his will made in 1922 his land was vested in trustees for persons other than the son. It was clear the father had forgotten to make provision for his son. The trustees of the will brought proceedings for possession of the bungalow. The county court judge granted them possession. The son appealed.

Held

As the son had expended money on the land of his father in the expectation, fostered and encouraged by the father, that he would be allowed to remain in occupation as long as he wished, there was an equity created in favour of the son under which he could occupy the bungalow as long as he desired.

Lord Denning MR:

> '... So in this case, even though there is no binding contract to grant any particular interest to the licensee, nevertheless the court can look at the circumstances and see whether there is an equity arising out of the expenditure of money. All that is necessary is that the licensee should, at the request or with the

encouragement of the landlord, have spent the money in the expectation of being allowed to stay there. If so, the court will not allow that expectation to be defeated where it would be inequitable so to do. In this case it is quite plain that the father allowed an expectation to be created in the son's mind that this bungalow was to be his home. It was to be his home for his life or, at all events, his home as long as he wished it to remain his home. It seems to me, in the light of that equity, that the father could not in 1932 have turned to his son and said: "You are to go. It is my land, my house." Nor could he at any time thereafter so long as the son wanted it as his home.

Mr Goodhart put the case of a purchaser. He suggested that the father could sell the land to a purchaser who could get the son out. But I think that any purchaser who took with notice would clearly be bound by the equity. So here, too, the present plaintiffs, the successors in title of the father, are clearly themselves bound by this equity. It is an equity well recognised in law. It arises from the expenditure of money by a person in actual occupation of land when he is led to believe that, as the result of that expenditure, he will be allowed to remain there. It is for the court to say in what way the equity can be satisfied. I am quite clear in this case it can be satisfied. I am quite clear in this case it can be satisfied by holding that the defendant can remain there as long as he desires to as his home …'

Jones (AE) v *Jones (FW)* [1977] 1 WLR 438 Court of Appeal (Lord Denning MR, Roskill and Lawton LJJ)

Proprietary estoppel: nature of relief

Facts
A father made a will after his second marriage in 1964 leaving his son George a house, his son Frederick a house and his new wife the residue of his estate which consisted of several properties. In 1967 the father's scrap merchant business in London was acquired under a compulsory purchase order so he retired and went to live in Suffolk in a house he bought there. The father wanted Frederick and his wife and children to come to Suffolk also and they agreed. The father bought them a house for £4,000. The conveyance of the house was taken in the father's name but Frederick believed that the father had given it to him after he had given him two payments of £500 each towards the house which the father accepted and said, 'The place is yours'. Every time Frederick asked the father about the house he received the same reply and he paid no rent only the rates. The father died in 1972 and his new wife took out letters of administration with the will annexed. She had the house vested in her and claimed it was hers and that Frederick ought to pay her rent. He refused so she served a notice to quit and took proceedings for possession. In the county court the judge found that the father intended Frederick to have the house 'lock, stock and barrel' and that he had a quarter share interest and the new wife a three quarters interest in the house because of his £1,000 payment.

In consequence he held that the new wife was entitled to three-quarters of a proper rent for the house representing her interest and that if he failed to do so the house should be sold and the proceeds divided accordingly. Frederick appealed claiming that the new wife was not entitled to an order for sale as the principle of proprietary estoppel applied.

Held
The father's conduct was such as to lead Frederick reasonably to believe that he could regard the house as his home for the rest of his life. On the basis of this belief he had given up his job and home in London and moved to Suffolk. He paid the £1,000 on this belief and had done work on the house as well. As the father would have been estopped from turning the son out the new wife was equally estopped from doing the same. She was, therefore, not entitled to an order that the property be sold as the son **was entitled to remain in the house rent free for the rest of his life.**

Karak Rubber Co Ltd v *Burden (No 2)* [1972] 1 WLR 602 Chancery Division (Brightman J)

This case had virtually similar facts to *Selangor United Rubber Estates Ltd* v *Cradock (No 3)* (in this Chapter), and followed it.

Lee v *Sankey* (1873) LR 15 Eq 204 Court of Chancery (Bacon V-C)

Strangers to the trust: constructive trustees

Facts

A firm of solicitors were employed by trustees to receive the proceeds of sale of part of the trust property. The solicitors handed over some of the proceeds of sale to one of the trustees who used them in unsuccessful speculative ventures and who eventually died insolvent. The other trustee and the beneficiaries sought to make the solicitors liable for the loss on the ground that they should have obtained a valid receipt for the money from both trustees before handing it over.

Held

The solicitors were liable; they had acted inconsistently with their duties in only obtaining a receipt from one of the trustees. As agents of the trustees they were accountable to the trustees.

Bacon V-C:

> 'It is well established by many decisions that a mere agent of trustees is answerable only to his principal and not to the cestui que trust in respect of trust moneys coming to his hands merely in his character of agent. But it is also not less clearly established that a person who receives into his hands trust moneys, and who deals with them in a manner inconsistent with the performance of trusts of which he is cognisant, is personally liable for the consequences which may ensue upon his so dealing.'

Lipkin Gorman v *Karpnale Ltd* [1987] 1 WLR 987 Queen's Bench Division (Alliott J); [1989] 1 WLR 1340 Court of Appeal (May, Parker and Nicholls LJJ); [1991] 3 WLR 10 House of Lords (Lord Bridge of Harwich, Lord Templeman, Lord Griffiths, Lord Ackner and Lord Goff of Chieveley)

Constructive trust – position of 'strangers' to a trust – conversion

Facts

C, a partner in a firm of solicitors misappropriated clients' money which he used in gambling. C was subsequently convicted of theft. The firm sought to recover the money from the casino where he gambled and from the firm's bank on the basis, inter alia, that each was a constructive trustee. The claim against the casino on the basis of knowing receipt failed at first instance as the staff there did not have actual knowledge that C was gambling with trust finds nor did they have constructive knowledge of his misuse of trust funds. But, the claim against the bank on the basis of knowing assistance succeeded at first instance, as the bank manager was, on the judge's findings at first instance, but see below, aware that C's gambling was out of control, that his personal accounts were operating irregularly and that he had access to clients' accounts but either shut his eyes to the obvious or wilfully and recklessly failed to make proper inquiries.

Held (on appeal (inter alia))

The evidence did not justify the judge's findings concerning the bank manager. Since it was on the footing of these findings that the judge had found the bank to be liable as a constructive trustee the Court of Appeal ruled that the bank's appeal must be allowed.

Further, as the Court of Appeal pointed out, the relationship between a bank and its customer is contractual and, accordingly, the bank cannot be liable as a constructive trustee of funds in its customer's account unless it is also in breach of its contractual duty of care towards its customers. In this case the Court of Appeal concluded that the evidence did not disclose a breach of the bank's duty of care (in contract or tort) towards its customer.

Held (on further appeal to the House of Lords)

The solicitors' claim against the casino must be allowed to the extent of the balance of the casino's winnings against the gambler – ie making allowance for the gambler's winnings against the casino. Although it was fully accepted that the casino had acted innocently and in good faith throughout, its case for retaining the money as against the solicitors depended on contracts which were rendered void by s18 of the Gaming Act 1845, for lack of consideration.

Commentary

The Court of Appeal's ruling makes clear, in particular, the basis of the relationship between a bank and its customer in respect of paying that customer's cheques drawn on a current account in credit. Note also that in this case May LJ stated, at page 1355, that in his opinion '… there is at least strong persuasive authority for the proposition that nothing less than knowledge, as defined in one of the first three categories stated by Peter Gibson J in *Baden, Delvaux and Lecuit* [1993] 1 WLR 509 (ie (i) actual knowledge; (ii) wilfully shutting one's eyes to the obvious; (iii) wilfully and recklessly failing to make such inquiries as an honest and reasonable man would make) of an underlying dishonest design is sufficient to make a stranger a constructive trustee of the consequences of that design.'

In allowing the solicitors' appeal against the casino to the extent of the casino's winning balance as against the gambler, the House of Lords recognised, per Lord Goff, that: 'Bona fide change of position should of itself be a good defence'. Accordingly, as Lord Goff also pointed out: '… it would be inequitable to require the casino to repay in full without bringing into account winnings paid by it to the gambler on any one or more of the bets so placed with it.'

Lloyds Bank plc v *Rosset* [1990] 2 WLR 867 House of Lords (Lords Bridge, Griffiths, Ackner, Oliver and Jauncey)

Extent of contribution necessary to raise a constructive trust

Facts

The husband provided funds from a trust of which he was beneficiary to purchase a house which was conveyed into his name. He then took a substantial overdraft to pay for considerable renovation work, and the charge was secured on the house. Repayment was demanded and not made, and the Bank sued for possession. The husband had left and did not contest the claim, but the wife claimed an equitable interest, both under the Land Registration Act and as beneficiary of a constructive trust as a result of work which she had done in the renovation.

Held

Following the decision the same day of *Abbey National Building Society* v *Cann* [1990] 2 WLR 833 the **wife failed in the claim under the Land Registration Act. On the trusts point, since the work she had** done did not amount to more than that which any wife would have done as part of her normal activities, and particularly as the evidence showed that much of it had been because she was anxious for the house to be ready by Christmas, her contribution was insufficient to give rise to a constructive trust.

In his speech, with which the other Law Lords present unanimously concurred, Lord Bridge explained the tests to be applied in these situations. In fact, his lordship indicated that the necessary agreement or common intention can arise in either of two categories of situation. Thus, as he stated:

> 'The first and fundamental question which must always be resolved is whether, independently of any inference to be drawn from the conduct of the parties in the course of sharing the house as their home and managing their joint affairs, there has at any time prior to acquisition or exceptionally at some later date, been any agreement, arrangement or understanding reached between them that the property is to be shared beneficially.'

A finding to this effect can, only in Lord Bridge's view, '...be based on evidence of express discussions between the partners, however imperfectly remembered and however imprecise their terms may have been'. His Lordship then pointed out that:

> 'Once a finding to this effect is made it will only be necessary for the partner asserting a claim to a beneficial interest against the partner entitled to the legal estate to show that he or she has acted to his or her detriment or significantly altered his or her position in reliance on the agreement in order to give rise to a constructive trust or a proprietary estoppel.'

As 'outstanding examples' of cases falling within this first category, his Lordship cited *Eves* v *Eves* [1975] 1 WLR 1338 and *Grant* v *Edwards* [1986] Ch 638. In these cases the 'excuses' given by the male partner to the female partner for not putting the shared house into joint names at least indicated that there was an understanding between them in this regard.

As Lord Bridge further pointed out:

> 'The subsequent conduct of the female partner in each of these cases, which the court rightly held sufficient to give rise to a constructive trust or proprietary estoppel supporting her claim to an interest in the property, fell far short of such conduct as would by itself have supported the claim in the absence of an express representation by the male partner that she was to have such an interest.'

The second 'very different' type of situation indicated by Lord Bridge is:

> '... where there is no evidence to support a finding of an agreement or arrangement to share, however reasonable it might have been for the parties to reach such an arrangement if they had applied their minds to the question, and where the court must rely entirely on the conduct of the parties, both as the basis from which to infer a common intention to share the property beneficially and as the conduct relied on to give rise to a constructive trust. In this situation direct contributions to the purchase price by the partner who is not the legal owner, whether initially or by payment of mortgage instalments, will readily justify the inference necessary to the creation of a constructive trust. But, as I read the authorities, it is at least extremely doubtful whether anything less will do.'

Lord Bridge cited as cases which demonstrate the second category of situation, as above *Pettitt* v *Pettitt* (4) and *Gissing* v *Gissing* [1970] AC 777.

In these latter two cases no agreement or understanding between the parties could be shown and the non-legal owner had made no *direct* contributions.

Lysaght v *Edwards* (1876) 2 Ch D 499 Chancery Division (Jessel MR)

Vendor of land as constructive trustee

Facts
By an agreement in writing, Edwards agreed to sell the Bury Mansion and estate, and Lysaght and another agreed to buy it. Edwards died before completion. By his will he had charged the estate with payment of his debts, and devised all his realty to trustees on trust to sell and invest the proceeds. He also devised all properties which he himself held on trust, to Hubbard, one of his trustees, subject to the trusts on which he had held them himself in his life.

Held
The Bury Mansion and estate was not within the realty of the will, but Hubbard held them on trust and could make a good title.

Jessel MR:

> '... The effect of a contract for sale has been settled for more than two centuries ... It is that the moment you have a valid contract for sale, in equity, the vendor becomes the trustee for the purchaser of the real estate sold; the beneficial ownership passes to the purchaser of the estate, the vendor retaining a right to the purchase money, ... and a right to retain possession of the estate until the purchase money is paid, in the absence of express contract as to the time of delivering it.'

Lyus v *Prowsa Developments* [1982] 1 WLR 104 Chancery Division (Dillon J)

Statute as an instrument of fraud: constructive trust

Facts
A development company had agreed to sell a plot of land to the plaintiffs together with a house which was to be built by the same company. Before the contract was completed the development company fell into financial difficulties and the land in question was acquired by a bank which had granted the company a secured loan. The bank sold the land under its mortgagee's statutory power of sale to the defendants, Prowsa Ltd, but in this sale contract the bank agreed with the purchaser that the purchaser would be bound by the plaintiffs' contractual rights to acquire the plot concerned in the original contract of sale.

Prowsa Ltd now considered that it was not bound by the plaintiffs' contractual rights against the land firstly because there was no privity of contract between the plaintiffs and itself and secondly because the plaintiffs had not registered their rights under the Land Registration Act 1925.

Held
The defendants were bound by the plaintiffs' contractual rights because of a constructive trust imposed on it similar to the one employed in the earlier cases of *Rochefoucauld* v *Boustead* [1897] 1 Ch 196 and *Bannister* v *Bannister* [1948] 2 All ER 133. The failure to register the plaintiffs' interest did not affect the claim.

Dillon J:

> '... in *Bannister* v *Bannister* Scott LJ in giving the judgment of a Court of Appeal, which included Jenkins J, said (at 136) that it was not necessary that the bargain on which an absolute conveyance was made should include any express stipulation that the grantee was in so many words to hold as trustee. It was enough that the bargain should have included a stipulation under which some sufficiently defined beneficial interest in the property was to be taken by another. If the bargain did include such a stipulation, then the equitable principle on which a constructive trust is raised would be applied against a person who insisted on the absolute character of the conveyance to himself for the purpose of defeating a beneficial interest which, according to the true bargain, was to belong to another. In as much as the constructive trust is raised to counter unconscionable conduct or fraud in the sense in which that term is used in a court of equity, the application of the equitable principle to which Scott LJ refers must depend on the facts of the

particular case rather than on the mere wording of the particular document. *Re Schebsman* [1944] Ch 83 is, therefore, concerned with a somewhat different problem ... It comes in, if at all, in that the absence of a clear declaration of trust may be one of the factors to be borne in mind in considering whether some beneficial interest was, according to the true bargain, to belong to a third party.

It may be added by way of a footnote to the judgment of Scott LJ that even if the beneficial interest of the claimant in the property concerned has not been fully defined, the court may yet intervene to raise a constructive trust on appropriate terms if to leave the defendant retaining the property free from all interest of the claimant would be tantamount to sanctioning a fraud on the part of the defendant: see *Pallant* v *Morgan* [1953] Ch 43. That is a further indication that the Schebsman test is not the criterion for the existence of a constructive trust.

It seems to me that the fraud on the part of the defendants in the present case lies not just in relying on the legal rights conferred by an Act of Parliament, but in the first defendant reneging on a positive stipulation in favour of the plaintiffs in the bargain under which the first defendant acquired the land. That makes, as it seems to me, all the difference. It has long since been held, for instance in *Rochefoucauld* v *Boustead* [1897] 1 Ch 196, that the provisions of the Statute of Frauds 1677, now incorporated in certain sections of the Law of Property Act 1925, cannot be used as an instrument of fraud, and that it is fraud for a person to whom land is agreed to be conveyed as trustee for another to deny the trust and relying on the terms of the statute to claim the land for himself. *Rochefoucauld* v *Boustead* was one of the authorities on which the judgment in *Bannister* v *Bannister* was founded.

It seems to me that the same considerations are applicable in relation to the Land Registration Act 1925. If for instance, the agreement of 18 October 1979 between the bank and the first defendant had expressly stated that the first defendant would hold plot 29 on trust to give effect for the benefit of the plaintiffs to the plaintiffs' agreement with the vendor company, it would be difficult to say that that express trust was overreached and rendered nugatory by the Land Registration Act 1925. The Land Registration Act 1925 does not, therefore, affect the conclusion which I would otherwise have reached in reliance on *Bannister* v *Bannister* and the judgment of Lord Denning MR in *Binions* v *Evans* [1972] Ch 359, had plot 29 been unregistered land.

The plaintiffs are, therefore, entitled to succeed in this action. The appropriate relief in that event is that specific performance should be ordered as against the second defendants of the sale to the plaintiffs of plot 29, with the completed house thereon, on the terms of the agreement of 30 January 1978 made between the plaintiffs and the vendor company.'

Mara v *Browne* [1896] 1 Ch 199 Court of Appeal (Lord Herschell, Rigby and A L Smith LJJ)

Agents of trustees as strangers with knowledge and constructive trustees

Facts
One of a partnership of two solicitors who were advisers to trustees received money belonging to the trust in his personal bank account and used the money to make advances to mortgagors to whom he had advised money should be lent, basing his loans on the authority of persons purporting to act as trustees. The mortgages were alleged to be speculative and an unjustified investment, and it was sought to make the partnership liable as constructive trustees.

Held
The mortgages were a breach of trust, but the solicitors' firm was not liable as constructive trustees since they had not handled the money.

It was also held that where a beneficiary is entitled to an interest both in possession and in remainder in the same trust property, the fact that a claim is statute-barred for the estate in possession will not prevent a claim for the estate in remainder when it finally falls in.

Montagu's Settlement Trusts, Re [1987] 2 WLR 1192 Chancery Division (Sir R Megarry V-C)

Constructive trust: knowledge

Facts

This case involved a settlement by the tenth Duke of Manchester. In 1923 he assigned such chattels as the trustees of the settlement should select on a trust designed to benefit the eleventh Duke, the plaintiff. The chattels to be put in trust for the plaintiff were to be selected by the trustees from a remainder interest due to the tenth Duke on the death of the ninth Duke.

When however the ninth Duke died in 1947 and the chattels in question vested in the tenth Duke the trustees failed to make the inventory and selection of chattels envisaged by the 1923 settlement. The trustees later released these chattels to the tenth Duke in 1948 and allowed him to treat the chattels as his own free of any trust.

The plaintiff, now the eleventh Duke, claimed that the trustees in failing to make the selection had committed a breach of trust and also that the chattels released by the trustees to the tenth Duke were held by him as a constructive trustee for the plaintiff. This constructive trust claim was based on the head of knowing receipt of trust property by a third party originally set out in the case of *Barnes* v *Addy* (1874) 9 Ch App 244.

Held

No constructive trust arose in this case.

Megarry V-C:

'That brings me to the essential question for decision. The core of the question (and I put it very broadly) is what suffices to constitute a recipient of trust property a constructive trustee of it. I can leave on one side the equitable doctrine of tracing: if the recipient of trust property still had the property or its traceable proceeds in his possession, he is liable to restore it unless he is a purchaser without notice. But liability as a constructive trustee is wider, and does not depend upon the recipient still having the property or its traceable proceeds. Does it suffice if the recipient had "notice" that the property he was receiving was trust property, or must he have not merely notice of this, but knowledge, or "cognisance", as it has been put?

In my previous judgment I provisionally took the view that mere notice was not enough, and that what was required was knowledge or cognisance. In saying this, I very much had in mind what was said in the Court of Appeal in *Carl Zeiss Stiftung* v *Herbert Smith & Co (No 2)* [1969] 2 Ch 276; and I shall not repeat what I have already said about that case. It is that question which Mr Taylor and Mr Chadwick have now explored before me, with an ample and helpful citation of authority, most of which had not been cited previously. It was common ground that it was impossible to contend that the law to be found in the cases was clear and not in something of a muddle. Part of the difficulty arises from the fact that in cases on constructive trusts in which there is clearly knowledge the term "notice" is often convenient to use, without any distinction between notice and knowledge being intended.

At the outset, I think that I should refer to *Baden, Delvaux and Lecuit* v *Société Générale pour Favoriser le Développement de Commerce et de l'Industrie en France SA* [1993] 1 WLR 509, a case which for obvious reasons I shall call "the *Baden* case". That case took 105 days to hear, spread over seven months, and the judgment of Peter Gibson J is over 120 pages long. It was a "knowing assistance" type of constructive trust, as distinct from the "knowing receipt or dealing" type which is in issue before me. I use these terms as a convenient shorthand for two of the principal types of constructive trust. Put shortly, under the first of these heads a person becomes liable as a constructive trustee if he knowingly assists in some fraudulent design on the part of a trustee. Under the second head, a person also becomes liable as a constructive trustee if he either receives trust property with knowledge that the transfer is a breach of trust, or else deals with the property in a manner inconsistent with the trust after acquiring knowledge of the trust. It will be seen that the word "knowledge" occurs under each head; and in the *Baden* case, at p407, the judge in effect said that "knowledge" had the same meaning under each head.

I pause at that point. In the books and the authorities the word "notice" is often used in place of the word "knowledge", usually without any real explanation of its meaning. This seems to me to be a fertile source of confusion; for whatever meaning the layman may attach to those words, centuries of equity jurisprudence have attached a detailed and technical meaning to the term "notice", without doing the same for "knowledge". The classification of "notice" into actual notice, constructive notice and imputed notice has been developed in relation to the doctrine that a bona fide purchaser for value of a legal estate takes free from any equitable interests of which he has no notice. I need not discuss this classification beyond saying that I use the term "imputed notice" as meaning any actual or constructive notice that a solicitor or other agent for the purchaser acquires in the course of the transaction in question, such notice being imputed to the purchaser. Some of the cases describe any constructive notice that as purchaser himself obtains as being "imputed" to him; but I confine "imputed" to notice obtained by another which equity imputes to the purchaser.

Now until recently I do not think there had been any classification of "knowledge" which corresponded with the classification of "notice". However, in the *Baden* case, at p407, the judgment sets out five categories of knowledge, or of the circumstances in which the court may treat a person as having knowledge. Counsel in that case were substantially in agreement in treating all five types as being relevant for the purpose of a constructive trust; and the judge agreed with them: p415. These categories are (i) actual knowledge; (ii) wilfully shutting one's eyes to the obvious; (iii) wilfully and recklessly failing to make such inquiries as an honest and reasonable man would make; (iv) knowledge of circumstances which would indicate the facts to an honest and reasonable man; and (v) knowledge of circumstances which would put an honest and reasonable man on inquiry. If I pause there, it can be said that these categories of knowledge correspond to two categories of notice: Type (i) corresponds to actual notice, and types (ii), (iii), (iv) and (v) correspond to constructive notice. Nothing, however, is said (at least in terms) about imputed knowledge. This is important, because in the case before me Mr Taylor strongly contended that Mr Lickfold's knowledge must be imputed to the Duke, and that this was of the essence of his case.

It seems to me that one must be very careful about applying to constructive trusts either the accepted concepts of notice or any analogy to them. In determining whether a constructive trust has been created, the fundamental question is whether the conscience of the recipient is bound in such a way as to justify equity in imposing a trust on him. The rules concerning a purchaser without notice seem to me to provide little guidance on this and to be liable to be misleading. First, they are irrelevant unless there is a purchase. A volunteer is bound by an equitable interest even if he has no notice of it; but in many cases of alleged constructive trusts the disposition has been voluntary and not for value, and yet notice or knowledge is plainly relevant. Second, although a purchaser normally employs solicitors, and so questions of imputed notice may arise, it is unusual for a volunteer to employ solicitors when about to receive bounty. Even if he does, he is unlikely to employ them in order to investigate the right of the donor to make the gift or of the trustees or personal representatives to make the distribution; and until this case came before me I had never heard it suggested that a volunteer would be fixed with imputed notice of all that his solicitors would have discovered had he employed solicitors and had instructed them to investigate his right to receive the property.

Third, there seems to me to be a fundamental difference between the questions that arise in respect of the doctrine of purchaser without notice and constructive trusts. As I said in my previous judgment, ante, p9D:

"The former is concerned with the question whether a person takes property subject to or free from some equity. The latter is concerned with whether or not a person is to have imposed upon him the personal burdens and obligations of trusteeship. I do not see why one of the touchstones for determining the burdens on property should be the same as that for deciding whether to impose a personal obligation on a man. The cold calculus of constructive and imputed notice does not seem to me to be an appropriate instrument for deciding whether a man's conscience is sufficiently affected for it to be right to bind him by the obligations of a constructive trustee."

I can see no reason to resile from that statement, save that to meet possible susceptibilities I would alter "man" to "person". I would only add that there is more to being made a trustee than merely taking property subject to an equity.

There is a further consideration. There is today something of a tendency in equity to put less emphasis on detailed rules that have emerged from the cases and more weight on the underlying principles that engendered those rules, treating the rules less as rules requiring complete compliance, and more as guidelines to assist the court in applying the principles. A good illustration of this approach is to be found in the judgment of Oliver J in *Taylors Fashions Ltd* v *Liverpool Victoria Trustees Co Ltd (Note)* [1982] QB 133. This view was adopted by Robert Goff J in *Amalgamated Investment & Property Co Ltd* v *Texas Commerce International Bank Ltd* [1982] QB 84, and it was, I think, accepted, though not cited, by the Court of Appeal in the latter case: see at pp116-132. Certainly it was approved in terms by the Court of Appeal in *Habib Bank Ltd* v *Habib Bank AG Zurich* [1981] 1 WLR 1265. The *Taylors Fashions* case concerned equitable estoppel and the five probanda to be found in the judgment of Fry J in *Willmott* v *Barber* (1880) 15 Ch D 96; and on the facts of the case before him Oliver J in the *Taylors Fashions* case concluded that the question was not whether each of those probanda had been satisfied but whether it would be unconscionable for the defendants to take advantage of the mistake there in question. Accordingly, although I readily approach the five categories of knowledge set out in the *Baden* case as useful guides, I regard them primarily as aids in determining whether or not the Duke's conscience was affected in such a way as to require him to hold any or all of the chattels that he received on a constructive trust.

There is one further general consideration that I should mention, and that is that "the court should not be astute to impute knowledge where no actual knowledge exists": see the *Baden* case at p415, per Peter Gibson J. This approach goes back at least as far as *Barnes* v *Addy* (1874) 9 Ch App 244. The view of James LJ, at p256, was that the court had in some cases

"gone to the very verge of justice in making good to cestuis que trust the consequences of the breaches of trust of their trustees at the expense of persons perfectly honest, but who have been, in some more or less degree, injudicious."

Of the five categories of knowledge set out in the *Baden* case, Mr Chadwick, as well as Mr Taylor, accepted the first three. What was in issue was nos (iv) and (v), namely, knowledge of circumstances which "would indicate the facts to an honest and reasonable man" or "would put an honest and reasonable man on inquiry". On the view that I take of the present case I do not think that it really matters whether or not categories (iv) and (v) are included, but as the matter has been argued at length, and further questions on it may arise, I think I should say something about it.

First, as I have already indicated, I think that one has to be careful to distinguish the notice that is relevant in the doctrine of purchaser without notice from the knowledge that suffices for the imposition of a constructive trust. This is shown by a short passage in the long judgment of the Court of Appeal in *In re Diplock* [1948] Ch 465 [see Chapter 18]. There, it was pointed out that on the facts of that case persons unversed in the law were entitled to assume that the executors were properly administering the estate, and that if those persons received money bona fide believing themselves to be entitled to it, "they should not have imposed upon them the heavy obligations of trusteeship". The judgment then pointed out:

"The principles applicable to such cases are not the same as the principles in regard to notice of defects in title applicable to transfers of land where regular machinery has long since been established for inquiry and investigation."

To that I may add the obvious point that the provisions about constructive notice in section 199 of the Law of Property Act 1925 apply only to purchasers (as defined in section 205(1)(xxi)) and are not in point in relation to a beneficiary who receives trust property from the trustees.

... I shall attempt to summarise my conclusions. In doing this, I make no attempt to reconcile all the authorities and dicta, for such a task is beyond me; and in this I suspect I am not alone. Some of the difficulty seems to arise from judgments that have been given without all the relevant authorities having been put before the judges. All I need do is to find a path through the wood that will suffice for the determination of the case before me, and to assist those who have to read this judgment.

(1) The equitable doctrine of tracing and the imposition of a constructive trust by reason of the knowing receipt of trust property are governed by different rules and must be kept distinct. Tracing is primarily a means of determining the rights of property, whereas the imposition of a constructive trust creates personal obligations that go beyond mere property rights.

(2) In considering whether a constructive trust has arisen in a case of the knowing receipt of trust property, the basic question is whether the conscience of the recipient is sufficiently affected to justify the imposition of such a trust.

(3) Whether a constructive trust arises in such a case primarily depends on the knowledge of the recipient, and not on notice to him; and for clarity it is desirable to use the word "knowledge" and avoid the word "notice" in such cases.

(4) For this purpose, knowledge is not confined to actual knowledge, but includes at least knowledge of types (ii) and (iii) in the *Baden* case, ie actual knowledge that would have been acquired but for shutting one's eyes to the obvious, or wilfully and recklessly failing to make such inquiries as a reasonable and honest man would make; for in such cases there is a want of probity which justifies imposing a constructive trust.

(5) Whether knowledge of the *Baden* types (iv) and (v) suffices for this purpose is at best doubtful; in my view, it does not, for I cannot see that the carelessness involved will normally amount to a want of probity.

(6) For these purposes, a person is not to be taken to have knowledge of a fact that he once knew but has genuinely forgotten: the test (or a test) is whether the knowledge continues to operate on that person's mind at the time in question.

(7)(a) It is at least doubtful whether there is a general doctrine of "imputed knowledge" that corresponds to "imputed notice". (b) Even if there is such a doctrine, for the purposes of creating a constructive trust of the "knowing receipt" type the doctrine will not apply so as to fix a donee or beneficiary with all the knowledge that his solicitor has, at all events if the donee or beneficiary has not employed the solicitor to investigate his right to the bounty, and has done nothing else that can be treated as accepting that the solicitor's knowledge should be treated as his own. (c) Any such doctrine should be distinguished from the process whereby, under the name "imputed knowledge", a company is treated as having the knowledge that its directors and secretary have.

(8) Where an alleged constructive trust is based not on "knowing receipt" but on "knowing assistance", some at least of these considerations probably apply; but I need not decide anything on that, and I do not do so.'

O'Sullivan v *Management Agency* [1985] 3 All ER 351 Court of Appeal (Waller, Dunn and Fox LJJ)

Fiduciary relationship: constructive trustees

Facts
The plaintiff, a well known composer and performer of popular music entered into several agreements with the defendants in 1970 with regard to recording, publishing and performing musical works composed by him. The agreements included, inter alia, the assignment of copyright in these works. At the time the agreements were entered into the plaintiff was a young man with no business experience and

he trusted the defendants implicitly. The plaintiff did not seek independent legal advice on the agreements nor was he encouraged to do so by the defendants. Consequently, the agreements were less advantageous to the plaintiff than might have been the case had they been negotiated at arm's length on independent legal advice. The plaintiff became very successful; by 1972 he had several hit records and was in considerable demand as a performer throughout the world. In 1976 the relationship between the plaintiff and the defendant broke down after a series of disagreements and because the plaintiff was unhappy with his contractual arrangements. The plaintiff eventually issued proceedings against the defendants claiming that the agreements were void because they had been obtained by undue influence and were also in restraint of trade. The trial judge held that the agreements were obtained by undue influence and were in restraint of trade and he also found that there was a fiduciary relationship between the defendants and the plaintiff arising from the confidence that had been reposed by the plaintiff in the defendants. Accordingly, the agreements were set aside, the copyrights were reconveyed to the plaintiff, and accounts ordered of the profits made by the defendants from the copyrights with compound interest to be paid on such profits. The defendants appealed against the judgment. Two issues which arose on appeal were (i) were the defendants in a fiduciary relationship with the plaintiff? and (ii) Whether they were liable to account for all the profits and compound interest thereon?

Held
1. Whenever two persons stand in a relationship whereby confidence is reposed by one in the other, this gives rise to a confidential relationship. Such relationship made the party in whom confidence was reposed a fiduciary. The defendants were, accordingly, in a fiduciary relationship to the plaintiff.
2. The defendants were liable to account for the profits they had made out of the fiduciary relationship. It was no bar to setting the contracts aside that restitutio in integrum was impossible because the contracts had been fully performed. The Court would set aside the contracts if this would lead to a just solution and order the defendants to account for the profits with due allowance being made for any work the defendants had performed under the contract and also reasonable remuneration.

Fox LJ:

'... It is said on behalf of the plaintiffs that if the principle of equity is that the fiduciary must account for profits obtained through the abuse of the fiduciary relationship, there is no scope for the operation of anything resembling restitutio in integrum. The profits must simply be given up. I think that goes too far and the law has for long had regard to the justice of the matter. If, for example, a person is by undue influence persuaded to make a gift of a house to another and that other spends money on improving the house, I apprehend that a credit could be given for the improvement. This is, I think recognised by Lord Blackburn in *Erlanger* v *New Sombrero Phosphate Co* (1878) 3 App Cas 1218.

... The next question is, it seems to me, the recompensing of the plaintiffs. The rules of equity against the retention of benefits by fiduciaries have been applied with severity. In *Boardman* v *Phipps* [1967] 2 AC 46 where the fiduciaries though in breach of the equitable rules, acted with complete honesty throughout, only succeeded in obtaining an allowance on a liberal scale for their work and skill.' (His Lordship then referred to Court of Appeal and House of Lords judgments in *Boardman* v *Phipps* and continued):

'... These latter observations ... accept the existence of a power in the court to make an allowance to a fiduciary. And I think it is clearly necessary that such a power should exist. Substantial injustice may result without it. A hard and fast rule that the beneficiary can demand the whole profit without an allowance for the work without which it could not have been created would be unduly severe. Nor do I think that the principle is only applicable in cases where the personal conduct of the fiduciary cannot be criticised. I think that the justice of the individual case must be considered on the facts of the case. Accordingly, where there has been dishonesty or surreptitious dealing or other improper conduct ... it might be appropriate to refuse relief ...

... Once it is accepted that the Court can make an appropriate allowance to a fiduciary for his skill and labour I do not see why, in principle, it should not be able to give him some part of the profit of the venture if it was thought that justice between the parties demanded that. To give the fiduciary any allowance for his skill and labour involves some reduction of the profits otherwise payable to the beneficiary. And the business reality may be that the profits could never have been earned at all, as between fully independent persons, except on a profit sharing basis ...'

Peso Silver Mines Ltd v *Cropper* (1966) 58 DLR (2d) 11 Canadian Supreme Court

Directors able to take benefit

Facts
The company had been negotiating for several prospecting claims but rejected them as being too expensive and speculative. Several directors, including Cropper, who had been in favour of the company's taking them then formed their own company and took them, and made a profit. The company claimed that the directors were liable to account to the company.

Held
The claims had been taken as private individuals and not as directors, therefore they were not obliged to account.

Regal (Hastings) Ltd v *Gulliver* [1942] 1 All ER 378 House of Lords (Lord Russell, Lord Sankey, Lord Macmillan, Lord Wright and Lord Porter)

Secret profits: directors of companies as constructive trustees

Facts
The company formed a subsidiary to acquire the leases of two cinemas. The landlord would not grant the leases unless all the company's shares were paid up, which the company could not do. The directors and the company solicitor therefore took them up personally, and on the taking over of the company made a substantial profit.

Held
The company's solicitor was a fiduciary, but since he had acted with the knowledge and consent of the directors he could keep the profit personally. The other directors had to account for the profit as constructive trustees for the company, since they had acted on inside knowledge.

Lord Russell of Killowen:

> 'Directors of a limited company are the creatures of statute. In some respects they resemble trustees: in others they do not. In some respects they resemble agents: in others they do not. In some respects they resemble managing partners: in others they do not. ... I am of the opinion that the directors standing in a fiduciary relationship to Regal in regard to the exercise of their powers as directors, and having obtained these shares by reason and only by reason of the fact that they were directors of Regal and in the course of the execution of that office, are accountable for the profits which they have made out of them. The equitable rules laid down in *Keech* v *Sandford* ... apply to them in full force.'

Risch v *McFee* (1990) The Times 6 July Court of Appeal (Balcombe and Butler-Sloss LJJ)

Interest-free loan by co-habitee – common intention

Facts

The plaintiff, who had cohabited with the defendant but had since separated from him, claimed a share in the house in which they had lived together.

Held

By the Court of Appeal, confirming the findings at first instance, that an unpaid interest-free loan made by the plaintiff to the male partner while she was living with him in his house, and in respect of which she had not sought repayment, should be taken into account in assessing her beneficial interest in the property. She had also made other contributions.

At first instance the judge had found that there was a common intention that the plaintiff should have a beneficial interest in the house and had concluded that she was entitled to 40 per cent of the net proceeds of sale. The Court of Appeal confirmed that once it had been established that the plaintiff was entitled to a beneficial interest in the house in which the couple had lived together, the judge was free to take into account the loan made by the plaintiff as part of her contribution ... 'as that in effect was what it had become'. The defendant's appeal was, accordingly, dismissed.

Commentary

Compare and contrast the position in *Re Sharpe* [1980] 1 WLR 219, which was distinguished in this case.

Royal Brunei Airlines Sdn Bhd v *Philip Tan Kok Ming* [1995] 3 All ER 97 Privy Council (Lord Goff, Lord Ackner, Lord Nicholls, Lord Steyn and Sir John May)

Intermeddlers – constructive trusts – knowing assistance

Facts

The defendant, T, was the principal director in, and shareholder of, Borneo Leisure Travel (BLT), a Brunei-incorporated travel agency. BLT acted as a ticket agent for the plaintiff, RBA, holding monies from ticket sales on trust for RBA under a standard form agreement. BLT became insolvent. Despite holding monies on trust for RBA, it was BLT's usual practice to pay part of the monies into its own bank account via a standing order, drawing from it for its own business purposes.

Held (on appeal to the Privy Council)

Per Lord Nicholls (giving the judgment of the Judicial Committee at p109c–e):

> 'The money paid to BLT on the sale of tickets for Royal Brunei Airlines was held by BLT upon trust for the airline. This trust, on its fact, conferred no power on BLT to use the money in the conduct of its business. The trust gave no authority to BLT to relieve its cash flow problems by utilising for this purpose the rolling 30-day credit afforded by the airline. Thus BLT committed a breach of trust by using the money instead of simply deducting its commission and holding the money intact until it paid the airline. Mr Tan accepted that he knowingly assisted in that breach of trust. In other words, he caused or permitted his company to apply the money in a way he knew was authorised by the trust of which the company was trustee. Set out in these bald terms, Mr Tan's conduct was dishonest. By the same token, and for good measure, BLT also acted dishonestly. Mr Tan was the company and his state of mind is to be imputed to the company.'

After a detailed review of case law, including the recent decision of Baden v Société Générale [1993] 1 WLR 509, the committee held that the test for determining whether or not a stranger to a trust should be held a constructive trustee by reason of knowing assistance required the following elements to be established:

1. the existence of a trust of fiduciary relationship;
2. the breach of trust (note, all that is required is a breach of trust, rather than a dishonest and fraudulent design on the trustee's behalf);
3. the assistance of the stranger; and
4. the dishonesty of the stranger in knowingly assisting in the breach of trust. This represents the keystone of the stranger's liability, mere knowledge being insufficient.

Lord Nicholls continued by stating that the 'five levels of knowledge' outlined in *Baden* v *Société Générale* (and relied on in earlier case law) were 'best forgotten'. Dishonesty required the stranger to act not as an honest person would, including taking into account the personal attributes, experience and intelligence of the stranger.

Commentary
The Privy Council's decision turns on its head earlier case law which required the dishonesty element of establishing a constructive trustee as being one pertaining to the trustee, rather than the stranger. Realistically, the shift towards the stranger having to have the dishonest design makes sense whilst arguably, representing a restriction on the circumstances in which a constructive trust will be imposed. However, the difficulty remains as to what will be deemed to be dishonest conduct on the part of the stranger. Lord Nicholls' test is likely to prove problematical insofar as it combines an objective test with the subjective attributes of the stranger. With this in mind, arguably, it will still be necessary (if not useful as a guide) to show one of the first three of the five levels of knowledge set out in the *Baden* v *Société Générale,* namely: (a) actual knowledge; or (b) wilfully shutting one's eyes to the obvious; or (c) wilfully and recklessly failing to make such enquiries as an honest and reasonable man would make.

The following, more general, comments can be made in respect of this decision. First, it is noteworthy that the opening sentence of Lord Nicholls' judgment is:

'The proper role of equity in commercial transactions is a topical question.'

Arguably, the new test is therefore limited to the context of 'commercial transaction', with the old test in *Baden* v *Société Générale* holding true for 'non-commercial transactions'. However, it is doubtful that such a fine distinction will be made. Second, again, in accordance with Lord Nicholls' suggestion, it is possible that the new test will also apply whether the stranger primarily in breach of trust or merely assisted in it. In this regard, a streamlining of the test of liabilities would be welcomed. Following on from the foregoing, the Privy Council avoided adding to the existing melee of judicial obiter dicta in respect of liability based upon 'knowing receipt' of trust property. Whilst the practical considerations of the two are different, there is no reason why the test for liability should not be the same.

Selangor United Rubber Estates Ltd v *Cradock (No 3)* [1968] 1 WLR 1555
Chancery Division (Ungoed-Thomas J)

Stranger to the trust: knowledge of illegal acts

Facts
The plaintiff company's rubber estates in Malaya were nationalised with the result that it had substantial assets totalling £232,000 but no business. Cradock decided to purchase the shares in the plaintiff company despite the fact that he had no money of his own, his plan being to use the company's assets to purchase its own shares through a series of complicated transactions. Such a scheme is unlawful under s54 Companies Act 1948. Cradock employed a banking company called Contanglo to purchase the shares. To pay for the shares Cradock instructed his own bank the District Bank to arrange for the plaintiff company's bank account, containing all the plaintiff's assets, to be transferred to his branch. The takeover of the plaintiff company was executed and Cradock appointed his nominees to the board. The

board resolved to lend all the plaintiff company's money to a company called Woodstock which in turn re-lent the money back to Cradock who paid it back into his own account at the District Bank. The result was that the District Bank had aided Cradock in his unlawful scheme. When the facts were discovered Cradock, Contanglo, Woodstock and Cradock's nominees were held to be constructive trustees. On the more difficult problem of whether the District Bank were constructive trustees:

Held
The District Bank were constructive trustees since a reasonable banker would have realised that, by allowing the company's money to be paid into Cradock's account, he was enabling Cradock to purchase the company with its own money.

Ungoed-Thomas J (talking of this category of constructive trusts):

> 'There are thus three elements (1) assistance by the stranger, (2) with knowledge, (3) in a dishonest and fraudulent design on the part of the trustees ...
>
>> (2) The knowledge required to hold a stranger liable as constructive trustee in a dishonest and fraudulent design, is knowledge of circumstances which would indicate to an honest, reasonable man that such a design was being committed or would put him on enquiry, which the stranger failed to make, whether it was being committed.
>> (3) What is "a dishonest and fraudulent design" is to be judged ... according to "plain principles of a court of equity" ... the governing consideration is to give effect to equitable rights, where it is not inequitable to do so, and when knowledge of the existence of those rights is material to granting equitable relief. In general, at any rate, it is equitable that a person with actual notice or constructive notice of those rights should be fixed with knowledge of them. This is in a context of producing equitable results in a civil action and not in the context of criminal liability.'

Stokes v *Anderson* (1991) The Independent 10 January Court of Appeal (Lloyd, Nourse and Ralph Gibson LJJ)

Quantum of co-habitee's interest in former shared house

Facts
An unmarried couple while living together had orally indicated their common intention that the woman should have a beneficial interest in the house in which they were living. However the quantum of that interest had never been discussed. When the couple separated a dispute arose between them as to the amount of that interest. At first instance, the judge held that each party should be entitled to one half of the beneficial interest. The man appealed to the Court of Appeal.

Held
The amount of the woman's interest should be one quarter of the value of the house, subject to a mortgage thereon, instead of the equal decision awarded at first instance. Since the parties had made clear their common intention to share the beneficial interest in the property and since certain payments by the female partner was conduct which amounted to acting on that common intention, then as Nourse LJ observed: 'The only real question for decision, a difficult one, was what was the extent of [the female partner's] beneficial interest.'

As regards this quantification of interest, Nourse LJ pointed out applying the view of Lord Diplock in *Gissing* v *Gissing* [1971] AC 886, at 909, to a more general proposition that '... all payments made and acts done by a claimant were to be treated as illuminating the common intention as to the extent of the beneficial interest. The court must supply the common intention by reference to that which all the material circumstances had shown to be fair'. On 'the fair view of all the circumstances' the Court of

Appeal's conclusion was that the woman's beneficial interest in the house should be reduced as stated above.

Thomson, Re [1930] 1 Ch 203 Chancery Division (Clauson J)

Fiduciary: constructive trustee

Facts
By his will a testator directed his executors to carry on his business of a yacht broker after his death. The testator died in August 1928 and the executors carried on the business as directed until February 1929 when the business was moved to new premises, the lease of those which it was in being about to expire. A lease of the new premises was granted to the defendant executor alone. This he kept secret for a few weeks and then claimed the right to hold the lease of the new premises for his own benefit and to set up and carry on on his own account a business similar to and in competition with the testator's business. The plaintiffs sought an injunction to restrain the defendant from carrying on such a business in his own name and a declaration that he held the new lease on trust for the estate.

Held
Having regard to the special nature of the business of a yacht broker, by starting such a business the defendant executor was entering into engagements which might conflict with the interests of the beneficiaries under the will, because he would be obtaining chances to earn commission as a yacht broker which, but for such competition, might be obtained for the beneficiaries under the will. This was a breach of his fiduciary duty.

Williams v *Barton* [1927] 2 Ch 9 Chancery Division (Russell J)

Fiduciary as constructive trustee

Facts
One of the two trustees of a will was employed as a clerk by a firm of stockbrokers on terms that his salary should consist of half the commission earned by the firm on business introduced by him. On the trustee's recommendation the firm was employed to value the testator's securities. The firm's charges were paid out of the testator's estate and under his contract of employment the trustee was paid half the fees earned. The trustee took no part in making the valuations or fixing the fees to be charged. The other trustee claimed that the commission should be paid to the testator's estate.

Held
It was the duty of the trustee to give the estate the benefit of his unfettered advice in choosing stockbrokers to act for the estate; as the recipient of half of the fees earned by the firm on business introduced by him, it was to his interest to choose his firm to act. The services rendered to the firm by the trustee remained unchanged but his remuneration for them increased and was increased by virtue of his trusteeship. That increase was a profit which the defendant would not have made but for his position as trustee and it was to be treated as part of the testator's estate accordingly.

Russell J:

> 'The point is not an easy one and there is little authority, if any, to assist in its determination ... it seems to me evident that the case falls within the mischief which is sought to be prevented by the rule. The case is clearly one where his duty as trustee and his interest in an increased remuneration are in direct conflict.

As a trustee it is his duty to give the estate the benefit of his unfettered advice in choosing the stockbrokers to act for the estate; as the recipient of half the fees to be earned by George Barnard & Co on work introduced by him his obvious interest is to choose or recommend them for the job.'

Williams v *Williams* (1881) 17 Ch D 437 Chancery Division (Kay J)

Stranger to the trust acting honestly: no constructive trust

Facts
A solicitor was instructed to sell certain lands and use the proceeds of sale in discharging the vendor's debts. The solicitor made enquiries as to whether the land was subject to a settlement but on these he came to the conclusion that it was not. In fact the lands were subject to a settlement. The beneficiaries under the settlement sought to make the solicitor liable for their loss.

Held
Although the solicitor was negligent in what he had done he had nevertheless acted honestly and no constructive trust would be imposed on him.

Williams-Ashman v *Price & Williams* [1942] Ch 219 Chancery Division (Bennett J)

Strangers to the trust acting honestly: no constructive trust

Facts
A firm of solicitors who at all times had a copy of the relevant trust deed paid out money to persons who were not beneficiaries and invested trust money in unauthorised investments on the instructions of the sole trustee.

Held
A claim that a constructive trust should be imposed on the solicitors must fail as they had acted honestly and had no actual knowledge of the terms of the trust (albeit that they did have a copy of it).

Willmott v *Barber* (1880) 15 Ch D 96 Court of Appeal (Jessel, Baggallay and Lush LJJ)

Proprietary estoppel

Facts
For present purposes the facts of the case are not required.

Held
Five elements had to be established for a plaintiff to succeed in a plea of proprietary estoppel:
1. He must have made a mistake as to his legal rights;
2. He must have expended some money or must have done some act (not necessarily on the other party's land) on the faith of his mistaken belief;
3. The possessor of the legal right which the plaintiff claims it would be inequitable for him to enforce must have known of the existence of his own right which is inconsistent with the right claimed by the plaintiff;

4. The possessor of the legal right must have known of the plaintiff's mistaken belief;
5. The possessor of the legal right must have encouraged the plaintiff in the expenditure of money or in the other acts which he had done, either directly or by abstaining from asserting his legal right.

Windeler v *Whitehall* (1990) 154 JP 29 Chancery Division (Millett J)

Facts

The plaintiff who had lived with the defendant but had declined to marry him, claimed, after the parties had separated, a share in the defendant's house and also in his business. While the parties were living together the defendant had made a will leaving his residuary estate to the plaintiff. The plaintiff had made no financial contribution towards the acquisition of the house.

Held

The plaintiff's claim must be dismissed. The fact that the defendant had made a will wherein the plaintiff was left his residuary estate was not evidence of a common intention that the plaintiff should have a share in the house which the defendant had bought and towards which the plaintiff had made no financial contribution. This testamentary provision was merely 'a recognition of some moral obligation at that time on his part to provide for her if he should die unexpectedly and while circumstances remained the same'. The judge also dismissed the plaintiff's claim to a share in the defendant's business. *Re Basham (deceased)* [1987] 1 All ER 405 was distinguished.

7 Trusts of Imperfect Obligation

Astor's Settlement, Re
See Chapter 1.

Bourne v *Keane* [1919] AC 815 House of Lords (Lord Birkenhead LC, Lord Buckmaster, Lord Atkinson, Lord Parmoor and Lord Wrenbury)

Purpose trust: masses

Facts
An Irish Roman Catholic testator domiciled in England bequeathed £200 to Westminster Cathedral for the saying of masses and £200 of his residuary personal estate to the Jesuit Fathers for the saying of masses. The question arose whether these gifts were valid since they were not charitable in the circumstances.

Held
These gifts for saying masses could stand as valid trusts.

Commentary
See also *Re Hetherington* in Chapter 8.

Caus, Re [1934] Ch 162 Chancery Division (Luxmoor J)

Trusts for the advancement of religion: purpose trusts

Held
A gift for saying masses was a valid charitable trust for the advancement of religion.

Commentary
See also *Gilmour* v *Coates* and *Bourne* v *Keane* (both in this Chapter) and *Re Hetherington* Chapter 8.

Conservative Central Office v *Burrell* [1982] 2 All ER 1 Court of Appeal (Lawton, Brightman and Fox LJJ)

Definition of an unincorporated association

Facts
The Conservative Party hierarchy consisted of the Parliamentary Party, Central Office and the rank and file membership. All of these fell under the general control of the Conservative Party leader. However,

Party funds were mainly derived from the rank and file membership albeit administered by the Central Office.

For tax purposes the rank and file membership was treated as an unincorporated association. Central Office appealed claiming that the money was theirs.

Held

Lawton LJ:

> '[Such an association is] two or more persons bound together for one or more common purposes, not being business purposes, by mutual undertakings, each having mutual duties and obligations, in an organisation which has rules which identify in whom control of it and its funds rests and on what terms, and which can be joined or left at will.'

On the facts there was no unincorporated association, hence the funds could not be taxed as if held by an unincorporated association.

Dalziel, Re [1943] Ch 277 Chancery Division (Cohen J)

Purpose trusts: monuments

Facts

The testatrix gave £20,000 to the governors of St Bartholomew's Hospital 'subject to the condition that they shall use the income' to maintain and, when necessary, rebuild the mausoleum and directed that 'if they shall fail to carry out this request I give the said sum of £20,000 to such other of the charities named in this my will as my trustees may select ...'

Held

The gift to the charity was not absolute but one on which a non-charitable purpose was charged, therefore both the gift to the hospital and the gift over were void. The difference between this case and *Re Tyler* [1891] 3 Ch 252 was that in *Re Tyler* the testator made a condition but in this case as Cohen J explained:

> 'Lady Dalziel has not only given power but directed the trustees to apply part of this gift, or if necessary, the whole of this gift in the maintenance of the tomb.'

Dean, Re (1889) 41 Ch D 552 Chancery Division (North J)

Purpose trusts: animal cases

Facts

A testator charged his estates with the payment of £750 pa to trustees for the period of 50 years if any of his horses and hounds should so long live for the maintenance of the same.

Held

Although the gift was non-charitable and its execution not enforceable by anyone, it was nevertheless a valid trust.

North J:

> 'The first question is as to the validity of the provision made by the testator in favour of his horses and dogs. It is said that it is not valid; because (for this is the principal ground upon which it is put) neither a horse nor a dog could enforce the trust; and there is no person who could enforce it. It is obviously not a

charity, because it is intended for the benefit of the particular animals mentioned and not for the benefit of animals generally, and it is quite distinguishable from the gift made in a subsequent part of the will to the Royal Society for the Prevention of Cruelty to Animals, which may well be a charity. In my opinion this provision for the particular horses and hounds referred to in the will is not, in any sense, a charity, and, if it were, of course the whole gift would fail because it is a gift of an annuity arising out of land alone. but, in my opinion, as it is not a charity, there is nothing in the fact that the annuity arises out of land to prevent its being a good gift.

Then it is said, that there is no cestui que trust who can enforce the trust, and that the Court will not recognise a trust unless it is capable of being enforced by some one. I do not assent to that view. There is not the least doubt that a man may if he pleases, give a legacy to trustees, upon trust to apply it in erecting a monument to himself, either in a church or in a churchyard, or even in unconsecrated ground, and I am not aware that such a trust is in any way invalid, although it is difficult to say who would be the *cestui que* trust of the monument. In the same way I know of nothing to prevent a gift of a sum of money to trustees, upon trust to apply it for the repair of such a monument. In my opinion such a trust would be good, although the testator must be careful to limit the time for which it is to last, because, as it is not a charitable trust, unless it is to come to an end within the limits fixed by the rule against perpetuities, it would be illegal. But a trust to lay out a certain sum in building a monument, and the gift of another sum in trust to apply the same to keeping that monument in repair, say, for ten years, is, in my opinion, a perfectly good trust, although I do not see who could ask the Court to enforce it. If persons beneficially interested in the estate could do so, then the present Plaintiff can do so; but, if such persons could not enforce the trust, still it cannot be said that the trust must fail because there is no one who can actively enforce it.

Is there then anything illegal or obnoxious to the law in the nature of the provision, that is, in the fact that it is not for human beings, but for horses and dogs? It is clearly settled by authority that a charity may be established for the benefit of horses and dogs, and, therefore, the making of a provision for horses and dogs, which is not a charity, cannot of itself be obnoxious to the law, provided, of course, that it is not to last for too long a period ...'

Denley's Trust Deed, Re [1969] 1 Ch 373 Chancery Division (Goff J)

Purpose trusts and ascertainable beneficiaries

Facts
The instrument provided a trust for the provision of a sports or recreation ground, for a period within the perpetuity rule, for the benefit of, primarily, employees of a company, and secondarily for the benefit of such other persons as the trustees allowed to use it.

Held
A distinction must be drawn between 'purpose or object trusts which are abstract or impersonal' and are void, and a trust for objects which 'though expressed as a purpose, is directly or indirectly for the benefit of an individual or group of individuals'. Such a trust is outside the mischief for which purpose trusts are held invalid, that is, that there is no cestui que trust. In this case there were ascertainable beneficiaries and therefore the trust was valid.

Gilmour v *Coates* [1949] AC 426 House of Lords (Lord Simonds, Lord Du Parcq, Lord Normand, Lord Morton and Lord Reid)

Trusts for the advancement of religion: purpose trusts

Facts

The income of a certain trust fund was to be applied for the purposes of a Carmelite convent, if those purposes were charitable. The convent housed a community of cloistered nuns who devoted themselves to prayers and meditation and who did not engage in any activities for the benefit of people outside the community. It was the belief of the Roman Catholic Church that the prayers and meditation benefited the public at large by causing the intervention of God on their behalf. Further, it was argued that there was an element of public benefit in that membership of the community was open to any woman in the world who had the necessary vocation.

Held

That prayers and meditation by a cloistered community was not for the public benefit and the trust was accordingly non-charitable. This was because intercessory prayer was not susceptible of legal proof and the court could only act on such proof. In any case, it was too vague and intangible to satisfy the test of public benefit. The fact that the community was open to any woman in the world was irrelevant; this was a matter of survival for the community needed recruits if it was to continue.

Lord Simonds:

"... I need not go back beyond the case of *Cocks* v *Manners* (1871) LR 12 Eq 574, which was decided nearly eighty years ago by Wickens V-C. In that case the testatrix left her residuary estate between a number of religious institutions, one of them being the Dominican Convent at Carisbrooke, a community not differing in any material respect from the community of nuns now under consideration. The learned judge, who was, I suppose, as deeply versed in this branch of the law as any judge before or since (for he had been for many years junior counsel to the Attorney-General in equity cases), used these words, which I venture to repeat, though they have already been cited in the court below: "On the Act (the statute of Elizabeth) unaffected by authority I should certainly hold that the gift to the Dominican convent is neither within the letter nor the spirit of it; and no decision has been referred to which compels me to adopt a different conclusion. A voluntary association of women for the purpose of working out their own salvation by religious exercises and self-denial seems to me to have none of the requisites of a charitable institution, whether the word 'charitable' is used in its popular sense or in its legal sense. It is said, in some of the cases, that religious purposes are charitable, but that can only be true as to religious services tending directly or indirectly towards the instruction or the edification of the public; an annuity to an individual, so long as he spent his time in retirement and constant devotion, would not be charitable, nor would a gift to ten persons, so long as they lived together in retirement and performed acts of devotion, be charitable. Therefore, the gift to the Dominican convent is not, in my opinion, a gift on a charitable trust."

No case, said the learned Vice-Chancellor, had been cited to compel him to come to a contrary conclusion, nor has any such case been cited to your Lordships. Nor have my own researches discovered one. But since that date the decision in *Cocks* v *Manners* has been accepted and approved in numerous cases ...

My Lords, I would speak with all respect and reverence to those who spend their lives in cloistered piety, and in this House of Lords, spiritual and temporal, which daily commences its proceedings with intercessory prayers, how can I deny that the Divine Being may in His Wisdom think fit to answer them? but, my Lords, whether I affirm or deny, whether I believe or disbelieve, what has that to do with the proof which the court demands that a particular purpose satisfies the test of benefit to the community? Here is something which is manifestly not susceptible of proof. But, then it is said this is a matter not of proof but of belief, for the value of intercessory prayers is a tenet of the Catholic faith, therefore, and in such a prayer, there is benefit to the community. But, it is just at this "therefore" that I must pause. It is, no doubt, true that the advancement of religion is, generally speaking, one of the heads of charity, but it does not follow from this that the court must accept as proved whatever a particular church believes. The faithful must embrace their faith believing where they cannot prove: the court can act only on proof. A gift to two or ten or a hundred cloistered nuns in the belief that their prayers will benefit the world at large does not from that belief alone derive validity any more than does the belief of any other donor for any other purpose. The importance of this case leads me to state my opinion in my own words but, having read again the judgment of the learned Master of the Rolls, I will add that I am in full agreement with what he says on this part of the case.

I then turn to the second of the alleged elements of public benefit, edification by example, and I think that this argument can be dealt with very shortly. It is, in my opinion, sufficient to say that this is something too vague and intangible to satisfy the prescribed test. The test of public benefit has, I think, been developed in the past two centuries. Today it is beyond doubt that that element must be present. No court would be rash enough to attempt to define precisely or exhaustively what its content must be. But it would assume a burden which it could not discharge if now for the first time it admitted into the category of public benefit something so indirect, remote, imponderable and I would add, controversial as the benefit which may be derived by others from the example of pious lives. The appellant called in aid the use by Wickens V-C of the word "indirectly" in the passage that I have cited from his judgment in *Cocks v Manners*, but I see no reason to suppose that that learned judge had in mind any such question as your Lordships have to determine ...'

Grant's Will Trusts, Re [1980] 1 WLR 360 Chancery Division (Vinelott J)

Trusts of imperfect obligation: unincorporated associations

Facts
A testator made a will devising 'all my real and personal estate to the Labour Party Property Committee for the benefit of the Chertsey Headquarters of (the new Chertsey Constituency Labour Party) providing that such headquarters remain in what was the Chertsey Urban District Council Area (1972); if not, I declare that the foregoing provision shall not take effect and in lieu thereof I give all my said estate to the National Labour Party absolutely.'

Held
The gift was void and failed because (1) it could not be construed as a gift to the members of the New Chertsey CLP at the date of the testator's death subject to a direction that it be used for headquarters purposes because the members of New Chertsey CLP did not control property given by subscription or otherwise to the New Chertsey CLP; they could not alter the rules so as to apply the bequest for some other purpose than that provided by the rules and they could not divide it among themselves on dissolution under the rules. (2) The gift was made in terms that the Labour Party Property Committee was to hold the property for the benefit of the Chertsey Headquarters of the New Chertsey CLP. This could not be construed as a gift to the members of the New Chertsey CLP at date. It had to be construed as a purpose trust and as it was non-charitable, it failed.

Hetherington, Re

See Chapter 8.

Hooper, Re [1932] 1 Ch 38 Chancery Division (Maugham J)

Purpose trust: monuments

Facts
A testator left property on trust to provide 'so far as they legally can do so and ... for as long as may be

practicable' for the care and upkeep of certain graves in a churchyard and a tablet and window in a church.

Held
The trusts for the upkeep of the window and tablet in the church were charitable. The gift for the particular graves was not charitable but it was a valid purpose trust since the words 'so far as they legally can do so' were indistinguishable from the phrase 'so long as the law for the time being permits'. The trust was, therefore, valid for a period of 21 years.

Maugham J:

> 'The point is one to my mind of doubt, and I should have felt some difficulty in deciding it if it were not for *Pirbright* v *Sawley* [1896] WN 86 a decision of Stirling J which unfortunately is reported, as far as I know, only in the Weekly Notes. The report is as follows: "A testator after expressing his wish to be buried in the inclosure in which his child lay in the churchyard of E, bequeathed to the rector and churchwardens for the time being of the parish church 890l consols, to be invested in their joint names, the interest and dividends to be derived therefrom to be applied, so long as the law for the time being permitted, in keeping up the inclosure and decorating the same with flowers. Held that the gift was valid for at least a period of 21 years from the testator's death, and *semble* that it was not charitable." That was a decision arrived at by Stirling J, after argument by very eminent counsel. The case does not appear to have attracted much attention in text-books, but it does not appear to have been commented upon adversely, and I shall follow it.
>
> The trustees here have the sum of £1,000 which they have to hold upon trust to "invest the same and to the intent that so far as they legally can do so and in any manner that they may in their discretion arrange they will out of the annual income thereof" do substantially four things: first, provide for the care and upkeep of the grave and monument in the Torquay cemetery; secondly, for the care and upkeep of a vault and monument there in which lie the remains of the testator's wife and daughter; thirdly, for the care and upkeep of a grave and monument in Shotley churchyard near Ipswich, where the testator's son lies buried; and, fourthly, for the care and upkeep of the tablet in Saint Matthias' Church at Ilsham to the memories of the testator's wife and children, and the window in the same church to the memory of his late father. All those four things have to be done expressly according to an arrangement made in the discretion of the trustees and so far as they legally can do so. I do not think that is distinguishable from the phrase "so long as the law for the time being permits", and the conclusion at which I arrive, following the decision I have mentioned, is that this trust is valid for a period of twenty-one years from the testator's death so far as regards the three matters which involve the upkeep of graves or vaults or monuments in the churchyard or in the cemetery. As regards the tablet in St Matthias' Church and the window in the same church, there is no question that that is a good charitable gift, and, therefore, the rule against perpetuities does not apply ...'

Leahy v *Attorney-General for New South Wales* [1959] AC 457 Privy Council (Viscount Simonds, Lord Morton, Lord Cohen, Lord Somervell and Lord Denning)

Trusts of imperfect obligation: unincorporated associations

Facts
By clause 3 of his will the testator left certain property 'upon trust for such order of nuns of the Catholic Church or the Christian Brothers as my executors and trustees shall select'. The trustees took out a summons to determine the effect of clause 3 since it was recognised that the words 'such order of nuns' might include contemplative orders, which were not charitable in the legal sense.

Held
The gift showed an intention to create a trust not merely for the benefit of existing members of the order selected but also for the benefit of the order as a continuing society, the gift infringed the rule against perpetual trusts. Therefore, if the order selected were non-charitable, the gift would fail for this reason.

Viscount Simonds:

> 'The prima facie validity of such a gift (by which term their Lordships intend a bequest or demise) is a convenient starting-point for the examination of the relevant law. For, as Lord Tomlin (sitting at first instance in the Chancery Division) said in *Re Ogden* [1933] Ch 678, a gift to a voluntary association of persons for the general purposes of the association is an absolute gift and prima facie a good gift. He was echoing the words of Lord Parker in *Bowman's* case [1917] AC 406 that a gift to an unincorporated association for the attainment of its purposes "may ... be upheld as an absolute gift to its members". These words must receive careful consideration, for it is to be noted that it is because the gift can be upheld as a gift to the individual members that it is valid, even though it is given for the general purposes of the association. If the words "for the general purposes of the association" were held to impart a trust, the question would have to be asked, "what is the trust and who are the beneficiaries?" A gift can be made to persons (including a corporation) but it cannot be made to a purpose or to an object: so, also, a trust may be created for the persons as cestuis que trust but not for a purpose or object unless the purpose or object be charitable. For a purpose or object cannot sue, but, if it is to be charitable, the Attorney-General can sue to enforce it ... It is, therefore, by disregarding the words "for the general purposes of the association" (which are assumed not to be charitable purposes) and treating the gift as an absolute gift to individuals that it can be sustained. The same conclusion had been reached fifty years before in *Cocks* v *Manners* (1871) LR 12 Eq 574, where a bequest of a share of residue to the ("Dominican Convent at Carisbrooke payable to the Superior for the time being") was held a valid gift to the individual members of that society. In that case no difficulty was created by the addition of words which might suggest that the community as a whole, not its members individually, should be the beneficiary. See also with *Re Smith* [1914] 1 Ch 397. There the bequest was to the society or institution known as the Franciscan Friars of Clevedon (in the) County of Somerset absolutely. Joyce J had no difficulty in construing this as a gift individually to the small number of persons who had associated themselves together at Clevedon under monastic vows. Greater difficulty must be felt when the gift is in such terms that though it is clearly not contemplated that the individual members shall divide it amongst themselves, yet it is prima facie a gift to the individuals and, there being nothing in the constitution in the Society to exhibit it, they can dispose of it as they think fit. Of this type of case *Re Clark* [1901] 2 Ch 110 may be taken as an example. There the bequest was to the committee for the time being of the Corps of Commissionaires in London to act in the purchase of their barracks, or in any other way beneficial to the Corps. The judge (Bryne J) was able to uphold this as a valid gift on the ground that all the members of the association could join together to dispose of the funds for the barracks. He assumed (however little the testator may have intended it) that the gift was to the individual members in the name of the society or of the committee of the society.'

Lipinski's Will Trusts, Re [1976] Ch 235 Chancery Division (Oliver J)

Trusts of imperfect obligation: unincorporated associations

Facts
A testator left half his residuary estate upon trust 'for the Hull Judeans (Maccabi) Association in memory of my late wife to be used solely in the work of constructing new buildings for the association and/or improvements to the said buildings'. The trustees took out a summons to determine the effect of the trust.

Held
The trust was a valid trust for the members of the unincorporated association.

Oliver J:

'There would seem to me to be, as a matter of common sense, a clear distinction between the case where a purpose is prescribed which is clearly intended for the benefit of ascertained or ascertainable beneficiaries, particularly where those beneficiaries have the power to make the capital their own, and the case where no beneficiary at all is intended (for instance, a memorial to a favourite pet) or where the beneficiaries are ascertainable (as for instance *Re Price* [1943] Ch 422). If a valid gift may be made to an unincorporated body as a simple accretion to the funds which are the subject-matter of the contract which the members have made inter se and *Neville Estates* v *Madden* [1962] Ch 832 and *Re Recher's Will Trusts* [1972] Ch 526 show that it may, I do not really see why such a gift, which specifies a purpose which is within the powers of the unincorporated body and of which the members of that body are the beneficiaries, should fail. Why are not the beneficiaries able to enforce the trust or, indeed, in the exercise of their contractual rights, to terminate the trust for their own benefit? Where the donee body is itself the beneficiary of the prescribed purpose, there seems to me to be the strongest argument in common sense for saying that the gift should be construed as an absolute one within the second category, the more so where, if the purpose is carried out, the members can by appropriate action vest the resulting property in themselves, for here the trustees and the beneficiaries are the same person ...

I have already said that, in my judgment, no question of perpetuity arises here, and accordingly the case appears to me to be one of the specification of a particular purpose for the benefit of ascertained beneficiaries, the members of the association for the time being. There is an additional factor. This is a case in which, under the constitution of the association, the members could, by the appropriate majority, alter their constitution so as to provide, if they wished, for the division of the association's assets among themselves. This has, I think, a significance. I have considered whether anything turns in this case on the testator's direction that the legacy shall be used 'solely' for one or other of the specified purposes. Counsel for the association has referred me to a number of cases where legacies have been bequeathed for particular purposes and in which the beneficiaries have been held entitled to override the purpose, even though expressed in mandatory terms.

Perhaps the most striking in the present context is the case of *Re Bowes* [1896] 1 Ch 507, where money was directed to be laid out in the planting of trees on a settled estate. That was a 'purpose' trust, but there were ascertainable beneficiaries, the owners for the time being of the estate; and North J held that the persons entitled to the settled estate were entitled to have the money whether or not it was laid out as directed by the testator. He said:

> "Then, the sole question is where this money is to go to. Of course, it is a perfectly good legacy. There is nothing illegal in the matter, and the direction to plant might easily be carried out; but it is not necessarily capable of being performed, because the owner of the estate might say he would not have any trees planted upon it at all. If that were the line he took, and he did not contend for anything more than that, the legacy would fail; but he says he does not refuse to have trees planted upon it; he is content that trees should be planted upon some part of it; but the legacy has not failed. If it were necessary to uphold it, the trees can be planted upon the whole of it until the fund is exhausted. Therefore, there is nothing illegal in the gift itself; but the owners of the estate now say 'It is a very disadvantageous way of spending this money; the money is to be spent for our benefit, and that of no one else; it was not intended for any purpose other than our benefit and that of the estate. That is no reason why it should be thrown away by doing what is not for our benefit, instead of being given to us; who want to have the enjoyment of it.' I think their contention is right. I think the fund is devoted to improving the estate, and improving the estate for the benefit of the persons who are absolutely entitled to it."

I can see no reason why the same reasoning should not apply in the present case simply because the beneficiary is an unincorporated non-charitable association. I do not think the fact that the testator has directed the application 'solely' for the specified purpose adds any legal force to the direction. The beneficiaries, the members of the association for the time being, are the persons who could enforce the purpose and they must, as it seems to me, be entitled not to enforce it or, indeed, to vary it.'

Macaulay's Estate, Re, Macaulay v *O'Donnell* [1943] Ch 435 House of Lords (Lord Buckmaster and Lord Tomlin)

Unincorporated associations and purpose trusts

Facts
A gift was made 'for the purposes' of an unincorporated association.

Held
A gift for such purposes was void for lack of a cestui que trust. An unincorporated association was defined, per Lord Buckmaster, as:

> 'A group of people defined and bound together by rules and called by a distinctive name'.

Morice v *Bishop of Durham*

See Chapter 1.

Neville Estates Ltd v *Madden* [1962] Ch 832 Chancery Division (Cross J)

Gifts to unincorporated associations

Facts
Catford Synagogue was established in 1937, comprising a Charities Commissioners' Scheme merging five London synagogues. During its existence various funds were raised and in 1952 a site was purchased on which a synagogue was built. In 1959 the synagogue obtained permission to develop part of the unused site. A prospective purchaser was found. However, the Charity Commissioners indicated that their permission to sell was required, and then compelled the synagogue to publicly offer the land after which higher offers than one by now accepted were received.

Held
On application by the prospective purchaser:
1. the funds originally raised, and therefore land, were held on trust for the synagogue as a quasi-corporation;
2. however, whilst the general presumption was that an unincorporated association would not be held to be a charity this rule as relaxed when the purposes had a religious element. The trust was for religious purposes and therefore the Charity Commissioners' authority over it was upheld.

Cross J:

> 'I turn now ... to the legal issues involved. The question of the construction and effect of gifts to or in trust for unincorporated associations was recently considered by the Privy Council, in *Leahy* v *A-G of New South Wales* [1959] AC 457. The position as I understand it, is as follows. Such a gift may take effect in one or other of three quite different ways.
>
> In the first place, it may, on its true construction, be a gift to the members of the association at the relevant date as joint tenants, so that any member can sever his share and claim it whether or not he continues to be a member of the association. Secondly, it may be a gift to the existing members not as joint tenants, but subject to their respective contractual rights and liabilities towards one another as members of the association. In such a case a member cannot sever his share. It will accrue to the other members on his death or resignation, even though such members include persons who became members after the gift

took effect. If this is the effect of the gift, it will not be open to objection on the score of perpetuity, unless there is something in its terms or in the rules of the association which precludes the members at any given time from dividing the subject of the gift between them on the footing that they are solely entitled to it in equity.

Thirdly, the terms or circumstances of the gift or the rules of the association may show that the property in question is not to be at the disposal of the members for the time being, but is to be held in trust so that it or its income may be enjoyed by the association or its members from time to time. In this case ... the gift will fail unless the association is a charitable body.'

Pirbright v *Sawley* [1896] WN 86 Chancery Division (Stirling J)

Purpose trusts and perpetuities

Facts
A gift of consols was left to maintain a burial enclosure 'for as long as the law permitted'.

Held
This was a valid gift which should endure for 21 years since the perpetuity rule was expressly accepted.

Recher's Will Trusts, Re [1972] Ch 526 Chancery Division (Brightman J)

Trusts of imperfect obligation: unincorporated associations

Facts
The testatrix made a bequest to 'The Anti-Vivisection Society, 76 Victoria Street, London SW1' by her will made in 1957. Until the end of 1956 a non-charitable unincorporated society, known as 'The London and Provincial Anti-Vivisection Society' had carried on its activities at 76 Victoria Street, but in 1957 it was amalgamated with the National Anti-Vivisection Society and the premises at 76 Victoria Street closed. In 1963 the society was amalgamated. The testatrix died in 1962 and the question arose whether the gift was valid.

Held
The gift could not be construed as a gift to the larger amalgamated society but only as a gift to the London and Provincial Society. If this society had remained in existence until the testatrix's death, the gift could have taken effect as a legacy to the members of the society beneficially, not so as to entitle each member to receive a share, but as an accretion to the funds which constituted the subject-matter of the contract by which the members bound themselves inter se.

Brightman J:

'Having reached the conclusion that the gift in question is not a gift to the members of the London and Provincial Society at the date of death, as joint tenants or tenants in common so as to entitle a member as of right to a distributive share, nor an attempted gift to present and future members beneficially, and is not a gift in trust for the purposes of the society, I must now consider how otherwise, if at all, it is capable of taking effect.

As I have already mentioned, the rules of the London and Provincial Society do not purport to create any trusts except insofar as the honorary trustees are not beneficial owners of the assets of the society, but are trustees on trust to deal with such assets according to the directions of the committee.

A trust for non-charitable purposes, as distinct from a trust for individuals, is clearly void because there is no beneficiary. It does not, however, follow that persons cannot band themselves together as an association or society, pay subscriptions and validly devote their funds in pursuit of some lawful non-charitable purpose. An obvious example is a members' social club. But it is not essential that the members should only intend to secure direct personal advantages to themselves. The association may be one in which personal advantages to the members are combined with the pursuit of some outside purpose. Or the association may be one which offers no personal benefit at all to the members, the funds of the association being applied exclusively to the pursuit of some outside purpose. Such an association of persons is bound, I would think, to have some sort of constitution; ie the rights and liabilities of the members of the association will inevitably depend on some form of contract inter se, usually evidenced by a set of rules.

In the present case it appears to me clear that the life members, the ordinary members and the associate members of the London Provincial Society were bound together by a contract inter se. Any such member was entitled to the rights and subject to the liabilities defined by the rules. If the committee acted contrary to the rules, an individual member would be entitled to take proceedings in the courts to compel observance of the rules or to recover damages for any loss he had suffered as a result of the breach of contract. As and when a member paid his subscription to the association, he would be subjecting his money to the disposition and expenditure thereof laid down by the rules. That is to say, the member would be bound to permit, and entitled to require, the honorary trustees and other members of the society to deal with that subscription in accordance with the lawful directions of the committee. Those directions would include the expenditure of that subscription, as part of the general funds of the association, in furthering the objects of the association. (The resultant situation, on analysis, is that the London and Provincial Society represented an organisation of individuals bound together by a contract under which their subscriptions became, as it were, mandated towards a certain type of expenditure as adumbrated in rI.). Just as the two parties to a bipartite bargain can vary or terminate their contract by mutual assent, so it must follow that the life members, ordinary members and associate members of the London and Provincial Society could, at any moment of time, by unanimous agreement (or by majority vote if the rules so prescribe), vary or terminate their multi-partite contract. There would be no limit to the type of variation or termination to which all might agree. There is no private trust or trust for charitable purposes or other trust to hinder the process. It follows that if all members agreed, they could decide to wind up the London and Provincial Society and divide the net assets among themselves beneficially. No one would have any locus standi to stop them so doing. The contract is the same as any other contract and concerns only those who are parties to it, that is to say, the members of the society.

The funds of such an association may, of course, be derived not only from the subscriptions of the contracting parties but also from donations from non-contracting parties and legacies from persons who have died. In the case of a donation which is not accompanied by any words which purport to impose a trust, it seems to me that the gift takes effect in favour of the existing members of the association as an accretion to the funds which are the subject-matter of the contract which such members have made inter se, and fails to be dealt with in precisely the same way as the funds which the members themselves have subscribed. So, in the case of legacy. In the absence of words which purport to impose a trust, the legacy is a gift to the members beneficially, not as joint tenants or as tenants in common so as to entitle each member to an immediate distributive share, but as an accretion to the funds which are the subject-matter of the contract which the members have made inter se.'

Shaw, Re [1957] 1 WLR 729 Chancery Division (Harman J)

Purpose trust

Facts
George Bernard Shaw left a bequest to inquire into the value of an improved phonetic alphabet to show the waste of time and labour in using the current alphabet.

Held
The gift was a non-charitable purpose trust which was void as it merely increased knowledge without providing for the dissemination of that knowledge by teaching and education.

Tyler, Re [1891] 3 Ch 252 Court of Appeal (Lindley, Fry and Lopes LJJ)

Purpose trusts: monuments

Facts
The testator bequeathed £42,000 Russian 5 per cent stock to the trustees of the London Missionary Society and committed to their care and charge the keys of his family vault at Highgate Cemetery 'the same to be kept in good repair, and name legible, and to rebuild when it shall require: failing to comply with this request, the money to go to the Bluecoat School, Newgate Street, London'. The question arose whether the gift was valid.

Held
The condition to repair the vault was valid, the rule against perpetuities had no application to a transfer, on the occurrence of a certain event, of property from one charity to another, as in this case.

Fry LJ:

> 'In this case the testator has given a sum of money to one charity with a gift over to another charity, upon the happening of a certain event. That event, no doubt, is such as to create an inducement or motive on the part of the first donee, the London Missionary Society, to repair the family tomb of the testator. Inasmuch as both the donees of this fund, the first donee and the second, are charitable bodies, and are created for the purposes of charity, the rule of law against perpetuities has nothing whatever to do with the donees. Does the rule of law against perpetuities create any object to the nature of the condition? If the testator had required the first donee, the London Missionary Society, to apply any portions of the fund towards the repair of the family tomb, that would, in all probability, at any rate, to the extent of the sum required, have been void as a perpetuity which was not charity. But he has done nothing of the sort. He has given the first donee no power to apply any part of the money. He has only created a condition that the sum shall go over to Christ's Hospital if the London Missionary Society do not keep the tomb in repair. Keeping the tomb in repair is not an illegal object. If it were, the condition tending to bring about an illegal act would itself be illegal; but to repair the tomb is a perfectly lawful thing. All that can be said is that it is not lawful to tie up property for the purpose. But the rule of law against perpetuities applies to property, not motives, and I know of no rule which says that you may not try to enforce a condition creating a perpetual inducement to do a thing which is lawful. That is the case.'

Vaughan, Re (1886) 33 Ch D 187 Chancery Division (North J)

Monuments and purpose trusts

Facts
A gift was left in trust for the maintenance of the upkeep of a burial ground in a churchyard.

Held
This was a charitable trust for the advancement of religion under the Statute of Elizabeth which allowed gifts for the upkeep of churches.

North J:

'I see no difference between a gift to keep in repair what is called "God's House" and a gift to keep in repair the churchyard round it, which is often called "God's Acre".'

Wedgwood, Re [1915] 1 Ch 113 Court of Appeal (Cozens-Hardy MR, Kennedy and Swinfen Eady LJJ)

Purpose trusts: animals

Facts
A testatrix gave her residue to her brother on a secret trust to apply it for the protection and benefit of animals. The testatrix had been particularly interested in more humane methods of slaughter.

Held
The gift was charitable because, as Cozens-Hardy MR said, 'it tends to promote public morality by checking the innate tendency to cruelty'.

8 Charitable Trusts

Atkinson, Re [1978] 1 WLR 586 Chancery Division (Megarry J)
Charitable trusts must be exclusively charitable

Facts
A testatrix directed the trustees of her will to pay and divide the residue of her will between such 'worthy causes as have been communicated by me to my trustees during my lifetime'.

Held
The gift was void for uncertainty because the term could not be confined within the bounds of charity, there being many causes which could be called 'worthy' without being charitable.

Attorney-General v *Ross* [1986] 1 WLR 252 Chancery Division (Scott J)
Charitable trusts with ancillary objects

Facts
A students' union was an integral part of a polytechnic, a registered charity, but its rules permitted its funds to be used for political purposes.

Held
The political purposes for which part of the funds were used were ancillary to the union's principal object, that of promoting the welfare of its members.

Scott J:

'It is well settled that an organisation may properly be regarded as established for charitable purposes only notwithstanding that some of its activities do not in themselves promote charitable purposes. Lord Reid in *Inland Revenue Commissioners* v *City of Glasgow Police Athletic Association* [1953] AC 380, said:

"It is not enough that one of the purposes of a body of persons is charitable: the Act requires that it must be established for charitable purposes only. This does not mean that the sole effect of the activities of the body must be to promote charitable purposes but it does mean that that must be its predominant object and that any benefits to its individual members of a non-charitable character which result from its activities must be of a subsidiary or incidental character."

Lord Cohen in the same case said, at p405:

"Certain principles appear to be settled. (a) If the main purpose of the body of persons is charitable and the only elements in its constitution and operations which are non-charitable are merely incidental to that main purpose, that body of persons is a charity notwithstanding the presence of those elements – *Royal College of Surgeons of England* v *National Provincial Bank Ltd* [1952] AC 631. (b) If, however, a non-charitable object is itself one of the purposes of the body of persons and is not merely incidental to the charitable purpose, the body of persons is not a body of persons formed for charitable purposes only within the meaning of the Income Tax Acts – *Oxford Group* v *Inland Revenue Commissioners* [1949] 2

All ER 537. (c) If a substantial part of the objects of the body of persons is to benefit its own members, the body of persons is not established for charitable purposes only – *Inland Revenue Commissioners* v *Yorkshire Agricultural Society* [1928] 1 KB 611."

Brightman J in the *London Hospital* case [1976] 1 WLR 613, after citing the passage that I have read from Lord Reid's judgment, commented, at p623: "In the end it seems to me that the question is to some extent a matter of degree."

In the present case Mr Lightman has concentrated on the affiliation of the union to the National Union of Students. This affiliation is expressly authorised under sub-clause (d) of clause 3 but is, I think, properly to be regarded as a means of pursuing the representational object expressed in sub-clause (a). Be that as it may, the union pays, it seems, affiliation fees in excess of £15,000 per annum at the current level to the National Union of Students. The National Union of Students expends its funds on purposes which are plainly not charitable. It is not, and could not be, suggested that the National Union of Students is charitable. How, argues Mr Lightman, can the union then be charitable? It is empowered to spend, and does spend, substantial sums out of its funds on a non-charitable purpose. But, as Brightman J observed, the question is one of degree. There is no reason in principle why, for the purpose of achieving its own charitable purposes, a charitable body should not ally itself with and contribute to the funds of a non-charitable organisation. I am sure that a number of charities do so as a matter of course.

There is, in my view, no reason in principle why a students' union being a charity should not affiliate itself to the National Union of Students, a non-charity, and pay the subscriptions or fees consequent upon the affiliation. It is an express object of this union, and consistent with an over-all charitable purpose, that it should represent its members on national student organisations. I do not, therefore, accept Mr Lightman's argument that affiliation to the National Union of Students and the payment of affiliation fees is inconsistent with the students' union having a charitable status.

A point was made by Mr Lightman concerning the reference in sub-clause (b) to political activities. The carrying on of political activities or the pursuit of political objectives cannot, in the ordinary way, be a charitable purpose. But I can see nothing the matter with an educational charity, in the furtherance of its educational purposes, encouraging students to develop their political awareness or to acquire knowledge of, and to debate, and to form views on, political issues. If the form of the encouragement involves provision of facilities for a students' Labour club, or Conservative club, or any other political club, I can see nothing in that which is necessarily inconsistent with the furtherance of educational purposes. Here, too, the question is, perhaps, one of degree. But the proposition that an educational charity, be it a school, polytechnic or university, cannot consistently with its charitable status promote and encourage the development of political ideas among its students has only to be stated to be seen to be untenable. The reference to political activities in sub-clause (b) is, in my judgment, no obstacle to the union's charitable status.

Finally, Mr Lightman prayed in aid the activities of the union. He submitted that the activities of the union since it was founded in 1970 could be prayed in aid in order to resolve the question whether the union was or was not charitable. He submitted that, on the facts of this case, I should conclude that the union existed primarily in order to express the political views and aspirations of its student members, and, further, that the main object of the union was to reflect and give effect to the political views of its student members. I am unable to accept these submissions.

The question whether under its constitution the union is or is not charitable must, in my view, be answered by reference to the content of its constitution, construed and assessed in the context of the factual background to its formation. This background may serve to elucidate the purpose for which the union was formed. But if the union was of a charitable nature when formed in 1971 it cannot have been deprived of that nature by the activities carried on subsequently in its name.

I must not be taken to be expressing the opinion that the activities of an organisation subsequent to its formation can never be relevant to the question whether the organisation was formed for charitable purposes only. The skill of Chancery draftsmen is well able to produce a constitution of charitable flavour intended to allow the pursuit of aims of a non-charitable or dubiously charitable flavour. In a case where the real purpose for which an organisation was formed is in doubt, it may be legitimate to take into account the nature of the activities which the organisation has since its formation carried on. It is, as I have remarked, settled by, among other cases, *Inland Revenue Commissioners* v *City of Glasgow Police Athletic Association* that, if the main purpose of an organisation is charitable, power to carry on incidental, supplementary non-charitable activities is not fatal to charitable status. The activities of an organisation after its formation may serve to indicate that the power to carry on non-charitable activities was in truth not incidental or supplementary at all but was the main purpose for which the organisation was formed. In such a case the organisation could not be regarded as charitable.'

Attorney-General of the Bahamas v *Royal Trust Co* [1986] 1 WLR 1001 Privy Council (Lord Keith, Lord Griffiths, Lord Goff, Lord Templeman and Lord Oliver)

Charitable trusts must be exclusively charitable

Facts
A testator left a will which included a bequest of the residue of his estate to be used 'for any purposes for and/or connected with the education and welfare of Bahamian children and young people ...' The trustee of the gift sought to determine if this was a valid charitable bequest. The Supreme Court of the Bahamas held that the gift was not charitable as the words 'and welfare' enlarged the purposes beyond those connected with education. This was upheld by the Bahamian Court of Appeal.

Held
The gift was not valid as a charitable trust.

Lord Oliver:

'The point is not one which is susceptible of a great deal of elaboration and their Lordships need say no more than that they agree with Blake CJ and the [Bahamian] Court of Appeal that the phrase "education and welfare" in this will inevitably falls to be construed disjunctively. It follows that, for the reasons which were fully explored in the judgements in the courts below, and as is now conceded on the footing of a disjunctive construction, the trusts ... do not constitute valid charitable trusts and that, accordingly, the residue of the trust estate falls into the residuary gift in ... the will.'

Blair v *Duncan* [1902] AC 37; (1901) 38 SLR 209 House of Lords (Earl of Halsbury LC, Lord Shand, Lord Davey, Lord Brampton and Lord Robertson)

Wholly and exclusively charitable

Facts
The testatrix bequeathed her residuary estate to two brothers, but if one or both predeceased her, their shares were to be applied for 'such charitable or public purposes as my trustee thinks proper'. One brother predeceased her, and the surviving brother brought an action for the whole claiming the charitable gift was void for uncertainty.

Held
The trust was not charitable, 'public' purposes being not necessarily charitable. As well as dealing with Scots law, Lord Davey said:

'There is no doubt that the English law has attached a wide and somewhat artificial meaning to the words "charity" and "charitable", derived, it is said, from the enumeration of objects in the well-known Act of

Elizabeth, but probably accepted by lawyers before that statute ... If ... the words in the present case were merely "charitable purposes" or were "charitable and public purposes", I think effect might be given to them, the words in the latter case being construed to mean "charitable purposes of a public character" ... The words we have here are "charitable or public purposes", and I think these words must be read disjunctively. It would therefore be in the power of the trustee to apply the whole of the fund for purposes which are not charitable, though they might be of a public character.'

British School of Egyptian Archaeology, Re [1954] 1 WLR 546 Chancery Division (Harman J)

Furtherance of education

Facts
A trust was set up to excavate, to discover antiquities, to hold exhibitions, to publish works and to promote the training and assistance of students – all in relation to Egypt.

Held
The purposes were charitable, they were for the diffusion of a certain branch of knowledge, namely, knowledge of the ancient past of Egypt; the purposes also had the effect of training students.

Bushnell, Re [1975] 1 WLR 1596 Chancery Division (Goulding J)

Political education not charitable

Facts
The testator, who died in 1941, left his residuary estate to his wife for life and after her death he directed his executors to hold the residue of the capital and income for four unincorporated associations for 'the advancement and propagation of the teaching of Socialised Medicine'. Eleven Managers were to be appointed to apply the income 'towards furthering the knowledge of the Socialist application of medicine to public and personal health and well-being and to demonstrating that the full advantage of Socialised Medicine can only be enjoyed in a Socialist State'. This was to be done by engaging lecturers and speakers to give public lectures on Socialised Medicine and printing and publishing for sale or free distribution books and pamphlets on the subject. The question arose whether the trust could take effect as a charitable trust for the advancement and propagation of the teaching of Socialised Medicine?

Held
The main or dominant or essential object of the trust was a political one. The testator was trying to promote his own theory of socialised medicine by education or propaganda; there was no desire to educate the public so that they could choose for themselves. The directions in the will showed that the dominant purpose was the promotion of the Socialist application of Medicine. The trust was therefore not charitable.

Caffoor Trustees v *Income Tax Commissioner, Colombo* [1961] AC 584 Privy Council (Lord Morton, Lord Radcliffe, Lord Morris and Rt Hon LMD De Silva)

Charitable trust: later limitations

Facts
The settlor left funds on trust for 'the education instruction or training in England or elsewhere abroad of deserving youths of the Islamic faith' in any department of human activity. The settlor went on to outline the eligible beneficiaries and gave a preference for 'male descendants along either the male or female line of the grantor or of any of his brothers or sisters ...'

Held
In view of the absolute priority conferred on the grantor's own family this was a family trust and not a trust of a public character.

Chichester Diocesan Fund and Board of Finance Inc v *Simpson* [1944] AC 341
House of Lords (Viscount Simonds LC, Lord Macmillan, Lord Porter, Lord Simonds and Lord Wright)

Charitable trusts must be exclusively charitable

Facts
Caleb Diplock who died in 1936 left a will by the terms of which his executors were directed to apply his residuary estate 'for such charitable institution or institutions or other charitable or benevolent object or objects in England' as they should in their absolute discretion think fit. The executors proceeded to distribute the estate among 139 charities of their choice. However, the next-of-kin challenged the validity of the gift on the grounds that it was void for uncertainty.

Held (Lord Wright dissenting)
'Charitable or benevolent' purposes resulted in the trust being not wholly and exclusively charitable. The gift was not charitable in these circumstances. Further, it was not a valid private trust either; there was uncertainty of objects.

Lord Porter:

> '... technical words must be interpreted in their technical sense and "charity" or "charitable" are technical words in English law and must be so construed unless it can be seen from the wording of the will as a whole that they are used in some other than their technical sense. For this purpose and in order to discover the testator's intention it is the duty of the court to take into consideration the whole of the terms of the will and not to confine itself to the disputed words or their immediate context.
>
> In the present case the words whose interpretation is contested are "charitable or benevolent". It is admitted on behalf of the appellants that, if the word "benevolent" stood alone, it would be too vague a term and the gift would be void: see *James* v *Allen* (1817) 3 Mer 17, but it is said that, when coupled with the word "charitable" even by the disjunctive "or", it either takes colour from its associate or is merely exegetical, and the phrase is used as implying either that "charitable" and "benevolent" are the same thing or that "benevolent" qualifies "charitable" so as to limit the gift to objects which are both charitable and benevolent.
>
> In my view, the words so coupled do not naturally bear any of the meanings suggested. The addition of "benevolent" to "charitable" on the face of it suggests an alternative purpose and I do not see why in this collocation "benevolent" should be read as "charitable benevolent". Nor do I think that it can be said to be merely exegetical. Prima facie, these are alternative objects ...'

Commentary
Further litigation in this case will be found in *Re Diplock* (Chapter 17) and *Ministry of Health* v *Simpson* (Chapter 18).

Clarke, Re [1923] 2 Ch 407 Chancery Division (Romer J)

Funds apportioned to charity

Facts
A testator left his residuary estate to be divided equally between four purposes, three of which were named charities and the fourth being 'such other funds, charities and institutions as my executors in their absolute discretion shall think fit'.

Held
The gift to the named charities was valid but the fourth share failed. The failure of one share did not affect the other shares.

Compton, Re [1945] Ch 123 Court of Appeal (Lord Greene MR, Finlay and Morton LJJ)

Public benefit

Facts
An educational trust was established for the benefit of members of three named families.

Held
This did not amount to a charitable trust as it was not for the public benefit. A group of persons may be numerous but if the nexus between them is their relationship to a single propositus or to several propositi, they were neither the community nor a section of it for charitable purposes. There was a distinction between personal and impersonal relationships. If the trust were based on the former, it was a private trust, but if on the latter, a public trust, satisfying the public benefit element.

Coxen, Re [1948] Ch 747 Chancery Division (Jenkins J)

Charitable trusts may have incidental non-charitable objects

Facts
A testator left £200,000 on trust for orthopaedic hospitals, with a direction that £100 was to be set aside each year for the fund to provide a dinner for the trustees when they met on trust business, and to pay a guinea to each trustee attending the whole meeting.

Held
The £100 for dinner and the attendance fee were essentially ancillary to the main charitable trusts for hospitals and should be considered as for the better administration of the trust and not for the personal benefit of the trustees.

Delius, Re [1957] Ch 299 Chancery Division (Roxburgh J)

Furtherance of education – public benefit

Facts
The widow of the composer Frederick Delius left money on trusts to advance his musical works.

Held
This was a valid charitable trust.

Roxburgh J:

'... if it is charitable to promote music in general it must be charitable to promote the music of a particular composer, presupposing (as in the case I can assume) that the composer is one whose music is worth appreciating.'

Dingle v *Turner* [1972] AC 601 House of Lords (Viscount Dilhorne, Lord MacDermott, Lord Hodson, Lord Simon and Lord Cross)

Charitable trusts for the relief of poverty: no public benefit required

Facts
A testator directed the trustees of his will to invest £10,000 and apply the income thereof 'in paying pensions to poor employees of E Dingle & Co Ltd ...' At the testator's death E Dingle & Co Ltd had 705 full-time employees and 189 part-time employees and was paying pensions to 89 ex-employees.

Held
The gift was a valid charitable gift. A gift for the relief of poverty would be charitable where as a matter of construction it was to relieve poverty amongst a particular description of poor persons. If, however, the trust is one to relieve poverty among named persons it is not a charitable trust but a private trust.

Lord Cross:

'Your Lordships, therefore, are now called on to give to the old "poor relations" cases and the more modern "poor employees" cases that careful consideration which, in his speech in the *Oppenheim* case [1951] AC 297, Lord Morton of Henryton said that they might one day require.

The contentions of the appellant and the respondents may be stated broadly as follows. The appellant says that in the *Oppenheim* case this House decided that in principle a trust ought not to be regarded as charitable if the benefits under it are confined either to the descendants of a named individual or individuals or the employees of a given individual or company and that although the "poor relations" cases may have to be left standing as an anomalous exception to the general rule because their validity has been recognised for so long, the exception ought not to be extended to "poor employees" trusts which had not been recognised for long before their status as charitable trusts began to be called in question. The respondents, on the other hand, say, first, that the rule laid down in the *Oppenheim* case with regard to educational trusts ought not to be regarded as a rule applicable in principle to all kinds of charitable trust and, secondly, that in any case it is impossible to draw any logical distinction between "poor relations" trusts and "poor employees" trusts, and, that as the former cannot be held invalid today after having been recognised as valid for so long, the latter must be regarded as valid also.

By a curious coincidence within a few months of the decision of this House in the *Oppenheim* case the cases on gifts to "poor relations" had to be considered by the Court of Appeal in *Re Scarisbrick* [1951] Ch 622. Most of the cases on this subject were decided in the eighteenth or early nineteenth centuries and are very inadequately reported but two things at least were clear. First, that it never occurred to the judges who decided them that in the field of "poverty" a trust could not be a charitable trust if the class of beneficiaries was defined by reference to descent from a common ancestor. Secondly, that the courts did not treat a gift or trust as necessarily charitable because the objects of it have to be poor in order to qualify, for in some of the cases the trust was treated as a private trust and not a charity. The problem in *Re Scarisbrick* was to determine on what basis the distinction was drawn. Roxburgh J – founding himself on some words attributed to Sir William Grant MR in *Att-Gen* v *Price* (1810) 17 Ves 371 – had held that the distinction lay in whether the gift took the form of a trust under which capital was retained and the income only applied for the benefit of the objects, in which case the gift was charitable, or whether the gift was one under which the capital was immediately distributable among the objects, in which case the gift was not a charity. The Court of Appeal rejected this ground of distinction. They held that in this field the distinction between a public or charitable trust and a private trust depended on whether as a matter of construction the gift was for the relief of poverty amongst a particular description of poor people or was merely a gift to particular poor persons, the relief of poverty among them being the motive of the gift. The fact that the gift took the form of a perpetual trust would no doubt indicate that the intention of the donor could not have been to confer private benefits on particular people whose possible necessities he had in mind; but the fact that the capital of the gift was to be distributed at once did not necessarily show that the gift was a private trust.

The appellant in the instant case, while of course submitting that the judges who decided the old cases were wrong in not appreciating that no gift for the relief of poverty among persons tracing descent from a common ancestor could ever have a sufficiently "public" quality to constitute a charity, did not dispute the correctness of the analysis of those cases made by the Court of Appeal in *Re Scarisbrick* ...

After this long – but I hope not unduly long – recital of the decided cases I turn to consider the arguments advanced by the appellant in support of the appeal. For this purpose I will assume that the appellant is right in saying that the *Compton* rule ought in principle to apply to all charitable trusts and that the "poor relations" cases, the "poor members" cases and the "poor employees" cases are all anomalous – in the sense that if such cases had come before the court for the first time after the decision in *Re Compton* [1945] Ch 123 the trusts in question would have been held valid as private trusts.

Even on that assumption – as it seems to me – the appeal must fail. The status of some of the "poor relations" trusts as valid charitable trusts was recognised more than 200 years ago and a few of those then recognised are still being administered as charities today. In *Re Compton*, Lord Greene MR said that it was "quite impossible" for the Court of Appeal to overrule such old decisions in the *Oppenheim* case. Lord Simonds in speaking of them remarked on the unwisdom of

"... (casting) doubt on decisions of respectable antiquity in order to introduce a greater harmony into the law of charity as a whole."

Indeed counsel for the appellant ventured to suggest that we should overrule the 'poor relations' cases. His submission was that which was accepted by the Court of Appeal in Ontario in *Re Cox (decd)* [1951] OR 205 – namely that while the "poor relations" cases might have to be left as long standing anomalies there was no good reason for sparing the "poor employees" cases which only date from *Re Gosling* (1900) 48 WR 300 decided in 1900 and which have been under suspicion ever since the decision in *Re Compton* in 1945. But the "poor members" and the "poor employees" decisions were a natural development of the "poor relations" decisions and to draw a distinction between different sorts of "poverty" trusts would be quite illogical and could certainly not be said to be introducing "greater harmony" into the law of charity. Moreover, although not as old as the "poor relations" trusts, "poor employees" trusts have been recognised as charities for many years; there are now a large number of such trusts in existence; and assuming, as one must, that they are properly administered in the sense that benefits under them are only given to people who can fairly be said to be, according to current standards, "poor persons", to treat such trusts as charities is not open to any practical objection. So as it seems to me it must be accepted that wherever else it may hold sway the *Compton* rule has no application in the field of trusts for the relief of poverty and that the dividing line between a charitable trust and a private trust lies where the Court of Appeal drew it in *Re Scarisbrick* ..."

Drummond, Re [1914] 2 Ch 90 Chancery Division (Eves J)

Relief of poverty

Facts
A gift was left in trust for holiday expenses of work people.

Held
Although employed at a low wage, the people concerned were not poor within the meaning of the Statute of Elizabeth and accordingly the gift was not charitable.

Dunne v *Byrne* [1912] AC 407 Privy Council (Lord Macnaghten, Lord Shaw, Lord Mersey and Lord Robson)

Exclusively charitable purposes required

Facts
A gift of residue was left 'to the Roman Catholic Archbishop of Brisbane and his successors to be used and expended wholly or in part as such Archbishop may judge most conducive to the good of religion.'

Held
The gift was not charitable since a thing may be conducive to the good of religion without being charitable in the legal sense or even religious.

Lord Macnaghten:

> '... We come to the real difficulty of the case. The fund is to be applied in such manner as the "Archbishop may judge most conducive to the good of religion" in his diocese. It can hardly be disputed that a thing may be "conducive", and in particular circumstances "most conducive", to the good of religion in a particular diocese or in a particular district without being charitable in the sense which the Court attaches to the word, and indeed without being in itself in any sense religious. In *Cocks* v *Manners* (1871) LR 12 Eq 574 there is the well-known instance of the dedication of a fund to a purpose which a devout Roman Catholic would no doubt consider "conducive to the good of religion", but which is certainly not charitable. In the present case the learned Chief Justice suggests by way of example several modes in which the fund now in question might be employed so as to be conducive to the good of religion though the mode of application in itself might have nothing of a religious character about it. As to what may be considered "most conducive to the good of religion" in the diocese of Brisbane the Archbishop is given an absolute and uncontrolled discretion. That being so, apart from a certain line of decisions cited at the Bar, there would be an end of the case. The language of the bequest (to use Lord Langdale's words) would be "open to such latitude of construction as to raise no trust which a Court of Equity could carry into execution": *Baker* v *Sutton* (1836) 1 Keen 224. If the property, as Sir William Grant said in *James* v *Allen* [1893] 2 Ch 41, "might consistently with the will be applied to other than strictly charitable purposes", the trust is too indefinite for the Court to execute.
>
> It was said: This is a gift for religious purposes, and the Court has held over and over again that a gift for religious purposes is a good charitable gift. That is true. But the answer is: This is not in terms a gift for religious purposes, nor are the words synonymous with that expression. Their Lordships agree with the opinion of the Chief Justice that the expression used by this testator is wider and more indefinite.'

Eastes, Re [1948] Ch 257 Chancery Division (Jenkins J)

Gifts for charitable purposes

Facts
A gift of residue was made to the Vicar and Churchwardens of St George's Church 'for any purposes in connection with the said church which they may select, it being my wish that they shall especially bear in mind the requirements of the children of the parish.'

Held
The gift was charitable. The word 'for any purposes in connection with the said church which they may select' did not allow the gift to be used for non-charitable purposes. The objects had to be construed as relating to the church, ie its fabric and services, and not the parish. The final words concerning the children were precatory and not legally binding.

Farley v *Westminster Bank Ltd* [1939] AC 430 House of Lords (Lord Atkin, Lord Russell and Lord Romer)

Gifts for charitable purposes

Facts
A testatrix bequeathed the residue of her estate in equal shares to the respective Vicars and Churchwardens of two named churches 'for parish work'.

Held
The gift was not charitable.

Lord Atkin:

'... "parish work" seems to me to be of such vague import as to go far beyond the ordinary meaning of charity, in this case in the sense of being a religious purpose. The expression covers the whole of the ordinary activities of the parish, some of which no doubt fall within the definition of religious purposes, and all of which no doubt are religious from the point of view of the person who is responsible for the spiritual care of the parish in the sense that they are conducive, perhaps, to the moral and spiritual good of his congregation. But that, I think, quite plainly is not enough; and the words are so wide that I am afraid that on no construction can they be brought within the limited meaning of "charitable" as used in the law ...'

Lord Russell:

'In my opinion, upon the true construction of this will, the words in brackets (for parish work) mean that the gift is not a gift for ecclesiastical or religious purposes in the strict sense, but it is a gift for the assistance and furtherance of those various activities connected with the parish church which are found, I believe, in every parish, but which, unfortunately for the donees here, include many objects which are not in any way charitable in the legal sense of that word.'

Good, Re [1905] 2 Ch 60 Chancery Division (Farwell J)

Trusts for the efficiency of the Forces

Facts
The testator left his residuary personalty upon trust for the officers' mess of his regiment to be used for maintaining a library for the officers' mess and purchasing plate for the mess.

Held
The gift was charitable as it tended to increase the efficiency of the Army and aid taxation. Further, it could be supported as a 'setting out of soldiers' within the meaning of those words in the Statute of Elizabeth.

Goodman v Saltash Corporation (1882) 7 App Cas 633 House of Lords (Lord Selborne LC, Earl Cairns, Lord Blackburn, Lord Watson, Lord Bramwell and Lord FitzGerald)

Public benefit: gift for inhabitants

Facts

A gift for the benefit of the inhabitants of Saltash was argued to be for the public benefit.

Held

A valid charity.

Lord Selborne LC:

> 'A gift subject to a condition or trust for the benefit of the inhabitants of a parish or town, or of any particular class of such inhabitants is (as I understand the law) a charitable trust.'

Gray, Re [1925] Ch 362 Chancery Division (Romer J)

Trusts for the efficiency of the Forces: trusts for sport

Facts

A testator made bequests to a regimental fund for the Carabiniers for 'the promotion of sport'.

Held

The bequests were charitable as they promoted the physical efficiency of the Army. Romer J observed:

> 'It was not the object of the testator in the present case to encourage or promote either sport in general or any sport in particular. I think it is reasonably clear that it was his intention to benefit the officers and men of the Carabiniers by giving them an opportunity of indulging in healthy sport ...'

Grove-Grady, Re [1929] 1 Ch 557 Court of Appeal (Lord Hanworth MR, Lawrence and Russell LJJ)

Animal cases must be for human benefit to be charitable

Facts

A testatrix left her residuary estate on trust to purchase some land to be used 'for the purpose of providing a refuge or refuges for the preservation of all animals and birds and other creatures not human ... so that all such animals, birds or other creatures not human shall there be safe from molestation or destruction by man ...'

Held

The trust was not charitable because it provided no benefit to the community in any way whatsoever.

Russell LJ:

> '... It is merely a trust to secure that all animals within the area shall be free from molestation or destruction by man. It is not a trust directed to ensure absence or diminution of pain or cruelty in the destruction of animal life. If this trust is carried out according to its tenor, no animal within the area may be destroyed by man no matter how necessary that destruction may be in the interests of mankind or in

the interests of the other denizens of the area or in the interests of the animal itself; and no matter how painlessly such destruction may be brought about. It seems to me impossible to say that the carrying out of such a trust necessarily involves benefit to the public. Beyond perhaps hearing of the existence of the enclosure the public does not come into the matter at all. Consistently with the trust the public could be excluded from the area or even looking into it. All the public need know about the matter would be that one or more areas existed in which all animals (whether good or bad from mankind's point of view) were allowed to live free from any risk of being molested or killed by man; though liable to be molested and killed by other denizens in the area. For myself I feel quite unable to say that any benefit to the community will necessarily result from applying the trust fund to the purposes indicated in the first object ...'

Guild (Executor Nominate of the late James Young Russell) v *IRC* [1992] 2 WLR 397 House of Lords (Lord Keith of Kinkel, Lord Roskill, Lord Griffiths, Lord Jauncey of Tullichettle and Lord Lowry)

Receational Charities Act 1958 – sports facilities – Scotland

Facts
The testator had left the residue of his estate to the council of North Berwick for '... use in connection with the sports centre in North Berwick or some similar purpose in connection with sport'. The IRC determined the transfer was not charitable and therefore liable to capital transfer tax.

Held
On appeal the term 'charity' and 'charitable purposes' were to be determined in Scotland, for tax purposes, as per their English meaning. Further, on applying s1(2)(a) of the Recreational Charities Act 1958, the provision of facilities for recreation or other leisure-time occupation could be provided with the view of improving the conditions of life of its intended recipients. This was so notwithstanding they were not in a position of relative social disadvantage or suffering from some degree of deprivation.

Gwyon, Re, Public Trustee v *Attorney-General* [1930] 1 Ch 255 Chancery Division (Eve J)

Relief of poverty

Facts
The testator left money for a trust to provide clothing for boys between certain ages, sons of parents resident in Farnham. No boy who was supported by a charitable institution or whose parents were on parish relief should be eligible. Any excess income was to be used for similar provision for boys from other designated areas.

Held
The provision was not for the relief of poverty as some poor boys were specifically excluded and rich boys were not. The provision for a particular community might save an otherwise charitable gift which was vague, but it could not save a gift which did not come within the heads of the Statute.

Eve J:

> 'Is the object of [the testator's] ... benefaction the relief of poverty? ... Apart from residential and age qualifications the only conditions imposed on a recipient ... [do not] necessarily import poverty, nor could

the recipient ... [do not] necessarily import poverty, nor could the recipients be accurately described as a class of aged, impotent or poor persons ... I think that ... the benevolence of the testator was intended for all eligible boys other than paupers ... In these circumstances I cannot hold this trust to be within the description of a legal charitable trust.

It was argued that the disposition might be treated as charitable by reason of its application being restricted to the area prescribed by the will ... Limitation or specification of locality may prevent a charitable trust from being avoided for vagueness and uncertainty, but only when it has first been shown to be a charitable trust. A trust which is not a charitable trust cannot be changed into a charitable one by limiting the area in which it is to operate.'

Hetherington, Re, Gibbs v *McDonnell* [1989] 2 All ER 129 High Court (Sir Nicolas Browne-Wilkinson V-C)

Public benefit and advancement of religion: saying of Masses

Facts
A devout Roman Catholic and regular worshipper at church, the testatrix included in her holograph will gifts as follows:

'I wish to leave two thousand pounds to the Roman Catholic Church Bishop of Westminster for masses for the repose of the souls of my husband and my parents and my sisters and also myself when I die.'

'Whatever is left over of my estate is to be given to the Roman Catholic Church St Edwards, Golders Green for masses for my soul.'

The administrator applied for a ruling whether these gifts established a valid charitable trust.

Held
They did as they were for a religious purpose and contained the necessary element of public benefit.

Sir Nicolas Browne-Wilkinson V-C:

'The grounds on which the trust in the present case can be attacked are that there is no *express* requirement that the Masses for souls which are to be celebrated are to be celebrated in public. The evidence shows that celebration in public is the invariable practice but there is no requirement of canon law to that effect. Therefore it is said the money could be applied to saying Masses in private which would not be charitable since there would be no sufficient element of public benefit.

In my judgment the cases establish the following propositions. A trust for the advancement of education, the relief of poverty or the advancement of religion is prima facie charitable and assumed to be for the public benefit: see *National Anti-Vivisection Society* v *IRC* [1948] AC 31. This assumption of public benefit can be rebutted by showing that in fact the particular trust in question cannot operate so as to confer a legally recognised benefit on the public, as in *Gilmour* v *Coats* [1948] AC 426 [see Chapter 7]. The celebration of a religious rite in public does confer a sufficient public benefit because of the edifying and improving effect of such celebration on the members of the public who attend. As Lord Reid said in *Gilmour* v *Coats*:

"A religion can be regarded as beneficial without it being necessary to assume that all its beliefs are true, and a religious service can be regarded as beneficial to all those who attend it without it being necessary to determine the spiritual efficacy of that service or to accept any particular belief about it."

... The celebration of a religious rite in private does not contain the necessary element of public benefit since any benefit by prayer or example is incapable of proof in the legal sense, and any element of edification is limited to a private, not public, class of those present at the celebration: see *Gilmour* v *Coats* itself; *Yeap Cheah Neo* v *Ong Cheng Neo* (1875) LR 6 PC 381 and *Hoare* v *Hoare* (1886) 56 LT 147.

Where there is a gift for a religious purpose which could be carried out in a way which is beneficial to the public (ie by public Masses) but could also be carried out in a way which would not have sufficient element of public benefit (ie by private Masses) the gift is to be construed as a gift to be carried out only by the methods that are charitable, all non-charitable methods being excluded: see *Re White, White v White* [1893] 2 Ch 41 and *Re Banfield (decd) Lloyds Bank Ltd v Smith* [1968] 2 All ER 276. Applying those principles to the present case, a gift for the saying of Masses is prima facie charitable, being for a religious purpose. In practice, those Masses will be celebrated in public, which provides a sufficient element of public benefit. The provision of stipends for priests saying the Masses, by relieving the Roman Catholic Church pro tanto of the liability to provide such stipends, is a further benefit. The gift is to be construed as a gift for public Masses only on the principle of *Re White*, private Masses not being permissible since it would not be a charitable application of the fund for a religious purpose.

Hopkins' Will Trusts, Re [1965] Ch 669 Chancery Division (Wilberforce J)

Research can be for the furtherance of education

Facts
A testatrix bequeathed one third of her residuary estate to the Francis Bacon Society Incorporated 'to be earmarked and applied towards finding the Bacon-Shakespeare Manuscripts ...' The main objects of the Society were, '(1) to encourage the study of the works of Francis Bacon as philosopher, lawyer, statesman and poet ... (2) to encourage the general study of the evidence in favour of Francis Bacon's authorship of the plays commonly ascribed to Shakespeare, and to investigate his connection with other works of the Elizabethan period.' The society was a registered charity and the question arose as to whether the bequest was a valid charitable gift.

Held
The gift was a valid charitable gift for education, a gift for search or research was charitable within this classification in *Pemsel*'s case. But where the trust was for research, the research must either (a) be of educational value to the researcher, or (b) must be so directed as to lead to something which will pass into the store of educational material, or (c) so as to improve the sum of communicable knowledge in an area which education may cover.

Wilberforce J:

> 'I come then to the only question of law: is the gift of a charitable character? The society has put its case in the alternative under two headings of education and of general benefit to the community and has argued separately for each. This compartmentalisation is derived from the accepted classification into four groups of the miscellany found in the Statute of Elizabeth (43 Eliz 1, c.4). That statute, preserved as to the preamble only by the Mortmain and Charitable Uses Act 1888, lost even that precarious hold on the Statute Book when the Act of 1888 was repealed by the Charities Act 1960, but the somewhat ossificatory classification to which it gave rise survives in the decided cases. It is unsatisfactory because the frontiers of "educational purposes" (as of the other divisions) have been extended and are not easy to trace with precision, and because, under the fourth head, it has been held necessary for the court to find a benefit to the public within the spirit and intendment of the obsolete Elizabethan statute. The difficulty of achieving that, while at the same time keeping the law's view of what is charitable reasonably in line with modern requirements, explains what Lord Simonds accepted as the case-to-case approach of the courts: see *National Anti-Vivisection Society v Inland Revenue Commissioners* [1948] AC 31. There are, in fact, examples of accepted charities which do not decisively fit into one rather than the other category. Examples are institutes for scientific research (see the *National Anti-Vivisection case*, per Lord Wright), museums (see *Re Pinion* [1965] Ch 85), the preservation of ancient cottages (*Re Cranstoun* [1932] 1 Ch

537), and even the promotion of Shakespearean drama (*Re Shakespeare's Memorial Theatre Trust* [1923] 2 Ch 398). The present may be such a case.

Accepting, as I have, the authority of Lord Simonds for so doing, that the court must decide each case as best it can, on the evidence available to it, as to benefit, and within the moving spirit of decided cases, it would seem to me that a bequest for the purpose of search, or research, for the original manuscripts of England's greatest dramatist (whoever he was) would be well within the law's conception of charitable purposes. The discovery of such manuscripts, or of one such manuscript, would be of the highest value to history and to literature. It is objected, against this, that as we already have the text of the plays, from an almost contemporary date, the discovery of a manuscript would add nothing worthwhile. This I utterly decline to accept. Without any undue exercise of the imagination, it would surely be a reasonable expectation that the revelation of a manuscript would contribute, probably decisively, to a solution of the authorship problem, and this alone is benefit enough. It might also lead to improvements in the text. It might lead to a more accurate dating.

Is there any authority, then, which should lead me to hold a bequest to achieve this objective is not charitable? By Mr Fox, for the next-of-kin, much reliance was placed on the decision on Bernard Shaw's will, the *"British Alphabet" case* (*Re Shaw, decd* [1957] 1 WLR 729 [see Chapter 7]). Harman J held that the gift was not educational because it merely tended to the increase of knowledge and that it was not within the fourth charitable category because it was not itself for a beneficial purpose but for the purpose of persuading the public by propaganda that it was beneficial. The gift was very different from the gift here. But that is not in itself a charitable object unless it be combined with teaching or education; and he referred to the House of Lords decision *Whicker* v *Hume* (1858) 7 HL Cas 124, where, in relation to a gift for advancement of education and learning, two of the Lords read "learning" as equivalent to "teaching", thereby in his view implying that learning, in its ordinary meaning, is not a charitable purpose.

This decision certainly seems to place some limits upon the extent to which a gift for research may be regarded as charitable. Those limits are that either it must be "combined with teaching or education", if it is to fall under the third head, or it must be beneficial to the community in a way regarded by the law as charitable, if it is to fall within the fourth category. The words "combined with teaching or education", though well explaining what the judge had in mind when he rejected the gift in *Shaw*'s case, are not easy to interpret in relation to other facts. I should be unwilling to treat them as meaning that the promotion of academic research is not a charitable purpose unless the researcher were engaged in teaching or education in the conventional meaning; and I am encouraged in this view by some words of Lord Greene MR in *Re Compton* [1945] Ch 123.

The testatrix there had forbidden the income of the bequest to be used for research, and Lord Greene MR treated this as a negative definition of the education to be provided. It would, he said, exclude a grant to enable a beneficiary to conduct research on some point of history or science. This shows that Lord Greene MR considered that historic research might fall within the description of "education". I think, therefore, that the word education' as used by Harman J in *Re Shaw, decd*, must be used in a wide sense, certainly extending beyond teaching, and that the requirement is that, in order to be charitable, research must either be of educational value to the researcher or must be so directed as to lead to something which will pass into the store of educational material, or so as to improve the sum of communicable knowledge in any area which education may cover – education in this last context extending to the formation of literary taste and appreciation (compare *Royal Choral Society* v *Inland Revenue Commissioners* [1943] 2 All ER 101). Whether or not the test is wider than this, it is, as I have stated it, amply wide enough to include the purposes of the gift in this case.

As regards the fourth category, Harman J is evidently leaving it open to the court to hold, on the facts, that research of a particular kind may be beneficial to the community in a way which the law regards as charitable. "Beneficial" here not being limited to the production of material benefit (as through medical or scientific research) but including at least benefit in the intellectual or artistic fields.

So I find nothing in this authority to prevent me from finding that the gift falls under either the third or fourth head of the classification of charitable purposes.'

Hummeltenberg, Re, Beatty v London Spiritualistic Alliance [1923] 1 Ch 237
Chancery Division (Russell J)

Public benefit: the purpose must be one which could come under court's control

Facts
The testator left a sum of money in trust to the London Spiritualist Alliance for the establishment of a college for the training of mediums.

Held
Not a valid charity.

Russell J:

> '... the primary meaning of the word medium is ... an individual who professes to act as an intermediary for communication between the living and the spirits of persons now dead.
>
> [It is said that this] is a trust beneficial to a section of the public, namely, that section which proposes or engages in the profession of medium ... [or] it is a trust beneficial to the whole community because its object is to increase the number of trained mediums in the world, and specially those trained for the purpose of diagnosing and healing disease. ... It is still ... necessary to show (1) that the gift will or may be operative for the public benefit and (2) that the trust is one the administration of which the court could if necessary undertake and control. ... [This] is a gift which ... could be wholly applied to the training ... of mediums other than what for convenience may be termed therapeutic mediums. I am not satisfied that a gift for that purpose is or may be in any sense of the words operative for the benefit of the public. Further, I am wholly unable to say, upon the evidence, that a trust for ... [this] purpose is a trust the administration of which the court could in any way undertake or control. It was contended that the court was not the tribunal to determine whether a gift ... was ... for the benefit of the public. It was said that the only judge of this was the donor ... So far as ... the personal or private view of the judge is immaterial, I agree; but so far as ... the donor ... is to determine whether the purpose is beneficial to the public, I respectfully disagree. If a testator by stating ... his view that a trust is beneficial to the public can establish that beyond question, trusts might be established in perpetuity for the promotion of all kinds of fantastic (though not unlawful) objects, of which the training of poodles to dance might be a mild example. In my opinion the question whether a gift is or may be operative for the public benefit is a question to be answered by the court by forming an opinion on the evidence before it ...'

Income Tax Special Purposes Commissioners v Pemsel [1891] AC 531 House of Lords (Lord Halsbury LC, Lord Macnaghten, Lord Watson, Lord Bramwell, Lord Herschell and Lord Morris)

Charity in law

Facts
Land was vested in the respondent on trust to apply the rents and profits for the missionary establishments of the Moravian Church. He applied to the Special Commissioners for Schedule A allowances extended to charitable trusts. The Commissioners refused, denying his was a charitable object, and the Queen's Bench Division refused him an order of mandamus. This was reversed in the Court of Appeal, and the Commissioners appealed to the Lords.

Held
The appeal would be dismissed.

Lord Halsbury LC:

'[The Statute 43 Eliz 1 c 4] is intituled "an Act to redress the misemployment of land goods and stocks of money heretofore given to charitable uses" ... [And] it is very intelligible ... that the Court of Chancery ... should have given the widest possible interpretation to an Act intended to remedy such abuses. The enumeration of charitable objects in the preamble ... was very soon interpreted not to be limited to the exact charities therein referred to. Where a purpose by analogy was deemed by the Court of Chancery to be within its spirit and intendment it was held to be "charitable".'

Lord Macnaghten:

'No doubt the popular meaning of the words "charity" and "charitable" does not coincide with their legal meaning: and no doubt it is easy enough to collect from the books a few decisions which seem to push the doctrine of the Court to the extreme, and to present a contrast between the two meanings in an aspect almost ludicrous. But, still, it is difficult to fix the point of divergence, and no one has yet succeeded in defining the popular meaning of the word "charity" ... How far, then, it may be asked, does the popular meaning of the word "charity" correspond with its legal meaning? "Charity" in its legal sense comprises four principal divisions: trusts for the relief of poverty; trusts for the advancement of education; trusts for the advancement of religion; and trusts for other purposes beneficial to the community, not falling under any of the preceding heads.'

Incorporated Council of Law Reporting for England and Wales v *Attorney-General* [1972] Ch 73 Court of Appeal (Russell, Sachs and Buckley LJJ)

Sources of the definition of charity

Facts

The object of the Council was 'The preparation and publication, in a convenient form, at a moderate price, and under gratuitous professional control, of Reports of Judicial Decisions of the Superior and Appellate Courts in England.' The Council was a non-profit making body whose reports were used by judges and the legal profession and others engaged in the study of law. The Charity Commissioners refused to register the Council as a charity. Foster J allowed an appeal by the Council against the Commissioners' decision.

Held

His decision would be affirmed. On the nature and definition of charity Sachs LJ said:

'The right of the Incorporated Council of Law Reporting to be registered as a charity under section 4 of the Charities Act 1960 depends on whether it is one "which is established for charitable purposes" (see the definition of "charity" in s45(1)). By section 46 "charitable purposes" is defined as meaning "purposes which are exclusively charitable according to the law of England and Wales". For the best part of four centuries the question whether the purposes of any given trust or institution are charitable has been decided by reference to the preamble of the Charitable Uses Act 1601 – "the Statute of Elizabeth I". Since 1891 the courts have followed the guidance given in the classic speech of Lord MacNaghten in *Income Tax Special Purposes Comrs* v *Pemsel* [1891] AC 531 where it is stated that "Charity" in its legal sense comprises four principal divisions. In every case since then the issue has been whether the purposes of any given trust or institution fell within one of those divisions. The result of the present case depends on whether the purposes of the council fall within the second – "trusts for the advancement of education", or alternatively within the fourth – "trusts for other purposes beneficial to the community" not falling within any of the other heads.

To come to a conclusion whether those purposes fall within either of the two above divisions – and, in particular, whether it falls within the fourth – it is necessary to have regard to what, since the judgment of Sir William Grant MR in *Morice* v *Bishop of Durham* (1805) 10 Ves 522 [see Chapter 1], has been termed "the spirit and intendment" of the above preamble, words commonly regarded as having the same meaning as "the equity of the statute". It so happens that there are available to use through judgments given in open court the contents of two documents substantially contemporaneous with the Statute of Elizabeth I which throw useful light both as to the spirit and intendment of that statute in relation to administration of the law in general and to the word "education" in reference thereto; the charters of an Inn of Chancery (Clifford's Inn) and an Inn of Court (Inner Temple) dated respectively 1618 and 1608. It is, however, preferable first to approach each of the questions that arise in the instant case apart from what can be learnt from these documents.

Before considering more closely what are the answers to these questions with the aid of the education to be derived from studying the judgments in the 41 reports cited to us and the mass of learning shown to have been devoted, at any rate, over the last two centuries to the relevant problems, it is convenient at the outset to mention some points which have often been repeated in those judgments. First, the word "charity" is "of all words in the English language ... one which more unmistakeably has a technical meaning in the strictest sense of the term ... peculiar to the law" (per Lord Macnaghten in *Pemsel*'s case), and that is "wide and elastic" (per Lord Ashbourne), and one that can include something quite outside the ordinary meaning the word has in popular speech (cf Lord Cozens-Hardy MR *Re Wedgewood* [1915] 1 Ch 113 [see Chapter 7].

It is thus necessary to eliminate from one's mind a natural allergy, stemming simply from the popular meaning of "charity", to the idea that law reporting might prove to be a charitable activity. Secondly, it is clear that the mere fact that charges on a commercial scale are made for services rendered by an institution does not of itself bar that institution from being held to be charitable – so long, at any rate, as all the profits must be retained for its purposes and none can ensure to the benefit of its individual members (cf *Scottish Burial Reform and Cremation Society Ltd* v *Glasgow City Corpn* [1968] AC 138. Thirdly, that there have, over at any rate the past century, been a number of references to the oddity that the tests by which the courts decide whether an institution is charitable depend entirely on the preamble of the Statute of Elizabeth I. The most recent is one opening that this state of affairs was "almost incredible to anyone not familiar with this branch of the English law" (per Lord Upjohn in the *Scottish Burial case*). To this I will return later.

... It would be odd indeed and contrary to the trend of judicial decisions if the institution and maintenance of a library for the study of a learned subject or of something rightly called a science did not at least prima facie fall within the phrase "advancement of education", whatever be the age of those frequenting it. The same reasoning must apply to the provision of books forming the raw material for that study, whether they relate to chemical data or to case histories in hospitals; and I can find no good reason for excluding case law as developed in the courts. If that is the correct approach, then when the institution is one whose individual members make no financial gain from the provision of that material and is one which itself can make no use of its profits except to provide further and better material, why is the purpose not charitable? ...

Where the purpose of producing a book is to enable a specified subject, and a learned subject at that to be studied, it is in my judgment, published for the advancement of education, as this, of course, includes as regards the Statute of Elizabeth I the advancement of learning. That remains its purpose despite the fact that professional men – be they lawyers, doctors or chemists – use the knowledge acquired to earn their living. One must not confuse the results, flowing from the achievement of a purpose with the purpose itself, any more than one should have regard to the motives of those who set that purpose in motion.'

Russell LJ took the view that it was a purpose beneficial to the community and explained the approach of the court in deciding if a trust fell within this category at p88:

'I come now to the question whether, if the main purpose of the Association is (as I think it is) to further the sound development and administration of the law in this country, and if (as I think it is) that is a purpose beneficial to the community or of general public utility, that purpose is charitable according to the law of England and Wales. On this point the law is rooted in the Statute of Elizabeth, a statute whose object was the oversight and reform of abuses in the administration of property devoted by donors to purposes which were regarded as worthy of such protection as being charitable. The preamble to the statute listed certain examples of purposes which were regarded as worthy of such protection. These were from an early stage regarded merely as examples, and have through the centuries been regarded as examples or guide-posts for the courts in the differing circumstances of a developing civilisation and economy. Sometimes recourse has been had by the courts to the instances given in the preamble in order to see whether in a given case sufficient analogy may be found with something specifically stated in the preamble, or sufficient analogy with some decided case in which already a previous sufficient analogy has been found. Of this approach perhaps the most obvious example is the provision of crematoria by analogy with the provision of burial grounds by analogy with the upkeep of churchyards by analogy with the repair of churches. On other occasions a decision in favour or against a purpose being charitable has been based on terms on a more general question whether the purpose is or is not within "the spirit and intendment" of the Elizabethan statute and in particular its preamble. Again (and at an early stage in development) whether the purpose is within "the equity" or within "the mischief" of the statute. Again whether the purpose is charitable "in the same sense" as purposes within the purview of the statute. I have much sympathy with those who say that these phrases do little of themselves to elucidate any particular problem. "Tell me", they say, "what you define when you speak of spirit, intendment, equity, mischief, the same sense, and I will tell you whether a purpose is charitable according to law. But you never define. All you do is sometimes to say that a purpose is none of these things. I can understand it when you say that the preservation of sea walls is for the safety of lives and property, and therefore by analogy the voluntary provision of lifeboats and fire brigades are charitable. I can even follow you as far as crematoria. But these other generalities teach me nothing." I say I have much sympathy for such an approach; but it seems to me to be unduly and improperly restrictive. The Statute of Elizabeth was a statute to reform abuses; in such circumstances and in that age the courts of this country were not inclined to be restricted in their implementation of Parliament's desire for reform to particular examples given by the statute, and they deliberately kept open their ability to intervene when they thought necessary in cases not specifically mentioned, by applying as the test whether any particular case of abuse of funds or property was within the "mischief" or the "equity" of the statute.

For myself I believe that this rather vague and undefined approach is the correct one, with analogy its handmaid, and that when considering Lord Macnaghten's fourth category in *Pemsel's* case of "other purposes beneficial to the community" (or as phrased by Sir Samuel Romilly "objects of general public utility") the courts, in consistently saying that not all such are necessarily charitable in law, are in substance accepting that if a purpose is shown to be so beneficial or of such utility it is prima facie charitable in law, but have left open a line of retreat based on the equity of the statute in case they are faced with a purpose (eg a political purpose) which could not have been within the contemplation of the statute even if the then legislators had been endowed with the gift of foresight into the circumstances of later centuries.

In a case such as the present, in which in my view the object cannot be thought otherwise than beneficial to the community and of general public utility, I believe the proper question to ask is whether there are any grounds for holding it to be outside the equity of the statute; and I think the answer to that is here in the negative. I have already touched on its essential importance to our rule of law. If I look at the somewhat random examples in the preamble to the statute I find in the repair of bridges, havens, causeways, sea banks and highways examples of matters which if not looked after by private enterprise must be a proper function and responsibility of government, which would afford strong ground for a statutory expression by Parliament of anxiety to prevent misappropriation of funds voluntarily dedicated to such matters. It cannot I think be doubted that if there were not a competent and reliable set of reports of judicial decisions, it would be a proper function and responsibility of government to secure their provision for the due administration of the law. It was argued that the specific topics in the preamble that I have mentioned are all concerned with concrete matters, and that so also is the judicially accepted opinion that the provision of a court house is a charitable purpose. But whether the search be for analogy or for the equity of the statute this seems to me to be too narrow or refined an approach. I cannot accept that the provision, in order to facilitate the proper administration of the law, of the walls and other physical facilities of a court house is a charitable purpose, but that the dissemination by accurate and selective reporting of knowledge of a most important part of the law to be there administered is not.

In my judgment accordingly the purpose for which the Association is established is exclusively charitable in the sense of Lord MacNaghten's fourth category.'

IRC v *Baddeley* [1955] AC 572 House of Lords (Viscount Simonds, Lord Porter, Lord Reid, Lord Tucker and Lord Somervell)

Wholly and exclusively charitable: public benefit

Facts
Two conveyances of land were made to trustees to permit it to be 'used by the leaders for the time being of the Stratford Newtown Methodist Mission for the promotion of the religious, social and physical well-being of persons resident in the County Boroughs of West Ham and Leyton ... by the provision of facilities ... for the social and physical training and recreation ... and by promoting and encouraging all forms of such activities as are calculated to contribute to the health and well being of such persons ...' The trustees claimed a reduced rate of stamp duty on the conveyance on the ground that these purposes were charitable.

Held
The objects of the trust were not wholly and exclusively charitable; the use of the word 'social' would permit the property to be used for non-charitable purposes. Further, the trust did not satisfy the public benefit requirement in any event.

Viscount Simonds:

'... The starting point of the argument must be, that this charity (if it be a charity) falls within the fourth class in Lord MacNaghten's classification. It must therefore be a trust which is, to use the words of Sir Samuel Romilly in *Morice* v *Bishop of Durham* (1805) 10 Ves 522 [see Chapter 1] of "general public utility" and the question is what these words mean. It is, indeed, an essential feature of all "charity" in the legal sense that there must be in it some element of public benefit, whether the purpose is educational, religious or eleemosynary: see the recent case of *Oppenheim* v *Tobacco Securities Trust Co Ltd* [1951] AC 297 and, as I have said elsewhere, it is possible, particularly in view of the so-called "poor relations cases", the scope of which may one day have to be considered, that a different degree of public benefit is requisite according to the class in which the charity is said to fall. But it is said that if a charity falls within the fourth class, it must be for the benefit of the whole community or at least of all the inhabitants of a sufficient area. And it has been urged with much force that, if, as Lord Greene said in *In re Strakosch* [1949] Ch 529, this fourth class is represented in the preamble to the Statute of Elizabeth by the repair of bridges, etc, and possibly by the maintenance of Houses of Correction, the class of beneficiaries or potential beneficiaries cannot be further narrowed down. Some confusion has arisen from the fact that a trust of general public utility, however general and however public, cannot be of equal utility to all and may be of immediate utility to few. A sea wall, the prototype of this class in the preamble, is of remote, if any, utility to those who live in the heart of the Midlands. But there is no doubt that a trust for the maintenance of sea walls generally or along a particular stretch of coast is a good charitable trust. Nor, as it appears to me, is the validity of a trust affected by the fact that by its very nature only a limited number of people are likely to avail themselves, or are perhaps even capable of availing themselves, of its benefits. It is easy, for instance, to imagine a charity which has for its object some form of child welfare, of which the immediate beneficiaries could only be persons of tender age. Yet this would satisfy any test of general public utility. It may be said that it would satisfy the test because the indirect benefit of such a charity would extend far beyond its direct beneficiaries, and that aspect of the matter has probably not been out of sight. Indirect benefit is certainly an aspect which must have influenced the decision of the 'cruelty to animal' cases. But, I doubt whether this sort of rationalisation helps to explain a branch of the law which has developed empirically and by analogy upon analogy.

It is, however, in my opinion, particularly important in cases falling within the fourth category to keep firmly in mind the necessity of the element of general public utility, and I would not relax this rule. For here is a slippery slope. In the case under appeal the intended beneficiaries are a class within a class; they are those of the inhabitants of a particular area who are members of a particular church: the area is comparatively large and populous and the members may be numerous. but, if this trust is charitable for them; does it cease to be charitable as the area narrows down and the numbers diminish? Suppose the area is confined to a single street and the beneficiaries to those whose creed commands few adherents: or suppose the class is one that is determined not by religious belief but by membership of a particular profession or by pursuit of a particular trade. These were considerations which influenced the House in the recent case of *Oppenheim*. That was a case of an educational trust, but I think that they have even greater weight in the case of trusts which by their nominal classification depend for their validity upon general public utility.

It is pertinent, then, to ask how far your Lordships might regard yourselves bound by authority to hold the trusts now under review valid charitable trusts, if the only question in issue was the sufficiency of the public element. I do not repeat what I said in the case of *Williams' Trustees* v *Inland Revenue Commissoners* [1947] AC 447 about *Goodman* v *Mayor of Saltash* (1882) 7 App Cas 633 and the cases that closely followed it. Further consideration of them does not change the view that I then expressed, which in effect indorsed the opinion of the learned editor of the last edition of Tudor on Charities. More relevant is the case of *Verge* v *Somerville* [1924] AC 496. In that case, in which the issue was as to the validity of a gift "to the trustees of the Repatriation Fund or other similar fund for the benefit of New South Wales returned soldiers", Lord Wrenbury, delivering the judgment of the Judicial Committee, said that, to be a charity, a trust must be "for the benefit of the community or of an appreciably important class of the community. The inhabitants", he said "of a parish or town or any particular class of such inhabitants, may, for instance, be the objects of such a gift, but private individuals, or a fluctuating body of private individuals, cannot." Here, my Lords, are two expressions: "an appreciably important class of the community" and "any particular class of such inhabitants", to which in any case it is not easy to give a precise quantitative or qualitative meaning. But I think that in the consideration of them the difficulty has sometimes been increased by failing to observe the distinction, at which I hinted earlier in this opinion, between a form of relief extended to the whole community yet by its very nature advantageous only to the few and a form of relief accorded to a selected few out of a larger number equally willing and able to take advantage of it. Of the former type repatriated New South Wales soldiers would serve as a clear example. To me it would not seem arguable that they did not form an adequate class of the community for the purpose of the particular charity that was being established. It was with this type of case that Lord Wrenbury was dealing, and his words are apt to deal with it. Somewhat different considerations arise if the form which the purporting charity takes is something of general utility which is nevertheless made available not to the whole public but only to a selected body of the public – an important class of the public it may be. For example, a bridge which is available for all the public may undoubtedly be a charity and it is indifferent how many people use it. But confine its use to a selected number of persons, however numerous and important: it is then clearly not a charity. It is not of general public utility: for it does not serve the public purpose which its nature qualifies it to serve.

Bearing this distinction in mind, though I am well aware that in its application it may often be very difficult to draw the line between public and private purposes, I should in the present case conclude that a trust cannot qualify as a charity within the fourth class in *Income Tax Commissioners* v *Pemsel* [1891] AC 531 if the beneficiaries are a class of persons not only confined to a particular area but selected from within it by reference to a particular creed. The Master of the Rolls in his judgment cites a rhetorical question asked by Mr Stamp in argument: "Who has ever heard of a bridge to be crossed only by impecunious Methodists?" The reductio ad absurdum is sometimes a cogent form of argument, and this illustration serves to show the danger of conceding the quality of charity to a purpose which is not a public purpose. What is true of a bridge for Methodists is equally true of any other public purpose falling within the fourth class and of the adherents of any other creed.

The passage that I have cited from *Verge* v *Somerville* refers also (not, I think, for the first time) to "private individuals" or a "fluctuating body of private individuals" in contradistinction to a class of the community or of the inhabitants of a locality. This is a difficult conception to grasp: the distinction between a class of the community and the private individuals from time to time composing it is elusive. But, if it has any bearing on the present case, I would suppose that the beneficiaries, a body of persons arbitrarily chosen and impermanent, fall more easily into the latter than the former category.'

Commentary
This case led to the passing of the Recreational Charities Act 1958.

IRC v *City of Glasgow Police Athletic Association* [1953] AC 380 House of Lords (Lord Cohen, Lord Morton, Lord Normand, Lord Reid and Lord Oaksey)

Recreational charities: public benefit

Facts
The Association provided recreation activities and facilities for members of the police. For tax purposes the question of its charitable status needed to be clarified.

Held (Lord Oaksey dissenting)
The Association had official importance and a public aspect, but the provision of recreation was not charitable in itself and could not be said to be for the maintenance of the services or conferring a public benefit, and accordingly was not charitable. Though this was so of recreational facilities, but Lord Normand said:

'I would hold further that gifts or contributions exclusively for the purpose of promoting the efficiency of the police forces and the preservation of public order are by analogy charitable gifts.'

IRC v *Educational Grants Association Ltd* [1967] Ch 123 Chancery Division (Pennycuick J)

Charitable trusts and public benefit

Facts
The association was established for the advancement of education and it had a close relation with Metal Box from which it received most of its income. On average 76-85 per cent of the association's income was applied for the education of children of persons having some tie with Metal Box Ltd. Tax relief was claimed on the ground that the association was charitable.

Held
There was no public benefit. Pennycuick J observed on *Re Koettgen's Will Trust* [1954] Ch 252:

'... I find considerable difficulty in the *Koettgen*'s decision. I should have thought that a trust for the public with preference for a private class comprised in the public might be regarded as a trust for the application of income at the discretion of the trustees between charitable and non-charitable objects. However, I am not concerned here to dispute the validity of the *Koettgen*'s decision.'

IRC v McMullen [1981] AC 1 House of Lords (Lord Hailsham LC, Lord Diplock, Lord Salmon, Lord Russell and Lord Keith)

Charity for the furtherance of education

Facts

The Football Association set up a trust known as the Football Association Youth Trust, the main objects of which were 'the furtherance of education of Schools and Universities in any part of the United Kingdom encouraging and facilitating the playing of Association Football or other games and sports at such Schools and Universities and thus assisting to ensure that due attention is given to the physical education and character development of pupils at such Schools and Universities ...'

Held

The trust was a valid charitable trust for the advancement of education as the purpose of the settlor was to promote the physical education and development of pupils at schools as an addition to such part of their education as related to their mental education. Education could not be restricted to mean formal instruction in the classrooms or the playground because the idea of education as set out by the Education Act 1944 expressly recognised the contribution extra-curricular activities and voluntary societies or bodies could make to the statutory system of education.

Lord Hailsham LC:

> 'But in deciding what is or is not an educational purpose for the young in 1980 it is not irrelevant to point out what Parliament considered to be educational for the young in 1944 when, by the Education Act of that year in ss7 and 53 (which are still on the statute book), Parliament attempted to lay down what was then intended to be the statutory system of education organised by the State, and the duties of the local education authorities and the Minister in establishing and maintaining the system. Those sections are so germane to the present issue that I cannot forbear to quote them both. Section 7 provides (in each of the sections the emphasis being mine):
>
> > "The statutory system of public education shall be organised in three progressive stages to be known as primary education, secondary education, and further education; and it shall be the duty of the local education authority for every area, so far as their powers extend, to contribute towards the spiritual, moral, mental, and *physical* development of the community by securing that efficient education throughout those stages shall be available to meet the needs of the population of their area."
>
> and in s53 of the same Act it is said:
>
> > "(1) It shall be the duty of every local education authority to secure that the facilities for primary, secondary and further education provided for their area include adequate facilities for recreation and social and physical training, and for that purpose a local education authority, with the approval of the Secretary of State, may establish, maintain and manage, or assist the establishment maintenance, and management of camps, holiday classes, playing fields, play centres, and other places (including playgrounds, gymnasiums, and swimming baths not appropriated to any school or college), at which facilities for recreation and for such training as aforesaid are available for persons receiving primary, secondary or further education, and may organise games, expeditions and other activities for such persons, and may defray or contribute towards the expenses thereof.
> >
> > (2) A local education authority, in making arrangements for the provision of facilities or the organisation of activities under the powers conferred on them by the last foregoing subsection shall, in particular, have regard to the expediency of co-operating with any voluntary societies or bodies whose objects include the provision of facilities or the organisation of activities of a similar character."
>
> There is no trace in these sections of an idea of education limited to the development of mental vocational or practical skills, to grounds or facilities the special perquisite of particular schools, or of any schools or colleges, or term time, or particular localities, and there is express recognition of the contribution which

extra-curricular activities and voluntary societies or bodies can play even in the promotion of the purely statutory system envisaged by the Act. In the light of s7 in particular I would be very reluctant to confine the meaning of education to formal instruction in the classroom or even the playground, and I consider them sufficiently wide to cover all the activities envisaged by the settlor in the present case. One of the affidavits filed on the part of the Crown referred to the practices of ancient Sparta. I am not sure that this particular precedent is an entirely happy one, but from a careful perusal of Plato's Republic I doubt whether its author would have agreed with Stamp LJ in regarding "physical education development" as an elusive phrase, or as other than an educational charity, at least when used in association with the formal education of the young during the period when they are pupils of schools or in statu pupillari at universities.

It is, of course, true that no authority exactly in point could be found which is binding on your Lordships in the instant appeal. Nevertheless, I find the first instance case of *Re Mariette* [1915] 2 Ch 284, a decision of Eve J both stimulating and instructive. Mr Morritt properly reminded us that this concerned a bequest effectively tied to a particular institution. Nevertheless, I cannot forbear to quote a phrase from the judgment, always bearing in mind the danger of quoting out of context. Eve J said:

> "No one of sense could be found to suggest that between those ages (10 to 19) any boy can be properly educated unless at least as much attention is given to the development of his body as is given to the development of his mind."

Apart from the limitation to the particular institution I would think that these words apply as well to the settlor's intention in the instant appeal as to the testator's in *Re Mariette*, and I regard the limitation to the pupils of schools and universities in the instant case as a sufficient association with the provision of formal education to prevent any danger of vagueness in the object of the trust or irresponsibility or capriciousness in application by the trustees. I am far from suggesting that either the concept of education or of physical education even for the young is capable of indefinite extension. On the contrary, I do not think that the courts have as yet explored the extent to which elements of organisation, instruction or the disciplined inculcation of information, instruction or skill may limit the whole concept of education. I believe that in some ways it will prove more extensive, in others more restrictive than has been thought hitherto. But it is clear at least to me that the decision in *Re Mariette* is not to be read in a sense which confines its application for ever to gifts to a particular institution. It has been extended already in *Re Mellody* [1918] 1 Ch 228 to gifts for annual treats for schoolchildren in a particular locality (another decision of Eve J), to playgrounds for children (*Re Chesters*, possibly *not* educational, but referred to in *Inland Revenue Comrs* v *Baddeley* [1955] AC 572); to a children's outing (*Re Ward's Estate* (1937) 81 Sol Jo 397), to a prize for chess to Boys and young men resident in the City of Portsmouth (*Re Dupree's Deed Trusts* [1945] Ch 16, a decision of Vaisey J), and for the furthering of the Boy Scouts movement by helping to purchase sites for camping, outfits etc (*Re Webber* [1954] 1 WLR 1500, another decision by Vaisey J). In that case Vaisey J is reported as saying:

> "I am very surprised to hear anyone suggest that the Boy Scouts Movement, as distinguished from the Boy Scouts Association or the Boy Scouts Organisation, is other than an educational charity. I should have thought that it was well-settled and well understood that the objects of the organisation of boy scouts were educational, and none the less educational by reason of the fact that the education is, no doubt, of a very special kind."

It is important to remember that in the instant appeal we are dealing with the concept of physical education and development of the young deliberately associated by the settlor with the status of pupillage in schools or universities (of which, according to the evidence, about 95% are within the age group 17 to 22). We are not dealing with adult education, physical or otherwise, as to which some considerations may be different. Whether one looks at the statute or the cases, the picture of education when applied to the young which emerges is complex and varied, but not, to borrow Stamp LJ's epithet, "elusive". It is the picture of a balanced and systematic process of instruction, training and practice containing, to borrow from s7 of the 1944 Act, both spiritual, moral, mental and physical elements, the totality of which, in any given case, may vary with, for instance, the availability of teachers and facilities, and the potentialities, limitations and individual preferences of the pupils. But the totality of the process consists as much in the balance between each of the elements as of the enumeration of the thing learned or the places in which the activities are carried on. I reject any idea which would cramp the education of the young within the school or university syllabus, confine it within the school or university campus, limit it to formal instruction, or render it devoid of pleasure in the exercise of skill. It is expressly acknowledged to be a subject in which the voluntary donor can exercise his generosity, and I can find nothing contrary to the law of charity which prevents a donor providing a trust which is designed to improve the balance between the various elements which go into the education of the young. That is what in my view the object of the instant settlement seeks to do.

I am at pains to disclaim the view that the conception of this evolving, and therefore not static, view of education is capable of infinite abuse or, even worse, proving void for uncertainty. Quite apart from the doctrine of the benignant approach to which I have already referred, and which undoubtedly comes to the assistance of settlors in danger of attack for uncertainty, I am content to adopt the approach of my predecessor Lord Loreburn LC in *Weir* v *Crum-Brown* [1908] AC 162, to which attention was drawn by counsel for the Attorney-General, that if the bequest to a class of persons, as here capable of application by the trustees, or, failing them, the court, the gift is not void for uncertainty. Lord MacNaghten also said:

> "The testator has taken pains to provide competent judges. It is for the trustees to consider and determine the value of the service on which a candidate may rest his claim to participate in the testator's bounty."

Mutatis mutandis, I think this kind of reasoning should apply here. Granted that the question of application may present difficulties for the trustees, or, failing them, for the court, nevertheless it is capable of being applied, for the concept in the mind of the settlor is an object sufficiently clear, is exclusively for the advancement of education, and, in the hands of competent judges, is capable of application.

I also wish to be on my guard against the "slippery slope" argument of which I see a reflection in Stamp LJ's reference to "hunting, shooting and fishing". It seems to me that that is an argument with which Vaisey J dealt effectively in *Re Dupree's Deed Trusts* in which he validated the chess prize. He said:

> "I think this case may be a little near the line, and I decide it without attempting to lay down any general propositions. One feels, perhaps, that one is on rather a slippery slope. If chess, why not draughts: if draughts, why not bezique, and so on, through to bridge, whist, and, by another route, stamp collecting and the acquisition of birds' eggs? When those particular pursuits come up for consideration in connection with the problem whether or not there is in existence a charitable trust, the problem will have to be faced and dealt with."

My Lords, for these reasons I reach the conclusion that the trust is a valid charitable gift for the advancement of education, which, after all, it what it claims to be. The conclusion follows that the appeal should be allowed, the judgments appealed from be reversed ...'

King, Re [1923] 1 Ch 243 Chancery Division (Romer J)

Motive of donor irrelevant

Facts
The testatrix left a gift for the erection of a memorial stained-glass window. It was contended her motive was to perpetuate her memory not to beautify the church.

Held
The motive was irrelevant. The objective result would be to beautify the church which was a valid charitable object for the advancement of religion and the gift was valid.

Koeppler's Will Trusts, Re [1985] 2 All ER 869 Court of Appeal (O'Connor, Slade and Robert Goff LJJ).

Condition precedent does not defeat charitable intention

Facts
The testator, who died in April 1979, left a share of his residuary estate '... for the Warden and the Chairman of the Academic Advisory Council for the time being of the institution known as Wilton Park ... for the benefit at their discretion of the said institution so long as Wilton Park remains a British contribution to the formation of an informed international public opinion and to the promotion of greater co-operation in Europe and the West in general ...'.

The question arose, inter alia, whether the gift was a valid charitable trust. The testator had used the term 'Wilton Park' as the name of conferences which he had personally organised in his lifetime. There was no such institution and 'Wilton Park' was neither a corporate nor an unincorporated body. The conferences organised by the testator had brought together politicians, academics, civil servants, industrialists and journalists from OECD countries so that they could exchange views on political, economic and social issues. The conferences were not intended to follow a particular party political line.

Held
1. The gift was on its true construction, a gift for the purposes of Wilton Park, as these purposes were for the advancement of education the gift was charitable.
2. The reference in the gift to 'the formation of an informed international public opinion and to the promotion of greater co-operation in Europe and the West in general' were not, on the true construction of the gift, the purpose or purposes for which the gift was made. These were merely conditions precedent to the gift taking effect.

Slade J:

'... There are two particular points which have caused me to hesitate before finally concluding that this gift is of a charitable nature. First, I have already mentioned the wide range of topics which are discussed at Wilton Park conferences, some of which could be said to have a political flavour. We were referred to a decision of my own in *McGovern* v *A-G* [1982] Ch 321 ...

However, in the present case, as I have already mentioned, the activities of Wilton Park are not of a party political nature. Nor, so far as the evidence shows are they designed to procure changes in the laws or governmental policy of this or any other country; even when they touch on political matters, they constitute, so far as I can see, no more than genuine attempts in an objective manner to ascertain and disseminate the truth. In these circumstances, I think that no objections to the trust arise on a political score similar to those which arose in the *McGovern* case ...

... Does the vague and accordingly non-charitable nature of these aims and aspirations (ie the conditions precedent to the gift: see above) prevent the gift from taking effect as charitable? ... In the present case ... there is no sufficient reason why the wide and vague scope of the testator's stated ultimate aims in doing the work which he did, and in making the testamentary gift which he did, should be held to destroy the otherwise admittedly educational nature of that work and that gift.'

Koettgen's Will Trusts, Re [1954] Ch 252 Chancery Division (Upjohn J)

Public benefit: later limitations

Facts
The testatrix bequeathed her residuary estate on trust 'for the promotion and furtherance of commercial education ...' She then outlined in wide terms who the eligible beneficiaries were to be and added 'it is my wish that the trustees shall give preference to any employees of John Batt & Co (London) Ltd or any members of the families of such employees ... Provided that the total income to be available for benefiting the preferred beneficiaries shall not in any one year be more than 75 per cent of the total available income for that year.'

Held
The gift to the primary class from whom the trustees could select the beneficiaries contained the necessary element of public benefit, and it was at the stage when the primary class of eligible persons was ascertained that the question of public benefit arose to be decided. Therefore, the direction to give preference to certain employees did not deprive the trust of charitable status.

London Hospital Medical College v *Inland Revenue Commissioners* [1976] 1 WLR 613 Chancery Division (Brightman J)

An association supporting an educational charity is itself charitable

Facts
The London Hospital Medical College had a students' union which had among its objects the promotion, encouragement and co-ordination of social, cultural and athletic activities of members and to add to the comfort and enjoyment of the students. Membership of the union was not confined to college students but included staff of the hospital and college such as newly qualified doctors and dentists. All members of the union were elected and paid subscriptions and there was never a case of anyone eligible not being elected. The union regarded itself as part of and incidental to and under the control of the college and the college made substantial contributions to it both directly and indirectly and maintained its premises. Up until 1971 the Inland Revenue treated the union as charitable but in that year and in 1972 they wrote to the college stating that they no longer considered the union's objects as exclusively charitable as it existed solely for the benefit of its members and not for anyone who was at the college as a medical student. It was submitted in defence that the union was a charity either because it formed an integral part of the college, itself a charity, or because its purposes were ancillary to those of the college.

Held
The union was charitable as it existed solely to further and did further the educational purpose of the college.

Brightman J:

> '... A club which provides athletic facilities and social activities for its members is not, per se charitable. Therefore, the union, standing alone is not charitable under the general law. But, if the union exists solely to further and does further, the educational purposes of the college, then in my judgment it is clearly charitable, *Re Coxen* [1948] Ch 747 was decided on this principle ... If, put shortly, the union existed for the benefit of the college, it would be immaterial that the union also provided a personal benefit for the individual students who were elected members of the union and chose to make use of its facilities. I would suppose that most schools of learning confer a personal benefit on the individual scholars who are admitted thereto. X, an individual scholar, is not per se an object of charity. The school of learning that X attends is nevertheless charitable if the school exists for the benefit of the community (ie public benefit). The fact that X receives a personal benefit is incidental to the implementation of the purposes of the charity ...'

Lucas, Re [1922] 2 Ch 52 Chancery Division (Russell J)

Charitable intent inferred from the nature of the gift

Facts
The income of a fund was to be given 'to the oldest inhabitants of Gunville to the amount of 5s per week each'.

Held
The gift was charitable because the smallness of the amount indicated that it was intended for the relief of the poor.

McGovern v *Attorney-General* [1982] Ch 321 Chancery Division (Slade J)

Primarily political objects cannot be charitable

Facts
In 1977 Amnesty International, an unincorporated, non-profit making body set up to ensure that prisoners of conscience throughout the world were treated in accordance with the United Nations declaration on human rights, set up a trust to administer those of its objects which were believed to be charitable. The objects of the trusts were (a) the relief of prisoners of conscience, (b) attempting to secure the release of prisoners of conscience (c) procuring the abolition of torture or inhuman or degrading treatment or punishment (d) research into the maintenance and observance of human rights (e) the dissemination of the results of such research (f) doing all such other things as would promote these charitable objects. The trust deed then stated that the objects were to be restricted to those things which were charitable according to United Kingdom law. The trustees applied to have the trust registered as a charity. This was refused by the Charity Commissioners so an application was made to the court seeking a declaration as to whether these objects were charitable.

Held
Charitable status could not be granted because (a), (b) and (c) were essentially political objects. However, (d) and (e) were charitable but as the trust was not 'wholly and exclusively' charitable it could not be registered.

Slade J:

'... Save in the case of gifts to classes of poor persons, a trust must always be shown to promote a public benefit of a nature recognised by the courts as being such, if it is to qualify as being charitable. The question whether a purpose will or may operate for the public benefit is to be answered by the court forming an opinion on the evidence before it; see *National Anti-Vivisection Society* v *Inland Revenue Comrs* per Lord Wright. No doubt in some cases a purpose may be so manifestly beneficial to the public that it would be absurd to call evidence on this point. In many other instances, however, the element of public benefit may be much more debatable. Indeed, in some cases the court will regard this element of being incapable of proof one way or the other and thus will inevitably decline to recognise the trust as being of a charitable nature.

Trusts to promote changes in the law of England are generally regarded as falling into the latter category and as being non-charitable for this reason. Thus Lord Parker said in *Bowman* v *Secular Society Ltd* [1917] AC 406:

"The abolition of religious tests, the disestablishment of the Church, the secularisation of education, the alteration of the law touching religion or marriage, or the observation of the Sabbath, are purely political objects. Equity has always refused to recognise such objects as charitable. It is true that a gift to an association formed for their attainment may, if the association be unincorporated, be upheld as an absolute gift to its members, or, if the association be incorporated, as an absolute gift to the corporate body; but a trust for the attainment of political objects has always been held invalid, not because it is illegal, for everyone is at liberty to advocate or promote by any lawful means a change in the law, but because the Court has no means of judging whether a proposed change in the law will or will not be for the public benefit, and therefore cannot say that a gift to secure the change is a charitable gift. The same considerations apply when there is a trust for the publication of a book. The Court will examine the book, and if its objects be charitable in the legal sense it will give effect to the trust as a good charity: *Thornton* v *Howe* (1862) 31 Beav 14; but if its objects be political it will refuse to enforce the trust: *De Themmines* v *De Bonneval* (1828) 5 Russ 288 ..."

... From the passages from the speeches of Lord Parker, Lord Wright and Lord Simonds which I have read, I extract the principle that the court will not regard as charitable a trust of which a main object is to procure an alteration of the law of the United Kingdom for one or both of two reasons. First, the court will ordinarily have no sufficient means of judging, as a matter of evidence, whether the proposed change will or will not be for the public benefit. Second, even if the evidence suffices to enable it to form a prima facie opinion that a change in the law is desirable, it must still decide the case on the principle that the law is right as it stands, since to do otherwise would be to usurp the functions of the legislature. I interpret the point made by Lord Simonds concerning the position of the Attorney-General as merely illustrating some of the anomalies and undesirable consequences that might ensue if the courts began to encroach on the functions of the legislature by ascribing charitable status to trusts of which a main object is to procure a change in the law of the United Kingdom, as being for the public benefit...

... Thus far, the only types of political trust to which I have directed specific attention have been those of which a main object is to procure a change in the law of this country. The principles established by *Bowman's* case and the *National Anti-Vivisection Society* case will render such trusts non-charitable, whether or not they are of a party political nature. Conversely, however, several cases cited to me illustrate that trusts of which a main object is to promote the interests of a particular political party in this country fail to achieve charitable status, even though they are not directed towards any particular change in English law: see, for example, *Bonar Law Memorial Trust* v *Inland Revenue Comrs* (1933) 49 TLR 220 and *Re Hopkinson (deceased)* (1949) 1 All ER 346. In my judgment any such trusts are plainly "political trusts" within the spirit, if not the letter, of Lord Parker's pronouncement, and the same reasons for the court's refusing to enforce them would apply, but a fortiori. Since their nature would ex hypothesi be very controversial, the court could be faced with even greater difficulties in determining whether the objects of the trust would be for the public benefit; correspondingly, it would be at even greater risk of encroaching on the functions of the legislature and prejudicing its reputation for political impartiality, if it were to promote such objects by enforcing the trust.

I now turn to consider the status of a trust of which a main object is to secure the alteration of the laws of a foreign country. The mere fact that the trust was intended to be carried out abroad would not by itself necessarily deprive it of charitable status. A number of trusts to be executed outside this country have been upheld as charities, though the judgment of Evershed MR in *Camille and Henry Dreyfus Foundation Inc* v *Inland Revenue Comrs* [1964] Ch 672 illustrates that certain types of trust, for example trusts for the setting out of soldiers or the repair of bridges or causeways, might be acceptable as charities only if they were to be executed in the United Kingdom. The point with which I am at present concerned is whether a trust of which a direct and main object is to secure a change in the laws of a foreign country can ever be regarded as charitable under English law. Though I do not think that any authority cited to me precisely covers the point, I have come to the clear conclusion that it cannot ...

... In my judgment, however, there remain overwhelming reasons why such a trust still cannot be regarded as charitable. All the reasoning of Lord Parker in *Bowman* v *Secular Society Ltd* seems to me to apply *a fortiori* in such a case. A fortiori the court will have no adequate means of judging whether a proposed change in the law of a foreign country will or will not be for the public benefit. Evershed MR in *Camille and Henry Dreyfus Foundation Inc* v *Inland Revenue Comrs* expressed the prima facie view that the community which has to be considered in this context, even in the case of a trust to be executed abroad, is the community of the United Kingdom. Assuming that this is the right test, the court in applying it would still be bound to take account of the probable effects of attempts to procure the proposed legislation, or of its actual enactment, on the inhabitants of the country concerned, which would doubtless have a history and social structure quite different from that of the United Kingdom. Whatever might be its view as to the content of the relevant law from the standpoint of an English lawyer, it would, I think, have no satisfactory means of judging such probable effects on the local community.

Furthermore, before ascribing charitable status to an English trust of which a main object was to secure the alteration of a foreign law, the court would also, I conceive, be bound to consider the consequences for this country as a matter of public policy. In a number of such cases there would arise a substantial prima facie risk that such a trust, if enforced, could prejudice the relations of this country with the foreign country concerned (cf *Habershon* v *Vardon* (1851) 4 De G & Sm 461. The court would have no satisfactory means of assessing the extent of such risk, which would not be capable of being readily dealt with by evidence and would be a matter more for political than for legal judgment. For all these reasons, I conclude that a trust of which a main purpose is to procure a change in the laws of a foreign country is a trust for the attainment of political objects within the spirit of Lord Parker's pronouncement and, as such, is non-charitable.

Thus far, I have been considering trusts of which a main purpose is to achieve changes in the law itself or which are of a party political nature. Under any legal system, however, the government and its various authorities, administrative and judicial, will have wide discretionary powers vested in them, within the framework of the existing law. If a principal purpose of a trust is to procure a reversal of government policy or of particular administrative decisions of governmental authorities, does it constitute a trust for political purposes falling within the spirit of Lord Parker's pronouncement? In my judgment it does. If a trust of this nature is to be executed in England, the court will ordinarily have no sufficient means of determining whether the desired reversal would be beneficial to the public, and in any event could not properly encroach on the functions of the executive, acting intra vires, by holding that it should be acting in some other manner. If it is a trust which is to be executed abroad, the court will not have sufficient means of satisfactorily judging, as a matter of evidence, whether the proposed reversal would be beneficial to the community in the relevant sense, after all its consequences, local and international, had been taken into account.

It may be added that Lord Normand, in the *National Anti-Vivisection Society* case specifically equated legislative change and changes by way of government administration in the present context. As he said:

"The society seems to me to proclaim that its purpose is a legislative change of policy towards scientific experiments on animals, the consummation of which will be an Act prohibiting all such experiments. I regard it as clear that a society professing these purposes is a political association and not a charity. If for legislative changes a change by means of government administration was substituted the result would be the same."

If the crucial test whether a trust is charitable formulated by Lord Simonds, namely the competence of the court to control and reform it, is applied, I think one is again driven to the conclusion that trusts of the nature now under discussion, which are to be executed abroad, cannot qualify as charities any more than if they are to be executed in this country. The court, in considering whether particular methods of carrying out or reforming them would be for the public benefit, would be faced with an inescapable dilemma, of which a hypothetical example may be given. It appears from the Amnesty International Report (1978 p270) that Islamic law sanctions the death penalty for certain well-defined offences, namely murder, adultery and brigandage. Let it be supposed that a trust were created of which the object was to secure the abolition of the death penalty for adultery in those countries where Islamic law applies and to secure a reprieve for those persons who have been sentenced to death for this offence. The court, when invited to enforce or to reform such a trust, would either have to apply English standards as to public benefit, which would not necessarily be at all appropriate in the local conditions, or it would have to attempt to apply local standards of which it knew little or nothing. An English court would not, it seems

Mariette, Re [1915] 2 Ch 284 Chancery Division (Eve J)
Advancement of education

Facts
A testator bequeathed (i) £1,000 to the Governors of Aldenham School for the purpose of building squash courts or for some similar purpose to be determined by the housemasters; (ii) £100 to the headmaster for the time being upon trust to use the interest to provide some prize for some event in the school athletic sports.

Held
The first gift was for the advancement of education and the contrary was not urged. The second gift was also for the advancement of education. They were both charitable. See the quote from this case in Lord Hailsham LC's speech in *IRC* v *McMullen* (above).

Mead's Trust Deed, Re [1961] 1 WLR 1244 Chancery Division (Cross J)
Public benefit

Facts
The gift was to members of a trade union

Held
The union did not constitute a section of the community sufficiently wide to make the gift a public benefit.

Cross J:

'Not only is this a very difficult question, but there appears to be no principle by reference to which it can be answered.'

Mills v Farmer (1815) 1 Mer 55 Lord Chancellor's Court (Lord Eldon LC)
Uncertainty of objects does not defeat a charitable trust

Facts
The testator bequeathed his residuary estate to his executor 'for such charitable purposes as I do intend to name hereafter', but died without ever having specified them. His next of kin asked for a declaration that the trust was void for uncertainty, and the property held on a resulting trust for them. The Master of the Rolls granted the declaration, but the Attorney-General appealed.

Held
The decree would be reversed and the Attorney-General ordered to bring in a scheme.

Lord Eldon LC:

'A ... principle which it is now too late to call in question, is, that in all cases where the testator has expressed an intention to give to charitable purposes, if that intention is declared absolutely, and nothing is left uncertain but the mode in which it is to be carried into effect, the intention will be carried into execution by this court, which will then supply the mode which alone was left deficient ... This is a bequest to charitable purposes. It therefore follows that a scheme must be laid before the Master.'

Moss, Re [1949] 1 All ER 495 Chancery Division (Romer J)

Animal cases: benefit to the community

Facts
The testatrix made bequests to a friend 'for her use at her discretion for her work for the welfare of cats and kittens needing care and attention'. The friend had for many years received, cared for and sheltered unwanted and stray cats.

Held
The gift was charitable because as Romer J observed:

> 'The care of and consideration for animals which through old age or sickness or otherwise are unable to care for themselves are manifestations of the finer side of human nature, and gifts in furtherance of these objects are calculated to develop that side and are, therefore, calculated to benefit mankind.'

National Anti-Vivisection Society v *Inland Revenue Commissioners* [1948] AC 31 House of Lords (Viscount Simon, Lord Wright, Lord Simonds, Lord Norman and Lord Porter)

Public benefit: animal cases

Facts
The appellants whose object was to have vivisection made illegal claimed exemption from income tax on the ground that they were charitable.

Held (Lord Porter dissenting)
They were not charitable because:

Lord Simonds:

> 'any assumed public benefit in the direction of the advancement of morals and education was far outweighed by the detriment to medical science and research and consequently to the public health which would result if the society succeeded in achieving its object, and that on balance, the object of the society, so far from being for the public benefit, was gravely injurious thereto.'

Further (Lord Porter again dissenting), as the Society was seeking changes in the law, its objects were essentially political so its claim to charitable status failed on that ground also.

Niyazi's Will Trusts, Re [1978] 1 WLR 910 Chancery Division (Megarry V-C)

Charity for the relief of poverty implied

Facts
A testator left the residue of his estate, worth about £15,000, to be used for 'the construction of or as a contribution towards the construction of a working men's hostel' in Famagusta, Cyprus. The next-of-kin challenged the gift on the ground that it was non-charitable and therefore failed.

Held

The terms 'working men's' and 'hostel' together had a sufficient connotation to make the residuary gift charitable. The size of the gift also implied that it would be restricted to the relief of poverty as it would only allow for the erection of a building with the basic requirements and therefore, those who occupied it were likely to be impoverished.

Megarry V-C:

'Certain points seem reasonably plain. First, "poverty" is not confined to destitution, but extends to those who have small means and so have to "go short". Second, a gift which in terms is not confined to the relief of poverty may by inference be thus confined. In *Re Lucas* [1922] 2 Ch 52 there was a gift of 5s per week to the oldest respectable inhabitants of a village. As the law then stood, Russell J was unable to hold that a gift merely to the aged was charitable; but he held that the limitation to 5s a week indicated quite clearly that only those to whom such a sum would be of importance and a benefit were to take, and so the gift was charitable as being for the relief of poverty. I do not think that it can be said that nothing save the smallness of the benefit can restrict an otherwise unrestricted benefit so as to confine it within the bounds of charity. I think that anything in the terms of the gift which by implication prevents it from going outside those bounds will suffice. In *Re Glyn's Will Trusts* [1950] 2 All ER 150 Danckwerts J held that a trust for building free cottages for old women of the working classes aged 60 or more provided a sufficient context to show an intention to benefit indigent persons, and so was charitable ...

... As the arguments finally emerged, Mr Mummery's main contention was that, even if neither "working men" nor "hostel", by itself, could be said to confine the trust to what in law was charity, the use of these expressions in conjunction sufficed for his purpose. They were enough to distinguish *Re Sanders' Will Trusts* [1954] Ch 265, especially as Harman J had not had the advantage which I have had of being able to consider what had been said in the *Guinness* case [1955] 1 WLR 872.

I think that the adjectival expression "working men's" plainly has some flavour of "lower income" about it, just as "upper class" has some flavour of affluence, and "middle class" some flavour of comfortable means. Of course, there are some "working men" who are at least of comfortable means, if not affluence: one cannot ignore the impact of such things as football pools. But in construing a will I think that I am concerned with the ordinary or general import of words rather than exceptional cases; and, whatever may be the future meaning of "working men" or "working class", I think that by 1967 such phrases had not lost their general connotation of "lower income". I may add that nobody has suggested that any difficulty arose from the use of "working men" as distinct from "working persons" or "working women".

The connotation of "lower income" is, I think, emphasised by the word "hostel". No doubt there are a number of hostels of superior quality; and one day, perhaps, I may even encounter the expression "luxury hostel". But without any such laudatory adjective the word "hostel" has to my mind a strong flavour of a building which provides somewhat modest accommodation for those who have some temporary need for it and are willing to accept accommodation of that standard in order to meet the need. When "hostel" is prefixed by the expression "working men's", then the further restriction is introduced of the hostel being intended for those with a relatively low income who work for their living, especially as manual workers. The need, in other words, is to be the need of working men, and not of students or battered wives or anything else. Furthermore, the need will not be the need of the better paid working men who can afford something superior to mere hostel accommodation, but the need of the lower end of the financial scale of working men, who cannot compete for the better accommodation but have to content themselves with the economies and shortcomings of hostel life. It seems to me that the word "hostel" in this case is significantly different from the word "dwellings" in *Re Sanders' Will Trusts*, a word which is appropriate to ordinary houses in which the well-to-do may live, as well as the relatively poor.

Has the expression "working men's hostel" a sufficient connotation of poverty in it to satisfy the requirements of charity? On any footing the case is desperately near the borderline, and I have hesitated in reaching my conclusion. On the whole, however, for the reasons that I have been discussing, I think that the trust is charitable, though by no great margin. This view is in my judgment supported by two further considerations. First, there is the amount of the trust fund, which in 1969 was a little under £15,000. I think one is entitled to assume that a testator has at least some idea of the probable value of his estate. The money is given for the purpose "of the construction of or as a contribution towards the cost of the construction of a working men's hostel". £15,000 will not go very far in such a project, and it seems improbable that contributions from other sources towards constructing a "working men's hostel" would enable or encourage the construction of any grandiose building. If financial constraints point towards the erection of what may be called an "economy hostel", decent but catering for only the more basic requirements, then only the relatively poor would be likely to be occupants. There is at least some analogy here to the 5s per week in *Re Lucas*. Whether the trust is to give a weekly sum that is small enough to indicate that only those in straitened circumstances are to benefit, or whether it is to give a capital sum for the construction of a building which will be of such a nature that it is likely to accommodate those only who are in straitened circumstances, there will in each case be an implied restriction to poverty.

The other consideration is that of the state of housing in Famagusta. Where the trust is to erect a building in a particular area, I think that it is legitimate, in construing the trust, to have some regard to the physical condition existing in that area. Quite apart from any question of the size of the gift, I think that a trust to erect a hostel in a slum or in an area of acute housing need may have to be construed differently from a trust to erect a hostel in an area of housing affluence or plenty. Where there is a grave housing shortage, it is plain that the poor are likely to suffer more than the prosperous, and that the provision of a "working men's hostel" is likely to help the poor and not the rich.'

Oppenheim v *Tobacco Securities Trust Co Ltd* [1951] AC 297 House of Lords (Lord Simonds, Lord Normand, Lord Oaksey, Lord Morton and Lord MacDermott)

Charitable trusts must be for public benefit

Facts
Certain investments were held on trust by the Tobacco Securities Trust to apply the income 'in providing for the ... education of children of employees or former employees of British-American Tobacco Co Ltd ...or any of its subsidiary or allied companies ... ' The question arose whether the trust was charitable. At first instance Roxburgh J held it was not charitable as it lacked the element of public benefit. The Court of Appeal affirmed his decision.

Held (Lord MacDermott dissenting)
The appeal would be dismissed.

Lord Simonds:

> 'It is a clearly established principle of the law of charity that a trust is not charitable unless it is directed to the public benefit. This is sometimes stated in the proposition that it must benefit the community or a section of the community. Negatively it is said that a trust is not charitable if it confers only private benefits. In the recent case of *Gilmour* v *Coats* [1949] AC 426 this principle was reasserted. It is easy to state and has been stated in a variety of ways, the earliest statement that I find being in *Jones* v *Williams* (1767) 2 Amb 651, in which Lord Hardwicke LC is briefly reported as follows: "Definition of charity: a gift to a general public use, which extends to the poor as well as to the rich ..." We are apt not to classify them by reference to Lord MacNaghten's decision in *Income Tax Special Purposes Commissioners* v *Pemsel* [1891] AC 531, and, as I have elsewhere pointed out, it was at one time suggested that the element of public benefit, was not essential except for charities falling within the fourth class, "other purposes beneficial to the community." This is certainly wrong except in the anomalous case of trusts for the relief of poverty, with which I must specifically deal. In the case of trusts for educational purposes the condition of public benefit must be satisfied. The difficulty lies in determining what is sufficient to satisfy the test, and there is little to help your Lordships to solve it.
>
> If I may begin at the bottom of the scale, a trust established by a father for the education of his son is

not a charity. The public element, as I will call it, is not supplied by the fact that from that son's education all may benefit. At the other end of the scale the establishment of a college or university is beyond doubt a charity. "Schools of learning and free schools and scholars of universities" are the very words of the preamble to the Charitable Uses Act 1601 (43 Eliz a, c.4). So also the endowment of a college, university or school by the creation of scholarships or bursaries is a charity, and nonetheless because competition may be limited to a particular class of persons. It is on this ground, as Lord Greene MR pointed out in *Re Compton* [1945] Ch 123, that the so-called "founder's kin" cases can be rested. The difficulty arises where the trust is not for the benefit of any institution either then existing or by the terms of the trust to be brought into existence, but for the benefit of a class of persons at large. Then the question is whether that class of persons can be regarded as such a "section of the community" as to satisfy the test of public benefit. These words "section of the community" have no special sanctity, but they conveniently indicate (1) that the possible (I emphasise the word "possible") beneficiaries must not be numerically negligible, and (2) that the quality which distinguishes them from other members of the community, so that they form by themselves a section of it, must be a quality which does not depend on their relationship to a particular individual. It is for this reason that a trust for the education of members of a family or, as in *Re Compton*, of a number of families cannot be regarded as charitable. A group of persons may be numerous, but, if the nexus between them is their personal relationship to a single propositus or to several propositi, they are neither the community nor a section of the community for charitable purposes.

I come, then, to the present case where the class of beneficiaries is numerous, but the difficulty arises in regard to their common and distinguishing quality. That quality is being children of employees of one or other of a group of companies. I can make no distinction between children of employees and the employees themselves. In both cases the common quality is found in employment by particular employers.

The latter of the two cases, by which the Court of Appeal held itself to be bound, the *Hobourn* case [1946] Ch 194, is a direct authority for saying that such a common quality does not constitute its possessors a section of the public for charitable purposes. In the former case, *Re Compton*, Lord Greene MR had by way of illustration placed members of a family and employees of a particular employer on the same footing, finding neither in common kinship nor in common employment the sort of nexus which is sufficient. My Lords, I am so fully in agreement with what was said by Lord Greene in both cases, and by my noble and learned friend, when Morton LJ, in the *Hobourn* case, that I am in danger of repeating without improving upon their words. No one who has been versed for many years in this difficult and very artificial branch of the law can be unaware of its illogicalities, but I join with my noble and learned friend in echoing the observations which he cited from the judgment of Russell LJ in *Re Grove-Grady* [1929] 1 Ch 557, and I agree with him that the decision in *Re Drummond* [1914] 2 Ch 90 "... imposed a very healthy check upon the extension of the legal definition of charity." It appears to me that it would be an extension, for which there is no justification in principle, or authority, to regard common employment as a quality which constitutes those employed a section of the community. It must not, I think, be forgotten that charitable institutions enjoy rare and increasing privileges, and that the claim to come within that privileged class should be clearly established. With the single exception of *Re Rayner* (1920) 89 LJ Ch 369, which I must regard as of doubtful authority, no case has been brought to the notice of the House in which such a claim as this has been made, where there is no element of poverty in the beneficiaries, but just this and no more, that they are the children of those in a common employment.

Learned counsel for the appellant sought to fortify his case by pointing to the anomalies that would ensue from the rejection of his argument. For, he said, admittedly those who follow a profession or calling – clergymen, lawyers, colliers, tobacco-workers and so on – are a section of the public; how strange then it would be if, as in the case of railwaymen, those who follow a particular calling are all employed by one employer. Would a trust for the education of railwaymen be charitable, but a trust for the education of men employed on the railways by the Transport Board not be charitable? And what of service of the Crown, whether in the civil service or the armed forces? Is there a difference between soldiers and soldiers of the King? My Lords, I am not impressed by this sort of argument and will consider on its merits if the occasion should arise, the case where the description of the occupation and the employment is in effect the same, where in a word, if you know what a man does, you know who employs him to do it. It is to me a far more cogent argument, as it was to my noble and learned friend in the *Hobourn* case, that, if a section of the public is constituted by the personal relation of employment, it is impossible to say that it is not constituted by a thousand as by 100,000 employees, and if by a thousand, then by a hundred, and if by a hundred, then by ten. I do not mean merely that there is a difficulty in drawing the line, though that, too, is significant. I have it also in mind that, though the actual number of employees at any one moment might be small, it might increase to any extent, just as, being large, it might decrease to any extent. If the number of employees is the test of validity, must the court take into account potential increase or decrease, and, if so, as at what date?'

Lord MacDermott:

'My Lords, it is not disputed that this trust is for the advancement of education. The question is whether it is of a public nature, whether, in the words of Lord Wrenbury in *Verge v Somerville* [1924] AC 496, "it is for the benefit of the community or of an appreciably important class of community".

The relevant class here is that from which those to be educated are to be selected. The appellant contends that this class is public in character; the respondent bank (as personal representative of the last surviving settlor) denies this and says that the class is no more than a group of private individuals.

Until comparatively recently the usual way of approaching an issue of this sort, at any rate where educational trusts were concerned, was, I believe, to regard the facts of each case and to treat the matter very much as one of degree. No definition of what constituted a sufficient section of the public for the purpose was applied, for none existed; and the process seems to have been one of reaching a conclusion on a general survey of the circumstances and considerations regarded as relevant rather than of making a single, conclusive test. The investigation left the course of the dividing line between what was and what was not a section of the community unexplored, and was concluded when it had gone far enough to establish to the satisfaction of the court whether or not the trust was public; and the decision as to that was, I think, very often reached by determining whether or not the trust was private.

If it is still permissible to conduct the present inquiry on these broad if imprecise lines, I would hold with the appellant. The numerical strength of the class is considerable on any showing. The employees concerned number over 110,000, and it may reasonably be assumed that the children, who constitute the class in question, are no fewer. The large size of the class is not, of course, decisive but in my view it cannot be left out of account when the problem is approached in this way. Then it must be observed that the propositi are not limited to those presently employed. They include former employees (not reckoned in the figure I have given) and are, therefore, a more stable category than would otherwise be the case. And, further, the employees concerned are not limited to those in the service of the "British American Tobacco Co Ltd or any of its subsidiary or allied companies" – itself a description of great width – but include the employees, in the event of the British American Tobacco Co Ltd being reconstructed or merged on amalgamation, of the reconstructed or amalgamated company or any of its subsidiary companies. No doubt the settlors here had a special interest in the welfare of the class they described, but, apart from the fact that this may serve to explain the particular form of their bounty, I do not think it material to the question in hand. What is material, as I regard the matter, is that they have chosen to benefit a class which is, in fact, substantial in point of size and importance and have done so in a manner which, to my mind, manifests an intention to advance the interests of the class described as a class rather than as a collection or succession of particular individuals...

The respondent bank, however, contends that the inquiry should be of quite a different character to that which I have been discussing. It advances as the sole criterion a narrower test derived from the decisions of the Court of Appeal in *In re Compton*, and in *In re Hobourn Aero Components Ltd's Air Raid Distress Fund*. The basis and nature of this test appear from the passage in the judgment of the court in *In re Compton*, where Lord Greene MR says: "In the case of many charitable gifts it is possible to identify the individuals who are to benefit, or who at any given moment constitute the class from which the beneficiaries are to be selected. This circumstance does not, however, deprive the gift of its public character. Thus, if there is a gift to relieve the poor inhabitants of a parish the class to benefit is readily ascertainable. But they do not enjoy the benefit, when they receive it, by virtue of their character as individuals but by virtue of their membership of the specified class. In such a case the common quality which unites the potential beneficiaries into a class is essentially an impersonal one."

It is definable by reference to what each has in common with the others, and that is something into which their status as individuals does not enter. Persons claiming to belong to the class do so not because they are AC, CD and EF, but because they are poor inhabitants of the parish. If, in asserting their claim, it were necessary for them to establish the fact that they were the individuals AB, CD, and EF, I cannot help thinking that on principle the gift ought not to be held to be a charitable gift, since the introduction into their qualification of a purely personal element would deprive the gift of its necessary public character. It seems to me that the same principle ought to apply when the claimants, in order to establish their status, have to assert and prove, not that they themselves are AB, CD and EF, but that they stand in some specified relationship to the individuals AB, CD and EF, such as that of children or employees. In that case, too, a purely personal element enters into and is an essential part of the qualification, which is defined by reference to something, ie personal relationship to individuals or an individual which is in its essence non-public.

The test thus propounded focuses upon the common quality which unites those within the class concerned and asks whether that quality is essentially impersonal or essentially personal. If the former, the class will rank as a section of the public and the trust will have the element common to and necessary for all legal charities; but, if the latter, the trust will be private and not charitable. It is suggested in the passage just quoted, and made clear beyond doubt in *In re Hobourn*, that in the opinion of the Court of Appeal employment by a designated employer must be regarded for this purpose as a personal and not as an impersonal bond of union. In this connection and as illustrating the discriminating character of what I may call 'the *Compton* test' reference should be made to that part of the judgment of the learned Master of the Rolls in *In re Hobourn*, in which he speaks of the decision in *Hall* v *Derby Borough Urban Sanitary Authority* (1885) 16 QBD 163. The passage runs thus:

> "That related to a trust for railway servants. It is said that if a trust for railway servants can be a good charity, so too a trust for railway servants in the employment of a particular railway company is a good charity. That is not so. The reason, I think, is that in the one case the trust is for railway servants in general and in the other case it is for employees of a particular company, a fact which limits the potential beneficiaries to a class ascertained on a purely personal basis."

My Lords, I do not quarrel with the result arrived at in the *Compton* and *Hobourn* cases, and I do not doubt that the *Compton* test may often prove of value and lead to a correct determination. But, with the great respect due to those who have formulated this test, I find myself unable to regard it as a criterion of general applicability and conclusiveness. In the first place I see much difficulty in dividing the qualities or attributes, which may serve to bind human beings into classes, into two mutually exclusive groups, the one involving individual status and purely personal, the other disregarding such status and quite impersonal. As a task this seems to me no less baffling and elusive than the problem to which it is directed, namely, the determination of what is and what is not a section of the public for the purposes of this branch of the law. After all, what is more personal than poverty or blindness or ignorance? Yet none would deny that a gift for the education of the children of the poor or blind was charitable; and I doubt if there is any less certainty about the charitable nature of a gift, for, say, the education of children who satisfy a specified examining body that they need and would benefit by a course of special instruction designed to remedy their educational defects.

But can any really fundamental distinction, as respects the personal or impersonal nature of the common link, be drawn between those employed, for example, by a particular university and those whom the same university has put in a certain category as the result of individual examination and assessment? Again, if the bond between those employed by a particular railway is purely personal, why should the bond between those who are employed as railwaymen be so essentially different? Is a distinction to be drawn in this respect between those who are employed in a particular industry before it is nationalised and those who are employed therein after that process has been completed and one employer has taken the place of many? Are miners in the service of the National Coal Board now in one category and miners at a particular pit or of a particular district in another? Is the relationship between those in the service of the Crown to be distinguished from that obtaining between those in the service of some other employer? Or, if not, are the children of, say, soldiers or civil servants to be regarded as not constituting a sufficient section of the public to make a trust for their education charitable?

It was conceded in the course of the argument that, had the present trust been framed so as to provide for the education of the children of those engaged in the tobacco industry in a named county or town, it would have been a good charitable disposition, and that even though the class to be benefited would have been appreciably smaller and no more important than is the class here. That concession follows from what the Court of Appeal has said. But if it is sound and a personal or impersonal relationship remains the universal criterion I think it shows, no less than the queries I have just raised in indicating some of the difficulties of the problem, that the *Compton* test is a very arbitrary and artificial rule. This leads me to the second difficulty that I have regarding it. If I understand it alright it necessarily makes the quantum of public benefit a consideration of little moment; the size of the class becomes immaterial and the need of its members and the public advantage of having that need met appear alike to be irrelevant. To my mind these are considerations of some account in the sphere of educational trusts for, as already indicated, I think the educational value and scope of the work actually to be done must have a bearing on the question of public benefit.

Finally, it seems to me that, far from settling the state of the law on this particular subject, the *Compton* test is more likely to create confusion and doubt in the case of many trusts and institutions of a character whose legal standing as charities has never been in question. I have particularly in mind gifts for the education of certain special classes such, for example, as the daughters of missionaries, the children of those professing a particular faith or accepted as ministers of a particular denomination, or those whose parents have sent them to a particular school for the earlier stages of their training. I cannot but think that in cases of this sort an analysis of the common quality binding the class to be benefited may reveal a relationship no less personal than that existing between an employer and those in his service. Take, for instance, a trust for the provision of university education for boys coming from a particular school. The common quality binding the members of that class seems to reside in the fact that their parents or guardians all contracted for their schooling with the same establishment or body. That the school in such a case may itself be a charitable foundation seems altogether beside the point and quite insufficient to hold the *Compton* test at bay if it is well founded in law.

My Lords, counsel for the appellant and for the Attorney-General adumbrated several other tests for establishing the presence or absence of the necessary public element. I have given these my careful consideration and I do not find them any more sound or satisfactory than the *Compton* test. I therefore return to what I think was the process followed before the decision in *Compton's* case, and, for the reasons already given, I would hold the present trust charitable and allow the appeal. I have only to add that I recognise the imperfections and uncertainties of that process. They are as evident as the difficulties of finding something better. But I venture to doubt if it is in the power of the courts to resolve those difficulties satisfactorily as matters stand. It is a long cry to the age of Elizabeth and I think what is needed is a fresh start from a new statute.'

Peggs v *Lamb* [1994] 2 WLR 1 Chancery Division (Morritt J)

Perpetuity rule – charitable trusts exemption – usage

Facts

Trustees of two registered trusts applied to implement a cy-près scheme. The trust property consisted of common land granted under a lost ancient charter to the freemen of Huntingdon. In 1835 the Municipal Corporations Act, of that year, transferred the property to the freemen of the borough subject to pre-existing rights. Following the decline in the number of freemen receiving the distributed income the trustees applied for a cy-près scheme in favour of all of the residents of Huntingdon.

Held

The charitable status of the trust would be upheld through past usage and to validate past payments that would otherwise have fallen foul of the perpetuity rule (applying *Goodman* v *Mayor of Saltash* (1882) 7 AC 633 (HL)). The cy-près scheme under s13(1)(d) of the Charities Act 1960 was justified in the circumstances.

Pinion, Re [1965] Ch 85 Court of Appeal (Harman, Davies and Russell LJJ)

Advancement of education: objective test

Facts

A testator left his studio and its contents, comprising pictures, antique furniture, some silver, china and miniatures etc to be offered to the National Trust, to be kept as a studio and maintained as a collection. He directed that if the Trust declined the gift then the executors were to appoint trustees to carry it out. The Trust declined the gift. The executors sought directions on the matter and the judge at first instance held that there was a valid charitable trust thus depriving the next-of-kin of any benefit. The next-of-kin appealed. Expert evidence showed that the studio was squalid and contained little of worth, the pictures were bad and the rest of the collection was of low quality, and there was no educational value in maintaining it for the public to see.

Held

The court would hear expert evidence on the educational value of a collection or other gift. In this case this evidence showed that the gift was of no educational value and it was therefore not a charitable gift for the advancement of education.

Harman LJ:

> 'Where a museum is concerned and the utility of the gift is brought into question it is, in my opinion, and herein I agree with the judge, essential to know at least something of the quality of the proposed exhibits in order to judge whether they will be conducive to the education of the public. So I think with a public library, such a place if found to be devoted entirely to works of pornography or of a corrupting nature, would not be allowable. Here it is suggested that education in the fine arts is the object. For myself a reading of the will leads me rather to the view that the testator's object was not to educate anyone, but to perpetuate his own name, and the repute of his family, hence perhaps the direction that the custodian should be a blood relation of his. However that may be, there is a strong body of evidence here that as a means of education this collection is worthless. The testator's own paintings of which there are over 50, are said by competent persons to be in an academic style and "atrociously bad" and the other pictures without exception worthless. Even the so-called "Lely" turns out to be a twentieth century copy.
>
> Apart from pictures there is a haphazard assembly – it does not merit the name collection for no purpose emerges, no time nor style is illustrated – of furniture and objects of so-called "art" about which expert opinion is unanimous that nothing beyond the third rate is found. Indeed one of the experts expresses his surprise that so voracious a collector should not by hazard have picked up even one meritorious object. The most that skilful cross-examination extracted from the expert witness was that there was a dozen chairs which might perhaps be acceptable to a minor provincial museum and perhaps another dozen not altogether worthless but two dozen chairs do not make a museum and they must, to accord with the will, be exhibited stifled by a large number of absolutely worthless pictures and objects.
>
> It was said that this is a matter of taste, and de gustibus non est disputandum, but here I agree with the judge that there is an accepted canon of taste on which the court must rely, for it has itself no judicial knowledge of such matters, and the unanimous verdict of the experts is as I have stated. The judge with great hesitation concluded that there was a scintilla of merit which was sufficient to save the rest. I find

myself on the other side of the line. I can conceive no useful object to be served in foisting upon the public this mass of junk. It has neither public utility nor educative value ...'

Resch's Will Trusts, Re [1969] 1 AC 514 Privy Council (Lord Hodson, Lord Guest, Lord Donovan, Lord Wilberforce LJJ and Sir Alfred North)

'Relief of the impotent', ie the sick, under the statute

Facts
A testator died in 1963 leaving a large bequest 'to the Sisters of Charity for a period of 200 years or for so long as they shall conduct St Vincent's Private Hospital whichever shall be the shorter period, to be applied for the general purposes of such hospital ...'

Held
The gift was a valid charitable bequest for the relief of the sick.

Lord Wilberforce:

> 'A gift for the purposes of a hospital is *prima facie* a good charitable gift. This is now clearly established both in Australia and England, not merely because of the use of the words 'impotent' in the preamble to 43 Eliz c.4, though the process of referring to the preamble is one often used for reassurance, but because the provision of medical care for the sick is, in modern times, accepted as a public benefit suitable to attract the privileges given to charitable institutions ...
>
> In spite of this general proposition, there may be certain hospitals, or categories of hospitals, which are not charitable institutions (see *Re Smith* [1962] 1 WLR 763). Disqualifying indicia may be either that the hospital is carried on commercially, ie with a view to making profits for private individuals, or that the benefits it provides are not for the public, or a sufficiently large class of the public to satisfy the necessary tests of public character. Each class of objection is taken in the present case. As regards the first, it is accepted that the private hospital is not run for profit, in any ordinary sense, of individuals. Moreover, if the purposes of the hospital are otherwise charitable, they do not lose this character merely because charges are made to the recipients of the benefits ...
>
> Their Lordships turn to the second objection. This, in substance, is that the private hospital is not carried on for "purposes beneficial to the community" because it provides only for persons of means who are capable of paying the substantial fees required as a condition of admission.
>
> In dealing with this objection it is necessary first to dispose of a misapprehension. It is not a condition of validity of a trust for the relief of the sick that it should be limited to the poor sick. Whether one regards the charitable character of trusts for the relief of the sick as flowing from the word "impotent" ("aged, impotent and poor people") in the preamble to 43 Eliz c.4 or more broadly as derived from the conception of benefit to the community, there is no warrant for adding to the condition of sickness that of poverty ... The proposition that relief of sickness was a sufficient purpose without adding poverty was accepted by the Court of Appeal in *Re Smith*. The appellants did not really contest this. They based their argument on the narrower proposition that a trust could not be charitable which excluded the poor from participation in its benefits. The purposes of the private hospital were, they said, to provide facilities for the well-to-do: an important section of the community was excluded: the trusts could not therefore be said to be for the benefit of the community. There was not sufficient "public element".
>
> To support this, they appealed to some well-known authorities.'

His Lordship referred to *Jones* v *Williams* (1767) Amb 651 and *Re Macduff* [1896] 2 Ch 451, where in a general discussion of such expressions as "charitable" or "philanthropic" Lindley LJ said (at p464):

> '"I am quite aware that a trust may be charitable though not confined to the poor; but I doubt very much whether a trust would be declared to be charitable which excluded the poor."

'... Their Lordships accept the correctness of what has been said in those cases, but they must be rightly understood. It would be a wrong conclusion from them to state that a trust for the provision of medical facilities would necessarily fail to be charitable merely because by reason of expense they could only be made use of by persons of some means. To provide, in response to public need, medical treatment otherwise inaccessible but in its nature expensive, without any profit motive, might well be charitable: on the other hand to limit admission to a nursing home to the rich would not be so. The test is essentially one of public benefit, and indirect as well as direct benefit enters into the account. In the present case, the element of public benefit is strongly present. It is not disputed that a need exists to provide accommodation and medical treatment in conditions of greater privacy and relaxation than would be possible in a general hospital and as a supplement to the facilities of a general hospital. This is what the private hospital does and it does so at, approximately, cost price. The service is needed by all, not only by the well-to-do. So far as its nature permits it is open to all: the charges are not law, but the evidence shows that it cannot be said that the poor are excluded: such exclusion as there is, is of some of the poor – namely, those who have (a) not contributed sufficiently to a medical benefit scheme or (b) need to stay longer in the hospital than their benefit will cover or (c) cannot get a reduction of or exemption from the charges. The general benefit to the community of such facilities results from the beds and medical staff of the general hospital, the availability of a particular type of nursing and treatment which supplements that provided by the general hospital and the benefit to the standard of medical care in the general hospital which arises from the juxtaposition of the two institutions ...'

Rowntree Housing Association v *Attorney-General* [1983] Ch 159 Chancery Division (Peter Gibson J)

Charity for 'the relief of aged, impotent and poor people' under the Statute of Elizabeth

Facts

The housing association was an incorporated charity whose objects included, inter alia, the provision of housing for elderly persons in need of such accommodation. The charity wished to build small self-contained houses, flats and bungalows to be sold to elderly people on long leases in consideration of a capital sum. Five different schemes were put forward for the sale of the dwellings, these schemes merely reflecting the needs of the persons who would benefit and containing suitable conditions as to payment for the dwellings, the provision of wardens and determination of the leases. The Charity Commissioners doubted if these schemes were charitable and raised four objections, namely: (1) they made provision for the aged on a contractual basis rather than by way of bounty; (2) the benefits were not capable of being withdrawn if a beneficiary at any time ceased to qualify; (3) they were for the benefit of private individuals rather than a charitable class; (4) they were a commercial enterprise capable of producing a profit for the beneficiary. The trustees of the charity sought the determination of the court as to whether all or any of the schemes were charitable in law.

Held

All the schemes were charitable being for the relief of the aged. As to the first objection there was nothing objectionable in giving a benefit by way of contract rather than bounty. As to the second objection, it depended very much on the circumstances and providing housing benefits for the elderly which were capable of being withdrawn at any time could have an unsettling effect on such people. As to the third objection, this must be rejected. The scheme was for the benefit of a charitable class and the fact the trustees selected people to obtain the benefits did not defeat the charitable nature of the gift. As to the fourth objection, if the elderly tenants profited because the dwellings increased in value this was purely incidental and was not a profit at the expense of the charity.

Peter Gibson J:

'... it is appropriate to consider the scope of the charitable purpose which the plaintiffs claim the scheme carries out, that is to say in the words of the preamble to the Statute of Elizabeth (43 Eliz 1 c.4 of the Charitable Uses Act 1601) "the relief of aged persons". That purpose is indeed part of the very first set of charitable purposes contained in the preamble: "the relief of aged, impotent and poor people". Looking at those words without going to authority and attempting to give them their natural meaning, I would have thought that two inferences therefrom were tolerably clear. First, the words "aged, impotent and poor" must be read disjunctively. It would be as absurd to require that the aged must be impotent or poor as it would be to require the impotent to be aged or poor, or the poor to be aged or impotent. There will no doubt be many cases where the objects of charity prove to have two or more of the three qualities at the same time. Second, essential to the charitable purpose is that it should relieve aged, impotent and poor people. The word "relief" implies that the persons in question have a need attributable to their condition as aged, impotent or poor persons which requires alleviating, and which those persons could not alleviate, or would find difficulty in alleviating, themselves from their own resources. The word "relief" is not synonymous with "benefit".

Those inferences are in substance what both counsel submit are the true principles governing the charitable purpose of the relief of aged persons. Mr Nugee stresses that any benefit provided must be related to the needs of the aged. Thus a gift of money to the aged millionaires of Mayfair would not relieve a need of theirs as aged persons. Mr McCall similarly emphasises that to relieve a need of the aged attributable to their age would be charitable only if the means employed are appropriate to the need. He also points out that an element of public benefit must be found if the purpose is to be charitable. I turn then to authority to see if there is anything that compels a different conclusion.

In *Re Lucas* [1922] 2 Ch 52, Russell J was concerned with a bequest to the oldest respectable inhabitants of Gunville of the amount of 5s per week each. He held that the amount of the gift implied poverty. But he said:

> "... I am not satisfied that the requirement of old age would of itself be sufficient to constitute the gift a good charitable bequest, although there are several dicta to that effect in the books. I can find no case, and none has been cited to me, where the decision has been based upon age and nothing but age."

In *Re Glyn's Will Trusts* [1950] 2 All ER 1150, Danckwerts J was faced with a bequest for building cottages for old women of the working classes of the age of 60 years or upwards. He said:

> "I have not the slightest doubt that this is a good charitable bequest. The preamble to the Statute of Elizabeth refers to the relief of aged, impotent and poor people. The words 'aged, impotent and poor' should be read disjunctively. It has never been suggested that poor people must also be aged to be objects of charity, and there is no reason for holding that aged people must also be poor to come within the meaning of the preamble to the Statute. A trust for the relief of aged persons would be charitable unless it was qualified in some way which would clearly render it not charitable."

He then went on say that there was a sufficient context to show that the testatrix intended to benefit indigent persons.

In *Re Sanders' Will Trusts* [1954] Ch 265, Harman J said that the ratio decidendi of *Re Glyn's Will Trusts* was that "out of 'old age' and 'working class' you might argue that poverty was a necessary qualification". But I share the views of the learned editor of Tudors on the Law of Charities that that is not what Danckwerts said.

In *Re Bradbury* [1950] 2 All ER 1150, Vaisey J followed *Re Glyn's Will Trusts* in holding that a bequest to pay sums for the maintenance of an aged person in a nursing home was charitable.

In *Re Robinson* [1951] Ch 198, a testator made a gift to the old people over 65 of a specified district to be given as his trustees though best. Vaisey J held that the words "aged, impotent and poor" in the preamble should be read disjunctively. He said it was sufficient that a gift should be to the aged, and commented on his decision in *Re Bradbury* that the aged person in a nursing home might be a person not at all in need of any sort of pecuniary assistance.

In *Re Cottam's Will Trusts* [1955] 1 WLR 1299, a gift to provide flats for persons over 65 to be let at economic rents was said by Danckwerts J to be a trust for the benefit of aged persons and therefore prima facie charitable, though he went on to find it was a trust for the aged of small means.

In *Re Lewis (decd)* [1955] Ch 104, there was a gift to ten blind girls, Tottenham residents if possible, of £100 each, and a similar gift to ten blind boys. Roxburgh J held that the words "aged, impotent and poor" in the preamble must be read disjunctively and that the trust was therefore charitable.

In *Re Neal* (1966) 110 SJ 549, a testator provided a gift for the founding of a home for old persons. Further directions provided for fees to be charged sufficient to maintain the home with sufficient staff to run it and cover the costs of the trustees. Goff J in a very briefly reported judgment, said that in order to conclude whether a trust was charitable or not it was not necessary to find in it an element of relief against poverty, but it was sufficient to find an intention to relieve aged persons. The form of the gift and the directions were a provision for succouring and supplying such needs of old persons as they had because they were old persons. Therefore he held it was a charitable bequest.

In *Re Adams (decd)* [1968] Ch 80, Danckwerts LJ again referred to the necessity of construing disjunctively the words "impotent and poor" in the preamble. By parity of reasoning he must be taken to have been of the view that "aged, impotent and poor" should be read disjunctively, too.

Lastly, in *Re Resch's Will Trusts* [1969] 1 AC 514 the Privy Council had to consider a gift of income to be applied for the general purposes of a named private hospital. The hospital charged substantial fees but was not run for the profit of individuals. Lord Wilberforce, delivering the judgment of the Board, referred to an objection that had been raised that the private hospital was not carried on for purposes beneficial to the community because it provided only for persons of means, capable of paying the fees required as a condition of admission. He said:

"In dealing with this objection, it is necessary first to dispose of a misapprehension. It is not a condition of the validity of a trust for the relief of the sick that it should be limited to the poor sick. Whether one regards the charitable character of trusts for the relief of the sick as flowing from the word 'impotent' (aged, impotent and poor people) in the preamble to 43 Eliz c.4 or more broadly as derived from the conception of benefit to the community, there is no warrant for adding to the condition of sickness that of poverty. As early as *Income Tax Special Purposes Comrs* v *Pemsel* [1891] AC 531 Lord Herschell was able to say: 'I am unable to agree with the view that the sense in which "charities" and "charitable purpose" are popularly used is so restricted as this. I certainly cannot think that they are limited to the relief of wants occasioned by lack of pecuniary means. Many examples may, I think, be given of endowments for the relief of human necessities, which would be as generally termed charities as hospitals or almshouses, where, nevertheless, the necessities to be relieved do not result from poverty in its limited sense of the lack of money'."

He returned to the question of public benefit and need.

"To provide, in response to public need, medical treatment otherwise inaccessible but in its nature expensive, without any profit motive, might well be charitable: on the other hand to limit admission to a nursing home to the rich would not be so. The test is essentially one of public benefit, and indirect as well as direct benefit enters into the account. In the present case, the element of public benefit is strongly present. It is not disputed that a need exists to provide accommodation and medical treatment in conditions of greater privacy and relaxation than would be possible in a general hospital and as a supplement to the facilities of a general hospital. This is what the private hospital does and it does so at, approximately, cost price. The service is needed by all, not only by the well-to-do. So far as its nature permits it is open to all; the charges are not low, but the evidence shows that it cannot be said that the poor are excluded ..."

These authorities convincingly confirm the correctness of the proposition that the relief of the aged does not have to be relief for the aged poor. In other words the phrase "aged, impotent and poor people" in the preamble must be read disjunctively. The decisions in *Re Glyn's Wills Trusts*, *Re Bradbury*, *Re Robinson*, *Re Cottam's Wills Trusts* and *Re Lewis* give support to the view that it is a sufficient charitable purpose to benefit the aged, or the impotent, without more. But these are all decisions at first instance and with great respect to the judges who decided them they appear to me to pay no regard to the word "relief". I have no hesitation in preferring the approach adopted in *Re Neal* and *Re Resch's Will Trusts* that there must be a need which is to be relieved by the charitable gift, such need being attributable to the aged or impotent condition of the person to be benefited ...'

Royal Choral Society v *IRC* [1943] 2 All ER 101 Court of Appeal (Lord Greene MR, MacKinnon and Du Parq LJJ)

Furtherance of education

Facts
A gift was made 'to promote the practice and performance of choral works whether by way of concerts or choral pageants in the Royal Albert Hall or elsewhere'.

Held
The gift was charitable.

Lord Greene MR:

'He (the Solicitor General) said that in the domain of art the only thing that could be educational in a charitable sense would be the education of the executants: the teaching of the painter, the training of the musician, and so forth. I protest against that narrow conception of education when one is dealing with aesthetic education. Very few people can become executants, or at any rate executants who can give pleasure either to themselves or to others; but a very large number of people can become instructed listeners with a trained and cultivated taste. In my opinion, a body of persons established for the purpose of raising the artistic taste of a country and established by an appropriate document which confines them to that purpose, is established for educational purposes, because the education of artistic taste is one of the most important things in the development of a civilised human being.'

Scarisbrick's Will Trusts, Re [1951] Ch 622 Court of Appeal (Sir Raymond Evershed MR, Jenkins and Hodson LJJ)

Charities for the relief of poverty exempt from public benefit requirement

Facts
The testatrix left her residuary estate to trustees to pay the income to her son and daughters for their lives, and after the death of the survivor, on trust 'for such relations of my son and daughters as in the opinion of the survivor of my son and daughters shall be in needy circumstances ...' At first instance it was held that the trust for the relations failed as they did not constitute a particular section of the poor. The Attorney-General appealed.

Held
Normally the restriction of beneficiaries to 'relations' of the testatrix's children would exclude the element of public benefit necessary for a charitable trust, but trusts for the relief of poverty were an exception to the requirement, whether the distribution was immediate or the trust were of a more permanent nature.

Jenkins LJ:

'(1) It is a general rule that a trust or gift in order to be charitable in the legal sense must be for the benefit of the public or some section of the public ...
(2) An aggregate of individuals ascertained by reference to some personal tie (eg of blood or contract) such as the relations of a particular individual, the members of a particular family, the employees of a

particular firm, the members of a particular association, does not amount to the public or a section thereof for the purposes of the general rule ...

(3) It follows that according to the general rule above stated a trust or gift under which the beneficiaries or potential beneficiaries are confined to some aggregate of individuals ascertained as above is not legally charitable even though its purposes are such that it would have been legally charitable if the range of potential beneficiaries had extended to the public at large or a section thereof ...

(4) There is, however, an exception to the general rule, in that trusts or gifts for the relief of poverty have been held to be charitable even though they are limited in their application to some aggregate of individuals ascertained as above, and are therefore not trusts or gifts for the benefit of the public or a section thereof. This exception operates whether the personal tie is one of blood ... or of contract ...

I see no sufficient ground in the authorities for holding that a gift for the benefit of poor relations qualifies as charitable only if it is perpetual in character ... If a gift or trust on its true construction does extend to those in need amongst relations in every degree even though it provides for immediate distribution, then, inasmuch as the class of potential beneficiaries becomes so wide as to be incapable of exhaustive ascertainment, the impersonal quality, if I may so describe it, supplied in continuing gifts by the element of perpetuity, is equally present.

... I am accordingly of opinion that as the law now stands the trust in question should be upheld as a valid charitable trust for the relief of poverty.'

Scottish Burial Reform and Cremation Society Ltd v *Glasgow Corporation* [1968] AC 138 House of Lords (Lord Reid, Lord Guest, Lord Upjohn, Lord Wilberforce and Lord Pearson)

Charitable trusts: benefit to the community

Facts

The appellants, a non-profit making limited company, were established for the general purpose of promoting methods of disposal of the dead which were both inexpensive and sanitary and the particular purpose of encouraging and providing facilities for cremation. They claimed a declaration that they were a charity in order to obtain relief from rates on their premises.

Held

This was a purpose which was beneficial to the community and within the spirit and intendment of the preamble of the Statute of Elizabeth.

Lord Reid:

'... the appellants must also show, however, that the public benefit is of a kind within the spirit and intendment of the Statute of Elizabeth. The preamble specifies a number of objects which were then recognised as charitable. But in more recent times a wide variety of other objects have come to be recognised as also being charitable. The courts appear to have proceeded first by seeking some analogy between an object mentioned in the preamble and the object with regard to which they had to reach a decision. Then they appear to have gone farther, and to have been satisfied if they could find an analogy between an object already held to be charitable and the new object claimed to be charitable. This gradual extension has proceeded so far that there are few modern reported cases where a bequest or donation was made or an institution was being carried on for a clearly specified object which was for the benefit of the public at large and not of individuals, and yet the object was held not to be within the spirit and intendment of the Statute of Elizabeth. Counsel in the present case were invited to search for any case having even the remotest resemblance to this case in which an object was held to be for the public benefit but not yet to be within that spirit and intendment; but no such case could be found.

There is, however, another line of cases where the bequest did not clearly specify the precise object to which it was to be applied, but left a discretion to trustees or others to choose objects within a certain field. There the courts have been much more strict, so that if it is possible that those entrusted with the discretion could, without infringing the testator's directions, apply the bequest in any way which would not be charitable (for example, because it did not benefit a sufficiently large section of the public) then the claim that the bequest is charitable fails. That line of cases, however, can have no application to the present case, and it is easy to fall into error if one tries to apply to a case like the present judicial observations made in a case where there was a discretion which could go beyond objects strictly charitable. In the present case the appellants make a charge for the services which they provide. It has never been held, however, that objects, otherwise charitable, cease to be charitable if beneficiaries are required to make payments for what they receive. It may even be that public demand for the kind of service which the charity provides becomes so large that there is room for a commercial undertaking to come in and supply similar services on a commercial basis; but no authority and no reason has been put forward for holding that when that stage is reached the objects and activities of the non-profit earning charitable organisation cease to be charitable.

If, then, all that is necessary to bring the objects and activities of the appellants within the spirit and intendment of the preamble to the Statute of Elizabeth is to find analogous decided cases, I think that there is amply sufficient analogy with the series of cases dealing with burial. I would therefore allow this appeal.'

Lord Wilberforce:

'On this subject, the law of England, though no doubt not very satisfactory and in need of rationalisation, is tolerably clear. The purposes in question, to be charitable, must be shown to be for the benefit of the public, or the community, in a sense or manner within the intendment of the preamble to the statute, 43 Eliz 1 c.4. The latter requirement does not mean quite what it says: for it is now accepted that what must be regarded is not the wording of the preamble itself, but the effect of decisions given by the courts as to its scope, decisions which have endeavoured to keep the law as to charities moving according as new social needs arise or old ones become obsolete or satisfied. Lord MacNaghten's grouping of the heads of recognised charity in *Income Tax Special Purposes Comrs* v *Pemsel* [1891] AC 531 is one that has proved to be of value and there are many problems which it solves. But three things may be said about it, which its author would surely not have denied: first that, since it is a classification of convenience, there may well be purposes which do not fit neatly into one or other of the headings: secondly, that the words used must not be given the force of a statute to be construed, and thirdly, that the law of charity is a moving subject which may well have evolved even since 1891.

With this in mind, approach may be made to the question whether the provision of facilities for the disposal of human remains, whether, generally, in an inexpensive and sanitary manner, or, particularly, by cremation, can be considered as within the spirit of the statute. Decided cases help us, at any rate to the point of showing that trusts for the repair or maintenance of burial grounds connected with a church are charitable. This was, if not decided, certainly assumed in *Vaughan* v *Thomas* (1886) 33 Ch D 187as it had been earlier assumed *Att-Gen* v *Blizard* (1855) 21 Beav 233.

More explicitly, in *Re Manser* [1905] 1 Ch 68, a trust for keeping in good order burial grounds for members of the Society of Friends was considered charitable. The opinion of Warrington J was that such trusts could be brought within the heading "advancement of religion" – "I think one naturally connects the burial of the dead with religion" he said. Then in *Re Eighmie* [1935] Ch 524, a trust for the maintenance of a cemetery owned and managed by a local authority was held charitable. The cemetery was an extension of a closed churchyard, so that the decision can be regarded as a logical step rather than a new departure. Now what we have to consider is whether to take the further step of holding charitable the purpose of providing burial, or facilities for the disposal of mortal remains, without any connection with a church, by an independent body. I have no doubt that we should. I would regard the earlier decisions as falling on the borderline between trusts for the advancement of religion and trusts otherwise beneficial to the community. One may say either that burial purposes fall within both, or that the categories themselves shade one into the other. So I find no departure in principle in saying that purposes such as the present – which, though the appellants in fact provide the means for religious observance, should be regarded as independent of any religious basis – are to be treated as equally within the charitable class.'

Appeal allowed.

Shakespeare Memorial Trust, Re [1923] 2 Ch 398 Chancery Division (PO Lawrence J)

Furtherance of education – public benefit

Facts
A trust had among its objects the performance of Shakespearean and other classical English plays and stimulating the art of acting.

Held
The gift was either educational or as for purposes beneficial to the community; it was clearly for the promotion of the works of Shakespeare or for improving our literary heritage.

Shaw's Will Trusts, Re [1952] Ch 163 Chancery Division (Vaisey J)

Furtherance of education

Facts
The widow of George Bernard Shaw bequeathed the residue of her estate upon trusts for 'the making of grants contributions and payments to any foundation ... having for its objects the bringing of the masterpieces of fine art within the reach of the people of Ireland of all classes in their own country ... The teaching, promotion and encouragement in Ireland of self-control, elocution, oratory, deportment, the arts of personal contact of social intercourse, and the other arts of public, private, professional and business life ...'

Held
The gift was a valid charitable trust for the advancement of education.

Vaisey J:
> I think that education includes ... not only teaching, but the promotion or encouragement of those arts and graces of life which are, after all, perhaps the finest and best part of the human character ... It is education of a desirable sort, and which, if corrected and augmented and amplified by other kinds of teaching and instruction, might have most beneficial results.'

South Place Ethical Society, Re, Barralet v Attorney-General [1980] 1 WLR 1565 Chancery Division (Dillon J)

Meaning of 'religion', education and benefit of the community

Facts
The South Place Ethical Society which was first established in 1824 had as objects (i) the study and dissemination of ethical principles and (ii) the cultivation of a rational religious sentiment. Ethics is concerned with belief in the excellence of truth, love and beauty, but not belief in anything supernatural. It also regards the object of human existence as being the discovery of truth by reason and not by

revelation. The society held regular Sunday meetings which were open to the public and also had as one of its objects the study and dissemination of ethical principles. The society asked the court for a declaration as to whether its objects were charitable. It contended that its purposes were for the advancement of religion but alternatively contended it was for the advancement of education.

Held

The society was not for the advancement of religion because religion is concerned with man's relations with God whereas ethics is concerned with man's relations with man. Further essential features of 'religion' were faith in a God and worship of that God. There could be no worship of ethical principles. However, the society could attain charitable status as being for the advancement of education and for the benefit of the community.

Dillon J:

'... I propose therefore to consider first the claim that the society is charitable because its objects are for the advancement of religion. In considering this, as in considering the other claims, I keep very much in mind the observation of Lord Wilberforce in the *Scottish Burial Reform and Cremation Society Ltd* v *Glasgow City Corpn* that the law of charity is a moving subject which may well have evolved even since 1891. The submissions of Mr Swingland seek to establish that this is indeed so, having regard to current thinking in the field of religion.

Of course it has long been established that a trust can be valid and charitable as for the advancement of religion although the religion which is sought to be advanced is not the Christian religion. In *Bowman* v *Secular Society Ltd* [1917] AC 406 Lord Parker of Waddington gave a very clear and valuable summary of the history of the approach of the law to religious charitable trusts. He said:

> "It would seem to follow that a trust for the purpose of any kind of monotheistic theism would be a good charitable trust."

Mr Swingland accepts that, so far as it goes, but he submits that Lord Parker should have gone further, even in 1917 (because the society's beliefs go back before that date) and the court should go further now. The society says that religion does not have to be theist or dependent on a god; and sincere belief in ethical qualities is religious, because such qualities as trust, love and beauty are sacred, and the advancement of any such belief is the advancement of religion.

I have been referred to certain decisions in the United States, which suggest that the arguments of Mr Swingland on this point would be likely to be accepted in the United States, and the society would there be regarded as a body established for the advancement of religion. One decision is the decision of the Supreme Court of the United States in *United States* v *Seeger* (1965) 380 US 163. That was concerned with the exemption of a conscientious objector from conscription on grounds of religion. The decision is not of course binding on me but the reasoning merits serious consideration, not least because it really states the substance of much of the argument that counsel for the society is putting forward, and states it with great clarity. The judgment of the court (delivered by Clark J), gives as the ratio (at 176) that in the opinion of the court -

> "A sincere and meaningful belief, which occupies in the life of its possessor a place parallel to that filled by the God of those admittedly qualifying for the exemption on the grounds of religion comes within the statutory definition."

In his separate opinion, concurring with the opinion of the court, Douglas J said (at 193):

> "... a sincere belief which in his life fills the same place as a belief in God fills in the life of an orthodox religionist is entitled to exemption ..."

There is also a decision of the United States Court of Appeals for the District of Columbia in *Washington Ethical Society* v *District of Columbia* (1957) 229 F 2d 127 in which it was held that the Washington Ethical Society was entitled to exemption from local taxes or rates in respect of its premises under an exemption accorded from buildings belonging to religious corporations or societies and used for religious worship. The report of the judgment of the court is brief. It seems, however, to have adopted a definition of the verb "to worship" as meaning to perform religious services, and to have adopted a dictionary definition of religion as "devotion to some principle; strict fidelity or faithfulness: conscientiousness; pious affection or attachment". In the *Washington Ethical Society* case the context of the Act undoubtedly weighed with the court. In *United States* v *Seeger* the judgments and the reasoning are much more thorough, and a great deal of weight has been placed on the views of modern theologians, including Bishop John Robinson and the views that he expressed in his book "Honest to God".

In a free country, and I have no reason to suppose that this country is less free than the United States, it is natural that the court should desire not to discriminate between beliefs deeply and sincerely held, whether they are beliefs in a god or in the excellence of man or in ethical principles or in Platonism or some other scheme of philosophy. But I do not see that that warrants extending the meaning of the word "religion" so as to embrace all other beliefs and philosophies. Religion, as I see it, is concerned with man's relations with God, and ethics are concerned with man's relations with man. The two are not the same, and are not made the same by sincere inquiry into the question, "What is God?". If reason leads people not to accept Christianity or any known religion, but they do believe in the excellence of qualities such as truth, beauty and love, or believe in the Platonic concept of the ideal, their beliefs may be to them the equivalent of a religion, but viewed objectively they are not religion. The ground of the opinion of the Supreme Court in *Seeger*'s case that any belief occupying in the life of its possessor a place parallel to that occupied by belief in God in the minds of theists is religion, prompts the comment that parallels, by definition, never meet.

In *Bowman* v *Secular Society Ltd* Lord Parker, in commenting on one of the objects of the society in that case, namely to promote the principle that human conduct should be based upon natural knowledge and not on supernatural belief, and that human welfare in this world is the proper end of all thought and action, said of that object:

"It is not a religious trust, for it relegates religion to a region in which it is to have no influence on human conduct."

That comment seems to me to be equally applicable to the objects of the society in the present case, and it is not to be answered in my judgment by attempting to extend the meaning of religion. Lord Parker has used the word "in its natural and accustomed sense".

Again, in *United Grand Lodge of Ancient, Free and Accepted Masons of England* v *Holborn Borough Council* [1957] 1 WLR 1080 Donovan J, delivering the judgment of the Divisional Court, after commenting that freemasonry held out certain standards of truth and justice by which masons were urged to regulate their conduct, and commenting that, in particular, masons were urged to be reverent, honest, compassionate, loyal, temperate, benevolent and chaste, said:

"Admirable though these objects are, it seems to us impossible to say that they add up to the advancement of religion."

Therefore I take the view that the objects of this society are not for the advancement of religion.

There is a further point. It seems to me that two of the essential attributes of religion are faith and worship; faith in a god and worship of that god. This is supported by the definitions of religion given in the Oxford English Dictionary, although I appreciate that there are other definitions in other dictionaries and books. The Oxford Dictionary gives as one of the definitions of religion:

"a particular system of faith and worship ... recognition on the part of man of some higher, unseen power as having control of his destiny and as being entitled to obedience, reverence and worship...".'

Sutton, Re, Stone v *Attorney-General* (1885) 28 Ch D 464 Chancery Division (Pearson J)

Wholly and exclusively charitable: 'charitable and deserving'

Facts
The testatrix directed that 'The whole of the money over which I have a disposing power be given in charitable and deserving objects.'

Held
The gift was good.

Pearson J:

'It is admitted that if the words were "be given in charitable objects" the bequest would be good, and, on the other hand, that if the words were "be given in deserving objects" the bequest would be bad. The question ... depends upon whether "charitable and deserving" is intended to describe one class of objects or two ... There can be no doubt as to the rule, that you ought so to construe a clause as to lean neither to the one side nor to the other; that you ought to give it its proper grammatical construction, not straining it in one direction in order to give more to charity, and not straining it in the other direction in order to give less to charity.

To my mind the words "charitable and deserving objects" means only one class of objects, and the word "charitable" governs the whole sentence. It means objects which are at once charitable and deserving ... Giving the best grammatical construction I can to this will, I think the testatrix has said that the objects of her bounty are to be charitable, but that they are at the same time to be deserving ... I must, therefore, hold that the gift is a good charitable gift.'

United Grand Lodge of Ancient Free and Accepted Masons of England v *Holborn Borough Council* [1957] 1 WLR 1080 Chancery Division (Donovan J)

Meaning of the 'advancement of religion'

Facts
The question was whether the objects of freemasonry were 'charitable or otherwise concerned with the advancement of religion'.

Held
They were not, and on what was for the advancement of religion Donovan J said:

'To advance religion means to promote it, to spread its message ever wider among mankind; to take some positive steps to sustain and increase religious belief; and these things are done in a variety of ways which may be comprehensively described as pastoral and missionary. There is nothing comparable to that in masonry. That is not said by way of criticism. For masonry really does something different. It says to a man, "whatever your religion or your mode of worship, believe in a Supreme Creator and lead a good moral life." Laudable as this precept is, it does not appear to us to be the same thing as the advancement of religion. There is no religious instruction, no programme for the persuasion of unbelievers, no religious supervision, to see that its members remain active and constant in the various religions they may profess, no holding of religious services, no pastoral or missionary work of any kind.'

Verge v *Somerville* [1924] AC 496 Privy Council (Lord Wrenbury, Lord Atkinson and Lord Darling)

Public benefit

Facts
The gift was for the repatriation of New South Wales soldiers returning from the First World War.

Held
The trust was good for the benefit of the community.

Lord Wrenbury:

> 'To ascertain whether a gift constitutes a valid charitable trust so as to escape being void on the ground of perpetuity, a first enquiry must be whether it is public – whether it is for the benefit of the community or of an appreciably important class of the community. The inhabitants of a parish or town, or any particular class of inhabitants, may for instance, be the objects of such a gift, but private individuals, or a fluctuating body of private individuals, cannot.'

Webb v O'Doherty and Others (1991) The Times 11 February Chancery Division (Hoffmann J)

Political campaign vis-à-vis educational charity

Facts
The plaintiff applied for an interlocutory injunction to restrain the defendants, ie, inter alios, the students' union of a College of Higher Education, from making disbursements out of student union funds to support a campaign to stop the Gulf War and also from affiliating with certain organisations which were themselves involved in such a campaign.

Held
The injunction so applied for would be granted. Thus, as Hoffmann J indicated, the students' union, being an educational charity, cannot use its funds for non-charitable purposes. Although, indeed, it has been accepted that educational purposes can include the discussion of political issues (see, in particular, *Attorney-General* v *Ross* [1986] 1 WLR 252, see ante, this chapter, such political aspect must be merely ancillary to the basic charitable purpose of the trust. As Hoffmann J pointed out in the instant case, there is '… a clear distinction between discussion of political matters and the dissemination or acquisition of information which might have a political content on the one hand and a campaign on a political issue on the other'. His Lordship stated that 'there was no doubt that campaigning in the sense of seeking to influence public opinion on political matters was not a charitable activity'. Although such campaigning was an activity which was completely open for students, as for anyone else '… it was not a proper object of the expenditure of charitable moneys'.

Commentary
This case is interesting in that it clearly indicates that a line must be drawn between political campaigning, which is not charitable, and ancillary political interest in an educational context, which remains charitable. Hoffmann J did, however, concede that 'There were some cases in which it was not altogether easy to distinguish between political discussion carried on for educational purposes and political campaigning'. As a case which exemplifies this difficulty his Lordship cited *McGovern* v *Attorney-General* [1982] Ch 321, see ante, this chapter.

Wedgwood, Re
See Chapter 7.

Williams v Kershaw (1835) 5 Cl & F 111n Chancery (Pepys MR)
Wholly and exclusively charitable: 'benevolent charitable and religious purposes'

Facts
The testator left his residuary estate to trustees 'to and for such benevolent, charitable and religious purposes as they in their discretion shall think most advantageous and beneficial'.

Held
The gift was void.

Pepys MR:

'It was argued, in order to prove the gift to be good, that the terms must be taken conjointly; if so, every application must be to a religious purpose, which would, no doubt, be benevolent, and, in a legal sense, charitable; but the question is, did the testator so consider it? Did he mean that there should be no application of any part of the residuary fund, except to religious purposes? Such does not appear to me to be his intention; he intended to restrain the discretion of the trustees, only within the limits of what was benevolent, or charitable, or religious.'

Williams' Trustees v *IRC* [1947] AC 447 House of Lords (Lord Simonds, Viscount Simon, Lord Wright, Lord Normand and Lord Porter)

Public benefit requirement

Facts
A trust was established for the benefit of Welsh people in London 'for promoting the moral social spiritual and educational welfare of Welsh people and fostering the study of the Welsh language and of Welsh history, literature music and art'. The question arose whether the trust was exempt from income tax on the ground that it was charitable.

Held
It was not: Welsh people in London did not form a section of the community but were a 'fluctuating body of private individuals'.

The following further cases are authority for the proposition that the object listed is or is not charitable (there are of course many others):

Case	*Gift to*
Attorney-General v *Mayor of Dartmouth* (1883) 48 LT 933	The use of the town of Dartmouth
Attorney-General v *Ockover* (1736) 1 Ves Sen 536	Church organ
Beaumont v *Oliviera* (1869) 4 Ch 309	Royal Humane Society – relief of distress
Bonar Law Memorial Trust v *IRC* (1933) 49 TLR 933	Political propaganda even when claimed to be educational
British Museum v *White* (1826) 2 S & S 594	Public libraries
Harrison v *Southampton Corporation* (1854) 2 Sm & G 387	Botanical Gardens
Hoare v *Osborne* (1866) LR 1 Eq 585	Monument in a church
Houston v *Burns* [1918] AC 337	Public purposes void – not exclusively charitable

IRC v *Yorkshire Agricultural Society* [1928] 1 KB 611	Agricultural show – public benefit
Liverpool City Council v *Attorney-General* (1992) The Times 1 May	Gift of park/recreational field – not a recreational charity
Re Barker (1909) 25 TLR 753	Prizes to be competed for by armed forces cadets
Re Christchurch Enclosure Act (1888) 36 Ch D 520	For residents of a certain area to graze cows
Re Clergy Society (1856) 2 K & J 65	Church Missionary Society
Re Cottam [1955] 1 WLR 1299	Flats for aged persons at low rents
Re Cranstoun's Will Trusts [1949] 1 Ch 523	The preservation of ancient buildings is educational and thus charitable
Re Gardom [1914] 1 Ch 662	Ladies of limited means – valid for relief of poverty
Re Lewis [1955] Ch 104	Ten blind girls and boys residents of Tottenham
Re Macduff [1896] 2 Ch 451	Trust for philanthropic purposes void
Re Manser [1905] 1 Ch 68	Quakers
Re Pleasants (1923) 39 TLR 675	Annual outing for children
Re Vagliano [1905] WN 179	Asylums
Re Verrall [1916] 1 Ch 100	National Trust
Re Wokingham Fire Brigade Trusts [1951] Ch 373	Fire Brigade
Thomas v *Howell* (1874) LR 18 Eq 198	Lifeboats – for the relief of distress

9 The Cy-près Doctrine

Biscoe v Jackson (1887) 35 Ch D 460 Court of Appeal (Cotton, Lindley and Fry LJJ)
General charitable intention

Facts
A testator bequeathed £40,000 to be used for charitable purposes. £10,000 of this was to be applied 'in the establishment of a soup kitchen in the parish of Shoreditch and a cottage hospital adjoining thereto …' It was impossible to obtain land for this purpose so the next-of-kin claimed the fund.

Held
A general charitable intention existed. Cotton LJ observed:

> 'We see an intention on the part of the testator to give £10,000 to the sick and poor of the parish of Shoreditch, pointing out how he desires that to be applied; and that particular mode having failed, as we must for the purposes of this appeal assume to be the case, then the intention to benefit the poor of Shoreditch, being a good charitable object, will have effect given to it according to the general principle laid down long ago by this court, by applying it cy-près.'

Dominion Students' Hall Trust, Re [1947] 1 Ch 183 Chancery Division (Evershed J)
Charity – fulfilment – impossibility

Facts
A company limited by guarantee maintained a hostel for male students of 'overseas' dominions of the British Empire. It applied to the court in respect of the administration of a scheme within it limited to 'European origin' dominion students. They requested that the reference to racial origin and in particular the term 'European origin' be removed.

Held
The term in question was likely to antagonise its potential beneficiaries whilst undermining its objects of promoting community of citizenship, culture and tradition. The effect was to make it 'impossible' to carry out the charity's terms and the offending clause would therefore be struck out.

Faraker, Re [1912] 2 Ch 488 Court of Appeal (Cozens-Hardy MR, Farwell and Kennedy LJJ)
Meaning of 'cease to exist' of a charity

Facts
Mrs Faraker died in 1911 and by her will she gave a legacy of £200 'to Mrs Bailey's Charity, Rotherhithe'. There had been a charity known as Mrs Hannah Bayly's Charity at Rotherhithe, founded in

1756, for the benefit of poor widows resident in the parish of St Mary's Rotherhithe. In 1905 the Charity Commissioners consolidated this and several other charities in Rotherhithe into one trust for the benefit of the poor of Rotherhithe but made no mention to the charity. The question arose whether the gift had lapsed (no question was raised on the spelling; it was agreed Mrs Faraker intended to refer to Hannah Bayly's charity). On appeal:

Held
The gift had not lapsed. Hannah Bayly's charity was still in existence subject to the alteration which had been made by the Charity Commissioners. The gift to the charity was one which simply identified the charity by name and therefore carried with it the application of it to the lawful objects of the charity funds for the time being.

Farwell LJ:

'... What is said is this: the Commissioners have in fact destroyed this trust because in the scheme which they have issued dealing with the amalgamation of the several charities the objects are stated to be poor persons of good character resident in Rotherhithe, not mentioning widows in particular – not of course excluding them, but not giving them that preference which I agree with the Master of the Rolls in thinking ought to have been given. But to say that this omission has incidentally destroyed the Bayly Trust is a very strained construction of the language and one that entirely fails, because the Charity Commissioners had no jurisdiction whatever to destroy the Charity. Suppose the Charity Commissioners or this Court were to declare that a particular existing charitable trust was at an end and extinct, in my opinion they would go beyond their jurisdiction is so doing. They cannot take an existing charity and destroy it: they are obliged to administer it. To say that this pardonable slip (I use the word with all respect to the draftsman) has the effect of destroying the charity appears to me to be extravagant. In all these cases one has to consider not so much the means to the end as the charitable end which is in view, and so long as that charitable end is well established the means are only machinery, and no alteration of the machinery can destroy the charitable trust for the benefit of which the machinery is provided.'

Finger's Will Trusts, Re [1972] Ch 286 Chancery Division (Goff J)
Lapse: difference between gifts to corporate and unincorporated bodies

Facts
The testatrix died in 1965 and by her will made in 1930, she left her residuary estate to be divided in equal shares among eleven named charities. One share was given to the 'National Radium Commission'. This was construed as a gift to the Radium Commission, an unincorporated charity set up by Royal Charter in 1929 but wound up in 1947 when its work was taken over by the National Health Service and carried on by it. Another share was given to the 'National Council for Maternity and Child Welfare', a corporate body which existed at the date of the will but which had been wound up in 1948 and its assets transferred to the 'National Association for Maternity and Child Welfare' which continued the Council's work. The question arose whether these charitable gifts had lapsed and if so, whether they could be applied by cy-près.

Held
1. The gift to the 'National Radium Commission' was a gift to an unincorporated body and therefore took effect per se as a gift for the purpose which it existed to serve. As the Commission's work was still being carried on and there was nothing in the terms of the gift to indicate that the gift was dependent on the continued existence of the Commission, the gift did not fail and could have effect given to it by way of scheme.

2. The gift to the 'National Council for Maternity for Child Welfare' was a gift to a corporate body and therefore took effect simply as a gift to that body beneficially unless there were circumstances to show that it was to take as trustee. There was no such circumstances shown in this case and as the Council had ceased to exist before the testatrix's death, the gift to it failed. However, it was possible to find a general charitable intention behind the gift because the testatrix regarded herself as having no relatives. Therefore, the gift could be applied cy-près as all the elements necessary for this in a case of initial impossibility were present.

Goff J:

'Accordingly I hold that the bequest to the National Radium Commission being a gift to an unincorporated charity is a purpose trust for the work of the commission which does not fail but is applicable under a scheme, provided (1) there is nothing in the context of the will to show – and I quote from *Re Vernon's Will Trusts* [1972] Ch 300 – that the testatrix's intention to make a gift at all was dependent upon the named charitable organisation being available at the time when the gift took effect to serve as the instrument for applying the subject-matter of the gift to the charitable purpose for which it was by inference given; (2) that charitable purpose still survives; but that the gift to the National Council for Maternity and Child Welfare, 117 Piccadilly, London being a gift to a corporate body fails notwithstanding the work continues, unless there is a context in the will to show that the gift was intended to be on trust for that purpose and not an absolute gift to the corporation.'

Harwood, Re [1936] Ch 285 Chancery Division (Farwell J)

Impossible gift

Facts
The testatrix made a will in 1925 leaving a bequest of £200 to the Wisbech Peace Society, Cambridge and a bequest of £300 to the Peace Society of Belfast. When the testatrix died in 1934 the Wisbech Peace Society had by that time ceased to exist. However, there was no evidence that there was a Peace Society of Belfast in existence or indeed that one had ever existed.

Held
The bequest to the Wisbech Peace Society lapsed and could not be applied cy-près, as there was no general charitable intention. But, the bequest to the Peace Society of Belfast could be applied cy-près, it indicated a means of benefiting a charity, there was a general charitable intention.

Farwell J:

'Then there is the gift to the "Peace Society of Belfast". The claimant for this legacy is the Belfast Branch of the League of Nations Union. I am quite unable on the evidence to say that that was the society which this lady intended to benefit, and I doubt whether the lady herself knew exactly what society she did mean to benefit. I think she had a desire to benefit any society which was formed for the purpose of promoting peace and was connected with Belfast. Beyond that, I do not think that she had any very clear idea in her mind. That is rather indicated by the pencil note which was found after her death. At any rate I cannot say that by the description, "the Peace Society of Belfast", the lady meant the Belfast Branch of the League of Nations Union; but there is enough in this case to enable me to say that, although there is no gift to any existing society, the gift does not fail. It is a good charitable gift and must be applied cy-près. The evidence suggests that at some time or other, possibly before the late War, there may have been a society called the Peace Society of Belfast. It is all hearsay evidence; there is nothing in the least definite about it, and it does not satisfy me that there ever was any society in existence which exactly fits the description in this case, and there being a clear intention on the part of the lady, as expressed in her will, to benefit societies whose object was the promotion of peace, and there being no such society as that named in her will, in this case there is a general charitable intent, and, accordingly, the doctrine of cy-près applies.'

Jenkins's Will Trusts, Re [1966] Ch 249 Chancery Division (Buckley J)

Construction of general charitable intention

Facts
A testatrix bequeathed her residuary estate in seven equal parts, six to charitable organisations and one to the British Union for the Abolition of Vivisection. The question arose whether the share to the British Union should be held on charitable trusts on the ground it disclosed a general charitable intention.

Held
Buckley J:

'The principle of noscitur a sociis does not in my judgment entitle one to overlook self-evident facts. If you meet seven men with black hair and one with red hair you are not entitled to say that here are eight men with black hair. Finding one gift for a non-charitable purpose among a number of gifts for charitable purposes the court cannot infer that the testator or testatrix meant the non-charitable gift to take effect as a charitable gift when in the terms it is not charitable, even though the non-charitable gift may have a close relation to the purposes for which the charitable gifts are made.'

Lepton's Charity, Re [1972] 1 Ch 276 Chancery Division (Pennycuick V-C)

Charities Act 1960 s13(1): meaning of 'original purposes'

Facts
In 1716 a testator devised funds on trust to pay out of the income up to £3 per annum to the Protestant dissenting minister at Pudsey, and the residue to the poor and aged of Pudsey. In 1716 the annual income was £5, but by 1967 it was £792 and the minister was still only receiving £3. The trustees applied to the court under s13 to raise the minister's payment to £100 per annum.

Held
Under the section (a)(ii), the original purpose could not be carried out 'according to the ... spirit of the gift'; and under (e)(iii), it had 'ceased to provide a suitable ... method of using the property ... regard being had to the spirit of the gift'. Where the income, as here, was to be distributed amongst two objects, the 'original purpose' as defined in the section was the trust as a whole. The testator had intended the bulk of the gift for the minister and only residue for the other object. The minister in 1716 had taken three fifths of the income, and under the circumstances the court would exercise its power under the section and approve the increase as requested.

Oldham Borough Council v Attorney-General (1992) The Times 5 August Court of Appeal (Dillon, Russell and Farquharson LJJ)

Cy-près doctrine – sale of land – original purposes – whether attaching to trust property – court's inherent jurisdiction

Facts
Oldham Borough Council (OBC) held playing fields, by deed of gift, under a trust to manage the fields

only as playing fields or for the benefit of local people. OBC planned to sell the land and use the proceeds to provide an alternative, better equipped, sports facility.

Held
By s13 Charities Act 1960, the alteration of 'original purposes' of a charitable gift required a cy-près scheme within the conditions of the Act. While, on the facts, the Act's conditions had not been met, 'original purposes' did not necessarily attach to property per se. Therefore, subject to the property not having any intrinsic charitable value linking it to the 'original purposes' (for example, an historical site) the property itself could be disposed of with the proceeds being applied to the original purposes. Accordingly the Court granted OBC permission to sell the land pursuant to its inherent powers.

Roberts, Re [1963] 1 WLR 406 Chancery Division (Wilberforce J)
Named institutions and lapse

Facts
The testator left a residuary gift for, inter alia, 'The Sheffield Boys' Working Home'. By the testator's death the Home had ceased to function.

Held
Although the physical entity had ceased to exist, the charitable work for which the home had existed continued. The gift accordingly did not lapse and could be applied cy-près.
Wilberforce J:
> 'The courts have gone very far in the decided cases to resist the conclusion that a legacy to a charitable institution lapses, and a number of very refined arguments have been found acceptable with a view to avoiding that conclusion.'

Rymer, Re [1895] 1 Ch 19 Court of Appeal (Lord Herschell LC, Lindley and AL Smith LJJ)
Gift to a particular body: lapse

Facts
The testator bequeathed a legacy of £5,000 'to the rector for the time being of St Thomas' Seminary for the education of priests in the diocese of Westminster for the purpose of such seminary'. At the date of the will the seminary was being carried on at Hammersmith but it ceased to exist and before the testator's death the students were transferred to Birmingham, to a seminary there. Chitty J held the gift had lapsed as there was no general charitable intention. On appeal:

Held
This was a gift to a particular seminary only which had lapsed and as there was no general charitable intention there could be no cy-près application.
Lindley LJ:
> '... We are asked to overrule the doctrine laid down by Vice-Chancellor Kindersley in *Clark* v *Taylor* (1853) 1 Drew 642 and followed in *Fisk* v *Attorney-General* (1867) LR 4 Eq 521. I think that the doctrine is perfectly right. There may be difficulty in arriving at the conclusion that there is a lapse. But when once you arrive at the conclusion that a gift to a particular seminary or institution, or whatever you may

call it, is "for the purposes thereof", and for no other purpose – if once you get to that, and it is proved that that institution or seminary, or whatever it is, has ceased to exist in the lifetime of the testator, you are driven to arrive at the conclusion that there is a lapse and then the doctrine of cy-près is inapplicable. That is in accordance with the law, and in accordance with all the cases that can be cited. I quite agree that in coming to that conclusion you have to consider whether the mode of attaining the object is only machinery, or whether the mode is not the substance of the gift. Here it appears to me that the gift to the seminary is in substance the whole of the thing. It is the object of the testator. I think it is plain from the language used.'

Satterthwaite's Will Trusts, Re [1966] 1 WLR 277 Court of Appeal (Harman, Diplock and Russell LJJ)

Construction of general charitable intention

Facts
The testatrix was known to have a hatred of the human race. By her will she left her estate to nine animal organisations which were apparently selected at random from a London telephone directory. Six were charities, one unidentifiable, one the National Anti-Vivisection Society and another the 'London Animal Hospital'. A veterinary surgeon who at one time practised under the name of the 'London Animal Hospital' but ceased practice before the testatrix made her will. He nevertheless claimed the gift.

Held
The bequest to the 'London Animal Hospital' was a gift by descriptive title and indicated an intention to benefit a charity and not the proprietor of a business. The nine bequests, by reason of the description of the beneficiaries showed a general charitable intention, being animal kindness, and therefore should be applied cy-près.

Russell LJ:

'My assumption is that the testatrix was pointing to a particular charitable application of this one-ninth of residue. If a particular mode of charitable application is incapable of being performed as such, but it can be discerned from his will that the testator has a charitable intention (commonly referred to as a general charitable intention) which transcends the particular mode of application indicated, the court has jurisdiction to direct application of the bequest to charitable purposes cy-près. Here I have no doubt from the nature of the other dispositions by this testatrix of her residuary estate that a general intention can be discerned in favour of charity through the medium of kindness to animals. I am not in any way given to an anti-vivisection society which in law – unknown to the average testator – is not charitable.'

Slevin, Re [1891] 2 Ch 236 Court of Appeal (Lindley, Bowen and Kay LJJ)

Supervening impossibility

Facts
The testator bequeathed several legacies to various charitable organisations including an orphanage which was run voluntarily by a lady at her own expense, by his will. The orphanage was in existence at the testator's death but was discontinued shortly afterwards and before the assets of his estate were administered. The question arose whether a charitable bequest to an institution which comes to an end after the death of the testator, but before the legacy is paid over, fails for the benefit of the residuary legatee, as in the case of lapse. Stirling J held that it did but the Attorney-General appealed claiming that the gift should be applied cy-près.

The Cy-près Doctrine

Held

The gift could be applied cy-près because lapse of the gift can only occur during the testator's lifetime except where the testator has provided for a resulting trust on failure of the charity or on its ceasing to exist.

Kay LJ:

'The orphanage did come to an end before the legacy was paid over. In the case of a legacy to an individual, if he survived the testator it could not be argued that the legacy would fall into the residue. Even if the legatee died intestate and without next-of-kin, still the money was his, and the residuary legatee would have no right whatever against the Crown. So, if the legatee were a corporation which was dissolved after the testator's death, the residuary legatee would have no claim.

Obviously it can make no difference that the legatee ceased to exist immediately after the death of the testator. The same view must be applicable whether it was a day, or month, or year, or as might well happen, ten years after; the legacy not having been paid either from delay occasioned by the administration of the estate or owing to part of the estate not having been got in. The legacy became the property of the legatee on the death of the testator, though he might not, for some reason, obtain the receipt of it till long after. When once it became the absolute property of the legatee, that is equivalent to saying that it must be provided for; and the residue is only what remains after making such provision. It does not for all purposes cease to be part of the testator's estate until the executors admit assets and appropriate and pay it over; but that is merely for their convenience and that of the estate. The rights as between the particular legatee and the residue are fixed at the testator's death ...

In the present case we think that the Attorney-General must succeed, not on the ground that there is such a general charitable intention that the fund should be administered cy-près even if the charity had failed in the testator's lifetime, but because, as the charity existed at the testator's death, this legacy became the property of that charity, and on its ceasing to exist its property fails to be administered by the Crown, who will apply it, according to custom, for some analogous purpose of charity.'

Spence's Will Trusts, Re [1979] Ch 483 Chancery Division (Megarry V-C)

Lapse: valid gift subject to limitation

Facts

A testatrix under the terms of her will left her residuary estate to be divided 'equally between The Blind Home Scott Street, Keighley and the Old Folk's Home at Hillworth Lodge, Keighley for the benefit of the patients'. The Keighley and District Association for the Blind was the only charity connected with the blind in the Keighley area. It ran a home in Scott Street which was often called 'The Blind Home', 'The Keighley and District Home for the Blind' and 'Keighley Home for the Blind'. A similar home was also run by the Association at Bingley. At the time the testatrix made her will an old people's home was run by the local authority at Hillworth Lodge but at the time of the testatrix's death the old people's home had been closed and was being converted into Council offices. The executors of the will sought a declaration as to whether the residuary gift was valid.

Held

1. In making a gift to 'The Blind Home' the testatrix was intending to make provision for the benefit of the patients at the Blind Home, Scott Street, Keighley. However, by the terms of the gift it was clear that she was not giving the money to augment the endowment of the charity which ran the home. Therefore, the charity could not apply the money for any of its objects but must limit the application of it for the benefit of the patients.
2. The gift to the 'Old Folk's Home' failed. It was a gift for a specific purpose behind which there was

no general charitable intention. Therefore, as the gift had become impossible before the testatrix died it had lapsed and there could be no application of the gift of cy-près.

Stemson's Will Trusts, Re [1970] Ch 16 Chancery Division (Plowman J)

Lapse: charity ceased to exist

Facts
The testator bequeathed his residuary estate to the Rationalist Endowment Fund Ltd (REF), an incorporated charity, by his will made in 1950. REF was dissolved in 1965 and its funds passed in accordance with its memorandum of association to the Rationalist Press Association Ltd also an incorporated charity but which, unlike REF, did not have the relief of poverty among its objects. The testator died in 1966 without having amended his will.

Held
Where funds come into the hands of a charitable organisation such as REF which was not a perpetual charity, but liable to termination, and its constitution provided for the disposal of its funds on termination, then, if it ceased to exist and its funds were disposed of the charity or charitable trust itself ceased to exist. Therefore, the gift of residuary estate could not take effect as directed; there was initial impossibility and because there was no general charitable intention the gift could not be applied cy-près.

Plowman J:

> 'I think that the true proposition was accurately formulated by Mr.Warner when he said that a charitable trust which no one has power to terminate retains its existence despite such vicissitudes as schemes, amalgamations and change of name so long as it has any funds. It follows, in my judgment that where funds come to the hands of a charitable organisation, such as REF, which is founded, not as a perpetual charity but as one liable to termination, and its constitution provides for the disposal of its funds in that event, then if the organisation ceases to exist and its funds are disposed of the charity or charitable trust itself ceases to exist and there is nothing to prevent the operation of the doctrine of lapse.'

Ulverston & District New Hospital Building Fund, Re [1956] Ch 622 Court of Appeal (Lord Evershed MR, Jenkins and Hodson LJJ)

Failure of object: resulting trust

Facts
Money had been collected for the building of a new hospital, but not enough was forthcoming and it became obvious that the purpose had failed.

Held
There had been no general charitable intent, only a specific object which was now unattainable. Accordingly the money raised was now held on resulting trust for return to the donors.

Commentary
The redistribution required in these cases has been made much simpler of administration by s14 Charities Act 1960.

Vernon's Will Trusts, Re [1972] Ch 300 (decided in 1962) Chancery Division (Buckley J)

Lapse: meaning of 'ceased to exist'

Facts

The testatrix died in 1960 and by her will made in 1937 she directed that her residuary estate should be divided 'among the following charitable institutions in equal shares: Coventry Crippled Children's Guild; The National Lifeboat Institution; The Royal Midland Counties Home for Incurables (at Leamington)'. At the date of the will there was in existence an institution called the 'Coventry and District Crippled Children's Guild'. This institution had been incorporated under the Companies Act 1919 and it provided orthopaedic clinics and convalescent homes for crippled children. By virtue of the National Health Act 1946 the assets of the Guild were vested in the Minister of Health in 1948. In 1952 the Guild was dissolved and its name struck off the register of companies but a hospital and a clinic which had been founded by the Guild continued in existence and were in existence at the testatrix's death in 1960.

However, in 1949 an unincorporated body known as The Coventry and District Cripples' Guild was formed. This charitable body had as its object the aid and support of cripples but it did not carry out any orthopaedic work. The question arose as to which institution was entitled to the share of residue and if it was the Coventry and District Crippled Children's Guild, whether the gift had lapsed.

Held

The testatrix clearly intended to refer to an institution which she believed to exist at the time she made her will in 1937. Her words were a misdescription of the Coventry and District Crippled Children's Guild and there was a valid gift to this body because there was no indication that it was to take the gift beneficially and not for the charitable purpose for which it existed. Therefore, although the institution had ceased to exist, the charity had not, as its work was being carried on at a hospital and clinic by the Minister of Health.

Buckley J:

> 'Every bequest to an unincorporated charity by name without more must take effect as a gift for a charitable purpose. No individual or aggregate of individuals could claim to take such a bequest beneficially. If the gift is to be permitted to take effect at all, it must be as a bequest for a purpose viz, that charitable purpose which the named charity exists to serve. A bequest which is in terms made for a charitable purpose will not fail for lack of a trustee but will be carried into effect either under the Sign Manual or by means of a scheme. A bequest to a named unincorporated charity, however, may on its true interpretation show that the testator's intention to make the gift at all was dependent upon the named charitable organisation being available at the time when the gift takes effect to serve as the instrument for applying the subject-matter of the gift to the charitable purpose for which it is by inference given. If so, and the named charity ceases to exist in the lifetime of the testator, the gift fails (*Re Ovey* (1885) 29 Ch D 560).
>
> A bequest to a corporate body, on the other hand, takes effect simply as a gift to that body beneficially, unless there are circumstances which show that the recipient is to take the gift as a trustee. There is no need in such a case to infer a trust for any particular purpose. The objects to which the corporate body can properly apply its funds may be restricted by its constitution, but this does not necessitate inferring as a matter of construction of the testator's will a direction that the bequest is to be held in trust to be applied for those purposes: the natural construction is that the bequest is made to the corporate body as part of its general funds, that is to say, beneficially and without the imposition of any trust. That the testator's motive in making the bequest may have undoubtedly been to assist the work of the incorporated body would be insufficient to create at trust.'

10 Appointment, Retirement and Removal of Trustees

Clout & Frewers Contract, Re [1924] Ch 230 Chancery Division (Lord Buckmaster for Astbury J)

Trustee – disclaimer by conduct

Facts
An executor trustee survived the testator for almost 30 years without proving or acting under the will or even applying for the legacy left to him in his official capacity.

Held
Discounting previous inconsistent case law, his conduct was held to amount to disclaimer.
  At p235, '… the mere fact that a trustee does nothing for three years is strong, though not conclusive, evidence that he does not intend to act. Surely a longer period of inaction would be still stronger evidence.'

Letterstedt* v *Broers (1884) 9 App Cas 371 Privy Council (Lord Blackburn, Sir Robert Collier, Sir Richard Couch and Sir Arthur Hobhouse)

Principles on which the court removes a trustee

Facts
The Board of Executors of Cape Town were the sole surviving executors and trustees of a will. The appellant beneficiary alleged misconduct in the administration of the trust and claimed that the board were unfit to act as trustees and should be removed and a new appointment made.

Held
The court had a jurisdiction to remove a trustee and replace him and the principal consideration in doing this would be the welfare of the beneficiaries. The board had not been guilty of misconduct but because of the hostility which had arisen it would be best to remove and replace them in the interest of the welfare of the beneficiaries.

Lord Blackburn:

'In exercising so delicate a jurisdiction as that of removing trustees, their Lords do not venture to lay down any general rule beyond the very broad principle above enunciated, that their main guide must be the welfare of the beneficiaries. Probably it is not possible to lay down any more definite rule in a matter so essentially dependent on details often of great nicety …
  It is quite true that friction or hostility between trustees and the immediate possessor of the trust estate is not itself a reason for the removal of the trustees. But where the hostility is grounded on the mode in

which the trust has been administered, where it has been caused wholly or partially by substantial overcharges against the trust estate, it is certainly not to be disregarded.

Looking, therefore, at the whole circumstances of this very peculiar case, the complete change of position, the unfortunate hostility that has arisen and the difficult and delicate duties that may yet have to be performed, their Lordships can come to no other conclusion than that it is necessary, for the welfare of the beneficiaries, that the Board should no longer be trustees.'

Tempest, Re (1866) Ch App 485 Court of Appeal in Chancery (Turner and Knight-Bruce LJJ)

Principles on which the Court appoints a trustee

Facts
A testator devised property to Stonor and Fleming on certain trusts. Stonor predeceased the testator and the persons with the power of appointing new trustees were unable to agree in the choice of a new trustee. A beneficiary petitioned the court for the appointment of Petre as a trustee. But another beneficiary opposed this petition on the ground that Petre came from a branch of the testator's family with which the testator was not on friendly terms and which he had excluded from the management of his property.

Held
Petre was not a person the court would appoint.

Turner LJ:

'The following rules and principles may, I think, safely be laid down as applying to all cases of appointments by the court of new trustees.

First, the court will have regard to the wishes of the persons by whom the trust has been created, if expressed in the instrument creating the trust, or clearly to be collected from it. I think this rule may be safely laid down, because if the author of the trust has in terms declared that a particular person, or a person filling a particular character, should not be a trustee of the instrument, there cannot, as I apprehend, be the least doubt that the court would not appoint to the office a person whose appointment was so prohibited, and I do not think that upon a question of this description any distinction can be drawn between express declarations and demonstrated intention.

The analogy of the course which the court pursues in the appointment of guardians affords, I think, some support to this rule. The court in those cases attends to the wishes of the parents, however informally they may be expressed.

Another rule which may, I think, safely be laid down is this – that the court will not appoint a person to be a trustee with a view to the interest of some of the persons interested under the trust, in opposition either to the wishes of the testator or to the interests of others of the cestius que trusts. I think so for this reason, that it is of the essence of the duty of every trustee to hold an even hand between the parties interested under the trust. Every trustee is duty bound to look to the interests of all, and not of any particular member or class of members of his cestuis que trusts.

A third rule which, I think may safely be laid down is this – that the court in appointing a trustee will have regard to the question, whether his appointment will promote or impede the execution of the trust, for the very purpose of the appointment is that the trust may be better carried into execution.'

11 Trustees' Fiduciary Duties

Biss, Re [1903] 2 Ch 40 Court of Appeal (Collins MR, Romer and Cozens-Hardy LJJ)

No fiduciary duty

Facts
A widow took out letters of administration on her husband's intestacy and she and her daughter and son continued to carry on the husband's profitable business as a lodging-house keeper in Westminster. The lodging house was held on a yearly tenancy and the widow applied for a renewal of the lease for the benefit of the estate. This the lessor refused to grant and he determined the yearly tenancy by notice. Afterwards, the lessor granted the son 'personally' a new lease for three years. The widow claimed that the son held the new lease for the benefit of the estate.

Held
No constructive trust arose; the son could keep the new lease for himself. Any chance of the estate receiving a renewal of the lease was extinguished by the refusal of the widow's application. Further, the son had not abused his position in any way and he did not stand in a fiduciary relationship to other persons interested in the estate because he was at most only a beneficiary of the estate.

Collins MR:

> '... In the present case the appellant is simply one of the next of kin of the former tenant, and had, as such, a possible interest in the term. He was not, as such, a trustee for the others interested, nor was he in possession. The administratrix represented the estate and alone had the right to renew incident thereto, and she unquestionably could renew only for the benefit of the estate. But is the appellant in the same category? Or is he entitled to go into the facts to shew that he had not, in point of fact, abused his position, or in any sense intercepted an advantage coming by way of accretion to the estate. He did not take under a will or a settlement with interests coming after his own, but simply got a possible share upon an intestacy in case there was a surplus of assets over debts. It seems to me that this obligation cannot be put higher than that of any other tenant in common against whom it would have to be established, not as a presumption of law but as an inference of fact, that he had abused his position. If he is not under a personal incapacity to take a benefit, he is entitled to shew that the renewal was not in fact an accretion to the original term, and that it was not until there had been an absolute refusal on the part of the lessor and after full opportunity to the administratrix to procure it for the estate if she could, that he accepted a proposal of renewal made to him by the lessor. These questions cannot be considered or discussed when the party is by his position debarred from keeping a personal advantage derived directly or indirectly out of his fiduciary or quasi-fiduciary position, but when he is not so debarred I think it becomes a question of fact whether that which he has received was in his hands an accretion to the interest of the deceased, or whether the connection between the estate and the renewal had not been wholly severed by the action of the lessor before the appellant accepted a new lease. This consideration seems to get rid of any difficulty that one of the next of kin was an infant. The right or hope of renewal incident to the estate was determined before the plaintiff intervened ...'

Boardman v Phipps

See Chapter 6.

Budgett v Budgett [1895] 1 Ch 202 Chancery Division (Kekewich J)

Indemnity

Facts
During taxation of solicitor and client costs it transpired that some costs and disbursements met by the solicitors as trustees had in fact been statute-barred. Similarly some unpaid costs which the solicitors wished to pay were now statute-barred.

Held
Trustees may pay statute-barred claims, and are still entitled to an indemnity, even if the beneficiaries did not wish the claims paid.

Chapple, Re (1884) 27 Ch D 584 Chancery Division (Kay J)

Fiduciary's power to receive remuneration will be construed strictly

Facts
A testatrix by her will appointed her solicitor as one of her two executors and trustees and stated that she desired him to continue to act as solicitor in relation to her property and affairs and that he should 'make the usual professional charges'. Under this direction the solicitor-trustee delivered bills of costs which included charges for all business done by him whether of a strictly professional nature or not.

Held
On the construction of the clause only items which were of a strictly professional character were allowed.

Kay J:

> 'Now a trustee or executor would not employ, and ought not to employ, a solicitor to do things which he could properly do himself. And any person whose fortune it is to be a trustee or executor has many things to do which he cannot properly throw on his solicitor. Accordingly, to return to the language of the will, when it says that the solicitor shall be "entitled to retain out of any trust money or to be allowed, and to receive from his co-trustees (if any) out of the same money the full amount of such charges" they must be charges for something in respect of which he has been properly employed.'

Corsellis, Re (1887) 34 Ch D 675 Court of Appeal (Cotton, Lindley and Lopes LJJ)

Solicitor/trustee's powers to charge for professional services

Facts
A solicitor who was one of the trustees of a will which contained no power to charge for professional services was, with his co-trustee, a respondent to an application for maintenance by a next friend on behalf of an infant, the maintenance to come out of the rent and profits of the testator's estate. As the application was to be heard in London, the solicitor employed London agents and made profit costs. The question arose whether his firm was entitled to these.

Held
The solicitor's firm was entitled to receive these as coming within the exception laid down in *Cradock v Piper* which applied not only to proceedings in a hostile suit, but to friendly proceedings in Chambers, such as an application for the maintenance of an infant.

Cotton LJ:

> '... The exception in *Cradock v Piper* is limited expressly to the costs incurred in respect of business done in an action or a suit, and it may be an anomaly that exception should apply to such a case, and should not apply to business done out of court by the solicitor for himself as trustee and his co-trustee. But there may be this reason for it, that in an action, although costs are not always hostilely taxed, yet there may be a taxation where parties other than the trustee-solicitor may appear and test the propriety of the costs, and the court can disallow altogether the costs of any proceedings which may appear to be vexatious or improperly undertaken. But whatever may be the principle, the question is whether that is not an established rule. In my opinion, as it is a rule laid down by Lord Cottenham so long ago as 1850, it would be wrong of this court, even if they would not originally have arrived at the same conclusion as Lord Cottenham did in that case, to disturb the rule and reverse the decision. He was Lord Chancellor sitting as a Court of Appeal, and a court of co-ordinate jurisdiction with our own court, and although learned Judges have expressed disapproval of that decision, it has been recognised as a rule in taxing costs from the time of the decision down to the present time. In *Broughton v Broughton* (1855) 5 De GM & G 160 Lord Cranworth said that he could not understand the decision, but he did not overrule the case; and Lord Justice Turner, when Vice-Chancellor, in *Lincoln v Windsor* (1851) 9 Hare 158, treated it as an established rule ...
>
> Then what is said to be the special difference in this case? It is said that the exception would only apply to costs in a hostile action, and that this was not an action at all, but only a summons, and that therefore the exception ought not to apply. Undoubtedly the proceeding was not in any hostile action, but was commenced, as I understand, by a summons; but in my opinion, it would be frittering away the decision, which we ought not to overrule, by saying that it only applied to a hostile action, no such limitation being laid down by Lord Cottenham. Therefore I am of opinion that the rule by way of exception established in *Cradock v Piper* (1850) 1 Mac & G 664 does apply to the first part of the costs, and we cannot agree with Mr Justice Kay as regards that part of his decision. Those costs, I think, the defendant, the trustee, ought not to be required to bring into account.'

Cradock v Piper (1850) 1 Mac & G 664 Chancery (Lord Cottenham LC)

Solicitor/trustee's remuneration

Facts
A trustee was also a solicitor. In his capacity as solicitor he represented the other trustees and beneficiaries in an action brought by creditors of the testator. The master taxing the costs disallowed all charges for professional work done by the trustee/solicitor.

Held
He could charge.

Lord Cottenham LC:

> '... the rule has been supposed to be founded upon the well known principle that a trustee cannot be permitted to make a profit of his office, which he would do, if, being party to a cause as trustee, he were permitted, being also a solicitor, to derive professional profits from acting for himself ... The rule ... is confined to cases in which the business or employment of the solicitor is the proper business or employment of the trustee; but it is no part of the business or employment of a trustee to assist other parties

in suits relative to trust property. If, therefore, the trustee acts as solicitor for such other parties, such business or employment is not any business or employment of the trustee; and the rule as hitherto laid down does not apply ... I am therefore of opinion that the rule does not extend beyond costs of the trustee, where he acts as solicitor for himself.'

Dougan v *McPherson* [1902] AC 197 House of Lords (Lord Halsbury LC, Lord Ashbourne, Lord Brampton, Lord Lindley, Lord Macnaghten and Lord Shand)

Trustee/beneficiary duty to other beneficiary

Facts
Two brothers A and B were beneficiaries under a trust. A was also a trustee but B was not. A purchased B's beneficial interest without showing him a valuation of the trust estate. In fact B's share was worth more than A paid for it and A knew this. B subsequently went bankrupt.

Held
The trustee in bankruptcy succeeded in setting aside the sale.

Dover Coalfield Extension Ltd, Re [1908] 1 Ch 65 Court of Appeal (Cozens-Hardy MR, Fletcher Moulton and Farwell LJJ)

Fiduciary need not account where remuneration acquired before he became a trustee

Facts
Cousins was a director of Dover Coalfield Extension Ltd. At the request of the company he became a director of the Consolidated Kent Collieries Corporation Ltd in order that he might look after the interests of the Dover company. In order to qualify himself for that appointment, after he had agreed to become a director of the Kent Corporation, certain shares in the Kent Corporation, the property of the Dover company, were transferred into his name. At the board meeting at which he was elected a director it was resolved that his qualification shares should be transferred to him by the Dover company. When the Dover company was wound up the liquidator claimed that the remuneration which Cousins had received from the Kent Corporation was the property of the Dover company.

Held
Cousins received the remuneration as a director of the Kent Corporation and not from use of property held by him on trust for the Dover company. He had not used his position as a trustee for the purpose of acquiring his directorship, he had been appointed a director before he became a trustee of the shares. The profit he gained was not procured by him by the use of his position as a trustee but was a profit earned by reason of work which he did for the Kent Corporation and which he would not have earned had he not been willing to do the work for which it was the remuneration. It was not a profit acquired solely by reason of his use of his position as trustee and he was entitled to keep it.

Dowse v *Gorton* [1891] AC 190 House of Lords (Lord Herschell, Lord Macnaghten and Lord Hannen)

Indemnity

Facts
The trust deed gave the trustees power to run a business. The trustee incurred expenses personally at a time when there was a cash-flow problem in the business.

Held
He could recover such expenses with priority over other creditors.

England's Settlement Trusts, Re [1918] 1 Ch 24 Chancery Division (Eve J)

A trustee is not indemnified for excessive or unnecessary expense

Facts
A trustee sued tenants of the trust estate for £193, a figure based on a surveyor's report of the tenants' liabilities but which in fact included many items for which the tenants were not legally responsible. The trustee refused to meet the tenants to discuss the matter and he also refused to accept £110 paid into court by the tenants to settle the matter. On counsel's advice the trustee continued the action and recovered only £90 by way of judgment but was ordered to pay costs of £600. The trustee did not consult his co-trustee or the beneficiary of the trust at any stage. He sought an indemnity for the costs of the action.

Held
The trustee was not entitled to any indemnity in relation to the costs of the action. Although he had not received competent advice from his legal advisers he was personally at fault in not consulting his co-trustee or the beneficiary to determine their views on whether the money paid into court should be accepted.

Hardoon v Belilios [1901] AC 118 Privy Council (Lord Hobhouse, Lord Robertson, Lord Lindley, Sir Francis Jeune and Sir Ford North)

Sole beneficiary absolutely entitled personally liable to indemnify trustee

Facts
A firm of sharebrokers placed some shares in the name of one of their employees, Hardoon, but he never had any beneficial interest in them. In the course of speculation the share certificates were pledged with Belilos who eventually became absolute owner of them but did not have them transferred into his own name. Calls on the shares were paid by Belilos through Hardoon and the payments debited to Hardoon without his knowledge. The company eventually went into liquidation and the liquidator made calls upon Hardoon for £402 12s 11d. He failed to pay and judgment was given against him for that amount so he brought an action against Belilos claiming an indemnity.

Hardoon failed in his action before the lower courts on the ground that there was no relationship of trustee and cestui que trust. He appealed to the Privy Council.

Held
There was a relationship of trustee and cestui que trust; all that was necessary to establish this was to prove that the legal title was in the plaintiff and the equitable title in the defendant. Further, where the cestui que trust was sui juris and solely entitled, the right of the trustee to an indemnity was not limited to the trust property but extended to the cestui que trust personally.

Hill v *Langley* (1988) The Times 28 January Court of Appeal (Balcombe, May and Stocker LJJ)

Trustee's duty of disclosure

Facts
The plaintiff was beneficiary under a will, and assigned her part of the property to the executor and trustee. He knew that the value was more than she appreciated but did not tell her so. Subsequently part of the property was sold and the plaintiff, realising her error, sued to have the assignment set aside.

Held
The trustee/executor was in breach of his duty to disclose, and therefore the assignment could be set aside, notwithstanding that restitutio in integrum was impossible because part of the property had been sold. The beneficiary's interest was in the proceeds of sale of the property and restitution could be made from that, though the plaintiff would be required to account for the consideration she had received on the assignment.

Holder v *Holder* [1968] Ch 353 Court of Appeal (Harman, Danckwerts and Sellers LJJ)

Fiduciary who has resigned may purchase trust property

Facts
A testator was the owner of two farms and his son Victor was tenant of both before his death. The testator appointed his wife, a daughter and Victor as executors and trustees of his estate and directed them to sell his property and divide the proceeds of sale between themselves and his eight other children. When the testator died Victor acted as an executor in the administration but renounced very shortly after the testator's death without having had any dealings with the farms as executor. The farms were put up for sale by public auction and Victor bought them. One of the beneficiaries claimed to have the transactions set aside.

Held
The rule preventing a trustee from purchasing the trust estate was based on the principle that no man may be both vendor and purchaser. Here Victor has renounced his executorship long before the sale. All the beneficiaries were aware of this and so could not have been looking to him to protect their interests. Thus the mischief which the rule was designed to prevent did not arise and the sale would not be set aside.

Harman LJ:

> 'The cross-appeal raises far more difficult questions, and they are broadly three. First, whether the actions of Victor before probate made his renunciation ineffective. Secondly, whether on that footing he was disentitled from bidding at the sale. Thirdly, whether the plaintiff is disentitled from taking this point because of his acquiescence.
>
> It was admitted at the bar in the court below that the acts of Victor were enough to constitute intermeddling with the estate and that his renunciation was ineffective. On this footing he remained a personal representative, even after probate had been granted to his co-executors, and could have been obliged by a creditor or a beneficiary to re-assume the duties of an executor. The judge decided in favour of the plaintiff because Victor at the time of the sale was himself still in a fiduciary position and like any other trustee could not purchase the trust property. I feel the force of this argument but doubt its validity in the very special circumstances of this case. The reason for the rule is that a man may not be both vendor and purchaser; but Victor was never in that position here. He took no part in instructing the

valuer who fixed the reserves or in the preparations for the auction. Everyone in the family knew that he was not a seller but a buyer. In this case Victor never assumed the duties of an executor. It is true that he concurred in signing a few cheques for trivial sums and endorsing a few insurance policies, but he never, so far as appears, interfered in any way with the administration of the estate. It is true he managed the farms, but he did that as tenant and not as executor. He acquired no special knowledge as executor. What he knew he knew as tenant of the farms.

Another reason lying behind the rule is that there must never be a conflict of duty and interest, but in fact there was none here in the case of Victor, who made no secret throughout that he intended to buy. There is of course ample authority that a trustee cannot purchase. The leading cases are decisions of Lord Eldon – *Ex parte Lacey* (1802) 6 Ves 625 and *Ex parte James* (1803) 8 Ves 337. In the former case the Lord Chancellor expressed himself thus:

> "The rule I take to be this; not, that a trustee cannot buy from his cestui que trust, but, that he shall not buy from himself. If a trustee will so deal with his cestui que trust, that the amount of the transaction shakes off the obligation, that attached upon him as trustee, then he may buy. If that case is rightly understood, it cannot lead to much mistake. The true interpretation of what is there reported does not break in upon the law as to trustees. The rule is this. A trustee, who is entrusted to sell and manage for others, undertakes in the same moment, in which he becomes a trustee, not to manage for the benefit and advantage of himself."

In *Ex parte James* the same Lord Chancellor said:

> "This doctrine as to purchases by trustees, assignees, and persons having a confidential character, stands much more upon general principle than upon the circumstances of any individual case. It rests upon this; that the purchase is not permitted in any case, however honest the circumstances; the general interests of justice requiring it to be destroyed in every instance."

These are no doubt strong words, but it is to be observed that Lord Eldon was dealing with cases where the purchaser was at the time of sale acting for the vendors. In this case Victor was not so acting: his interference with the administration of the estate was of a minimal character and the last cheque he signed was in August before he executed the deed of renunciation. He took no part in the instructions for probate, nor in the valuations or fixing of the reserves. Everyone concerned knew of the renunciation and of the reason for it, namely, that he wished to be a purchaser. Equally, everyone, including the three firms of solicitors engaged, assumed that the renunciation was effective and entitled Victor to bid. I feel great doubt whether the admission made at the bar was correct, as did the judge, but assuming it was right, the acts were only technically acts of intermeddling and I find no case where the circumstances are parallel. Of course, I feel the force of the judge's reasoning that if Victor remained an executor he is within the rule, but in a case where the reasons behind the rule do not exist I do not feel bound to apply it. My reasons are that the beneficiaries never looked to Victor to protect their interests. They all knew he was in the market as purchaser; that the price paid was a good one and probably higher than anyone not a sitting tenant would give. Further, the first two defendants alone acted as executors and sellers; they alone could convey; they were not influenced by Victor in connection with the sales.

I hold, therefore, that the rule does not apply in order to disentitle Victor to bid at the auction, as he did. If I be wrong on this point and the rule applies so as to disentitle Victor to purchase there arises a further defence, namely, that of acquiescence, and this requires some further recital of the facts.'

Holding and Management Ltd v *Property Holding and Investment Trust plc and Others* [1989] 1 WLR 1313 Court of Appeal (Lloyd, Nicholls and Farquharson LJJ)

Section 30(2) of the Trustee Act 1925

Facts and decision
Section 30(2) of the Trustee Act 1925 provides:

'A trustee may reimburse himself or pay or discharge out of the trust premises all expenses incurred in or about the execution of the trusts or powers.'

In this case, however, the plaintiff company, as maintenance trustee in respect of a block of flats, was held not to be entitled to the reimbursement of its litigation costs under the above subsection (inter alia) in the following outline circumstances. The trustee company had put forward a programme of works which was opposed by the tenants and in respect of which the company applied to the court for directions as to whether the proposed scheme was within its powers. In the course of the hearing a compromise was reached which was advantageous to the tenants. The judge made no order for costs inter partes but he also ruled that the trustee was not entitled to an indemnity for costs from the maintenance fund.

The trustee's appeal was dismissed by the Court of Appeal. As Nicholls LJ pointed out:

'So long as a trust continues, beneficiaries may not control the trustee in the exercise of his powers: in *Re Brockbank* [1948] Ch 206 [see Chapter 16]. But that is a far cry from saying that if a trustee incurs costs without regard to the wishes of his beneficiaries he will always be entitled to an indemnity out of the trust fund.'

The Court of Appeal also agreed with the judge that the plaintiff's claim fell outside the indemnity provisions of RSC Ord 62 r6(2).

Commentary
This case demonstrates the limits which the courts will apply to the operation of s30(2) of the TA 1925.

The proceedings concerned, per the Court of Appeal:

'... in substance were not a conventional application by a trustee for directions.'

In fact, the proceedings were 'in a very real sense ... adversarial'.

Macadam, Re [1946] Ch 73 Chancery Division (Cohen J)

Fiduciary must account when has used office to obtain remuneration

Facts
The trustees of a trust had power under the articles of a company by virtue of their office to appoint two directors to the company. The trustees appointed themselves and received directors' fees. The question arose whether they were entitled to retain these or if they held them for the trust.

Held
They were liable to account for these fees as they had received them by the use of their powers as trustees.

Cohen J:

'I think that the root of the matter really is: Did he acquire the position in respect of which he drew the remuneration by virtue of his position as trustee? In the present case there can be no doubt that the only way in which the plaintiffs became directors was by exercise of the powers vested in the trustees of the will under art. 68 of the articles of association of the company. The principle is one which has always been regarded as of the greatest importance in these courts, and I do not think I ought to do anything to weaken it. As I have said, although the remuneration was remuneration for services as director of the company, the opportunity to receive that remuneration was gained as a result of the exercise of a discretion vested in the trustees, and they had put themselves in a position where their interest and duty conflicted. In those circumstances, I do not think this court can allow them to make a profit out of doing so, and I do not think the liability to account for a profit can be confined to cases where the profit is derived directly from the trust estate.'

Norfolk's (Duke of) Settlement Trusts, Re [1981] 3 WLR 455 Court of Appeal (Cumming-Bruce, Brightman and Fox LJJ)

The court has inherent jurisdiction to increase or award remuneration

Facts

The trust was set up in 1958 and was comprised large holdings of real estate, stock and shares. There were three trustees of the trust, one of whom was a trust corporation. The trust instrument authorised the trust corporation to charge remuneration for its services at the level of its fees in force at the date of the settlement, ie 2 shillings or 10 pence per £100 of capital annually. The acquisition of further real estate redevelopment of properties belonging to the trust in London involved the trust corporation in an exceptional amount of extra work whilst resulting in substantial increases in the value of the trust. When Capital Transfer Tax was introduced in 1975 the trust corporation rearranged the trust's affairs so as to minimise tax liability. In all these circumstances the trust corporation found that the levels of remuneration fixed were inadequate, mainly because of inflation, and it was therefore operating the trust at a loss to itself. Accordingly, an application was made to the Court under its inherent jurisdiction that the trust corporation (i) be allowed to raise the general level of remuneration under the trust instrument backdated to 31 March 1977, (ii) receive £25,000 for services performed outside the scope of its duties in redeveloping trust property (iii) receive £50,000 for rearranging trust liability so as to reduce CTT liability (iv) receive remuneration for services of an exceptional nature performed in the future. Walton J at first instance found, as regards (ii), 'the work of redeveloping trust property was outside the scope of the trustees' duties and was only executed on the basis of an implied promise to pay, thus remuneration would be ordered. As regards (iii), this was a matter inherent in a trustee's duties and no remuneration would be ordered accordingly. The claims under (i) and (iv) would be dismissed as the court had no power to increase the general level of remuneration. The trust company appealed to the Court of Appeal seeking a declaration that the court had power under its inherent jurisdiction to increase the level of remuneration.

Held

The court did have power to increase the level of remuneration where this was beneficial to the trust and the case would be remitted to the Chancery Division to decide if the jurisdiction should be exercised.

Fox LJ:

> '... If it be the law, as I think it clearly is, that the court has inherent jurisdiction on the appointment of a trustee to authorise payment of remuneration to him, is there any reason why the court should not have jurisdiction to increase the remuneration already allowed by the trust instrument?
>
> Two reasons are suggested. First, it is said that a trustee's right to remuneration under an express provision of the settlement is based on a contract between the settlor and the trustee which the trustee is not entitled to avoid; the benefit of that contract is to be regarded as settled by the trust instrument for the benefit of the beneficiaries. I find that analysis artificial. It may have some appearance of reality in relation to a trustee who, at the request of the settlor, agrees to act before the settlement is executed and approves the terms of the settlement. But very frequently executors and trustees of wills know nothing of the terms of the will until the testator is dead; sometimes in the case of corporate trustees such as banks, they have not even been asked by the testator whether they will act. It is difficult to see with whom, in such cases, the trustees are to be taken as contracting. The appointment of a trustee by the court also gives rise to problems as to the identity of the contracting party.

The position, if seems to me, is this. Trust property is held by the trustees on the trusts and subject to the powers conferred by the trust instrument and by law. One of those powers is the power to the trustee to charge remuneration. That gives the trustee certain rights which equity will enforce in administering the trust. How far those rights can properly be regarded as beneficial interests I will consider later. But it seems to me to be quite unreal to regard them as contractual. So far as they derive from any order of the court they simply arise from the court's jurisdiction and so far as they derive from the trust instrument itself they derive from the settlor's power to direct how this property should be dealt with ...

I conclude that the court has an inherent jurisdiction to authorise the payment of remuneration of trustees and that that jurisdiction extends to increasing the remuneration authorised by the trust instrument. In exercising that jurisdiction the court has to balance two influences which are to some extent in conflict. The first is that the office of trustee is, as such, gratuitous; the court will accordingly be careful to protect the interests of the beneficiaries against claims by the trustees. The second is that it is of great importance to the beneficiaries that the trust should be well administered. If therefore the court concludes, having regard to the nature of the trust, to the experience and skill of a particular trustee and to the amounts which he seeks to charge when compared with what other trustees might require to be paid for their services and to all the other circumstances of the case, that it would be in the interests of the beneficiaries to increase the remuneration, then the court may properly do so.'

Protheroe v *Protheroe* [1968] 1 WLR 519 Court of Appeal (Lord Denning MR, Danckwerts and Widgery LJJ)

Trustee under constructive trust may not purchase trust property

Facts
A husband bought the leasehold of the matrimonial home in 1954 in which both he and his wife had a joint beneficial interest. The lease was purchased in the husband's name. In 1964 after they had separated the husband purchased the freehold of the property for £200. The wife claimed that she was entitled to share in the proceeds of sale of the freehold on the sale of the house. The husband claimed that her interest was limited to the leasehold.

Held
The husband was trustee for both his wife and himself as regards their beneficial interests in the matrimonial home and like all trustees he was not allowed to purchase the freehold of leasehold properties because of his advantageous position. Therefore, his purchase of the freehold resulted in it becoming trust property in which the wife was entitled to share equally.

Lord Denning MR:

'... Although the house was in the husband's name, he was a trustee of it for both. It was a family asset which the husband and wife owned in equal shares. Being a trustee, he had an especial advantage in getting the freehold. There is a long established rule of equity from *Keech* v *Sandford* (1726) 2 Eq Cas 741 [see Chapter 1] downwards that if a trustee, who owns the leasehold, gets in the freehold, that freehold belongs to the trust and he cannot take the property for himself.'

Queensland Mines Ltd v *Hudson* (1978) 18 ALR 1 Judicial Committee of the Privy Council

Fiduciaries – incidental profits

Facts
Queensland Mines had been interested in developing a mine. Hudson, its managing director, successfully obtained mining licences for the mine. However, the company ran into cash flow problems and could not proceed. Hudson then, with full knowledge of the company, resigned and successfully developed the mine.

Held
Hudson would not be compelled to return his profits. Two reasons were given, the first being that the rejection of the opportunity due to the company's financial difficulties took the final venture outside of Hudson's fiduciary duties. Alternatively Hudson, acting with full knowledge of the company, had effectively obtained the company's full consent to his actions.

Sargeant and Another v *National Westminster Bank plc and Another* (1990) The Times 10 May Court of Appeal (Nourse and Bingham LJJ and Sir George Waller)

The rule that a trustee must not place himself in a position where his interest and duty conflict not infringed in this case

Facts
The plaintiff trustees held land (three farms) on trust for sale under their late father's will, for the benefit of themselves and of their deceased brother's estate. They had previously been granted agricultural tenancies by their father. The trustees now wished to purchase the freehold of one of the farms (the father's will expressly permitted trustees to purchase trust property) and to sell the other farms. The defendants, who were the personal representatives of the deceased brother, claimed that the plaintiffs were not entitled to sell the property, either to themselves or to a third party, subject to agricultural tenancies in their favour. Clearly, the sale price of the farms free from the tenancies would be considerably higher than it would be if the farms were sold subject to these tenancies.

Held
The rule that a trustee must not put himself in a position where his interest and duty conflict had not been infringed in the instant case. Thus, as Hoffmann J pointed out at first instance:

> 'As landlords and trustees [the plaintiffs] can only sell what they have, which is the freehold interest subject to the tenancies.'

They were under no obligation in these circumstances to give up the tenancies. This decision was confirmed by the Court of Appeal. As Nourse LJ observed:

> '... it was not [the plaintiffs] who had put themselves in that position. They had been put there mainly by the testator's grant of the tenancies and by the provision of his will ...'

So long as the trustees in selling got the best price for the freeholds subject to the tenancies they were not in breach of their fiduciary duty.

Commentary
This is an important case in that, in effect, it points out the limits to the principle enunciated by Lord Herschell in *Bray* v *Ford* [1896] AC 44; see in this Chapter).

Spurling's Will Trusts, Re [1966] 1 All ER 745 Chancery Division (Ungoed – Thomas J)

Indemnity

Facts
Allegations of breach of trust were made against a trustee, and he successfully defended an action against him. He claimed indemnity for the costs of the action.

Held
He should be indemnified.

Ungoed-Thomas J:

> 'If costs of successfully defending claims to make good to a trust fund for alleged breach of trust were excluded, it would drive a coach and four through the very raison d'etre which [the Master of the Rolls] ... invoked for the principle he lays down; namely the safety of trustees, and the need to encourage persons to act as such by protecting them "if they have done their duty or even if they have committed an innocent breach of trust".'

Thompson's Settlement, Re [1985] 2 All ER 720 Chancery Division (Vinelott J)

Fiduciary self-dealing

Facts
In 1954 the settlor created a settlement for the benefit of his grandchildren and appointed his two sons, A and B, and his son-in-law as trustees. The settlement comprised substantial agricultural estates including, inter alia, an estate in Scotland 'the Coupar estate' and an estate in Norfolk 'the Brancaster estate'. The conveyances of these estates to the trustees provided that a trustee could purchase the estates concerned either at public auction or by private contract provided that in the case of a private contract the sale was conducted by the trustees other than the purchasing trustee. At the date of the settlement the estates were let to a farming company 'the old company' of which the settlor, his wife and A and B were the directors. When the settlor died in 1964 it was agreed by the settlor's family and the directors that the old company should be wound up. On the dissolution of the old company the lease of the Coupar estate was taken over by a new company belonging to A and his family and the lease of the Brancaster estate was taken over by a partnership between B and his sons. The old company did not assign the leases in either case. In 1969 A and B, as trustees of the settlement, executed a lease of the Coupar estate in favour of the new company belonging to A and his family. B and his sons had taken possession of the Brancaster estate on the assumption that there had been a valid transfer of the lease to them by the old company. The possibility of appropriating the various trust estates between the three branches of the settlor's family subsequently arose. An issue which emerged from this possibility was whether the Coupar estate and the Brancaster estate should be valued for the purposes of appropriation as being subject to farming tenancies or with vacant possession. In this context the question whether the self-dealing rule had been broken by A and B arose because of their positions as trustees of the settlement and as respective members of the new company and partnership to which leases of the estates had been granted. As trustees of the settlement their concurrence in the assignment of leases in the trust property was necessary.

Held
A and B, as trustees, had put themselves in a position where their interest and duty conflicted because

they were interested in the company and the partnership which had taken over the leases. Consequently they were precluded from dealing in their capacity as trustees with themselves in their respective capacities as managing director of the company and a member of the partnership.

Vinelott J:

'... The first submission of Mr Price was that the self-dealing rule has no application to a sale by trustees to a company, although if any of the trustees has an interest in the company the transaction falls within the fair-dealing rule. He founded this submission on the well-known case of *Farrar v Farrars Ltd* (1888) 40 Ch D 395. In that case three mortgagees were in possession of the mortgaged property. One of them, JR Farrar, was also solicitor to the mortgagees. The property was sold to a company which was to some extent promoted by JR Farrar and in which he took a small shareholding and for which he also acted as solicitor. He took no part in the negotiations. An action to set aside the transaction failed. Lindley LJ said:

"A sale by a person to a corporation of which he is a member is not, either in form or in substance, a sale by a person to himself. To hold that it is, would be to ignore the principle which lies at the root of the idea of a corporate body, and that idea is that the corporate body is distinct from the persons composing it. A sale by a member of a corporation to the corporation itself is in every sense a sale valid in equity as well as at law. There is no authority for saying that such a sale is not warranted by any ordinary power of sale ... Mr Farrar was not a trustee selling to himself, or to others for him, nor was he buying directly or indirectly for himself, and although a sale by a mortgagee to a company promoted by himself, of which he is the solicitor, and in which he has shares, is one the company must prove to have been bona fide and at a price at which the mortgagees could properly sell, yet, if such proves to be the fact, there is no rule of law which compels the Court to set aside the sale. *Ex parte Lacey* (1802) 6 Ves 625 does not require the Court to hold the sale invalid, however fair and honest it may be, although the judgment in that case does throw upon the company the burden of shewing that the sale was fair and honest."

I do not think that this case assists Mr Price. (A) was not at the material time simply a shareholder in the new company. He and his wife were directors of the new company and he was its managing director. Their duty as directors was to further the interests of the new company in which, as it happened, they held a majority of shares at the time of the purported assignment of the lease of the Coupar Grange estate. The position as between the trustees of the grandchildren's settlement and the directors of the new company is the same as it would have been if (A) had been a trustee of a settlement instead of a director of a company ... (B), of course, as a partner in a farming partnership, was ...

... In the instant case the concurrence of the trustees of the grandchildren's settlement was required if the leases were to be assigned to or new tenancies created in favour of the new company or partnership. The beneficiaries were entitled to ask that the trustees should give unprejudiced consideration to the question whether they should refuse to concur in the assignments in the expectation that a surrender of the leases might be negotiated from the old company and the estates sold or let on the open market ...

... As I have said, no assignment of the leases was ever executed. In the case of the Brancaster estate the legal title to the lease remained with the old company which has long since been dissolved. Apart from the operation of the self-dealing rule the oral agreement of 5th July 1966 coupled with the subsequent taking of possession of the estate by the partnership would have given rise to a contract enforceable by specific performance. The effect of the application of the rule is that no enforceable contract came into existence. Accordingly there is no valid lease of the estate in favour of the partnership...'

Thomson, Re

See Chapter 6.

Tito v *Waddell (No 2)* [1977] Ch 106 Chancery Division (Megarry V-C)

The self-dealing rule

Facts
This was a complex case described by Megarry V-C as 'litigation on a grand scale', involving the inhabitants of Banaba Island, known as Ocean Island, a former British Protectorate. Phosphates were mined from the islands and a royalty paid to the islanders, which was considerably less than the islanders believed it should be. In these proceedings they claimed that the Crown as responsible authority was subject to a trust for the benefit of the islanders, and was in breach of trust.

Held
If there was a trust it was not a trust in the legal sense, in that it was not one enforceable by the courts. In the course of a wide-ranging judgment, Megarry V-C said on the subject of the self-dealing rule, which he called a disability rather than a duty of the trustee:

> 'The ... rule is that if a trustee purchases the beneficial interest of any of his beneficiaries, the transaction is not voidable ex debito justitiae, but can be set aside by the beneficiary unless the trustee can show that he has taken no advantage of his position and has made full disclosure to the beneficiary, and that the transaction is fair and honest.'

Williams v *Barton*

See Chapter 6.

12 Investment of Trust Funds

Bartlett* v *Barclays Bank Trust Co (No 1) [1980] Ch 515 Chancery Division (Brightman J)

Trustee's duty of care: special expertise

Facts
The bank was the trustee of a trust which consisted of 99.8 per cent of the shares in a private company. The trust was created in 1920 and in 1960 the bank needed to raise money to pay death duties on interests in the settlement. It asked the board of the private company to consider the possibility of going public to raise the necessary money. The board said going public would be easier if the company went into property development. The bank did not object to this and subsequently the company engaged in two projects in property development. One project was a disaster while the other was quite profitable, but not sufficient to prevent an overall loss on both projects. The beneficiaries brought an action against the bank, claiming it was liable to make good the loss in that it never should have allowed the board of the company to go into property development. In the circumstances, the bank claimed it was entitled to rely on the calibre of the board for investment information and further, that if it could not it ought fairly to be excused under s61 of the Trustee Act 1925.

Held
It was a trustee's duty to conduct trust business with the care of a reasonably prudent businessman. In the case of a professional corporate trustee, such as the bank, the duty of care was higher and the bank was liable for loss caused to a trust by neglect to exercise the special care and skill it professed to have. The bank was under a duty as trustee to ensure it received an adequate flow of information concerning the activities of the board to ensure that it did not embark on hazardous projects and to prevent these becoming a disaster. In this case, the bank had confined itself to such information as it received from the board at annual general meetings. The bank was, therefore, in breach of trust and liable for the loss. Furthermore, the bank was not entitled to rely on s61 of the Trustee Act 1925 as a defence for, although it was acted 'honestly', it had not acted 'reasonably' within s61 and it would in any case be unfair to excuse the bank at the expense of the beneficiaries.

Brightman J considered *Re Lucking* [1968] 1 WLR 866 and concluded:

'I do not understand Cross J to have been saying that in every case where trustees have a controlling interest in a company, it is their duty to ensure that one of their number is a director or that they have a nominee on the board who will report from time to time on the affairs of the company. He was merely outlining convenient methods by which a prudent man of business (as also a trustee) with a controlling interest in a private company, can place himself in a position to make an informed decision whether any action is appropriate to be taken for the protection of his asset. Other methods may be equally satisfactory and convenient, depending on the circumstances of the individual case ...'

British Museum (Trustees of the) v Attorney-General [1984] 1 All ER 337 Chancery Division (Megarry V-C)

Court's power to change powers of investment in changing circumstances

Facts

In 1960 the Court approved a scheme relating to the investment of funds belonging to the British Museum. By this scheme a number of separate funds were consolidated into three pools, each pool being earmarked for different purposes with special provisions relating to the capital and income thereof. The result of these arrangements was that the fund was until about 1983 able to keep pace with inflation. However, steep rises in the price of museum pieces and the reduction of grants from public funds meant that this could no longer be done and the trustees asked the court to approve a new scheme to enable the balance to be restored to some extent.

Held

A revised version of the scheme would be approved. Megarry V-C summarised his views on the approach to be adopted to such applications as follows:

> '... From what I have said it will be seen that much of what I say depends to a greater or lesser extent on the special position of the trustees and the trust funds in the case before me. On the other hand, there is much that is of more general application, and it may be convenient if I attempt to summarise my views.
>
> 1) In my judgment, the principle laid down in the line of cases headed by *Re Kolb's Will Trusts* [1961] 3 WLR 1034 is one that should no longer be followed, since conditions have changed so greatly in the last 20 years. Though authoritative, those cases were authorities only rebus sic stantibus; and in 1983 they bind no longer. However, if Parliament acts on the recommendation of the Law Reform Committee and replaces the 1961 Act with revised powers of investment, the *Kolb* principle may well become applicable once more. Until then, the court should be ready to grant suitable applications for the extension of trustees' powers of investment, judging each application on its merits, and without being constrained by the provisions of the 1961 Act.
>
> 2) In determining what extended powers of investment should be conferred, there are many matters which will have to be considered. I shall refer to five, without in any way suggesting that this list is exhaustive, or that anything I say is intended to fetter the discretion that the court has to exercise in each case.
>
> > i) The court is likely to give great weight to the width and efficacy of any provisions for advice and control. The wider the powers, the more important these provisions will be. An existing system of proven efficacy, as here, is likely to be especially cogent.
> >
> > ii) Where the powers are of great width, as in the present case, there is much to be said for some scheme of fractional division, confining part of the fund to relatively safe investments, and allowing the other part to be used for investments in which the greater risks will be offset by substantial prospects of a greater return. On the other hand, when the powers are appreciably less wide than they are in the present case, I would in general respectfully concur with the views expressed by the Law Reform Committee that no division of the fund into fractions should be required, and that the only division should be into investments which require advice and those which do not. Nevertheless, although a division of the fund into fractions should not be essential, there may well be cases where such a division may be of assistance in obtaining the approval of the court.
> >
> > iii) The width of the powers in the present scheme seems to me to be at or near the extreme limit for charitable funds. Without the fractional division of the fund and the assurance of effective control and advice I very much doubt whether such a scheme could have been approved. What the court has to judge is the combined effect of width, division, advice and control, which all interact, together with the standing of the trustees.
> >
> > iv) The size of the fund in question may be very material. A fund that is very large may well justify a

latitude of investment that would be denied to a more modest fund; for the spread of investments possible for a larger fund may justify the greater risks that wider powers will permit to be taken.

v) The object of the trust may be very material. In the present case, the desirability of having an increase of capital value which will make possible the purchase of desirable acquisitions for the museum despite soaring prices does something to justify the greater risks whereby capital appreciation may be obtained ...'

Chapman v Browne [1902] 1 Ch 785 Court of Appeal (Collins MR, Romer and Matthew LJJ)

Second mortgages as investment: breach of trust

Facts
The trustees invested in a second mortgage which technically they should not have done. They sought a declaration that they had not acted imprudently, or alternatively relief by the court for having merely acted reasonably if mistakenly.

Held
Even where trustees were given unlimited powers of investment in the trust instrument, they could not invest in anything which a prudent man of business would eschew. Second mortgages were notoriously risky investments; the rule that a trustee should not invest in them was a good one although the basis was not necessarily, as formerly thought, that the trustee did not get the legal estate. There were other objections, such as that if the first mortgagee were to foreclose, the security might be lost if he went into possession when there were no funds in the trust to redeem him. The trustees therefore were in breach of trust, and as they seemed not to have considered at all whether the mortgage was a suitable investment, they would not be relieved.

Commentary
Some of the old objections to a second mortgage as a trustee investment have been overtaken by the Land Charges Act's providing for registration of successive interests. Moreover the Law Reform Committee has recommended that investment in second mortgages should now be permitted.

Harari's Settlement Trust, Re [1949] 1 All ER 430 Chancery Division (Jenkins J)

Express powers of investment to be construed reasonably

Facts
By a settlement made in 1938 the settlor gave the trustees power to retain or sell or invest all capital moneys held upon the trust 'in or upon such investments as to them may seem fit'.

Held
That giving the words their plain meaning, the trustees were not restricted to the statutory list of authorised investment, but could choose any investment that they honestly thought desirable. There was no reason to construe the authorising words restrictively in spite of the fact that this had been done in several preceding cases. The clause gave a power to invest in the purchase of land.

Jenkins J:

'There is, however, a good deal of authority ... to the effect that investment clauses should be strictly construed and should not be construed as authorising investments outside the trustee range unless they clearly and unambiguously indicate an intention to that effect.' (He then referred to a number of cases and continued). 'That, I think, is a representative collection of the authorities bearing on this topic, and having given them the best consideration I can, it seems to me that I am left free to construe this settlement according to what I consider to be the natural and proper meaning of the words used in their context, and, so construing the words "in or upon such investments as to them may seem fit", I see no justification for implying any restriction. I think the trustees have power, under the plain meaning of these words, to invest in any investments which, to adopt Kekewich J's observation, they "honestly think" are desirable investments for the investment of moneys subject to the trusts of the settlement which are not there ...'

Khoo Tek Keong v *Ching Joo Tuan Neoh* [1934] AC 529 Privy Council (Lord Blanesborough, Lord Thankerton and Lord Russell)

Powers of investment – relief of a trustee who has acted reasonably and honestly

Facts

The testator appointed his son Khoo Tek Keong and another trustees of funds for accumulation for twelve years and then to be distributed among his widow and descendants. The trustees were given power to invest ' ... in such investments as they in their absolute discretion think fit with liberty to vary the same from time to time'. The distribution in the event was made to the widow and three named sons, one of whom joined with the widow to allege breaches of trust by Khoo Tek Keong. The first allegation concerned 'lending out trust funds on personal loans on security of jewellery without valuation'; and the second 'lending out trust funds to Chetties without securities'.

Held

The loans upon the security of the jewellery, in the absence of proof that the jewellery was insufficient security, were not breaches of trust. However, the unsecured loans were breaches of trust.

Lord Russell of Killowen:

'Their Lordships find it impossible, in the face of the extraordinarily wide scope of the investment clause, to hold that the loans on the security of the jewellery have been proved to be breaches of trust by the appellant. They were loans made upon the security of property, and carrying interest; they were accordingly investments within the meaning of clause 11 of the will.

... As regards the loans to Chetties, these stand upon a different footing. Their Lordships agree with the Appellate Court that these do constitute breaches of trust by the appellant ... upon the ground that being loans upon no security beyond the liability of the borrower to repay, they are not investments within the meaning of clause 11 of the will ... Their Lordships agree with the view that the appellant has failed to establish any claim to be relieved from personal liability. Section 60 of the Ordinance No 14 of 1929 is in the following terms: "If it appears to the court that a trustee ... is or may be personally liable for any breach of trust ... but has acted honestly and reasonably, and ought fairly to be excused for the breach of trust ... the court may relieve him either wholly or partly from personal liability for the same".

The ... trial judge vouches for the appellant's honesty, but he must further establish that he acted reasonably ... His main contention is that he merely pursued the same course of conduct as the testator had pursued in his lifetime ... He never considered the question of these dealings with the trust funds in the light of his duty as a trustee.

... In the result the appeal ought in their Lordships' opinion to succeed as to the loans on the security of jewellery, and fail as to the loans to Chetties ...'

Kolb's Will Trusts, Re [1961] 3 WLR 1034 Chancery Division (Cross J)

Altering powers of investment: the Trustee Investment Act

Facts

The testator by clause 6 of his will bequeathed the residue of his estate to his trustees to invest the proceeds of sale in 'such stocks, shares and/or convertible debentures in the "blue chip" category' as his trustees thought fit. After setting aside £5,000 on trust for three named beneficiaries he directed that the ultimate residue be held on charitable trusts. The trustees asked the court to declare the meaning of clause 6, while the Attorney-General on behalf of the charities objected to any extension of the power of investment as far as the ultimate residue was concerned.

Held

The investment clause was void for uncertainty.

Cross J:

> 'The summons ... [asks] that the trustees may be given power to invest all or any part of the capital in fully paid ordinary shares or convertible debentures of companies operating in the UK, the USA or Canada with a paid-up capital of at least £1,000,000. There is no doubt that the court has jurisdiction to make such an order in the case of a charitable trust ... and if this summons had come on last term and the Attorney-General had raised no objection to the proposed extension of the investment powers, the order asked for would probably have been made. But on 3 August the Trustee Investment Act 1961, was passed, under which trustees who have no power to invest in ordinary shares are given power to invest up to half of their trust fund in such shares if the company and the shares fulfil the conditions laid down in Parts III and IV of the First Schedule to the Act. Section 15 of the Act preserves the power of the court to widen the investment powers of trustees beyond those conferred by the Act; but the powers given by the Act must, I think, be taken to be prima facie sufficient and ought only to be extended if, on the particular facts, a special case for extending them can be made out.
>
> It is suggested that this case is a special case because here the testator clearly wished his trustees to invest the whole fund in equities and nothing else, and it is only because of the unfortunate wording of clause 6 that his trustees have not the power to do so. For myself, I doubt very much whether the wishes of the testator standing alone would constitute such special circumstances.'

Learoyd v Whiteley (1887) 12 App Cas 727 House of Lords (Lord Halsbury LC, Lord Watson and Lord Fitzgerald)

Standard of care in investing trust funds

Facts

The trustees of a settlement were authorised to invest money in real securities. On the advice of a competent firm of valuers they invested £3,000 of trust money in a brickfield near Pontefract. The valuers had experience in advising on the value of brickfields and their report stated that the property was a good security for the amount invested. In consequence the trustees lent the money at 5 per cent. In fact the report did not state that it was based on the assumption that the brickfield was a going concern when it was not. Further, the report did not make any distinction between the value of the land and the value of the machines and buildings. The trustees accepted the report and acted on it in good faith without making any further inquiries. The brickfield failed and when it was sold the proceeds were insufficient to cover the outstanding mortgage debt.

Held
Although the trustees had acted bona fide they were liable for the loss. They had not acted with ordinary prudence because as trustees they were not entitled to act with trust money as if they were ordinary persons sui juris but must confine themselves to making such investments which were permitted by the trust but were not hazardous.

Lord Watson:

> 'As a general rule the law requires of a trustee no higher degree of diligence in the execution of his office than a man of ordinary prudence would exercise in the management of his own private affairs. Yet he is not allowed the same discretion in investing the moneys of the trust as if he were a person sui juris dealing with his own estate. Business men of ordinary prudence may, and frequently do, select investments which are more or less of a speculative character, but it is the duty of a trustee to confine himself to the class of investments which are permitted by the trust, and likewise to avoid all investments of that class which are attended with hazard. So, so long as he acts in the honest observance of these limitations, the general rule already stated will apply.'

Lucking's Will Trusts, Re [1968] 1 WLR 866 Chancery Division (Cross J)

Trustee's liabilities

Facts
Nearly 70 per cent of the shares in a prosperous family company manufacturing show accessories were held by two trustees Lucking and Block as part of the estate of the deceased; about 29 per cent belonged to Lucking in his own right, and 1 per cent belonged to Lucking's wife. In 1954 the directors of the company were Lucking, his wife and an old Army friend of Lucking's, a Lt Col Dewar, whom he had appointed as manager also. In 1956 Block was appointed co-trustee with Lucking. Lt Col Dewar wrongfully drew some £15,000 from the company's bank account in excess of his remuneration, and later he became bankrupt. The money was lost and one of the beneficiaries under the trust sued the trustees for the loss.

Held
In the circumstances Lucking was liable for the loss; Block would not be held liable as he relied entirely on what Lucking told him.

Cross J:

> 'The conduct of the defendant trustees is, I think, to be judged by the standard applied in *Speight* v *Gaunt* (1883) 9 App Cas 1, namely, that a trustee is only bound to conduct the business of the trust in such a way as an ordinary prudent man would conduct a business of his own.
>
> Now what steps, if any, does a reasonably prudent man who finds himself a majority shareholder in a private company take with regard to the management of the company's affairs? He does not, I think, content himself with such information as to the management of the company's affairs as he is entitled to as shareholder, but ensures that he is represented on the board. He may be prepared to run the business himself as managing director or, at least, to become a non-executive director while having the business managed by someone else. Alternatively, he may find someone who will act as his nominee on the board and report to him from time to time as to the company's affairs. In the same way, as it seems to me, trustees holding a controlling interest ought to ensure so far as they can that they have such information as to the progress of the company's affairs as directors would have. If they sit back and allow the company to be run by the minority shareholder and receive no more information than shareholders are entitled to, they do so at their risk if things go wrong. In this case, of course, the trust was represented on the board by Mr Lucking. As I see it, however, one ought not to regard him as performing a duty to the trust which

it was incumbent on the trustees to perform personally, so that Mr Block became automatically responsible for any deficiencies in Mr Lucking, as does a passive trustee who allows his co-trustee to exercise alone discretions which it is their duty to exercise jointly. If these trustees had decided, as they might have done, to be represented on the board by a nominee they would have been entitled to rely on the information given them by that nominee as to the way in which the company's affairs were being managed even though such information was inaccurate or inadequate, unless they had some reason to suspect that it was inaccurate or inadequate. Mr Block, as I see it, cannot have been in a worse position because his co-trustee was the trust's representative on the board than he would have been if the trust's representative had not been a trustee at all. The position of Mr Lucking, on the other hand, as I see it, was quite different. He cannot say that what he knew or ought to have known about the company's affairs he knew or ought to have known simply as a director with a duty to the company and no one else. He was in the position he was partly as a representative of the trust and, in and so far as he failed in his duty to the company, he also failed in his duty to the trust.'

Mason v *Fairbrother* [1983] 2 All ER 1078 Chancery Division (Blackett-Ord V-C)

Court's powers to widen investment powers in special circumstances

Facts
The Co-operative Society applied to have the powers of investment of its pension and death benefit fund altered. In this case the fund was limited to investing in the Co-operative Society and those investments specified by the TIA 1961. In 1982 the fund was worth £127 million and the trustees wished to have wider investment powers more appropriate to a modern pension fund. They applied, inter alia, to have their investment powers widened under s57(1) TA 1925.

Held
In the light of the dicta in *Re Kolb*, *Re Cooper* and *Re Porritt* to the effect that wider powers could only be given in special circumstances, the fact of inflation and that the fund was a public fund rather than a private fund were special circumstances. The scheme would therefore be approved.

Power's Will Trusts, Re [1947] Ch 572 Chancery Division (Jenkins J)

Express power of investment restricted to property which yields an income

Facts
An investment clause required 'All moneys requiring to be invested ... may be invested by the trustee in any manner which he may in his absolute discretion think fit in all respects as if he were the sole beneficial owner of such moneys including the purchase of freehold property in England and Wales.' The trustees wished to purchase a house with vacant possession for the principal beneficiary to reside in rent free.

Held
The clause did not permit this because the use of the word 'investment' connoted a yield of income. It did not authorise the purchase of a house for occupation by the beneficiaries because that part of the purchase price paid for the advantage of vacant possession would not be laid out in income-producing property for the sale of the income it would yield.

Shaw v *Cates* [1909] 1 Ch 389 Chancery Division (Parker J)

Standard of care in investing trust funds

Facts

A surveyor valued land at Folkestone, upon which two houses were built and two others in the course of construction, at £9,180 and recommended a mortgage of up to two thirds of that sum. A schedule to the report gave separate values for each of the properties. The trustees inspected the houses and decided to invest £4,400, this being exactly two thirds of the sum shown in the schedule. The surveyor was also the rent-collector for the mortgagor who failed to keep the premises in proper repair and, as a result, nine years later he went bankrupt and the security for the mortgage proved insufficient. The beneficiaries sued the trustees for the whole loss.

Held

The trustees were liable for the loss. They had failed to comply with the requirements of s4 TA 1888 (now s8 TA 1925). They did not employ an independent valuer as the section required since they knew that the surveyor was the agent of the mortgagor. Further, they had made an advance which was not actually recommended in the surveyor's report by advancing on the values in the schedule and not on the values in the main report.

Parker J:

> 'The principle involved seems to be that within the limits of what is often called the "two thirds" rule a prudent man may, as to the amount which can properly be advanced on any proposed security, whether the property be agricultural land or house or buildings used for trade purposes, rely on expert advice obtained with certain precautions, it being of course assumed that in giving the advice the expert will consider all the circumstances of the case, including the nature of the property, and will not advise a larger advance than under all the circumstances can be prudently made. I dissent entirely from the position taken up by some of the defendants' expert witnesses, that when once they have ascertained the value of the property that they have adopted, they are at least prima facie justified in advising an advance of two thirds of its value. Such a position in my opinion defeats the object of the section by making what the Legislature has recognised as the standard of the minimum protection which a prudent man will require into a standard of the normal risk which, whatever the nature of the property, a prudent man will be prepared to run; and it deprives the expert advice on which the trustee is to rely as to the margin of protection to be required, of all its value. It is as true now as it was before the Act that the maximum sum which a prudent man can be advised to lend upon a mortgage depends on the nature of the property and upon all the circumstances of the case. If the property is liable to deteriorate or is specially subject to fluctuations in value, or depends for its value on circumstances the continual existence of which is precarious, a prudent man will now, as much as before the Act, require a larger margin for his protection than he would in the case of property attended by no such disadvantages, and an expert who does his duty will take this into consideration ...
>
> In my opinion the advance which was actually made was not the advance which Mr Barton advised, and his report, therefore, cannot be relied on as within s8 of the Trustee Act 1893. Again, I do not think that Mr Barton was in fact instructed and employed independently of the mortgagor. He was suggested by the mortgagor, instructed by the mortgagor's solicitors, referred to the mortgagor both as to his fee and as to the properties he was to value, and was accompanied by the mortgagor when he made his survey. I am not suggesting that he was consciously influenced by the mortgagor or that he acted otherwise than honestly in the matter, but I do not think that he in fact fulfilled the conditions mentioned in the section as to his instructions and employment. If, according to the true meaning of the section, the belief of the trustees is the material point, I am unable to hold that the trustees did reasonably believe that Mr Barton was instructed and employed independently of the mortgagor. They left the instruction to be given by

Beckingsale & Co, who were also the mortgagor's solicitors, and after ascertaining that Mr Barton was a competent person took no further trouble in the matter.'

Stuart, Re, Smith v *Stuart* [1897] 2 Ch 583 Chancery Division (Stirling J)

Relief of trustee where acting on agent's advice

Facts
The trust instrument contained power to invest in leasehold mortgages. Acting on the advice of a solicitor who had worked for him before, who had also worked for the testator, and who continued to act satisfactorily for the trust, the trustee invested in four mortgages. The solicitor also acted for the lessees and instructed the surveyors. He did not in all cases secure a valuation, and where he did in one case it was of the security without stating the value of the property. The mortgages proved insufficient security. The trustee contended that he had acted honestly and reasonably and should be relieved.

Held
He should not be relieved.

Stirling J:

> 'The effect of [the section] appears to me to be this ... a jurisdiction is given to the court under special circumstances, the court being satisfied as to several matters mentioned in the section, to relieve the trustee of the consequences of a breach of trust as regards his personal liability. But the court must first be satisfied that he has acted honestly and reasonably. As to the honesty of the trustee in this case there is no question; but that is not the only condition to be satisfied ... In my opinion the burden lies on the trustee who asks the court to exercise [this] ... jurisdiction to show that he has acted reasonably; and ... it is fair ... to consider whether ... [the defendant] would have acted with reference to these investments as he did, if he had been lending money of his own ... I think a man dealing with his own money would not act upon the opinion of his solicitor alone in a question as to the value of a property proposed as security, though, no doubt, he might do so as to any question of title or law which may be involved ... In making a loan the trustee ... [should] act on a valuation made by a person whom the trustee reasonably believed to be a ... surveyor ... employed independently of any owner of the property. The surveyors on whose valuations ... [the defendant] acted were not employed independently ... [though he] was not aware ... that ... [the solicitor] had acted for the mortgagors ... I confess I do not think that if ... [the defendant] had been dealing with money of his own he would under these circumstances have advanced it without further enquiry.'

Tollemache, Re [1903] 1 Ch 955 Court of Appeal (Cozens-Hardy, Romer and Vaughan-Williams LJJ)

Extension of the trustees' powers

Facts
The tenant for life's income under the trust was small and could be increased by mortgaging her interest at a higher rate than she received from authorised investments. The mortgage was not however permitted under the trust deeds. The remainderman's interest would not, it was contended, be prejudiced.

Held
The court would be reluctant to interfere in any way with the trust deed as laid down by the settlor. In this case, though the change would be in the interest of one beneficiary, it was not an emergency which the court would feel justified in meeting.

Wakeman, Re [1945] Ch 177 Chancery Division (Uthwatt J)

Power of investment of trustees for sale

Held
LPA 1925 s28(1) gives trustees for sale the same powers of investment as trustees of other trusts, but in this case the trustees had disposed of all the land they held on trust for sale and therefore the section did not apply.

Walker, Re, Walker v *Walker* (1890) 59 LJ Ch 386 Chancery Division (Kekewich J)

Investment in mortgages

Facts
Trustees applied for relief under what became s9 of the Trustee Act 1925, 'When a trustee shall have improperly advanced money on a mortgage security which would at the time of the investment, have been a proper investment ... for a less sum than actually advanced'.

Held
Kekewich J:

'... Supposing, for instance, a man invests £100 on property that would bear only £80; he is not to lose the whole £100 because of that. That is a reasonable provision on behalf of trustees ... I understand [the section] to mean that the impropriety consists in the amount invested. If the investment is otherwise improper, ... he cannot claim the benefit of the section ... He must establish the propriety of the investment independently of the value, and then he has the benefit of the section to save him from any loss greater than that which would have been incurred by advancing too large a sum on what would otherwise be a proper security.'

Wragg, Re [1919] 2 Ch 58 Chancery Division (P O Lawrence J)

Definition of investment

Facts
The testator left property on trust for his children with power to the trustees to invest in any stocks, shares, funds or securities or such other investments as they in their absolute discretion thought fit, as if they were absolutely entitled to the property.

Held
The clause authorised the purchase of real property for the sake of the income it would produce.

P O Lawrence J:

'To invest includes as one of its means to apply money in the purchase of some property from which interest or profit is expected and which property is purchased in order to be held for the sake of the income it will yield.'

13 Conversion and Apportionment

Allhusen v *Whittell* (1867) LR 4 Eq 295 Chancery (Page-Wood V-C)
Apportionment on postponed payment of debts

Facts
The testator left his residuary personal estate to successive interests, and there were considerable debts of the estate. Many were not paid until after the end of the executor's year, and the successor interests applied for an order on the question of apportionment.

Held
In order that the life tenant should not be unjustly enriched, he would be required to pay interest on sums in excess of what he would have received if the debts had been paid.

Page-Wood V-C:

> ' ... supposing a testator has a large sum, £50,000 or £60,000, say, in the funds, and has only £10,000 worth of debts, the executors will be justified, as between themselves and the whole body of persons interested in the estate, in dealing with it as they think best in the administration. But, the executors, when they have dealt with the estate, will be taken by the court as having applied in payment of the debts such a portion of the fund as, together with income of that portion for one year, was necessary for payment of debts.'

Bartlett v *Barclays Bank Trust Co (No 1)*
See Chapter 12.

Chesterfield's (Earl of) Trusts, Re (1883) 24 Ch D 643 Chancery Division (Chitty J)
Apportionment of a reversion and life interest; when an asset falls into possession the value of investments needed at T's death to produce its value should be calculated: this amount becomes capital for the reversioner and the rest income for the life tenant

Facts
The testator left his residuary personal estate in trust for conversion with power to postpone during the first life, with remainders. One of the assets was a mortgage, which fell into possession some time later, with arrears of interest. Quaere: how to apportion the sum as between capital and income?

Held
Chitty J:

> 'This court is of opinion that the said ... monies are apportionable between principal and income by ascertaining the respective sums which, when [invested]... at 4% per annum on 1 December 1871, the day

of the death of the [testator] ... and accumulating at compound interest, calculated at that rate, would, with the accumulations of interest, have produced at the respective dates of receipt the amounts actually received, and that the aggregate of the sums so ascertained ought to be treated as principal, and be applied accordingly, and the residue should be treated as income.'

Fawcett, Re [1940] Ch 402 Chancery Division (Farwell J)

Unauthorised investments: life tenant is entitled to a 'Fair yield'

Facts
The testatrix left her residuary personal estate in trust for her nephews and nieces for life with remainders to their children. There was no power to postpone. Part of the residue was unauthorised investments.

Held
After the first year the tenant for life is entitled to a fair, but not necessarily the actual, income from the unauthorised investments. Any excess goes to capital.

Farwell J:

> 'The rule in *Howe* v *Lord Dartmouth* (1802) 7 Ves 137 in my judgment, was based upon the equitable idea of treating that which ought to have been done as having been done, and accordingly, in the early cases the general rule was that the tenant for life was entitled to whatever the investments, if they were sold and reinvested in Consols, would produce.
>
> ... The general, though not the universal, rule is now to allow four per cent, and I see no reason in the present case to depart from that modern practice. In order to give effect to the rule it appears to me that in a case of this kind it is the duty of the trustees to have the unauthorised investments valued as at the end of the first year after the testatrix's death. During that year the executors are given time to deal with the estate as a whole. At the end of it comes the time when, in my judgment, any unauthorised investments which they still retain should be valued and the tenant for life becomes entitled to be paid four per cent on the valuation of the whole of the unauthorised investments. To that extent these tenants for life are entitled to receive income in each year and that income, four per cent on the capital value of the unauthorised investments, must be paid out of the actual income received from the unauthorised investments; that is to say, the trustees will receive the whole of the dividends which the unauthorised investments pay and there will be no apportionment. Those dividends will be applied in the first instance in paying, so far as they go, four per cent on the capital value of the unauthorised investments. If the income received on the unauthorised investments is more than sufficient to pay the four per cent, then the balance will ... form part of the whole fund in the hands of the trustees. If, on the other hand, the income actually received from the unauthorised investments is not sufficient to pay four per cent in each year to the tenants for life, they will not be entitled to immediate recoupment out of the capital, but when the unauthorised investments are sold the trustees will then have in their hands a fund representing the proceeds of sale of the unauthorised investments, together with any surplus income which may have accrued in earlier years; out of those proceeds of sale the tenants for life will be entitled to be recouped so as to provide them with the full four per cent during the whole period, and they will be entitled to be refunded the deficit calculated at four per cent simple interest but less tax. In that way it appears to me the rule can be worked out satisfactorily as between capital and income and the balance will be held as evenly as possible between those two opposing interests.'

Howe v *Earl of Dartmouth* (1802) 7 Ves 137 Lord Chancellor's Court (Lord Eldon LC)

Duty of trustees of residuary personal estate given to successive interests to hold the balance evenly between life tenant and remainderman

Facts
The Earl of Strafford left the residue of his estate to his wife for life, then to X for life, and after her death to various persons in succession. The personal estate consisted in part of bank stock and long annuities and short annuities. The Countess of Strafford predeceased her husband, the testator. The estate remained in the original investments for some years and on the death of X the then tenant for life contended that X had received, by way of income from the bank stock and the long and short annuities, more than she would have been entitled to, if these assets had been sold immediately after the testator's death and the proceeds invested in a permanent form.

Held
As the bank stock was subject to fluctuations in trade, it was an unauthorised security, and the annuities, being of a wasting nature, were also an unauthorised investment. The assets in question were, therefore, correctly converted into authorised investments and from that time the tenant for life was entitled to all the income produced thereby.

Lord Eldon LC:

> 'It is given as all his personal estate, and the mode, in which he says it is to be enjoyed, is to one for life, and to the others afterwards. Then the court says, it is to be construed as to the perishable parts, so that the one shall take for life, and the others afterwards; and unless the testator directs the mode so that it is to continue, as it was, the court understands, that it shall be put in such a state that the others may enjoy it after the decease of the first; and the thing is quite equal; for it may consist of a vast number of particulars: for instance, a personal annuity, not to commence in enjoyment till the expiration of twenty years from the death of the testator, payable upon a contingency ... If in this case it is equitable, that long or short annuities should be sold, to give everyone an equal chance, the court acts equally in the other case; for those future interests are for the sake of the tenant for life to be converted into a present interest; being sold immediately, in order to yield an immediate interest for the tenant for life. As in the one case that which the tenant for life has too great an interest, is melted for the benefit of the rest, in the other that, of which, if it remained in specie, he might never receive anything, is brought in; and he has immediately the interest of its present worth.'

Parry, Re, Brown v Parry [1947] Ch 23 Chancery Division (Romer J)

Date of valuation where there is power to postpone

Facts
The testator left his residue on trust for sale with power to postpone, to successive interests. There was no direction as to income pending conversion, and the estate included unauthorised investments which greatly increased in value in the first year after the testator's death. The date for apportionment was therefore referred to the court.

Held
The date should be that of the testator's death, since a power to postpone meant sale could take place at any time.

Romer J:

> '[Counsel for the life tenants] ... objects to that part of the rule which fixes the date of death as the appropriate time for valuing the unauthorised investments. The proper time for valuing investments which were retained unsold, they say, was the first anniversary of the testator's death. Their argument is that from the first appearance of the rule ... in *Howe v Dartmouth* (1802) 7 Ves 137 nobody ever thought of the

testator's death as being the proper date for valuing unauthorised investments until ... *Brown* v *Gellatly* (1867) 2 Ch App 751 ... [That] has given rise to an anomaly, [and] ... should not be allowed to prevail.'

His Lordship reviewed the early authorities extensively, quoting Lord Cairns:

' "It was the duty of the trustees to convert [unauthorised investments] ... at the earliest moment at which they could properly be converted. I do not mean that the trustees were by any means open to censure for not having converted them within the year, but I think the rights of the parties must be regulated as if they had been so converted".'

He continued:

'It was submitted ... that Lord Cairns' decision was wrong ... and ... inconsistent with ... *Yates* v *Yates* (1860) 28 Beav 637 and *Re Llewellyn's Trust* (1861) 29 Beav 171 ...
In *Yates* v *Yates* the Master of the Rolls said:

"When a testator gives property to trustees, with an absolute trust for conversion, and with a direction as to the time at which the conversion shall take place, if, from any causes whatever, arising from the exercise of the discretion and judgment of the trustees, the conversion is delayed, then the tenant for life is not to be prejudiced by that delay, but is to have the benefit as if the conversion had taken place within a reasonable time from the death of the testator, which is usually fixed at twelve months from that period."

In *Re Llewellyn's Trust* a testator settled his real and personal estate on his wife for life with remainder to his children and authorised his trustees at their discretion, with a view to facilitating the ultimate distribution of his property, to convert into money his residuary personal estate ... The Master of the Rolls expressed himself as follows:

"It appears there are certain assets which cannot be realised instantly, that is to say, the purchase money for the partnership in which the testator was engaged, his share of which, with interest, is payable by instalments from time to time. With respect to that ... it must be treated as if the whole were realised at once, and the tenant for life allowed 4 per cent upon the value; because the court cannot realise it, like mere outstanding personal estate, and it is for the benefit of the estate that the instalments should be paid in the manner arranged. They are payable with interest at 5 per cent, but the tenant for life will not be entitled to the whole interest, only to 4 per cent. The period for ascertaining the value of the property will be twelve months after the death of the testator, but the tenant for life will get her income as from the testator's death."

Now, so far as the point now in issue is concerned, it is certainly difficult to reconcile these views, expressed and acted upon by Sir John Romilly, with the decision of Lord Cairns as to the ships in *Brown* v *Gellatly*. I am inclined, however, to prefer the latter case to *Yates* v *Yates* and *Re Llewellyn's Trust* for more than one reason. In the first place, it was later in date, and, having regard to the fact that the principles now in question were somewhat laboriously built up by the process of trial and error over a long period of time, this consideration is not without weight. Secondly, there can be no certainty that Sir John Romilly had present to his mind, as Lord Cairns assuredly did to his, the contrast between cases where trustees had an immediate duty to convert and cases where they had not. Thirdly, Lord Cairns' treatment of the ships was in entire accord with the order of Lord Eldon in relation to the retained leaseholds in *Gibson* v *Bott*. Fourthly, *Brown* v *Gellatly* has been frequently approved and was cited without any adverse comment by the Privy Council in *Wentworth* v *Wentworth* [1900] AC 163. And finally, not only was the order regarding the ships not inconsistent with previous authority, but it seems to me that it was plainly right. Notional conversion is very understandable when the executors are under a duty, express or implied, to sell; such a duty readily lets in the doctrine that equity regards that as done which ought to be done, and the notional conversion arising from the doctrine (subject only to a year's grace) acted as a convenient medium for procuring a balance between life tenant and remainderman. If no duty exists, however, the medium is not available, and another has to be found in its place. If there is no duty upon the executors to sell at once, or within a year, or at any other time, I can see no reason for assuming a notional conversion at once, or within a year, or at any other time. The essential equity, however – the balance between the successive interests – remains equally compelling even where there is no immediate obligation to convert, and property is retained for the benefit of the estate as a whole. It is accordingly rational, and indeed obvious, to substitute a valuation of the testator's assets in the place of a hypothetical sale; and if so, it is difficult to think of a better date for the valuation than the day when the testator died and the assets passed to his executors.'

14 Duty to Distribute

Allen-Meyrick's Will Trusts, Re [1966] 1 WLR 499 Chancery Division (Buckley J)

Trustees' duty to distribute cannot be exercised from day to day by the court

Facts
A testatrix gave her residue to trustees in trust to apply the income thereof 'in their absolute discretion for the maintenance of my husband', and subject thereto she gave the residue to her two godchildren equally on trust. The trustees made payments to the husband who was bankrupt, but were unable to agree if any further income should be applied. They wished to surrender their discretion to the court. Among the payments which the trustees made were the rent of a house for the husband and certain debts of the husband.

Held
The court would not accept the surrender of the discretion since it involved considering from time to time changing circumstances and could not be exercised in advance. However, it would be prepared to give the trustees directions when required.

Obiter: the trustees could validly expend the whole or any part of the fund for the maintenance of the husband, for instance, in paying an hotel keeper to give him a dinner, or in paying the rent of a house in which he is living and in respect of these the trustee in bankruptcy has no claim.

Benjamin, Re [1902] 1 Ch 723 Chancery Division (Joyce J)

The Benjamin Order

The testator left his estate to be divided between those of his children living at his death. One of his sons had disappeared ten months before the testator's death.

Held
On the evidence before the court, the probability was that the son was dead. An order was made for distribution on the footing that he was dead, although no declaration of death was made and should he return, his entitlement would revive.

Eaves v *Hickson* (1861) 30 Beav 136 Chancery (Romilly MR)

Duty to find correct beneficiary

Facts
The trustees were shown a marriage certificate which would have made the holder of it a beneficiary, and on the strength of it they paid over money. In fact the marriage certificate was a forgery and the true beneficiary later appeared.

Held
The trustees were liable to the true beneficiary.

Commentary
Note that the trustees may now seek relief under s61 TA 1925.

Marshall, Re [1914] 1 Ch 192 Chancery Division (Cozens-Hardy MR)
Beneficiary's right to claim distribution

Facts
One of several beneficiaries who was sui juris wished to claim his share transferred to him.

Held
In the absence of special circumstances a beneficiary was entitled to absolute possession of property held on trust for him if that property (ie the beneficiary's share) is severable from other property also held on trust or belonging to other parties.

Cozens-Hardy MR:

> 'The right of a person, who is entitled indefeasibly in possession to an aliquot share of property, to have that share transferred to him is one which is plainly established by law.
>
> There is also another case which is equally plain and established by law, that where real estate is devised in trust for sale and to divide the proceeds of sale between A, B, C and D – some of the shares being settled and some of them not – A has no right to say 'Transfer to me my undivided fourth of the real estate because I would rather have it as real estate than personal estate'. The court has long ago said that it is not right because it is a matter of notoriety, of which the court will take judicial notice, that an individual share of real estate never fetches quite its proper proportion of the proceeds of sale of the entire estate; therefore to allow an individual share to be elected to be taken as real estate by one of the beneficiaries would be detrimental to the other beneficiaries.'

Saunders v *Vautier*

See Chapter 1.

15 Miscellaneous Duties of Trustees

Bishopsgate Investment Management Ltd (In Liquidation) v *Maxwell (No 2)* [1994] 1 All ER 261 Court of Appeal (Ralph Gibson, Leggatt and Hoffmann LJJ)

Director – fiduciary duty – transfer of shares – failure to enquire

Facts
The defendant (Ian Maxwell, 'M') was a director of the plaintiff company (BI). M had signed various share transfer forms whereby shares held by BI were transferred to Robert Maxwell Group plc for a nominal consideration. Whilst the forms, in accordance with BI's memorandum and articles, had also been signed by Kevin Maxwell (another director) the liquidator of BI sought to have M held liable for breach of trust.

Held
It was acknowledged that M had no positive duty to agree to the transfer of the shares. However, having taken the decision to agree to the transfer M had a duty to make proper enquiries and had failed to discharge the burden of proof of establishing the propriety of the transaction.

Hoffmann LJ:

'If a director chooses to participate in the management of the company and exercise it powers on its behalf, he owes a duty to act bone fide in the interest of the company. He must exercise the power solely for the purpose for which it was conferred. To exercise the power for another purpose is a breach of his fiduciary duty. It is no answer that he was under no duty to act in the first place. Nor can Mr Ian Maxwell be excused on the ground that he blindly followed the lead of his brother Kevin. If one signature was sufficient, the articles [of BI] would have said so. The company was entitled to have two officers independently decide that it was proper to sign the transfer. Mr Ian Maxwell was in breach of his fiduciary duty because he gave away the company's assets for no consideration to a private family company of which he was a director. This was prima facie a use of his powers as a director for an improper purpose and in my judgment the burden was upon him to demonstrate the propriety of the transaction.'

Commentary
The case, arising out of the almost endless 'Maxwell' litigation, emphasises that fiduciaries, eg company directors and trustees, whilst not necessarily having a duty to exercise their rights as directors/trustees if they decide to do so they must first make the proper and necessary enquiries. It is not sufficient for a director/trustee to 'rubber stamp' decisions of its fellow directors/trustees.

Cowan v *Scargill* [1984] 3 WLR 501 Chancery Division (Megarry V-C)

Trustee's duty to act in the interests of the beneficiaries in all matters

Facts
The Mineworkers' Pension Scheme was a trust to provide pensions and lump sums on retirement, injury

and certain diseases, and payments for widows and children of those involved in coal mining. The scheme had wide powers of investment and had over £200 million for investment each year. There were ten trustees of the scheme, five appointed by the National Coal Board (the plaintiffs) and five appointed by the National Union of Mineworkers (the defendants). In 1982 the defendants refused to approve an annual investment plan unless it was amended so that (a) there was no increase in the percentage of overseas investment; (b) overseas investments already made be withdrawn at the most opportune time and (c) that there should be no investment in energy industries which were in direct competition with coal. The plaintiffs sought directions as to whether the defendants were in breach of their fiduciary duties.

Held
1. The defendants, as trustees of a pension fund, were governed by the ordinary law of trusts. But as trustees of a pension fund the duty to do the best they could for their beneficiaries had particular relevance because many of those who benefited from the pension scheme had contributed to the pension fund. Further, they could not restrict their range of investments but were under a duty to take advantage of the full range of investment powers granted to them. Accordingly, the defendants, as trustees, could not refuse to concur in making an investment for social or political reasons, as here, when such an investment was in the financial interest of the beneficiaries of the pension fund;
2. The defendants' policy was to further the interests of the mining industry by refusing to concur in investments in energy industries in direct competition with coal. This was not in the best interests of the beneficiaries of the pension fund because most of them had retired from the coal industry or were women and children who had never been engaged in the industry. The defendants were, thus, in breach of their fiduciary duties.

Megarry V-C:

'... I turn to the law. The starting point is the duty of trustees to exercise their powers in the best interests of the present and future beneficiaries of the trust, holding the scales impartially between different classes of beneficiaries. The duty of the trustees towards their beneficiaries is paramount. They must, of course, obey the law; but subject to that, they must put the interests of the beneficiaries first. When the purpose of the trust is to provide financial benefits for the beneficiaries, as is usually the case, the best interests of the beneficiaries are normally their best financial interests. In the case of a power of investment, as in the present case, the power must be exercised so as to yield the best return for the beneficiaries, judged in relation to the risks of the investments in question; and the prospects of the yield of income and capital appreciation both have to be considered in judging the return from the investment ...

... This leads me to the second point, which is a corollary of the first. In considering what investments to make trustees must put on one side their own personal interests and views. Trustees may have strongly held social or political views. They may be firmly opposed to any investment in South Africa or other countries, or they may object to any form of investment in companies concerned with alcohol, tobacco, armaments or many other things. In the conduct of their own affairs, of course, they are free to abstain from making any such investments. Yet under a trust, if investments of this type would be more beneficial to the beneficiaries than other investments, the trustees must not refrain from making the investments by reason of the views that they hold.

Trustees may even have to act dishonourably (though not illegally) if the interests of the beneficiaries require it. Thus where trustees for sale struck a bargain for the sale of trust property but had not bound themselves by a legally enforceable contract, they were held to be under a duty to consider and explore a better offer that they received and not to carry through the bargain to which they felt in honour bound: see *Buttle* v *Saunders* [1950] 2 All ER 193 ...

... Third, by way of caveat I should say that I am not asserting that the benefit of the beneficiaries which a trustee must make his paramount concern inevitably and solely means their financial benefit, even if the only object of the trust is to provide financial benefits. Thus, if the only actual or potential beneficiaries of a trust are all adults with very strict views on moral and social matters, condemning all forms of alcohol, tobacco and popular entertainment, as well as armaments, I can well understand that it might not be for the "benefit" of such beneficiaries to know that they are obtaining rather larger financial returns under the trust by reason of investments in those activities than they would have received if the trustees had invested the trust funds in other investments. The beneficiaries might well consider that it was far better to receive less than to receive more money from what they consider to be evil and tainted sources. "Benefit" is a word with a very wide meaning, and there are circumstances in which arrangements which work to the financial disadvantage of a beneficiary may yet be for his benefit ...'

Harries and Others v *Church Commissioners for England and Another* [1992] 1 WLR 1241 Chancery Division (Sir Donald Nicholls V-C)

Trustees' investment duties – profitability of investments vis-a-vis ethical, non-monetary considerations

Facts
The Bishop of Oxford and others applied, by originating summons, for a declaration that the Church Commissioners in administering the funds for which, in effect, they were trustees should operate their investment policy by bearing in mind that 'the underlying purpose for which they held their assets was the promotion of the Christian faith through the Church of England'. The plaintiffs thus argued that the Commissioners should not invest '... in a manner which would be incompatible with that purpose even if it involved a risk of incurring significant financial detriment.'

Held
The declaration sought must be refused. The Vice-Chancellor pointed out that: 'Where trustees held property as an investment to generate money, prima facie the purposes of the trust would be best served by the trustees seeking to obtain therefrom the maximum return, whether by way of income or capital growth, which was consistent with commercial prudence.'

The Commissioners already had an investment policy whereby they eschewed investments in companies, the main business of which was armaments, gambling, alcohol, tobacco and newspapers. They had considered themselves at liberty to exclude those investments '... because there had remained open an adequate width of alternative investments'. His Lordship found nothing to criticise in the Commissioners' approach in this regard. But to take the approach advocated by the plaintiffs, ie investment decisions involving the taking into consideration of non-financial matters, when this could put investment profits at risk '... would involve a departure by the commissioners from their legal obligations'.

Londonderry's, Settlement Re [1965] Ch 918 Court of Appeal (Harman, Danckwerts and Salmon LJJ)

Beneficiaries not entitled to see documents relating to trustees' exercise of their discretion

Facts
The trustees of a settlement created by the seventh Marquess of Londonderry decided to exercise a power under the settlement to bring it to an end and distribute the capital among the beneficiaries. The settlor's daughter was dissatisfied with the amounts the trustees proposed to appoint to her under their powers in bringing the settlement to an end. She asked the trustees to supply her with copies of various documents

relating to the settlement. The trustees gave her copies of the appointments and of the accounts but refused to disclose any other documents. The settlor's daughter was not satisfied and she issued a summons asking whether the trustees could be required to disclose (a) minutes of meetings of the trustees (b) agendas and other documents for trust meetings (c) correspondence relating to the administration of the trust.

Held
The beneficiaries are prima facie entitled to production and inspection of all trust documents in the possession of the trustees – including title deeds and documents relating to the nature and content of their own beneficial interest. But the beneficiaries under a discretionary trust such as this are not entitled to see documents containing confidential information as to the exercise of the discretion where this 'might cause infinite trouble in the family out of all proportion to the benefit which might be received from inspection of the same'.

Harman LJ:

> 'I have found this a difficult case. It raises what, in my judgment, is a novel question on which there is no authority exactly in point although several cases have been cited to us somewhere near it. The court is really required here to resolve two principles that come into conflict, or at least apparent conflict. The first is that, as the defendant beneficiary admits, trustees exercising a discretionary power are not bound to disclose to their beneficiaries the reasons actuating them in coming to a decision. This is a long-standing principle and rests largely, I think, on the view that nobody could be called upon to accept a trusteeship involving the exercise of a discretion unless, in the absence of bad faith, he were not liable to have his motives to reasons called in question either by the beneficiaries or by the court. To this there is added a rider, namely, that if trustees do give reasons, their soundness can be considered by the court. Compare the observations of James LJ in *Re Gresham Life Assurance Society, Ex parte Penney* (1872) 8 Ch App 466 on the analogous position of directors.
>
> It would seem on the face of it that there is no reason why this principle should be confined to decisions orally arrived at and should not extend to a case like the present, where owing to the complexity of the trust and the large sums involved, the trustees, who act subject to the consent of another body called the appointors, have brought into existence various written documents, including, in particular, agenda for and minutes of their meetings from time to time held in order to consider distributions made of the fund and its income ...'

Tempest v *Lord Camoys* (1882) 21 Ch D 571 Court of Appeal (Jessel MR, Brett and Cotton LJJ)

Exercise of discretion

Facts
The testator gave his trustees a discretionary power to sell certain property and a discretionary power to purchase some other property with the proceeds. The property was sold and some of the beneficiaries wished to purchase a property known as Bracewell Hall, for £60,000 using £30,000 trust monies available and raising the remainder by mortgage. One of the two trustees supported this idea, the other opposed it. A petition was brought that the purchase might nevertheless be ordered.

Held
The court would not intervene to compel the dissenting trustee to concur in the purchase as it was a bona fide exercise of his discretion.

Jessel MR:

'It is very important that the law of the court on this subject should be understood. It is settled law that when a testator has given a pure discretion to trustees as to the exercise of a power, the court does not enforce the exercise of the power against the wish of the trustees, but it does prevent them from exercising it improperly. The court says that the power, if exercised at all, is to be properly exercised. This may be illustrated by the case of persons having a power to appoint new trustees. Even after a decree in a suit for administering the trusts has been made they may still exercise the power, but the court will see that they do not appoint improper persons.

'But in all cases where there is a trust or duty coupled with the power the court will then compel the trustees to carry it out in a proper manner and within a reasonable time. In the present case there was a power which amounts to a trust to invest the fund in question in the purchase of land. The trustees would not be allowed by the court to disregard that trust, and if Mr Fleming (the dissenting trustee) had refused to invest the money in land at all, the court would have found no difficulty in interfering. But that is a very different thing from saying that the court ought to take from the trustees their uncontrolled discretion as to the particular time for the investment and the particular property which should be purchased. In this particular case it appears to me that the testator in his will has carefully distinguished between what is to be at the discretion of his trustees and what is obligatory on them.'

16 Powers of Trustees

Bartlett v *Barclays Bank Trust Co (No 1)*
See Chapter 12.

Belchier, ex parte (1754) Amb 218 (Hardwicke LC)
Power to delegate

Facts
Mrs Parsons was a trustee in bankruptcy, and assigned property to a broker to sell. The broker sold the property but died insolvent a few days later without having handed over the proceeds of sale. The creditors of the first bankrupt tried to make Mrs Parsons personally liable for the money which the broker had never paid. The evidence was that it was trade custom for property of that sort to be sold using a broker.

Held
She was not liable.

Hardwicke LC:

'If Mrs Parsons is chargeable in this case, no man in his senses would act as assignee under commission of bankruptcy. This court has laid down a rule with regard to the transactions of assignees, and more so of trustees, so as not to strike a terror into mankind acting for the benefit of others and not their own.
... Where trustees act by other hands either from necessity or conformable to the common usage of mankind, they are not answerable for losses.'

Berry v *Green* [1938] AC 575 House of Lords (Lord Maugham LC, Lord Macmillan, Lord Thankerton, Lord Russell and Lord Atkin)
Right to transfer of share

Facts
The testator died establishing various annuities out of his estate. Whilst the recipients of the annuities remained alive the balance of the testator's residuary estate and income was to be accumulated. On the death of the last recipient of the annuities the testator's accumulated estate was bequeathed to the Congregational Union of England and Wales ('CUEW'). The CUEW applied for an order to determine the trust for accumulation and for the funds to be held for them absolutely, or alternatively paid to them immediately by virtue of their absolute entitlement.

Held
Where a beneficiary is sui juris and entitled absolutely to a known share of a trust fund he may apply for it to be transferred to him even if there are others entitled to a known share; but not where others are

entitled to a share of the accumulation. On the facts one of the recipients might survive the 21-year accumulations period causing the fund to fall into intestacy as being undisposed of, thereby defeating the CUEW's claim on it. Therefore the application was refused.

Brockbank, Re [1948] Ch 206 Chancery Division (Vaisey J)

Trustees' discretionary power cannot be controlled by beneficiaries or the Court

Facts
A testator left his residuary estate to be held on trust for his wife for life and after her death for his children, and appointed Ward and Bates as trustees. Ward wished to retire. The widow and children wished Lloyds Bank to be appointed a trustee along with Bates, but he refused to join with Ward in exercising the statutory power under s36(1) to appoint the bank as he believed that this would impose an unnecessary charge on the small estate. The widow and children took out a summons asking that Bates should be directed to concur in appointing the bank as trustee.

Held
The beneficiaries are not entitled to control the discretion of their trustees in appointing new trustees. They must either put an end to the trust or if the trust continued abide by the decision of the trustees as to who was selected.

Vaisey J:

> '... It is said that where all the beneficiaries concur, they may force a trustee to retire, compel his removal and direct the trustees, having the power to nominate their successors, to appoint as such successors such persons or person or corporation as may be indicated by the beneficiaries, and it is suggested that the trustees have no option but to comply.
>
> I do not follow this. The power of nominating a new trustee is a discretionary power, and, in my opinion, is no longer exercisable and, indeed, can no longer exist if it has become one of which the exercise can be dictated by others ...
>
> It seems to me that the beneficiaries must choose between two alternatives. Either they must keep the trusts of the will on foot, in which case those trusts must continue to be executed by trustees duly appointed pursuant either to the original instrument or to the powers of s36 of the Trustee Act 1925, and not by trustees arbitrarily selected by themselves; or they must, by mutual agreement, extinguish and put an end to the trusts ...'

Chapman v *Chapman* [1954] AC 429 House of Lords (Lord Simonds LC, Lord Oaksey, Lord Morton, Lord Asquith and Lord Cohen)

Power to compound: Court's inherent jurisdiction to vary trusts

Facts
The trustees of certain settlements sought, in order to minimise death duties and taxation, to rearrange the trusts of the settlement, or to release the property from certain of the trusts. Some of the beneficiaries or potential beneficiaries were infants or unborn persons, and for this reason the consent of the court was necessary for any variation.

Held
The court had no power either inherently or under statute to sanction a rearrangement where there was no

real dispute as to rights under the settlement, even where the interests of unborn persons or infants were concerned.

Lord Simonds LC:

'... The major proposition I state in the words of one of the great masters of equity. "I decline" said Farwell J in *Re Walker* [1901] 1 Ch 879 at p885 "to accept any suggestion that the court has an inherent jurisdiction to alter a man's will because it thinks it beneficial. It seems to me it is quite impossible." ... What are the exceptions to this rule? ... They are reasonably clearly defined. There is no doubt that the Chancellor ... had and exercised the jurisdiction to change the nature of an infant's property from real to personal estate and *vice versa*, though this jurisdiction was generally so exercised as to preserve the rights of testamentary disposition and of succession ... The court assumed power, sometimes for that purpose ignoring the direction of a settlor, to provide maintenance for an infant, and, rarely, for an adult, beneficiary ... The court had power in the administration of trust property to direct that by way of salvage some transaction unauthorised by the trust instrument should be carried out. Nothing is more significant than the repeated assertions by the court that mere expediency was not enough to found the jurisdiction. Lastly, and I can find no other than these four categories, the court had power to sanction a compromise by an infant in a suit to which that infant was party by his next friend or guardian *ad litem* ...'

Lord Asquith:

'... Counsel ... [proposed] an ambitious general principle of law, namely: that there resided in the Court of Chancery an inherent jurisdiction to vary the trusts of a settlement or will, in every case in which two conditions are satisfied, viz (1) that all adults interested in the trust dispositions consented, and (2) that the variation was plainly for the benefit of all interested parties other than adults, viz infants and unborn persons ... I ... think this principle is too broadly stated.

In practice, Courts of Chancery have asserted this jurisdiction mainly, if not indeed solely, in three classes of cases:

(a) Where the trust dispositions have provided for accumulations of income in favour of an infant during his minority without providing for his maintenance during that period: but this provision would be stultified if the infant was not maintained while the income was accumulating. The court has in such cases refrained from enforcing the letter of the trusts, and by authorising maintenance has saved the infant from starving while the harvest designed for him was in the course of ripening.

(b) Where some event or development unforeseen, perhaps unforeseeable, and anyhow unprovided against by the settlor or testator, threatened to make shipwreck of his intentions: and it was imperative that something should be saved from the impending wreck. These are often referred to as the "salvage" cases: and many of the "maintenance" cases which I have classified separately could properly be subsumed under this wider class.

(c) Where there has been a *compromise* of rights (under the settlement or will) which are the subject of doubt or dispute. It is then often to the interest of all interested parties, adult or infant or unborn, to have certainty substituted for doubt, even if the supersession of a dubious right by an undoubted one may be doing beneficent violence to the terms of the trust.'

Delamere's Settlement Trusts, Re [1984] 1 All ER 588 Court of Appeal (Slade, Waller and Robert Goff LJJ)

Trustee Act 1925 s31: power of maintenance

Facts

The trustees held £122,000 of accumulated income for the benefit of six infant beneficiaries. For tax reasons they wished to know what to do with accumulations accruing for any infant should he die before the age of 18.

Held

On the particular facts, the section did not apply.

Slade LJ:

'The principal function of s31 appears to be to supply a code of rules governing the disposal of income, especially during a minority, in cases where a settlor or testator has made dispositions of capital and either (a) being an unskilled draftsman, has not thought about income, or, (b) being a skilled draftsman, has been content to let the statutory code apply.

[S]31(2)(ii) ... [would] defeat the interest (albeit a vested interest) of the infant in the accumulations if he dies before attaining 18 or marrying, and cause them to rejoin the general capital of the trust property from which they arose.'

Fry v *Tapson* (1884) 23 Ch D 268 Chancery Division (Kay J)

Power to delegate: trustees' agents must be chosen with care

Facts

Trustees with power to invest in mortgages took their solicitor's advice and lent on a mortgage on a property in Liverpool which failed. The solicitor had introduced them to a surveyor who was in fact employed by the mortgagor and inflated the value of the property. The trustees defended an action to make them liable, claiming they had used ordinary care and acted on proper advice.

Held

They were jointly and severally liable.

Kay J:

'There is no substantial dispute among the witnesses that the loan was an extremely improvident one for trustees to make ... But the most incautious act was to employ Mr Kerr to value for the mortgagees and to accept his report ... He was a London surveyor, not shown to have any of the local knowledge which was so important in this case, and his employment was inexpedient for that reason; ... he was employed by the mortgagor to find a borrower ... He had written recommending the property in terms which read more like the language of an auctioneer puffing what he had to sell than of a man exercising a calm judgment upon its value as a security for a loan of trust money; and solicitors of experience, who have been called on the part of the defendants, have all confirmed my impression that no prudent lender, whether a trustee or not, would have been satisfied with his valuation ... But it has been argued, ... [if] it was improper to act upon any valuation by him, the trustees employed competent solicitors, who instructed Mr Kerr, and this absolves them. *Speight* v *Gaunt* (1883) 9 App Cas 1 ... illustrated ... that trustees acting according to the ordinary course of business, and employing agents as a prudent man of business would on his own behalf, are not liable for the default of an agent so employed. But an obvious limitation of that rule is that the agent must not be employed out of the ordinary scope of his business. If a trustee employs an agent to do that which is not the ordinary business of such an agent, and he performs that unusual duty improperly, and loss is thereby occasioned, the trustee would not be exonerated ... Some eminent solicitors have been called on behalf of the defendants, and they all agree that this is not the solicitor's business, but if asked to name a valuer, the ordinary course is to submit a name or names to the trustees, and to tell them everything which the solicitor knows to guide their choice, but to leave the choice to them ...'

Jones v *Jones*

See Chapter 1.

Lowther v *Bentinck* (1875) LR 19 Eq 166 Chancery Division (Jessel MR)

Purpose of advancement

Facts
The testator bequeathed a fund to L for life, and remainder to L's children as L appointed by his will. Further provisions applied in the event of default with the trustees having a power of advancement in favour of L. L had substantial debts which nearly absorbed his entire income and the trustees wished to advance funds to discharge these debts.

Held
The discharge of his debts is not necessarily for the benefit of the beneficiary unless there are special circumstances; in the circumstances the monies could be advanced.

McGeorge, Re [1963] Ch 544 Chancery Division (Cross J)

A deferred gift of residuary realty carries intermediate income under s175 LPA

Facts
By his will, a testator devised land to his daughter on the condition that the devise 'shall not take effect until after the death of my wife should she survive me'. But, if the daughter should die before the wife leaving issue the issue were on attaining 21 to take by substitution the devise to the daughter. The testator also bequeathed his residuary estate on trust for his wife for life and on her death to divide it equally between his son and daughter.

Held
The devise to the daughter was a future specific devise which was deferred within the meaning of s175 LPA and it carried the intermediate income of the land devised. However, as the devise was subject to defeasance during the lifetime of the testator's widow, the income should be accumulated during the shorter of the two periods of the widow's lifetime or 21 years from the testator's death. The daughter was not entitled to payment of the income under s31(1) because she had a vested interest in the income, and in any case the will showed an intention to exclude s31.

Cross J:

> 'The devise ... is, it is said, a future specific devise within the meaning of the section (LPA 1925 s175); the testator has not made any express disposition of the income accruing from it between his death and the death of his widow, therefore that income is carried by the gift. At first sight it is hard to see how Parliament could have enacted a section which produces such a result. If a testator gives property to A after the death of B, then whether or not he disposes of the income accruing during B's life he is at all events showing clearly that A is not to have it. Yet if the future gift to A is absolute and the intermediate income is carried with it by force of this section, A can claim to have the property transferred to him at once, since no one else can be interested in it. The section, that is to say, will have converted a gift in remainder into a gift in possession in defiance of the testator's wishes. The explanation for the section taking the form it does is, I think, probably as follows. It has long been established that a gift of residuary personalty to a legatee on being on a contingency or to an unborn person at birth, carries the intermediate income so far as the law will allow it to be accumulated, but that rule had been held for reasons depending on the old land law not to apply gifts of real property, and it was apparently never applied to specific dispositions of personalty. Section 175 of the Law of Property Act was plainly intended to extend the rule to residuary devises and to specific gifts whether of realty or of personalty. It is now, however, established at all events

in court of first instance that the old rule does not apply to residuary bequests whether vested or contingent which are expressly deferred to a future date which must come sooner or later. See *Re Oliver* [1947] 2 All ER 162, (*Re Gillett's Will Trusts* [1956] Ch 102) and *Re Geering* [1964] Ch 136. There is a good reason for this distinction. If a testator gives property to X contingently on his attaining the age of 30 it is reasonable to assume, in the absence of a direction to the contrary, that he would wish X if he attains 30 to have the income produced by the property between his death and the happening of the contingency. If, on the other hand, he gives property to X for any sort of interest after the death of A, it is reasonable to assume that he does not wish X to have the income accruing during A's lifetime unless he directs that he is to have it. But this distinction between an immediate gift on a contingency and a gift which is expressly deferred was not drawn until after the Law of Property Act 1925 was passed. There were statements in textbooks and even in judgments to the effect that the rule applied to deferred as well as to contingent gifts of residuary personalty. (See Jarman, 7th Edn (1930) p1006).

The legislature, when it extended this rule to residuary devises and specific gifts, must, I think, have adopted this erroneous view of the law. I would have liked, if I could, to construe the reference to "future specific devises" and "executory interest" in the section in such a way as to make it consistent with the recent cases on the scope of the old rule applicable to residuary bequests. But to do that would be to rectify the Act, not to construe it, and I see no escape from the conclusion that whereas before 1926 a specific gift or a residuary devise which was not vested in possession did not prima facie carry intermediate income at all, now such a gift may carry intermediate income in circumstances in which a residuary bequest would not carry it.

It was argued in this case that the fact that the will contained a residuary gift constituted an express disposition of the income of the land in question which prevented the section from applying. I am afraid that I cannot accept this submission. I have little doubt that the testator expected the income of the land to form part of the income of residue during his widow's lifetime, but he has made no express disposition of it. I agree with what was said in this connection by Eve J in *Re Raine*[1929] 1 Ch 716.

As the devise is not vested indefeasibly in the daughter but is subject to defeasance during the mother's lifetime the intermediate income which the gift carried by virtue of s175 ought prima facie to be accumulated to see who eventually becomes entitled to it. It was, however, submitted by counsel for the daughter that she could claim payment of it under s31(1) of the Trustee Act 1925. So far as material, that subsection provides that where any property is held by trustees in trust for any person for any interest whatsoever, whether vested or contingent, then, subject to any prior interests or charges affecting that property, if such person on attaining the age of 21 years has not a vested interest in such income, the trustees shall thenceforth pay the income of that property and of any accretion of such income made during his infancy to him until he attains a vested interest therein or dies or until failure of his interest. There are, as I see it, two answers to the daughter's claim. The first – and narrower – answer is that her interest in the income of the devised land is in a vested interest. It is a future interest liable to be divested but it is not contingent. Therefore, s31(1)(ii) does not apply to it. the second – and wider – answer is that the whole framework of s31 shows that it is inapplicable to a future gift of this sort and that a will containing such a gift expresses a contrary intention within s69(2) which prevents the section from applying. By deferring the enjoyment of the devise until after the widow's death the testator has expressed the intention that the daughter shall not have the immediate income. It is true that as he has not expressly disposed of it in any other way, s175 of the Law of Property Act 1925, defeats that intention to the extent of making the future devise carry the income so that the daughter will get it eventually if she survives her mother or dies before her leaving no children to take by substitution. But even if the words of s31 fitted the case, there would be no warrant for defeating the testator's intention still further by reading it into the will and thus giving the daughter an interest in possession in the income during her mother's lifetime. In the result, in my judgment, the income of the fund must be accumulated for 21 years if the widow so long lives.'

Marley and Others v Mutual Security Merchant Bank and Trust Co Ltd [1991] 3 All ER 198 Judicial Committee of the Privy Council (Lord Bridge of Harwich, Lord Oliver of Aylmerton, Lord Goff of Chieveley, Lord Jauncey of Tullichettle and Sir Robin Cooke)

Position of trustees who ask the court's approval in the exercise of discretions (note the administrators in this case were in the position of trustees as regards their administrative duties)

Facts

This case was concerned with the estate of the performer and composer Bob Marley, who died intestate in Jamaica in 1981, leaving very considerable assets in the form of music rights as well as tangible assets including real property in Jamaica. The respondents were at all material times the sole administrators of the deceased's estate and the appellants were his widow and children who, between them, were the sole beneficiaries of his estate under the relevant Jamaican legislation.

The administrators had issued an originating summons (to which they made the beneficiaries parties) before a judge in chambers in the Jamaican Supreme Court, seeking approval of a conditional contract for the sale of the deceased's main assets. The administrators wished to effect such sale, subject to any modification the court might require, in the course of the administration of the deceased's estate. The judge granted the administrators the order they sought but the beneficiaries, who had opposed the originating summons, appealed to the Jamaican Court of Appeal. The Court of Appeal confirmed the judge's order, subject to certain variations, and dismissed the appeal. The beneficiaries appealed to the Judicial Committee.

Held

The appeal must be allowed. The judgment of the Judicial Committee was delivered by Lord Oliver. His Lordship set out early in his speech '... the position and duties of a trustee who applies to the court for directions'. Thus, as his Lordship explained, 'A trustee who is in genuine doubt about the propriety of any contemplated course of action in the exercise of his fiduciary duties and discretions is always entitled to seek proper professional advice and, if so advised, to protect his position by seeking the guidance of the court. If, however, he seeks the approval of the court to an exercise of his discretion *and thus surrenders his discretion to the court* [emphasis inserted], he has always to bear in mind that it is of the highest importance that the court should be put into possession of all the material necessary to enable that discretion to be exercised. It follows that, if the discretion which the court is now called upon to exercise in place of the trustee is one which involves for its proper execution the obtaining of expert advice or valuation, it is the trustee's duty to obtain that advice and place it fully and fairly before the court ...'

His Lordship further went on to state that '... it should be borne in mind that in exercising its jurisdiction to give directions on a trustee's application the court is essentially engaged solely in determining what ought to be done in the best interests of the trust estate and not in determining the rights of adversarial parties'. In cases of the type covered by the instant appeal his Lordship pointed out that '... the real questions at issue ... are what directions ought to be given in the interests of the beneficiaries and whether the court has before it all the material appropriate to enable it to give those directions'.

It was thus necessary, in the instant appeal, to remit the matter to the Jamaican Supreme Court '... for further consideration, on the basis of accurate and up-to-date figures, of expert advice and appraisals so far as necessary, and of sufficient evidence to demonstrate that the potential market for these very valuable assets [ie assets of the deceased's estate] has been fully and effectively explored'. His Lordship also stressed that there was no question whatever raised as to the good faith of the respondents or their advisers.

Marshall, Re
See Chapter 14.

Pauling's Settlement Trusts, Re (No 1) [1964] Ch 303 Court of Appeal (Upjohn, Harman and Willmer LJJ)

Trustees must ensure that advances are used for the purpose intended

Facts
Under the marriage settlement of Commander and Mrs Younghusband made in 1919 moneys were held upon trust for Mrs Younghusband for life, remainder on her death to her children. The settlement contained an express power of advancement by which the trustees, Coutts & Co, could raise with the written consent of Mrs Younghusband, up to half the expectant or presumptive or vested share of any child of the wife and pay to him for his own absolute use, or advancement or benefit in such manner as the trustees should think fit. Between 1945 and 1948 the family lived beyond their means and the Commander was always in need of money. Between 1948 and 1954 the trustees made several advances to the children (Francis, George, Ann and Anthony). One advance of £8,450 was made to Francis and George on a written request of Mrs Younghusband and with the written authority of Francis and George, both of whom were over 21 years at the time. The money was used to buy a house in the Isle of Man. The house was conveyed into the Commander's name and was not settled. Subsequently the house was mortgaged by the Commander for £5,000 and eventually it was sold for less than it was purchased for, with the result that all the money was lost. Further advances were made, a total of four in all; on some, though not all occasions, the children received independent legal advice as to their rights under the settlement. Most of the money advanced was used to purchase and furnish houses for the family and to pay off loans of Commander and Mrs Younghusband. In 1958 the children brought an action against the bank for breach of trust, claiming £29,160 on the ground that it had been improperly advanced and that they had been subject to undue influence since they had been under parental control at the time.

Held
1. The power of advancement can only be exercised if it is for the benefit of the child to have a share of the capital before his or her due time. It should only be used where there is some good reason for it and not capriciously or without some other benefit in view.
2. When making an advance for a particular stated purpose, the bank could properly pay it to the child advanced if the bank reasonably thought that the child could be trusted to carry out the prescribed purpose, but the bank could not properly leave the child entirely free, legally and morally, to apply the sum for that purpose, or to spend it in any way that he or she chose, without any responsibility on their part to enquire as to its application.
3. Where the trust was advanced for a particular purpose, the child advanced was under a duty to apply it for that purpose and could not apply it to any other purpose. If any misapplication came to the bank's notice, they could not safely make further advances for a particular purpose without ensuring that the money would be applied for that purpose first.
4. Where a trustee carried out a transaction in breach of trust with the apparent consent of the beneficiary he would still be liable if he knew or ought to have known that the beneficiary was acting under undue influence.
5. The presumption of undue influence of a parent over his child could endure for a "short time" after the child attained 21.

On these principles the bank was liable in breach of trust for all but two of the advances. In one case a defence under s61 Trustee Act succeeded and in the other the children were at an age when they could have no longer been under undue influence, when they consented.

Peters v *Chief Adjudication Officer* [1989] Fam Law 318 Court of Appeal (Croome Johnson, Glidewell and May LJJ)

Control over trustees powers and social security claimants

Facts
The plaintiff was in receipt of social security benefits, and had three dependent daughters living at home. Under their grandmother's will in 1984 the girls each received £1,455, which in the case of the two who were under 18 years of age, was held in trust for them during their minority. The Social Security authorities treated the whole of all three sums as resources available to the plaintiff and cut her social security benefit.

Held
The claimant's appeal was allowed. The money held on trust for a minor was properly treated as a capital resource, but the value of the resource to be taken into account must be the actual value of the minor's present equitable interest, not the total value of the fund which she would receive on attaining majority.

Commentary
For the position with discretionary trusts, see *Jones* v *Jones* in Chapter 1.

Pilkington v *Inland Revenue Commissioners* [1964] AC 612 House of Lords (Viscount Radcliffe, Lord Reid, Lord Jenkins, Lord Hodson and Lord Devlin)

Advancement can include tax avoidance

Facts
William Norman Pilkington made a will in 1934 by which he left his residuary estate to trustees upon protective trusts for all his nephews and nieces living at his death in equal shares for life. The trust contained a provision that any consent which the nephews and nieces might give during their lifetime to an advancement would not cause a forfeiture of their life interests. There was no provision replacing or excluding s32 of the Trustee Act. When the testator died in 1935 he had one nephew, Richard. Richard had three children, one of whom was the defendant Penelope Pilkington in whose favour he wished the trustees to exercise the statutory power of advancement under s32 in order to avoid estate duty. This scheme involved the setting up of a fresh trust to which half of Penelope's presumptive share would be advanced and the income of the same applied for her maintenance until she was 21. From then until she was 30 the income was to be paid to her and on attaining 30 the capital would become hers absolutely. However, if she died under 30, the capital was to be held on trust for her children who attained 21. The trustees sought a declaration whether they could exercise the power of appointment in the manner proposed.

Held
1. Provided the advancement was for the benefit of the person in whose favour it was made, it was no

objection that other persons benefited incidentally as a result of the advancement, nor that the money advanced was settled on fresh trusts.
2. There was nothing in s32 which restricted the manner or purpose of an advancement. However, in the circumstances of the case the exercise of the power of advancement would infringe the rule against perpetuities and could not lawfully be made.

Viscount Radcliffe:

'So much for "advancement", which I now use for brevity to cover the combined phrase "advancement or benefit". It means any use of the money which will improve the material situation of the beneficiary. It is important, however, not to confuse the idea of "advancement" with the idea of advancing the money out of the beneficiary's expectant interest. The two things have only a casual connection with each other. The one refers to the operation of finding money by way of anticipation of an interest not yet absolutely vested in possession or, if so vested, belonging to a infant; the other refers to the status of the beneficiary and the improvement of his situation. The power to carry out the operation of anticipating an interest is not conferred by the word "advancement" but by those other words of the section which expressly authorise the payment or application of capital money for the benefit of a person entitled "whether absolutely or contingently on his attaining any specified age or on the occurrence of any other event, or subject to a gift over on his death under any specified age or on the occurrence of any other event, and whether in possession or in remainder or reversion," etc.

I think, with all respect to the Commissioners, a good deal of their argument is infected with some of this confusion. To say, for instance, that there cannot be a valid exercise of a power of advancement that results in a deferment of the vesting of the beneficiary's absolute title (Miss Penelope, it will be remembered, is to take at 30 under the proposed settlement instead of at 20 under the will) is in my opinion to play upon words. The element of anticipation consists in the raising of money for her now before she has any right to receive anything under the existing trusts: the advancement consists in the application of that money to form a trust fund, the provisions of which are thought to be for her benefit. I have not forgotten, of course, the references to powers of advancement which are found in such cases as *Re Joicey* [1915] 2 Ch 115, *Re May's Settlement* [1926] Ch 136 and *Re Mewburn's Settlement* [1934] Ch 112 to which our attention is called, or the answer supplied by Cotten LJ in *Re Aldridge* (1886) 55 LT 554 to his own question "What is advancement?"; but I think that it will be apparent from what I have already said that the description that he gives (it cannot be a definition) is confined entirely to the aspect of anticipation or acceleration which renders the money available and not to any description or limitation of the purposes for which it can then be applied.'

Raine, Re [1929] 1 Ch 716 Chancery Division (Eve J)

Pecuniary contingent legacies do not carry maintenance under s175 LPA

Facts
The testatrix bequeathed £2,000 to her god-child, 'if and when she shall attain the age of twenty-one years', and she bequeathed a similar legacy of £100 to another infant. Subject to this the testatrix gave all her real and personal estate to trustees upon trust for her sister-in-law. The will contained no express power of maintenance and there was no express disposition of the income of the legacies.

Held
The income of these contingent legacies was not applicable for the maintenance of the legatees, as a pecuniary legacy does not come within the words of s175.

Saunders v Vautier

See Chapter 1.

Smith, Re Public Trustee v Aspinall [1928] Ch 915 Chancery Division (Romer J)

Control over trustees' powers: control by beneficiaries: discretionary trusts

Facts

The testator established a fund in favour of A and thereafter in favour of A's children. Provisions were made for the maintenance of A and A's children, accumulation of the fund and division on A's death; all of which had a discretionary trust overcoat whereby the trustees had a discretion to apply funds for the maintenance of A after A's children had reached 21.

A and A's children (on their all reaching 21) executed a mortgage to enable them to purchase a property. The Public Trustee (sole trustee) applied for the court's assistance, specifically to determine whether he was obliged to exercise his discretion in favour of the mortgagee bank (as assignee of the fund) or if he could still pay monies direct to A for her maintenance.

Held

The Public Trustee was bound to pay the monies to the mortgagee bank until the mortgage was discharged.

Romer J:

> 'Where there is a trust under which trustees have a discretion as to applying the whole or part of a fund to or for the benefit of a particular person, [A], that ... person cannot come to the trustees, and demand the fund; for the whole fund has not been given to him, but only so much as the trustees think fit to let him have ... Where ... A has assigned his interest under the trust, or become bankrupt, ... his assignee or his trustee in bankruptcy stand in no better position than he does and cannot demand that the funds shall be handed to them, yet they are in a position to say to A: "Any money which the trustees do in the exercise of their discretion pay to you, passes by the assignment or under the bankruptcy". But they cannot say that in respect of any money which the trustees have not paid to A or invested in purchasing goods or other things for A, but which they apply for the benefit of A in such a way that no money or goods ever gets into the hands of A.'

Speight v Gaunt (1883) 9 App Cas 1 Court of Appeal (Jessel MR, Lindley and Bowen LJJ)

Trustees may delegate and conduct trust affairs as a prudent man would his own

Facts

Gaunt was the trustee of a trust. He employed one Cooke, a stockbroker, to invest £15,000 of the trust funds in stock or shares in companies quoted on the Stock Exchange, on the suggestion of the beneficiaries. Cooke had been in partnership in a firm of stockbrokers of high repute at the time. In accordance with the usual course of business Cooke entered into a contract to buy the shares from a jobber on the Stock Exchange on the next account-day. He brought Gaunt a bought-note stating that he required the money to pay for the stock and shares on the following day as he was liable to pay for them on the account-day. Cheques totalling £15,000 were drawn in favour of and handed to Cooke who left the bought-note with Gaunt. In fact Cooke did not complete the transaction to purchase the stocks and shares but instead appropriated the cheques to his own use. On being questioned by Gaunt on the matter he made various excuses. Shortly afterwards Cooke was adjudicated bankrupt. The cestuis que trust claimed that Gaunt was liable for breach of trust with respect to the transaction and was personally liable for the loss since he should have paid the £15,000 directly to the bankers of the companies in which the shares had been bought. Gaunt, in defence, argued that he could not be held liable unless it was shown that he had not acted as a prudent man of business would have acted on his own behalf.

Held
Gaunt was not liable; he had acted as a prudent man of business had done and nothing more could have been expected of him as trustee for otherwise no one would become a trustee if a higher standard was imposed on them with regard to trust affairs than they should apply in dealing with their own affairs.

Jessel MR:

> '... It seems to me that on general principles a trustee ought to conduct the business of the trust in the same manner that an ordinary prudent man of business would conduct his own, and that beyond that there is no liability, or obligation on the trustee. In other words, a trustee is not bound because he is a trustee to conduct business in other than the ordinary and usual way in which similar business is conducted by mankind in transactions of their own. It never could be reasonable to make a trustee adopt further and better precautions than an ordinary prudent man of business would adopt, or to conduct business in any other way. If it were otherwise, no one would be a trustee at all. He is not paid for it. He says, "I take all reasonable precautions, and all the precautions which are deemed reasonable by prudent men of business, and beyond that I am not required to go.".'

Commentary
The House of Lords dismissed an appeal from the decision of the Court of Appeal and affirmed the decision of Jessel MR and the other members of the Court of Appeal (Bowen and Lindley LJJ) on this point.

Stafford (Earl of), Re [1980] Ch 28 Court of Appeal (Buckley, Goff and Lawton LJJ)

Power to compound

Facts
T died in December 1951 two months after his wife. He settled his mansion house on a strict settlement, with all his chattels, the limitations being to his two daughters for life, remainder for one grandson, remainder for the other grandson. By her will, T's wife left her estate between the two daughters equally. The daughters divided the valuable chattels (of which there were many) as they thought correct between the two estates, and these allocations were acted on. Later evidence showed that many of the chattels allocated to the wife's estate in fact had belonged to T. The beneficiaries other than the daughters put forward a compromise, and the trustees sought the decision of the court, surrendering to the court their powers under s15 of the Trustee Act 1925.

Held
The section conferred wide and flexible powers of compounding disputes. In exercising them the trustees had to take into account the interests of the beneficiaries and the value of the assets likely to be recovered, balanced against the costs and other disadvantages of continuing the dispute. In the circumstances the compromise would be approved.

Vickery, Re [1931] 1 Ch 572 Chancery Division (Maugham J)

Trustees's powers and liability in employing agents under Trustee Act

Facts
A missionary called Mr Stephens who had no knowledge of business affairs was appointed sole executor of Mrs Vickery's estate by her will. Stephens appointed a solicitor, Mr Jennens, to wind up the estate and also to collect £214 14s 5d in the Post Office Savings Bank and £62 4s in Savings Certificates in May 1927. In September 1927 Stephens was informed that Jennens had at one time been suspended from practice by one of the testatrix's sons who asked Stephens to instruct a different solicitor. Stephens did not do so as Jennens repeatedly promised him that matters would be settled quickly. Eventually another solicitor was employed in December 1927 as the estate had not been settled but Jennens absconded without handing over the moneys he had collected and these were lost. The testatrix's sons claimed that Stephens was guilty of a breach of trust and since they were entitled to the moneys under the will they claimed them from Stephens who relied on s23(1) and s30(1) in defence.

Held
1. Stephens was not liable. Section 23(1) revolutionised the position of a trustee as regards employment of agents and there did not have to be a necessity for the employment as previously required.
2. Under s23(1) a trustee was only liable for loss caused by the misconduct of the agent where such losses occurred because of the trustee's 'default'. Stephens was not guilty of default but only of an error of judgment at the most in appointing Jennens to wind up the estate.
3. Stephens was not liable under s30(1) either, because he had only committed an error of judgment.

Maugham J:

'The question that arises is whether in the circumstances, and in view of my findings as to the facts, the defendant is liable to make good these sums with interest by reason of his negligence either in employing Jennens to receive the sums, or in permitting those sums to remain in his hands, in the circumstances of the case, for a longer period than necessary.

In considering this question the Court has to bear in mind in particular two sections of the Trustee Act 1925. Section 23, subsection (1) is as follows: [His Lordship read the sub-section and continued:] This sub-ection is new and, in my opinion, authorised the defendant in signing the authorities to Jennens and Jennens to collect the two sums in question; for I do not think it can be doubted that the defendant acted in good faith in employing Jennens for the purpose. It will be observed that the subsection has no proviso or qualification to it such as we find in relation to section 23, subsection (3). It is hardly too much to say that it revolutionises the position of a trustee or an executor so far as regards the employment of agents. He is no longer required to do any actual work himself, but he may employ a solicitor or other agent to do it, whether there is any real necessity for the employment or not. No doubt he should use his discretion in selecting an agent, and should employ him only to do acts within the scope of the usual business of the agent; but, as will be seen, a question arises whether even in these respects he is personally liable for a loss due to the employment of the agent unless he has been guilty of wilful default.

Section 23, subsection 3, is in the following terms: [His Lordship read the subsection and continued:] This subsection is a reproduction with amendments of section 17 of the Trustee Act 1893, which replaced section 2 of the Trustee Act 1888. It will be observed that para (a) of the subsection related to the production of a deed having endorsed thereon a receipt for money or other property, and that para (1) refers to the receipt of money payable to the trustee under a policy of insurance. In these cases, no doubt, there is no reason why the banker or the solicitor should do anything more than receive the money and pay the same to the trustee or as he shall direct. The proviso must, I think, be limited to these two cases; and, of course, it is not intended to preclude a trustee from keeping trust funds at his bank pending investment or proper use of them; and it has nothing to do, in my opinion, with the case I have to decide, in which the powers given by paras (a) and (c) were not utilised by the defendant. There was no doubt a good reason for not making the proviso extend to subsection 1 of section 23, since in many cases where, for example, a banker or other agent is employed by a trustee to receive money, the money cannot at once be conveniently paid to the trustee, but has to be employed by the banker or other agent in a number of ways.

I have now to consider section 30 subsection 1 of the Trustee Act 1925, a section which replaces section 24 of the Trustee Act 1893, which in its turn re-enacted Lord Cranworth's Act, section 31. It is in the following terms: [His Lordship read the subsection and continued]: Reliance has been placed on the words concluding the sub-section "nor for any other loss, unless the same happens through his own wilful default". To avoid misconception I wish to say that, having regard to the numerous decisions since the enactment of Lord Cranworth's Act in relation to the liability of trustees for innocent breaches of trust, it is impossible now to hold that the words 'for any other loss' are quite general, with the result that no trustee is ever liable for breach of trust unless the breach is occasioned by his own wilful default. In my opinion the words are confined to losses for which it is sought to make the trustee liable occasioned by his signing receipts for the sake of conformity or by reason of the wrongful acts or defaults of another trustee or of an agent with whom trust money or securities have been deposited, or for the insufficiency or deficiency of securities of some other analogous loss. It may be noted that if the phrase is not so limited it is difficult to see how there could have been any need for section 3 of the Judicial Trustee Act 1896 now re-enacted as section 61 of the Trustee Act 1925 or for section 29 of the Act; nor would it be possible to explain the numerous cases before 1896 where trustees were made liable for honest mistakes either of construction or fact: see, for example, *Learoyd* v *Whiteley* (1887) 12 App Cas 727 [see Chapter 12], *National Trustees Co of Australasia* v *General Finance Co of Australasia* [1905] AC 373 [see Chapter 17], and cases there cited.

On the other hand, since section 30 subsection 1 expressly refers to the defaults of bankers, brokers, or other persons with whom any trust money or other securities may be deposited, I am unable – dealing here with the more limited case – to escape the conclusion that the trustee cannot be made liable for the default of such a person unless the loss happens through the "wilful default" of the trustee. Before considering the meaning of the words "wilful default" in this connection, I would observe that in the case of *Re Brier* (1884) 26 Ch D 238 the Court of Appeal, consisting of Lord Selborne LC, and Cotton and Fry LJJ, gave effect to Lord Cranworth's Act section 31, and held the trustees and executors not liable inasmuch as it had not been established that the loss occasioned by the agent's insolvency (in a case where, as the law then required, it was shown that the employment of the agent was a proper one) was due to the wilful default of the trustees and executors.

Now the meaning of the phrase "wilful default" has been expounded by the Court of Appeal in the case of *Re Trusts of Leeds City Brewery Ltd's Deed* [1925] Ch 532n and in the case of *Re City Equitable Fire Insurance Co* [1925] Ch 407. It should be noted that in both those cases the indemnity given to the trustees in the first case and to the directors and officers of the company in the second case, was worded in a general form so that it could not be contended that they were liable for any matter or thing done or omitted unless it could be shown that the loss so occasioned arose from their own wilful default. This, as I have said, is not true of an ordinary executor or trustee; but the exposition of the phrase "wilful default" is not the less valuable. The Court of Appeal held, following the case of *Re City Equitable Fire Insurance Co* the decision of Romer J that a person is not guilty of wilful default or default unless he is conscious that, in doing the act which is complained of or in omitting to do the act which it is said he ought to have done, he is committing a breach of his duty, or is recklessly careless whether it is a breach of duty or not. I accept with respect what Warrington LJ said – namely, that in the case of trustees there are definite and precise rules of law as to what a trustee may or may not do in the execution of his trust, and that a trustee in general is not excused in relation to a loss occasioned by a breach of trust merely because he honestly believed that he was justified in doing the act in question. But for the reasons which I have given I think that, where an executor employs a solicitor or other agent to receive money belonging to the estate in reliance on section 23 subsection 1 of the Trustee Act 1925, he will not be liable for a loss of the money occasioned by misconduct of the agent unless the loss happens through the wilful default of the executor, using those words as implying, as the Court of Appeal have decided, either a consciousness of negligence or breach of duty, or a recklessness in the performance of a duty ...'

17 Breach of Trust I: Personal Remedies

Bahin* v *Hughes (1886) 31 Ch D 390 Court of Appeal (Cotton, Bowen and Fry LJJ)

Active trustee does not indemnify others unless a solicitor or acting for personal gain

Facts
The testator left a legacy of £2,000 to his three daughters, Miss Hughes, Mrs Edwards and Mrs Burden on trust to pay the income to Mrs Bahin for life remainder to her children. Miss Hughes, who managed the business of the trust, invested in an unauthorised investment, namely a mortgage of leasehold premises. The security proved insufficient and there was a loss to the trust. Mrs Bahin sought to hold all the trustees liable. As Mrs Edwards had died her husband was added as a party. Both Mr Edwards and Mrs Burden claimed to be indemnified by Miss Hughes for the loss on the grounds that she had instigated the purchase of the investment and told them it was a good investment.

Held
The trustees were jointly and severally liable to make good the loss and none could claim an indemnity. The mere fact Miss Hughes had managed the trust affairs alone and in doing so had committed a breach of trust did not of itself entitle the other trustees to an indemnity. They would only be entitled to an indemnity where an active trustee, such as Miss Hughes, was a solicitor or had obtained personal gain from the breach of trust.

Cotton LJ:

'… It would be laying down a wrong rule that where one trustee acts honestly, though erroneously, the other trustee is to be held entitled to indemnity who by doing nothing neglects his duty more than the acting trustee. That Miss Hughes made an improper investment is true, but she acted honestly, and intended to do the best she could, and believed that the property was sufficient security for the money, although she made no inquiries about their being leasehold houses. In my opinion the money was lost just as much by the default of Mr Edwards as by the innocent thought erroneous action of his co-trustee Miss Hughes. All the trustees were in the wrong, and every one is equally liable to indemnify the beneficiaries.'

Bartlett v *Barclays Bank Trust Co (No 1)*

See Chapter 12.

Bell's Indenture, Re [1980] 1 WLR 1217 Chancery Division (Vinelott J)

Breach of trust: constructive trustees and measure of liability

Facts
A marriage settlement was made in 1907 and a voluntary settlement in 1930. Alexander was trustee and beneficiary under both. In 1947 the trustees of the marriage settlement improperly sold a farm to the

trustees of the voluntary settlement for £8,200. In 1949 the trustees of the voluntary settlement sold the farm for £12,400 to a stranger. If the trustees of the marriage settlement had not sold the farm in 1947 they could and would have sold it in 1949.

In the course of these manoeuvres, a solicitor in partnership with another knowingly allowed money which had been paid into his firm's client account to be paid out again in breach of trust. His partner knew of the payment in and that it was by trustees, but did not know of the breach of trust. He died before the action and it was sought to make his estate liable, as partners are jointly and severally liable.

Held
The trustees of the marriage settlement were clearly in breach of trust. The value of the loss was to be assessed at the date of judgment, and in this case would be limited to what the trustees of the marriage settlement would have made if they had sold in 1949. No account should be taken of what the income would have been if they had sold the farm and reinvested in another farm, but nor was the defaulting trustee able to reduce the amount he had to pay by the amount of death duty which would have been payable if such an investment had taken place.

On the liability of the solicitor who had knowingly been involved, there was no question but that he had become constructive trustee of the money received. However, his partner could not be made liable because although the knowing partner had implied authority from his partner to receive trust money, he did not have implied authority to constitute himself constructive trustee. Where he did in fact do so, his partner was not liable for misapplications in which he had taken no part and of which he was ignorant.

Chillingworth v *Chambers* [1896] 1 Ch 685 Court of Appeal (Lindley, Kay and A L Smith LJJ)

The right of contribution does not include a trustee who is also a beneficiary

Facts
The plaintiff and the defendant were both trustees of a will. They advanced trust money to secure mortgages of certain property, a form of investment which was not authorised by the will. The plaintiff became a beneficiary under the will and after this both he and the defendant advanced more money on mortgage. The properties proved to be inadequate security for the loans and there was a loss of £1,580. Both the plaintiff and defendant were declared jointly and severally liable to make good the loss. However, the whole loss was made good out of the plaintiff's share of the trust fund. The plaintiff claimed a contribution from the defendant.

Held
The normal rules as to the right of contribution between trustees where all or some were liable for a breach of trust and of whom one had made good the loss, does not apply where the trustee who has made good the loss is also a beneficiary. The plaintiff was not entitled to a contribution.

A L Smith LJ:

> 'There appear to be three rules which have application to a case like the present, and may be shortly stated as follows: (1) that a cestui que trust cannot make a trustee liable for losses occasioned to him by a breach of trust which that cestui que trust has authorised and consented to; (2) that in such a case a trustee is entitled to be recouped out of the interest of the cestui que trust in the trust funds any loss he may sustain by reason of his having to make good such breach of trust; and (3) that, as between two trustees who are in pari delicto, the one who has made good a loss occasioned by a breach of trust for which the two are jointly and severally liable may obtain contribution to that loss from the other.
>
> The question is how these rules are to be applied in the present case.

As to the existence of the 1st rule, Lord Eldon, as long ago as the year 1818, in *Walker* v *Symonds* (1818) 3 Swans 164, states: "It is established by all the cases, that if the cestui que trust joins with the trustees in that which is a breach of trust, knowing the circumstances, such a cestui que trust can never complain of such a breach of trust." And in 1841 Lord Langdale, in *Fyler* v *Fyler* (1841) 3 Beav 560, states the rule as follows: "If all this has taken place" – that is, the breach of trust – "with the consent of the parties now complaining, it certainly appears to me that they would not have any right to maintain this suit, for volenti non fit injuria. If they have authorised this course of dealing with their own fund, it would be in the highest degree unjust, to permit them to establish a claim against those who have acted under their authority."

As to the 2nd rule, this was held by Lord Hardwicke in the year 1746, in *Trafford* v *Boehm* (1746) 3 Atk 444: "The rule of the Court in all cases is, that if a trustee errs in the management of the trust, and is guilty of a breach, yet if he goes out of the trust with the approbation of the cestui que trust, it must be made good first out of the estate of the person who consented to it." And Lord Langdale, in *Lincoln* v *Wright* (1844) 4 Beav 432, states the rule thus: "Now, nothing can be more clear than the rule which is adopted by the Court in these cases; that if one party, having a partial interest in the trust fund, induces the trustee to depart from the direction of the trust for his own benefit, and enjoys that benefit, he shall not be permitted, personally, to enjoy the benefit of the trust, whilst the trustees are subjected to a serious liability which he has brought upon them. What the Court does, in such a case, is to lay hold of the partial interest to which that person is entitled, and apply it, so far as it will extend, in exoneration of the trustees, who by his request and desire or acquiescence, or by any other mode of concurrence, have been induced to do the improper act."

The judgment of Turner LJ in *Raby* v *Ridehalgh* (1851) 7 De GM & G 104, appears to me to proceed upon the same principle, for he held cestuis que trust who had been privy to and instigated a breach of trust liable out of the trust shares to recoup the trustees.

A question has arisen under this judgment as to what amount of the cestui que trust interest the trustee is entitled to impound.

For the reasons given by Lindley LJ I am of opinion that Turner LJ did not intend to cut down the rule which had theretofore, in my opinion, existed, namely, that a trustee may be entitled to impound the cestui que trustee's interest in so far as it will go to recoup him for the losses he has had to make good. It is not stated whether the amount impounded in this case was not sufficient to indemnify the trustee.

I do not doubt, that had the plaintiff in the present case not been a co-trustee with the defendant, but only a cestui que trust of the estate of which the defendant was trustee, that, inasmuch as the plaintiff had authorised and consented to the breach of trust which is now complained of, he could not have claimed contribution from the defendant to make good the loss he had sustained; and, what is more, that the defendant would have been entitled to impound the plaintiff's interest in his one-fifth share to exonerate him from any loss he might have been called upon to make good by reason of the breach of trust ...

... I now come to the 3rd rule, which is, that, where two trustees concur in committing a breach of trust and are in pari delicto, the one, if he has made good the loss occasioned thereby to the trust estate, can obtain contribution from the other. The existence of this rule is not disputed at the bar: see *Lingard* v *Bromley* (1812) 1 V & B 114.

The real question is, how is this rule to be applied in the present case, which arises, not between two trustees who are merely trustees, but between a trustee who is also a cestui que trustee and his co-trustee who is not?

In my judgment, the true view is that the plaintiff in this case can only bring into play the 3rd rule (that is, the rule as to contribution between co-trustees) if and when he has made good to the cestuis que trust any loss they have sustained by reason of the breach of trust complained of over and above his share in the trust property; but this he has not done.

As before stated, if he had not made good this loss, and the defendant had, the plaintiff's share could have been impounded for that purpose by the defendant until he had been recouped what he had paid; and the plaintiff, therefore, is not in a position to ask for contribution from the defendant until the plaintiff had paid more than the amount of his share. When he had done so, then, it seems to me, he would have been entitled to ask for contribution towards what he had paid over and above his interest in the trust funds. But there yet remains to the plaintiff of his share in the trust funds the sum of £1,50l, and, consequently, in my judgment, there is nothing upon which the plaintiff can bring into play the operation of rule 3.

For these reasons, I think that North J was quite right in deciding as he did, that the plaintiff was entitled to no contribution from the defendant. This appeal must be dismissed.'

Diplock, Re [1948] Ch 465 (Lord Greene MR, Wrottesley and Evershed LJJ)

Remedies in rem and in personam for breach of trust

Facts

Caleb Diplock, who died in March 1936, left a will by the terms of which the executors were directed to apply his residuary estate 'for such charitable institution or institutions or other charitable or benevolent object or objects in England' as they should in their absolute discretion think fit. The residuary estate amounted to approximately £263,000 and the executors proceeded to distribute it among 139 charities of their choice without obtaining any directions from the court. However, the next-of-kin challenged the validity of the bequest on the grounds of uncertainty and in *Chichester Diocesan Fund and Board of Finance Ltd* v *Simpson* [1944] AC 341 the House of Lords upheld their challenge.

The next-of-kin then proceeded to recover the funds which had been wrongfully distributed by the executors. First, they made a claim in personam against the executors or their estates and these were compromised with the approval of the court. Then they brought actions against a number of the institutions who had benefited under the distribution. In most cases the institutions had been sent cheques which they had paid into their accounts. Some had put the money to one side in a special account and earmarked it for a particular purpose. Others had used the money to alter and enlarge buildings and land owned by them. The next-of-kin made two claims against the institutions: (i) a claim in personam based on an alleged equity in an unpaid creditor, legatee or next-of-kin to recover from an overpaid beneficiary or, a stranger to the estate who was not entitled to any payment; (ii) a claim in rem to trace identifiable assets, whether mixed or unmixed, into the hands of a volunteer who had wrongly received them.

Held

1. As to the claim in personam:

    This was available to the next-of-kin in the circumstances alleged. There was established the existence of an equity to recover from an over-paid or wrongly paid recipient and this equity might be available equally to an unpaid or underpaid creditor, legatee or next-of-kin.

    a) this claim was not defeated by the fact that the payment to the recipient had been made under a mistake of law as opposed to a mistake of fact.
    b) the next-of-kin should claim first against the personal representatives and the claim against the institutions should give credit for the amount recovered from the personal representatives.
    c) the claim lay only for the principal; interest was not recoverable.
    d) the period of limitation applicable to the claim was 12 years under s20 Limitation Act 1939. This ran from the date when the right to receive the share or interest accrued (normally one year from death).

2. As to the claim in rem:

    a) Where money in the hands of a trustee or other fiduciary agent had been mixed with that of another, the person with an equitable interest in that money could trace this money into the mixed fund, or any assets purchased out of the mixed fund. It did not matter whether the fund had been mixed by an innocent volunteer or the trustee or fiduciary agent or whether the money had been passed on mixed by the trustee or fiduciary agent to the volunteer. For this remedy to apply three conditions must be satisfied:

i) There must be a fiduciary relationship between the claimant and the original holder of the money, ie the next-of-kin and the personal representative in this case. This gave the claimant an equitable interest in the money.

ii) The money or any asset purchased out of it must still be in existence either separately or as part of a mixed fund.

iii) The imposition of a charge in favour of the claimant must not cause an injustice to the volunteer.

b) Where the money had been passed to the innocent volunteer unmixed and he had kept it apart from his own funds then the innocent volunteer held the money on behalf of the claimant, ie the next-of-kin.

c) If the money had been passed to the innocent volunteer and he had mixed it with his own money, then the claimant and the innocent volunteer ranked pari passu as regards the mixed fund. If the mixing had taken place in an active banking account then the rule in *Clayton*'s case (1816) 1 Mer 529 [see Chapter 18] applied. If the mixing had taken place through the innocent volunteer applying the money he had received to alter, improve or extend his own property, no tracing would be allowed as a charge in favour of the claimant would work an injustice to the innocent volunteer. Similarly, if the money had been used by the innocent volunteer to clear a blot on his title to certain property, tracing would not be allowed as this would also work an injustice to the volunteer.

Lord Greene MR (who gave the judgment of the court):

The claim in personam

At pp502–504 he gave the court's conclusions on the next-of-kin's claim in personam based on an alleged equity to recover from an overpaid beneficiary or a stranger who was not entitled to any payment:

'What then is the conclusion to be drawn on this part of the appellants' claim from what we fear has been a long citation of the authorities? It is not, we think, necessary or desirable that we should attempt any exhaustive formulation of the nature of the equity invoked which will be applicable to every class of case. But it seems to us, first, to be established and that the equity may be available equally to an unpaid or underpaid creditor, legatee, or next-of-kin. Second, it seems to us that a claim by a next-of-kin will not be liable to be defeated merely (a) in the absence of administration by the court: or (b) because the mistake under which the original payment was made was one of law rather than fact; or (c) because the original recipient, as things turn out, had no title at all and was a stranger to the estate; though the effect of the refund in the last case will be to dispossess the original recipient altogether rather than to produce equality between him and the claimant and other persons having a like title to that of the recipient. In our judgment there is no authority either in logic or in the decided cases for such limitations to the equitable right of action. In our judgment also there is no justification for such limitations to be found in the circumstances which gave rise to the equity. And as regards the conscience of the defendant upon which, in this as in other jurisdictions equity is said to act, it is prima facie at least a sufficient circumstance that the defendant, as events have proved, has received some share of the estate to which he was not entitled. "A party", said Sir John Leach in *David* v *Frowd* (1833) 1 My & K 200 "claiming under such circumstances has no great reason to complain that he is called upon to replace what he has received against his right."

On the other hand, to such a claim by an unpaid beneficiary, there is, in our judgment, at least in circumstances such as the present, one important qualification. Since the original wrong payment was attributable to the blunder of the personal representatives, the right of the unpaid beneficiary is in the first instance against the wrongdoing executor or administrator; and the beneficiary's direct claim in equity against those overpaid or wrongly paid should be limited to the amount which he cannot recover from the party responsible. In some cases the amount will be the whole amount of the payment wrongly made, eg where the executor or administrator is shown to be wholly without assets or is protected from attack by having acted under an order of the court.

Authority for this qualification is to be found in the judgment of Sir J Strange in the case of *Orr v Kanes* (1750) 2 Ves Sen 194, where be observed that, if the executor is insolvent, an unpaid legatee is admitted to claim direct from the wrongly paid recipient because "the principal case went upon the insolvency of the executor". It is true that no direct authority for the qualification is to be found in any of the other decided cases; but in none of those cases where the direct claim was allowed, did it appear in fact that there was an executor or administrator against whom a claim might have been made or successfully made. Roper in the passage which we have cited from his text book treats the qualification as established by the authority of *Orr v Kanes*: where the unpaid legate "can have no redress against" the personal representative the direct claim is justified since otherwise he would be without a remedy.'

The distinction between tracing at common law and tracing at equity
At pp518–521 the distinctions between the claim in rem at common law and at equity were explained:

'Before passing to a consideration of the case of *Sinclair v Brougham* (4) we may usefully make some observations of our own as to the distinction between the attitude of the common law and that of equity to these questions.

The common law approached them in a strictly materialistic way. It could only appreciate what might almost be called "physical" identity of one thing with another. It could treat a person's money as identifiable so long as it had not been mixed with other money. It could treat as identifiable as the money, other kinds of property acquired by means of it, provided that there was no admixture of other money. But it is noticeable that in this latter case the common law did not base itself on any known theory of tracing such as that used in equity. It proceeded on the basis that the unauthorised act of purchasing was one capable of ratification by the owner of the money (see per Lord Parker in *Sinclair v Brougham* [1914] AC 398 [see Chapter 18]). Certain words of Lord Haldane in *Sinclair v Brougham* may appear to suggest a further limitation, that "money" as we have used that word was not regarded at common law as identifiable once it had been paid into a bank account. We do not, however, think it necessary to discuss this point at length.

We agree with the comments of Wynn-Parry J upon it and those of Atkin LJ (as he then was) in *Banque Belge v Hambrouk* [1921] 1 KB 321. If it is possible to identify a principal's money with an asset purchased exclusively by means of it we see no reason for drawing a distinction between a chose in action such as a banker's debt to his customer and any other asset. If the principal can ratify the acquisition of the one, we see no reason for supposing that he cannot ratify the acquisition of the other.

We may mention three matters which we think are helpful in understanding the limitation of the common law doctrine and the reasons why equity was able to take a more liberal view. They are as follows:

(1) The common law did not recognise equitable claims to property, whether money or any other form of property. Sovereigns in A's pocket either belonged in law to A or they belonged to B. The idea that they could belong in law to A and that they should nevertheless be treated as belonging to B was entirely foreign to the common law. This is the reason why the common law doctrine finds its typical exemplification in cases of principal and agent. If B, a principal, hands cash to A, his agent, in order that it may be applied in a particular manner, the cash, in the eyes of the common law, remains the property of B. If, therefore, A, instead of applying it in the authorised manner, buries it in a sack in his garden and uses it for an unauthorised purchase, B can, in the former case, recover the cash as being still his own property and in the latter case, affirm the purchase of something bought with his money by his agent. If, however, the relationship of A and B was not one which left the property in the cash in B but merely constituted a relationship of debtor and creditor between them, there could, of course, have been no remedy at law under this head, since the property in the cash would have passed out of B into A.

(2) The narrowness of the limits within which the common law operated may be linked with the limited nature of the remedies available to it. Specific relief as distinct from damages (the normal remedy at

common law) was confined to a very limited range of claims as compared with the extensive uses of specific relief developed by equity. In particular, the device of a declaration of charge was unknown to the common law and it was the availability of that device which enabled equity to give effect to its wider conception of equitable rights.

(3) It was the materialistic approach of the common law coupled with and encouraged by the limited range of remedies available to it that prevented the common law from identifying money in a mixed fund. Once the money of B became mixed with the money of A its identification in a physical sense became impossible; owing to the fact of mixture there could be no question of ratification of an unauthorised act; and the only remedy of B, if any, lay in a claim for damages.

Equity adopted a more metaphysical approach. It found no difficulty in regarding a composite fund as an amalgam constituted by the mixture of two or more funds each of which could be regarded as having, for certain purposes, a continued separate existence. Putting it in another way, equity regarded the amalgam as capable, in proper circumstances, of being resolved into its component parts.

Adapting, for the sake of contrast, the phraseology which we have used in relation to the common law, it was the metaphysical approach of equity coupled with and encouraged by the far-reaching remedy of a declaration of charge that enabled equity to identify money in a mixed fund. Equity, so to speak, is able to draw up a balance sheet on the right-hand side of which appears the composite fund and on its left-hand side the two or more funds of which it is to be deemed to be made up.

Regarded as a pure piece of machinery for the purpose of tracing money into a mixed fund or into property acquired by means of a mixed fund, a declaration of charge might be thought to be suitable means of dealing with any case where one person has, without legal title, acquired some benefit by the use of the money or another – in other words, any case of what is often called "unjust enrichment". The opinion of Lord Dunedin in *Sinclair* v *Brougham* appears to us to come very nearly to this, for he appears to treat the equitable remedy as applicable in any case where a superfluity, expressed or capable of being expressed in terms of money, is found to exist. Such a view would dispense with the necessity of establishing as a starting point the existence of a fiduciary or quasi-fiduciary relationship or of a continuing right of property recognised in equity. We may say at once that, apart from the possible case of Lord Dunedin's speech, we cannot find that any principle so wide in its operation is to be found enunciated in English law. The conditions which must exist before the equitable form of relief becomes available will be considered later in this judgment. But one truism may be stated here in order to get it out of the way. The equitable form of relief whether it takes the form of an order to restore an unmixed sum of money (or property acquired by means of such a sum) or a declaration of charge upon a mixed fund (or upon property acquired by means of such a fund) is, of course, personal in the sense that its efficacy is founded upon the jurisdiction of equity to enforce its rules by acting upon the individual. But it is not personal in the sense that the person against whom an order of this nature is sought can be made personally liable to repay the amount claimed to have belonged to the claimant. The equitable remedies pre-suppose the continued existence of the money either as a separate fund or as part of a mixed fund or as latent in property acquired by means of such a fund. If, on the facts of any individual case, such continued existence is not established, equity is as helpless as the common law itself. If the fund, mixed or unmixed, is spent upon a dinner, equity, which dealt only in specific relief and not in damages, could do nothing. If the case was one which at common law involved breach of contract the common law could, of course, award damages but specific relief would be out of the question. It is, therefore, a necessary matter for consideration in each case where it is sought to trace money in equity, whether it has such a continued existence, actual or notional, as will enable equity to grant specific relief.'

Innocent volunteers
At p523 the judgment dealt with the question of whether tracing was permitted by equity into a mixed fund where the fund had been given already mixed to the innocent volunteer or where the mixing had been carried out by the innocent volunteer. At first instance Winn-Parry J held that such a claim must fail in limine. The Court of Appeal disagreed with him and set out the principles applicable in such a case at pp524–526:

'Where an innocent volunteer (as distinct from a purchaser for value without notice) mixes "money" of his own with "money" which in equity belongs to another person, or is found in possession of such a mixture, although that other person cannot claim a charge on the mass superior to the claim of the volunteer, he is entitled nevertheless to a charge ranking pari passu with the claim of the volunteer. And Lord Parker's reasons for taking this view appear to have been on the following lines: Equity regards the rights of the equitable owner as being "in effect rights of property" though not recognised as such by the common law, just as a volunteer is not allowed by equity in the case, eg of a conveyance of the legal estate in land, to set up his legal title adversely to the claim of a person having an equitable interest in the land, so in the case of a mixed fund of money the volunteer must give such recognition as equity considers him in conscience (as a volunteer) bound to give to the interest of the equitable owner of the money which has been mixed with the volunteer's own. But this burden on the conscience of the volunteer is not such as to compel him to treat the claim of the equitable owner as paramount. That would be to treat the volunteer as strictly as if he himself stood in a fiduciary relationship to the equitable owner which ex hypothesi he does not. The volunteer is under no greater duty of conscience to recognise the interest of the equitable owner than that which lies upon a person having an equitable interest on one of two trust funds of "money" which have become mixed towards the equitable owner of the other. Such a person is not in conscience bound to give precedence to the equitable owner of the other of the two funds.

We may enlarge upon the implications which appear to us to be contained in Lord Parker's reasoning. First of all, it appears to us to be wrong to treat the principle which underlies *Hallett*'s case (1880) 13 Ch D 696 [see Chapter 18] as coming into operation only where the person who does the mixing is not only in a fiduciary position but is also a party to the tracing action. If he is a party to the action he is, of course, precluded from setting up a case inconsistent with the obligations of his fiduciary position. But supposing that he is not a party? The result cannot surely depend on what equity would or would not have allowed him to say if he had been a party. Suppose that the sole trustee of (say) five separate trusts draws £100 out of each of the trust banking accounts, pays the resulting £500 into an account which he opens in his own name, draws a cheque for £500 on that account and gives it as a present to his son. A claim by the five sets of beneficiaries to follow the money of their respective trusts would be a claim against the son. He would stand in no fiduciary relationship to any of them. We recoil from the conclusion that all five beneficiaries would be dismissed empty handed by a court of equity and the son left to enjoy what in equity was originally their money. Yet that is the conclusion to which the reasoning of the learned judge would lead us. Lord Parker's reasoning, on the other hand, seems to us to lead to the conclusion that each set of beneficiaries could set up its equitable interest which would prevail against the bare legal title of the son as a volunteer and that they would be entitled to share pari passu in so much of the fund or its proceeds as remained identifiable.

An even more striking example was admitted by Mr Pennycuick to be the result of his argument, and he vigorously maintained that it followed inevitably from the principles of equity involved. If a fiduciary agent takes cash belonging to his principal and gives it to his son, who takes it innocently, then so long as the son keeps it unmixed with other cash in one trouser pocket, the principal can follow it and claim it back. Once, however, the son, being under no fiduciary duty to the principal, transfers it to his other trouser pocket in which there are reposing a coin or two of his own of the same denominations, the son, by a sort of process of accretion, acquires an indefeasible title to what the moment before the transfer he could not have claimed as his own. This result appears to us to stultify the beneficent powers of equity to protect and enforce what it recognises as equitable rights of property which subsist until they are destroyed by the operation of a purchase for value without notice.

The error into which, we respectfully suggest, the learned judge has fallen is in thinking that what, in *Hallett*'s case was only the method (there appropriate) of bringing a much wider-based principle of equity into operation – viz the method by which a fiduciary agent, who has himself wrongfully mixed the funds, is prohibited from asserting a breach of his duty – is an element which must necessarily be present before equity can afford protection to the equitable rights which it has brought into existence. We are not prepared to see the arm of equity thus shortened.'

Innocent volunteers using money to improve their assets
At pp546–54 the judgment dealt with the situation where the volunteer has used the money in the alteration or improvement of assets and whether tracing would be permitted in such circumstances:

'In the present cases, however, the charities have used the Diplock money, not in combination with money of their own to acquire new assets, but in the alteration and improvement of assets which they already owned. The altered and improved asset owes its existence, therefore, to a combination of land belonging to the charity and money belonging to the Diplock estate. The question whether tracing is possible and if so to what extent, and also the question whether an effective remedy by way of declaration of charge can be granted consistently with an equitable treatment of the charity as an innocent volunteer, present quite different problems from those arising in the simple case above stated. In the case of the purchase of an asset out of a mixed fund, both categories of money are, as we have said, necessarily present throughout the existence of the asset in an identifiable form. In the case of adaptation of property of the volunteer by means of trust money, it by no means necessarily follows that the money can be said to be present in the adapted property. The beneficial owner of the trust money seeks to follow and recover that money and claims to use the machinery of a charge on the adapted property in order to enable him to do so. But in the first place the money may not be capable of being followed. In every true sense, the money may have disappeared. A simple example suggests itself. The owner of a house who, as an innocent volunteer, has trust money in his hands given to him by a trustee uses that money in making an alteration to his house so as to fit it better to his own personal needs. The result may add not one penny to the value of the house. Indeed, the alteration may well lower its value; for the alteration, though convenient to the owner, may be highly inconvenient in the eyes of a purchaser. Can it be said in such cases that the trust money can be traced and extracted from the altered asset? Clearly not, for the money will have disappeared leaving no monetary trace behind: the asset will not have increased (or may even have depreciated) in value through its use.

But the matter does not end here. What, for the purposes of the inquiry, is to be treated as "the charity property"? Is it to be the whole of the land belonging to the charity? or is it to be only that part of it which was altered or reconstructed or on which a building has been erected by means of Diplock money? If the latter, the result may well be that the property, both in its original state and as altered or improved, will, when taken in isolation, have little or no value. What would be the value of a building in the middle of Guy's Hospital without any means of access through other parts of the hospital property? If, on the other hand, the charge is to be on the whole of the charity land, it might well be thought an extravagant result if the Diplock estate, because Diplock money had been used in reconstructing a corner of it, were to be entitled to a charge on the entirety.

But it is not merely a question of locating and identifying the Diplock money. The result of a declaration of charge is to disentangle trust money and enable it to be withdrawn in the shape of money from the complex in which it has become involved. This can only be done by sale under the charge. But the equitable owner of the trust money must in this process submit to equality of treatment with the innocent volunteer. The latter too, is entitled to disentangle his money and to withdraw it from the complex. Where the complex originates in money on both sides there is no difficulty and no inequity. Each is entitled to a charge. But if what the volunteer had contributed is not money but other property of his own such as land, what then? You cannot have a charge for land. You can, it is true, have a charge for the value of land, an entirely different thing. Is it equitable to compel the innocent volunteer to take a charge merely for the value of the land when what he has contributed is the land itself? In other words, can equity, by the machinery of a charge, give to the innocent volunteer that which he has contributed so as to place him in a position comparable with that of the owner of the trust fund? In our opinion it cannot.

In the absence of authority to the contrary our conclusion is that as regards the Diplock money used in these cases it cannot be traced in any true sense; and, further, that even if this were not so, the only remedy available to equity, viz, that of a declaration of charge, would not produce an equitable result and is inapplicable accordingly.'

Innocent volunteer using money to clear a blot on his title
At pp549–550 the Court of Appeal considered the position where a volunteer had used the money given to him to clear off a blot on his title to land or to extinguish an encumbrance. The conclusion was that the position was in principle no different from that where the money had been used by the volunteer to make alterations or improvements. In the case before the court the Leaf Homoeopathic Hospital had been given £6,000 to pay off a bank loan secured on its property:

> 'Here, too, we think that the effect of the payment to the bank was to extinguish the debt and the charge held by the bank ceased to exist. The case cannot, we think, be regarded as one of subrogation, and if the appellants were entitled to a charge it would have to be a new charge created by the court. The position in this respect does not appear to us to be affected by the fact that the payment off of this debt was one of the objects for which the grant was made. The effect of the payment off was that the charity, which had previously held only an equity of redemption, became the owners of unencumbered property. That unencumbered property derived from a combination of two things, the equity of redemption contributed by the charity and the effect of the Diplock money in getting rid of the encumbrance. If equity is now to create a charge (and we say "create" because there is no survival of the original charge) in favour of the judicial trustee, it will be placing him in a position to insist upon a sale of what was contributed by the charity. The case, as it appears to us, is in effect analogous to the cases where Diplock money is expended on improvements on charity land. The money was in this case used to remove a blot on the title; to give the judicial trustee a charge in respect of the money, so used, would, we think, be equally unjust to the charity who, as the result of such a charge, would have to submit to a sale of the interest in the property which it brought in. We may point out that if the relief claimed were to be accepted as a correct application of the equitable principle, insoluble problems might arise in a case where in the meanwhile fresh charges on the property had been created or money had been expended upon it.'

Commentary
For the full history of this litigation, see also *Chichester Diocesan Board* v *Simpson* (Chapter 8) and *Ministry of Health* v *Simpson* (Chapter 18).

Docker v *Somes* (1834) 2 My & K 655 Court of Chancery (Lord Brougham LC)

Breach of trust: measure of liability

Facts
A testator bequeathed property to his two sons who were also his executors, on trust, after legacies, for the benefit of his children. His will contained a proviso that the trustees might carry on the shipping business for up to six years after his death. They did carry on the business, and at the end of the six years an account was called for. The question was, which profits were to be accounted for?

Held
The trustees were liable to account for the property, and profits made from that property, even though this had been increased in value through the carrying on of a shipping business as expressly permitted.

Lord Brougham LC:

> 'Wherever a trustee, or one standing in the relation of a trustee, violates his duty, and deals with the trust estate for his own behalf, the rule is, that he shall account to the cestui qui trust for all the gain which he has made. Thus, if trust money is laid out in buying and selling land, and a profit was made by the transaction, that shall not go to the trustee who has so applied the money, but to the cestui qui trust whose money has been thus applied. In like manner (and cases of this kind are more numerous) where a trustee

or executor has used the fund committed to his care in stock speculations, though the loss, if any, must fall upon himself, yet for every farthing of profit he may make he shall be accountable to the trust estate.'

Fletcher v *Collis* [1905] 2 Ch 24 Court of Appeal (Vaughan Williams, Romer and Stirling LJJ)

A beneficiary who consents to a breach of trust cannot claim from trustees for any loss

Facts
By a marriage settlement property was settled on a husband for life, remainder to the wife for life, remainder to the children. At the request of the wife and with the husband's consent, the whole of the trust property was sold and the proceeds given to the wife who spent them. Subsequently the husband was adjudicated bankrupt. The children brought an action against the trustee to make him replace the trust property. The trustee agreed to do so and the action was stayed. When the trustee died in 1902 the trust fund had been replaced and there was a considerable surplus representing income. The personal representative of the trustee claimed the surplus as part of the trustee's estate on the grounds that it represented a partial indemnity from the husband to the trustee. The trustee in bankruptcy contested this claim saying the husband was entitled to the surplus as income as if there had been no breach of trust.

Held
The husband had consented to the breach of trust; he was not entitled to require the trustee to make good the loss of income resulting from such breach, to which he would have otherwise been entitled. As the husband was not entitled to anything his trustee in bankruptcy stood in no better position.

Romer LJ:

> '... In the case I have before referred to in respect to the general proposition, the beneficiary who knowingly consented to the breach could not, if of full consulting age and capacity, and in the absence of special circumstances, afterwards be heard to say that the conduct of the trustee in committing the breach of trust was, as against him the particular beneficiary, improper so as to make the trustee liable to the beneficiary for any damage suffered in respect of that beneficiary's interest in the trust estate by reason of the loss occasioned by the breach ...'

Commentary
The case to which Romer LJ referred was *Sawyer* v *Sawyer* (1885) 28 Ch D 595 which, it was argued, was authority for the view that a beneficiary's interest in the estate would only be impoundable if he instigated or requested a breach of trust, rather than merely consented to it. Romer LJ held it was subject to the right of the trustee set out above.

Head v *Gould* [1898] 2 Ch 250 Chancery Division (Kekewich J)

Liability of retired trustees: liability of solicitor trustees

Facts
Under a marriage settlement property was settled on Mrs Head for life remainder to her children. There were three children and the trustees had an express power of advancement in favour of them. Mrs Head was in financial difficulties and her daughter asked the trustees for advances so that she could help her. When the whole of the daughter's share was advanced to her mother she pressed for more. The trustees said that they wished in the circumstances to be released from trusteeship and that new trustees should be found who were willing to make further advances. Under a power of appointment the trustees were

replaced by the daughter and Gould, a solicitor. The new trustees sold a house belonging to the trust and, in breach of trust, handed the proceeds to Mrs Head. They then, in breach of trust, surrendered life insurance policies belonging to Mrs Head which she had mortgaged as security for a loan from the trust fund made by the previous trustees. As a result of these the beneficial interest of one of the other children was lost and he sought to make both the old trustees and the new trustees liable.

Held
1. The old trustees were not liable for the breaches of trust committed by the new trustees. In order to make a retiring trustee liable for a breach of trust committed by his successor it must be shown that the breach of trust which was in fact committed was contemplated by the former trustee when the change in trustees took place, and was not merely the outcome of or rendered easy by the change in trustees.
2. The new trustees were liable for the breaches of trust and, further, the daughter could not claim an indemnity from Gould, even though he was a solicitor and had acted as such to the trust in advising on the matters which were in fact breaches, because she had actively participated in the breaches and not participated only in consequence of Gould's advice.

Knott v *Cottee* (1852) 16 Beav 77 Court of Chancery (Romilly MR)

Breach of trust: measure of liability

Facts
A testator bequeathed property to C and two others on trust to invest the product in 'the public or Government Stocks or Funds of Great Britain or upon real security in England or Wales' and to hold on certain trusts during his widow's life, and after on trust for his infant children and their families. The executor C invested part of the estate in Russian, Dutch, Belgian and other foreign stocks. The court decreed these investments improper, and further directions were sought.

Held
The trustees were held liable for the original amount invested less the sum received as proceeds of sale in 1846.

Romilly MR:

> 'Here is an executor who has a direct and positive trust to perform, which was to invest the money upon government stocks or funds, or upon real securities, and accumulate at compound interests all the balances after maintaining the children. He has made certain investments, which the court has declared to be improper. The case must either be treated as if these investments had not been made, or had been made for his own benefit out of his own monies, and that he had at the same time retained monies of the testator in his hands. I think, therefore, that there must be a reference back, to ascertain what balances the executor retained from time to time, it being clear that he has retained some balances.
>
> The next question is, at what rate of interest ought he to be charged? The usual course is to charge an executor 4 per cent, where he has simply retained the balances; but where he has acted improperly, or has employed the trust money in trade for his own benefit, or has been guilty of other acts of misconduct, the court visits him with interest at 5 per cent. In this case there does not appear to me to have been any such misconduct as to make him answerable at 5 per cent. It appears simply a case in which an executor has retained monies, which he has not properly invested. I am therefore of opinion that he ought to be charged with interest at 4 per cent and with annual rests: for there is an express trust for accumulations, of which he was aware when he retained the trust monies.'

Mara v Browne

See Chapter 6.

Milligan v Mitchell (1833) 1 My & K 446 Chancery Division (Lord Brougham LC)

Breach of trust: remedies: injunction

Facts
A trust of money, collected for the purpose, existed to build and maintain a chapel in Woolwich as a place of worship in accordance with the usage of the Church of Scotland. Two of the trustees applied for an injunction against the others, alleging that the recent minister had conducted services in a way not consistent with the usage of the Church of Scotland, and that, there now being another vacancy, they were proposing to appoint a minister who was not an authorised minister of the Church of Scotland.

Held
The interim injunction would be granted.

Lord Brougham LC:

> 'I am of opinion that the apprehensions of the plaintiffs are fully justified by the facts, which stand wholly uncontradicted, no affidavits having been filed against the motion ... Enough appears undenied to warrant the court in holding that ... a part of the trustees are acting ... in a manner inconsistent with their trust as regards the ecclesiastical concerns of Woolwich Chapel. The injunction must therefore issue to prevent the election of any person to be minister of the church who is not regularly licensed as a preacher or probationer of the established Church of Scotland.'

National Trustees Executors and Agency Company of Australasia Ltd v General Finance etc Company of Australasia Ltd [1905] AC 373 Privy Council (Lord Davey, Lord Lindley, Sir Alfred North and Sir Arthur Wilson)

Breach of trust: honest and reasonable mistake: relief of paid trustee

Facts
The professional trust company had received and followed the advice of competent legal advisors, but been held liable for the wrongful distribution of trust funds by the Supreme Court of Victoria, Australia. They sought relief under s3 of the Australian Trusts Act 1901, which is similar to s61 of the Trustee Act 1925.

Held
Relief was granted on the grounds, as per Sir Alfred North, that:

> 'Section 3 of the Trusts Act ... is as follows: "If it appears to the Supreme Court that a trustee is ... personally liable for any breach of trust ... but has acted honestly and reasonably and ought fairly to be relieved ... then the court may relieve the trustee either wholly or in part from personal liability ..." The courts in ... [Australia] have found that the appellants acted honestly and reasonably ... [Counsel] contended that, these two things having been established, the right to relief followed as a matter of course; but that is clearly not the construction of the Act. Unless both are proved, the court cannot help the trustees; but if both are made out, there is then a case for the court to consider whether the trustees ought fairly to be excused ... looking at all the circumstances. It is a very material circumstance that the appellants are a limited joint-stock company formed for the purpose of earning profits for their

shareholders ... What they now ask the court to do is to allow them to retain a sum of money to which the respondent's title is clear, in order thereby to relieve the trust company from a loss they have incurred in the course of their business ... The position of a ... company which undertakes to perform for reward services it can only perform through its agents, and which has been misled by those agents to misapply a fund under its charge, is widely different from that of a private person acting as a gratuitous trustee. And without saying that the remedial provisions of the section should never be applied to a trustee in the position of the appellants, their Lordships think it is a circumstance to be taken into account, and they do not find here any fair excuse for the breach of trust, or any reason why the respondents, who have committed no fault, should lose their money to relieve the appellants, who have done a wrong ...'

*Perrin*s v *Bellamy* [1899] 1 Ch 797 Chancery Division (Kekewich J) Court of Appeal (Lindley MR, Rigby and Romer LJJ) affirming

Breach excused under s61 TA 1925

Facts
The trustees of a settlement erroneously assumed that they had a power of sale and sold off some of the leaseholds comprised in the settlement. In consequence the income of the tenant for life was diminished and he sought to make the trustees liable for the income.

Held
As the trustees had acted honestly and reasonably, they were entitled under s3 of the Judicial Trustee Act 1896 (now s61 Trustee Act 1925) to be relieved from personal liability in respect of the breach of trust.

Kekewich J:

'Broadly speaking, these trustees have committed a breach of trust, and they are responsible for it. But then the statute comes in, and the very foundation for the application of the statute is that the trustee whose conduct is in question "is or may be personally liable for any breach of trust". I am bound to look at the test of the section by the light of those words, and with the view that, in cases falling within the section, the breach of trust is not of itself to render the trustee personally liable. Leaving out the intervening words, which merely make the section retrospective, I find when in general the trustee is to be relieved from personal liability. He is not to be held personally liable if he "has acted honestly and reasonably, and ought to be excused for the breach of trust". In this case, as in the large majority of cases of breach of trust which come before the court, the word "honestly" may be left out of consideration. Cases do unfortunately occur from time to time in which trustees, and even solicitors in whom confidence has been reposed, run away with the money of their cestuis que trust, and where such flagrant dishonesty occurs breach of trust becomes a minor consideration. In the present case there is no imputation or ground for imputation of any dishonesty whatever. The legislature has made the absence of all dishonesty a condition precedent to the relief of the trustee from liability. But that is not the grit of the section. The grit is in the words "reasonably, and ought fairly to be excused for the breach of trust". How much the latter words add to the force of the word "reasonably" I am not at present prepared to say. I suppose, however, that in the view of the Legislature there might be cases in which a trustee, though he had acted reasonably, ought not fairly to be excused for the breach of trust. Indeed, I am not sure that some of the evidence adduced in this case was not addressed to a view of that kind, as, for instance, the evidence by which it was attempted to shew that these trustees, though they acted reasonably in selling the property, ought not fairly to be excused because the plaintiff Mrs Perrins objected to their selling, and her objection was brought to their notice. In the section the copulative 'and' is used, and it may well be argued that in order to bring a case within the section it must be shewn not merely that the trustee has acted "reasonably", but also, that he ought "fairly" to be excused for the breach of trust. I venture, however, to think that, in general and in the absence of special circumstances, a trustee who has acted "reasonably" ought to be relieved, and that it is not incumbent on the court to consider whether he ought "fairly" to be excused, unless there is evidence of a special character shewing that the provisions of the section ought not to be applied in his favour. I need not pursue that subject further, because in the present case I find no ground whatever for saying that these trustees, if they acted reasonably, ought not to be excused. The question, and the only question, is whether they acted reasonably. In saying that, I am not unmindful of the words of the section which follow, and which require that it should be shewn that the trustee ought "fairly" to be excused, not only "for the breach of trust", but also "for omitting to obtain the direction of the court in the matter in which he committed such breach of trust". I find it difficult to follow that. I do not see how the trustee can be excused for the breach of trust without being also excused for the omission referred to, or how he can be excused for the omission without also being excused for the breach of trust. If I am at liberty to guess, I should suppose that these words were added by way of amendment, and crept into the statute without due regard being had to the meaning of the context. The fact that a trustee has omitted to obtain the directions of the court has never been held to be a ground for holding him personally liable, though it may be a reason guiding the court in the matter of costs, or in deciding whether he has acted reasonably or otherwise, and especially so in these days, when questions of difficulty, even as regards the legal estate, can be decided economically and expeditiously on originating summons. But if the court comes to the conclusion that a trustee has acted reasonably I cannot see how it can usefully proceed to consider as an independent matter, the question whether he has or has not omitted to obtain the directions of the court.'

Shaw v *Cates*

See Chapter 12.

Somerset, Re [1894] 1 Ch 231 Court of Appeal (Lindley, A L Smith and Davey LJJ)

Section 62 TA 1925: Consent of the beneficiary must include knowledge that the act is a breach of trust

Facts
Under a marriage settlement the trustees had power to sell the trust property, with the consent of the husband and wife, or the survivor, and to reinvest it in, among other things, mortgages of freehold and leasehold land. The husband wished to have some of the property sold and the proceeds invested in a mortgage of an estate. The trustees lent an excessive sum on the mortgage. The money was lent at the instigation, request and consent in writing of the husband. When the security for the mortgage proved to be inadequate the husband, as tenant for life, and the children of the marriage sued the trustees for the loss. The trustees admitted liability to the children but claimed to be entitled to impound the life interest of the husband for the purposes of meeting the claim under s6 Trustee Act 1888 (now replaced by s62 TA 1925).

Held
The husband had clearly instigated, requested and consented to the investment but it did not appear that he had intended to be a party to a breach of trust and in effect he had left it to the trustees to determine whether the security was sufficient for the money advanced. The trustees could not in these circumstances impound the husband's life interest under s8 TA 1888 (s62 TA 1925).

Lindley LJ:

'Did the trustees commit the breach of trust for which they have been made liable at the instigation or request, or with the consent in writing, of the appellant? The section is intended to protect trustees, and ought to be construed so as to carry out that intention. But the section ought not, in my opinion, to be construed as if the word "investment" had been inserted instead of "breach of trust". An enactment to that effect would produce great injustice in many cases. In order to bring a case within this section the cestui que trust must instigate, or request or consent in writing to some act or omission which is itself a breach of trust, and not to some act or omission which only becomes a breach of trust by reason of want or care on the part of the trustees. If a cestui que trust instigates, requests or consents in writing to an investment not in terms authorised by the power of investment, he clearly falls within the section: and in such a case his ignorance or forgetfulness of the terms of the power would not, I think, protect him – at all events, not unless he could give some good reason why it should, eg that it was caused by the trustee. But if all that a cestui que trust does is to instigate, request or consent in writing to an investment which is authorised by the terms of the power, the case is, I think, very different. He has a right to expect that the trustees will act with proper care in making the investment, and if they do not they cannot throw the consequences on him unless they can show that he instigated, requested or consented in writing to their non-performance of their duty in this respect. This is, in my opinion, the true construction of this section.'

Strahan, Re (1856) 8 De GM & G 291 Court of Appeal in Chancery (Turner and Knight-Bruce LJJ)

Trustee's liability for breaches of trust before his appointment

Facts
P was one of the trustees of a marriage settlement. In breach of trust he invested £13,000 trust money in the mortgage of bonds, an unauthorised investment under the trust instrument, and he paid £3,000 of trust money into his own bank account. In 1852 and subsequent to these events S was appointed a trustee of the settlement. After S was appointed P paid a further £1,000 trust money into his own account. S did not enquire when appointed that all sums required to be settled under the marriage settlement had been settled, if he had done so he would have found the sums P had paid into his bank account outstanding. In 1855 new trustees were appointed when the banking business in which S and P were partners became bankrupt. The new trustees sued S.

Held
As regards the £13,000 in unauthorised investments S was liable because on assuming trusteeship it was his duty to ensure all trust investments were proper ones. As to the £3,000 P had paid into his bank account S was not liable because he was under no duty to look back to see whether his co-trustees had received any funds which ought to have been settled, in the absence of any reason for supposing that they had not. As regards the £1,000 which P had paid into his account after S's appointment, S was not liable for this because he was under no duty to enquire whether any property covenanted to be settled had fallen in when there was nothing to lead him to suppose that there was such property.

Target Holdings Ltd v *Redfern (a firm) and Another* [1995] 3 All ER 785 House of Lords (Lord Browne-Wilkinson, Lord Keith, Lord Ackner, Lord Jauncey and Lord Lloyd)

Duties of a solicitor acting for mortgagor – breach of trust – remedy – restitution

Facts
TH advanced £1,525,000 by way of a mortgage to P, with R acting as solicitor for both TH and P. The loan was to be used to finance the purchase of a property declared to TH to have a value of £2 million and

a purchase price also of £2 million. However, unknown to TH but known to R, the purchase price was in fact only £775,000. P therefore created, with the assistance of R, a string of companies to purchase the land which resulted in P ultimately appearing to buy it for £2 million. P subsequently defaulted on the mortgage. TH took possession, sold the property for £500,000 and, after discovery of the full facts, sought to claim against R for breach of trust. In defence, R argued that TH had lost nothing through their conduct as TH had always been prepared to advance the loan amount of £2 million.

TH applied for summary judgment against R. At first instance this was refused, with R being granted leave to defend, conditional upon an interim payment of £1 million to TH. On appeal by both TH (in respect of the refused summary judgment) and R (in respect of the conditional leave to defend) the Court of Appeal held R to be in breach of trust and liable to TH by way of restitution of the full loan as if it had never been advanced, less any credit by TH following it having repossessed and then sold the property.

Held (unanimously by the House of Lords on appeal by R)
R's breach of trust could only be said to have caused the actual loss ultimately suffered by TH (ie the shortfall between the money advanced and the amount recovered on realisation of the property) if it could be shown that, but for the breach of trust, the transactions would not have gone ahead. This was not a matter for Order 14 proceedings and pending a full trial it was appropriate to assume that the transaction would have gone ahead; R would be given unconditional leave to defend. As to the merits Lord Browne-Wilkinson (who gave the only judgment) thought it highly likely that the money had been essential to enable the transaction to go ahead and but for R's breach of trust TH would probably not have advanced any money and, therefore, not have suffered any loss.

18 Breach of Trust II: Tracing

Agip (Africa) Ltd* v *Jackson [1989] 3 WLR 1367 Chancery Division (Millett J)
Tracing money in equity – constructive trustees

Facts
The plaintiffs sued the first (Mr J) and second (Mr B) defendants (in partnership as chartered accountants under the name of J & Co) and the third defendant (one of their employees, Mr G) for a total sum of over US $500,000 plus interest: the plaintiffs had been deprived of the money as a result of fraud on the part of one of their employees, a Mr Z. Some US $45,000 had been paid into court; the defendants made no claim to it. The plaintiffs sought recovery of funds telegraphically transferred by their bank in Tunisia, as a result of forged instructions, not from the recipient company (BOS Ltd) but from the persons who controlled the recipient company and caused it to part with them (the first and third defendants) or from the persons through whose hands the funds subsequently passed (the first and second defendants). The greater part of the money was paid away and probably found its way to confederates of the fraudulent employee. It was not alleged that the defendants were parties to the fraud or that they had actual knowledge of it. The plaintiffs brought an action at common law for money had and received; alternatively they claimed that the defendants were liable to account in equity as constructive trustees. As against the first and second defendants the plaintiffs relied on the mere receipt of the money. In addition, however, they also alleged that all the defendants, and in particular the first and third defendants, were guilty of wilful and reckless failure to make the inquiries which honest men would have made in order to satisfy themselves that they were not acting in furtherance of a fraud.

Held
The claim to recover the money from J & Co as money had and received and without proof of dishonesty or want of probity must fail as to the sum in court because of the impossibility of tracing the money at common law. It also failed as to the balance for this and for the additional reason that J & Co accounted to their principals before they had notice of the plaintiffs' claim. However, there was no difficulty in tracing the plaintiffs' money in equity which had well developed principles by which the proceeds of fraud could be followed and recovered from those whose hands they passed.

Millett J said that the only restriction on the ability of equity to follow assets was the requirement that there must be some fiduciary relationship which permitted the assistance of equity to be invoked: see *In re Diplock* [1948] Ch 465. That requirement may sometimes be circumvented since it is not always necessary that there should be an initial fiduciary relationship in order to start the tracing process; it is sufficient that the payment to the defendant itself gives rise to a fiduciary relationship: see *Chase Manhattan Bank NA* v *Israel-British Bank (London) Ltd* [1981] Ch 105. However, the requirement is readily satisfied in most cases of commercial fraud. In the present case there was a fiduciary relationship between Mr Z and the plaintiffs.

The tracing remedy
The tracing claim in equity gave rise to a proprietary remedy which depended on the continued existence of the trust property in the hands of the defendant. Unless he was a bona fide purchaser for value without

notice he must restore the trust property to its rightful owner if he still had it; but even a volunteer could not be made subject to a personal liability to account for it as a constructive trustee if he had parted with it without having previously acquired some knowledge of the existence of the trust; *In re Montagu's Settlement Trust* [1987] Ch 264. The plaintiffs were entitled to the money in court which rightfully belonged to them. To recover the money which the defendants had paid away, the plaintiffs must subject them to a personal liability to account as constructive trustees and prove the requisite degree of knowledge to establish liability.

Knowing receipt
Much confusion had been caused by treating 'knowing receipt or dealing' as a single category: see *Baden, Delvaux and Lecuit v Société Générale* [1983] BCLC 325, 505 per Peter Gibson J. It was necessary to distinguish between two main classes of case under that heading.

The first was concerned with the person who received for his own benefit trust property transferred to him in breach of trust. He was liable as a constructive trustee if he received it with notice, actual or constructive, that it was trust property and that the transfer to him was a breach of trust; or if he received it without such notice but subsequently discovered the facts. In either case he was liable to account for the property, in the first case as from the time he received it and in the second as from the time he acquired notice.

The second distinct class of case in respect of trust property received lawfully did not need to be considered further since the transfer to BOS was not lawful. In either class it was immaterial whether the breach of trust was fraudulent or not. The essential feature of the first class was that the recipient must have received the property for his own use and benefit.

Mr B did not deal with the money or give instructions in regard to it. It would not be just to hold him liable. Mr G did not receive the money at all and Mr J and Mr B did not receive or apply it for their own use and benefit. None of them could be made liable to account as a constructive trustee on the basis of knowing receipt.

Knowing assistance
A stranger to the trust would also be liable to account as a constructive trustee if he knowingly assisted in the furtherance of a fraudulent and dishonest breach of trust. It was not necessary that the party sought to be made liable as a constructive trustee should have received any part of the trust property but the breach must have been fraudulent: see *Barnes v Addy* (1874) 9 Ch App 244. In *Baden*, Peter Gibson J accepted that constructive notice was sufficient for liability under that head and there was no distinction between cases of 'knowing receipt' and 'knowing assistance'. His Lordship was unable to agree. The basis of liability in the two types of cases was quite different. Tracing and cases of 'knowing receipt' were both concerned with rights of priority in relation to property taken by a legal owner for his own benefit; cases of 'knowing assistance' were concerned with the furtherance of fraud. In *Belmont Finance Corporation Ltd v Williams Furniture Ltd* [1979] Ch 250 the Court of Appeal held that the breach must be a fraudulent and dishonest one. It followed that constructive notice was not enough to make him liable. Knowledge might be proved affirmatively or inferred from circumstances.

The various mental states which might be involved were analysed by Peter Gibson J in the *Baden* case as comprising: (i) actual knowledge, (ii) wilfully shutting one's eyes to the obvious, (iii) wilfully and recklessly failing to make such inquiries as an honest and reasonable man would make, (iv) knowledge of circumstances which would indicate the facts to an honest and reasonable man, and (v) knowledge of circumstances which would put an honest and reasonable man on inquiry. According to Peter Gibson J a person in category (ii) or (iii) would be taken to have actual knowledge, while a person in categories (iv) and (v) had constructive knowledge only.

While adopting the classification his Lordship warned against over-refinement or too ready an assumption that categories (iv) and (v) were necessarily cases of constructive notice only. The true distinction was between honesty and dishonesty. If a man did not draw the obvious inferences or make the obvious inquiries the question was: why not? If it was because, however foolishly, he did not suspect wrongdoing or having suspected it had his suspicions allayed, however unreasonably, that was one thing. But if he did suspect wrong doing yet failed to make inquiries because 'he did not want to know' (ii) or because he regarded it as 'none of his business' (iii) that was quite another. Such conduct was dishonest.

Mr B did not participate in the furtherance of the fraud and could not be held directly liable on that ground. But Mr J and Mr G clearly did. Mr J set up the arrangements and employed Mr G to carry them out. They plainly assisted in the fraud but did they do so with the requisite degree of knowledge?

The defendants' state of mind
His Lordship was led to the conclusion on the evidence that Mr J and Mr G were at best indifferent to the possibility of fraud. The made no inquiries of the plaintiffs because they thought it was none of their business. That was not honest behaviour. The sooner that those who provided the services of nominee companies for the purpose of enabling their clients to keep their activities secret realised that the better. It was quite enough to make them liable as constructive trustees. Although Mr B could not be held directly liable, he was vicariously liable for the acts of his partner, Mr J, and his employee, Mr G.

The ruling at first instance was confirmed by the Court of Appeal (Fox, Butler-Sloss and Beldam LJJ) (1991) The Times 9 January. See Chapter 6.

Bishopsgate Investment Management Ltd (In Liquidation) v *Homan and Others*
[1994] 3 WLR 1270 Court of Appeal (Dillon, Leggatt and Henry LJJ)

Tracing – overdrawn bank account

Facts
The liquidators of BI were seeking to trace funds improperly paid from various pension schemes, of which they were trustees, to M plc. In addition BI was also seeking to claim an equitable charge in priority to M plc's unsecured creditors (M plc was now in liquidation).

Held
At the time that the funds were paid to M plc the account receiving the funds was in credit. However, following M plc's liquidation the account had become overdrawn. Prior to M plc's liquidation there had been no intention to impress a trust on the credit balance of the account. In conjunction with this, equitable tracing was not possible through an overdrawn and therefore non-existent fund.

Leggatt LJ:

'... it is only possible to trace in equity money which has continued existence, actual or notional.'

Commentary
The Court of Appeal's decision highlights the inherent limitation of equitable tracing, namely that the actual dissipation – of the asset sought to be traced into is an absolute bar to the proprietary remedy leaving the 'victim' to seek recompense against the assets of the party at fault (often impossible if, for example, that party has no assets against which to act).

Boardman v *Phipps*
See Chapter 6.

Clayton's Case, Devaynes v Noble (1816) 1 Mer 529 Rolls Court (Grant MR)

The "first in, first out" rule

Facts
Clayton was the client of a firm of bankers in which Devaynes was a senior partner. When Devaynes died Clayton continued to deal with the firm but it went bankrupt owing Clayton money. Clayton claimed money owing to him at the time of Devaynes death from his estate. However, payments by the bank to Clayton after Devaynes' death were more than sufficient to satisfy the balance owing to him at Devaynes' death. However, Clayton argued that these should be appropriated to satisfy payments made by him after Devaynes' death.

Held
In the case of a current account such as a banking account, there was a presumption that the payments made were appropriated to the various debts as they were incurred.

Commissioner of Stamp Duties (Queensland) v Livingston

See Chapter 2.

Diplock, Re

See Chapter 17.

Hallett's Estate, Re (1880) 13 Ch D 696 Court of Appeal (Jessel MR, Baggallay and Thesiger LJJ)

Priorities in tracing where trustee/fiduciary has mixed different funds

Facts
Hallett, a solicitor, was one of the trustees of a marriage settlement made for the benefit of himself, his wife and children. He also acted as solicitor to a trust of which a Mrs Cotterill was a beneficiary, but he was not a trustee of the Cotterill trust. Hallett mixed money belonging to the marriage settlement and money he had received on behalf of the Cotterill trust together with his own money in his private banking account. He drew on this account for his own purposes and paid in sums to the account subsequently. At his death his estate was insolvent so there was insufficient to meet his personal debts and the claims of the two funds. Two matters were put before the court: (i) could Mrs Cotterill trace the funds belonging to the trust under which she was a beneficiary even though Hallett had not been a trustee of that trust and (ii) if she was entitled to trace, how payments from the fund should be allocated as between the creditors of Hallett's estate, the Cotterill trust and the marriage settlement.

Held
1. There was a fiduciary relationship between Hallett and Mrs Cotterill. He had received trust property with knowledge that it was trust property and mixed it with his own money improperly. Mrs Cotterill was therefore entitled to trace.
2. Where a trustee had mixed beneficiary's monies with his own in one fund the beneficiary had a first charge on the whole fund for the trust money.
3. Where a trustee mixes trust monies with his own monies, as between the trustee and the beneficiary, the rule in Clayton's case does not apply. Instead, it is presumed that the trustee acted with an honest

intention and therefore exhausted his own money in the account first. Therefore, if any moneys remained in the account after all the trustee's money had been withdrawn this belonged to the beneficiary.
4. As there were sufficient monies in the estate to satisfy the claims of Mrs Cotterill and the marriage settlement it was unnecessary to consider the position in tracing as between the claimants themselves.

Jessel MR:

'The modern doctrine of Equity as regards property disposed of by persons in a fiduciary position is a very clear and well-established doctrine. You can, if the sale was rightful, take the proceeds of the sale, if you can indentify them. If the sale was wrongful, you can still take the proceeds of the sale, in a sense adopting the sale for the purpose of taking the proceeds, if you can identify them. There is no distinction, therefore, between a rightful and a wrongful disposition of the property, so far as regards the right of the beneficial owner to follow the proceeds. But it very often happens that you cannot identify the proceeds. The proceeds may have been invested together with money belonging to the person in a fiduciary position, in a purchase. He may have bought land with it, for instance, or he may have bought chattels with it. Now, what is the position of the beneficial owner as regards such purchases? I will, first of all, take his position when the purchase is clearly made with what I will call, for shortness, the trust money, although it is not confined, as I will shew presently, to express trusts. In that case, according to the now well-established doctrine of Equity, the beneficial owner has a right to elect either to take the property purchased, or to hold it as a security for the amount of the trust money laid out in the purchase; or, as we generally express it, he is entitled at his election either to take the property, or to have a charge on the property for the amount of the trust money. But in the second case where a trustee has mixed the money with his own, there is this distinction, that the cestui que trust, or beneficial owner, can no longer elect to take the property, because it is no longer bought with the trust money simply and purely, but with a mixed fund. He is, however, still entitled to a charge on the property purchased, for the amount of the trust money laid out in the purchase; and that charge is quite independent of the fact of the amount laid out by the trustee. The moment you get a substantial portion of it furnished by the trustee, using the word "trustee" in the sense I have mentioned, as including all persons in a fiduciary relation, the right to the charge follows. That is the modern doctrine of equity.'

Ministry of Health v *Simpson* [1951] AC 251 House of Lords (Lord Simonds, Lord Normand, Lord Oaksey, Lord Morton and Lord MacDermott)

Personal remedy against a recipient of funds under a breach of trust

Facts
This was an appeal from the judgment of the Court of Appeal in *Re Diplock* [1948] Ch 465 (see Chapter 17) where the facts are set out in full. The relevant point, and decision, of the appeal is best set out in Lord Simonds' judgment.

Held
Lord Simonds:

'The problem for determination can be simply stated and it is perhaps surprising that the sure answer to it is only to be found by examination of authorities which go back nearly three hundred years. Acting under a mistake the personal representatives of a testator whose residuary disposition is invalid distribute his residuary estate upon the footing that it is valid. Have the next of kin a direct claim in equity against the persons to whom it has been wrongfully distributed? I think that the authorities clearly establish that, subject to certain qualifications, ... they have such a claim.

I think it is important in a discussion of this question to remember that the particular branch of the jurisdiction of the Court of Chancery with which we are concerned relates to the administration of the assets of a deceased person. While in the development of this jurisdiction certain principles were established which were common to it and to the comparable jurisdiction in the execution of trusts, I do not find in history or logic any justification for an argument which denies the possibility of an equitable right in the administration of assets because, as it is alleged, no comparable right existed in the execution of trusts. I prefer to look solely at the authorities which are strictly germane to the present question: it is from them alone that the nature and extent of the equity are to be ascertained.

Before I turn back to the seventeenth century when the Court of Chancery was gradually wresting from the spiritual courts the jurisdiction in administering the assets of deceased persons and framing apt rules to that end, I will refer first to a statement made by Lord Davey early in this century which, as I think, illuminated the position. In *Harrison* v *Kirk* [1904] AC 1 at p7, Lord Davey says this:

> "But the Court of Chancery, in order to do justice and to avoid the evil of allowing one man to retain what is really and legally applicable to the payment of another man, devised a remedy by which, where the estate had been distributed either out of court or in court without regard to the rights of a creditor, it has allowed the creditor to recover back what has been paid to the beneficiaries or the next of kin who derive from the deceased testator or intestate."

The importance of this statement is manifold. It explains the basis of the jurisdiction, the evil to be avoided and its remedy: its clear implication is that no such remedy existed at common law: it does not suggest that it is relevant whether the wrong payment was made under error of law or of fact: it is immaterial whether those who have been wrongly paid are beneficiaries under a will or next of kin, it is sufficient that they derive title from the deceased. It is true that Lord Davey expressly dealt with a claimant creditor, not a beneficiary or next of kin. I shall show your Lordships that what he said of the one might equally be said of the other. It would seem strange if a Court of equity, whose self-sought duty it was to see that the assets of a deceased person were duly administered and came into the right hands and not into the wrong hands, devised a remedy for the protection of the unpaid creditor but left the unpaid legatee or next of kin unprotected ...

Finally, my Lords, I must say some words on an argument of a more general character put forward on behalf of the appellant. The Court of Chancery, it was said, acted upon the conscience, and, unless the defendant had behaved in an unconscientious manner, would make no decree against him. The appellant or those through whom he claimed, having received a legacy in good faith and having spent it without knowledge of any flaw in their title, ought not in conscience to be ordered to refund ... Upon the propriety of a legatee refusing to repay to the true owner the money that he has wrongly received I do not think it necessary to express any judgment ... The broad fact remains that the Court of Chancery, in order to mitigate the rigour of the common law or to supply its deficiencies, established the rule of equity which I have described and this rule did not excuse the wrongly paid legatee from repayment because he had spent what he had been wrongly paid. No doubt the plaintiff might by his conduct and particularly by laches have raised some equity against himself; but if he had not done so, he was entitled to be repaid. In the present case the respondents have done nothing to bar them in equity from asserting their rights.'

Oatway, Re [1903] 2 Ch 356 Chancery Division (Joyce J)

Rights to trace give a charge over all property purchased until the money is restored

Facts

Oatway was the trustee under a will. He paid £3,000 trust moneys into his private banking account which already contained a substantial sum of money belonging to him. Shortly afterwards he purchased shares in a company for £2,137 paying for them by a cheque drawn on his banking account. After purchasing the shares he dissipated the whole of the remainder of the funds in the account. Later he sold the shares for £2,474 and shortly afterwards died insolvent. The beneficiaries under the trust claimed that the proceeds of sale of the shares should be treated as trust money while Oatway's personal representatives claimed that as there was sufficient money belonging to Oatway in the account when he purchased the shares that he should be deemed to have used his own money to buy the shares and that the proceeds of sale of the shares belonged to his estate accordingly.

Held
The trust had a first charge on the shares or the proceeds of sale thereof for trust money paid into the account. The charge attached to each and every part of the account in which the trust funds had been mixed until such time as the money was restored to the trust.

Joyce J:

> 'Trust money may be followed into land or any other property in which it has been invested; and when a trustee has, in making any purchase or investment, applied trust money together with his own, the cestuis que trust are entitled to a charge on the property purchased for the amount of the trust money laid out in the purchase or investment. Similarly, if money held by any person in a fiduciary capacity be paid into his own banking account, it may be followed by the equitable owner, who as against the trustee, will have a charge for what belongs to him upon the balance to the credit of the account. If, then, the trustee pays in further sums, and from time to time draws out money by cheques, but leaves a balance to the credit of the account, it is settled that he is not entitled to have the rule in *Clayton's* case (1816) 1 Mer 572 applied so as to maintain that the sums which have been drawn out and paid away so as to be incapable of being recovered represented *pro tanto* the trust money, and that the balance remaining is not trust money, but represents only his own moneys paid into the account. *Brown* v *Adams* (1869) 4 Ch App 764 to the contrary ought not to be followed since the decision in *Re Hallett's Estate* (1880) 13 Ch D 696. It is, in my opinion, equally clear that when any of the money drawn out has been invested, and the investment remains in the name or under the control of the trustee, the rest of the balance having been afterwards dissipated by him, he cannot maintain that the investment which remains represents his own money alone, and that what has been spent and can no longer be traced and recovered was the money belonging to the trust. In other words, when the private money of the trustee and that which he held in a fiduciary capacity have been mixed in the same banking account, from which various payments have from time to time been made, then, in order to determine to whom any remaining balance or any investment that may have been paid for out of the account ought to be deemed to belong, the trustee must be debited with any sums taken out and duly invested in the names of the proper trustees. The order of priority in which the various withdrawals and investments may have been respectively made is wholly immaterial. I have been referring, of course, to cases where there is only one fiduciary owner or set of cestuis que trust claiming whatever may be left as against the trustee.'

Roscoe (James) (Bolton) Ltd v *Winder* [1915] 1 Ch 62 Chancery Division (Sargent J)

Limits to right of tracing in a general account

Facts
Wigham agreed to buy a company and as part of the agreement he was to collect certain debts owing to the company and pay them to the company. Debts totalling £623 were collected and of this sum Wigham paid £455 into his private bank account and subsequently drew all of it out, except £25, for private expenditure. Later, he paid money of his own into the account and drew on it. At his death there was £358 in the account. The company claimed it had a charge on the £358 for the £623 it was owed.

Held
Where trust money is paid into a general account and then withdrawn and subsequently more is paid in,

there is no presumption that the moneys paid in are intended to replace the trust moneys which have been drawn out. The company was only entitled to recover the £25 which had not been withdrawn.

Sinclair v *Brougham* [1914] AC 398 House of Lords (Lord Haldane LC, Lord Dunedin, Lord Sumner, Lord Atkinson and Lord Parker)

Tracing where two beneficiaries' funds have been mixed

Facts
A building society operated a banking business which was held to be ultra vires. When the building society was wound up there were competing claims by the bank customers and the shareholders. The bank customers claimed a right to trace their funds into the assets of the society.

Held
The bank customers did have a right to trace because there was a fiduciary relationship between them and the directors who had mixed the funds. However, the House of Lords also held that the right to trace did not give the bank customers priority over the shareholders. They ranked pari passu.

Tilley's Will Trusts, Re [1967] Ch 1179 Chancery Division (Ungoed-Thomas J)

Tracing may extend to a share of profits from property purchased with mixed funds

Facts
The testatrix died in 1959 leaving an estate valued at £94,000. On her husband's death in 1932 the testatrix was appointed sole trustee of his estate which was to be held in trust for herself for life with remainder to their two children Charles and Mabel equally. The testatrix engaged in property speculation after her husband's death. She sold off properties belonging to the testator's estate in 1933, 1939, 1951 and 1952 receiving a total of £2,237 for them which was paid into her personal bank account and mixed with her own moneys. Up until 1951 the testatrix's bank account was heavily overdrawn and her property investments were financed by overdraft facilities, and there was no need for her to rely on the trust money for this purpose; it merely went to reduce the size of the overdraft. From 1951 onwards the testatrix's bank account was in credit and she was able to pay for her property investments without having to rely on the £2,237 trust moneys in the account. When the testatrix died in 1959 the personal representatives of Mabel, who died in 1955 claimed one half of the proportion of profits made on purchases of property by the testatrix to the extent which the testatrix's personal representatives could not show that those properties were purchased out of the widow's personal moneys.

Held
1. Where a trustee mixes trust property with his own and purchases property with it the beneficiary can claim a charge on the property for the amount of trust money expended on the purchase. Where there is an increase in the value of the property the beneficiary can claim that proportion of the profit attributable to the amount of trust money expended in the purchase.
2. On the facts of the case the testatrix had ample overdraft facilities at all times to render any contribution from the trust funds negligible and they only had the effect of slightly reducing the overdraft. Therefore, looking objectively at the situation, the trust money had not been used to finance the property purchases and the profit could not be recovered.

Ungoed-Thomas J:

'It seems to me that if, having regard to all the circumstances of the case objectively considered, it appears that the trustee has in fact, whatever his intention, laid out trust moneys in or towards a purchase, then the beneficiaries are entitled to the property purchased and any profits which it produces to the extent to which it has been paid for out of the trust moneys ...'

Vaughan v *Barlow Clowes International Ltd* (1992) The Times 6 March Court of Appeal (Dillon, Woolf and Leggatt LJJ)

Tracing – mixing of investment funds – re *Clayton's Case*

Facts
The appellant was appealing against a decision holding that certain assets remaining after the BCI liquidation be distributed in accordance with the rule in *Clayton's Case*, ie that money deposited into an account, and mixed, be distributed on the assumption that withdrawals were in the same order as deposits.

Held
The appeal was allowed. The express wording of the investment applications forms indicated all monies would form part of a common fund. It would be inappropriate to apply the rule in *Clayton's Case* as this would conflict with the investor's express, or implied, expectations as to how the fund would be distributed.

THE LAW OF CONTRACT

19 Contents of Contracts

Bentley (Dick) Productions Ltd* v *Harold Smith (Motors) Ltd [1965] 1 WLR 623
Court of Appeal (Lord Denning MR, Danckwerts and Salmon LJJ)

Sale of car – misrepresentation as to mileage

Facts
The defendants, car dealers, sold a Bentley to the plaintiffs and stated that the car had only done 20,000 miles since being fitted with a replacement engine and gear box. In truth, the mileage was nearer 100,000 and the car repeatedly broke down.

Held
The defendants were in breach of warranty and the plaintiffs were entitled to damages. Although the statement was made innocently, the defendants were in a position, as dealers, to check its accuracy and, having made the statement to induce the plaintiffs to enter into the contract, they would not be allowed to resile from it.

Lord Denning MR:

'The first point is whether this representation, namely that it had done 20,000 only since it had been fitted with a replacement engine and gear box, was an innocent misrepresentation (which does not give rise to damages), or whether it was a warranty. It was said by Holt CJ, and repeated in *Heilbut, Symons & Co* v *Buckleton* that: "An affirmation at the time of the sale is a warranty, provided it appear on evidence to be so intended". But that word "intended" has given rise to difficulties. I endeavoured to explain, in *Oscar Chess Ltd* v *Williams* that the question whether a warranty was intended depends on the conduct of the parties on their words and behaviour, rather than on their thoughts. If an intelligent bystander would reasonably infer that a warranty was intended, that will suffice. What conduct, then? What words and behaviour lead to the inference of a warranty?

Looking at the cases once more, as we have done so often, it seems to me that if a representation is made in the course of dealings for a contract for the very purpose of inducing the other party to act upon it, and actually inducing him to act upon it by entering into the contract, that is prima facie ground for inferring that it was intended as a warranty. It is not necessary to speak of it as being collateral. Suffice it that it was intended to be acted upon and was, in fact, acted upon. But the maker of the representations can rebut this inference if he can show that it really was an innocent misrepresentation, in that he was in fact innocent of fault in making it, and that it would not be reasonable in the circumstances for him to be bound by it ... in the present case it is very different. The inference is not rebutted. Here we have a dealer, Smith, who was in a position to know, or at least to find out, the history of the car. He could get it by writing to the makers. He did not do so. Indeed, it was done later. When the history of this car was examined, his statement turned out to be quite wrong. He ought to have known better. There was no reasonable foundation for it.'

Commentary
Applied in *Evans (J) & Son (Portsmouth) Ltd* v *Andrea Merzario Ltd* [1976] 1 WLR 1078. Distinguished: *Oscar Chess Ltd* v *Williams* [1957] 1 WLR 370.

Bettini v *Gye* (1876) 1 QBD 183 High Court (Blackburn, Quain and Archibald JJ)

Condition precedent?

Facts
The defendant director of the Royal Italian Opera in London engaged the plaintiff tenor for the period 30 March to 13 July 1875: it was a term of the agreement that the plaintiff would 'be in London without fail at least six days before the commencement of this engagement for ... rehearsals'. Because of temporary illness, he said, he did not arrive until 28 March. Was the defendant justified in refusing to proceed with the engagement?

Held
He was not as the stipulation in question was not a condition precedent.

Blackburn J:

> 'The answer ... depends on whether this part of the contract is a condition precedent to the defendant's liability or only an independent agreement, a breach of which will not justify a repudiation of the contract, but will only be a cause of action for a compensation in damages ... We think the answer ... depends on the true construction of the contract taken as a whole. Parties may think some matter apparently of very little importance essential, and if they sufficiently express an intention to make the literal fulfilment of such a thing a condition precedent, it will be one, or they may think that the performance of some matter apparently of essential importance, and prima facie a condition, is not really vital, and may be compensated for in damages, and if they sufficiently express such an intention, it will not be a condition precedent ...
>
> If the plaintiff's engagements had been only to sing in operas at the theatre it might very well be that previous attendance at rehearsals with the actors in company with whom he was to perform was essential. If the engagement had only been for a few performances, or for a short time, it would afford a strong argument that attendance for the purpose of rehearsals during the six days immediately before the commencement of the engagement was a vital part of the agreement. But we find on looking to the agreement that the plaintiff was to sing in theatres, halls, and drawing rooms, public and private, from Mar. 30 to July 13 1875, and that he was to sing in concerts as well as in operas ... As far as we can see the failure to attend at rehearsals during the six days immediately before Mar. 31, could only affect the theatrical performances, and, perhaps, the singing in duets or concerted pieces during the first week or fortnight of this engagement, which is to sing in theatres, halls, and drawing rooms, and concerts for fifteen weeks. We think, therefore, that it does not go to the root of the matter so as to require us to consider it a condition precedent. The defendant must, therefore, we think, seek redress by a cross claim for damages.'

British Crane Hire Corporation Ltd v *Ipswich Plant Hire Ltd* [1974] 2 WLR 856 Court of Appeal (Lord Denning MR, Megaw LJ and Sir Eric Sachs)

Incorporation of terms in contract – common understanding

Facts
Both the plaintiffs and the defendants were in the business of hiring out heavy earth-moving equipment. The defendants were carrying out drainage work and urgently needed a dragline crane. By telephone, they agreed to hire one from the plaintiffs and although the hiring rate was agreed, nothing was said about the conditions of hire. As was their custom, the plaintiffs sent their written standard terms to be signed by the defendants, but before the latter did so, due to the fault of neither party, the crane sank into marshy ground. The plaintiffs' standard terms contained an indemnity clause, making the defendants liable for

any expense incurred in recovering the crane. The trial judge held that the plaintiffs' terms were incorporated into the contract and that the defendants were liable under the indemnity clause. He also found, as a fact, that there had been only two previous transactions between the parties.

Held
The contract was made on the plaintiffs' terms, not by the course of dealing, but on the common understanding of the parties.

Lord Denning MR:

> 'The judge found that the printed conditions were incorporated into the contract. The defendants appeal from that finding. The facts are these. The arrangements for the hire of the crane were all on the telephone. The plaintiffs agreed to let the defendants hire this crane. It was to be delivered on the Sunday. The hiring charges and transport charges were agreed. Nothing was said about conditions. There was nothing in writing. But soon after the crane was delivered, the plaintiffs, in accordance with their practice, forwarded a printed form to be signed by the hirer. It set out the order, the work to be done and the hiring fee, and that it was subject to the conditions set out on the back of the form. The defendants would ordinarily have sent the form back signed; but this time they did not do so. The accident happened before they signed it. So they never did so. But the plaintiffs say, nevertheless, from the previous course of dealing, the conditions on the form govern the relationship between the parties. They rely on condition 6:
>
>> "SITE CONDITIONS: The Hirer shall take all reasonable precautions to ensure that the Crane can safely be taken onto and kept upon or at the site and in particular to ensure that the ground is in a satisfactory condition to take the weight of the Crane and/or its load. The Hirer shall where necessary supply and lay timber or other suitable material for the crane to travel over and work upon and shall be responsible for the recovery of the Crane from soft ground".
>
> Also on condition 8:
>
>> "… The Hirer shall be responsible for and indemnify the Owner against … All … expenses in connection with or arising out of the use of the plant … "
>
> In support of the course of dealing the plaintiffs relied on two previous transactions in which the defendants had hired cranes from the plaintiffs. One was 20 February 1969 and the other 6 October 1969. Each was on a printed form which set out the hiring of a crane, the price, the site, and so forth; and also setting out the conditions the same as those here. There were thus only two transactions, many months before, and they were not known to the defendants' manager who ordered this crane. In the circumstances, I doubt whether those two would be sufficient to show a course of dealing.'

Bunge Corpn v *Tradax SA* [1981] 1 WLR 711 House of Lords (Lord Wilberforce, Lord Fraser of Tullybelton, Lord Scarman, Lord Lowry and Lord Roskill)

Shipping contract – right to terminate

Facts
Under a contract for the sale and purchase of soya bean meal, it was agreed that a shipment was to be made in June. The buyers had to provide a vessel and to give at least 15 days' notice of its probable readiness. In the event, they gave such notice on 17 June and the sellers contended that the late notice was a breach of contract amounting to a repudiation.

Held
The sellers' view would be upheld and they were also entitled to damages.

Lord Scarman:

'I wish, however, to make a few observations on the topic of "innominate" terms in our contract law. In *Hong Kong Fir Shipping Co Ltd* v *Kawasaki Kisen Kaisha Ltd* the Court of Appeal rediscovered and reaffirmed that English law recognises contractual terms which, on a true construction of the contract of which they are part, are neither conditions nor warranties but are, to quote Lord Wilberforce's words in *Bremer Handelsgesellschaft mbH* v *Vanden Avenne-Izegem*, "intermediate". A condition is a term the failure to perform which entitles the other party to treat the contract as at an end. A warranty is a term breach of which sounds in damages but does not terminate, or entitle the other party to terminate, the contract. An innominate or intermediate term is one the effect of non-performance of which the parties expressly or (as is more usual) impliedly agree will depend on the nature and the consequences of breach. In the *Hong Kong Fir* case the term in question provided for the obligation of seaworthiness, breach of which it is well known may be trivial (eg one defective rivet) or very serious (eg a hole in the bottom of the ship). It is inconceivable that parties when including such a term in their contract could have contemplated or intended (unless they expressly say so) that one defective rivet would entitle the charterer to end the contract or that a hole in the bottom of the ship would not. I read the *Hong Kong Fir* case as being concerned as much with the construction of the contract as with the consequences and effect of breach. The first question is always, therefore, whether, on the true construction of a stipulation and the contract of which it is part, it is a condition, an innominate term, or only a warranty. If the stipulation is one which on the true construction of the contract the parties have not made a condition, and breach of which may be attended by trivial, minor or very grave consequences, it is innominate, and the court (or an arbitrator) will, in the event of dispute, have the task of deciding whether the breach that has arisen is such as the parties would have said, had they been asked at the time they made their contract, "It goes without saying that, if that happens, the contract is at an end" ... The seller needed sufficient notice to enable him to choose the loading port; the parties were agreed that the notice to be given him was 15 days; this was a mercantile contract in which the parties required to know where they stood not merely later with hindsight but at once as events occurred. Because it makes commercial sense to treat the clause in the context and circumstances of this contract as a condition to be performed before the seller takes his steps to comply with bargain, I would hold it to be not an innominate term but a condition.'

Cehave NV v *Bremer Handelsgesellschaft mbH, The Hansa Nord* [1975] 3 WLR 447 Court of Appeal (Lord Denning MR, Roskill and Ormrod LJJ)

Cattle food – shipment 'in good condition'

Facts
A German company agreed to sell a Dutch company a quantity of pellets to be used in cattle food at a price of approximately £100,000. The contract provided 'shipment to be made in good condition'. Upon arrival, it was discovered that part of the cargo in one hold of the ship had been severely damaged by overheating and the buyers purported to reject the whole cargo. Because the sellers refused to return the purchase price, the pellets were sold by order of a Dutch Court and subsequently repurchased at a substantially reduced price by the buyers because of a fall in the market price. The buyers used the cargo in almost the same manner and quantity to make cattle food as they would have done with sound pellets. The arbitrator and Commercial Court judge held the 'shipment in good condition' clause to be a condition of the contract.

Held
The clause was not a condition but an intermediate stipulation: the Sale of Goods Act did not require a rigid division of terms in contracts for the sale of goods into 'conditions' and 'warranties' only.

Lord Denning MR:

'1 *The general law apart from the sale of goods*

For the last 300 or 400 years, the courts have had to grapple with this problem: in what circumstances can a party, who is in breach himself of a stipulation of the contract, call on the other side to perform his part or sue him for non-performance? At one time the solution was thought to depend on the nature of the stipulation itself and not on the extent of the breach or its consequences. Under the old form of pleading, a plaintiff had to aver and prove that he had performed all conditions precedent or that he was ready and willing to perform them. The question, therefore, was whether the stipulation (which he had broken) was a condition precedent or not, or, in the terminology of the 18th century, whether it was an *independent* covenant (the breach of which did not debar him from suing the other side), or a *dependent* covenant (the breach of which did debar the plaintiff, because the performance by the other was *dependent* on the plaintiff performing his).

This distinction was well stated by Serjeant Williams in his notes to *Pordage* v *Cole:*

> "... Where there are several covenants, promises, or agreements, which are independent of each other, one party may bring an action against the other for a breach of his covenant etc, without averring a performance of the covenants, etc on his, the plaintiff's part, and it is no excuse for the defendants to allege in his plea a breach of the covenants, etc on the part of the plaintiff ... But where the covenants etc are *dependent*, it is necessary for the plaintiff to aver and prove a performance of the covenants etc on his part, to entitle himself to an action for the breach of the covenants on the part of the defendant ..."

Although that division was treated as exhaustive, nevertheless, when the courts came to apply it, they had regard to the extent of the breach. This was done by Lord Mansfield in 1777 in the great case of *Boone* v *Eyre*, of which there was no satisfactory record until Lord Kenyon, in 1796, produced a manuscript note of it: see *Campbell* v *Jones* and *Glazewood* v *Woodrow*. It is summarised in the notes to *Cutter* v *Powell*. The plaintiff conveyed to the defendant a plantation in the West Indies, together with the stock of negroes on it, in consideration of £500 down and an annuity of £100 a year, and covenanted that he had a good title to the plantation and was lawfully possessed of the negroes. Some time later, the defendant discovered that the plaintiff had no title to the negroes and stopped paying the annuity. The court held that the defendant was liable to pay the annuity. He could not escape simply because the plaintiff had not "a title to a few negroes". His remedy was to bring a cross-action for damages. It would be different "if the plaintiff had no title to the plantation itself", for then the plaintiff could not have recovered the annuity. In the language of those times, if the breach went to the whole consideration, the covenant was considered to be a condition precedent and the defendant could plead the breach in bar of the action, but if the breach went "only to a part, where a breach may be paid for in damages, there the defendant has a remedy on his covenant, and shall not plead it as a condition precedent". In short, if the breach went to the root of the matter, the stipulation was to be considered a condition precedent; but if the breach did not go to the root, the stipulation was considered to be an independent covenant which could be compensated for in damages: see *Davidson* v *Gwynne* per Lord Ellenborough, *Ellen* v *Topp* and *Graves* v *Legg*.

Apart from those cases of "breach going to the root", the courts at the same time were developing the doctrine of "anticipatory breach". When one party, before the day when he is obliged to perform his part, declares in advance that he will not perform it when the day comes, or by his conduct evinces an intention not to perform it, the other may elect to treat his declaration or conduct as a breach going to the root of the matter and to treat himself as discharged from further performance: see *Hochster* v *De La Tour*. By his prior declaration or conduct, the guilty party is said to repudiate the contract. The word "repudiation" should be confined to those cases of an anticipatory breach, but it is also used in connection with cases of an actual breach going to the root of the contract: see *Heyman* v *Darwins Ltd* per Lord Wright. All of them were gathered together by Lord Blackburn in his famous speech in *Mersey Steel and Iron Co* v *Naylor Benzon & Co*:

> "The rule of law, as I have always understood it, is that where there is a contract in which there are two parties, each side having to do something (it is so laid down in the notes to *Pordage* v *Cole*), if you see that the failure to perform one part of it goes to the root of the contract, goes to the foundation of the

whole, it is a good defence to say, 'I am not going on to perform my part of it when that which is the root of the whole and the substantial consideration for my performance is defeated by your misconduct' ... I repeatedly asked Mr Cohen whether or not he could find any authority which justified him in saying that every breach of contract ... must be considered to go to the root of the contract, and he produced no such authority. There are many cases in which the breach may do so: it depends upon the construction of the contract."

Those last words are clearly a reference to a "condition" strictly so called, in which any breach entitled the other to be discharged from further performance. But the earlier words are quite general. They refer to all terms other than conditions strictly so called.

2 The Sale of Goods Act 1893

Such was the state of the law when the Sale of Goods Act 1893 was passed on 20 February 1894. I have studied the then current edition of Benjamin on Sale and the little books which Judge Chalmers wrote before and after the Act, and the proceedings in Parliament. These show that until the year 1893, there was much confusion in the use of the words "condition" and "warranty" But that confusion was removed by the Act itself and by the judgment of Bowen LJ in *Bentsen* v *Taylor & Sons & Co*. Thenceforth those words were used by lawyers as terms of art. The difference between them was this: if the promisor broke a condition in any respect, however slight, it gave the other party a right to be quit of his obligations and to sue for damages, unless he, by his conduct, waived the condition, in which case he was bound to perform his future obligations but could sue for the damage he had suffered. If the promisor broke a warranty in any respect, however serious, the other party was not quit of his future obligations. He had to perform them. His only remedy was to sue for damages: see *The Mihalis Angelos. Wickman Machine* Tool *Sales Ltd* v *L Schuler AG*.

Now that division was not exhaustive. It left out of account the vast majority of stipulations which were neither "conditions" nor "warranties", strictly so called, but were intermediate stipulations, the effect of which depended on the breach. The cases about these stipulations were legion. They stretched continuously from *Boone* v *Eyre* in 1777 to *Mersey Steel* v *Naylor* in 1884. I cannot believe that Parliament, in 1893, intended to give the go-by to all these cases, or to say that they did not apply to the sale of goods. Those cases expressed the rules of the common law. They were preserved by Section 61(2) of the 1893 Act which said:

> "The rules of the common law, including the law merchant, save in so far as they are inconsistent with the express provisions of this Act ... shall continue to apply to contracts for the sale of goods."

There was nothing in the Act inconsistent with those cases. So they continued to apply.

In 1962, in *Hong Kong Fir Shipping Co Ltd* v *Kawasaki Kisen Kaisha Ltd* the Court of Appeal drew attention to this vast body of case law. They showed that, besides conditions and warranties, strictly so called, there are many stipulations of which the effect depends on this: if the breach goes to the root of the contract, the other party is entitled to treat himself as discharged: but if it does not go to the root, he is not. In my opinion, the principle embodied in these cases applies to contracts for the sale of goods just as to all other contracts.

The task of the court can be stated simply in the way in which Upjohn LJ stated it. First, see whether the stipulation, on its true construction, is a condition strictly so called, that is a stipulation such that, for any breach of it, the other party is entitled to treat himself as discharged. Second, if it is not such a condition, then look to the extent of the actual breach which has taken place. If it is such as to go to the root of the contract, the other party is entitled to treat himself as discharged; but otherwise not. To this may be added an anticipatory breach. If the one party, before the day on which he is due to perform his part, shows by his words or conduct that he will not perform it in a vital respect when the day comes, the other party is entitled to treat himself as discharged.

"Shipped in good condition"

This brings me back to the particular stipulation in this case: "shipped in good condition". Was this a condition strictly so called, so that any breach of it entitled the buyer to reject the goods? Or was it an intermediate stipulation so that the buyer cannot reject unless the breach is so serious as to go to the root of the contract?

If there was any previous authority holding it to be a condition strictly so called, we should abide by it, just as we did with the clause "expected ready to load": see *Finnish Government (Ministry of Food)* v *H Ford & Co Ltd* and *The Mihalis Angelos*. But there is no such authority with the clause "shipped in good condition". I regard this clause as comparable to a clause as to quality, such as "fair and average quality". If a small portion of the goods sold was a little below that standard, it would be met by commercial men by an allowance off the price. The buyer would have no rights to reject the whole lot unless the divergence was serious and substantial: see *Biggin & Co Ltd* v *Permanite Ltd* by Devlin J and *Ashington Piggeries Ltd* v *Christopher Hill Ltd* by Lord Diplock. That is shown in this very case by clause 5 in Form 100 of the Cattle Food Trade Association which contains percentages of contamination, below which there is a price allowance and above which there is a right in the buyer to reject. Likewise with the clause "shipped in good condition"; if a small portion of the whole cargo was not in good condition and arrived a little unsound, it should be met by a price allowance. The buyers should not have a right to reject the whole cargo unless it was serious and substantial. This is borne out by the difficulty which often arises (as in this case) on a cif contract as to whether the damage was done before shipment or took place after shipment; for in the latter case, the buyer would have no claim against the seller but would be left to his claim against the insurers. So, as a matter of good sense, the buyer should be bound to accept the goods and not reject them unless there is a serious and substantial breach, fairly attributable to the seller.

In my opinion, therefore, the term "shipped in good condition" was not a condition strictly so called; nor was it a warranty strictly so called. It was one of those intermediate stipulations which gives no right to reject unless the breach goes to the root of the contract.

On the facts stated by the Board of Appeal, I do not think the buyers were entitled to reject these instalments of the contract. The board only said that "not all the goods in hold Number 1 were shipped in good condition". That does not say how many were bad. In any case, their condition cannot have been very bad, seeing that all of them were, in fact, used for the intended purpose. The breach did not go to the root of the contract. The buyer is entitled to damages, but not to rejection.'

Chelsea Football & Athletic Co Ltd v *SB Property Co Ltd* [1992] TLR 175 Court of Appeal (Dillon, Leggatt and Nolan LJJ)

Sale of land contract – implied terms – delay

Facts

In August 1982 a lease for premises, including the Stamford Bridge stadium, was granted by the company to the club, for a period of seven years. At the same time Chelsea Football Club sold the freehold of certain of this land to SB Property. The idea was to give the property company six years to find a developer, the club having an option to purchase the land back if a developer was not found. Exactly three days before the end of the six year period, the company granted a lease of all the land to a company called Crest Homes Ltd for 210 years. Notwithstanding this fact, a week later, the club gave notice that they proposed to exercise their option to purchase the freehold. The property company challenged the validity of this move. By 1991 the property market had collapsed and Crest Homes decided it was expedient to surrender their lease, and SB conceded, contrary to their earlier arguments, that the football club had indeed validly exercised its option.

In late 1991, Chelsea Football Club began a new action, alleging that the property company's delaying tactics amounted to a breach of an implied term and that the club had suffered substantial damages as a result of this delay, because the property market had now collapsed.

Held

There was no indication in the lease that time was to be of the essence. The Court of Appeal could find no justification at all for implying any such term (that the parties would do nothing which might have the effect of preventing or delaying completion of the contract). The need for urgency had arisen largely because of the collapse of the property market, which neither party anticipated when drawing up the lease. The lease contained no indication of urgency at all, and the court would not imply any such term.

De Lassalle v *Guildford* [1901] 2 KB 215 Court of Appeal (Sir A L Smith MR, Henn Collins and Romer LJJ)

Collateral warranty

Facts

The plaintiff said he would not take up the lease of a house unless the defendant owner assured him that the drains were in good order. The defendant gave that assurance: the plaintiff took up the lease (which was silent as to the condition of the drains): the drains turned out not to have been in good order.

Held

The plaintiff was entitled to damages for breach of the collateral warranty as to the condition of the drains.

Sir A L Smith MR:

> 'In the present case, did the defendant assume to assert a fact, or merely to state an opinion or judgment upon a matter of which he had no special knowledge and upon which the plaintiff ... might be expected also to have an opinion. What is it the defendant asserts? I paraphrase the evidence: "You need have no certificate of a sanitary inspector; it is quite unnecessary; the drains are in perfect condition, I give you my word upon the subject. Will that satisfy you? If so, hand me over the counterpart." What more deliberate and emphatic assertion of a fact could well be made during the course of the dealing which led up to the counterpart lease being handed over to the defendant? That the question asked and the answer given were seriously intended ... to be the basis of the contractual relation between the parties, I cannot doubt. There is the evidence that the plaintiff would not take the lease unless the drains were guaranteed, and surely the statements made by the defendant were not made on the assumption that they were to be of no avail to the plaintiff except they were made fraudulently. In my judgment, everything necessary to establish a warranty has in this case been proved.
>
> The next question is: Was the warranty collateral to the lease so that it might be given in evidence and given effect to? It appears to me in this case clear that the lease did not cover the whole ground, and that it did not contain the whole of the contract between the parties. The lease is entirely silent about the drains ... There is nothing in the lease as to the then condition of the drains – i e, at the time of the taking of the lease, which was the vital point in hand. Then why is not the warranty collateral to anything which is to be found in the lease? The present contract or warranty by the defendant was entirely independent of what was to happen during the tenancy. It was what induced the tenancy, and in no way affected the terms of the tenancy during the three years which was all the lease dealt with. The warranty in no way contradicts the lease, and without the warranty the lease never would have been executed.'

Esso Petroleum Co Ltd v *Mardon* [1976] 2 WLR 583 Court of Appeal (Lord Denning MR, Ormrod and Shaw LJJ)

Lease of petrol station – estimate of sales

Facts

The plaintiffs acquired a busy main street site for a petrol station on the basis of calculations showing an estimated annual consumption of 200,000 gallons from the third year. The planning authority insisted on access only from side streets: this falsified the calculations but, through lack of care, the plaintiffs failed to revise their original estimate. During negotiations for a tenancy, the plaintiffs' representative, a person of 40 years' experience, told the defendant in good faith that throughput had been estimated at 200,000 gallons in the third year. This the defendant doubted, but in the light of the representative's greater expertise he took the tenancy. It turned out that the site was capable only of an annual throughput of some 70,000 gallons and, although he took a new tenancy at a reduced rent, the defendant lost heavily. In response to the plaintiffs' claim for possession and petrol supplied, the defendant claimed damages for breach of warranty and negligent misrepresentation.

Held

He was entitled to succeed and the measure of damages was the loss he had suffered by having been induced to enter into a disastrous contract. By taking a new tenancy, he had acted reasonably in attempting to mitigate his losses.

Lord Denning MR:

> 'Counsel for Esso retaliated, however, by citing *Bisset* v *Wilkinson* where the Privy Council said that a statement by a New Zealand farmer that an area of land "would carry 2,000 sheep" was only an expression of opinion. He submitted that the forecast here of 200,000 gallons was an expression of opinion and not a statement of fact; and that it could not be interpreted as a warranty or promise.
>
> Now, I would quite agree with counsel for Esso that it was not a warranty – in this sense – that it did not *guarantee* that the throughput *would* be 200,000 gallons. But, nevertheless, it was a forecast made by a party, Esso, who had special knowledge and skill. It was the yardstick ... by which they measured the worth of a filling station. They knew the facts. They knew the traffic in the town. They knew the throughput of comparable stations. They had much experience and expertise at their disposal. They were in a much better position than Mr Mardon to make a forecast. It seems to me that if such a person makes a forecast – intending that the other should act on it and he does act on it – it can well be interpreted as a warranty that the forecast is sound and reliable in this sense that they made it with reasonable care and skill. It is just as if Esso said to Mr Mardon. "Our forecast of throughput is 200,000 gallons. You can rely on it as being a sound forecast of what the service station should do. The rent is calculated on that footing." If the forecast turned out to be an unsound forecast, such as no person of skill or expierence should have made, there is a breach of warranty ... It is very different from the New Zealand case where the land had never been used as sheep farm and both parties were equally able to form an opinion as to its carrying capacity.
>
> In the present case it seems to me that there was a warranty that the forecast was sound, that is that Esso had made it with reasonable care and skill. That warranty was broken. Most negligently Esso made a "fatal error" in the forecast they stated to Mr Mardon, and on which he took the tenancy. For this they are liable in damages ...
>
> It seems to me that *Hedley Byrne*, properly understood, covers this particular proposition: if a man, who has or professes to have special knowledge or skill, makes a representation by virtue thereof to another – be it advice, information or opinion – with the intention of inducing him to enter into a contract with him, he is under a duty to use reasonable care to see that the representation is correct, and that the advice, information or opinion is reliable. If he negligently gives unsound advice or misleading information or expresses an erroneous opinion, and thereby induces the other side into a contract with him, he is liable in damages ...
>
> Applying this principle, it is plain that Esso professed to have – and did in fact have – special knowledge or skill in estimating the throughput of a filling station. They made the representation – they forecast a throughput of 200,000 gallons – intending to induce Mr Mardon to enter into a tenancy on the faith of it.

They made it negligently. It was a "fatal error". And thereby induced Mr Mardon to enter into a contract of tenancy that was disastrous to him. For this misprepresentation they are liable in damages.'

Evans (J) & Son (Portsmouth) Ltd v *Andrea Merzario Ltd* [1976] 1 WLR 1078 Court of Appeal (Lord Denning MR, Roskill and Geoffrey Lane LJJ)

Collateral contract – consideration

Facts

The plaintiffs had, from 1959-1967, used the defendants' services as forwarding agents for the import of machines from Italy to England. During that period, the plaintiffs' machines were stored below deck. In 1967, the defendants changed to containers, but orally assumed the plaintiffs that the latter's machines would be shipped below deck. On one voyage in 1968, they were not and, due to rough seas, several machines were lost overboard. The defendants sought to rely on their written standard terms which permitted them to carry cargo howsoever they wished and exempted them from liability in the case of loss.

Held

There was a collateral contract between the parties that the plaintiffs' machines would be carried below deck; the plaintiffs furnished consideration for the defendants' promise by entering into the main contract of carriage.

Lord Denning MR:

'The judge quoted largely from the well known case of *Heilbut, Symons & Co* v *Buckleton*, in which it was held that a person is not liable in damages for an innocent misrepresentation; and that the courts should be slow to hold that there was a collateral contract. I must say that much of what was said in that case is entirely out of date ... When a person gives a promise or an assurance to another, intending that he should act on it by entering into a contract, we hold that it is binding: *Dick Bentley Productions*.'

Commentary

Applied: *Bentley (Dick) Productions Ltd* v *Harold Smith (Motors) Ltd* [1965] 1 WLR 623

Eyre v *Measday* [1986] 1 All ER 488 Court of Appeal (Slade, Purchas LJJ and Sir Ronaleyn Cumming-Bruce)

Sterilisation – collateral warranty

Facts

The plaintiff consulted the defendant gynaecologist in order to have a sterilisation operation. The defendant, in explaining the procedure involved, informed the plaintiff that it was a permanent procedure and that the operation was irreversible. He did not advise the plaintiff that there was a small risk of her becoming pregnant after the operation. The plaintiff (and her husband) believed that the operation would render her absolutely sterile. After the operation, however, the plaintiff became pregnant and gave birth to a child.

The plaintiff brought an action against the defendant alleging that, in informing her that the operation was irreversible but failing to inform her of the small risk that the operation would be unsuccessful, the defendant had been in breach of a contractual term, or an express or implied collateral warranty, that the operation would render her absolutely sterile.

Held

The defendant's contractual undertaking was to perform a particular operation rather than to render the plaintiff absolutely sterile. When a medical practitioner contracts to carry out a particular operation, the court would imply a term into the contract that the operation would be performed with reasonable skill and care. But the court would be reluctant to imply a term or collateral warranty that the expected result would actually be achieved. On the present facts, applying the doctrine of *The Moorcock* (1889) 14 PD 64, no intelligent lay bystander could have drawn the inference that the defendant was intending to give such a warranty.

Federal Commerce and Navigation Ltd v *Molena Alpha Inc, The Nanfri, The Benfri, The Lorfri* [1978] 3 WLR 991 House of Lords (Lord Wilberforce, Viscount Dilhorne, Lord Fraser of Tullybelton, Lord Russell of Killowen and Lord Scarman)

Charterparties – right to terminate

Facts

Under three identical charterparties, the charterers were entitled to make deductions from the hire in certain events, including slow steaming, and to give instructions to the masters of the vessels relating to certain matters. A dispute arose as to slow steaming deductions and the owners threatened to withdraw the charterers' ability to give instructions to the masters, knowing that this would place them in serious difficulties. The charterers alleged that the owners' conduct amounted to a repudiation of the charterparties.

Held

It did as it went to the root of the contracts.

Lord Fraser of Tullybelton:

> 'Treating the [relevant clause] then as an innominate or intermediate term, I proceed to consider whether the threatened breach of it here was so fundamental as to amount to repudiation of the contract. The test of repudiation has been formulated in various ways by different judges. I shall adopt the formulation by Buckley LJ in *Decro-Wall International SA* v *Practitioners in Marketing Ltd* as follows:
>
>> " ... will the consequences of the breach be such that it would be unfair to the injured party to hold him to the contract and leave him to his remedy in damages as and when a breach or breaches may occur? If this would be so, then a repudiation has taken place."
>
> Judged by that test I have no doubt that the breach here was repudiatory. The whole purpose of the contract from the charterers' point of view was that they should have the use of the ship for carrying on their trade ... but if the owner's threat had been carried out it would have been ruinous to that trade. I need not repeat the umpire's findings as to the consequences in full but I attach particular importance to his finding ...
>
>> "The Charterers were likely to be blacklisted as grain carriers by Continental Grain, which is one of the world's largest shippers of grain. In consequence the Charterers' reputation would be very seriously damaged and they would probably have been unable to obtain business for the vessels from other major shippers of grain."
>
> Such damage to their reputation might well have been lasting and not limited to the duration of actual interruption of the trade. In face of that finding, I am, with all respect to Kerr J, unable to agree with his view that the owners were only creating a "temporary impasse". It was said that the breach was not repudiatory because the owners were merely reacting against the charterers' unilateral deductions from the hire, and particularly against their revival of a stale claim for deductions. This is really a plea in mitigation

but it does not affect the result. If the owners' reaction involved committing a breach that went to the root of the contract, they cannot in my opinion escape the legal consequences by pleading that they had been provoked. I would therefore hold that the breach was repudiatory.'

Ferguson v *John Dawson & Partners (Contractors) Ltd* [1976] 1 WLR 1213 Court of Appeal (Megaw, Lawton and Browne LJJ)

Contract of services or for services?

Facts

The defendant building contractors orally engaged the plaintiff as a general labourer, 'purely working as a lump labour force'. Both parties regarded the plaintiff as a 'self-employed labour only sub-contractor'. The plaintiff was injured in the course of his work and the defendants were liable if he had been working for them under a contract of service as opposed to a contract for services.

Held (Lawton LJ dissenting)

The plaintiff's action would succeed.

Megaw LJ:

'I reject the defendants' contention that on legal analysis there were no contractual terms governing the relationship between the plaintiff and the defendants other than a term "self-employed labour only sub-contractor". There were such other contractual terms. For this purpose it does not matter whether they were originally incorporated by implication when the plaintiff was taken on by Mr Murray [the defendants' site agent], or were added thereafter by the acceptance of the parties by conduct. What the relevant terms were was sufficiently proved by the evidence of Mr Murray himself, the defendants' site agent, in cross-examination. His evidence, except in minor respects, is not, as the defendants suggest, merely evidence of what was done in performance of the contract. It is evidence of what the contractual rights and obligations were throughout the plaintiff's work for the defendants. True, it is not expressed in the questions and answers as being agreed terms of a contract. But I have no doubt that Mr Murray understood, and everyone understood, that what he was being asked about was the relationship between the parties – the rights and obligations of the defendants and the workman, including the plaintiff, which were understood and accepted to exist, that is, on legal analysis, the contractual terms.

James Miller & Partners Ltd v *Whitworth Street Estates (Manchester) Ltd* and *L Schuler AG* v *Wickman Machine Tool Sales Ltd*, House of Lords authorities relied on by the defendants, are not relevant. They hold that, subject to certain exceptions, you may not look at what has been done in pursuance of a contract in order to construe that contract. There are a number of other reasons, also, why I think those decisions are not relevant here. But the main reason is that we are not here concerned with construing a contract, but with evidence as to what the terms of a contract were – the implication of terms ...

Mr Murray accepted that he was responsible for "hiring and firing". In other words, as between the defendants and the workmen, including the plaintiff, he, Mr Murray, could dismiss them. There would be no question of his being able to determine a contract between the defendants and a sub-contractor. He could move men from site to site, if he was so minded; and, in support of the existence of that contractual right on behalf of the defendants, he gave instances of having done so. If tools were required for the work, it was for the defendants to provide them. Again, as confirmation of that contractual obligation, Mr Murray gave evidence of instances where the plaintiff had required tools for the work which he had been required to do, and the defendants had provided them. It was for Mr Murray to tell the workmen, including the plaintiff, what particular work they were to do: "I tell him what to take and what to do". The centurian in St Matthew's gospel says to the man under him "Do this, and he doeth it". The man under him is a servant, not an independent contractor. All these things are in relation to the contractual relationships existing. "I tell him what to do" and he does it on Mr Murray"s instructions because, when legal analysis has to be applied, it is a term of the contract that the plaintiff shall carry out the defendants' instructions what to do when they tell him to do it. The men, including the plaintiff, were employed on an hourly basis. The money paid to them would be correctly described as a "wage".

In my judgment, on the tests laid down in the authorities, all of this indicates beyond doubt that the reality of the relationship was employer and employee: a contract of service ...

My own view would have been that a declaration by the parties, even if it be incorporated in the contract, that the workman is to be, or is to be deemed to be, self-employed, an independent contractor, ought to be wholly disregarded – not merely treated as not being conclusive – if the remainder of the contractual terms, governing the realities of the relationship, show the relationship of employer and employee ... I find difficulty in accepting that the parties, by a mere expression of intention as to what the legal relationship should be, can in any way influence the conclusion of law as to what the relationship is. I think that it would be contrary to the public interest if that were so: for it would mean that the parties, by their own whim, by the use of a verbal formula, unrelated to the reality of the relationship, could influence the decision on whom the responsibility for the safety of workmen, as imposed by statutory regulations, should rest.'

G A Estates v *Caviapen Trustees Ltd* (1991) The Times 22 October Court of Session (Lord Coulsfield)

Construction of contracts

Facts
In this Scottish case, the plaintiffs, in a sale of land, warranted to the defendants that the land was fit for the purpose of constructing a particular development. The defendants, when they discovered that the land was not suitable for the purpose stated, refused to pay. The plaintiffs sought payment relying on the contra proferentem rule, contending the warranty had been drafted specifically in favour of the defendants and should, if ambiguous, be construed in the manner least favourable to them. The defendants, counterclaiming, argued that the clause was not conceived as a favour to them and was not intended to benefit one party more than another. The contra proferentem rule had no relevance.

Held
In order for the contra proferentem rule to be justified, the argument that the warranty was a special feature and was never normally included in contracts for sale of land was to be rejected. No special rule of construction (such as contra proferentem) applied here.

Graham v *Pitkin* [1992] 1 WLR 403 Privy Council (Lords Keith of Kinkel, Roskill, Templeman and Jauncey of Tullichettle)

Conditional contracts – purchaser entitled to waive condition?

Facts
In a sale of land contract the defendants, the vendors, agreed to sell property to the plaintiffs. A special condition of the contract was that the sale was subject to the plaintiff purchasers obtaining a ten-year mortgage of $19,000. The building society agreed to a mortgage, but for a lower amount. Then breaches of covenant were discovered, and there was a long delay while the building society argued that they would not advance funds until the breaches were corrected. At this point, three years on, the purchaser indicated she would probably buy for cash. The vendor, without serving notice to complete, announced that due to delays she was rescinding the contract.

Held

The condition as to the obtaining of a mortgage was solely for the purchaser, and she could waive it if she wished. It was not a condition precedent. The delays were more the fault of the vendor, in refusing to rectify breaches of covenant discovered by the building society. The fact that the building society would not advance a loan, until these had been put right, did not entitle the vendor to claim that as the mortgage was not forthcoming the contract must be considered at an end. At no point had the purchaser shown any signs of wishing to repudiate the contract and it was for the purchaser to decide whether she wished to adhere to the condition.

Heilbut, Symons & Co v *Buckleton* [1913] AC 30 House of Lords (Viscount Haldane LC, Lord Atkinson and Lord Moulton)

Purchase of shares – warranty

Facts

The respondent enquired of the appellants, rubber merchants in London, 'I understand you are bringing out a rubber company' and was told, 'We are'. He asked 'if it was alright' (ie financially sound) and was told, 'We are bringing it out.' The company was not a rubber company properly so called and the respondent lost a considerable amount of money when the value of the shares in the company, which he had purchased, fell heavily. He claimed damages for breach of contract, for breach of warranty that the company was a rubber company.

Held

There was no breach of contract. The appellants' statements were not intended to be a contractual undertaking; nor had either party so regarded them.

Lord Moulton:

> 'There is no controversy between the parties as to certain points of fact and of law. It is not contested that the only company referred to was the Filisola Rubber and Produce Estates Limited, or that the reply of Mr Johnston to the plaintiff's question over the telephone was a representation by the defendants that the company was a "rubber company", whatever may be the meaning of that phrase; nor is there any controversy as to the legal nature of that which the plaintiff must establish. He must show a warranty, ie a contract collateral to the main contract to take the shares, whereby the defendants, in consideration of the plaintiff taking the shares, promised that the company itself was a rubber company. The question in issue is whether there was any evidence that such a contract was made between the parties.
>
> It is evident, both on principle and on authority, that there may be a contract, the consideration for which is the making of some other contract. "If you will make such and such a contract, I will give you one hundred pounds", is, in every sense of the word, a complete legal contract. It is collateral in the main contract, but each has an independent existence and they do not differ in respect of their possession to the full character and status of a contract. But such collateral contracts must, from their very nature, be rare. The effect of a collateral contract, such as that which I have instanced, would be to increase the consideration of the main contract by £100 and the more natural and usual way of carrying this out, would be by so modifying the main contract, and not by executing a concurrent and collateral contract. Such collateral contracts, the sole effect of which is to vary or add to the terms of the principal contract, are therefore viewed with suspicion by the law. They must be proved strictly. Not only the terms of such contracts, but the existence of an animus contrahendi on the part of all the parties to them, must be clearly shown. Any laxity on these points would enable parties to escape from the full performance of the obligations of contracts unquestionably entered into by them and, more especially, would have the effect of lessening the authority of written contracts by making it possible to vary them by suggesting the existence of verbal collateral agreements relating to the same subject matter.

There is, in the present case, an entire absence of any evidence to support the existence of such a collateral contract. The statement of Mr Johnston, in answer to the plaintiff's question, was beyond controversy, a mere statement of fact, for it was in reply to a question for information and nothing more. No doubt it was a representation as to fact and, indeed, it was the actual representation upon which the main case of the plaintiff rested. It was this representation which he alleged to have been false and fraudulent and which, he alleged, induced him to enter into the contracts and take the shares. There is no suggestion throughout the whole of his evidence that he regarded it as anything but a representation. Neither the plaintiff, nor the defendants, were asked any question, or gave any evidence, tending to show the existence of any animus contrahendi, other than as regards the main contracts. The whole case for the existence of a collateral contract therefore rests on the mere fact that the statement was made as to the character of the company, and if this is to be treated as evidence sufficient to establish the existence of a collateral contract of the kind alleged, the same result must follow with regard to any other statement relating to the subject matter of a contract made by a contracting party prior to its execution. This would negate entirely the firmly established rule that an innocent representation gives no right to damages. It would amount to saying that the making of any representation prior to a contract relating to its subject matter is sufficient to establish the existence of a collateral contract that the statement is true and therefore to give a right to damages if such should not be the case.

In the history of English law we find many attempts to make persons responsible in damages by reason of innocent misrepresentations and, at times, it has seemed as though the attempts would succeed. On the Chancery side of the Court, the decisions favouring this view usually took the form of extending the scope of the action for deceit. There was a tendency to recognise the existence of what was sometimes called "legal fraud", ie that the making of an innocent statement of fact without reasonable grounds, or of one which was inconsistent with information which the person had received or had the means of obtaining, entailed the same legal consequences as making it fraudulently. Such a doctrine would make a man liable for forgetfulness or mistake or even for honestly interpreting the facts known to him or drawing conclusions from them in a way which the Court did not think to be legally warranted. The high-water mark of these decisions is to be found in the judgment pronounced by the Court of Appeal in the case of *Peek v Derry*, when they laid down that where a defendant has made a mis-statement of fact and the Court is of the opinion that he had no reasonable grounds for believing that it was true, he may be made liable in an action of deceit if it has materially tended to induce the plaintiff to do an act by which he has incurred damage. But on appeal to your Lordships' House, this decision was unanimously reversed and it was definitely laid down that, in order to establish a cause of action sounding in damages for misrepresentation, the statement must be fraudulent or what is equivalent thereto, must be made recklessly, not caring whether it be true or not. The opinions pronounced in your Lordships' House in that case, show that both in substance and in form the decision was, and was intended to be, a reaffirmation of the old common law doctrine that actual fraud was essential to an action for deceit and it finally settled the law that an innocent misrepresentation gives no right of action sounding in damages.

On the Common Law side of the Court, the attempts to make a person liable for an innocent misrepresentation have usually taken the form of attempts to extend the doctrine of warranty beyond its just limits and to find that a warranty existed in cases where there was nothing more than an innocent misrepresentation. The present case is, in my opinion, an instance of this. But in respect of the question of the existence of a warranty, the Courts have had the advantage of an admirable enunciation of the true principle of law which was made in very early days by Holt CJ with respect to the contract of sale. He says: "An affirmative at the time of the sale is a warranty, provided it appears on evidence to be so intended." So far as decisions are concerned, this has, on the whole, been consistently followed in the courts of Common Law. But, from time to time, there have been dicta inconsistent with it which have, unfortunately, found their way into text books and have given rise to confusion and uncertainty in this branch of the law. For example, one often sees quoted the dictum of Bayley J in *Cave v Coleman*, where, in respect of a representation made verbally during the sale of a horse, he says that "being made in the course of dealing, and before the bargain was completed, it amounted to a warranty" – a proposition that is far too sweeping and cannot be supported. A still more serious deviation from the correct principle is to be found in a passage in the judgment of the Court of Appeal in *De Lassalle* v *Guildford* which was cited to us in the argument in the present case. In discussing the question whether a representation amounts to a warranty or not, the judgment says:

> "In determining whether it was so intended, a decisive test is whether the vendor assumes to assert a fact of which the buyer is ignorant, or merely states an opinion or judgment upon a matter of which the vendor has no special knowledge, and on which the buyer may be expected also to have an opinion and to exercise his judgment."

With all deference to the authority of the Court that decided that case, the proposition which it thus formulates cannot be supported. It is clear that the Court did not intend to depart from the law laid down by Holt CJ and cited above, for, in the same judgment, that dictum is referred to and accepted as a correct statement to the law. It is therefore evident that the use of the phrase "decisive test" cannot be defended. Otherwise it would be the duty of a judge to direct a jury that if a vendor states a fact of which the buyer is ignorant, they must, as a matter of law, find the existence of a warranty, whether or not the totality of the evidence shows that the parties intended the affirmation to form part of the contract; and this would be inconsistent with the law as laid down by Holt CJ. It may well be that the features thus referred to in the judgment of the Court of Appeal in that case, may be criteria of value in guiding a jury in coming to a decision whether or not a warranty was intended; but they cannot be said to furnish decisive tests, because it cannot be said, as a matter of law, that the presence or absence of those features is conclusive of the intention of the parties. The intention of the parties can only be deduced from the totality of the evidence and no secondary principles of such a kind can be universally true.

It is, my Lords, of the greatest importance, in my opinion, that this House should maintain, in its full integrity, the principle that a peson is not liable in damages for an innocent misrepresentation, no matter in what way or under what form the attack is made. In the present case, the statement was made in answer to an enquiry for information. There is nothing which can, by any possibility, be taken as evidence of an intention on the part of either or both of the parties that there should be a contractual liability in respect of the accuracy of the statement. It is a representation as to a specific thing and nothing more. The judge, therfore, ought not to have left the question of warranty to the jury and if, as a matter of prudence, he did so in order to obtain their opinion in case of appeal, he ought then to have entered judgment for the defendants, notwithstanding the verdict.'

Hong Kong Fir Shipping Co Ltd v *Kawasaki Kisan Kaisha Ltd* [1962] 2 WLR 474
Court of Appeal (Sellers, Upjohn and Diplock LJJ)

Charter – vessel breakdowns

Facts
The defendants chartered the vessel 'Hong Kong Fir' from the plaintiffs for 24 months; the charter party provided 'she being fitted in every way for ordinary cargo service'. It transpired that the engine room staff were incompetent and the vessel spent less than nine weeks of the first seven months of the charter at sea because of breakdowns and consequent repairs required to make her seaworthy. The defendants repudiated the charter party and claimed that the term as to seaworthiness was a condition of the contract, any breach of which entitled them so to do.

Held
The term was neither a condition nor a warranty and in determining whether the defendants could terminate the contract, it was necessary to look at the consequences of the breach to see if they deprived the innocent party of substantially the whole benefit he should have received under the contract. On the facts, this was not the case, because the charter party still had a substantial time to run.

Diplock LJ:

'No doubt there are many simple contractual undertakings, sometimes express but more often, because of their very simplicity ("It goes without saying"), to be implied, of which it can be predicted that every breach of such an undertaking must give rise to an event which will deprive the party not in default of substantialy the whole benefit which it was intended that he should obtain from the contract. And such a stipulation, unless the parties have agreed that breach of it shall not entitle the non-defaulting party to treat the contract as repudiated, is a "condition". So too, there may be other simple contractual undertakings of which it can be predicted that *no* breach can give rise to an event which will deprive the party not in default of substantially the whole benefit which it was intended that he should obtain from the contract; and such a stipulation, unless the parties have agreed that breach of it shall entitle the non-defaulting party to treat the contract as repudiated, is a "warranty".

There are, however, many contractual undertakings, of a more complex character which cannot be categorised as being "conditions" or "warranties" if the late nineteenth-century meaning adopted in the Sale of Goods Act 1893 and used by Bowen LJ in *Bentsen* v *Taylor Sons & Co* be given to those terms. Of such undertakings, all that can be predicted is that some breaches will, and others will not, give rise to an event which will deprive the party not in default of substantially the whole benefit which it was intended that he should obtain from the contract; and the legal consequences of a breach of such an undertaking, unless provided for expressly in the contract, depend upon the nature of the event to which the breach gives rise and do not follow automatically from a prior classification of the undertaking as a "condition" or a "warranty". For instance, to take Bramwell B's example in *Jackson* v *Union Marine Insurance Co Ltd* itself, breach of an undertaking by a shipowner to sail with all possible dispatch to a named port, does not necessarily relieve the charterer of further performance of his obligation under the charter party, but if the breach is so prolonged that the contemplated voyage is frustrated, it does have this effect.

In 1874, when the doctrine of frustration was being foaled by "impossibility of performance" out of "condition precedent", it is not surprising that the explanation given by Bramwell B should give full credit to the dam by suggesting that, in addition to the express warranty to sail with all possible dispatch, there was an implied *condition precedent* that the ship should arrive at the named port in time for the voyage contemplated. In *Jackson* v *Union Marine Insurance Co Ltd* there was no breach of the express warranty; but if there had been, to engraft the implied condition upon the express warranty would have been merely a more complicated way of saying that a breach of a shipowner's undertaking to sail with all possible dispatch may, but will not necessarily, give rise to an event which will deprive the charterer of substantially the whole benefit which it was intended that he should obtain from the charter. Now that the doctrine of frustration has matured and flourished for nearly a century, and the old technicalities of pleading "conditions precedent" are more than a century out of date, it does not clarify but, on the contrary, obscures the modern principle of law where such an event *has* occurred as a result of a breach of an express stipulation in a contract, to continue to add the now unnecessary colophon "Therefore it was an implied *condition* of the contract that a particular 'kind of breach' of an express *warranty* should not occur". The common law evolves not merely by breeding new principles but also, when they are fully grown, by burying their progenitors.

As my brethren have already pointed out, the shipowner's undertaking to tender a seaworthy ship has, as a result of numerous decisions as to what can amount to "unseaworthiness", become one of the most complex of contractual undertakings. It embraces obligations with respect to every part of the hull and machinery, stores and equipment, and the crew itself. It can be broken by the presence of trivial defects easily and rapidly remediable, as well as by defects which must inevitably result in a total loss of the vessel.

Consequently, the problem in this case is, in my view, neither solved nor soluble by debating whether the shipowner's express or implied undertaking to tender a seaworthy ship is a "condition" or a "warranty". It is like so many other contractual terms; an undertaking, one breach of which may give rise to an event which relieves the charterer of further performance of his undertakings if he so elects, and another breach of which may not give rise to such an event but entitle him only to monetary compensation in the form of damages. It is, with all deference to Mr Ashton Roskill's skilful argument, by no means surprising that among the many hundreds of previous cases about the shipowner's undertaking to deliver a seaworthy ship, there is none where it was found profitable to discuss in the judgments the question whether that undertaking is a "condition" or a "warranty"; for the true answer, as I have already indicated, is that it is neither, but one of that large class of contractual undertakings, one breach of which may have the same effect as that ascribed to a breach of "condition" under the Sale of Goods Act 1893 and a different breach of which may have only the same effect as that ascribed to a breach of "warranty" under that Act. The cases referred to by Sellers LJ illustrate this and I would only add that in the dictum which he cites from *Kish* v *Taylor* it seems to me, from the sentence which immediately follows it, as from the actual decision in the case, and the whole tenor of Lord Atkinson's speech itself, that the word "will" was intended to be "may".'

Commentary

Applied in *Decro-Wall International SA* v *Practitioners in Marketing Ltd* [1971] 1 WLR 361.

Liverpool City Council v *Irwin* [1976] 2 WLR 562 House of Lords (Lord Wilberforce, Lord Cross of Chelsea, Lord Salmon, Lord Edmund Davies and Lord Fraser of Tullybelton)

Landlord and tenant – covenant implied?

Facts

The council owned a tower block containing some 70 dwelling units, access to which was by a common staircase and two lifts. Mr and Mrs Irwin were tenants of one unit: their tenancy agreement imposed certain obligations on them, but none on the council. Over the years the condition of the block deteriorated; there were defects in the stairs and lifts and internal rubbish chutes became blocked. The Irwins alleged, inter alia, a breach on the part of the council of its implied covenant for their quiet enjoyment of the property.

Held

Such a covenant was to be implied but, on the facts, the council had not been in breach of it.

Lord Wilberforce:

'The court here is simply concerned to establish what the contract is, the parties not having themselves fully stated the terms. In this sense the court is searching for what must be implied.

What then should this contract be held to be? There must first be implied a letting, ie a grant of the right of exclusive possession to the tenants. With this there must, I would suppose, be implied a covenant for quiet enjoyment, as a necessary incident of the letting. The difficulty begins when we consider the common parts ...

There can be no doubt that there must be implied (i) an easement for the tenants and their licensees to use the stairs, (ii) a right in the nature of an easement to use the lifts and (iii) an easement to use the rubbish chutes.

But are these easements to be accompanied by any obligation on the landlord, and what obligation?

My Lords, ... it is necessary to define what test is to be applied, and I do not find this difficult. In my opinion such obligation should be read into the contract as the nature of the contract iself implicitly requires, no more, no less; a test in other words of necessity. The relationship accepted by the corporation is that of landlord and tenant; the tenant accepts obligations accordingly, in relation, inter alia, to the stairs, the lifts and the chutes. All these are not just facilities, or conveniences provided at discretion; they are essentials of the tenancy without which life in the dwellings, as a tenant, is not possible. To leave the landlord free of contractual obligation as regards these matters, and subject only to administrative or political pressure, is, in my opinion, totally inconsistent with the nature of this relationship. The subject matter of the lease (high-rise blocks) and the relationship created by the tenancy demands, of its nature, some contractual obligation on the landlord ...

It remains to define the standard. My Lords, if, as I think, the test of the existence of the term is necessity the standard must surely not exceed what is necessary having regard to the circumstances. To imply an absolute obligation to repair would go beyond what is a necessary legal incident and would indeed be unreasonable. An obligation to take reasonable care to keep in reasonable repair and usability is what fits the requirements of the case. Such a definition involves – and I think rightly – recognition that the tenants themselves have their responsibilities. What it is reasonable to expect of a landlord has a clear relation to what a reasonable set of tenants should do for themselves ...

I would hold therefore that the corporation's obligatioin is as I have described. And in agreement, I believe, with your Lordships, I would hold that it has not been shown in this case that there was any breach of that obligation.'

Lombard North Central plc v *Butterworth*

See Chapter 25.

London Export Corpn Ltd v *Jubilee Coffee Roasting Co Ltd* [1958] 1 WLR 661
Court of Appeal (Jenkins, Parker and Pearce LJJ)

Incorporation of custom

Facts
An association's rules provided, inter alia, that an umpire who had made an award at an arbitration should not be a member of the board of appeal hearing an appeal from his decision. After hearing the parties, the board asked the umpire to join them while they deliberated on their decision: such attendance was customary in the trade.

Held
The board's ultimate decision had been rightly set aside.

Jenkins LJ:

'It appears to me, when all have been looked at, that the relevant principle or law cannot be stated with any greater precision than this: That an alleged custom can be incorporated into a contract only if there is nothing in the express or necessarily implied terms of the contract to prevent such inclusion and, further, that a custom will only be imported into a contract where it can be so imported consistently with the tenor of the document as a whole.'

Luxor (Eastbourne) Ltd v *Cooper* [1941] AC 108 House of Lords (Viscount Simon LC, Lord Thankerton, Lord Russell of Killowen, Lord Wright and Lord Romer)

Estate agent's commission – implied term?

Facts
Wishing to dispose of two cinemas, the appellants agreed to pay the respondent commission on completion of the sales. Although the respondent introduced a willing and able purchaser, the appellants

decided that they would not proceed with the transactions. The respondent claimed as damages for breach of contract the amount that he would have received by way of commission.

Held

He was not entitled to succeed.

Viscount Simon LC:

> 'I find it impossible to formulate with adequate precision the tests which should determine whether or not a "just excuse" exists for disregarding the alleged implied term, and this leads me to consider whether there really is any such implied term at all. The matter may be tested in this way. If such an implied term must be assumed, then this amounts to saying that, when the owner gives the agent the opportunity of earning commission on the express terms thus stated, the agent might have added: "From the moment that I produce a duly qualified offeror, you must give up all freedom of choice, and carry through the bargain, if you reasonably can, with my nominee." The vendor must reply: "Of course. That necessarily follows." However, I am by no means satisfied that the vendor would acquiesce in regarding the matter in this light. I doubt whether the agent is bound, generally speaking, to exercise any standard of diligence in looking for a possible purchaser. He is commonly described as "employed", but he is not "employed" in the sense in which a man is employed to paint a picture or to build a house, with the liability to pay damages for delay or want of skill. The owner is offering to the agent a reward if the agent's activity helps to bring about an actual sale, but that is no reason why the owner should not remain free to sell his property through other channels. The agent necessarily incurs certain risks, eg the risk that his nominee cannot find the purchase price, or will not consent to terms reasonably proposed to be inserted in the contract of sale. I think that, upon the true construction of the express contract in this case, the agent also takes the risk of the owner not being willing to conclude the bargain with the agent's nominee. This last risk is ordinarily a slight one, for the owner's reason for approaching the agent is that he wants to sell.
>
> If it really were the common intention of owner and agent that the owner should be bound in the manner suggested, there would be no difficulty in so providing by an express term of the contract, but, in the absence of such an express term, I am unable to regard the suggested implied term as "necessary".'

Malcolm v Chancellor, Masters and Scholars of the University of Oxford (1990) The Times 23 March High Court (Gavin Lightman QC)

Terms of contract incomplete

Facts

The plaintiff had received from the defendant publishers an 'absolute commitment' to publish his book but they subsequently declined to do so. The plaintiff sought specific performance or damages for breach of contract.

Held

His action would be dismissed. With considerable regret, his Lordship came to the conclusion that no completed contract could be spelt out of what had passed between the parties: for example, how many copies were to be printed, in hardback or paperback or both, at what price and yielding what royalty? Too much was missing. In any case, his Lordship would not have regarded specific performance as a proper or practicable remedy in a case like the present, where close co-operation between author and publisher was clearly essential. Had he been able to find a binding contract to publish, his Lordship would have been minded to award substantial damages.

Maredelanto Compania Naviera SA v *Bergbau-Handel Gmbh, The Mihalis Angelos* see *Mihalis Angelos, The*

Mihalis Angelos, The [1970] 3 WLR 601 Court of Appeal (Lord Denning MR, Edmund Davies and Megaw LJJ)

Charter – breach of condition

Facts

On 25 May 1965 the owners of the 'Mihalis Angelos' let the vessel to charterers for the voyage from Haiphong, Vietnam, to Hamburg, the vessel being 'expected ready to load under the charter about 1 July 1965'. At the time the charter was made, she was on her way to Hong Kong to discharge and to be surveyed, and she only completed discharging on 23 July. It was found as a fact that the owners had no reasonable grounds for believing her to be ready to load about 1 July.

Held

Law and practice had established that an 'expected ready to load' clause was a condition, any breach of which gave the charterer the right to terminate the contract.

Lord Denning MR:

'The contest resolved itself simply into this: was the "expected ready to load" clause a condition, such that for breach of it the charterers could throw up the charter? Or was it a mere warranty, such as to give rise to damages if it was broken but not a right to cancel, seeing that cancellation was expressly dealt with in the cancelling clause? Sir Frederick Pollock divided the terms of the contract into two categories, conditions and warranties. The difference between them was this: if the promisor broke a *condition* in *any* respect, however slight, it gave the other party a right to be quit of his future obligations and to sue for damages, unless he, by his conduct, waived the condition, in which case he was bound to perform his future obligations but could sue for the damage he suffered. If the promisor broke a *warranty* in *any* respect, however serious, the other party was not quit of his future obligations. He had to perform them. His only remedy was to sue for damages.

This division was adopted by Sir MacKenzie Chalmers when he drafted the Sale of Goods Act and by Parliament when it passed it. It was stated by Fletcher Moulton LJ, in his celebrated dissenting judgment in *Wallis, Son & Wells* v *Pratt & Haynes*, which was adopted in its entirety by the House of Lords. It would be a mistake, however, to look on that division as exhaustive. There are many terms of many contracts which cannot be fitted into either category. In such cases, the courts, for nigh on 200 years, have not asked themselves: was the term a condition or a warranty? But rather was the breach such as to go to the root of the contract? If it was, then the other party is entitled, at his election, to treat himself as discharged from any further performance. That is made clear by the judgment of Lord Mansfield in *Boone* v *Eyre* and by the speech of Lord Blackburn in *Mersey Steel and Iron Co* v *Naylor, Benzon & Co* and the notes to *Cutter* v *Powell*. *Hong Kong Fir Shipping Co Ltd* v *Kawasaki Kisen Kaisha Ltd* is a useful reminder of this large category.

Although this large category exists, there is still remaining a considerable body of law by which certain stipulations have been classified as "conditions" so that any failure to perform, however slight, entitles the other to treat himself as discharged. Thus a statement in a charter party on 19 October 1860 that the ship is "now in the port of Amsterdam" was held to be a "condition". On that date she was just outside Amsterdam and could not get in owing to strong gales; but she got in a day or two later when the gales abated. The Court of Exchequer Chamber held that the charterer was entitled to call off the charter; see *Behn* v *Burness*, overruling the Court of Exchequer.

The question in this case is whether the statement by the owner, "expected ready to load under this charter about 1 July 1965" is likewise a "condition". The meaning of such a clause is settled by a decision of this court. It is an assurance by the owner that he honestly expects that the vessel will be ready to load on that date and that his expectation is based on reasonable grounds: see *Samuel Sanday & Co* v *Keighley, Maxted & Co*. The clause with that meaning has been held in this court to be a "condition", which, if not fulfilled, entitled the other party to treat himself as discharged; see *Finnish Government (Ministry of Food)* v *H V Ford & Co Ltd*. Those were sale of goods cases; but I think that the clause should receive the same interpretation in charter party cases. It seems to me that if the owner of a ship, or his agent, states in a charter that she is "expected ready to load about 1 July 1965", he is making a representation as to his own state of mind, ie of what he himself expects; and what is more, he puts it in the contract as a term of it, binding himself to its truth. If he or his agent breaks that term by making the statement without any honest belief in the truth, or without any reasonable grounds for it, he must take the consequences. It is, at lowest, a misrepresentation, which entitles the other party to rescind and, at highest, a breach of contract, which goes to the root of the matter. The charterer who is misled by the statement is entitled, on discovering its falsity, to throw up the charter. It may therefore properly be described as a "condition". I am confirmed in this view by the illustration given by Scrutton LJ himself in all the editions of his work on charter parties:

> "A ship was chartered 'expected to be at X about the 15 December ... shall with all convenient speed sail to X'. The ship was in fact then on such a voyage that she could not complete it and be at X by 15 December. *Submitted*, that the charterer was entitled to throw up the charter."

I do not regard *Associated Portland Cement Manufacturers [1900] Ltd* v *Houlder Brothers & Co Ltd* as any authority to the contrary. The facts are too shortly reported for any guidance to be got from it.

I hold, therefore, that on 17 July 1965 the charterers were entitled to cancel the contract on the ground that the owners had broken the "expected ready to load" clause.'

Megaw LJ:

'In my judgment, such a term ought to be regarded as being a condition of the contract, in the old sense of the word "condition": that is, that when it has been broken, the other party can, if he wishes, by intimation to the party in breach, elect to be released from performance of his further obligations under the contract; and he can validly do so without having to establish that, on the facts of the particular case, the breach has produced serious consequences which can be treated as "going to the root of the contract" or as being "fundamental", or whatever other metaphor may be thought appropriate for a frustration case.'

Commentary
Applied in *Decro-Wall International SA* v *Practitioners in Marketing Ltd* [1971] 1 WLR 361.

Moorcock, The (1889) 14 PD 64 Court of Appeal (Lord Esher MR, Bowen and Fry LJJ)

Contract – implied term as to use of wharf

Facts
By agreement between the parties, the plaintiffs' vessel proceeded to the defendants' wharf to discharge and load a cargo. Both parties knew that when the tide ebbed a vessel at the wharf would be grounded. When the plaintiffs' ship was moored there, she took ground and, owing to inequalities in the river bed, sustained damage. Although the defendants had no legal control over the river bed, they could ascertain its state but they had not done so.

Held
The defendants were liable in respect of the damage suffered by the plaintiffs' vessel.

Lord Esher MR:

'Whether they can see the actual bottom of the river or not at low water is not, to my mind, the least material. Supposing at low water there were two feet of water always over the mud; it makes no difference that they cannot see the bottom. They can feel for the bottom by sounding, or in some similar way, and find out its condition with as much accuracy, may, with a great deal more accuracy, than if they could see it with their own eyes. When it is so easy to do this, and when, in order to earn money, business requires a ship to be brought alongside their wharf, in my opinion honesty of business requires, and we are bound to imply it, that the defendants have undertaken to see that the bottom of the river is reasonably fit for the purpose, or that they ought, at all events, take reasonable care to find out whether the bottom of the river is reasonably fit for the purpose for which they agree that their jetty should be used, and then if not, either procure it to be made reasonably fit for the purpose, or inform the persons with whom they have contracted that it is not so. That, I think, is the least that can be implied as the defendants' duty, and that is what I understand the learned judge has implied. He then goes on to say that, as a matter of fact, they did not take such reasonable measures in this case. I myself have not the least doubt in making this implication as part of the contract. I, therefore, have no doubt that the defendants broke the contract, and they are, therefore, liable to the plaintiffs for the injury which the vessel sustained.'

Commentary
See also *Associated Japanese Bank (International) Ltd v Crédit du Nord SA* [1988] 1 WLR 255.

Neilson v *Stewart* 1991 SLT 523 House of Lords (Lord Keith, Lord Brandon, Lord Ackner, Lord Oliver, Lord Jauncey)

Formation – uncertainty – severance

Facts
A sale of shares was agreed between seller and purchaser. The agreement included a loan repayment which was to be deferred for one year 'after which time repayment shall be negotiated to our mutual satisfaction'. The purchaser failed to complete the agreement and subsequently argued that the phrase in question rendered the whole agreement unenforceable by reason of uncertainty. The seller's argument was that there were two severable agreements, one for the sale of shares, which was enforceable, and one for the arrangements of the loan, which was not enforceable.

Held
The House of Lords held that in fact both parts of the agreement were enforceable. The parties did not apparently intend the loan to be fixed as to time and manner of payment, all loans were repayable on demand and it was not essential that interest should be payable. Any apparent ambiguities could thus be resolved. The seller's action for damages for breach of contract by the buyer was successful.

Commentary
As a Scottish case this was of general interest, but not necessarily a binding precedent for English contractual law. As now confirmed by the House of Lords, it is, of course, of more far-reaching significance

Oscar Chess Ltd v *Williams* [1957] 1 WLR 370 Court of Appeal (Denning, Hodson and Morris LJJ)

Age of car – condition or representation?

Facts

In May 1955, the defendant acquired a new car from the plaintiffs, who were motor car dealers and who took the defendant's Morris in part exchange. The defendant said it was a 1948 model, as per the registration document, and the plaintiffs made him an allowance of £290. The registration book had been altered by an unknown third party and the car was, in reality, a 1939 model worth £175. The County Court judge held that it was a condition of the contract that the car was a 1948 model.

Held (Morris LJ dissenting)

The defendant's statement as to the age of the car was a mere representation, not a term of the contract. He had no special knowledge as to its age and the plaintiffs knew that he was relying on the date in the registration book. Therefore the defendant was not liable.

Denning LJ:

> 'I entirely agree with the judge that both parties assumed that the Morris was a 1948 model and that this assumption was fundamental to the contract. But this does not prove that the representation was a term of the contract. The assumption was based by both of them on the date given in the registration book as the date of first registration. They both believed it was a 1948 model when it was only a 1939 one. They were both mistaken and their mistake was of fundamental importance.
>
> The effect of such a mistake is this: It does not make the contract a nullity from the beginning, but it does, in some circumstances, enable the contract to be set aside in equity. If the buyer had come promptly, he might have succeeded in getting the whole transaction set aside in equity on the ground of this mistake: see *Solle* v *Butcher*; but he did not do so and it is too late for him to do it: see *Leaf* v *International Galleries*. His only remedy is in damages and, to recover these, he must prove a warranty.
>
> In saying that he must prove a warranty, I used the word "warranty" in its ordinary English meaning to denote a binding promise. Everyone knows what a man means when he says "I guarantee it" or "I warrant it" or "I give you my word on it". He means that he binds himself to it. That is the meaning it has borne in English Law for 300 years, from the leading case of *Chandelor* v *Lopus* (1603) Cro Jac 4 onwards. During the last fifty years, however, some lawyers have come to use the word "warranty" in another sense. They use it to denote a subsidiary term in contract, as distinct from a vital term, which they call a "condition". In so doing, they depart from the ordinary meaning, not only of the word "warranty" but also of the word "condition". There is no harm in their doing this, so long as they confine this technical use to its proper sphere, namely to distinguish between a vital term, the breach of which gives the right to treat the contract as at an end, and a subsidiary term which does not. But the trouble comes when one person uses the word "warranty" in its ordinary meaning and another uses it in its technical meaning. When Holt CJ in *Crosse* v *Gardner* (1689) Carth 90 (as glossed by Buller J in *Pasley* v *Freeman* (1789) 3 Term Rep 51, 57) and *Medina* v *Stoughton* (1700) 1 Salk 210 made his famous ruling that an affirmation at the time of a sale is a warranty, provided it appears on evidence to be so intended, he used the word "warranty" in its ordinary English meaning of a binding promise: and when Lord Haldane LC and Lord Moulton in 1913 in *Heilbut, Symons & Co* v *Buckleton* adopted his ruling, they used it likewise in its ordinary meaning. These different uses of the word seem to have been the source of confusion in the present case. The judge did not ask himself, "Was the representation (that it was a 1948 Morris) intended to be a warranty?" He asked himself "Was it fundamental to the contract?" He answered it by saying that it was fundamental; and therefore it was a condition and not a warranty. By concentrating on whether it was fundamental, he seems to me to have missed the crucial point in the case, which is whether it was a term of the contract at all. The crucial question is: was it a binding promise or only an innocent misrepresentation? The technical distinction between a "condition" and a "warranty" is quite immaterial in this case, because it is far too late for the buyer to reject the car. He can, at best, only claim damages. The material distinction here is between a statement which is a term of the contract and a statement which is only an innocent misrepresentation. This distinction is best expressed by the ruling of Lord Holt: Was it intended as a warranty or not? Using the word "warranty" there in its ordinary English

meaning: because it gives the exact shade of meaning that is required. It is something to which a man must be taken to bind himself.

In applying Lord Holt's test, however, some misunderstanding has arisen by the use of the word "intended". It is sometimes supposed that the tribunal must look into the minds of the parties to see what they themselves intended. That is a mistake. Lord Moulton made it quite clear that "the intention of the parties can only be deduced from the totality of the evidence". The question whether a warranty was intended depends on the conduct of the parties, on their words and behaviour, rather than on their thoughts. If an intelligent bystander would reasonably infer that a warranty was intended, that will suffice. And this, when the facts are not in dispute, is a question of law. That is shown by *Heilbut, Symons & Co* v *Buckleton* itself, where the House of Lords upset the finding by a jury of a warranty.

It is instructive to take some recent instances to show how the courts have approached this question. When the seller states a fact which is or should be within his own knowledge and of which the buyer is ignorant, intending that the buyer should act on it and he does so, it is easy to infer a warranty: see *Couchman* v *Hill*, where the farmer stated that the heifer was served, and *Harling* v *Eddy*, where he stated that there was nothing wrong with her. So also, if he makes a promise about something which is or should be within his own control: see *Birch* v *Paramount Estates Ltd* [1958] 167 EG 396, decided on 2 October 1956, in this court, where the seller stated that the house would be as good as the show house. But if the seller, when he states a fact, makes it clear that he has no knowledge of his own, but has got his information elsewhere and is merely passing it on, it is not so easy to imply a warranty. Such a case was *Routledge* v *McKay* [1954] 1 WLR 615, 636, where the seller "stated that it was a 1942 model and pointed to the corroboration found in the book", and it was held that there was no warranty.

Turning now to the present case; much depends on the precise words that were used. If the seller says "I believe it is a 1948 Morris, here is the registration book to prove it", there is clearly no warranty. It is a statement of belief, not a contractual promise. But if the seller says "I guarantee that is a 1948 Morris. This is borne out by the registration book, but you need not rely solely on that. I give you my own guarantee that it is ", there is clearly a warranty. The seller is making himself contractually responsible, even though the registration book is wrong.

In this case, much reliance was placed by the judge on the fact that the buyer looked up *Glass's Guide* and paid £290 on the footing that it was a 1948 model: but that fact seems to me to be neutral. Both sides believed the car to have been made in 1948 and, in that belief, the buyer paid £290. That belief can be just as firmly based on the buyer's own inspection of the log book as on a contractual warranty by the seller.

Once that fact is put on one side, I ask myself: What is the proper inference from the known facts? It must have been obvious to both that the seller had himself no personal knowledge of the year when the car was made. He only became owner after a great number of changes. He must have been relying on the registration book. It is unlikely that such a person would warrant the year of manufacture. The most he could do would be to state his belief and then produce the registration book in verification of it. In these circumstances, the intelligent bystander would, I suggest, say that the seller did not intend to bind himself so as to warrant that it was a 1948 model. If the seller was asked to pledge himself to it, he would at once have said "I cannot do that. I have only the log book to go by, the same as you."

The judge seems to have thought that there was a difference between written contracts and oral contracts. He thought that the reason why the buyer failed in *Heilbut, Symons & Co* v *Buckleton* and *Routledge* v *McKay* was because the sales were afterwards recorded in writing and the written contracts contained no reference to the representation. I agree that that was an important factor in those cases. If an oral representation is afterwards recorded in writing, it is good evidence that it was intended as a warranty. If it is not put into writing, it is evidence against a warranty being intended. But it is by no means decisive. There have been many cases where the courts have found an oral warranty collateral to a written contract, such as *Birch* v *Paramount Estates*. But when the purchase is not recorded in writing at all, it must not be supposed that every representation made in the course of the dealing is to be treated as a warranty. The question then is still: Was it intended as a warranty? In the leading case of *Chandelor* v *Lopus* in 1603 a man, by word of mouth, sold a precious stone for £100 affirming it to be a bezar stone, whereas it was not. The declaration averred that the seller affirmed it to be a bezar stone, but did not aver that he warranted it to be so. The declaration was held to be ill because "the bare affirmation that it was a bezar stone, without warranting it to be so, is no cause of action". That has been the law from that day to this and it was emphatically reaffirmed by the House of Lords in *Heilbut, Symons & Co* v *Buckleton*.

One final word: It seems to me clear that the motor dealers who bought the car relied on the year stated in the log book. If they had wished to make sure of it, they could have checked it then and there by taking the engine number and chassis number and writing to the makers. They did not do so at the time, but only eight months later. They are experts and, not having made that check at the time, I do not think they should now be allowed to recover against the innocent seller, who produced to them all the evidence he had, namely the registration book. I agree that it is hard on the dealers to have paid more than the car is worth: but it would be equally hard on the seller to make him pay the difference. He would never have bought the Hillman at all unless he had got the allowance of £290 from the Morris. The best course in all these cases would be to "shunt" the difference down the train of innocent sellers until one reaches the rogue who perpetrated the fraud: but he can rarely be traced or, if he can, he rarely has the money to pay the damages. So one is left to decide between a number of innocent people who is to bear the loss. That can only be done by applying the law about representations and warranties as we know it: and that is what I have tried to do. If the rogue can be traced, he can be sued by whomsoever has suffered the loss: but if he cannot be traced, the loss must lie where it falls. It should not be inflicted on innocent sellers, who sold the car many months, perhaps many years, before and have forgotten all about it and have conducted their affairs on the basis that the transaction was concluded. Such a seller would not be able to recollect, after all this length of time, the exact words he used, such as whether he said "I believe it is a 1948 model", or "I warrant it is a 1948 model". The right course is to let the buyer set aside the transaction if he finds out the mistake quickly and comes promptly, before other interests have irretrievably intervened; otherwise the loss must lie where it falls: and that is, I think, the course prescribed by law. I would allow this appeal accordingly.'

Commentary
Applied: *Routledge* v *McKay* [1954] 1 WLR 615. Distinguished in *Bentley (Dick) Productions Ltd* v *Harold Smith (Motors) Ltd* [1965] 1 WLR 623.

Prenn v *Simmonds* [1971] 1 WLR 1381 House of Lords (Lord Reid, Lord Donovan, Lord Wilberforce, Lord Pearson and Lord Diplock)

Contract – construction

Facts
Following detailed negotiations, agreement was reached for the sale and purchase of shares if 'profits' reached a certain level. Did this refer to profits of the group or just of the holding company?

Held
In the light of the aim of the agreement and commercial good sense, the reference to 'profits' was to the consolidated profits of the group.

Lord Wilberforce:

'There were prolonged negotiations between solicitors, with exchanges of draft clauses, ultimately emerging in ... the agreement. The reason for not admitting evidence of these exchanges is not a technical one or even mainly one of convenience ... It is simply that such evidence is unhelpful. By the nature of things, where negotiations are difficult, the parties' positions, with each passing letter, are changing and until the final agreement, although converging, still divergent. It is only the final document which records a consensus. If the previous documents use different expressions, how does construction of those expressions, itself a doubtful process, help on the construction of the contractual words? If the same expressions are used, nothing is gained by looking back; indeed, something may be lost since the relevant surrounding circumstances may be different. And at this stage there is no consensus of the parties to appeal to. It may be said that previous documents may be looked at to explain the aims of the parties. In a limited sense this is true; the commercial, or business object, of the transaction, objectively ascertained, may be a surrounding fact ... And if it can be shown that one interpretation completely frustrates that object, to the extent of rendering the contract futile, that may be a strong argument for an alternative interpretation, if that can reasonably be found. But beyond that it may be difficult to go; it may be a matter of degree, or of judgment, how far one interpretation, or another, gives effect to a common intention; the parties, indeed, may be pursuing that intention with differing emphasis, and hoping to achieve it to an extent which may differ, and in different ways. The words used may, and often do, represent a formula which means different things to each side, yet may be accepted because that is the only way to get "agreement" and in the hope that disputes will not arise. The only course then can be to try to ascertain the "natural" meaning. Far more, and indeed totally, dangerous it is to admit evidence of one party's objective – even if this is known to the other party. However strongly pursued this may be, the other party may only be willing to give it partial recognition, and in a world of give and take, men often have to be satisfied with less than they want. So, again, it would be a matter of speculation how far the common intention was that the particular objective should be realised ... In my opinion, then, evidence of negotiations, or of the parties' intentions ... ought not to be received, and evidence should be restricted to evidence of the factual background known to the parties at or before the date of the contract, including evidence of the "genesis" and objectively the "aim" of the transaction.'

Reardon Smith Line Ltd v *Yngvar Hansen-Tangen* [1976] 1 WLR 989 House of Lords (Lord Wilberforce, Viscount Dilhorne, Lord Simon of Glaisdale, Lord Kilbrandon and Lord Russell of Killowen)

Charter – words of identification or contractual description?

Facts

In order to perform a charter, a steamship company nominated a vessel 'to be built by Osaka Shipbuilding Co Ltd and known as Hull No 354 until named'. Osaka was unable to build the ship in its own yard and so subcontracted the work to Oshima, a newly created company in which it held 50 per cent of the shares. Osaka provided a large part of Oshima's work force and managerial staff. In Osaka's books the ship was numbered 354; in Oshima's 004. Although the vessel when built complied fully with the physical specifications in the charter and was fit for the contemplated service, delivery was refused.

Held

The charterers were not entitled to refuse delivery.

Lord Wilberforce:

'The appellants sought, necessarily, to give to the ... provision in the ... charter contractual effect. They argued that these words formed part of the "description" of the future goods contracted to be provided, that, by analogy with contracts for the sale of goods, any departure from the description entitled the other party to reject, that there were departures in that the vessel was not built by Osaka and was not Hull No 354. I shall attempt to deal with each of these contentions.

In the first place, I am not prepared to accept that authorities as to "description" in sale of goods cases are to be extended, or applied, to such a contract as we have here. Some of these cases either in themselves (*Re Moore & Co and Landauer & Co*) or as they have been interpreted (eg *Behn* v *Burness*) I find to be excessively technical and due for fresh examination in this House. Even if a strict and technical view must be taken as regards the description of unascertained future goods (eg commodities) as to which each detail of the description must be assumed to be vital, it may be, and in my opinion is, right to treat other contracts of sale of goods in a similar manner to other contracts generally, so as to ask whether a particular item in a description constitutes a substantial ingredient of the "identity" of the thing sold, and only if it does to treat it as a condition ... It is one thing to say of given words that their purpose is to state (identify) an essential part of the description of the goods. It is another to say that they provide one party with a specific indication (identification) of the goods so that he can find them and if he wishes sub-dispose of them. The appellants wish to say of words which "identify" the goods in the second sense, that they describe them in the first. I have already given reasons why I can only read the words in the second sense. The difference is vital. If the words are read in the first sense, then, unless I am right in the legal argument above, each element in them has to be given contractual force. The vessel must, as a matter of contract, and as an essential term, be built by Osaka and must bear their yard number 354; if not, the description is not complied with and the vessel tendered is not that contracted for. If in the second sense, the only question is whether the words provide a means of identifying the vessel. If they fairly do this, they have fulfilled their function ...

So the question becomes simply whether, as a matter of fact, it can fairly be said that – as a means of identification – the vessel was ... "built by Osaka Shipping Co Ltd and known as Hull No 354, until named". To answer this, regard may be had to the actual arrangements for building the vessel and numbering it before named. My Lords, I have no doubt ... that an affirmative answer must be given. I shall not set out the evidence which clearly makes this good. The fact is that the vessel always was Osaka Hull No 354 – though also Oshima No 004 – and equally it can fairly be said to have been "built" by Osaka as the company which planned, organised and directed the building and contractually engaged ... to build it, though also it could be said to have been built by Oshima. For the purpose of the identificatory clause, the words used are quite sufficient to cover the facts. No other vessel could be referred to: the reference fits the vessel in question.

There are other facts not to be overlooked. (1) So long as the charterers could identify the nominated vessel they had not the slightest interest in whatever contracting or sub-contracting arrangements were made in the course of the building ... (2) In making the arrangements they did for building the vessel, Osaka acted in a perfectly straightforward and open manner. They cannot be said to be substituting one vessel for another; they have not provided any ground on which the charterers can claim that their bargain has not been fulfilled. The contracts all down the chain were closely and appropriately knitted into what Osaka did. (3) If the market had risen instead of falling, it would have been quite impossible for Osaka ... to refuse to tender the vessel in accordance with the charters on the ground that it did not correspond with that contracted for. No more on a falling market is there, in my opinion, any ground on which the charterers can reject the vessel. In the end I find this a simple and clear case.'

Commentary
See also *Staffordshire Area Health Authority* v *South Staffordshire Waterworks Co* [1978] 1 WLR 1387.

Reigate v *Union Manufacturing Co (Ramsbottom) Ltd* [1918] 1 KB 592 Court of Appeal (Pickford, Bankes and Scrutton LJJ)

Agency – right of principal to terminate

Facts
The defendants appointed the plaintiff sole agent for the sale of certain goods for an initial period of seven years. During that period the defendants became insolvent, went into voluntary liquidation and ceased to carry on business. The plaintiff claimed damages for breach of contract.

Held
He was entitled to succeed.

Scrutton LJ:

'I think these principles have been clearly established. Before you consider what has been decided in other cases, the first thing is to see what the parties have agreed to in the case under consideration; and, secondly, before troubling about seeing what you are to imply into the contract, the first thing is to see what the parties have expressed in the contract; and, when you have understood what the parties have expressed in the words there used, you are not to add implications because you think it would have been a reasonable thing to have put in the contract, or because you think you would have insisted on such a term being in the contract. You must only imply a term if it is necessary in the business sense to give efficacy to the contract – that is, if it is such a term that you can be confident that if at the time the contract was being negotiated someone had said to the parties: "What will happen in such a case?" they would have both replied, "Of course, so and so. We did not trouble to say that: it is too clear"' Unless you can come to some such conclusion as that, we ought not to imply a term which the parties themselves have not expressed when they have expressed other terms ... As I understand, it is suggested that the contract is only to remain in force so long as the company carry on their business. Is that a necessary implication? Supposing that the parties had been asked this: "You have not said so, but I suppose if the company ceases to carry on business this contract is at an end," would they both have said, "Yes, of course"? I should be very much surprised if they would. I expect they would immediately have found that they disagreed as to what the position was; and, unless I am satisfied that it is a necessary implication which must have been in the minds of both of them, I have no business to imply a term which they themselves have not expressed, particularly when I find they have thought sufficiently about the matter to express the conditions on which the agreement was to be determined – first, the obvious one that it was to be determined if the agent died; secondly, they assumed it might be determined after seven years if a particular notice was given. For these reasons I find an express condition that the contract is to continue for seven years, subject to the company refusing orders that they had reasonable ground to refuse, and no ground for implying a term that the seven years shall be subject to the implied condition that the company is carrying on business.'

Richco International Ltd v *Bunge and Co Ltd* [1991] 2 Lloyd's Rep 93 Queen's Bench Division (Phillips J)

Construction of terms – contracts in a string

Facts
Several contracts were negotiated in string. Among the clauses were conditions as to ports of shipment and loading arrangements. The charterers sought to interpret clauses differently in certain aspects of the contract.

Held
Where contracts are in a string, exactly the same meaning must be given to clauses in contracts throughout the chain. The same weighting should also be given to the importance (or lack of it) of similar clauses.

Sagar v *H Ridehalgh & Son Ltd* [1931] 1 Ch 310 Court of Appeal (Lord Hanworth MR, Lawrence and Romer LJJ)

Wages – deduction for bad work

Facts
The plaintiff weaver was employed by the defendants and trade union wage rates were incorporated in the contract of employment. For more than thirty years, the defendants had made reasonable deductions

for bad work and most other mills did the same. For bad work the defendants deducted one shilling from the plaintiff's pay.

Held
They were entitled to do so.

Lawrence LJ:

> 'The employers based their contention on two alternative grounds, either that the established practice of making reasonable deductions for bad work in the defendants' mill was incorporated into the plaintiff's contract of service by reason of his having agreed to be employed upon the same terms as the other weavers in that mill or else that the general usage of making reasonable deductions for bad work prevailing in the cotton weaving trade of Lancashire was so well known and understood that every weaver engaging in that trade must be taken to have entered upon his employment on the footing of that usage.
>
> As regards the first of these grounds. It is clearly established by the evidence ... that the practice of making reasonable deductions for bad work has continuously prevailed at the defendants' mill for upwards of thirty years, and that during the whole of that time all weavers employed by the defendants have been treated alike in that respect. The practice was, therefore, firmly established at the defendants' mills when the plaintiff entered upon his employment there. Further, I think that it is clear that the plaintiff accepted employment in the defendant's mill on the same terms as the other weavers employed at that mill. I draw this inference not only from the statement of claim (as explained by the particulars) and from the plaintiff's own evidence, but also from the fact that this action is avowedly brought to test the legality of the practice prevailing at the defendants' mill and not to determine whether this particular plaintiff was employed upon some special terms which would make that practice inapplicable to his contract of service. Although I entirely agree with the learned judge in finding it difficult to believe that the plaintiff did not know of the existence of the practice at the mill, I think that it is immaterial whether he knew of it or not, as I am satisfied that he accepted his employment in the same terms as to deductions for bad work as the other weavers at the mill.
>
> In the result I have come to the conclusion that the practice of making reasonable deductions for bad work prevailing at the defendants' mill was incorporated in the plaintff's contract of service. Further, I am of opinion that the second ground is also established by the evidence, namely, that the practice in the defendants' mill is in accordance with the general usage of making reasonable deductions for bad work prevailing in the weaving trade of Lancashire, which usage in the absence of any stipulation to the contrary would be incorporated into every contract of service as a weaver in a Lancashire cotton mill without special mention.'

Schawel v *Reade* [1913] 2 Ir Rep 81 House of Lords (Lord Moulton, Lord Atkinson and Lord Macnaghten)

Sale of horse – warranty

Facts
The plaintiff, who required a stallion for stud purposes, went to the defendant's stables to look for a horse. While he was inspecting a horse the defendant said: 'You need not look for anything: the horse is perfectly sound. If there was anything the matter with the horse, I would tell you.' The plaintiff thereupon terminated his examination and a few days later a price was agreed upon. Three weeks later the plaintiff bought the horse. It was totally unfit for stud purposes. The judge left the following question to the jury: 'Did the defendant at the time of the sale represent to the plaintiff in order that the plaintiff might purchase the horse that the horse was fit for stud purposes and did the plaintiff act upon that representation in the purchase of the horse?' The issue before the House of Lords was whether the jury's affirmative answer amounted to a finding of a warranty.

Held
It did.

Lord Moulton:

> 'It would be impossible, in my mind, to have a clearer example of an express warranty where the word "warranty" was not used. The essence of such warranty is that it becomes plain by the words and action of the parties that it is intended that in the purchase the responsibility of the soundness shall rest upon the vendor; and how in the world could a vendor more clearly indicate that he is prepared and intends to take upon himself the responsibility of the soundness than by saying: "You need not look at that horse, because it is perfectly sound," and sees that the purchaser thereupon desists from his immediate independent examination?'

Schuler (L) AG v *Wickman Machine Tool Sales Ltd* [1973] 2 WLR 683 House of Lords (Lord Reid, Lord Morris of Borth-y-Gest, Lord Wilberforce, Lord Simon of Glaisdale and Lord Kilbrandon)

Breach of 'condition' – right to terminate

Facts
The respondents were the exclusive selling agents in the UK for the appellants' presses. The agency agreement provided:

> 'It shall be a condition of this agreement that (the respondent) shall send its representative to visit (the six largest UK motor manufacturers) at least once every week.'

The respondents committed some minor breaches of this term and the appellants terminated the agreement, claiming that by reason of the term being a condition, they were entitled so to do.

Held (Lord Wilberforce dissenting)
The parties could not have intended that the appellants should have the right to terminate the agreement if the respondents failed to make one of the obliged number of visits which, in total, amounted to nearly 1,500. A provision elsewhere in the agreement gave the appellants the right to determine the agreement if the respondents committed a 'material' breach: this indicated that the parties had not intended to use the word 'condition' in its technical sense.

Lord Reid:

> 'Schuler maintain that the word "condition" has now acquired a precise legal meaning; that particularly since the enactment of the Sale of Goods Act 1893, its recognised meaning in English law is a term of a contract any breach of which by one party gives to the other party an immediate right to rescind the whole contract. Undoubtedly the word is frequently used in that sense. There may, indeed be some presumption that in a formal legal document it has that meaning. But it is frequently used with a less stringent meaning. One is familiar with printed "conditions of sale" incorporated into a contract, and with the words "for conditions see back" printed on a ticket. This simply means that the "conditions" are terms of the contract.
>
> In the ordinary use of the English language "condition" has many meanings, some of which have nothing to do with agreements. In connection with an agreement, it may mean a pre-condition: something which must happen or be done before the agreement can take effect. Or it may mean some state of affairs which must continue to exist if the agreement is to remain in force. The legal meaning on which Schuler rely is, I think, one which would not occur to a layman; a condition in that sense is not something which has an automatic effect. It is a term, the breach of which by one party gives to the other an option either to terminate the contract or to let the contract proceed and, if he so desires, sue for damages for the breach.
>
> Sometimes a breach of a term gives that option to the aggrieved party because it is of a fundamental

character going to the root of the contract, sometimes it gives that option because the parties have chosen to stipulate that it shall have that effect. Blackburn J said in *Bettini* v *Gye*:

> "Parties may think some matter, apparently of very little importance, essential; and if they sufficiently express an intention to make the literal fulfilment of such a thing a condition precedent, it will be one."

In the present case it is not contended that Wickman's failure to make visits amounted, in themselves, to fundamental breaches. What is contended is that the terms of clause 7 "sufficiently express an intention" to make any breach, however small, of the obligation to make visits a condition, so that any breach shall entitle Schuler to rescind the whole contract if they so desire.

Schuler maintain that the use of the word "condition" is, in itself, enough to establish this intention. No doubt some words used by lawyers do have a rigid inflexible meaning. But we must remember that we are seeking to discover intention as disclosed by the contract as a whole. Use of the word "condition" is an indication – even a strong indication – of such an intention, but it is by no means conclusive. The fact that a particular construction leads to a very unreasonable result must be a relevant consideration. The more unreasonable the result, the more unlikely it is that the parties can have intended it and if they do intend it, the more necessary it is that they shall make that intention abundantly clear.

Clause 7(b) requires that over a long period, each of the six firms shall be visited every week by one or other of two named representatives. It makes no provision for Wickman being entitled to substitute others, even on the death or retirement of one of the named representatives. Even if one could imply some rights to do this, it makes no provision for both representatives being ill during a particular week. And it makes no provision for the possibility that one or other of the firms may tell Wickman that they cannot receive Wickman's representative during a particular week. So if the parties gave any thought to the matter at all, they must have realised the probability that in a few cases out of the 1,400 required visits, a visit as stipulated would be impossible. But if Schuler's contention is right, failure to make even one visit entitles them to terminate the contract, however blameless Wickman might be. This is so unreasonable that it must make me search for some other possible meaning of the contract. If none can be found, then Wickman must suffer the consequences. But only if that is the only possible interpretation.

If I have to construe clause 7 standing by itself, then I do find difficulty in reaching any other interpretation. But if clause 7 must be read with clause 11, the difficulty disappears. The word "conditions" would make any breach of clause 7(b), however excusable, a material breach. That would then entitle Schuler to give notice under clause 11(a)(i), requiring the breach to be remedied. There would be no point in giving such a notice if Wickman were clearly not in fault, but if it were given, Wickman would have no difficulty in showing that the breach had been remedied. If Wickman were at fault, then on receiving such a notice, they would have to amend their system so that they could show that the breach had been remedied. If they did not do that within the period of the notice, then Schuler would be entitled to rescind.

In my view, that is a possible and reasonable construction of the contract and I would therefore adopt it. The contract is so obscure that I can have no confidence that this is its true meaning, but for the reasons which I have given, I think that it is the preferable construction. It follows that Schuler were not entitled to rescind the contract as they purported to do. So I would dismiss this appeal.'

Shell UK Ltd **v** ***Lostock Garage Ltd*** [1976] 1 WLR 1187 Court of Appeal (Lord Denning MR, Ormrod and Bridge LJJ)

Agreement for supply of petrol – implied term?

Facts

The defendants operated a garage and they entered into a solus agreement with the plaintiffs for the supply of petrol. After 20 years, there was a petrol price 'war': the plaintiffs introduced a support scheme of subsidies which they applied to two other of their garages in the neighbourhood, but not to the defendants. Erroneously believing that the tie to the plaintiffs had ended, the defendants obtained petrol from Mansfield at a lower cost. The plaintiffs threatened Mansfield with proceedings for inducing a breach of contract, so they (Mansfield) ceased supplying the defendants and they (the defendants) resumed taking supplies from the plaintiffs. In proceedings for damages and an injunction, the defendants argued that the solus agreement was subject to an implied term that the plaintiffs would not abnormally discriminate against the defendants so as to render their (the defendants') sales uneconomic.

Held (Bridge LJ dissenting)
This was not the case.

Lord Denning MR:

'Implied terms
It was submitted by counsel for Lostock that there was to be implied in the solus agreement a term that Shell, as the supplier, should not abnormally discriminate against the buyer and/or should supply petrol to the buyer on terms which did not abnormally discriminate against him. He said that Shell had broken that implied term by giving support to the two Shell garages and refusing it to Lostock; that, on that ground, Shell were in breach of the solus agreement; and that Lostock were entitled to terminate it.

This submission makes it necessary once again to consider the law as to implied terms. I ventured with some trepidation to suggest that terms implied by law could be brought within one comprehensive category, in which the courts could imply a term such as was just and reasonable in the circumstances: see *Greaves & Co (Contractors) Lrt* v *Baynham Meikle & Partner; Liverpool City Council* v *Irwin*. But, as I feared, the House of Lords have rejected it as quite unacceptable. As I read the speeches, there are two broad categories of implied terms.

(i) *The first category*
The first category comprehends all those relationships which are of common occurrence, such as the relationship of seller and buyer, owner and hirer, master and servant, landlord and tenant, carrier by land or by sea, contractor for building works, and so forth. In all those relationships the courts have imposed obligations on one party or the other, saying they are implied terms. These obligations are not founded on the intention of the parties, actual or presumed, but on more general considerations: see *Luxor (Eastbourne) Ltd* v *Cooper* per Lord Wright; *Lister* v *Romford Ice and Cold Storage Co* per Viscount Simonds and Lord Tucker (both of whom give interesting illustrations); *Liverpool City Council* v *Irwin* per Lord Cross of Chelsea and Lord Edmund-Davies. In such relationships the problem is not solved by asking: what did the parties intend? or, would they have unhesitatingly agreed to it, if asked? It is to be solved by asking; has the law already defined the obligation or the extent of it? If so, let it be followed. If not, look to see what would be reasonable in the general run of such cases (see per Lord Cross of Chelsea) and then say what the obligation shall be. The House in *Liverpool City Council* v *Irwin* went through that very process. They examined the existing law of landlord and tenant, in particular that relating to easements, to see if it contained the solution to the problem; and, having found that it did not, they imposed an obligation on the landlord to use reasonable care. In these relationships the parties can exclude or modify the obligation by express words, but unless they do so, the obligation is a legal incident of the relationship which is attached by the law itself and not by reason of any implied term.

Likewise, in the general law of contract, the legal effect of frustration does not depend on an implied term. It does not depend on the presumed intention of the parties, nor on what they would have answered, if asked, but simply on what the court iself declares to amount to a frustration: see *Davis Contractors* v *Fareham Urban District Council* per Lord Radcliffe.

(ii) *The second category*
The second category comprehends those cases which are not within the first category. These are cases, not of common occurrence, in which from the particular circumstances a term is to be implied. In these cases the implication is based on an intention imputed to the parties from their actual circumstances: see *Luxor (Eastbourne) Ltd* v *Cooper* per Lord Wright. Such an imputation is only to be made when it is necessary to imply a term to give efficacy to the contract and make it a workable agreement in such manner as the parties would clearly have done if they had applied their mind to the contingency which has arisen.

These are the "officous bystander" type of case: see *Lister* v *Romford Ice & Cold Storage Co* per Lord Tucker. In such cases a term is not to be implied on the ground that it would be reasonable, but only when it is necessary and can be formulated with a sufficient degree of precision. This was the test applied by the majority of this court in *Liverpool City Council* v *Irwin*; and they were emphatically upheld by the House on this point; see per Lord Cross of Chelsea and Lord Edmund Davies.

There is this point to be noted about *Liverpool City Council* v *Irwin*. In this court the argument was only about an implication in the second category. In the House of Lords that argument was not pursued. It was only the first category.

Into which of the two categories does the present case come? I am tempted to say that a solus agreement between supplier and buyer is of such common occurrence nowadays that it could be put into the first category; so that the law could imply a term based on general considerations. But I do not think this would be found acceptable. Nor do I think the case can be brought within the second category. If Shell had been asked at the beginning: "Will you agree not to discriminate abnormally against the buyer?" I think they would have declined. It might be a reasonable term, but it is not a necessary term. Nor can it be formulated with sufficient precision. On this point I agree with Kerr J. It should be noticed that in *Esso Petroleum Co Ltd* v *Harper's Garage (Stourport) Ltd* Mocatta J also refused to make such an implication and there was no appeal from his decision.

In the circumstances, I do not think any term can be implied ...

"He who comes to equity"
There is another way of reaching the same result. As I have already said, I do not think there was any implied term that Shell would not abnormally discriminate against Lostock. So there was no breach of contract by Shell. Nevertheless, there was conduct by Shell which was unfair to Lostock. It was not done by Shell deliberately so as to injure Lostock. It was done to avoid the impact of the Price Code; so as not to break the code in the overall conduct of their business. But, whatever the reason, the fact is that Shell insisted on maintaining the tie in circumstances where it was unfair and unreasonable for them to do so. To my mind this frees the garage from the tie during the time when the support scheme was operated by Shell to the prejudice of the garage. At any rate no court would grant Shell an injunction against the garage. It is well settled that "he who comes to equity must do equity". I need only refer to such cases as *Stickney* v *Keeble*; *Measures Brothers Ltd* v *Measures*; and *Chappell* v *Times Newspapers Ltd*. So long as Shell were operating the support scheme to the prejudice of Lostock, a court of equity would not grant Shell any equitable relief by way of injunction or otherwise. And a court of law would not grant Shell any damages because they could prove no loss, and in any case they were themselves the cause of any loss. If Shell had continued the support scheme for any substantial length of time – so that it struck at the root of the consideration for the tie – Lostock might have been relieved altogether from the tie. But, as the support scheme was short-lived, Lostock were only relieved of the tie during its continuance.'

Shirlaw v Southern Foundries (1926) Ltd see Southern Foundries (1926) Ltd v Shirlaw

Southern Foundries (1926) Ltd v Shirlaw [1940] AC 701 House of Lords (Viscount Maugham, Lord Atkin, Lord Wright, Lord Romer and Lord Porter)

Contract appointing managing director – act of third party

Facts
The respondent was appointed the appellants' managing director for a period of ten years. At that time, the appellants' articles provided that the power to remove the managing director was 'subject to the provisions of any contract between him and the company'. Three years later FF Ltd acquired financial

control of the appellants: new articles were adopted giving FF Ltd the power to remove any of the appellants' directors: they removed the respondent. Was there a term to the effect that the appellants would not remove the respondent from office?

Held (Viscount Maugham and Lord Romer dissenting)
There was and he was entitled to damages for breach of it.

Lord Wright:

> 'As I follow the appellant company's case, it is that a contract between A and B can, apart from any express or implied condition in the contract, be dissolved at the will of C, a stranger to the contract, without the consent of B, one of the contracting parties. It is contended that this is so because, by an arrangement between A and C, A has vested this power in C. No authority is cited to justify such a proposition. A contract is a consensual agreement between A and B, between whom the rights and liabilities exist. I do not understand on what principle B can be ejected from his contractual rights by the stranger C, with whom he has no privity. The appellants promised that the respondent should hold the office of managing director for ten years, subject to the express or implied conditions. The appellants now have to justify his removal while the contract period was running. No doubt there might be cases in which, apart from the contract provisions, the appellants could resist a claim for damage. There might, for instance, be a change in the law, or there might be a requisition by the government of the works and undertaking of the appellant company which might in certain events frustrate and dissolve the contract irrespective of the will of the parties. Even in such cases, however, it has been held that the requisition must not be self-induced ... Apart from government interference, or the like, the contract can only rightfully be dissolved by the will of the parties who entered into it. That will may be evinced by the conditions, express or implied, which were originally agreed to, and by action in accordance with them, or by a subsequent agreement to rescind the contract. Nothing of the sort, however, can be shown by the appellants. They have to justify the determination of the contract, or the case will be one of breach or repudiation. If their only justification is the action of Federated, that, in my opinion, is no defence. The alteration of the articles did not constitute a breach of contract by the appellant company as against the respondent, but his removal the following year did, and entitled him to damages. In my opinion, the appellant company fail in their defence, and the appeal should be dismissed.'

Commentary
See also *Associated Japanese Bank International Ltd* v *Crédit du Nord SA* (1988) NLJ Law Reports 109.

Thake v *Maurice* [1986] 2 WLR 337 Court of Appeal (Kerr, Neill and Nourse LJJ)

Vasectomy – failure to warn

Facts
A differently constituted Court of Appeal had, shortly after the hearing of *Eyre* v *Measday*, to consider an appeal on similar facts. Here a man had undergone a vasectomy; his wife, nevertheless, fell pregnant. There were, however, a number of differences between the facts in the two cases. Firstly, there were differences in the consent forms signed by the plaintiffs in the two cases. Secondly, it was felt, particularly by Slade LJ in the former case, that different considerations may apply to sterilisation operations on men and women. The third, and most important difference, was that here it was common ground that there was a need for warning to be given that the operation might not have the desired result and no such warning had been given.

Held (Kerr LJ dissenting)

Whilst the defendant had not been in breach of contract, nevertheless, on the particular facts, on the claim in negligence, the failure by the defendant to give his usual warning amounted to a breach of the duty of care which he owed to the plaintiff.

In his dissenting judgment, Kerr LJ found that, in the unusual circumstances of the case, the revival of the plaintiff's fertility also gave rise to a breach of contract on the part of the defendant.

Wells (Merstham) Ltd v *Buckland Sand and Silica Co Ltd* [1964] 2 WLR 453 High Court (Edmund Davies J)

Warranty – third party purchasing sand

Facts

The defendants warranted to the plaintiffs that their 'B W Sand' conformed to a certain analysis. Such sand would be suitable for chrysanthemum growing and the defendants knew that this was why the plaintiffs wanted it. To save costs, the plaintiffs placed their order through a third party, but they (the third party) did not tell the defendants that the sand was for re-sale to the plaintiffs. The sand delivered to the plaintiffs did not conform to the warranty: the plaintiffs chrysanthemums suffered disastrously.

Held

The plaintiffs were entitled to damages for breach of warranty and it was irrelevant that the order had been placed through a third party.

Edmund Davies J:

> 'Fundamental to the conception of a collateral contract is "an intention on the part of either or both parties that there should be a contractual liability in respect of the accuracy of the statement" But in this connexion it is well to bear in mind the cautionary words of Denning LJ in *Oscar Chess Ltd* v *Williams* that,
>
>> "It is sometimes supposed that the tribunal must look into the minds of the parties to see what they themselves intended. That is a mistake ... The question whether a warranty was intended depends on the conduct of the parties, on their words and behaviour, rather than on their thoughts. If an intelligent bystander would reasonably infer that a warranty was intended, that will suffice. And this, when the facts are not in dispute, is a question of law."
>
> Approaching in this way the facts as I have found them, in my judgment a warranty was here intended and expressed that the constituents of B W sand were (and would be found to be) as set out in the analysis supplied, and on the basis of that warranty the plaintiffs entered into contracts to buy such sand ...
>
> Then does it make any difference that, the warranty having been given to the plaintiffs, all the purchases other than the first were made by the plaintiffs from a third party? ... it would be absurd in the circumstances of the case to regard that warranty as being impliedly restricted to orders placed directly by the plaintiffs with the defendants.
>
> As between A (a potential seller of goods) and B (a potential buyer), two ingredients, and two only, are in my judgment required in order to bring about a collateral contract containing a warranty: (1) a promise or assertion by A as to the nature, quality or quantity of the goods which B may reasonably regard as being made animo contrahendi, and (2) acquisition by B of the goods in reliance on that promise or assertion ... A warranty may be enforceable notwithstanding that no specific main contract is discussed at the time when it is given, though obviously an animus contrahendi (and, therefore, a warranty) would be unlikely to be inferred unless the circumstances show that it was within the present contemplation of the parties that a contract based on the promise would shortly be entered into. Furthermore, the operation of the warranty must have a limitation in point of time which is reasonable in all the circumstances.'

20 Misrepresentation

Armstrong v *Jackson* [1917] 2 KB 822 High Court (McCardie J)

Broker selling own shares to client – rescission

Facts
The plaintiff instructed the defendant broker to purchase some shares for him and the defendant sent a contract note purporting to show that these instructions had been carried out. The plaintiff did not take up the shares immediately but eventually, on the defendant's advice, he did so, duly paying the defendant for them. Some years later (the value of the shares having fallen) it appeared that the contract note was fictitious and that the shares in question had previously been owned by the defendant.

Held
The plaintiff was entitled to have the whole transaction set aside.

McCardie J:

> '... in the present case, the plaintiff is prima facie entitled to a decree setting aside the transaction in question. But counsel for the defendant vigorously contended that no such decree can be made here. In the first place, it was argued that, inasmuch as the contract between the parties was executed no rescission can be granted unless fraud can be proved against the defendant ... The position of principal and agent gives rise to particular and onerous duties on the part of the agent, and the high standard of conduct required from him springs from the fiduciary relationship between his employers and himself. His position is confidential, and readily lends itself to abuse. Hence, a strict and salutary rule is required to meet the specific situation. The rules of English law, as they now exist, spring from the original strictness of the requirements of equity when the fiduciary relationship exists. These requirements are superadded to the common law obligations of diligence and skill ... It is, I think, immaterial that the plaintiff in the present case took a transfer of the shares and became the registered holder thereof. Such facts do not impair his right to rescission. So to hold would impair, gravely and injuriously, the powers of the court ... If, however, a finding against the defendant of personal deceit be essential to the plaintiff's claim for rescission, then I regret to say that I feel no doubt that such a case has been established.'

Bell v *Lever Brothers Ltd* [1932] AC 161 House of Lords (Lord Hailsham, Lord Blanesburgh, Lord Warrington, Lord Atkin and Lord Thankerton)

Mistake – belief that contract not otherwise terminable

Facts
Lever Bros owned 99.5 per cent of the issued share capital of the Niger Company Ltd, a firm that had, inter alia, an extensive cocoa business. The Niger Company was making heavy losses which were being met by Lever Bros. Bell and another were made executive officers of Niger Company in an effort to 'turn it around'. Within five years, the company was so successful it was considering amalgamation with its main competitor. Bell's position was redefined; a new contract drawn up, terminating his contract with

Niger and transferring him to Lever Bros. The renegotiated contract made allowance for substantial compensation and recognition of his exceptional work. Later Lever Bros discovered that Bell had engaged in private dealings in breach of his original contract of employment. At the time of the transfer Lever Bros could thus have terminated Bell's contract of employment. They claimed the new contract transferring Bell was void for mistake.

Held
The plaintiffs were not entitled to avoid the agreement as the mistake was not sufficiently fundamental in character.

Lord Warrington:

> 'The final question ... is only relevant to the issue of whether there was a mutual mistake ... I will assume for the present that ... the learned judge was entitled to deal with the matter of the footing of mutual mistake ... The learned judge thus describes the mistake involved in this case as sufficient to justify a court in saying that there was no true consent – namely:
>
>> "Some mistake or misapprehension as to some facts ... which, by the common intention of the parties, whether expressed or more generally implied, constitute the underlying assumption, without which the parties would not have made the contract they did."
>
> That a mistake of this nature, common to both parties, is, if proved, sufficient to render a contract void is, I think, established law. This principle, however, is confined to cases in which "the mistake is as to the substance of the whole consideration, going, as it were, to the root of the matter" (*Kennedy* v *Panama etc Mail Co* (1867) LR 2 QB 580, 588 ...) ... [In] the present case [it] is, in my opinion, clear that each party believed that the remunerative offices, compensation for the loss of which was the subject of the negotiations, were offices which could not be determined except by the consent of the holder thereof and further believed that the other party was under the same belief and was treating on that footing. The real question, therefore, is whether the erroneous assumption on the part of both parties to the agreements that the service contracts were indeterminable except by agreement, was of such a fundamental character as to constitute an underlying assumption without which the parties would not have made the contract they in fact made, or whether it was only a common error as to a material element, but one not going to the root of the matter and not affecting the substance of the consideration.'

Lord Atkin:

> 'Mistake as to quality of the thing contracted for raises more difficult questions. In such a case, a mistake will not affect assent unless it is the mistake of both parties and is as to the existence of some quality which makes the thing without the quality essentially different from the thing as it was believed to be ...'

Commentary
Distinguished in *Grist* v *Bailey* [1966] 3 WLR 618. Aplied in *Magee* v *Pennine Insurance Co Ltd* [1969] 2 WLR 1278. See also *Associated Japanese Bank (International) Ltd* v *Crédit du Nord SA* [1988] 1 WLR 255.

Bissett v *Wilkinson* [1927] AC 177 Privy Council (Viscount Dunedin, Lord Atkinson, Lord Phillimore, Lord Carson and Lord Merrivale)

Expression of opinion – number of sheep land would carry

Facts
A vendor admitted that he had told prospective purchasers that certain land in New Zealand 'would

carry 2,000 sheep' and that they bought the land in this belief. It turned out that the land did not have this capacity and, inter alia, the purchasers claimed rescission of the agreement.

Held
Their claim would fail.

Lord Merrivale:

'In an action for rescission, as in an action for specific performance of an executory contract, when misrepresentation is the alleged ground of relief of the party who repudiates the contract, it is, of course, essential to ascertain whether that which is relied on is a representation of a specific fact, or a statement of opinion, since an erroneous opinon stated by the party affirming the contract, though it may have been relied on and have induced the contract on the part of the party who seeks rescission, gives no title to relief unless fraud is established ...

In the present case, as in those cited, the material facts of the transaction, the knowledge of the parties respectively, and their relative positions, the words of representation used, and the actual condition of the subject-matter spoken of, are relevant to the two inquiries necessary to be made. What was the meaning of the representation? Was it true? ...

As was said by Sim J [the trial judge]:

"In ordinary circumstances, any statement made by an owner who has been occupying his own farm as to its carrying capacity would be regarded as a statement of fact ... This, however, is not such a case. The purchasers knew all about Hogan's block and knew also what sheep the farm was carrying when they inspected it. In these circumstances ... the purchasers were not justified in regarding anything said by the vendor as to the carrying capacity as being anything more than an expression of his opinion on the subject."

In this view of the matter their Lordships concur.

Whether the vendor honestly and in fact held the opinion which he stated remained to be considered. This involved examination of the history and condition of the property. If a reasonable man with the vendor's knowledge could not have come to the conclusion he stated, the description of that conclusion as an opinion would not necessarily protect him against rescission for misrepresentation, but what was actually the capacity in competent hands of the land the purchasers purchased had never been, and never was, practically ascertained ...

It is of dominant importance that Sim J negatived the purchasers' charge of fraud.

After attending to the close and very careful examination of the evidence which was made by learned counsel for each of the parties, their Lordships entirely concur in the view which was expressed by the learned judge who heard the case. The purchasers failed to prove that the farm, if properly managed, was not capable of carrying 2,000 sheep.'

Brikom Investments Ltd v *Seaford Estates Ltd* [1981] 1 WLR 863 Court of Appeal (Ormrod and Griffiths LJJ)

Landlord and tenant – implied covenant to repair

Facts
The plaintiff let a flat to the defendant for a term of seven years. Under s32 of the Housing Act 1961, where a lease was for 'a term of less than seven years' the landlord was impliedly liable for certain internal repairs. A fair rent was assessed and registered on the basis that the plaintiffs were liable for those repairs and in correspondence they accepted that liability. When they failed to carry out some of such repairs, the defendant carried them out himself and deducted the cost from his rent. The plaintiffs claimed, inter alia, arrears of rent on the basis of the full registered rent.

Held
They were not entitled to succeed.

Ormrod LJ:

> 'In our judgment it would clearly be inequitable to hold that the tenant was liable for the full amount of the arrears of a rent which reflects, in part, that the landlords were liable for the repairs, and at the same time that the tenant was liable for the cost of such repairs.
>
> This is the classic situation which the doctrine of estoppel was designed to meet. Counsel for the tenant put his case in alternative ways. Either the landlords, by demanding a rent fixed on the basis of the rent officer's allocation of liability for repairs, represented that they accepted liability accordingly, or the landlords, by not taking steps to have the registered rent changed so as to reflect the true position and suing for the enhanced rent, had made their election and could not be heard, in these proceedings, to assert a claim inconsistent with the position they had adopted.
>
> Counsel for the landlords, however, contended that the representation was a representation of law and not of fact, and therefore could not give rise to an estoppel, and that the tenant was seeking to use the estoppel as a sword, that is to recover the cost of the repairs, and not, in the classic phrase, as a shield. He relied on two cases ... in neither of which had the party alleging estoppel acted to his detriment, nor had the other party gained any advantage from the representation.
>
> These dichotomies are dangerously neat and apt to mislead. Representations of fact shade into representations of law, and swords, with a little ingenuity, can be beaten into shields, or shields into swords. In this case the shield may have quite a sharp edge but it is nonetheless a shield and the representation was essentially one of fact, ie that the landlords accepted liability for the s32 repairs to the tenant's flat in return for the enhanced rent. We would hold that so long as the enhanced rent is claimed the landlords cannot put the burden of the s32 repairs on the tenant. But they can take immediate action to have the fair rent corrected so as to reflect the true position in regard to repairs, and will then be entitled to the benefit of the tenant's covenant. The tenant, therefore, succeeds on this point.'

Brown v *Raphael* [1958] Ch 636 Court of Appeal (Lord Evershed MR, Romer and Ormrod LJJ)

Implied representation

Facts
Auction particulars of the reversion in a trust fund stated that the annuitant was 'believed to have no aggregable estate': this belief was held honestly but mistakenly and the eventual purchaser sought, inter alia, rescission of the contract. The name of the vendor's solicitors appeared at the foot of the auction particulars.

Held
The purchaser was entitled to succeed as it was impliedly represented that there were reasonable grounds for the material belief.

Lord Evershed MR:

> 'In order that the plaintiff may succeed ... it is necessary that three things should be established: (i) he must show that the language relied on imports or contains a representation of some material fact; (ii) he must show that the representation is untrue; and (iii) he must show that, in entering into the contract, he was induced so to do in reliance on it. The learned judge concluded all those three matters in the plaintiff's favour ... in my judgment there is no ground shown for this court to disturb the learned judge's conclusions. ...
>
> The first point is, to my mind, the most significant and perhaps the most difficult: Is there here a representation of a material fact? ...

I am ... entirely of the same opinion as was the learned judge, namely, that this is a case in which there was not merely the representation that the defendant entertained the belief, but also, inescapably, the further representation that he, being competently advised, had reasonable grounds for supporting that belief. The learned judge put the matter thus in his judgment. He first observed that, if the purchaser was not entitled to suppose that the vendor was in possession of facts which enabled him to express an opinion which was based on reasonable grounds, that would, he thought (and I agree with him) make business dealings, certainly in this class of business, almost impossible. He said:

> "It must be remembered that in this case the purchaser going to the auction had no means whatever of finding out anything about the annuitant's means. When the contract was signed, the purchaser did not even know the name of the annuitant. On the other hand, the vendor must be expected to be in possession of facts unavailable to the purchaser and the purchaser is entitled to suppose that he is in possession of facts which enable him to express an opinion which is based on reasonable grounds. As I have already said, if that is not so, business relationships become quite impossible. It may be different where the facts on which the opinion is expressed are equally available to both parties. Then the opinion may be no more than an expression of opinion, but, where the opinion is expressed on facts assumed to be available to the vendor, which certainly are not available to the purchaser, and that opinion is expressed to induce the contract, in my judgment the purchaser is entitled to expect that the opinion is expressed on reasonable grounds."

The learned judge, using that general language in relation to this case, was reflecting the language of Bowen LJ in *Smith* v *Land & House Property Corpn* (1884) 28 Ch D 7. I, therefore, am satisfied that the relevant language int he present case involved the representation that there were reasonable grounds for the belief, and certainly that was a representation of a most material fact.'

Clarke v *Dickson* (1858) EB & B 148 Court of Queen's Bench (Crompton J)

Misrepresentation – restitution impossible

Facts
In 1850 the plaintiff was induced to take shares in a company by the defendants' misrepresentation. Four years later, when the company was in bad circumstances, with the plaintiff's assent it was registered as a company with limited liability. Subsequently it was wound up and the plaintiff then discovered the falsity of the representations. He sued to recover the money he had paid for the shares.

Held
His action would fail.

Crompton J:

> 'When once it is settled that a contract induced by fraud is not void, but voidable at the option of the party defrauded, it seems to me to follow that, when that party exercises his option to rescind the contract, he must be in a state to rescind; that is, he must be in such a situation as to be able to put the parties into their original state before the contract. Now here I will assume ... that the plaintiff bought his shares from the defendants and not from the company, and that he might at one time have had a right to restore the shares to the defendants if he could, and demand the price from them. But then what did he buy? Shares in a partnership with others. He cannot return those; he has become bound to those others. Still stronger, he has changed their nature: what he now has and offers to restore are shares in a quasi corporation now in process of being wound up ... The plaintiff must rescind in toto or not at all; he cannot both keep the shares and recover the whole price. That is founded on the plainest principles of justice. If he cannot return the article he must keep it, and sue for his real damage in an action on the deceit. Take the case I put in the argument, of a butcher buying live cattle, killing them, and even selling the meat to his customers. If the rule of law were as the plaintiff contends, that butcher might, upon discovering a fraud on the part of the grazier who sold him the cattle, rescind the contract and get back

the whole price: but how could that be consistently with justice? The true doctrine is, that a party can never repudiate a contract after, by his own act, it has become out of his power to restore the parties to their original condition.'

Derry v *Peek* (1889) 14 App Cas 337 House of Lords (Lord Halsbury LC, Lord Watson, Lord Bramwell, Lord FitzGerald and Lord Herschell).

Misrepresentation – belief in truth in an action for deceit

Facts
A special Act incorporating a tramway company provided that the carriages might be moved by animal power and, with the consent of the Board of Trade, by steam power. The directors issued a prospectus containing a statement that by this special Act the company had the right to use steam instead of horses. The plaintiff bought shares on the strength of this statment. The Board of Trade later refused to consent to the use of steam and the company was wound up. The plaintiff brought an action for deceit.

Held
1. In an action for deceit, it is not enough to establish misrepresentation alone; something more must be proved to cast liability on the defendant.
2. There is an essential difference between the case where the defendant honestly believes in the truth of a statement although he is careless, and where he is careless with no such honest belief.
3. A mere statement by the defendant that he believed something to be true is not conclusive proof that it was so. Fraud is established where it is proved that a false statement is made:
   a) knowingly;
   b) without belief in its truth;
   c) recklessly, careless as to whether it be true or false. There must, to prevent fraud, always be an honest belief in its truth.

   If fraud is proved, the motive of the person making the statement is irrelevant. It matters not that there was no intention to cheat or injure the person to whom the statement was made.
4. The defendants were not fraudulent in this case. They made a careless statement but they honestly believed in its truth.

Doyle v *Olby (Ironmongers) Ltd* [1969] 2 WLR 673 Court of Appeal (Lord Denning MR, Winn and Sachs LJ)

Fraudulent misrepresentations – measure of damages

Facts
After buying an ironmonger's business, things turned out to be very different from what the vendors had led the plaintiff to believe. He was awarded damages for fraudulent misrepresentations and the appeal concerned, inter alia, the measure of damages.

Held
The defendants were bound to make reparation for all the actual damage directly flowing from the fraudulent inducements.

Lord Denning MR:

'On principle the distinction seems to be this: in contract, the defendant has made a promise and broken it. The object of damages is to put the plaintiff in as good a position, as far as money can do it, as if the promise has been performed. In fraud, the defendant has been guilty of a deliberate wrong by inducing the plaintiff to act to his detriment. The object of damages is to compensate the plaintiff for all the loss he has suffered, so far, again, as money can do it. In contract, the damages are limited to what may reasonably be supposed to have been in the contemplation of the parties. In fraud, they are not so limited. The defendant is bound to make reparation for all the actual damage directly flowing from the fraudulent inducement. The person who has been defrauded is entitled to say: "I would not have entered into this bargain at all but for your representation. Owing to your fraud, I have not only lost all the money I paid you, but what is more, I have been put to a large amount of extra expense as well and suffered this or that extra damages." All such damages can be recovered: and it does not lie in the mouth of the fraudulent person to say that they could not reasonably have been foreseen. For instance, in this very case the plaintiff has not only lost money which he paid for the business, which he would never have done if there had been no fraud; he put all that money in and lost it; but also has been put to expense and loss in trying to run a business which has turned out to be a disaster for him. He is entitled to damages for all his loss subject, of course, to giving credit for any benefit that he has received. There is nothing to be taken off in mitigation: for there is nothing more that he could have done to reduce his loss. He did all that he could reasonably be expected to do.'

Commentary

See also *Naughton* v *O'Callaghan* [1990] 3 All ER 191 in Chapter 25 and *East* v *Maurer* following.

East v *Maurer* [1991] 2 All ER 733 Court of Appeal (Mustill, Butler-Sloss, and Beldam LJJ)

Fraudent misrepresentation – assessment of damages

Facts

In 1979, the defendant who owned two hair salons agreed to sell one to the plaintiffs. The plaintiffs were induced to buy, in part by a representation from the defendant to the effect that he hoped in future to work abroad, and that he did not intend to work in the second salon, save in emergencies. In fact, the defendant who had built up a considerable reputation in the area, continued to work regularly at the second salon and many of his clients followed him. The result of this was that the plaintiffs saw a steady fall-off in business and never made a profit. They were finally forced to sell it in 1989, for considerably less than they paid. The plaintiffs sued for breach of contract and fraudulent misrepresentation. The court at first instance found that the defendant's representations were false. The defendant appealed on the basis that damages awarded were assessed on the wrong basis.

Held

The Court of Appeal held that the proper approach was to assess the profit the plaintiff might have made had the defendant not made the representation(s).

'Reparation for all actual damage' as indicated by Lord Denning in *Doyle* v *Olby* (above) would include loss of profits. The assessment of profits was however to be on a tortious basis. The effect of such an approach may well result in the amount of damages awarded being reduced (as they were here, by one third).

Commentary
See also *Royscott Trust* v *Rogerson* [1991] 3 WLR 57 (below).

Edgington v *Fitzmaurice* (1885) 29 Ch D 459 Court of Appeal (Cotton, Bowen and Fry LJJ)

Prospectus – representation as to object of loan

Facts
The plaintiff, who was a shareholder of the Army and Navy Provision Market (Limited), ('the company'), received a circular issued by the directors inviting subscriptions for debenture bonds to the amount of £25,000 with interest. The circular stated that the company had bought a lease of a valuable property and that the company had spent various sums of money on it. The debentures were being issued to raise money for alterations of and additions to the property and to transport fish from the coast for sale in London. The circular was challenged as being misleading in certain respects. It was alleged that it was framed in such a way as to lead to the belief that the debentures would be a charge on the property of the company, that the prospectus omitted any reference to a second mortgage, that the whole balance of the mortgage which was referred to might be called in within four years and that the real object of the issue was to pay off pressing liabilities of the company, not to complete the alterations, etc. The plaintiff, who had taken debentures, claimed repayment of the sum he had advanced with interest on the ground that it had been obtained from him by fraudulent mis-statements; alternatively, for damages for failure to so charge the property. The defendants, who were the directors and certain officers of the company, claimed that the temporary nature of the second mortgage meant that it was not necessary to mention it, that they were not aware that the first mortgage could be called in as alleged, that the secretary and manager had no authority to represent that the debenture holders would have any charge and that they believed that the money would be used as set out in the circular and, indeed, some of it had been so expended.

Held
The mis-statement as to the objects of the loan was a material misrepresentation of intention involving a mis-statement of fact upon which the plaintiff had acted to his detriment. It followed that the directors were liable to an action for deceit, even though the plaintiff was also influenced by his belief that he was entitled to a charge on the company's property.

Bowen LJ:

> 'There must be a mis-statement of an existing fact: but the state of a man's mind is as much a fact as the state of his digestion. It is true that it is very difficult to prove what the state of a man's mind at a particular time is, but if it can be ascertained, it is as much a fact as anything else. A misrepresentation as to the state of a man's mind is, therefore, a mis-statement of fact.'

Erlanger v *New Sombrero Phosphate Co* (1878) 3 App Cas 1218 House of Lords (Lord Cairns LC, Lord Hatherley, Lord Penzance, Lord O'Hagan, Lord Selbourne, Lord Blackburn and Lord Gordon)

Rescission – promoters' breach of duty

Facts
The respondents sought the rescission of a contract for the purchase of a small island in the West Indies on the ground that all the circumstances attending the transaction had not been disclosed by the vendors,

a syndicate of which the appellants were members. The syndicate had formed a company – the respondents – and had sold the island to it, but they had not appointed competent officials to enable the company to form an independent judgment as to the propriety of the purchase.

Held

The contract had rightly been set aside.

Lord Penzance:

'... I think it is clear that the company having, in the first instance, a right to relieve itself from this contract, which the promoters have unfairly fastened upon it, it is for the vendors to show affirmatively that the company has forfeited that right. The actual lapse of time before commencing the suit was not very great. Delay, as it seems to me, has two aspects. Lapse of time may so change the condition of the thing sold, or bring about such a state of things, that justice cannot be done by rescinding the contract subject to any amount of allowances or compensations. This is one aspect of delay, and it is in many cases particularly applicable to property of a mining character. But delay must also imply acquiescence, and in this aspect it equally bars the respondent company's right, for such a contract as is now under consideration is only voidable, and not void ... And so dealing with the facts of the present case, I find myself unable to conclude affirmatively that it has been made out by the argument that either the character of the property, or the way in which the company had dealt with it, did in point of fact preclude the possibility of justice being worked out on the basis of the contract being rescinded ... The substantial question, therefore, is whether there was such delay as fairly imports acquiescence ... On the whole I am unable to satisfy myself, either that it is not practicable to do justice on the basis of the contract being rescinded, or that the company has by any laches or delay laid itself fairly open to the imputation of having acquiesced in the contract which they now seek to set aside.'

Esso Petroleum Co Ltd v *Mardon*

See Chapter 19.

Gran Gelato Ltd v *Richcliff (Group) Ltd* [1992] 1 All ER 865 Chancery Division (Nicholls VC)

Solicitors' negligence – misrepresentation – damages

Facts

In 1984 the defendant granted to the plaintiffs an underlease of basement and ground floor shop premises for a term of almost 10 years. The underlease was carved out of two headleases. Unknown to either the plaintiffs or their solicitors both headleases contained 'break' clauses giving the main lessor the right to terminate the lease prematurely. In the course of the preliminary negotiations the plaintiffs' solicitors sent 'inquiries before lease' (enquiring about the existence of these or similar clauses) to the defendant's solicitors. They answered that such clauses did 'not to the lessor's knowledge' exist. Three years later the head lessor exercised the break clause and terminated the head lease – the plaintiffs' underlease was of course terminated also, though it still had about 4 and a half years to run.

Held

The defendant's solicitors' response to the inquiries before lease was a misrepresentation. Under normal conveyancing rules, the solicitor acting for the seller did not in general owe the buyer a duty of care when answering questions, because the buyer has a remedy against the seller for misrepresentation. Here the defendants had clearly intended that the plaintiff would act on the accuracy of the answers provided.

The onus was therefore on the vendors to establish that their solicitors had acted in some way outside the norm to create a special duty of care towards the plaintiff, since they were unable to do this the plaintiff's claim against the vendor's solicitors would fail. Regardless of any element of contributory negligency on the part of their own solicitors, however, they would have a right of action against the vendors.

Howard Marine & Dredging Co Ltd v *A Ogden & Sons (Excavations) Ltd* [1978] 2 WLR 515 Court of Appeal (Lord Denning MR, Bridge and Shaw LJJ)

Misrepresentation as to capacity of barges

Facts

In 1974, the Northumbrian Water Authority was planning to construct a large sewage works and it invited contractors to tender for the excavation works. The defendants were invited to tender. They were experienced excavators but, in this particular case, the material was to be dumped at sea, and this they knew nothing about. Furthermore, they would be obliged to hire barges to carry the material. The defendants invited, inter alia, the plaintiffs to tender for the hire of the barges and the plaintiffs, who owned some barges which were potentially suitable, sent their manager to the site to look at the material to be carried. He formed the view that the barges would be suitable and offered them to the defendants for £1,800 per week, stating that they would carry 850 cubic metres of material each. He said nothing about the weight each would carry. The defendants asked him about this and he gave an explanation which the defendants did not properly understand, so that they retained the impression that 850 cubic metres could be carried. In fact, the capacity did also depend upon the density of the material. The defendants, using the plaintiffs' tender, tendered for and won the Authority contract. The price of barge hire was later reduced to £1,724 per week. Howards asked Ogdens to confirm the order for the barges and, at this time, the manager was asked about the capacity in tonnes and he stated it to be 1,600. This was wrong, but he had innocently relied on a mistaken entry in the Lloyd's Register for the two barges. Eventually a firm order was given for £1,500 per week and the barges put to work. Later, Ogdens discovered that the payload was only 1,055 tonnes and they refused to pay more than £2,000 hire. Howards withdrew the barges and Ogdens hired others to complete the work. Howards issued a writ for the outstanding hire and Ogdens counter claimed for misrepresentation.

Held (Lord Denning dissenting)

The defendants were entitled to succeed on their counterclaim by virtue of s2(1) of the Misrepresentation Act 1967.

Bridge LJ:

'...It does not appear to me that Howards ever intended to bind themselves by ... a collateral warranty ... The first question then is whether Howards would be liable in damages in respect of (the) misrepresentation if it had been made fraudulently ... An affirmative answer to that question is inescapable ... Howards must be liable unless they proved that (the Manager) had reasonable ground to believe what he said ... the onus passes to the representor ... In the course of negotiations leading to a contract, the 1967 Act imposes an absolute obligation not to state facts which the representor cannot prove he had a reasonable ground to believe ... the question remains whether his evidence, however benevolently viewed, is sufficient to show that he had an objectively reasonable ground to disregard the figure in the ship's documents and to prefer the Lloyd's Register figure. I think it is not ... I would accordingly allow the appeal.'

Shaw LJ:

'... It must have been apparent to everyone concerned ... that the profitability of Ogden's contract ... must depend on the payload of the barges. So the question, though swamped by a number of others, must, or should have stood out by its content, as relating to a matter of substance and importance. It called for an answer ... which could be relied on ... What was asked for was a specific fact. Ogdens had not themselves ... such ready and facile means (of ascertaining what the fact was) as was available to (the manager) ... I would venture to hold that Ogdens have a cause of action in negligence at common law ... '

Laurence v *Lexcourt Holdings Ltd* [1978] 1 WLR 1128 High Court (Brian Dillon QC)

Misrepresentation – planning permission

Facts
The plaintiffs claimed specific performance of an agreement for a lease. The premises were unoccupied at the time when the freehold was bought by the plaintiffs in 1970. They comprised a pair of shops with living accommodation above. The plaintiffs used the ground floor and part of the first as offices, having had planning permission to do so. The rest of the first and second floors were not covered by the permission and were unoccupied until the defendants took possession after the agreement for the lease had been made. The defendants were an accounting company. Before the agreement for the lease was made, nothing at all was said about the restricted planning permission. The plaintiff had forgotten about it. The defendants were in a great hurry to get possession and they failed to make the usual enquiries. Afterwards, enquiries were made and the terms of the permission were discovered. They also revealed that the property was affected by a new road plan. Proposals had existed for some time and were known to both parties, but they did not attach any importance to them as they did not believe that they would come to fruition. The parties agreed that the plaintiffs would apply for planning permission for office user of the remaining part of the first floor and of the second floor. Application was made, but permission granted for a limited period of three years. The lease was for fifteen years. The defendants and plaintiffs could not agree on alternative leasehold arrangements and the defendants gave up possession and ceased paying rent. The defendants claimed to rescind on the ground of, inter alia, misrepresentation.

Held
The defendants were entitled to rescission.

Brian Dillon QC:

' ... where there has been a misrepresentation it is well settled that it is no defence to the person who has made the misrepresentation to say, "Oh well, the party who was misled could have checked and found out the facts for himself and he really has only himself to blame that he relied on me and did not make the enquiries that he might have made ...". I think the defendants are entitled to succeed on the ground of misrepresentation because it is not right, in my view, to describe property as offices and offer them for a 15 year letting as offices when the only planning permission as offices which is available is for ... two years ...'

I turn to the alternative submissions of the defendants on the ground of mistake. I find as a fact that there was a common mistake between the parties in that when the agreement of February 1974 was made, both (parties) believed that there was planning permission available without restriction for the use of the first and second floors of no 50 as offices. The law on the question of common mistake and relief in equity was stated by Denning LJ in a well known passage in *Solle* v *Butcher*, where he said:

"A contract is also liable in equity to be set aside if the parties were under a common misapprehension either as to facts or as to their relative and respective rights, provided that the misapprehension was fundamental and that the party seeking to set it aside was not himself at fault."

There are, therefore, the two requirements to be considered. Was the misapprehension fundamental and were the defendants who are seeking to set the agreement aside, themselves at fault?

The question of fault was considered by Goff J in *Grist* v *Bailey* [1967] Ch 532. He said:

"There remains one other point and that is the condition laid down by Denning LJ that the party seeking to take advantage of the mistake must not be at fault. Denning LJ did not develop that at all and it is not, I think, with respect, absolutely clear what it comprehends. Clearly there must be some degree of blameworthiness beyond the mere fault of having made a mistake; but the question is how much, or in what way? Each case must depend on its own facts ..."

In the present case, there is no doubt that the defendants were imprudent in proceeding without making the usual searches and enquiries, but they did not owe any duty of care to the plaintiffs to make those searches and their mistake did not bring about Mr Laurence's mistake. In a sense, if they had searched and obtained the information and mentioned to Mr Laurence what they had discovered, Mr Laurence's memory would have been jogged and he would then not have made a mistake, but I do not think that makes the defendants responsible for Mr Laurences' mistake or forgetfulness. It seems to me that whatever Denning LJ did have in mind in his qualification in *Solle* v *Butcher* does not cover the failure to search on the part of the defendants in this case and I do not think, therefore, that they were disentitled from relying on the mistake because they failed to search. Was the mistake, then, a fundamental mistake? *Solle* v *Butcher* and *Grist* v *Bailey* were both cases in which the mistake concerned whether a tenancy of the premises was a protected tenancy under the Rent Acts and I think they show that a mistake of that nature is a fundamental mistake, whether it be the case that the premises are being sold on the footing that they are subject to a protected tenancy when, in truth, because the tenant has died, they are not so subject, or whether it be the case that the premises are being sold on the basis that they are subject to a tenancy which is not protected when, in truth, it is protected for some of the rather technical reasons that arise under the Rent Acts. I do not see any real difference in point of importance between the Rent Acts and the Planning Acts, which are both major acts affecting land. I think it is fundamental to people who are taking land for a term as long as 15 years with a view to their use as offices, that planning permission should be available for more than a mere two or three years and I think, therefore, that this mistake, which was common to both parties, was a fundamental mistake which entitles the defendants to avoid the agreement. I do not see that it matters that the mistake was as to the legal suitability of the land for a particular use, rather than as to its physical description. Whether the case be put on mistake or misrepresentation, I think the absence of the planning permission was fundamental ...'

Leaf v *International Galleries* [1950] 2 KB 86 Court of Appeal (Sir Raymond Evershed MR, Denning and Jenkins LJJ)

Misrepresentation – right to rescind

Facts
The plaintiff bought from the defendants an oil painting of Salisbury Cathedral which was represented to him as a painting by Constable, a representation which was held to be one of the terms of the contract. Five years later he discovered that it was not a Constable and he sought rescission of the contract on the ground of innocent misrepresentation.

Held
He could not succeed.

Denning LJ:

'The question is whether the buyer is entitled to rescind the contract on that account. I emphasise that this a claim to rescind only. There is no claim in this action for damages for breach of condition or breach of warranty. The claim is simply one for rescission ... The only question is whether the buyer is entitled to rescind. The way in which the case is put by counsel for the buyer is this. He says this was an innocent misrepresentation and that in equity he is entitled to claim rescission even of an executed contract of sale on that account. He points out that the judge has found that it is quite possible to restore the parties to the same position that they were in originally, by the buyer simply handing back the picture to the sellers in return for the repayment of the purchase price.

In my opinion, this case is to be decided according to the well known principles applicable to the sale of goods. This was a contract for the sale of goods. There was a mistake about the quality of the subject-matter, because both parties believed the picture to be a Constable, and that mistake was in one sense essential or fundamental. Such a mistake, however, does not avoid the contract. There was no mistake about the subject-matter of the sale. It was a specific picture of "Salisbury Cathedral". The parties were agreed in the same terms on the same subject-matter, and that is sufficient to make a contract: see *Solle* v *Butcher*. There was a term in the contract as to the quality of the subject-matter, namely, as to the person by whom the picture was painted – that it was by Constable. That term of the contract was either a condition or a warranty. If it was a condition, the buyer could reject the picture for breach of the condition at any time before he accepted it or was to be deemed to have accepted it, whereas, if it was only a warranty, he could not reject it but was confined to a claim for damages.

I think it right to assume in the buyer's favour that this term was a condition, and that, if he had come in proper time, he could have rejected the picture, but the right to reject for breach of condition has always been limited by the rule that once the buyer has accepted, or is deemed to have accepted, the goods in performance of the contract, he cannot therefore reject, but is relegated to his claim for damages ... In this case this buyer took the picture into his house, and five years passed before he intimated any rejection. That, I need hardly say, is much more than a reasonable time. It is far too late for him at the end of five years to reject this picture for breach of any condition. His remedy after that length of time is for damages only, a claim which he has not brought before the court.'

Commentary
Distinguished in *Peco Arts Inc* v *Hazlitt Gallery Ltd* [1983] 1 WLR 1315.

Long v *Lloyd* [1958] 1 WLR 753 Court of Appeal (Jenkins, Parker and Pearce LJJ)

Misrepresentation – right to rescind

Facts
The defendant haulage contractor advertised for sale a lorry as being in 'exceptional condition' and he told the plaintiff, a prospective purchaser, that it did 11 miles to the gallon and that he had told him, after a trial run, all that was wrong with the vehicle. The plaintiff purchased the lorry and, two days later, on a short run, further faults developed and the plaintiff noticed that it did only about 5 miles to the gallon. That evening he reported these things to the defendant and the plaintiff accepted the defendant's offer to pay for some of the repairs. The next day the lorry set out on a longer journey – to Middlesbrough – and it broke down: the following day the plaintiff wrote to the defendant asking for the return of his money. The lorry had not been in a roadworthy condition, but the defendant's representations concerning it had been honestly made.

Held
The plaintiff was not entitled to rescission of the contract as he had finally accepted the lorry before he had purported to rescind.

Pearce LJ:

'On the following day the plaintiff, knowing all that he did about the condition and performance of the lorry, despatched it, driven by his brother, on a business trip to Middlesbrough. That step, at all events, appears to us to have amounted, in all the circumstances of the case, to a final acceptance of the lorry by the plaintiff for better or for worse, and to have conclusively extinguished any right of rescission remaining to the plaintiff after completion of the sale. Accordingly, even if the plaintiff should be held ... to have had a right to rescission which survived the completion of the contract, we think that on the facts of this case he lost any such right before his purported exercise of it.'

Museprime Properties Ltd v *Adhill Properties Ltd* [1990] 36 EG 114 High Court (Scott J)

Misrepresentation – rescission

Facts
In a sale by auction of three properties the particulars wrongly represented the rents from the properties as being open to negotiation. The statements in the auction particulars and made later by the auctioneer himself misrepresented the position with regard to rent reviews. In fact on two of the three properties rent reviews had been triggered and new rents agreed. The plaintiff company successfully bid for the three properties – commercial and residential premises in Finchley – and discovered the true situation. They commenced an action for rescission. The defendant company countered with the defence that the misrepresentations were not such as to induce any reasonable person to enter into a contract.

Held
The plaintiffs had established, and indeed the defendants conceded, that misrepresentation had occurred and any material misrepresentation is a ground for rescission. The judge referred, with approval, to the view of Goff and Jones: *Law of Restitution* (3rd edn (1986) p168) as follows:

> 'In our view any misrepresentation which induces a person to enter into a contract should be a ground for rescission of that contract. If the misrepresentation would have induced a reasonable person to enter into the contract, then the court will ... presume that the representee was so induced, and the onus will be on the representor to show that the representee did not rely on the misrepresentation either wholly or in part. If, however, the misrepresentation would not have induced a reasonable person to contract, the onus will be on the misrepresentee to show that the misrepresentation induced him to act as he did. But these considerations go to the question of the onus of proof. To disguise them under the cloak of "materiality" is misleading and unnecessary.'

Here the plaintiffs had established their claim to rescission of the contract on the ground of material misrepresentation because the inaccurate statements had induced them to buy the properties. They would therefore be awarded the return of their deposit, damages in respect of lost conveyancing expenses and interest.

Peyman v *Lanjani* [1985] 2 WLR 154 Court of Appeal (Stephenson, May and Slade LJJ)

Breach of contract – election to affirm or rescind

Facts
In October 1978 the defendant agreed to take an assignment of the lease of a restaurant. The assignment required the landlord's consent and the defendant arranged for his agent to impersonate him at an interview with the landlord's agent, believing that he would give a better impression. Consent was given and the lease duly assigned. In February, the defendant agreed, through his agent, to sell the lease to the plaintiff, taking the plaintiff's house in part exchange. Contracts were exchanged, subject to the

landlord's consent and the defendant's agent again impersonated him in seeking to obtain it. After learning of the original impersonation, and before the landlord's consent had been given, the plaintiff paid £10,000 under the agreement and took possession as a licensee. After consulting a new solicitor, and still before the landlord had given his consent, the plaintiff purported to rescind the contract.

Held
He was entitled to do so.

May LJ:

'... the doctrine of election comes into play when at a particular stage of a relationship or transaction between two parties the conduct of one is held as a matter of law to entitled the other to a choice between two mutually inconsistent courses of action. We are concerned with the choice which arose as a result of Mr Lanjani's breach of contract resulting from his inability to provide a good title to his leasehold interest in the restaurant. A similar choice arises in law when a party to a contract becomes entitled to rescind it by reason of the discovery of fraud on the part of the other party. Other instances arise when a landlord becomes entitled to forfeit a lease because of his tenant's breach of covenant ... For the purposes of this judgment I will confine myself to the case where a party to a contract becomes entitled either to rescind it or to affirm it as the result of some conduct on the part of the other party to it, but in my opinion the same principles apply where as a result of the application of the relevant law to the material facts such a choice becomes available.

The next feature of the doctrine of election in these cases which in my opinion is important is that when the person entitled to make the choice does so one way or the other, and this has been communicated to the other party to the contract, then the choice becomes irrevocable even though, if and when the first person seeks to change his mind, the second cannot show that he has altered his position in any way.

This being so, I do not think that a party to a contract can realistically or sensibly be held to have made this irrevocable choice between rescission and affirmation unless he has actual knowledge not only of the facts of the serious breach of the contract by the other party which is the precondition of his right to choose, but also of the fact that in the circumstances which exist he does have that right to make that choice which the law gives him. To hold otherwise ... would in my opinion not only be unjust, it would be contrary to the principles of law which one can extract from the decided cases.'

Phillips v *Brooks Ltd* [1919] 2 KB 243 High Court (Horridge J)

Contract induced by fraud – property passed?

Facts
North entered the shop of the plaintiff jeweller and selected an emerald ring. When writing a cheque (which he signed 'George Bullough') he said: 'You see who I am; I am Sir George Bullough' and he gave the plaintiff an address in St James' Square. The plaintiff had heard of Sir George Bullough as a man of means and a directory told him that Sir George lived at the address North had given. The plaintiff allowed North to take the ring (as it was, he said, his wife's birthday tomorrow), but the cheque was returned marked 'No account' and North was subsequently convicted of obtaining the ring by false pretences. Meanwhile, though, he had pledged the ring with the defendant pawnbrokers and the plaintiff now sought its return.

Held
His action would fail.

Horridge J:

'I think the seller intended to contract with the person present, and there was no error as to the person with whom he contracted, although the plaintiff would not have made the contract if there had not been a fraudulent misrepresentation ... In this case there was a passing of the property and the purchaser had a good title, and there must be judgment for the defendants, with costs.'

Commentary
Followed in *Lewis* v *Averay* [1971] 3 WLR 603 and *Dennant* v *Skinner* [1948] 2 KB 164. Distinguished in *Ingram* v *Little* [1960] 3 WLR 504.

Redgrave v *Hurd* (1881) 20 Ch D 1 Court of Appeal (Sir George Jessel MR, Baggallay and Lush LJJ)

Misrepresentation – opportunity to discover

Facts
A solicitor, the plaintiff, was contemplating retirement and he advertised for a partner who would also purchase his house. The defendant responded and, amongst other things, agreed to purchase the plaintiff's house. However, he refused to complete the purchase as he alleged that he had discovered that the practice, of which he was now a partner, was 'utterly worthless' and that representations made in regard thereto by the plaintiff were false. The plaintiff sought specific performance, the defendant rescission.

Held
The defendant was entitled to succeed.

Lush LJ:

'In one part of the judgment of the learned judge in the court below he appears to hold that, where a false representation has been made and papers are handed to the party to whom it is made, from which, if he chose, he might detect the falsehood, and he does not do so, he is in the same position as if he had done so. I entirely differ from that view, and think what my learned borther said is the correct view of the law – that where a false representation has been made, it lies on the party who makes it to show that, although he made the false representation, the defendant – the other party – did not rely on it. The onus probandi is on him to show that the other party waived it, and relied on his own knowledge. Nothing of that kind appears here.'

Resolute Maritime Inc v *Nippon Kaiji Kyokai, The Skopas* see *Skopas, The*

Royscott Trust v *Rogerson* [1991] 3 WLR 57 Court of Appeal (Balcombe and Ralph Gibson LJJ)

Measure of damages – innocent misrepresentation

Facts
A car dealer agreed to sell a car on HP to a customer for a cash price of £7,600, of which the customer was to pay a deposit of £1,200. These amounts were mistakenly stated as £8,000 and £1,600 respectively to the finance company and all future transactions were based on these figures.

The customer paid part of the sum due to the finance company, but in 1987 he dishonestly sold the car; and later ceased to make any payments. The amount unpaid by that time was, the finance company claimed, £3,625. They based this figure on the difference between the amount repaid to them by the customer and the amount £6,400 which they had advanced to the car dealer. The figures supplied to the finance company, however, had been mistakenly set too high, and the finance company sued the car dealer for innocent misrepresentation and claimed damages under s2(1) of the Misrepresentation Act (MA) 1967.

Held
The measure of damages recoverable under s2(1) of the MA 1967 was a tortious rather than contractual one. The finance company was entitled to recover damages in respect of all losses occurring as a natural consequence, including unforeseeable losses, subject to the normal rules on remoteness. It was in any event a foreseeable event that a customer buying a car on HP might dishonestly sell the car. The act by the customer was not a novus actus, the chain of causation was unbroken.

The car dealers were liable for innocent misrepresentation and the finance company could claim the £3,625 plus interest.

St Marylebone Property Co Ltd v *Payne* (1994) 45 EG 156 Mayors and City of London Court (Assistant Recorder Boggis QC)

Misrepresentation – use of a photograph to convey statements of fact

Facts
At a sale by auction, separate brochures were circulated for each property. The plaintiffs' company, relying on the brochure, made a successful bid, but discovered subsequently that there was actually less land than the picture/brochure portrayed. The contract of sale contained a clause excluding liability for all errors in the brochure. The company, alleging misrepresentation, claimed the return of their deposit.

Held
The photograph, together with arrows purporting to indicate the extent of the property, constituted misrepresentation of fact. There was inducement, as the company relied on the photograph. Despite the clause excluding liability for errors, it was unfair and unreasonable to allow the vendor to rely on the clause. The auction had been dominated by the (completely misleading) photograph. The plaintiffs were entitled to repudiate the contract and their deposit would be returned.

Sharneyford Supplies Ltd v *Edge* [1987] 2 WLR 363 Court of Appeal (Kerr, Parker and Balcombe LJJ)

Breach of contract – amount of damages

Facts
The defendant agreed to sell a maggot farm to the plaintiff with vacant possession. However the tenants on the land had security of tenure and it was impossible therefore to convey good title to the plaintiff. The plaintiff claimed against the tenant for breach of contract and sought damages under two heads:
1. cost of investigating title and other expenses in the sum of £472.05; and
2. loss of profits from December 1979 to June 1982, that being the date when the plaintiff found other premises at which to carry on the business of breeding maggots. The loss of profits amounted to £131,544 with interest.

Mervyn Davies J followed strictly the rule in *Bain* v *Fothergill* and thus in essence all the plaintiff received for the defendant's negligent misrepresentation was the expenses. The plaintiff appealed.

Held

The appeal would be allowed as the defendant had failed to satisfy the requirement engrafted on the rule in *Bain* v *Fothergill*, ie that the vendor must show that he did all that he reasonably could to perform the contract by removing any defect in title which he agreed to transfer.

Balcombe LJ:

'The question then arises: did Mr Edge establish that he had done all that he reasonably could to mitigate the effect of his breach of contract by trying to remove this defect on his title? The judge held that he had ... He summarised in numbered paragraphs what Mr Edge had done ... Of these numbered paragraphs, paras (i) to (v) inclusive dealt with events up to and including the exchange of contracts. I fail to see how these can have any relevance to the question at issue. Of the events subsequent to the date of contract, the only steps which it could be said that Mr Edge (or his solicitor, whose acts or omissions for this purpose must be attributed to Mr Edge) took to try and remove the defect on his title were the telephone conversation with Mr Hill between 14 and 19 November 1979 and the letters of 6 and 29 February 1980. The one striking omission is that at no time did Mr Edge give to Messrs Meek and Holt notice to determine their tenancy, either at common law or under s25 of the Landlord and Tenant Act 1954. In the absence of such notices having been given, I find it impossible to say that Mr Edge had done all that he reasonably could to try and remove the defect on his title and acquire vacant possession of the farm. Counsel for the third party submitted that such notices would have been to no avail, since under s25 of the 1954 Act a notice of not less than six months is necessary, and any such notice would necessarily have expired long after the date fixed for completion; further, there was no likelihood that Mr Edge could have successfully resisted an application by Messrs Meek and Holt for a new tenancy. However, it is by no means certain that Messrs Meek and Holt, if served with formal notice to determine their tenancy, and thereby realising the seriousness with which Mr Edge treated the matter, would have sought to resist giving up possession. It is significant that neither Mr Meek nor Mr Holt was called to give evidence at the trial and, as has already been said, the burden of proof to establish that he had taken all reasonable steps rested on Mr Edge. But in any event that argument is similar to that which was rejected in both *Day* v *Singleton* and *Malhotra* v *Choudhury*: that it matters not that the attempt to clear the title might have failed: it must at least have been tried. It follows that I am unable to accept the judge's conclusion that Mr Edge had, by himself or his solicitor, done what he reasonably could to try to acquire vacant possession of the farm ... I also disagree with his conclusion that there was no bad faith on the part of Mr Edge ... if one adopts the definition of "bad faith" in this context given by Stephenson LJ in *Malhotra* v *Choudhury* ... On this ground alone I would allow this appeal.

However, it was argued before us, as it was before the judge, that Mr Edge's obligation to use his best endeavours to clear the defect on his title extended to an obligation on his part to pay the £12,000 to buy out Messrs Meek and Holt, if that was a reasonable sum in all the circumstances. It is not clear from his judgment whether the judge accepted this submission as a matter of principle. He said that he had "taken account" of the suggestion that the £12,000 offer ought to have been pursued, at any rate in the sense that there should have been negotiations to reduce that figure. However, he then went on to say that, in view of the intimation that the figure was not negotiable, he did not think that Mr Edge was obliged to take that course ...

If a vendor is liable to use his best endeavours to clear any defect from his title, I can see the logic of the argument that those endeavours could include, in an appropriate case, the payment of a sum of money to a third party. However, logic has played little part in the development of this particular branch of the law, and to apply it strictly in this instance would only serve to demonstrate the illogicality of some of the earlier distinctions. The particular difficulty I find in following this argument to its logical conclusion is that the rule in *Bain* v *Fothergill* would then cease to exist, since there would be few cases in which a defect in title could not be removed if the sum offered were large enough. While I accept that it would be no bad thing if the rule were to cease to exist, I cannot believe that this is a valid way of removing it. Further, the practical problems would be great. How would the court determine, in any given case, whether the sum which an incumbrancer might require to surrender the incumbrance which constituted a defect on the title was reasonable? In a case, such as *JW Cafés Ltd* v *Brownlow Trust Ltd* ..., when the defect consists of restrictive covenants affecting the title, how far would the vendor have to go in trying to procure the removal of these restrictive covenants, and at what price? To extend the principle of *Day* v *Singleton* [1899] 2 Ch 320 to this extent, logical though it might otherwise appear, could be productive of endless litigation. Although there is no authority directly in point, I am fortified in my view by a passage in the leading textbook, *Williams on Vendor and Purchaser* (4th edn, 1936) p 1020:

> "And where his [the vendor's] title is imperfect, he is of course not liable to pay substantial damages if he declines to buy in any outstanding estate or incumbrance. Such an act as this would depend on others' consent, and does not lie entirely within his own power."

It was also argued before us that the continued acceptance by Mr Edge of the supply of maggots from Messrs Meek and Holt, and the 1982 negotiations for the grant of a new lease to them, in some way amounted to a failure by Mr Edge to use his best endeavours to clear the defect in his title. I am unable to follow this argument. While there appears to have been no evidence to justify the judge's finding ... that the maggots were being produced and had to be used (impliedly by Mr Edge and no one else), so long as the tenancy had not been determined there was no reason why Mr Edge should not accept the rent payable under it; his failure was to take the necessary steps to terminate the tenancy. Similarly, the 1982 negotiations were not of themselves of any significance; the most that can be said about them is that they were inconsistent with any attempt by Mr Edge to recover vacant possession from Messrs Meek and Holt.

The notice of appeal also included as a ground of appeal that the judge ought to have followed the decision of Graham J in *Watts* v *Spence* ... Counsel for the plaintiff very wisely did not attempt to argue this ground before us. In the circumstances I need only say that, like the judge, I find the criticism of *Watts* v *Spence* in *McGregor on Damages* (14th edn, 1980) pp 1000–1002, paras 1486–1489 entirely convincing.

In the circumstances I would allow this appeal and substitute for the second declaration made by the judge on the preliminary issues a declaration that the quantum of damages recoverable by the plaintiff for breach of contract be assessed in accordance with the general law but so that the plaintiff may also recover such further damages (if any) in tort for innocent misrepresentation as the court shall determine.'

Commentary

Applied: *Bain* v *Fothergill* (1874) LR 7 HL 158 and *Wroth* v *Tyler* [1973] 2 WLR 405.

The rule in *Bain* v *Fothergill* was abolished by s3 of the Law of Property (Miscellaneous Provisions) Act 1989 as from 27 September 1989.

Skopas, The [1983] 1 WLR 857 High Court (Mustill J)

Agent's liability

Facts

In an action arising out of the sale and purchase of the vessel *The Skopas,* there arose this preliminary question of law: If an agent, acting in his express or ostensible authority, makes a statement which is untrue in circumstances where he did not have reasonable ground to believe that it was true, can he be held liable under the Misrepresentation Act 1967?

Held

He could not.

Mustill J:

> 'It may ... be objected that ... there is ... room to read s2(1) [of the 1967 Act] as creating an additional liability in the agent. I do not agree. The 1967 Act is concerned with representations made in the particular

context of a contract, and it seems to me that it was aimed at the position of the parties to the contract. It was therefore natural that there should be created under subss(1) and (2) rights which are prima facie absolute, and independent of any general duty of care, a concept which plays no part in the law of contract. The purpose of the 1967 Act was to fill a gap which existed, or was believed to exist, in the remedies of one contracting party for an innocent representation by the other. But there was no such gap in the case of the agent; he was already subject to the ordinary liabilities in fraudulent negligence, the doctrine of *Hedley Byrne & Co Ltd* v *Heller & Partners Ltd* [1964] AC 465 having been recognised before the 1967 Act was passed. What purpose would there be in creating an entirely new absolute liability, independent of proof that the representee fell within the scope of a duty of care, simply because the representor happened to be an agent, concerned in the making of a contract, but not himself a party to it? I can see none; and, since, as I have suggested, the words of s2(1) must be read as extending to the principal, I consider that their operation should be confined to him alone …'

Smith v *Hughes* (1871) LR 6 QB 597 Court of Queen's Bench (Sir Alexander Cockburn CJ, Blackburn and Hannen JJ)

Sale of oats – buyer's mistaken belief

Facts
A trainer of racehorses bought some oats. He thought, he said, that he had purchased old oats; in fact they were new so he refused to pay for them and the county court decided that right was on his side.

Held
There must be a new trial.

Blackburn J:

'… on the sale of a specific article, unless there be a warranty making it part of the bargain that it possesses some particular quality, the purchaser must take the article he has bought, though it does not possess that quality. And I agree that, even if the vendor was aware that the purchaser thought that the article possessed that quality, and would not have entered into the contract unless he had so thought, still the purchaser is bound, unless the vendor was guilty of some fraud or deceit upon him. A mere abstinence from disabusing the purchaser of that impression is not fraud or deceit, for, whatever may be the case in a court of morals, there is no legal obligation on the vendor to inform the purchaser that he is under a mistake which has not been induced by the act of the vendor.'

Smith New Court Securities Ltd v *Scrimgeour Vickers (Asset Management) Ltd and Another* [1994] 4 All ER 225 Court of Appeal (Nourse, Rose and Hoffmann LJJ)

Fraudulent misrepresentation – assessment of damages – open market values

Facts
On 21 July 1989, the plaintiff purchased a parcel of shares in company F at a price of 82.25p per share – a deal totalling over £23 million. It subsequently was found that this transaction had been induced by a fraudulent misrepresentation. In September 1989, the shares in company F fell dramatically in value, because of a (totally unconnected) fraud. The plaintiff eventually sold the shares in company F at a great loss, and pursued an action against Scrimgeour Vickers and other defendants claiming that they had been induced to enter the contract by fraudulent misrepresentation. The main problem arose as to the value of the shares and assessment of damages.

Held
Accepting that there had been a fraudulent misrepresentation, the court would assess damages as being the difference in price between what was actually paid and what the shares would have fetched on the open market. The court held that though rather arbitrary, the only rational way to proceed was to assume the market knew everything it did know, save for the fact of the misrepresentation. Had the parcel of shares been offered on 21 July, and making this assumption as to the market's state of knowledge, the value of the shares would be 4.25p lower than that paid on the basis of the misrepresentation. Damages would therefore be £1,196,010.

Nourse J:

> 'What assumptions as to information should be made for the purposes of determining the loss caused by fraudulent misrepresentation? It seems to us that there are only two possibilities. The first is to assume that the market knew everything it did know, but was not influenced by the misrepresentation itself. The second is to assume the market was omniscient ... it (omniscience) seems to us such an arbitrary and irrational assumption that we are reluctant to declare it English law unless clearly bound by authority to do so.'

Sybron Corp v *Rochem Ltd* [1983] 3 WLR 713 Court of Appeal (Stephenson, Fox and Kerr LJJ)

Mistake – fraud discovered after pension awarded

Facts
Having opted for early retirement, the appellant manager was awarded a discretionary pension by the respondent employers. It was subsequently discovered that the appellant had been a party, with other employees subordinate to him, to fraudulent misconduct. The respondents sought, in effect, to have the pension arrangements set aside.

Held
There were entitled to succeed as the pension arrangements had been made under a mistake of fact induced by the appellant's breach of duty.

Kerr LJ:

> 'Since mistake induced by misrepresentation has not been pleaded, although I think that, in the circumstances of this case, it might well have been, the issue is whether or not [the appellant] was in breach of a duty to his employers which induced the mistake on their part. As to this, it seems to me that there can only be one answer. [The appellant] was throughout in fraudulent breach of a clear duty owed to his employers to put an end to the activities of ... the ... conspirators, who were engaged in seeking to destroy the employers' business for their own purposes, and this continuing breach of his duty induced the mistake. His duty was to report the activities of the conspirators in any event, and to dismiss them forthwith in so far as it lay within his powers to do so. Covering up and deliberately concealing their activities, which is what he was doing throughout, was the clearest possible breach of duty for a person in his position, and equally clearly it induced the mistake in question. All that *Bell* v *Lever Bros Ltd* [1932] AC 161 decides in this regard, at most, is that [the appellant] was under no duty to disclose his own misconduct. I say "at most" because I am far from convinced that *Bell* v *Lever Bros Ltd* applies, even to this extent, to cases where the concealment is fraudulent, as here, since the absence of fraud was stressed throughout the appellate proceedings in that case, including the speeches of Lord Atkin and Lord Thankerton ... with which Lord Blanesburgh agreed. On no view, however, can *Bell* v *Lever Bros Ltd* be invoked by [the appellant] to a greater extent than this. The fact that compliance by [the appellant] with his duties in this regard would in this case inevitably have revealed his own fraudulent complicity is irrelevant ...

'I therefore do not accept that it makes any difference that the pension arrangements as such were not directly induced by misrepresentation or breach of duty on the part of [the appellant]. What matters is that when these arrangements were concluded and acted on by his employers, he was in clear breach of his duty to his employers, and indeed in fraudulent breach, and that these breaches induced the mistake on their part, which caused them not to exercise their rights under ... the scheme.'

With v *O'Flanagan* [1936] Ch 575 Court of Appeal (Lord Wright MR, Romer LJ and Clauson J)

Continuing representation – sale of medical practice

Facts
Desiring to sell his medical practice, the defendant truthfully told the plaintiff that it brought in £2,000 pa and that he had a panel of 1,480 persons. During the four months of negotiations before the contract of sale was signed the defendant was ill: takings dwindled to practically nothing and the number of panel patients fell to 1,260. These facts were not disclosed to the plaintiff, but he discovered them immediately after completion and he sought rescission of the contract.

Held
He was entitled to succeed.

Romer LJ:

'The only principle invoked by the [plaintiff] in this case is as follows. If A, with a view to inducing B to enter into a contract makes a representation as to a material fact, then if at a later date and before the contract is actually entered into, owing to a change of circumstances, the representation then made would to the knowledge of A be untrue and B subsequently enters into the contract in ignorance of that change of circumstances and relying upon that representation, A cannot hold B to the bargain. There is ample authority for that statement and, indeed, I doubt myself whether any authority is necessary, it being, it seems to me, so obviously consistent with the plainest principles of equity.'

21 Exclusion Clauses

Ailsa Craig Fishing Co Ltd* v *Malvern Fishing Co Ltd [1983] 1 WLR 964 House of Lords (Lord Wilberforce, Lord Elwyn-Jones, Lord Salmon, Lord Fraser of Tullybelton and Lord Lowry)

Exception clause – loss of fishing boat

Facts
The appellants' fishing boat sank in Aberdeen harbour and was a complete loss. The judge found that the loss had been caused by negligence on breach of contract on the part of the respondent security company, but the respondents sought to rely on the clause that limited their liability to £1,000 or £10,000, according to the circumstances. The appellants contended, inter alia, that the clause could not apply because there had been a total failure by the respondents to perform the contract.

Held
This contention would be rejected.

Lord Fraser of Tullybelton:

'The question whether Securicor's liability has been limited falls to be answered by construing the terms of the contract in accordance with the ordinary principles applicable to contracts of this kind. The argument for limitation depends on certain special conditions attached to the contract prepared on behalf of Securicor and put forward in their interest. There is no doubt that such conditions must be construed strictly against the proferens, in this case Securicor, and that in order to be effective they must be "most clearly and unambiguously expressed" ... It has sometimes apparently been regarded ... as a proposition of law, that a condition excluding liability can never have any application where there has been a total breach of contract, but I respectfully agree with the Lord President (Lord Emslie) who said in his opinion in the present case that that was a misunderstanding ...

There are later authorities which lay down very strict principles to be applied when considering the effect of clauses of exclusion or of indemnity ... In my opinion these principles are not applicable in their full rigour when considering the effect of conditions merely limiting liability. Such conditions will of course be read contra proferentem and must be clearly expressed but there is no reason why they should be judged by the specially exacting standards which are applied to exclusion and indemnity clauses.'

Commentary
Applied in *Mitchell (George) (Chesterhall) Ltd* v *Finney Lock Seeds Ltd* [1983] 3 WLR 163.

British Crane Hire Corporation Ltd v *Ipswich Plant Hire Ltd*

See Chapter 19.

Computer and Systems Engineering plc v John Lelliott Ltd (1991) The Times 21 February Court of Appeal (Purchas, Taylor and Beldam LJJ)

Standard form contracts – exclusion clauses – strict interpretation

Facts
A standard form contract excluded liability for 'flooding or burst pipes'. Damage was caused to the plaintiff's property by a fractured sprinkler pipe. The question was whether the subcontractor's negligence was within the exclusion clause.

Held
The damage caused was not within the meaning of the exclusion clause, which would be interpreted strictly, and the plaintiff could claim.

Curtis v Chemical Cleaning & Dyeing Co Ltd [1951] 1 KB 805 Court of Appeal (Somervell, Singleton and Denning LJJ)

Damage to wedding dress – exclusion clause

Facts
The plaintiff took a white satin wedding dress to the defendants to be cleaned. On being asked to sign a 'receipt' which stated, inter alia, that articles were 'accepted on condition that the company is not liable for any damage howsoever arising', she asked why her signature was required: she was told it was because the defendants did not accept liability for damages to beads and sequins. When the dress was returned to the plaintiff, there was a stain on it: her action for damages was successful and the defendants appealed.

Held
The appeal would be dismissed.

Denning LJ:

> 'If the party affected signs a written document, knowing it to be a contract which governs the relations between him and the other party, his signature is irrefragable evidence of his assent to the whole contract, including the exempting clauses, unless the signature is shown to be obtained by fraud or misrepresentation: see *L'Estrange* v *Graucob* [1934] 2 KB 394. What is a sufficient misrepresentation for this purpose? ...
>
> In my opinion, any behaviour by words or conduct is sufficient to be a misrepresentation if it is such as to mislead the other party about the existence or extent of the exemption. If it conveys a false impression, that is enough. If the false impression is created knowingly, it is a fraudulent misrepresentation; if it is created unwittingly, it is an innocent misrepresentation ... by failing to draw attention to the width of the exemption clause, the assistant created the false impression that the exemption related to the beads and sequins only, and that it did not extend to the material of which the dress was made. It was done perfectly innocently, but, nevertheless, a false impression was created ... it was a sufficient misrepresentation to disentitle the cleaners from relying on the exemption, except in regard to the beads and sequins ... In my opinion, when a condition, purporting to exempt a person from his common law liabilities, is obtained by an innocent misrepresentation, the party who has made that misrepresentation is disentitled to rely on the exemption. Whether one calls that a rule of law or one of equity does not matter in these days.'

Dillon v Baltic Shipping Co, The Mikhail Lermontov [1991] 2 Lloyd's Rep 155
NSW Court of Appeal Australia

Exclusion clauses – ticket terms and conditions part of contract?

Facts
The plaintiff and her daughter booked a cruise on the 'Mikhail Lermontov' by paying a deposit. One week later they received a document headed 'Booking Form CTC Cruises'. This form contained, inter alia, the clause:

> 'Contract of Carriage for travel as set out ... will be made only at the time of issuing the tickets and will be subject to conditions and regulations printed on the tickets ...'

Having paid the balance, the plaintiff received tickets containing terms and conditions, limiting the shipping line's liability for personal injury and death. Just over a week into the cruise, the liner struck a rock and sank. The plaintiff suffered personal injury and nervous shock.

The plaintiff claimed damages for personal injuries, loss of property and loss of the enjoyment of the holiday. The defendants argued that limitation clauses, referred to on the ticket, formed part of the conditions of the contract and that they were entitled to rely on them.

Held
The statement in the initial brochure (supplied on receipt of the deposit) was insufficient to draw the attention of the customer to the fact that limitation clauses were contained in the ticket terms and conditions. The issue of a ticket with terms and conditions printed in full occurred after payment of the balance and a firm contract of carriage was already in existence. At the time the contract of carriage came into force, the plaintiff had not had a reasonable opportunity to see and agree to conditions and terms referred to, and which the defendants sought to impose on all the passengers when tickets were delivered, which was about a month or more later.

Exclusion or limitation clauses thus referred to, on the ticket, could not be said to be incorporated into the contract and could not be relied upon.

Flamar Interocean Ltd v Denmac Ltd, The Flamar Pride and The Flamar Progress [1990] 1 Lloyd's Rep 434 High Court (Potter J)

Exclusion clause – UCTA 1977 – reasonableness

Facts
The owners of the two vessels claimed damages for breach of contract against the defendants, the technical managers of the vessels. The contract(s) in question was a ship's management contract for each vessel, pertaining to pre-delivery inspection of the vessels, maintenance inspections, insurance and so on. The question arose as to whether the technical managers (the defendants) could rely on an exclusion clause in the contract.

Held
Under s2(2) of the Unfair Contract Terms Act 1977 a person could not exclude or restrict his liability for negligence, save insofar as the clause might satisfy the test of reasonableness. It was incontestable that there had been negligence, in (inter alia): (a) failure to require adequate and thorough pre-delivery tests to be carried out; (b) failure to engage someone with experience of refrigerated vessels; and (c) failure to provide liability insurance cover. The clauses in question did not satisfy the test of reasonableness as

laid out in s11(1) of the 1977 Act, providing that the term shall be fair and reasonable having regard to the circumstances 'which were, or ought reasonably to have been, known to or in the contemplation of the parties when the contract was made'. The exclusion clause could not be relied on by the defendants.

George Mitchell (Chesterhall) Ltd v *Finney Lock Seeds Ltd* [1983] 3 WLR 163 House of Lords (Lord Diplock, Lord Scarman, Lord Roskill, Lord Bridge of Harwich and Lord Brightman)

Clause limiting liability – fundamental breach

Facts
The plaintiffs orally ordered 30 lbs of late cabbage seed from the defendant. An invoice was presented on which conditions were printed and which the plaintiff knew were there. One of these conditions sought to limit the defendant's liability for defective seed to the price paid for that seed. Owing to the defendant's negligence, the seed was of the wrong type and was commercially useless. The price of the seed was £192; and the loss suffered by the plaintiff exceeded £61,000.

Held
1. On their true construction, the conditions limited the liability of the defendants to a refund of the price paid. *Photo Productions*; *Ailsa Craig Fishing* applied.

Lord Bridge:

'The *Photo Productions* case gave the final quietus to the doctrine that a "fundamental breach" of contract deprived the party in breach of the benefit of clauses in the contract excluding or limiting his liability.'

2. But that in all the circumstances, including the fact of the clear recognition in the seed trade that reliance on the conditions would not be fair or reasonable and that the defendants could insure against crop failure without materially increasing the price of seeds, it would not be fair or reasonable to allow reliance on the conditions, which were accordingly unenforceable.

Harris v *Wyre Forest District Council* see *Smith* v *Eric S Bush*

Hollier v *Rambler Motors (AMC) Ltd* [1972] 2 WLR 401 Court of Appeal (Salmon and Stamp LJJ and Latey J)

Exemption clause – previous dealings

Facts
The plaintiff sent his motor car to the defendants' garage for repairs. There had been three or four previous such transactions over a period of five years and, on at least two occasions, the plaintiff had signed an invoice containing an exemption clause in favour of the defendants, but on this occasion did not. The car was damaged by fire caused by the defendants' negligence.

Held
There was not sufficient previous course of dealing between the parties to impart the exemption clause into the present oral contract.

Salmon LJ:

> 'I am bound to say that ... I do not know of any other case in which it had been decided, or even argued, that a term could be implied into an oral contract on the strength of a course of dealing (if it can be so called) which consisted, at the most, of three or four transactions over a period of five years.'

Commentary

Applied: *McCutcheon* v *David MacBrayne Ltd* [1964] 1 WLR 125. Distinguished: *Kendall (Henry) & Sons* v *William Lillico & Sons Ltd* [1968] 3 WLR 110.

L'Estrange v *Graucob (F) Ltd* [1934] 2 KB 394 Court of Appeal (Scrutton and Maugham LJJ)

Exemption clause – sale of automatic machine

Facts

The plaintiff purchased an automatic machine from the defendants by a contract contained in the defendants' written 'Sale Agreement' which she signed. The machine proved faulty and the defendants sought to rely on an exemption clause in the agreement.

Held

Having signed the agreement, the plaintiff was bound by it.

Scrutton LJ:

> 'In this case the plaintiff has signed a document headed "Sales Agreement" which she admits had to do with an intended purchase and which contained a clause excluding all conditions and warranties. That being so, the plaintiff, having put her signature to the document, and not having been induced to do so by any fraud or misrepresentation, cannot be heard to say that she is not bound by the terms of the document because she did not read them.'

Levison v *Patent Steam Carpet Cleaning Co Ltd* [1977] 3 WLR 90 Court of Appeal (Lord Denning MR, Orr LJ and Sir David Cairns)

Exemption clause – fundamental breach

Facts

By telephone, the plaintiffs asked the defendants to collect their Chinese carpet worth £900 for cleaning. When the defendants' van driver called, he asked for the owner's signature on one of their order forms: one of the plaintiffs obliged, without reading the terms and conditions set out in small print above his signature. One of those conditions provided that the carpet's maximum value was deemed to be £40; another that all merchandise was 'expressly accepted at the owner's risk'. The carpet was never returned and, eventually, the defendants said that it had been stolen. The plaintiffs sued successfully to recover the carpet's full value: the defendants appealed.

Held

The appeal would be dismissed: there had been a fundamental breach of contract against which the defendants' exemption clauses did not afford them protection.

Orr LJ:

> 'On the first of the major issues in this appeal I agree with both Lord Denning MR and Sir David Cairns that the only contract between the parties was a written contract ... incorporating the printed terms and conditions; and like Sir David Cairns I should have reached the same conclusion in the absence of any previous dealing between the parties.
>
> As to the second major issue, whether the effect of ... the contract is to exclude liability of the defendants, for fundamental breach, I am content, following the decision of this court in *Alderslade* v *Hendon Laundry Ltd* [1945] KB 189 and the observations made in the House of Lords in *Suisse Atlantique Société d' Armament Maritime SA* v *NV Rotterdamsche Kolen Centrale* [1966] 2 WLR 944, to hold that it has no such effect because the words "All merchandise is expressly accepted at the owner's risk" are in my judgment, in the context of this contract, insufficiently clear or strong to be so construed, and having reached this conclusion I do not find it necessary to consider the factor of relative bargaining power.
>
> On the final and crucial issue as to the burden of proof I agree that as a matter both of justice and of common sense the burden ought to rest on the bailee who, if the goods have been lost while in his possession, is both more likely to know the facts and in a better position to ascertain them than the bailor, and I would on this issue follow the decision of McNair J in *Woolmer* v *Delmer Price Ltd* [1955] 1 QB 291, and the view expressed by Denning LJ in *J Spurling Ltd* v *Bradshaw* [1956] 1 WLR 461.'

McCutcheon v *David MacBrayne Ltd* [1964] 1 WLR 125 House of Lords (Lord Reid, Lord Hodson, Lord Guest, Lord Devlin and Lord Pearce)

Oral contract – previous transactions

Facts

At the appellant's request, his brother-in-law took his car to the respondents' office in Islay where he was quoted the freight for shipping to the mainland. Brother-in-law paid and was given a receipted invoice which he did not read. On the voyage, the ship sank, as a result of the respondents' negligent navigation, and the car was lost. The appellant claimed damages for negligence and the respondents relied on an exclusion clause exhibited in their office and on the ship: on the invoice was a statement, too, that goods were carried subject to the conditions specified on the respondents' notices. It was the respondents' usual practice to ask consignors to sign a risk note, but due to an oversight brother-in-law was not asked to sign one on this occasion. Both the appellant and brother-in-law had shipped goods through the respondents before: sometimes risk notes had been signed and, although the appellant knew that conditions of some kind existed, neither of them had ever read them. The respondents contended that, by reason of the previous dealings, the conditions were imported into the contract of carriage.

Held

This was not the case.

Lord Reid:

> 'The respondents contend that, by reason of the knowledge thus gained by the appellant and his agent in these previous transactions, the appellant is bound by their conditions. But this case differs essentially from the ticket cases. There, the carrier in making the contract hands over a document containing or referring to conditions which he intends to be part of the contract. So if the consignor or passenger, when accepting the document, knows or ought as a reasonable man to know that this is the carrier's intention, he can hardly deny that the conditions are part of the contract, or claim, in the absence of special circumstances, to be in a better position than he would be if he had read the document. But here, in making the contract neither party referred to, or indeed had in mind, any additional terms, and the contract was complete and full effective without any additional terms. If it could be said that when making the

contract [brother-in-law] knew that the respondents always required a risk note to be signed and knew that the purser was simply forgetting to put it before him for signature, then it might be said that neither he nor his principal could take advantage of the error of the other party of which he was aware. But counsel frankly admitted that he could not put his case as high as that. The only other ground on which it would seem possible to import these conditions is that based on a course of dealing. If two parties have made a series of similar contracts each containing certain conditions, and then they make another without expressly referring to those conditions it may be that those conditions ought to be implied. If the officious bystander had asked them whether they had intended to leave out the conditions this time, both must, as honest men, have said "of course not". But again the facts here will not support that ground. According to [brother-in-law], there had been no consistent course of dealing; sometimes he was asked to sign and sometimes not. And, moreover, he did not know what the conditions were. This time he was offered an oral contract without any reference to conditions, and he accepted the offer in good faith.

The respondents also rely on the appellant's previous knowledge. I doubt whether it is possible to spell out a course of dealing in his case. In all but one of the previous cases he had been acting on behalf of his employer in sending a different kind of goods and he did not know that the respondents always sought to insist on excluding liability for their own negligence. So it cannot be said that, when he asked his agent to make a contract for him, he knew that this or, indeed, any other special term would be included in it. He left his agent a free hand to contract, and I see nothing to prevent him from taking advantage of the contract which his agent in fact made.

"The judicial task is not to discover the actual intentions of each party: it is to decide what each was reasonably entitled to conclude from the attitude of the other." [*Law of Contract* by William M Gloag].

In this case I do not think that either party was reasonably bound or entitled to conclude from the attitude of the other as known to him that these conditions were intended by the other party to be part of this contract. I would therefore allow the appeal ...'

Commentary
Distinguished: *Parker* v *South Eastern Railway Co* (1877) 2 CPD 416. Applied in *Hollier* v *Rambler Motors (AMC) Ltd* [1972] 2 WLR 401.

Melrose v *Davidson* 1993 SLT 611 Inner House: First Division

Unfair contract term – exclusion clause

Facts
The plaintiffs applied for a loan to buy a house. They signed an application form in which the building society undertook to provide a copy of the mortgage valuation survey on the property. The same application form contained a clause purporting to exclude all liability for the mortgage survey report. The survey estimated that the property was in good condition and no essential repairs were needed. The plaintiffs proceeded with the purchase of the house, but defects were subsequently found in the property and the plaintiffs sued the surveyors.

Held
The 1977 Unfair Contract Terms Act applied to the contract. The contract was concerned with the valuation of the property as a preliminary to the provision of a loan. The exclusion clause would therefore have no effect.

Micklefield v SAC Technology Ltd [1990] 1 WLR 1002 High Court (John Mowbray QC)

Option lost if wrongfully dismissed?

Facts
The plaintiff director was entitled to subscribe for shares in the company under a share option scheme. The scheme provided that if he 'ceases to be employed [by the company] for any reason whatsoever, any option granted to him shall ... lapse and not be exercisable'. Further, the scheme provided that if he ceases to be so employed 'he shall not be entitled, and by applying for an option ... shall be deemed irrevocably to have waived any entitlement by way of compensation for loss of office or otherwise howsoever to any sum or other benefit to compensate him for the loss of any rights under the scheme'. The plaintiff gave notice of his intention to exercise the option; eight days later (and eight days before, in accordance with the terms of the scheme, he would have purchased the shares) his employment was terminated and he was given six months' salary in lieu of notice. Assuming (as the plaintiff contended) that he had been wrongfully dismissed, was he entitled to damages for loss of the option?

Held
He was not so entitled.

John Mowbray QC:

> '... the principle that a man cannot be permitted to take advantage of his own wrong (that is, in this context, from a breach by him of the contract), is subject to an exception. I refer to the speech of Lord Jauncey, with which all the rest of their Lordships agreed, in *Alghussein Establishment* v *Eton College* [1988] 1 WLR 587 at 595 where he said:
>
>> "For my part, I have no doubt that the weight of authority favours the view that, in general, the principle is embodied in a rule of construction rather than in an absolute rule of law."
>
> If that is correct, and the rule is only one of construction, then it can be excluded by a sufficiently clear contrary provision in the contract ... It follows that, so long as ... the scheme is sufficiently clear, it will exclude the principle.
>
> In my judgment, ... the scheme is clear and decisive enough to exclude the principle as well as to operate as an exemption clause. It expressly applies if an option holder ceases to be an executive for any reason. That, on its terms, includes the case of his being wrongly dismissed. If the clause stopped there, one might perhaps doubt whether it was meant to apply to a wrongful dismissal. As I see it, the rest of the clause, though, makes it clear that it can only apply in the case of a wrongful dismissal. It goes on with a waiver of any entitlement by way of compensation for loss of office. Such an entitlement could only arise in a case of wrongful dismissal and the word "waiver" makes it clear that it is some right of the plaintiff's that is being removed from him. Counsel for the plaintiff said it would be necessary to refer openly to a wrongful dismissal, but I do not take that view. I think this is a clause which is intended and clearly sufficient to enable the company to escape part of its liability.'

His Lordship also decided that s3 of the Unfair Contract Terms Act 1977 did not apply to share option schemes: see ibid, Schedule 1, para 1(e).

Commentary
Alghussein Establishment v *Eton College* [1988] 1 WLR 587: see Chapter 26.

Olley v *Marlborough Court Ltd* [1949] 1 KB 532 Court of Appeal (Bucknill, Singleton and Denning LJJ)

Hotel – notice in bedroom

Facts
The plaintiffs arrived at a hotel, booked in at reception and paid in advance. They went up to their room where a notice purported to exempt the proprietors for articles lost or stolen unless handed to the manageress for safe custody. During their stay some clothing was stolen from their room.

Held
The contract had been concluded when the plaintiffs booked and paid for their room and the defendants could not unilaterally vary the contract to include as a term the notice in the bedroom, which the plaintiffs only saw at a later stage.

Denning LJ:

> 'The only other point in the case is whether the hotel company are protected by the notice which they put in the bedrooms, "The proprietors will not hold themselves responsible for articles lost or stolen, unless handed to the manageress for safe custody". The first question is whether that notice formed part of the contract. Now people who rely on a contract to exempt themselves from their common law liability, must prove that contract strictly. Not only must the terms of the contract be clearly proved, but also the intention to create legal relations – the intention to be legally bound – must also be clearly proved. The best way of proving it is by a written document, signed by the party to be bound. Another way is by handing him, before or at the time of the contract, a written notice specifying its terms and making it clear to him that the contract is on those terms. A prominent public notice which is plain for him to see when he makes the contract, or an express oral stipulation would, no doubt, have the same effect. But nothing short of one of these three ways will suffice. It has been held that mere notices put on receipts for money do not make a contract. (See *Chapelton* v *Barry Urban District Council*). So also, in my opinion, notices put up in bedrooms do not of themselves make a contract. As a rule, the guest does not see them until after he has been accepted as a guest. The hotel company no doubt hopes that the guest will be bound by them, but the hope is vain unless they clearly show that he agreed to be bound by them, which is rarely the case.'

Parker v *South Eastern Railway Co* (1877) 2 CPD 416 Court of Appeal (Mellish, Baggallay and Bramwell LJJ)

Clause on back of ticket – effect

Facts
The plaintiff deposited a bag in a cloakroom of a railway station owned by the defendants. He was given a ticket which stated on its face, 'see back'. On the back was a clause limiting the defendants' liability to £10. The plaintiff's bag, worth £24 10s, was lost.

Held
The plaintiff was bound by the clause, even though he had not read it; the defendants had done all that was reasonably necessary to bring the clause to his attention.

Mellish LJ:

> 'The question then is, whether the plaintiff was bound by the conditions contained in the ticket. In an ordinary case, where an action is brought on a written agreement which is signed by the defendant, the

agreement is proved by proving his signature and, in the absence of fraud, it is wholly immaterial that he has not read the agreement and does not know its contents. The parties may, however, reduce their agreement into writing, so that the writing constitutes the sole evidence of the agreement, without signing it; but in that case, there must be evidence independently of the agreement itself to prove that the defendant has assented to it. In that case also, if it is proved that the defendant has assented to the writing constituting the agreement between the parties, it is, in the absence of fraud, immaterial that the defendant had not read the agreement and did not know its contents. Now if, in the course of making a contract, one party delivers to another a paper containing writing and the party receiving the papers knows that the papers contain conditions which the party delivering it intends to constitute the contract, I have no doubt that the party receiving the paper does, by receiving and keeping it, assent to the conditions contained in it, although he does not read them and does not know what they are. I hold, therefore, that the case of *Harris* v *Great Western Railway* was rightly decided, because in that case, the plaintiff admitted, on cross examination, that she believed there were some conditions on the ticket. On the other hand, the case of *Henderson* v *Stevenson* LR 2 Sc & Div 470, is a conclusive authority that if the person receiving the ticket does not know that there is any writing upon the back of the ticket, he is not bound by a condition printed on the back. The facts in the cases before us differ from those in both *Henderson* v *Stevenson* and *Harris* v *Great Western Railway* because, in both the cases which have been argued before us, though the plaintiffs admitted that they knew there was writing on the back of the ticket, they swore not only that they did not read it, but that they did not know or believe that the writing contained conditions, and we are to consider whether, under those circumstances, we can lay down, as a matter of law, either that the plaintiff is bound or that he is not bound by the conditions contained in the ticket, or whether his being bound depends on some question of fact to be determined by the jury and, if so, whether, in the present case, the right question was left to the jury.

Now I am of the opinion that we cannot lay down, as a matter of law, either that the plaintiff was bound or that he was not bound by the conditions printed on the ticket, from the mere fact that he knew there was writing on the ticket but did not know that the writing contained conditions. I think there may be cases in which a paper containing writing is delivered by one party to another in the course of a business transaction, where it would be quite reasonable that the party receiving it should assume that the writing contained in it no condition and should put it in his pocket unread. For instance, if a person driving through a turnpike gate received a ticket upon paying the toll, he might reasonably assume that the object of the ticket was that by producing it, he might be free from paying toll at some other turnpike gate and might put it in his pocket unread. On the other hand, if a person who ships goods to be carried on a voyage by sea receives a bill of lading signed by the master, he would plainly be bound by it, although afterwards, in an action against the shipowners for the loss of the goods, he might swear that he had never read the bill of lading and that he did not know that it contained the terms of the contract of carriage and that the shipowner was protected by the exception contained in it. Now the reason why the person receiving the bill of lading would be bound, seems to me to be that in the great majority of cases, persons shipping goods do know that the bill of lading contains the terms of the contract of carriage; and the shipowner, or the master delivering the bill of lading, is entitled to assume that the person shipping goods has that knowledge. It is, however, quite possible to suppose that a person who is neither a man of business nor a lawyer might, on some particular occasion, ship goods without the least knowledge of what a bill of lading was, but in my opinion, such a person must bear the consequences of his own exceptional ignorance, it being plainly impossible that business could be carried on if every person who delivers a bill of lading had to stop to explain what a bill of lading was.

Now the question we have to consider is whether the railway company was entitled to assume that a person depositing luggage and receiving a ticket in such a way that he could see that some writing was printed on it, would understand that the writing contained the conditions of contract; this seems to me, to depend upon whether people in general would, in fact, and naturally, draw that inference. The railway company, as it seems to me, must be entitled to make some assumptions respecting the person who deposits luggage with them: I think they are entitled to assume that he can read and that he understands the English language and that he pays such attention to what he is about as may be reasonably expected from a person in such a transaction as that of depositing luggage in a cloakroom. The railway company must, however, take mankind as they find them and if what they do is sufficient to inform people in general that the ticket contains conditions, I think that a particular plaintiff ought not to be in a better position than other persons on account of his exceptional ignorance or stupidity or carelessness. But if what the railway company do is not sufficient to convey to the minds of people in general that the ticket contains conditions, then they have received goods on deposit without obtaining the consent of the persons depositing them to the conditions limiting their liability. I am of the opinion, therefore, that the proper direction to leave to the jury in these cases is, that if the person receiving the ticket did not see or know that there was any writing on the ticket, he is not bound by the conditions; that if he knew there was writing and knew or believed that the writing contained conditions, then he is bound by the conditions; that if he knew there was writing on the ticket, but did not know or believe that the writing contained conditions, nevertheless he would be bound if the delivering of the ticket to him was in such a manner that he could see there was writing upon it was, in the opinion of the jury, reasonable notice that the writing contained conditions.

I have, lastly, to consider whether the direction of the learned judge was correct, namely, "Was the plaintiff, under the circumstances, under any obligation in the exercise of reasonable and proper caution, to read, or to make himself aware, of the condition?" I think that this direction was not strictly accurate and was calculated to mislead the jury. The plaintiff was certainly under no obligation to read the ticket, but was entitled to leave it unread if he pleased; and the question does not appear to me to direct the attention of the jury to the real question, namely whether the railway company did what was reasonably sufficient to give the plaintiff notice of the condition.

On the whole, I am of the opinion that there ought to be a new trial.'

Commentary
Distinguished in *McCutcheon* v *David MacBrayne Ltd* [1964] 1 WLR 125.

Phillips Products v *Hyland see Thompson* v *T Lohan (Plant Hire) Ltd*

Photo Production Ltd v *Securicor Transport Ltd* [1980] 2 WLR 283 House of Lords (Lord Wilberforce, Lord Diplock, Lord Salmon, Lord Keith and Lord Scarman)

Exception clause – fundamental breach

Facts
The plaintiffs employed the defendants to provide security services at their factory, including night patrols. While on such a patrol, an employee of the defendants deliberately lit a small fire, which got out of control and completely destroyed the factory and its contents, of value £615,000. The defendants in their defence, relied on an exemption clause; the Court of Appeal followed and applied *Harbutt's Plasticine* and found for the plaintiffs.

Held
There was no rule of law preventing the defendants from relying on the clause and, on its true construction, it exempted them from liability.

Lord Wilberforce:

'Much has been written about the *Suisse Atlantique Case*. Each speech has been subjected to various degrees of analysis and criticism, much of it constructive. Speaking for myself, I am conscious of imperfections of terminology, though sometimes in good company. But I do not think that I should be conducing to the clarity of the law by adding to what was already too ample a discussion, a further analysis which, in turn, would have to be interpreted. I have no second thoughts as to the main proposition that the question whether, and to what extent, an exclusion clause is to be applied to a fundamental breach, of a breach of a fundamental term, or, indeed, to any breach of contract, is a matter of construction of the contract. Many difficult questions arise and will continue to arise in the infinitely varied situations in which contracts come to be breached: by repudiatory breaches, accepted or not, anticipatory breaches, by breaches of conditions or of various terms and whether by negligent or deliberate action, or otherwise. But there are ample resources in the normal rules of contract law for dealing with these, without the superimposition of a judicially invented rule of law. I am content to leave the matter there with some supplementary observations.

1. The doctrine of "fundamental breach", in spite of its imperfections and doubtful parentage, has served a useful purpose. There were a large number of problems, productive of injustice, in which it was worse than unsatisfactory to leave exception clauses to operate. Lord Reid referred to these in the Suisse Atlantique Case, pointing out at the same time that the doctrine of fundamental breach was a dubious specific. But since then, Parliament has taken a hand: it has passed the Unfair Contract Terms Act 1977. This Act applies to consumer contracts and those based on standard terms and enables exception clauses to be applied with regard to what is just and reasonable. It is significant that Parliament refrained from legislating over the whole field of contract. After this Act, in commercial matters generally, when the parties are not of unequal bargaining power and when risks are normally borne by insurance, not only is the case for judicial intervention undemonstrated, but there is everything to be said, and this seems to have been Parliament's intention, for leaving the parties free to apportion the risks as they think fit and for respecting their decisions.

At the stage of negotiation as to the consequences of a breach, there is everything to be said for allowing the parties to estimate their respective claims according to the contractual provisions they have themselves made, rather than for facing them with a legal complex so uncertain as the doctrine of fundamental breach must be. What, for example, would have been the position of Photo Productions' factory if, instead of being destroyed, it had been damaged, slightly or moderately or severely? At what point does the doctrine (with logical justification I have not understood) decide, ex post facto, that the breach was (factually) fundamental before going on to ask whether, legally, it is to be regarded as fundamental? How is the date of "termination" to be fixed? Is it the date of the incident causing the damage, or the date of the innocent party's election, or some other date? All these difficulties arise from the doctrine and are left unsolved by it.

At the judicial stage there is still more to be said for leaving cases to be decided straightforwardly on what the parties have bargained for, rather than on analysis which becomes progressively more refined, of decisions in other cases on normal principles of contractual law with minimal citation of authority. I am sure that most commercial judges have wished to be able to do the same (cf *Angelia, (The) Trade and Transport Inc* v *Iino Kaiun Kaisha Ltd* per Kerr J). In my opinion they can and should.

2. *Harbutt's Plasticine Ltd* v *Wayne Tank and Pump Co Ltd* must clearly be overruled. It would be enough to put that on its radical inconsistency with the *Suisse Atlantique Case*. But even if the matter were res integra, I would find the decision to be based on unsatisfactory reasoning as to the "termination" of the contract and the effect of "termination" on the plaintiffs' claim for damage. I have, indeed, been unable to understand how the doctrine can be reconciled with the well accepted principle of law stated by the highest modern authority that when, in the context of a breach of contract, one speaks of "termination", what is meant is no more than that the innocent party or, in some cases, both parties, are excused from further performance. Damages in such cases are then claimed under the contract, so what reason in principle can there be for disregarding what the contract itself says about damages, whether it "liquidates", them, or limits them, or excludes them? These difficulties arise in part from uncertain or inconsistent terminology. A vast number of expressions are used to describe situations where a breach has been committed by one party, of such a character as to entitle the other party to refuse further performance; discharge, rescission, termination, the contract is at an end, or dead, or displaced; clauses cannot survive, or simply go. I have come to think that some of these difficulties can be avoided; in particular the use of "rescission", even if distinguished from rescission ab initio as an equivalent for discharge, though

justifiable in some contexts (see *Johnson* v *Agnew*) may lead to confusion in others. To plead for complete uniformity may be to cry for the moon. But what can and ought to be avoided is to make use of these confusions in order to produce a concealed and unreasoned legal innovation: to pass, for example, from saying that a party, victim of a breach of contract, is entitled to refuse further performance, to saying that he may treat the contract as at an end, or as rescinded, and to draw from this the proposition, which is not analytical but one of policy, that all or (arbitrarily) some of the clauses of the contract lose, automatically, their force, regardless of intention.

If this process is discontinued, the way is free to use such words as "discharge" or "termination" consistently with principles as stated by modern authority which *Harbutt's Case* disregards. I venture, with apology, to relate the classic passages. In *Heyman* v *Darwins Ltd* Lord Porter said:

> "To say that the contract is rescinded or has come to an end or has ceased to exist may, in individual cases, convey the truth with sufficient accuracy, but the fuller expression that the injured party is thereby absolved from future performance of his obligations under the contract, is a more exact description of the position. Strictly speaking, to say that upon acceptance of the renunciation of a contract the contract is rescinded, is incorrect. In such a case the injured party may accept the renunciation as a breach going to the root of the whole of the consideration. By that acceptance he is discharged from further performance and may bring an action for damages, but the contract itself is not rescinded."

Similarly Lord Macmillan: see also *Boston Deep Sea Fishing and Ice Co Ltd* v *Ansell* per Bowen LJ. In *Moschi* v *Lep Air Services Ltd* my noble and learned friend, Lord Diplock drew a distinction (relevant for that case) between primary obligations under a contract, which on "rescission" generally comes to an end, and secondary obligations which may then arise. Among the latter, he included an obligation to pay compensation, ie damages. And he stated in terms that this latter obligation "is just as much an obligation arising from the contract as are the primary obligations that it replaces". My noble and learned friend has developed this line of thought in an enlightening manner in his opinion, which I have now had the benefit of reading.

These passages, I believe to state correctly the modern law of contract in the relevant respects; they demonstrate that the whole foundation of Harbutt's Case is unsound. A fortiori, in addition to *Harbutt's Case* there must be overruled *Wathes (Western) Ltd* v *Austins (Menswear) Ltd*, which sought to apply the doctrine of fundamental breach to a case where, by election of the innocent party, the contract had not been terminated, an impossible acrobatic, yet necessarily engendered by the doctrine. Similarly, *Charterhouse Credit Co Ltd* v *Tolly* must be overruled, though the result might have been reached on construction of the contract.

3. I must add to this, by way of exception to the decision not to "gloss" the *Suisse Atlantique*, a brief observation on the deviation cases, since some reliance has been placed on them, particularly on the decision of this House in *Hain Steamship Co Ltd* v *Tate & Lyle Ltd* (so earlier than the *Suisse Atlantique*) in the support of the *Harbutt* doctrine. I suggested in the *Suisse Atlantique* that these cases can be regarded as proceeding on normal principles applicable to the law of contract generally, viz that it is a matter of the parties' intentions whether and to what extent clauses in shipping contracts can be applied after a deviation, ie a departure from the contractually agreed voyage or adventure. It may be preferable that they should be considered as a body of authority sui generis, with special rules derived from historical and commercial reasons. What, on either view, they cannot do is to lay down different rules as to contracts generally from those later stated by this House in *Heyman* v *Darwins Ltd*. The ingenious use by Donaldson J in *Kenyon, Son & Craven Ltd* v *Baxter Hoare & Co Ltd* of the doctrine of deviation in order to reconcile the *Suisse Atlantique* case with *Harbutt's Case*, itself based in part on the use of the doctrine of deviation, illustrates the contortions which that case has made necessary and would be unnecessary if it vanished as an authority.

4. It is not necessary to review fully the numerous cases in which the doctrine of fundamental breach has been applied or discussed. Many of these have now been superseded by the Unfair Contract Terms Act 1977. Others, as decisions, may be justified as depending on the contract (cf *Levison* v *Patent Steam*

Carpet Cleaning Co Ltd) in the light of well-known principles such as that stated in *Alderslade* v *Hendon Laundry Ltd.*

In this situation, the present case has to be decided. As a preliminary, the nature of the contract has to be understood. Securicor undertook to provide a service of periodical visits for a very modest charge, which works out at 26p per visit. It did not agree to provide equipment. It would have no knowledge of the value of Photo Productions' factory; that, and the efficacy of their fire precautions, would be known to Photo Productions. In these circumstances, nobody could consider it unreasonable that as between these two equal parties, the risk assumed by Securicor should be a modest one and that Photo Productions should carry the substantial risk of damage or destruction.

The duty of Securicor was, as stated, to provide a service. There must be implied an obligation to use care in selecting their patrolmen, to take care of the keys and, I would think, to operate the service with due and proper regard to the safety and security of the premises. The breach of duty committed by Securicor lay in a failure to discharge this latter obligation. Alternatively, it could be put on a vicarious responsibility for the wrongful act of Musgrove, viz starting a fire on the premises; Securicor would be responsible for this on the principle stated in *Morris* v *C W Martin & Sons Ltd*. This being the breach, does condition 1 apply? It is drafted in strong terms: "Under no circumstances, any injurious act or default by any employee". These words have to be approached with the aid of the cardinal rules of construction that they must be read contra proferentem and that in order to escape from the consequences of one's own wrongdoing, or that of one's servants, clear words are necessary. I think that these words are clear. Photo Productions in fact relied on them for an argument, that since they exempted from negligence, they must be taken as not exempting from the consequence of deliberate acts. But this is a perversion of the rule that if a clause can cover something other than negligence, it will not be applied to negligence. Whether, in addition to negligence, it covers other, eg deliberate acts, remains a matter of construction, requiring, of course, clear words. I am of the opinion that it does and, being free to construe and apply the clause, I must hold that liability is excluded. On this part of the case I agree with the judge and adopt his reasons for judgment. I would allow the appeal.'

Commentary
Applied: *Suisse Atlantique Société d'Armement Maritime SA* v *NV Rotterdamsche Kolen Centrale* [1966] 2 WLR 944. Overruled: *Harbutt's Plasticine Ltd* v *Wayne Tank and Pump Co Ltd* [1970] 2 WLR 198. Applied in *Mitchell (George) (Chesterhall) Ltd* v *Finney Lock Seeds Ltd* [1983] 3 WLR 163 and *Aforos Shipping Co SA* v *Pagnan, The Aforos* [1983] 1 WLR 195.

R & B Customs Brokers Co Ltd v *United Dominions Trust Ltd* [1987] 1 WLR 659n
Court of Appeal (Dillon and Neill LJJ)

Exclusion clause – 'dealing as consumer'

Facts
The plaintiffs bought from the defendant finance company a Colt Shogun ('the car'), the car having been supplied by the third party motor dealer who took the plaintiffs' Volvo in part exchange. The plaintiffs took the car on 21 September but, for some unknown reason, the defendants did not sign the conditional sale agreement ('the agreement') until 3 November and this was accepted to be the date of the contracts between the dealer and the defendants and the defendants and the plaintiffs respectively. Between these dates, the plaintiffs discovered that the car's roof leaked and the dealer took it in for repair on 5 November. The leak was not cured then or subsequently and in the following February the plaintiffs rejected the car and claimed their money back. The car was the second or third vehicle which the plaintiffs had acquired on credit terms and the agreement provided, inter alia, that any implied conditions

as to the condition or quality of the car or its fitness for any particular purpose in relation to business transactions were excluded.

Held
Unless excluded by the agreement's express terms, the sale was subject to an implied condition as to fitness under s14(3) of the Sale of Goods Act 1979. On the facts, this was a consumer transaction (as opposed to a business transaction) and the implied condition was not excluded. It followed that the plaintiffs were entitled to judgment.

Dillon LJ:

> '... I have no doubt that the requisite degree of regularity is not made out on the facts. [The plaintiff's] evidence that the car was the second or third vehicle acquired on credit terms was in my judgment and in the context of this case not enough. Accordingly, I agree with the judge that, in entering into the conditional sale agreement with the defendants, the company was "dealing as consumer". The defendants' [agreement] is thus inapplicable and the defendants are not absolved from liability under s14(3).'

Rutter v *Palmer* [1922] 2 KB 87 Court of Appeal (Bankes, Scrutton and Atkin LJJ)

Exclusion clause – sale of car

Facts
The plaintiff placed his car with the defendant dealer for sale on commission and the deposit note stated that 'customers' cars are driven by your staff at customers' sole risk'. While showing the car to a prospective purchaser, one of the defendant's drivers negligently caused the vehicle to collide with a lamp post.

Held
The defendant was effectively exempt from liability.

Scrutton LJ:

> 'The contract here is a contract by a garage proprietor to sell a car on commission. In order to bring about a purchase, a trial of the car may be necessary, and this involves the driving of the car by one of the servants of the garage proprietor. What is the liability of the latter in these circumstances? He is only liable for his own negligence, and for that of his servants. If an accident happens without any negligence on his part or on the part of his servants, he would not be liable; but if there has been negligence on his or his servants' part, which has caused the accident, he would be liable. That being so, this clause has been introduced into the contract, which he makes with his customer: "Customers' cars are driven by your staff at customers' sole risk". It seems to me that two obvious limitations must be put upon the meaning of these words. In the first place, "staff" must mean "staff of qualified drivers" – it does not include a typist or a charwoman – and, secondly, "driven" does not include joy-riding, but must mean driven for the purpose of the bailment, that is to say, for the purpose of selling the car. The clause cannot mean that the garage proprietor is to be exempt from liability if an accident happens while it is being taken out by a member of his clerical staff for pleasure. Thus limited, the clause, which is regularly inserted in all contracts by garage proprietors to sell customers' cars on commission and for that purpose to take them out for a trial run, can only have one meaning, and that is that the owner of the car must effect his own insurance against accidents due to the negligence of the garage proprietor's servants – that is to say, accidents for which without the clause the garage proprietor would be liable.
>
> It was contended on behalf of the plaintiff that the clause was ambiguous and must, therefore, be construed strictly against the party relying upon it ... I can find no ambiguity in this clause.'

St Albans City and District Council* v *International Computers Ltd (1994) The Times 11 November Queen's Bench Division (Scott Baker J)

Exclusion clause – reasonableness

Facts

A computer firm was sued by the local authority that had hired them to assess population figures on which to base community charges. The standard contract used by the computer firm contained an exclusion/limitation clause restricting liability to £100,000. The database supplied to the plaintiffs was seriously inaccurate and resulted ultimately in the local authority sustaining a loss of £1.3m.

Held

The limitation clause was unenforceable and unreasonable. Section 11(4) of the Unfair Contract Terms Act 1977 listed various criteria to be taken into account when assessing reasonableness. These included, inter alia, the defendants' resources, whether they had insurance cover and general equality of bargaining power. The defendant company, though internationally well-known, was not on an equal footing, but they could not justify the very low limitation (which was small in relation to potential loss) and most importantly they had aggregate insurance of £50 million. The Act placed the burden of proof on the defendants to establish the clause as fair and reasonable, and this the computer firm had failed to do. The court also took into account the practical consequences, ie that the loss, if not paid for by the defendants or their insurers, would fall on the ordinary population of St Albans. The defendants could not rely on the clause and must pay damages in full.

Scott Baker J:

'On whom was it better that a loss of that size should fall, a local authority or an international computer company? The latter was well able to insure and in the instant case was insured ... If the loss was to fall the other way it would ultimately be borne by the local population ... Those factors outweighed the facts that bodies should be free to make their own bargains, that the plaintiffs contracted with their eyes open, that such limitations were commonplace in the computer industry and that the software involved was an area of developing technology.'

Smith* v *Eric S Bush*, *Harris* v *Wyre Forest District Council [1989] 2 WLR 790 House of Lords (Lord Keith of Kinkel, Lord Brandon of Oakbrook, Lord Templeman, Lord Griffiths and Lord Jauncey of Tullichettle)

Surveyor's report – disclaimer of liability

Facts

The cases were heard together: their facts were similar and they involved the same points of law. In *Smith* the plaintiff applied to the Abbey National Building Society to enable her to buy a terraced house in Norwich for £17,500. She paid an inspection fee and signed an application form which stated that a copy of the survey report and mortgage valuation obtained by the society would be given to her. The form also contained a disclaimer to the effect that neither the society nor its surveyor warranted that the report and valuation would be accurate and that the report and valuation would be supplied without any acceptance of responsibility. The society instructed the defendant surveyors: in due course the plaintiff received a copy of their report and it contained a disclaimer in similar terms. On the strength of the report, the plaintiff completed the purchase, but the defendants had failed to notice that chimney breasts had been removed and 18 months later the house flues collapsed, causing substantial damage. The plaintiff sued for negligence and the defendants, inter alia, relied on the disclaimer which the plaintiff admitted she had read.

Held

The plaintiff was entitled to succeed. The defendants had owed her a duty of care, they had been in breach of that duty and in view of the Unfair Contract Terms Act 1977, they could not rely on the disclaimer.

Lord Templeman:

> 'It was submitted ... that the valuation ... obtained by the Abbey National was essential to enable them to fulfil their statutory duty imposed by the Building Societies Act 1962. But in *Candler* v *Crane Christmas & Co* [1951] 1 All ER 426 the draft accounts were prepared for the company, which was compelled by statute to produce accounts.
>
> In the present appeals ... the contractual duty of a valuer to value a house for the Abbey National did not prevent the valuer coming under a tortious duty to Mrs Smith, who was furnished with a report of the valuer and relied on the report.
>
> In general, I am of the opinion that in the absence of a disclaimer of liability the valuer who values a house for the purpose of a mortgage, knowing that the mortgagee will rely and the mortgagor will probably rely on the valuation, knowing that the purchaser mortgagor has in effect paid for the valuation, is under a duty to exercise reasonable skill and care and that duty is owed to both parties to the mortgage for which the valuation is made. Indeed, in both the appeals now under consideration the existence of such a dual duty is tacitly accepted and acknowledged because notices excluding liability for breach of the duty owed to the purchaser were drafted by the mortgagee and imposed on the purchaser. In these circumstances it is necessary to consider the second question which arises in these appeals, namely whether the disclaimers of liability are notices which fall within the Unfair Contract Terms Act 1977 ...
>
> Section 11(3) of the 1977 Act provides that, in considering whether it is fair and reasonable to allow reliance on a notice which excludes liability in tort, account must be taken of "all the circumstances obtaining when the liability arose or (but for the notice) would have arisen". Section 13(1) of the Act prevents the exclusion of any right or remedy and (to that extent) s2 also prevents the exclusion of liability "by reference to ... notices which exclude ... the relevant obligation or duty". ... In my opinion both these provisions support the view that the 1977 Act requires that all exclusion notices which would in common law provide a defence to an action for negligence must satisfy the requirement of reasonableness.
>
> The answer to the second question involved in these appeals is that the disclaimer of liability made by ... the Abbey National on behalf of the appellant surveyors in *Smith's* case constitute notices which fall within the 1977 Act and must satisfy the requirement of reasonableness.
>
> The third question is whether in relation to each exclusion clause it is, in the words of s11(3) of the 1977 Act:
>
>> "fair and reasonable to allow reliance on it, having regard to all the circumstances obtaining when the liability arose or (but for the notice) would have arisen." ...

Counsel for the surveyors ... urged on behalf of his clients in this appeal, and on behalf of valuers generally, that it is fair and reasonable for a valuer to rely on an exclusion clause, particularly an exclusion clause which is set forth so plainly in building society literature. The principal reasons urged by counsel for the surveyors are as follows. (1) The exclusion clause is clear and understandable and reiterated and is forcefully drawn to the attention of the purchaser. (2) The purchaser's solicitors should reinforce the warning and should urge the purchaser to appreciate that he cannot rely on a mortgage valuation and should obtain and pay for his own survey. (3) If valuers cannot disclaim liability they will be faced by more claims from purchasers, some of which will be unmeritorious but difficult and expensive to resist. (4) A valuer will become more cautious, take more time and produce more gloomy reports, which will make house transactions more difficult. (5) If a duty of care cannot be disclaimed the cost of negligence insurance for valuers and therefore the cost of valuation fees to the public will be increased.

Counsel for the surveyors also submitted that there was no contract between a valuer and a purchaser and that, so far as the purchaser was concerned, the valuation was "gratuitous", and the valuer should not be forced to accept a liability he was unwilling to undertake. My Lords, all these submissions are, in my view, inconsistent with the ambit and thrust of the 1977 Act ...

It is open to Parliament to provide that members of all professions or members of one profession providing services in the normal course of the exercise of their profession for reward shall be entitled to exclude or limit their liability for failure to exercise reasonable skill and care. In the absence of any such provision valuers are not, in my opinion, entitled to rely on a general exclusion of the common law duty of care owed to purchasers of houses by valuers to exercise reasonable skill and care in valuing houses for mortgage purposes.'

Lord Griffiths:

'It must ... be remembered that this is a decision in respect of a dwelling house of modest value in which it is widely recognised by surveyors that purchasers are in fact relying on their care and skill. It will obviously be of general application in broadly similar circumstances. But I expressly reserve my position in respect of valuations of quite different types of property for mortgage purposes, such as industrial property, large blocks of flats or very expensive houses. In such cases it may well be that the general expectation of the behaviour of the purchaser is quite different. With very large sums of money at stake prudence would seem to demand that the purchaser obtain his own structural survey to guide him in his purchase and, in such circumstances with very much larger sums of money at stake, it may be reasonable for the surveyors valuing on behalf of those who are providing the finance either to exclude or limit their liability to the purchaser.'

Smith v *South Wales Switchgear Ltd* [1978] 1 WLR 165 House of Lords (Lord Wilberforce, Viscount Dilhorne, Lord Salmon, Lord Fraser of Tullybelton and Lord Keith of Kinkel)

Conditions – indemnity

Facts

The respondents engaged the appellants to overhaul the electrical equipment in their factory, which contract was stated to be subject to the respondents' General Conditions. These conditions contained a clause purporting to make the appellants liable to indemnify the respondents against 'Any liability, loss, claim or proceedings whatsoever ... (i) in respect of personal injury to, or death of, any person whosoever ... (ii) in respect of any injury or damage whatsoever to any property, real or personal, arising out of or in the course of ... the execution of (the) order'. An employee of the appellants was seriously injured, due to the negligence of the respondents, who claimed against the appellant to be indemnified against his claim for damages.

Held

The clause did not, in its true construction, apply to the respondents' negligence.

Lord Fraser of Tullybelton:

'I come now to the question of construction. The indemnity clause is as follows:

"23 In the event of this order involving the carrying out of work by the Supplier and its sub-contractors on land and/or premises of the Purchaser, the Supplier will keep the Purchaser indemnified against: (a) all losses and costs incurred by reason of the Supplier's breach of any statute, bye-law or regulation. (b) Any liability, loss, claim or proceedings whatsoever under Statute or Common Law (i) in respect of personal injury to, or death of, any person whomsoever, (ii) in respect of any injury or damage whatsoever to any property, real or personal, arising out of or in the course of or caused by the execution of this order. The

Supplier will insure against and cause all sub-contractors to insure against their liability hereunder, and will produce to the Purchaser on demand the policies of insurance with current renewal receipts therefor."

The principles which are applicable to clauses which purport to exempt one party to a contract from liability, were stated by Lord Greene MR in *Alderslade* v *Hendon Laundry Ltd* and were quoted with approval by Lord Morton of Henryton in the Privy Council in *Canada Steamship Lines Ltd* v *R* where he summarised them as follows:

> "(i) If the clause contains language which expressly exempts the person in whose favour it is made (hereafter called 'the proferens') from the consequences of the negligence of his own servants, effect must be given to that provision ... (ii) if there is no express reference to negligence, the court must consider whether the words used are wide enough, in their ordinary meaning, to cover negligence on the part of the servants of the proferens. If a doubt arises at this point, it must be resolved against the proferens ... (iii) if the words used are wide enough for the above purpose, the court must then consider whether 'the head of damage may be based on some ground other than that of negligence', to quote again Lord Greene MR in the *Alderslade Case*. The 'other ground' must not be so fanciful or remote that the proferens cannot be supposed to have desired protection against it, but subject to this qualification, which is, no doubt, to be implied from Lord Greene's words, the existence of a possible head of damage other than that of negligence is fatal to the proferens even if the words used are, prima facie, wide enough to cover negligence on the part of his servants."

These rules were stated in relation to clauses of exemption, but they are, in my opinion, equally applicable to a clause of indemnity which in many cases, including *Canada Steamship Lines Ltd* v *R* is merely the obverse of the exemption. The statement has been accepted as authoritative in the law of Scotland: see *North of Scotland Hydro-Electric Board* v *D & R Taylor*, which was concerned with a clause of indemnity and it was accepted by both parties, rightly in my opinion, as being applicable to the present appeal.

The argument based on the first of Lord Morton of Henryton's tests can be disposed of quickly. Counsel for the respondents argued that paragraph (b) in the present indemnity clause contained language which "expressly" entitled the respondents to indemnity against the consequence of their own negligence and that the first test was satisfied. The argument was that the words "any liability, loss, claim or proceedings whatsoever", amounted to an express reference to such negligence because they covered any liability however caused. The argument was supported by reference to the opinions of Buckley and Orr LJJ in *Gillespie Brothers & Co Ltd* v *Roy Bowles Transport Ltd,* where great emphasis was placed on the word "whatsoever" occurring in an indemnity clause as showing that the indemnity was intended to apply to all claims and demands however caused, including claims for negligence. I agree with the decision in that case and with the statement by Buckley LJ that the clause was one "which cannot sensibly be construed as subject to an implied qualification", but I am unable to agree with Buckley LJ's conclusion that the clause contained "an agreement in express terms" to indemnify the proferens. I do not see how a clause can "expressly" exempt or indemnify the proferens against his negligence unless it contains the word "negligence" or some synonym for it and I think that is what Lord Morton of Henryton must have intended, as appears from the opening words of his second test ("If there is no express reference to negligence"). On this point I agree with the opinion of the Lord Justice Clerk (Lord Wheatley) in the present case and of Lord Maxwell in *Clark* v *Sir William Arrol & Co Ltd*. The word "whatsoever" occurs in paragraph (b) of clause 23 here, but, in my opinion, it is no more than a word of emphasis and it cannot be read as equivalent to an express reference to negligence. To hold that it could, would be to invest it with the same sort of magic property as the word "allernarly" used to have in relation to an alimentary literent in Scotland and there is no justification for that. In the present case. I am clearly of the opinion that there is no express provision that the respondents are to be indemnified against the results of their own negligence and that the Second Division were right in so holding.

I pass then to consider the second test. The words "Any liability ... whatsoever under ... Common Law ... in respect of personal injury" which occur near the beginning of clause 23(b), if read in isolation, are of course wide enough to cover liability arising from negligence of the respondents or their servants. But they cannot properly be read in isolation from their context in clause 23 and in the general conditions.

I have reached the opinion that clause 23(b), read as a whole, does not apply to liability arising from negligence by the respondents or their servants. The general conditions are evidently intended to apply to many contracts where the respondents are "the Purchaser" and some other party is the supplier of goods or service to them. But clause 23 applies only "in the event of (the particular contract) involving the carrying out of work by the supplier *and* its sub-contractors on" the respondents' premises. (Counsel for the appellants accepted, rightly in my opinion, that the word "and" which I have italicised, must be read as if it were, or included, "or". Otherwise, in a case such as the present, where no sub-contractors were involved, the clause would not apply at all. That seems absurd.) The clause is thus looking to cases where the employees of the supplier will be working on the respondents' premises and it very naturally provides for an indemnity against the consequences of negligence by those employees while working there. But the employees of the respondents would not require to do any work in carrying out the contract and it seems unlikely that the parties intended that the respondents were to be indemnified by the appellants against liability as occupiers of the factory, especially as the indemnity is against claims in respect of injury to any person whomsoever and is not limited to servants of the suppliers or sub-contractors. Moreover, the indemnity is, in the final words of paragraph (b), in respect of injuries etc, "arising out of or in the course of or caused by the execution of this order" and the only parties who will be concerned in "execution" of the order are the appellants and any sub-contractors. "In the course of" must convey some connection with execution of the order beyond the merely temporal; and thus they appropriately apply to activities of the party who is carrying out work under the order.

The scope of the indemnity is defined in paragraphs (a) and (b) of clause 23. It was accepted by both parties in argument that paragraph (a) is concerned only with breaches of criminal law. That appears rather less clearly in the March 1970 version ("all losses and costs incurred by reason of the Suppliers' breach of any statute, by-law or regulation") than in the original version ("all fines, penalties and loss incurred ...") but I think it is clear enough. Paragraph (b) is evidently concerned with civil liability. In contrast with paragraph (a) it is not expressly limited to liabilities incurred by reason of the acts or omissions of the supplier. So far as it goes, that contrast is in favour of the respondents, but it is not, in my opinion, enough to overcome the other indications that I have mentioned, which point in favour of the appellants.

Some further support for the appellants' argument is to be derived from the final part of clause 23 dealing with insurance. No doubt these provisions are obscure and the reference to sub-contractors insuring against "their liability hereunder" (which I read as meaning "under this clause") is inept, as no liability was imposed on sub-contractors under the clause, nor could it have been, as no sub-contractors were parties to the contract. But it evidently contemplates both suppliers and sub-contractors, if any, having liabilities under paragraph (b) of the clause; these must, I think, be separate liabilities arising from the respective acts or omissions. Otherwise the effect of the insurance provisions would be to require double (or multiple) insurance by suppliers and (apparently all) sub-contractors against liability arising from acts or omissions of any part, including the respondents; it seems to me most unlikely that that can have been intended.

For these reasons, the construction of clause 23 goes, in my opinion, further than raising a doubt to be resolved against the respondents as the proferens under the second test and leads to a positive conclusion adverse to them. That is enough for the decision of the appeal, but if it were necessary to go on to consider the third test, I would hold that the head of damage under liability at common law for personal injury, may be based on some ground other than the respondents' own negligence. The possibility of common law liability falling on the respondents, as occupiers of the premises, through the fault of the suppliers' servants, is, in my opinion, not fanciful or remote. Nor is the possibility of claims for nuisance or for breach of contract caused by defective work by the suppliers. No doubt the respondents would have a right of relief against the supplier in most, if not all, of these cases, but that is not a sufficient answer, as they might well prefer to rely on the protection of an express right of indemnity rather than on their right to raise an action of relief with all its inevitable hazards. See *North of Scotland Hydro Electric Board* v *D & R Taylor* per the Lord Justice Clerk (Thomson) and Lord Patrick.'

Spurling (J) Ltd v *Bradshaw* [1956] 1 WLR 461 Court of Appeal (Denning, Morris and Parker LJJ)

Exemption clause – loss howsoever caused

Facts
The defendant bought eight barrels of orange juice and sent them to the plaintiff warehousemen to be stored. The plaintiffs sent a 'landing account' acknowledging receipt and stating: 'The company's conditions as printed on the back hereof cover the goods ...' Those conditions included: 'We will not in any circumstances ... be liable for any loss ... howsoever ... occasioned ... even when such loss ... may have been occasioned by the negligence ... of ourselves or our servants or agents ...' On the same day the plaintiffs sent an invoice for storage fees and there appeared on the invoice: 'All goods are handled ... in accordance with the conditions as over and warehoused at owner's risk ...': there were no conditions 'as over'. When eventually released by the plaintiffs, the juice was in bad condition. At the trial, the defendant conceded that he had received many landing accounts from the plaintiffs in respect of other goods but he said that he had never read the conditions on the back of them.

Held
The conditions formed part of the contract as the defendant had sufficient notice of them and the plaintiffs were protected by the exempting clause.

Denning LJ:

'Another thing to remember about these exempting clauses is that in the ordinary way the burden is on the bailee to bring himself within the exception. A bailor, by pleading and presenting his case properly, can always put the burden of proof on the bailee. In the case of non-delivery, for instance, all he need plead is the contract and a failure to deliver on demand. That puts on the bailee the burden of proving either loss without his fault (which would be a complete answer at common law) or, if the loss was due to his fault, that it was a fault from which he is excluded by the exempting clause ... I do not think that the Court of Appeal in *Alderslade* v *Hendon Laundry Ltd* ... had the burden of proof in mind at all. Likewise, with goods that are returned by the bailee in a damaged condition, the burden is on him to show that the damage was done without his fault: or that, if fault there was, it was excused by the exempting clause. Nothing else will suffice. Where, however, the only charge made in the pleadings – or the only reasonable inference on the facts – is that the damage was due to negligence and nothing more, then the bailee can rely on the exempting clause without more ado. That was, I think, the case here. As I read the pleadings, and the way in which the case was put to the judge, the defendant was complaining of negligence and nothing more. The clause therefore avails to exempt the plaintiffs provided that it was part of the contract.

This brings me to the question whether this clause was part of the contract. Counsel for the defendant urged us to hold that the plaintiffs did not do what was reasonably sufficient to give notice of the conditions within *Parker* v *South Eastern Ry Co*. I agree that the more unreasonable a clause is, the greater the notice which must be given of it. Some clauses which I have seen would need to be printed in red ink on the face of the document with a red hand pointing to it before the notice could be held to be sufficient. The clause in this case, however, in my judgment, does not call for such exceptional treatment, especially when it is construed, as it should be, subject to the proviso that it only applies when the warehouseman is carrying out his contract and not when he is deviating from it or breaking it in a radical respect. So construed, the judge was, I think, entitled to find that sufficient notice was given. It is to be noticed that the landing account on its face told the defendant that the goods would be insured if he gave instructions; otherwise they were not insured. The invoice, on its face, told him they were warehoused "at owner's risk". The printed conditions, when read subject to the proviso which I have mentioned, added little or nothing to those explicit statements taken together. Next it was said that the landing account and invoice were issued after the goods had been received and could not therefore be part of the contract of bailment:

but the defendant admitted that he had received many landing accounts before. True he had not troubled to read them. On receiving this account, he took no objection to it, left the goods there, and went on paying the warehouse rent for months afterwards. It seems to me that by the course of business and conduct of the parties, these conditions were part of the contract.

In these circumstances, the plaintiffs were entitled to rely on this exempting condition.'

Suisse Atlantique Société d'Armement Maritime SA v *NV Rotterdamsche Kolen Centrale* [1966] 2 WLR 944 House of Lords (Viscount Dilhorne, Lord Reid, Lord Hodson, Lord Upjohn and Lord Wilberforce)

Exception clause – fundamental breach

Facts

A charter party was arranged for a ship to be hired for two years. The time was to be spent in consecutive voyages between North America and Europe. Payment was to be made on the basis of the number of voyages completed. In fact eight round trips were completed altogether, though the owners alleged that six more trips could have been made had the ship not spent an inordinate number of lay-days in port. (This may have had something to do with the sudden fall in freight charges following the re-opening of the Suez Canal.) One clause in the charter purported to restrict compensation for each lay-day to US $1,000. The owners claimed that they had suffered substantially higher losses and said that they were not bound by the exclusion/limitation clause because the charterers had committed a fundamental breach of contract.

Held

The clause was found not to be an exclusion clause at all but a liquidated damages clause, and as such the parties were bound by it. But, obiter, the Lords in discussing exclusion clauses and fundamental breach made it clear that the doctrine of fundamental breach should not, as a matter of policy, be permitted to nullify exclusion or limitation clauses.

Lord Upjohn:

'At the conclusion of his main argument, counsel for the owners endeavoured to take a new point not raised in the courts below, namely that the charterers had committed a fundamental breach of the contract which amounted to a repudiation and, upon that footing, it was urged that the owners were entitled to general damages for lack of profitability and were not confined to demurrage.

Your Lordships, in the special circumstances of this case, permitted this appeal to be reargued de novo after supplemental cases have been lodged by each side. The owner's basic argument on this new case is that after the first voyage, there were such delays beyond the lay days each time that the ship entered port for loading or discharge, that the delays, each admittedly a breach of the charter party, amounted cumulatively to a repudiation of the contract which entitled the respondents, at their option, to accept and to treat the contract as at an end and sail away. This appeal comes before your Lordships on a consultative case by the arbitrators and the relevant facts have not yet been found on this point, so for the purposes of this point, it is necessary to make the double assumption in favour of the owners, first that it is open to the arbitrators on the facts to find that there has been a breach of contract by the charterers which goes to its root and entitled the owners to treat the contract as at an end and secondly, that in fact they will so find ... for the purpose solely of dealing with the argument, I am prepared to make the assumptions desired by the owners.

But what seems to be quite clear, making these assumptions, is that there has been no acceptance by the owners of the repudiation which brought the contract to an end. On the contrary, it seems to me clear that, by their conduct, the owners expressly affirmed the contract. The relevant facts were known at all material times to them, for they must have been currently aware of the excessive delays in port; they had already sailed away once – I say nothing about that for it is still sub judice – but it was for the owners, knowing of the delays, to make up their minds whether to sail away again. They did not do so and with full knowledge of the facts, elected to treat the contract as on foot until the expiry of the charter party by effluxion of time. It is this feature which gives rise to the whole difficulty in this interesting case. For it is common ground that had the owners accepted the assumed repudiation and sailed away, thereby terminating the contract, none of its terms survived and damages for breach of contract would have been at large, including damages for loss of profitable employment of the ship for the term of the charter party.

In general it cannot be disputed that where a party, having an option to treat a contract at an end nevertheless affirms it, that contract and all its terms must remain in full force and effect for the benefit of both parties during the remainder of the period of performance, for it is not possible even for the innocent party to make a new contract between the parties without the concurrence of the other ... Now it is, in my opinion, quite clear that as a matter of construction of the charter party, the demurrage clause both as to loading and discharging is expressed without limitation of time and therefore applies throughout the term of the contract ... Therefore, to succeed in this appeal, the owner must displace the demurrage clause. He seeks to do in reliance on the well known doctrine that in certain circumstances a party to a contract cannot rely on an exception or limitation clause inserted solely for his benefit. But before examining this doctrine, the first question which logically must be asked is, surely, whether this demurrage clause is a clause of exception or limitation. Whatever the ultimate ambit of the doctrine may be found to be, it is, in my opinion, confined to clauses which are truly inserted for the purpose only of protecting one contracting party from the legal consequences of other express terms of the contract, or from terms which would otherwise be implied by law, or from the terms of the contract regarded as a whole; just as one party may waive a clause which is inserted solely for his benefit ... so per contra there are occasions when a party cannot be permitted to rely on such a clause. But if the clause is inserted for the benefit of both, I know of no authority – and none has been cited – which entitles one party unilaterally to disregard its provisions. In my opinion, the demurrage with which we are concerned is a clause providing for agreed damages and is different from a clause excluding or limiting liability for damages by breach of contract by one party. An agreed damages clause is for the benefit of both; the party establishing breach by the other need prove no damage in fact; the other must pay that, no less but no more. But where liability for damages is limited by a clause, then the person seeking to claim damages must prove them at least up to the limit laid down by the clause; the other party, whatever may be the damage in fact, can refuse to pay more if he can rely on the clause. As Greer J said in relation to a demurrage clause in *Aktieselskabet Reidar* v *Arcos Ltd* [1926] 2 KB 83, 86: "this clause was put in for my benefit as well as yours; it measures the damages I have to pay ... " Counsel for the owners sought to say that the agreed damages of $1,000 a day were much too low to be an estimate of damage and that it might be open to the arbitrators to hold that in truth this was in the nature of a penalty clause or a limitation clause, limiting liability. I do not think it is open now to the owners to make this submission. It is quite clear on the authorities that the parties need not agree on a true estimate of damage. They are perfectly entitled to agree on a low rate. See *Cellulose Acetate Silk Co Ltd* v *Widnes Foundry (1926) Ltd* [1933] AC 20.

Accordingly, in my opinion, the demurrage clause is a clause which, the contract being affirmed, remains an agreed damages clause for the benefit of both parties and it is not a clause of exception or limitation inserted for the benefit of one party only to which the doctrine under consideration can properly be applied. That is sufficient to dispose of this appeal.

But in view of the arguments that have been addressed to your Lordships, I think it is right that I should express my views thereon upon the footing that the demurrage clause in this case is, indeed, a clause of exception or limitation of liability inserted solely for the benefit of the charterer and that it is therefore a clause to which, in certain circumstances, the doctrine relied upon by the appellants applies. That the doctrine exists is not in doubt, but it is necessary to examine the authorities to understand the principle upon which it is based.

There was much discussion during the argument upon the phrases "fundamental breach" and "breach of a fundamental term" and I think it is true that in some of the cases these terms have been used interchangeably; but in fact they are quite different. I believe that all your Lordships are agreed and, indeed, it has not seriously been disputed before us that there is no magic in the words "fundamental breach"; this expression is no more than a convenient shorthand expression for saying that a particular breach or breaches of contract by one party is or are such as to go to the root of the contract, which entitles the other party to treat such breach or breaches as a repudiation of the whole contract. Whether such breach or breaches do constitute a fundamental breach depends on the construction of the contract and on all the facts and circumstances of the case. The innocent party may accept that breach or those breaches as a repudiation and treat the whole contract as at an end and sue for damages generally, or he may, at his option, prefer to affirm the contract and treat it as continuing on foot, in which case he can sue only for damages for breach or breaches of the particular stipulations in the contract which has or have been broken.

But the expression "fundamental term" has a different meaning.

A fundamental term of a contract is a stipulation which the parties have agreed either expressly or by necessary implication, or which the general law regards as a condition which goes to the root of the contract, so that any breach of that term may at once, and without further reference to the facts and circumstances, be regarded by the innocent party as a fundamental breach and this is conferred on him by the alternative remedies at his option that I have just mentioned ...

... the law is now quite clearly established that unless the parties otherwise agree, the usual and customary course on any voyage described in a charter party is a fundamental term and therefore any breach of it (however, for practical purposes, irrelevant) is a fundamental breach ...

... the necessary result, in my opinion, is that the principle upon which one party to a contract cannot rely on the clause of exception or limitation of liability inserted for his sole protection, is not because they are regarded as subject to any special rule of law applicable to such clauses as being in general opposed to the policy of the law for some other reason but ... it is the consequence of the application of the ordinary rules applicable to all contracts that if there is a fundamental breach accepted by the innocent party, the contract is at an end; the guilty party cannot rely on any special terms in the contract. If not so accepted, the clauses of exception or limitation remain in force like all the other clauses of the contract ...

... as, in my opinion, the owners have expressly affirmed the contract, they cannot escape the consequences of the demurrage clause unless, as a matter of construction of that clause, they can show that it has no application to the events of this clause; this they cannot do for the reasons I have already given. Accordingly upon the footing that the demurrage clause is a clause of exclusion or limitation, this does not avail the owners in this case.

But, my Lords, again having regard to the arguments addressed to your Lordships, I think I ought to make one or two observations upon the question of construction of exclusion or limitation clauses.

It cannot be doubted that even while the contract continues in force (that is, there has been no fundamental breach, but only some lesser breach), exclusion clauses are strictly construed. Why this should be so is largely a matter of history and I think probably stems from the fact that in so many cases exception clauses are to be found in rather small print, sometimes on the back of the main terms of the contract and that the doctrine of "contra proferentes" has been applied. But whatever the reason, that they are strictly construed against the contracting party seeking protection, even during the currency of the contract, cannot be doubted ...

But where there is a breach of a fundamental term, the law has taken an even firmer line, for there is a strong, though rebuttable, presumption that in inserting a clause of exclusion or limitation in their contract, the parties are not contemplating breaches of fundamental terms and such clauses do not apply to relieve a party from the consequences of such a breach even where the contract continues in force. This result has been achieved by a robust use of a well known canon of construction that wide words which, taken in isolation, would bear one meaning must be so construed as to give business efficacy to the contract and the presumed intention of the parties upon the footing that both parties are intending to carry out the contract fundamentally ...

My Lords, in view of the introduction in the questions posed by the arbitrator of the impact of a presumed wilful default, for my part, I think it is only necessary to say that it seems to me as a matter of general principle that wilful default in connection with the matter we are now considering is relevant and relevant only to one matter, that is to say whether, in fact, the owners can establish a fundamental breach. In cases such as this, where there has been no breach of any fundamental term, the question as to whether there has been a fundamental breach must be a question of fact and degree in all the circumstances of the case, but one of the elements in reaching a conclusion upon that matter is necessarily the question as to whether there has been a wilful breach, for as a practical matter it cannot be doubted that it is easier to find as a fact, for such it primarily is, that the charterers are evincing an intention no longer to be bound by the terms of the contract and are therefore guilty of repudiatory conduct if it can be established that the breaches have been wilful and not innocent. I say no more than that. My Lords, I would dismiss this appeal.'

Commentary
Applied in *Photo Production Ltd* v *Securicor Transport Ltd* [1980] 2 WLR 283.

Thompson v *T Lohan (Plant Hire) Ltd* [1987] 1 WLR 649 Court of Appeal (Fox, Dillon and Woolf LJJ)

Exclusion clause – unfair term?

Facts
The second defendants (hirers) hired an excavator with a driver from the first defendants. Clause 8 of the contract of hire provided that the driver then became the agent of the hirer who was totally responsible for all their acts. Whilst performing his duties negligently the driver killed the plaintiff's husband, who was an employee of the first defendants. The plaintiff recovered damages against the first defendants [the driver's employers]. The first defendants sought to recoup the money they had paid out from the second defendants. The second defendants argued that Clause 8 of the contract was contrary to s2(1) of the Unfair Contract Terms Act 1977 and thus invalid.

Held
This argument could not succeed.

Fox LJ:

'I come now to the final question, which concerns the operation of s2(1) of the Unfair Contract Terms Act 1977. Section 2 provides:

> "(1) A person cannot by reference to any contract term or to a notice given to persons generally or to particular persons exclude or restrict his liability for death or personal injury resulting from negligence.
> (2) In the case of other loss or damage, a person cannot so exclude or restrict his liability for negligence except in so far as the term or notice satisfies the requirement of reasonableness."

I should also refer to s4(1):

> "A person dealing as consumer cannot by reference to any contract term be made to idemnify another person (whether a party to the contract or not) in respect of liability that may be incurred by the other for negligence or breach of contract, except in so far as the contract term satisfies the requirement of reasonableness."

It is said on behalf of the third party that, assuming clause 8 to be otherwise valid and effective according to its tenor (as I have found), it operates to exclude or restrict a liability for death or personal injury resulting from negligence; and that therefore it offends in this case the provisions of s2(1) of the Act and is struck down.

We were referred to the decision of this court in *Phillips Product Ltd* v *Hyland (Note)* [1987] 1 WLR 659. The case is concerned with the construction of the Act of 1977. So far as material the facts were these.

In 1980 Phillips, who were steel stockholders, were carrying out extensions to their factory. They arranged with a builder, Mr Pritchard, that he should do the building work but they themselves were to be responsible for buying materials and arranging for the provision of plant, so far as necessary. However, they gave Mr Pritchard permission to place an order with the defendants, Hamstead (Plant Hire) Co Ltd, for the hiring of a JCB excavator. Mr Pritchard made arrangements on the telephone for the hire of a JCB excavator with a driver. The first defendant, Mr Hyland, arrived at Phillip's premises with a JCB machine, of which he was the driver.

Kenneth Jones J found Mr Hyland had made it perfectly plain to Mr Pritchard that he would brook no interference in the way in which he operated the JCB. However, during the course of his operating the JCB excavator, Mr Hyland collided with a part of Phillips's building, doing a good deal of damage to it. In consequence, Phillips issued a writ against Mr Hyland and Hamstead, and claimed damages against both defendants. It was conceded on behalf of the defendants that Mr Hyland had driven the JCB excavator without reasonable care and that the cost of making good the damage was £3,000. Accordingly, the judge gave judgment for Phillips against him in that sum.

At the trial the argument centred on the liability or otherwise of Hamstead in tort. It was conceded on their behalf that, apart from any special terms in the contract of hire, they were liable for the negligence of Mr Hyland as their employee so as to entitle Phillips to judgment against them for such sum as was awarded against Mr Hyland. However, it was contended on behalf of Hamstead that clause 8 of the terms of hire which, for all practical purposes are the same as clause 8 in the general terms and conditions in the present appeal, gave a complete defence to the claim. In giving the judgment of the Court of Appeal, Slade LJ said, post, p 665(g)–(h).

> "Certainly there is nothing which leads to the conclusion that a plant owner who uses the general conditions is not excluding his liability for negligence in the relevant sense by reference to the contract term clause 8. We are unable to accept that in the ordinary sensible meaning of words in the context of s2 and the Act as a whole, the provisions of clause 8 do not fall within the scope of s2(2). A transfer of liability from A to B necessarily and inevitably involves the exclusion of liability so far as A is concerned."

It was held that, in the circumstances, of that case, clause 8 could not operate, having regard to the provisions of s2(2), to give an indemnity as claimed.

Mr Samuels, for the third party, says that is the same in this case, and that the words from the judgment of Slade LJ to which I have referred exactly cover the position here. It is said that there is a transfer of liability from Lohan to the third party, and that that is exactly what s2(1) of the Act of 1977 is effective to prevent. In my view the comparison of this case with the *Phillips* case is not justified. It seems to me that the *Phillips* case was a quite different case, and the Court of Appeal was not addressing its mind to the problem which we have to determine in the present case.

In the *Phillips* case there was a tortfeasor, Hamstead, who were vicariously liable to Phillips for the damage done by their servant, Hyland. Thus Hamstead were liable to Phillips for negligence, but were seeking to exclude that liability by relying upon clause 8. If that reliance had been successful, the result in the *Phillips* case would be that the victim would be left with no remedy by virtue of the operation of clause 8. Prima facie the victim was entitled to damages for negligence against Hamstead, because Hamstead were vicariously liable in negligence for the acts of their own servant. So one starts from that point. There was a plain liability of Hamstead to Phillips. That was, as Slade LJ said, a case of a plant owner excluding his liability for negligence in the relevant sense by reference to the contract term, clause 8. I should mention that the *Phillips* case turned upon s2(2) of the Act, but that is of no consequence in the present case.

If one then turns to the present case, the sharp distinction between it and the *Phillips* case is this, that whereas in the *Phillips* case there was a liability in negligence of Hamstead to Phillips (and that was sought to be excluded), in the present case there is no exclusion or restriction of the liability sought to be achieved by reliance upon the provisions of clause 8. The plaintiff has her judgment against Lohan and can enforce it. The plaintiff is not prejudiced in any way by the operation sought to be established of clause 8. All that has happened is that Lohan and the third party have agreed between themselves who is to bear the consequences of Mr Hill's negligent acts. I can see nothing in s2(1) of the Act of 1977 to prevent that. In my opinion, s2(1) is concerned with protecting the victim of negligence and, of course, those who claim under him. It is not concerned with arrangements made by the wrongdoer with other persons as to the sharing or bearing of the burden of compensating the victim. In such a case it seems to me there is no exclusion or restriction of the liability at all. The liability has been established by Hodgson J. It is not in dispute and is now unalterable. The circumstance that the defendants have between themselves chosen to bear the liability in a particular way does not affect that liability; it does not exclude it, and it does not restrict it. The liability to the plaintiff is the only relevant liability in the case, as it seems to me, and that liability is still in existence and will continue until discharge by payment to the plaintiff. Nothing is excluded in relation to the liability, and the liability is not restricted in any way whatever. The liability of Lohan to the plaintiff remains intact. The liability of Hamstead to Phillips was sought to be excluded.

In those circumstances it seems to me that, looking at the language of s2(1), this case does not fall within its prohibition. I reach that conclusion on the language of s2 itself, and without reference to s4, to which I have referred and on which Mr Judge, for Lohan, relied. I do not find it necessary to consider it further, having regard to the conclusion which I have reached upon the language of s2 itself.

For the reasons which I have given, it seems to me that the judge came to the correct conclusion in this case, and I would therefore dismiss this appeal.'

Tudor Grange Holdings Ltd v *Citibank NA* [1991] 4 All ER 1; [1991] TLR 217
Chancery Division (Browne-Wilkinson VC)

Contractual exclusion clauses – previous settlements

Facts
At a hearing in chambers the defendant bank and others applied to have an action by the plaintiff company struck out. Judgment was given in open court.

By a deed of release, dated March 1989, the plaintiffs purported to release Citibank and its associates from 'all claims, demands and causes of action prior to the date hereof'.

The question arose as to whether this release was, under s10 of Unfair Contract Terms Act 1977, reasonable. The argument lay that it was not, and since it failed to satisfy the test of reasonableness it could not be binding.

Held
Section 10 was held not to be intended to cover the present situation; it did not cover settlements and compromises on events that had already occurred. In the view of the court the Act was aimed solely at exemption clauses, clauses modifying future liability – it was not concerned with retrospective claims or settlements. The claim by the plaintiffs was accordingly struck out and the release which they had agreed remained binding on them.

22 Undue Influence and Restraint of Trade

Allcard v *Skinner* (1887) 36 Ch D 145 Court of Appeal (Cotton, Lindley and Bowen LJJ)

Undue influence – gift to sisterhood

Facts
In 1867 an unmarried woman aged 27 sought a clergyman as a confessor. The following year she became an associate of the sisterhood of which he was spiritual director and in 1871 she was admitted a full member, taking vows of poverty, chastity and obedience. Without independent advice, she made gifts of money and stock to the mother superior on behalf of the sisterhood. She left the sisterhood in 1879 and in 1884 claimed the return of the stock. Proceedings to recover the stock were commenced in 1885.

Held
Although the plaintiff's gifts were voidable, (Cotton LJ dissenting) she was disentitled to recover because of her conduct and the delay.

Lindley LJ:

'... I believe that in this case there was in fact no unfair or undue influence brought to bear upon the plaintiff other than such as inevitably resulted from the training she had received, the promise she had made, the vows she had taken, and the rules to which she had submitted herself. But her gifts were in fact made under a pressure which, while it lasted, the plaintiff could not resist, and were not, in my opinion, past recall when the pressure was removed. When the plaintiff emancipated herself from the spell by which she was bound she was entitled to invoke the aid of the court in order to obtain the restitution from the defendant of so much of the plaintiff's property as had not been spent in accordance with the wishes of the plaintiff but remained in the hands of the defendant. The plaintiff now demands no more.

I proceed to consider the second point which arises in this case, viz, whether it is too late for the plaintiff to invoke the assistance of the court. More than six years had elapsed between the time when the plaintiff left the sisterhood and the commencement of the present action. The action is not one of those to which the Statute of Limitations in terms applies, nor is that statute pleaded. But this action very closely resembles an action for money had and received, laches and acquiescence are relied upon as a defence, and the question is whether this defence ought to prevail. In my opinion, it ought ...

It is not, however, necessary to decide whether this delay alone would be a sufficient defence to the action. The case by no means rests on mere lapse of time. There is far more than inactivity and delay on the part of the plaintiff. There is conduct amounting to confirmation of her gift. Gifts liable to be set aside by the court on the ground of undue influence have always been treated as voidable, and not void ... such gifts are voidable on equitable grounds only. A gift intended when made to be absolute and irrevocable, but liable to be set aside by a court of justice, not on the ground of change of mind on the part of the donor, but on grounds of public policy based upon the fact that the donor was not sufficiently free relatively to the donee – such a gift is very different from a loan which the borrower knows he is under an obligation to repay, and is also different from a gift expressly made revocable, and never intended to be absolute and unconditional. A gift made in terms absolute and unconditional naturally leads the donee to regard it as his own, and the longer he is left under this impression the more difficult it is justly to deprive him of what he has naturally so regarded.

So long as the relation between the donor and the donee which invalidates the gifts lasts, so long is it necessary to hold that lapse of time affords no sufficient ground for refusing relief to the donor. But this necessity ceases when the relation itself comes to an end; and if the donor desires to have his gift declared invalid and set aside, he ought, in my opinion, to seek relief within a reasonable time after the removal of the influence under which the gift was made. If he does not, the inference is strong, and if the lapse of time is long the inference becomes inevitable and conclusive – that the donor is content not to call the gift in question or, in other words, that he elects not to avoid it, or, what is the same thing in effect, that he ratifies and confirms it ... In this particular case the plaintiff considered, when she left the sisterhood, what course she should take, and she determined to do nothing, but to leave matters as they were. She insisted on having back her will, but she never asked for her money until the end of five years or so after she left the sisterhood. In this state of things I can only come to the conclusion that she deliberately chose not to attempt to avoid her gifts but to acquiesce in them, or, if the expression be preferred, to ratify or confirm them. I regard this as a question of fact, and upon the evidence I can come to no other conclusion than that which I have mentioned. Moreover, by demanding her will and not her money, she made her resolution known to the defendant.'

Amoco Australia Pty Ltd v *Rocca Bros Motor Engineering Co Pty Ltd* [1975] 2 WLR 779 Privy Council (Lord Morris of Borth-y-Gest, Lord Cross of Chelsea, Lord Kilbrandon, Lord Salmon and Lord Edmund Davies)

Restraint of trade – separate agreements

Facts
Arising from a lease and underlease, Rocca was to obtain petrol at a rebate price from Amoco which in turn was to obtain a trade tie in return for its investment in Rocca's service station. The two leases, it was found, were parts of a single commercial transaction.

Held
Both leases were unenforceable.

Lord Cross of Chelsea:

'The appellant argued that what was true of a mortgage – which takes effect by way of lease to the mortgagee – must also be true of an ordinary lease and that where a lease contains a covenant which is unenforceable as being in restraint of trade the covenantor – in this case the respondent – most [sic] elect either to give up the lease or to perform the covenant notwithstanding its unenforceability.

It is clear – as counsel indeed conceded – that no such election is required of the covenantor when the unenforceable promise is contained in a bare contract. Provided that the unenforceable part is severable the rest of the contract remains in force and either party can rely on its terms. It would be odd if the position should be different when the promise in question is contained in a lease. The fact that a covenantor has obtained and will continue to enjoy benefits under the relevant agreement which formed part of the consideration for the covenant which he claims to be unenforceable is no doubt pro tanto a reason for holding that the covenant is not in unreasonable restraint of trade. But once it is held that it is in unreasonable restraint of trade, there seems to be no reason for drawing any distinction with regard to the consequences between provisions in contracts and covenants in leases. If in a case where severance was possible the party who had entered into a covenant in a lease which was unenforceable because it was in unreasonable restraint of trade was forced to make the election suggested by counsel he would be put under pressure to observe a promise which public policy said he should be free to disregard. Lord Reid [in *Esso Petroleum* v *Harper's Garage (Stourport) Ltd*] was not expressing any opinion on the point and as at present advised their Lordships do not think that the assumption which he was prepared to make was justified. But even if the appellant was right in saying that had the covenants been severable the respondent would have been put to his election either to observe the unenforceable restraint or to give up the lease its case would not be advanced in the least since the covenants are not severable and the respondent has always been willing – indeed anxious – to give up the underlease provided that the headlease also disappears from the scene.

Finally their Lordships turn to consider whether the headlease can remain on foot if the provisions of the underlease disappear ... It is not possible to regard the two leases as separate dispositions of property. The agreement [for the leases] shows clearly that they were parts of a single commercial transaction under which the respondent was to get a supply of petrol at an agreed rebate and the appellant a trade tie with security for its investment in the station. The statements to the contrary in ... the headlease are simply untrue and it may well be that they were inserted in order to strengthen the position of the appellant in the event of the valdity of the trade tie in the underlease being challenged. If there was no question of public policy in the case then no doubt the respondent would be estopped from denying that the headlease was independent of the underlease but if there was such an estoppel here it would deter the respondent from asserting that the trade tie was unenforceable on grounds of public policy, since ... its position if the underlease went but the headlease remained in force would be far worse than if it acquiesced in the trade tie and retained the benefit of the underlease.'

Attwood v *Lamont* [1920] 3 KB 571 Court of Appeal (Lord Sterndale MR, Atkin and Younger LJJ)

Restraint of trade – tailor

Facts
The contract of employment of a cutter and head of the tailoring department of the plaintiff's general outfitter business provided:

'In consideration of the employers employing him in the capacity and at the salary aforesaid, the [employee] hereby agrees with the employers that he will not at any time hereafter, either on his own account or that of any wife of his, or in partnership with, or as assistant, servant, or agent, to any other person, persons, or company, carry on or be in any way directly or indirectly concerned in any of the following trades or businesses, that is to say, the trade or business of a tailor, dressmaker, general draper, milliner, hatter, haberdasher, gentlemen's, ladies', or children's outfitter, at any place within a radius of ten miles of the employers' place of business ...'

Held
The covenant was too wide to be enforced.

Lord Sterndale MR:

'... I think it is quite clear that this agreement was part of a scheme by which every head of a department was to be restrained from competition with the plaintiff, even in the business of departments with which he had no connection and with the customers of which he was never brought into contact.

If this be the true meaning of the agreement, it was, as it is described, an agreement not to trade in opposition, and not an agreement to restrain the unfair use of secrets or knowledge of customers acquired by the servants in the employers' service. To effect this object the retention of the restraint regarding the business of all the departments is necessary, and I think that to strike out references to all but the tailoring department is not merely to remove one of several covenants each directed to the legitimate object of preventing unfair competition, but to alter entirely the scope and intention of the agreement. It is thereby sought to be converted from an agreement to restrain general competition into an agreement which will conform to the requirements of the cases to which I have referred. I am of opinion that ... this agreement should not be severed. If this be right, the agreement is invalid, for, as it stands, it is far too wide, and it is unnecessary to consider whether, if severed, it could be upheld.'

Backhouse v *Backhouse* [1978] 1 WLR 243 High Court (Balcombe J)

Unequal bargaining power – husband and wife

Facts
Following the breakdown of their marriage, a husband was anxious to have the matrimonial home transferred into his sole name. He did not advise the wife to take independent legal advice and she received no consideration for the transfer except release from her liability under the mortgage of the property.

Held
Financial arrangements between the parties would be made on the basis that the transfer to the husband had not taken place.

Balcombe J:

'Counsel for the husband says that the wife was not poor or ignorant. She was certainly not wealthy ... She was not in my view "ignorant" in the sense that, as I said, she was an intelligent woman, but she certainly was given no value for her transfer, merely the release from her liability on the mortgage, and she received no independent advice. As for this last, I accept that no one can make a person go to solicitors if they do not wish to do so, but this wife was never even invited to do so before she signed away what was her only substantial capital asset ... When a marriage has broken down, both parties are liable to be in an emotional state. The party remaining in the matrimonial home, as the husband did in this case, has an advantage. The wife is no doubt in circumstances of great emotional strain. It seems to me that she should at least be encouraged to take independent advice so that she may know whether or not it is right for her, whatever the circumstances of the breakdown of the marriage may be, to transfer away what is her only substantial capital asset. It is possible that this is something which may come under the general heading which Lord Denning MR referred to in *Lloyds Bank Ltd* v *Bundy* as "inequality of bargaining power" where he summarised the various categories in which transactions can be set aside: duress, unconscionable transactions and so on, and suggested that through all these instances runs a single thread, that they rest on inequality of bargaining power. If that be right then it seems to me that this transaction is an example of something which is done where the parties did not have equal bargaining power and should not be at any rate encouraged by the courts. I consider too that counsel for the wife had a valid point when she said that by analogy with s34 of the Matrimonial Causes Act 1973, which precludes parties from contracting out of their right to apply to the court for an order containing financial arrangements, the court should not look with favour on assignments of proprietary interests in the matrimonial home made without the benefit of legal advice.

As it happens I do not have before me the issue whether the transfer should be set aside. In the end it may make very little difference, having regard to the very wide powers that are given to the court to produce a just result under ss23, 24 and 25 of the 1973 Act. I propose to approach the problem in this case on the basis that the transfer in question had not been made.'

Bank of Baroda v *Shah* [1988] 3 All ER 24 Court of Appeal (Dillon, Neill and Stocker LJJ)

Undue influence – bank's position

Facts
By way of a legal charge, the defendant husband and wife charged their property with the payment to the plaintiffs of all moneys at any time owed to the bank by Seasonworth Ltd ('Seasonworth'). The defendants entered into the charge as a result of misrepresentation and undue influence exerted by the wife's brother, one of two directors of Seasonworth whose solicitors (Shah & Burke) acted for the defendants in connection with the charge although they (the defendants) had not instructed them to do so. Seasonworth defaulted in its obligations to the bank: the bank sought possession of the defendants' property.

Held
An order for possession would be made.

Dillon LJ:

> 'Specifically, the defendants assert that, whatever the bank may have supposed: (i) they did not in fact have any solicitors, independent or not, to act for them or advise them; (ii) Shah & Burke were in fact only acting for Seasonworth and Jayantilal Shah [the wife's brother]; and (iii) accordingly, when Singh & Ruparell [the bank's solicitors] sent the legal charge ... to Shah & Burke for execution, that was tantamount to sending it to Jayantilal Shah himself to get it executed by the defendants for the bank, and if so was a direct parallel to the situation in *Avon Finance Co Ltd* v *Bridger* [1985] 2 All ER 281 given the bank's knowledge of Jayantilal Shah's influence or possible influence over the defendants ...
>
> It is impossible, in the light of *Coldunell Ltd* v *Gallon* [1986] 1 All ER 429 for this court to hold that there was an obligation in law on the bank or its solicitors to ensure that the defendants had entirely independent legal advice before the defendants executed the legal charge ... If therefore solicitors were acting for the defendants, who were also the solicitors acting for Seasonworth, that was not a situation which Singh & Ruparell were able to challenge or were required to challenge. They were entitled to assume that Shah & Burke would act honestly and would give proper advice to the defendants, if Shah & Burke were, as they represented, acting for the defendants ... Beyond that, however I do not see how Singh & Ruparell could have asked Shah & Burke for proof that Shah & Burke were indeed authorised by the defendants to act for the defendants; that was something that Singh & Ruparell had to take on trust, and when the legal charge executed by the defendants was returned to them by Shah & Burke they were entitled to treat the return of it as confirmation that Shah & Burke had indeed been acting as solicitors for the defendants.
>
> Against that background it is plain, in my judgment, that Singh & Ruparell never intended for a moment to leave it to Jayantilal Shah or Seasonworth to get the legal charge executed by the defendants. They left that to Shah & Burke in the capacity of solicitors for the defendants which Shah & Burke had represented themselves as holding and which Singh & Ruparell believed them to hold. The fact that, unknown to Singh & Ruparell, Shah & Burke had no authority from the defendants does not lead to the conclusion that Singh & Ruparell are to be treated as having entrusted the task of getting the legal charge executed by the defendants to Shah & Burke in the capacity which they actually did hold, namely as agents for Jayantilal Shah and solicitors for Seasonworth.
>
> Accordingly in my judgment the defendants fail to bring this case within the *Turnbull* v *Duval* [1902] AC 429 and *Chaplin* v *Brammall* [1908] 1 KB 233 line of authorities.
>
> In reaching the opposite conclusion the judge relied in particular on my judgment in *Kingsnorth Trust Ltd* v *Bell* [1986] 1 All ER 423. But the facts of that case are, in my judgment, significantly different from the facts of the present case, in that in that case there had been no suggestion at all that the husband's solicitors, Messrs Burnetts, had ever been instructed to act for the wife, before the lender's solicitors, Messrs Trump & Partners, asked Messrs Burnetts to get the mortgage executed by the wife.'

Bank of Credit and Commerce International SA v *Aboody* [1989] 2 WLR 759 Court of Appeal (Slade, Balcombe and Woolf LJJ)

Undue influence – husband and wife

Facts
A husband and wife owned a family company (Eratex Ltd) and the company's liabilities to its bank were secured, inter alia, by charges of the wife's house. The bank sought to enforce the securities and the wife pleaded actual undue influence by the husband. Although the judge found that such influence had been established, he refused to set aside the charges as it had not been proved that they were manifestly disadvantageous to the wife. The wife appealed.

Held
The appeal would be dismissed as the judge's conclusion that there had been no manifest disadvantage was correct and, further, it was probable that the wife would have entered into the charges even in the absence of undue influence.

Slade LJ:

'We now turn to consider the point of law which constitutes the first ground of appeal, namely that a party who proves that a transaction was induced by the actual exercise of undue influence is entitled to have it set aside without also proving that the transaction was manifestly disadvantageous to him or her.

Ever since the judgments of this court in *Allcard* v *Skinner* (1887) 36 Ch D 145 a clear distinction has been drawn between (1) those cases in which the court will uphold a plea of undue influence only if it is satisfied that such influence has been affirmatively proved on the evidence (commonly referred to as cases of "actual undue influence" and, in argument before us, as "class 1" cases); (2) those cases (commonly referred to as cases of "presumed undue influence," and, in argument before us, as "class 2" cases) in which the relationship between the parties will lead the court to presume that undue influence has been exerted unless evidence is adduced proving the contrary, eg by showing that the complaining party has had independent advice.

There are well established categories of relationship, such as a religious superior and inferior and doctor and patient where the relationship as such will give rise to the presumption (frequently referred to in argument before us as "class 2A" cases). The relationship of husband and wife does not as such give rise to the presumption: see *National Westminster Bank plc* v *Morgan* [1985] AC 686, 703B, and *Bank of Montreal* v *Stuart* [1911] AC 120. Nor does the normal relationship of banker and customer as such give rise to it. Nevertheless, on particular facts (frequently referred to in argument as "class 2B" cases) relationships not falling within the class 2A category may be shown to have become such as to justify the court in applying the same presumption.

> "the presumption of undue influence, like other presumptions, is a tool of the lawyer's trade whose function it is to enable him to arrive at a just result by bridging a gap in the evidence at a point where, in the nature of the case, evidence is difficult or impossible to come by:" see *In re The Estate of Brocklehurst, decd* [1978] Ch 14, 43, per Bridge LJ.

In the majority of reported cases on undue influence successful plaintiffs appear to have succeeded in reliance on the presumption. If on the facts both pleas are open to him, a plaintiff in such a case may well be advised to rely on actual and presumed undue influence cumulatively or in the alternative.

In the present case, however, no doubt after carefully considered advice, no attempt has been made to plead or submit that Mrs Aboody is entitled to the benefit of any presumption. Her case throughout has been pleaded and argued on the footing that it is a class 1 case, so that the onus falls on her to establish undue influence – an onus which, subject to the question of manifest disadvantage, the judge considered that she had discharged ...

... we must reject the first ground of appeal. In our judgment, and in the light of *National Westminster Bank plc* v *Morgan* [1985] AC 686, even a party who affirmatively proves that a transaction was induced by the exercise of undue influence is not entitled to have it set aside in reliance on the doctrine of undue influence without proving that the transaction was manifestly disadvantageous to him or her.

Since Mrs Aboody's claim in the present case is based exclusively on undue influence, it thus becomes necessary to consider whether, contrary to the judge's view, she has shown that all or any of the six transactions were manifestly disadvantageous to her ... Eratex Ltd was the family business and the sole or principal means of support of Mr and Mrs Aboody. Eratex Ltd might still have collapsed with or without the facilities covered by the six transactions. But at least these facilities gave it some hope of survival. The judge found that ... it had "more than an equal chance of surviving," and that, [later], it had "at least a reasonably good chance of surviving." If it had survived, the potential benefits to Mrs Aboody would have been substantial.

In the end, we can see no sufficient grounds for disagreeing with his conclusion that on balance a manifest disadvantage has not been shown by Mrs Aboody in respect of any of the six transactions ...

... in our judgment ... the jurisdiction exercised by the court in such cases is not essentially of a punitive nature; its purpose is to do justice to the complainant in suitable circumstances giving him or her relief from a disadvantageous transaction. We think that, at least in ordinary circumstances, it would not be appropriate for the court to exercise this jurisdiction in a case where the evidence establishes that on balance of probabilities the complainant would have entered into the transaction in any event. In the present case there is the additional factor that the transactions under attack are relied on not by Mr Aboody himself but by the bank, which was not personally responsible for exerting the undue influence. Even if Mrs Aboody had succeeded on all the other issues in this case, we are therefore disposed to think that it would not have been right to grant her equitable relief as against the bank, our decision being based not merely on narrow considerations of causation.'

Barclays Bank plc v *O'Brien* [1993] 3 WLR 786 House of Lords (Lord Templeman, Lord Lowry, Lord Browne-Wilkinson, Lord Slynn of Hadley and Lord Woolf)

Misrepresentation by husband – bank's constructive knowledge

Facts
Husband and wife made a joint application for overdraft facilities for a company in which the husband had an interest. The overdraft was secured on their home. The husband misrepresented the situation to the wife saying the facility was short-term and for a fixed low sum. The wife appealed on the basis that she had not read any of the documents and was unaware of the extent of the overdraft because of her husband's misrepresentation.

Held
A wife who stood surety for her husband's debt and who had been induced by undue influence, misrepresentation or similar wrong had a right to have the transaction set aside if the third party (in this case the bank) had actual or constructive knowledge.

The House of Lords held that unless reasonable steps were taken to ascertain a) whether the transaction was of financial advantage to the wife, and b) if there were reasons to suspect that the husband had committed a legal or equitable wrong which had induced the wife into the transaction, then there would be, at the least, constructive knowledge. The bank, having failed to take any such steps to verify the situation, had constructive knowledge of the husband's wrongful misrepresentation. The wife was entitled to have the charge set aside.

Briggs v *Oates* [1991] 1 All ER 407 High Court (Scott J)

Restraint of trade – geographical & chronological limits in employer – employee contracts

Facts
The defendant was employed by a firm of solicitors. The plaintiff was the senior partner of that firm. On 3 September 1979 the defendant was employed as salaried partner in the firm. The agreement

contained a clause preventing the defendant from practising as a solicitor for five years from the date of the termination of the agreement within a radius of five miles from the firm's office. In 1983 the senior partners dissolved the partnership according to the terms of their partnership and the defendant and one senior partner set up in practice only 120 yards from their old offices.

Held
Because the partners, in dissolving the partnership, committed a breach of contract the defendant was effectively released from his contractual obligations. But in any case, the clause would not satisfy the reasonableness criteria.

Scott J:

> 'It is well settled that the reasonableness of a restraint clause is to be tested by reference to the position as at the date of the contract of which it forms part. If the submissions of counsel for the plaintiff are right I would regard the cl 8 restraint as unreasonable as between the parties. A contract under which an employee could be immediately and wrongfully dismissed, but would nevertheless remain subject to an anti-competitive restraint, seems to me to be grossly unreasonable. I would not be prepared to enforce the restraint in such a contract.'

CIBC Mortgages plc v *Pitt* [1993] 3 WLR 802 House of Lords (Lord Templeman, Lord Lowry, Lord Browne-Wilkinson, Lord Slynn of Hadley and Lord Woolf)

Joint loan to husband and wife – undue influence by husband

Facts
The husband wished to buy stock market shares and borrowed money on the security of his and his wife's home. They jointly applied for a loan, stating that the purpose of the loan was to purchase a second home. The wife read none of the documents she signed and was 'pressured' by her husband into making the application in the first place. The husband defaulted on the loan repayments.

Held
While a claimant who could prove actual undue influence was entitled to have the impugned transaction set aside, the plaintiffs would only be affected if it could be established that they had actual or implied notice of the undue influence. In this case there was nothing to indicate that this was anything other than a normal loan to husband and wife's joint benefit.

Clarke v *Newland* [1991] 1 All ER 397 Court of Appeal (Neill and Balcombe LJJ)

Facts
The plaintiff was a general practitioner in London. In 1982 the defendant joined his practice as an assistant and in 1985 became a salaried partner. In the partnership agreement a clause provided that the defendant undertook not to practise in the practice area (which was geographically defined) within three years of the termination of the agreement. In 1988, the plaintiff gave notice to the defendant that he was terminating the agreement as he was, under the terms of the agreement, permitted to do. The defendant decided to set up in practice as a GP about 100 yards from the plaintiff's surgery. At first instance the court held that the covenant 'not to practise' was too wide and refused to grant an injunction to the plaintiff to enforce the covenant.

Held

The clause was so ambiguous as to be meaningless. Not only was the exact practice area not defined, but it was not clear whether it referred to practising as any sort of medical practitioner or just as a GP. Even the alternative spellings (practice/practise) created confusion.

Neill LJ:

> 'From these cases [*Haynes* v *Doman* [1899] 2 Ch 13, *Home Counties Dairies Ltd* v *Skilton* [1970] 1 All ER 1227 and *Littlewoods Organisation* v *Harris* [1978] 1 All ER 1026 (in which *Mills* v *Dunham* [1891] 1 Ch 576 and *Moenich* v *Fenestre* (1892) 67 LT 602 were cited)] and the other cases in the same field it is possible to collect certain rules: (1) that the question of construction should be approached in the first instance without regard to the question of legality or illegality; (2) that the clause should be construed with reference to the object sought to be obtained; (3) that in a restraint of trade case the object is the protection of one of the partners against rivalry in trade. To these rules can be added a fourth; (4) that the clause should be construed in its context and in the light of the factual matrix at the time when the agreement was made. One bears in mind the speech of Lord Wilberforce in *Prenn* v *Simmonds* [1971] 3 All ER 237 at 239 where he said:
>
>> "The time has long passed when agreements, even those under seal, were isolated from the matrix of facts in which they were set and interpreted purely on internal linguistic considerations." '

Cleveland Petroleum Co Ltd v *Dartstone Ltd* [1969] 1 WLR 116 Court of Appeal (Lord Denning MR, Russell and Salmon LJJ)

Restraint of trade – solus agreement

Facts

An underlease granted by the plaintiffs provided that the underlessee would sell only their petrol. The underlease was assigned to the defendants and they undertook to observe and perform the convenants in it. The defendants challenged the validity of the ties.

Held

They were bound by them.

Lord Denning MR:

> 'The law on this subject was fully considered by the House of Lords in *Esso Petroleum Co Ltd* v *Harper's Garage (Stourport) Ltd*. I need not go through all the judgments today, but it seems plain to me that in three at least of the speeches of their Lordships a distinction is taken between a man who is already in possession of the land before he ties himself to an oil company and a man who is out of possession and is let into it by an oil company. If an owner in possession ties himself for more than five years to take all his supplies from one company, that is an unreasonable restraint of trade and is invalid. But if a man, who is out of possession, is let into possession by the oil company on the terms that he is to tie himself to that company, such a tie is good. Lord Reid said:
>
>> "Restraint of trade appears to me to imply that a man contracts to give up some freedom which otherwise he would have had. A person buying or leasing land had no previous right to be there at all, let alone to trade there, and, when he takes possession of that land subject to a negative restrictive covenant, he gives up no right or freedom which he previously had."
>
> Lord Morris of Borth-y-Gest said:
>
>> "If one who seeks to take a lease of land knows that the only lease which is available to him is a lease with a restriction, then he must either take what is offered (on the appropriate financial terms) or he must

seek a lease elsewhere. No feature of public policy requires that, if he freely contracted, he should be excused from honouring his contract."

Lord Pearce said:

"It would be intolerable if, when a man chooses of his own free will to buy, or take a tenancy of, land which is made subject to a tie (doing so on terms more favourable to himself owing to the existence of the tie) he can then repudiate the tie while retaining the benefit."

It seems to me that in this court, on an interlocutory application, we should go by those sayings in the House of Lords. We should hold that when a person takes possession of premises under a lease, not having been in possession previously; and on taking possession, he enters into a restrictive covenant tying him to take all his supplies from the lessor, prima facie, the tie is valid. It is not an unreasonable restraint of trade. Such was the case here, because [the original underlessees] did not, so far as we know, have possession before the underlease ... So the tie in the original underlease was valid. In any case, however, it is to be observed that the defendants took possession themselves with their eyes open. They knew that there was this restrictive covenant on the land and nevertheless entered into this assignment binding themselves to it. Prima facie it is valid.'

Cornish v *Midland Bank plc* [1985] 3 All ER 513 Court of Appeal (Kerr, Croom-Johnson and Glidewell LJJ)

Undue influence – banker and customer

Facts
The plaintiff, a customer of the defendant bank, signed a second mortgage in favour of the bank without appreciating, and without being informed by the bank, that it was so worded as to secure not only a loan of £2,000 for house renovations, but also unlimited further advances made to her husband.

Held
Although the plaintiff was entitled to damages as the defendants had been in breach of their duty to her, the mortgage itself would not be set aside.

Croom-Johnson LJ:

'... between the trial by Taylor J and the hearing of this appeal the judgment in *National Westminster Bank plc* v *Morgan* has been reversed in the House of Lords (see ... [1985] 2 WLR 588). Lord Scarman, who made the principal speech, stated that to raise the presumption of undue influence it was necessary to show that the transaction had itself been wrongful in that it amounted to one in which an unfair advantage had been taken of another person. He considered the facts and held that there was no evidence that the bank had taken advantage of Mrs Morgan. The transaction had not been disadvantageous to her or gone beyond the normal business relationship of banker and customer.

Lord Scarman said ... [1985] 2 WLR 588 at 600:

"It was, as one would expect, conceded by counsel for the wife that the relationship between banker and customer is not one which ordinarily gives rise to a presumption of undue influence; and that in the ordinary course of banking business a banker can explain the nature of the proposed transaction without laying himself open to a charge of undue influence."

Faced with that fresh authority, counsel for the present plaintiff has properly conceded that the judge's decision on undue influence cannot stand. In this case the only relationship between the plaintiff and the bank was that of banker and customer. No unfair advantage was taken of her. The transaction of taking a second mortgage of the farm was not disadvantageous to her. That part of this appeal which submits that the mortgage should not be set aside must be allowed.'

Commentary
Followed: *National Westminster Bank plc* v *Morgan* [1985] 2 WLR 588. Applied: *Hedley Byrne & Co Ltd* v *Heller & Partners Ltd* [1963] 3 WLR 101.

Cresswell v *Potter* [1978] 1 WLR 255n High Court (Megarry J)

Unconscionable bargain – matrimonial home

Facts
The matrimonial home had been conveyed to a husband and wife as joint tenants at law and in equity. After the marriage had broken down the wife was handed a document to execute by an enquiry agent who acted on behalf of the husband and his solicitor. This document was described as a conveyance. By it, in return for an indemnity against the liabilities under a mortgage of the property but for no other consideration, the wife released and conveyed to the husband all her interest in the matrimonial home. She believed, according to her evidence, that she was signing a document that would make it possible to sell the property without affecting her rights in it. The enquiry agent, for his part, could remember very little about the execution of the document. Megarry J considered the three requirements laid down in *Fry* v *Lane* poverty and ignorance of the plaintiff; sale at an undervalue, and lack of independent advice.

Held
These three requirements – or their modern equivalents – were here satisfied so the conveyance would be set aside.

Esso Petroleum Co Ltd v *Harper's Garage (Stourport) Ltd* [1967] 2 WLR 871 House of Lords (Lord Reid, Lord Morris of Borth-y-Gest, Lord Hodson, Lord Pearce and Lord Wilberforce)

Petrol solus agreement – restraint of trade

Facts
Harper (respondents) owned two garages. Under an agreement with Esso the respondents agreed to buy all their requirements of motor fuels from the appellants at current list prices. One agreement was to last for 4 years 5 months and the other for 21 years. The respondents wished to shift to another brand of petrol and the appellants sought an injunction to prevent them from doing so.

Held
The test being reasonableness, the shorter agreement was enforceable but the longer was not.

Lord Reid:

> 'In my view this agreement is within the scope of the doctrine of restraint of trade as it had been developed in English law. Not only have the respondents agreed negatively not to sell other petrol but they have agreed positively to keep this garage open for the sale of the appellants' petrol at all reasonable hours throughout the period of the tie. It was argued that this was merely regulating the respondent's trading and rather promoting than restraining his trade. But regulating a person's existing trade may be a greater restraint than prohibiting him from engaging in a new trade. And a contract to take one's whole supply from one source may be much more hampering than a contract to sell one's whole output to one buyer. I would not attempt to define the dividing line between contracts which are and contracts which are not in

restraint of trade, but in my view this contract must be held to be in restraint of trade. So it is necessary to consider whether its provisions can be justified ...

Where two experienced traders are bargaining on equal terms and one has agreed to a restraint for reasons which seem good to him the court is in grave danger of stultifying itself if it says that it knows that trader's interest better than he does himself. But there may well be cases where, although the party to be restrained has deliberately accepted the main terms of the contract, he has been at a disadvantage as regards other terms: for example where a set of conditions has been incorporated which has not been the subject of negotiation – there the court may have greater freedom to hold them unreasonable ...

When petrol rationing came to an end in 1950 the large producers began to make agreements, now known as solus agreements, with garage owners under which the garage owner, in return for certain advantages, agreed to sell only the petrol of the producer with whom he made the agreement. Within a short time three-quarters of the filling stations in this country were tied in that way and by the dates of the agreements in this case over 90 per cent had agreed to ties. It appears that the garage owners were not at a disadvantage in bargaining with the large producing companies as there was intense competition between these companies to obtain these ties. So we can assume that both the garage owners and the companies thought that such ties were to their advantage. And it is not said in this case that all ties are either against the public interest or against the interest of the parties. The respondents' case is that the ties with which we are concerned are for too long periods.

The advantage to the garage owner is that he gets a rebate on the wholesale price of the petrol which he buys and also may get other benefits or financial assistance. The main advantages for the producing company appear to be that distribution is made easier and more economical and that it is assured of a steady outlet for its petrol over a period. As regards distribution, it appears that there were some 35,000 filling stations in this country at the relevant time, of which about a fifth were tied to the appellants. So they only have to distribute to some 7,000 filling stations instead of to a very much larger number if most filling stations sold several brands of petrol. But the main reason why the producing companies want ties for five years and more, instead of ties for one or two years only, seems to be that they can organise their business better if on the average only one fifth or less of their ties come to an end in any one year. The appellants make a point of the fact that they have invested some £200 millions in refineries and other plant and that they could not have done that unless they could foresee a steady and assured level of sales of their petrol. Most of their ties appear to have been made for periods of between five and 20 years. But we have no evidence as to the precise additional advantage which they derive from a five-year tie as compared with a two-year tie or from a 20-year tie as compared with a five-year tie.

The Court of Appeal held that these ties were for unreasonably long periods. They thought that, if for any reason the respondents ceased to sell the appellants' petrol, the appellants could have found other suitable outlets in the neighbourhood within two or three years. I do not think that that is the right test. In the first place there was no evidence about this and I do not think that it would be practicable to apply this test in practice. It might happen that when the respondents ceased to sell their petrol, the appellants would find such an alternative outlet in a very short time. But, looking to the fact that well over 90% of existing filling stations are tied and that there may be great difficulty in opening a new filling station, it might take a very long time to find an alternative. Any estimate of how long it might take to find suitable alternatives for the respondents' filling stations could be little better than guesswork.

... do not think that the appellants' interest can be regarded so narrowly. They are not so much concerned with any particular outlet as with maintaining a stable system of distribution throughout the country so as to enable their business to be run efficiently and economically. In my view there is sufficient material to justify a decision that ties of less than five years were insufficient, in the circumstances of the trade when these agreements were made, to afford adequate protection to the appellants' legitimate interests .... A tie for 21 years stretches far beyond any period for which developments are reasonably foreseeable. Restrictions on the garage owner which might seem tolerable and reasonable in reasonably foreseeable conditions might come to have a very different effect in quite different conditions: the public interest comes in here more strongly.'

Commentary
Distinguished: *Petrofina (Great Britain) Ltd* v *Martin* [1966] 2 WLR 318. Applied in *Alec Lobb (Garages) Ltd* v *Total Oil Great Britain Ltd* [1983] 1 WLR 87 and *Cleveland Petroleum Co Ltd* v *Dartstone Ltd* [1969] 1 WLR 116.

Fitch v *Dewes* [1921] 2 AC 158 House of Lords (Lord Birkenhead LC, Viscount Cave, Lord Sumner, Lord Parmoor and Lord Carson)

Restraint of trade – solicitor's managing clerk

Facts
The plaintiff employed the defendant as a managing clerk and the contract provided that the defendant would:

> '... not directly or indirectly become engaged or manage or be concerned in the office, profession or business of a solicitor within a radius of 7 miles of the Town Hall of Tamworth'

after the expiration of his term of service.

Held
Although unlimited in point of time, the clause would be enforced.

Lord Birkenhead LC:

> 'The controversy is the old one between freedom of contract and certain considerations of public policy, which have received much attention at the hands of the courts in the last few years. It is sufficient for me to say at this point that the contract was entered into between two solicitors: that at its date the appellant had reached the age of twenty-seven years; that he had been for some thirteen years employed in a solicitor's office; and it is reasonable to infer from the promotion which he had received and from the evident appreciation which his employer had formed of his services, that he was a young man alert and very competent both to understand and to safeguard his own interests. The agreement then into which he entered, and in respect of which he has accepted for a lengthy period the consideration which was to move from the covenantee towards himself, will naturally stand unless he satisfies your Lordships that it is bad as being in restraint of trade.
>
> What then is said by the appellant under that head? He does not complain of the restriction of space, and indeed it would have been very difficult for him to do so. The clause only restricts him from being directly or indirectly engaged in the office profession or business of a solicitor within a radius of seven miles of the Town Hall of Tamworth. We need not therefore trouble ourselves with any question of the restriction in respect of space but may confine ourselves to the complaint which is made that the agreement cannot stand, because the restriction in respect of time is unlimited and is against the public interest. But it is to be noticed here, as has been said in more than one of the earlier cases, that guidance may be derived in dealing with a restriction relating to time from an examination of the restriction which is made in respect of space. And the converse remark is of course equally true. For instance, if the restriction in respect of space is extremely limited, it is evident that a very considerable restriction in respect of time may be more acceptable than would otherwise have been the case.
>
> The courts have been generous in elucidating these matters by the enunciation of general principles in the course of the last few years, and I am extremely anxious not to carry this process further today; therefore I say plainly and, I hope, simply, that it has for long now been accepted that such an agreement as this, if it is impeached, is to be measured by reference to two considerations: first, is it against the public interest? And, second, does that which has been stipulated for exceed what is required for the protection of the convenantee? It might perhaps be more properly stated, as it has sometimes been with the highest authority stated, does it exceed what is necessary for the protection of both the parties? But the impeachment which

is in fact made in this case demands the consideration of the earlier question only, does the restriction which is attacked exceed that which was reasonably necessary for the protection of the convenantee?

My Lords, it is not contended that there is anything which is open to attack in clause 8 except that part of the clause which for all time excludes the appellant from carrying on practice within seven miles of Tamworth. Are we then to say that such a restriction so unlimited goes farther than is permitted in relation to the standard which I have restated? I am of opinion that it does not go too far. One of your Lordships asked Mr Clayton in the course of his argument what period in his judgment would be a reasonable period, and Mr Clayton replied that he thought that ten years might be a reasonable period. My Lords why? Why is it to be said than ten years is a reasonable period? I can quite easily understand that at the end of a period of ten years the appellant in this case, who by this very clause is not prevented from maintaining and even developing his business acquaintance with the clients of the firm so long as he does not practise within a range of seven miles, might have retained all these circumstances of special, and as I think of illegitimate, advantage for the purpose of competing with the business of the respondent, and then might come forward and do that very thing against which in my judgment the covenantee is abundantly entitled to be protected. Therefore I should dismiss a period of ten years and I should even say of twenty or thirty years that it was quite impossible to be dogmatic upon the period proper to each individual case. Some men live very long lives, and it might easily be that in a case in which two men were both tenacious of life the very same danger which applies at this moment in this case would present itself, in a more striking and formidable shape, at the end of twenty years or at the end of an even longer period. I have no doubt that it is for this reason that the courts long since determined that they would lay down no hard and fast rule either in relation to time or in relation to space, but that they would treat the question alike of time and of space as one of the elements by the light of which they would measure the reasonableness of the restriction taken as a whole.

I am therefore, for the reasons I have stated, of opinion that the attack which has been made upon this restriction fails. I find that it is not opposed to the public interest and that it does not exceed what is reasonably required under the circumstances of this case for the protection of this covenantee.'

Fry v *Lane* (1888) 40 Ch D 312 High Court (Kay J)

Undue influence – sale by 'poor, ignorant men'

Facts
Two men had sold their reversionary interests in certain property, according to them at a greatly undervalued price, and they sought to have the transactions set aside.

Held
They should succeed.

Kay J:

'On the evidence before me, I cannot hesitate to conclude that the price of £170 in J B Fry's case and £270 in George Fry's case, were both considerably below the real value ... Both J B Fry and his brother George were poor, ignorant men, to whom the temptation of the immediate possession of £100 would be very great. Neither of them in the transaction of the sale of his share was, in the words of Sir John Leach, "on equal terms" with the purchaser. Neither had independent advice. The solicitor who acted for both parties in each transaction seems, from the Law List, to have been admitted in March 1877. In October 1878, the time of completing the sale of J B Fry's share, he had not been more than a year and a half on the roll. His inexperience probably in some degree accounts for his allowing himself to be put in the position of solicitor for both parties in such a case. I think that in each transaction he must have been considering the purchaser's interest too much properly to guard that of the vendors. Nothing could be more obvious than to test the value by obtaining an offer from one or more of the leading offices in London which deal in purchases of this kind ...

I regret that I must, on the evidence, come to the conclusion that, though there was a semblance of bargaining by the solicitor in each case, he did not properly protect the vendors, but gave a great advantage to the purchasers who had been former clients, and for whom he was then acting. The circumstances illustrate the wisdom and necessity of the rule that a poor, ignorant man selling an interest of this kind should have independent advice, and that a purchase from him at an undervalue should be set aside if he has not. The most experienced solicitor acting for both sides, if he allows a sale at an undervalue, can hardly have duly performed his duty to the vendor. To act for both sides in such a case and permit a sale at an undervalue is a position in which no careful practitioner would allow himself to be placed.'

Commentary
Applied in *Cresswell* v *Potter* [1978] 1 WLR 255n

Goldsoll v *Goldman* [1915] 1 Ch 292 Court of Appeal (Lord Cozens-Hardy MR, Kennedy and Swinfen Eady LJJ)

Covenant in restraint of trade – severability

Facts
The plaintiff dealers substantially in imitation jewellery convenated with the defendant, a competitor, that he would not for two years 'either solely or jointly with or as agent or employee for any person or company, directly or indirectly carry on or be engaged, concerned, or interested in or render services (gratuitously or otherwise) to the business of a vendor of or dealer in real or imitation jewellery in the county of London, England, Scotland, Ireland, Wales or any part of the United Kingdom of Great Britain and Ireland and the Isle of Man, or in France, the United States of America, Russia, or Spain, or within twenty-five miles of Potsdamerstrasse, Berlin, or St Stefan's Kirche, Vienna.'

Notwithstanding this covenant, the defendant assisted and rendered services to a co-defendant carrying on a business identical with the plaintiffs' in the same street. There had been a breach of the covenant – could the covenant he had infringed be treated as good, either in whole or in part, and enforced?

Held
It could, by limiting the area of restraint to the United Kingdom and the Isle of Man and the extent of the restraint to imitation jewellery.

Lord Cozens-Hardy MR:

'On the question of the space covered by the covenant, Neville J, has held, and I entirely agree with him, that it is unreasonably large, in so far as it is intended to cover not merely the United Kingdom and the Isle of Man, but also the foreign countries mentioned in the covenant. He has also held – and his decision is consistent with a long series of authorities – that the covenant can be severed as regards the space covered by it. It is clear that part of the covenant dealing with the area is reasonable, and the learned judge in the court below has limited the injunction which he has granted to "the county of London, England, Scotland, Ireland and Wales, or any part of the United Kingdom of Great Britain and Ireland and the Isle of Man". That such a covenant is severable in this respect has been decided by authorities nearly two hundred years old.

No objection is taken, or could be taken, with regard to the limit of time. But the further difficulty has been raised that while the business of the plaintiffs was, as I have said, a business in imitation jewellery, the covenant is against carrying on or being engaged, concerned, or interested in "the business of a vendor of or dealer in real or imitation jewellery". It is admitted that the business of a dealer in real jewellery is not the same as that of a dealer in imitation jewellery. There are many shopkeepers who would be insulted if they were asked whether they sold imitation jewellery. That being so, it is difficult to support the whole of this provision, for the covenant must be limited to what is reasonably necessary for the protection of the covenantee's business.

Then comes the question whether the doctrine of severability is applicable to this part of the covenant. In my opinion it is, and the covenant is good in so far as it purports to restrain the covenantor from carrying on business in imitation jewellery.'

Home Counties Dairies Ltd v *Skilton* [1970] 1 WLR 526 Court of Appeal (Harman, Salmon and Cross LJJ)

Restraint of trade – milkman

Facts
The plaintiffs employed the defendant as a milk roundsman and he covenanted that he would not, during the year following the determination of his contract of service, sell or solicit orders for 'milk or dairy produce' from any person who had been a customer during the last six months of his service. After five years' service, he left and immediately began to work the same round for a competitor. It was argued by the defendant that the clause was too wide in that, on its literal meaning it would prevent him from entering into employment with a grocer who sold butter and cheese.

Held
The restraint was valid and would be enforced, inter alia, because the words 'dairy produce' would be construed as limited to the sort of dairy produce with which he had been concerned in his employment.

Harman J:

'… Agreements in restraint of trade, like other agreements, must be construed with reference to the object sought to be attained by them. In cases such as the one before us, the object is protection of one of the parties against rivalry in trade. Such agreement cannot be properly held to apply to cases which although covered by words of the agreement, cannot be reasonably supposed ever to have been contemplated by the parties and which on a rational view of the agreement are excluded from its operation by falling in truth, outside and not within its real scope.'

Kingsnorth Trust Ltd v *Bell* [1986] 1 WLR 119 Court of Appeal (Sir John Donaldson MR, Dillon LJ and Mustill J)

Undue influence – husband and wife

Facts
The defendant executed a mortgage deed in favour of the plaintiffs, induced so to do by a fraudulent misrepresentation made by her husband as to the purpose of the loan. The Court of Appeal observed that there is no presumption in law that a transaction between husband and wife for the husband's benefit was procured by undue influence (see *Bank of Montreal* v *Stuart* [1911] AC 120). In the instant case, however, it was established that the execution of the document by the defendant was procured by undue influence on the part of the husband and that she had not had independent advice. The plaintiffs argued that they were not bound by the fraudulent misrepresentation made by the husband.

Held
They were under the law of agency, a creditor who instructed a husband as agent to obtain the signing

of a document by his wife, was liable for any fraudulent misrepresentation made by the husband to obtain his wife's signature, irrespective of how personally innocent the creditor was.

It was observed, per curiam, that in circumstances such as these, the creditor ought, for his own protection, to insist that the person liable to be influenced had independent advice.

Commentary

Distinguished in *Coldunell Ltd* v *Gallon* [1986] 2 WLR 466 and *Midland Bank plc* v *Perry* (1987) The Times 28 May. See also *Midland Bank plc* v *Shephard* [1988] 3 All ER 17.

Levison v *Patent Steam Carpet Cleaning Co Ltd*

See Chapter 21.

Lloyds Bank Ltd v *Bundy* [1974] 3 WLR 501 Court of Appeal (Lord Denning MR, Cairns LJ and Sir Eric Sachs)

Undue influence – banker and customer

Facts

The defendant was an elderly farmer who was not well versed in business affairs: his farmhouse was his only asset. Both he and his son banked with the plaintiffs, as did the son's company. The defendant charged his houses to the bank to secure the company's overdraft and subsequently signed a further guarantee and charge. An assistant manager of the plaintiff bank, with the son, later told the defendant that they would only continue to support the company if he increased the guarantee and charge: he did so, the assistant manager appreciating that the defendant relied on him implicitly to advise him about the transaction 'as bank manager'.

Held

The guarantee and charge would be set aside.

Lord Denning MR:

> 'Gathering all together, I would suggest that through all these instances there runs a single thread. They rest on "inequality of bargaining power". By virtue of it, the English law gives relief to one who, without independent advice, enters into a contract on terms which are very unfair or transfers property for a consideration which is grossly inadequate, when his bargaining power is grievously impaired by reason of his own needs or desires, or by his own ignorance or infirmity, coupled with undue influences or pressures brought to bear on him by or for the benefit of the other. When I use the word "undue" I do not mean to suggest that the principle depends on proof of any wrongdoing. The one who stipulates for an unfair advantage may be moved solely by his own self-interest, unconscious of the distress he is bringing to the other. I have also avoided any reference to the will of the one being "dominated" or "overcome" by the other. One who is in extreme need may knowingly consent to a most improvident bargain, solely to relieve the straits in which he finds himself. Again, I do not mean to suggest that every transaction is saved by independent advice. But the absence of it may be fatal. With these explanations, I hope this principle will be found to reconcile the cases. Applying it to the present case, I would notice these points.
>
> 1. The consideration moving from the bank was grossly inadequate. The son's company was in serious difficulty ... The bank considered that their existing security was insufficient. In order to get further security, they asked the father to charge the house – his sole asset – to the uttermost ... That was for the benefit of the bank. But not at all for the benefit of the father, or indeed for the company. The bank did not promise to continue the overdraft or to increase it. On the contrary, they required the overdraft to be reduced. All that the company gained was a short respite from impending doom.

2. The relationship between the bank and the father was one of trust and confidence. The bank knew that the father relied on them implicitly to advise him about the transaction. The father trusted the bank. This gave the bank much influence on the father. Yet the bank failed in that trust. They allowed the father to charge the house to his ruin.
3. The relationship between the father and the son was one where the father's natural affection had much influence on him.
4. He would naturally desire to accede to his son's request. He trusted his son. There was a conflict of interest between the bank and the father. Yet the bank did not realise it. Nor did they suggest that the father should get independent advice. If the father had gone to his solicitor – or to any man of business – there is no doubt that any one of them would say: "You must not enter into this transaction. You are giving up your house, your sole remaining asset, for no benefit to you. The company is in such a parlous state that you must not do it."

These considerations seem to me to bring this case within the principles I have stated. But, in case that principle is wrong, I would also say that the case falls within the category of undue influence of the second class stated by Cotton LJ in *Allcard* v *Skinner*. I have no doubt that the assistant bank manager acted in the utmost good faith and was straightforward and genuine. Indeed the father said so. But beyond doubt he was acting in the interests of the bank – to get further security for a bad debt. There was such a relationship of trust and confidence between them that the bank ought not to have swept up his sole remaining asset into their hands – for nothing – without his having independent advice. I would therefore allow this appeal.'

Commentary
Distinguished in *Avon Finance Co Ltd* v *Bridger* [1985] 2 All ER 281.
See also *Backhouse* v *Backhouse* [1978] 1 WLR 243 and *Alec Lobb (Garages) Ltd* v *Total Oil GB Ltd* [1985] 1 WLR 173.

Mason v *Provident Clothing and Supply Co Ltd* [1913] AC 724 House of Lords (Viscount Haldane LC, Lord Dunedin, Lord Shaw and Lord Moulton)

Restraint of trade – canvasser

Facts
The plaintiffs were a clothing and supply company with branches all over England. The defendant was employed by them as a canvasser. In the contract of employment the defendant agreed to a restraint of trade clause which stated:

'... that the [defendant] would not within three years after termination of employment be in the employ of any person, firm or company carrying on or engaged in a business the same as or similiar to that of the [plaintiff company], or assist any person employed or assisting in any such business within 25 miles of London.'

Held
The clause was wider than was reasonably required for the plaintiffs' protection and it would not therefore be enforced.

Lord Moulton:

'... The law as to covenants in restraint of trade was so carefully and authoritatively formulated in this House in the *Nordenfelt* case that I do not think it necessary to discuss the numerous authorities cited in the course of the argument in order to ascertain what is the critical question which the Court ought to put to itself in such a case as this. It is as follows: Are the restrictions which the covenant imposes upon the freedom of action of the servant after he has left the service of the master greater than are reasonably necessary for the protection of the master in his business? ...

The nature of the employment of the appellant in this business was solely to obtain members and collect their instalments. A small district in London was assigned to him, which he canvassed and in which he collected the payments due, and outside that small district he had no duties. His employment was therefore that of a local canvasser and debt collector, and nothing more.

Such being the nature of the employment, it would be reasonable for the employer to protect himself against the danger of his former servant canvassing or collecting for a rival firm in the district in which he had been employed. If he were permitted to do so before the expiry of a reasonably long interval he would be in a position to give to his new employer all the advantages of that personal knowledge of the inhabitants of the locality, and more especially of his former customers, which he had acquired in the service of the respondents and at their expense. Against such a contingency the master might reasonably protect himself, but I can see no further or other protection which he could reasonably demand. If the servant is employed by a rival firm in some district which neither includes that in which he formerly worked for the respondents, nor is immediately adjoining thereto, there is no personal knowledge which he has acquired in his former master's service which can be used to that master's prejudice ...

These, then being the limits of the protection which the master might reasonably insist on, I turn to the covenant in order to see whether it exceeds these limits ... [I]t prohibits the appellant from entering into a similar employment within 25 miles of [London] for a period of three years ... such an area is very far greater than could be reasonably required for the protection of his former employers.

It was suggested in the argument that even if the covenant was, as a whole, too wide, the Court might enforce restrictions which it might consider reasonable (even though they were not expressed in the covenant), provided they were within its ambit. My Lords, I do not doubt that the Court may, and in some cases will, enforce a part of a covenant in restraint of trade, even though taken as a whole the covenant exceeds what is reasonable. But, in my opinion, that ought only to be done in cases where the part so enforceable is clearly severable, and even so only in cases where the excess is of trivial importance, or merely technical, and not a part of the main purport and substance of the clause. It would in my opinion be pessimi exempli if, when an employer had exacted a covenant deliberately framed in unreasonably wide terms, the Courts were to come to his assistance and, by applying their ingenuity and knowledge of the law, carve out of this void covenant the maximum of what he might validly have required. It must be remembered that the real sanction at the back of these covenants is the terror and expense of litigation, in which the servant is usually at a great disadvantage, in view of the longer purse of his master. It is sad to think that in this present case this appellant, whose employment is a comparatively humble one, should have had to go through four courts before he could free himself from such unreasonable restraints as this covenant imposes, and the hardship imposed by the exaction of unreasonable covenants by employers would be greatly increased if they could continue the practice with the expectation that, having exposed the servant to the anxiety and expense of litigation, the Court would in the end enable them to obtain everything which they could have obtained by acting reasonably. It is evident that those who drafted this covenant aimed at making it a penal rather than a protective covenant, and that they hoped by means of it to paralyse the earning capabilities of the man if and when he left their service, and were not thinking of what would be a reasonable protection to their business, and having so acted they must take the consequences.'

Midland Bank plc v *Shephard* [1988] 3 All ER 17 Court of Appeal (Neill and Balcombe LJJ)

Husband and wife – presumption of undue influence?

Facts
The husband's account with the plaintiffs was overdrawn so he arranged to transfer the overdraft to a new joint account with his wife: the mandate, which they both signed, provided, inter alia, that 'any loan or

overdraft [was] our joint and several responsibility'. Needing a loan for business purposes, the husband arranged a £10,000 overdraft on the joint account: although the wife knew of her husband's intention to borrow the money, she was not told that it would be a liability on the joint account. The husband became bankrupt; the plaintiffs sued the wife.

Held

They were entitled to succeed as there was no evidence that the husband had induced the wife to sign the mandate by means of fraudulent misrepresentation or by some fraudulent concealment or that he had induced the wife to sign by exercising undue influence over her.

Neill LJ:

'... counsel for the defendant confined himself to submitting that she had an arguable defence based upon the undue influence of Mr Shephard. The submission was developed on the following lines. (a) There was no direct communication between the bank and the defendant before the joint account was opened. (b) The defendant was never told that by signing the mandate she would immediately become personally liable for the existing overdraft transferred from Mr Shephard's previous account, nor was it explained to her that she might become personally liable for a future overdraft on the joint account. (c) Mr Shephard acted as the agent for the bank in obtaining the defendant's signature to the mandate. (d) Mr Shephard misled the defendant by failing to inform her of her actual and potential liability. (e) Mr Shephard abused the trust which his wife had in him. (f) Though fraud had not hitherto been alleged, the conduct of Mr Shephard amounted to fraudulent misrepresentation or fraudulent concealment. (g) There was no evidence that the defendant herself had any business knowledge or experience.

In support of these submissions counsel for the defendant referred to several authorities, including *Turnbull & Co v Duval* [1902] AC 429 and *Kingsnorth Trust Ltd v Bell* [1986] 1 All ER 423. In addition we were referred by counsel for the bank to the decision of the House of Lords in *National Westminster Bank plc v Morgan* [1985] 1 All ER 821. From these authorities the following relevant propositions can be extracted.

1. The confidential relationship between husband and wife does not give rise by itself to a presumption of undue influence ...
2. Even if the relationship between the parties gives rise to a presumption of undue influence, the transaction will not be set aside unless it was to the manifest disadvantage of the person influenced ...
3. The court should examine the facts to see whether the relevant transaction had been, or should be presumed to have been, procured by undue influence, and if so whether the transaction was so disadvantageous to the person seeking to set it aside as to be unfair.
4. The court will not enforce a transaction at the suit of a creditor if it can be shown that the creditor entrusted the task of obtaining the alleged debtor's signature to the relevant document to someone who was, to the knowledge of the creditor, in a position to influence the debtor and who procured the signature of the debtor by means of undue influence or by means of fraudulent misrepresentation ...

I come now to apply these propositions and the authorities to the facts of the present case. In order to establish a defence of undue influence it would be necessary for the defendant to prove (a) that she was induced or must be presumed to have been induced to sign the mandate by the undue influence of Mr Shephard, or by his fraudulent misrepresentations or fraudulent concealment of material facts; (b) that the contract into which she was induced to enter was manifestly disadvantageous to her; and (c) that in the circumstances the acts of Mr Shephard are to be attributed to the bank.

I propose to deal first with point (b). It was strongly argued by counsel for the bank that the contract was for the opening of a joint account from which the defendant was intended to and did obtain a substantial benefit herself ... In my judgment it can properly be argued that the signing of the mandate was potentially disadvantageous to the defendant and therefore I would not myself reject the defence of undue influence on the ground that this element of the defence was not even arguable.

As to the other elements of the defence, however, I take a different view. In the first place I consider that there is no basis whatever for the suggestion that Mr Shephard induced the defendant to sign the mandate by means of any fraudulent misrepresentation, or by some fraudulent concealment. This suggestion was put forward at a comparatively late stage of the argument before us, but it is not supported by any of the evidence, nor can I find in any of the three affidavits sworn by the defendant any hint that the defendant was charging her husband with fraud. It may also be noticed that Mr Shephard has sworn two affidavits in support of the defendant's case and, we were told, they are living together as man and wife.

Secondly, I cannot see in the evidence any support for the proposition that Mr Shephard induced the defendant to sign the mandate by exercising some dominating influence over her. The facts of this case are far removed from those which were examined by the Court of Appeal in *Kingsnorth Trust Ltd* v *Bell* or those considered in the earlier case of *Avon Finance Co Ltd* v *Bridger* [1985] 2 All ER 281 where elderly parents were induced to sign a legal charge at the behest of their son and by means of his deception. In the present case the defendant signed the standard joint account mandate which was required to be signed by every customer who wished to operate a joint account. The document was in no way unusual and I can see no evidence whatever that the defendant was pressed or unduly influenced to sign it.

Finally I should deal with the suggestion that the bank are disentitled to enforce the mandate because they sent or gave the document to Mr Shephard and did not themselves obtain the defendant's signature. The defence must fail in any event in the absence of any proof that the defendant was unduly influenced to sign the mandate, but even if Mr Shephard had exercised some dominating influence over her, there is no evidence to show that the bank knew that he would or might bring such influence to bear, or that they used Mr Shephard in order that he should exert pressure on his wife (compare the judgment of Brightman LJ in *Avon Finance Co Ltd* v *Bridger*). As I said earlier, this was an ordinary document, which was signed as a matter of routine when a joint account was opened. It will be remembered that in her first affidavit ... the defendant said that she was made a party to the account in order to pay the household expenses when her husband was abroad on business.

In my judgment the evidence in this case does not disclose even a shadowy defence of undue influence.'

National Westminster Bank plc v *Morgan* [1985] 2 WLR 588 House of Lords (Lord Scarman, Lord Keith of Kinkel, Lord Roskill, Lord Bridge of Harwich and Lord Brandon of Oakbrook)

Undue influence – banker and customer

Facts

Mrs Morgan and her husband owned a house. It was mortgaged to the building society, who threatened to seek possession for unpaid debts. The defendant bank offered to 'refinance' the couple and to relieve the pressure put on them by the society. This was to be done by way of a loan, secured by a further mortgage, this time in favour of the bank. Mr Morgan readily agreed, but when the bank manager visited Mrs Morgan to obtain her signature to the mortgage deed, she wanted reassurance that the loan to be made would not be used by her husband for the purpose of his business, but would go to pay off the society. The manager reassured her and she signed the deed. The loan was not repaid and the bank, in turn, sued for possession of the house. Mrs Morgan argued that the bank manager exercised undue influence over her and that a special relationship existed between her and the bank which required it to ensure that she receive independent legal advice before entering into a further mortgage. She also sought to rely upon the remarks of Lord Denning in *Lloyd's Bank* v *Bundy*.

Held

The bank was entitled to possession.

Lord Scarman:

> '... the relationships which may develop a dominating influence of one over another are infinitely various. There is no substitute in this branch of the law for a "meticulous examination of the facts."
>
> A meticulous examination of the facts of the present case reveals that [the bank] never "crossed the line". Nor was the transaction unfair to the wife. The bank was, therefore, under no duty to ensure that she had independent advice. It was an ordinary banking transaction whereby the wife sought to save her home; and she obtained an honest and truthful explanation of the bank's intention which, notwithstanding the terms of the mortgage deed which in the circumstances the trial judge was right to dismiss as "essentially theoretical", was correct; for no one has suggested that ... the bank sought to make the wife liable, or to make her home the security, for any debt of her husband other than the loan and interest necessary to save the house from being taken away from them in discharge of their indebtedness to the building society.
>
> For these reasons, I would allow the appeal. In doing so, I would wish to give a warning. There is no precisely defined law setting limits to the equitable jurisdiction of a court to relieve against undue influence. This is the world of doctrine, not of neat and tidy rules. The courts of equity have developed a body of learning enabling relief to be granted where the law has to treat the transaction as unimpeachable unless it can be held to have been procured by undue influence. It is the unimpeachability at law of a disadvantageous transaction which is the starting point from which the court advances to consider whether the transaction is the product merely of one's own folly or of the undue influence exercised by another. A court in the exercise of this equitable jurisdiction is a court of conscience. Definition is a poor instrument when used to determine whether a transaction is or is not unconscionable: this is a question which depends on the particular facts of the case.'

Commentary

Followed in *Cornish* v *Midland Bank plc* [1985] 3 All ER 513. See also *Midland Bank plc* v *Shephard* [1988] 3 All ER 17 and *Bank of Credit and Commerce International SA* v *Aboody* [1989] 2 WLR 759.

Nordenfelt v *Maxim Nordenfelt Guns and Ammunition Co Ltd* [1894] AC 535 House of Lords (Lord Herschell LC, Lord Watson, Lord Ashbourne, Lord Macnaghten and Lord Morris)

Restraint of trade – validity

Facts

Nordenfelt was a maker and inventor of guns and ammunition. It was a specialised trade and although customers were few in number the business extended worldwide. Mr Nordenfelt sold the business in 1888 to the respondent company and entered into a covenant (later to be repeated in a contract of service) that he would not for 25 years 'engage ... either directly or indirectly in the trade or business of a manufacturer of guns, gun mountings or carriages, gunpowder explosives or ammunition or in any business competing or liable to compete in any way with that for the time being carried on by the company'. After some years Nordenfelt entered into a business with a rival company dealing with guns and ammunition and the respondents sought an injunction to restrain him from doing so.

Held

The injunction would be granted as the covenant was valid.

Lord Macnaghten:

> 'The true view at the present time I think, is this: the public have an interest in every person's carrying on his trade freely: so has the individual. All interferences with individual liberty of action in trading and all restraints of trade of themselves, if there is nothing more, are contrary to public policy and therefore void.

That is the general rule. But there are exceptions: restraints of trade and interferences with individual liberty of action may be justified by the special circumstances of a particular case. It is a sufficient justification, and indeed it is the only justification, if the restriction is reasonable – reasonable, that is, in reference to the interests of the parties concerned and reasonable in reference to the interests of the public, so framed and so guarded as to afford adequate protection to the party in whose favour it is imposed, while at the same time, it is in no way injurious to the public... Now, in the present case it was hardly disputed that the restraint was reasonable, having regard to the interests of the parties at the time when the transaction was entered into. It enabled Mr Nordenfelt to obtain the full value of what he had to sell; without it the purchasers could not have been protected in the possession of what they wished to buy. Was it reasonable in the interests of the public? It can hardly be injurious to the public, that is, the British public, to prevent a person from carrying on a trade in weapons of war abroad. But apart from that special feature in the present case, how can the public be injured by the transfer of a business from one hand to another? If a business is profitable there will be no lack of persons ready to carry it on. In this particular case the purchasers brought in fresh capital, and had at least the opportunity of retaining Mr Nordenfelt's services. But then it was said there is another way in which the public maybe injured. Mr Nordenfelt has "committed industrial suicide" and as he can no longer earn his living at the trade which he has made peculiarly his own, he may be brought to want and become a burden to the public. My lords, this seems to be very far-fetched. Mr Nordenfelt received over £200,000 for what he sold. He may have got rid of the money. I do not know how that is. But even so, I would answer the argument in the words of Tindal CJ:

> "If the contract is a reasonable one at the time it is entered into we are not bound to look out for improbable and extravagant contingencies in order to make it void." '

Schroeder (A) Music Publishing Co Ltd v *Macaulay* [1974] 1 WLR 1308 House of Lords (Lord Reid, Viscount Dilhorne, Lord Diplock, Lord Simon of Glaisdale and Lord Kilbrandon)

Music publishers – agreement in restraint of trade?

Facts
The respondent, an unknown songwriter, entered an agreement with the appellants to given them copyright of all compositions for a five-year period. The agreement was terminable by the employers on one month's notice but not by the respondent. The publishers were under no obligation to publish any of the songs. The respondent sought a declaration that the contract was contrary to public policy.

Held
He was entitled to succeed.

Lord Reid:

> '... The public interest requires in the interests both of the public and of the individual that everyone should be free so far as practicable to earn a livelihood and to give to the public the fruits of his particular abilities. The main question to be considered is whether and how far the operation of the terms of this agreement is likely to conflict with this objective. The respondent is bound to assign to the appellants during a long period the fruits of his musical talent. But what are the appellants bound to do with those fruits? Under the contract nothing. If they do use the songs which the respondent composes they must pay in terms of the contract. But they need not do so. As has been said they may put them in a drawer and leave them there ...
>
> It was argued that there must be read into this agreement an obligation on the publisher to act in good faith. I take that to mean that he would be in breach of contract if by reason of some oblique or malicious motive he refrained from publishing work which he would otherwise have published. I very much doubt

this but even if it were so it would make little difference. Such a case would seldom occur and then would be difficult to prove.

I agree with the appellants' argument to this extent. I do not think that a publisher could reasonably be expected to enter into any positive commitment to publish future work by an unknown composer. Possibly there might be some general undertaking to use his best endeavours to promote the composer's work. But that would probably have to be in such general terms as to be of little use to the composer.

But if no satisfactory positive undertaking by the publisher can be devised, it appears to me to be an unreasonable restraint to tie the composer for this period of years so that his work will be sterilised and he can earn nothing from his abilities as a composer if the publisher chooses not to publish. If there had been in clause 9 any provision entitling the composer to terminate the agreement in such an event the case might have had a very different appearance. But as the agreement stands not only is the composer tied but he cannot recover the copyright of work which the publisher refuses to publish.'

Lord Diplock:

'Standard forms of contracts are of two kinds. The first, of very ancient origin, are those which set out the terms on which mercantile transactions of common occurrence are to be carried out. Examples are bills of lading, charterparties, policies of insurance, contracts of sale in the commodity markets. The standard clauses in these contracts have been settled over the years by negotiation by representatives of the commercial interests involved and have been widely adopted because experience has shown that they facilitate the conduct of trade. Contracts of these kinds affect not only the actual parties to them but also others who may have a commercial interest in the transactions to which they relate, as buyers or sellers, charterers or shipowners, insurers or bankers. If fairness or reasonableness were relevant to their enforceability the fact that they are widely used by parties whose bargaining power is fairly matched would raise a strong presumption that their terms are fair and reasonable.

The same presumption, however, does not apply to the other kind of standard form of contract. This is of comparatively modern origin. It is the result of the concentration of particular kinds of business in relatively few hands. The ticket cases in the 19th century provide what are probably the first examples. The terms of this kind of standard form of contract have not been the subject of negotiation between the parties to it, or approved by any organisation representing the interests of the weaker party. They have been dictated by that party whose bargaining power, either exercised alone or in conjunction with other providing similar goods or services, enables him to say: "If you want these goods or services at all, these are the only terms on which they are obtainable. Take it or leave it."

To be in a position to adopt this attitude towards a party desirous of entering into a contract to obtain goods or services provides a classic instance of superior bargaining power. It is not without significance that on the evidence in the present case, music publishers in negotiating with song-writers whose success has been already established do not insist on adhering to a contract in the standard form they offered to the respondent. The fact that the appellants' bargaining power vis-à-vis the respondent was strong enough to enable them to adopt this take-it-or-leave it attitude raises no presumption that they used it to drive an unconscionable bargain with him, but in the field of restraint of trade it calls for vigilance on the part of the court to see that they did not.'

Watson v *Prager* [1991] 1 WLR 726 Chancery Division (Scott J)

Restraint of trade – whether terms of boxer-manager agreement reasonable

Facts

The plaintiff, a professional boxer, signed a boxer-manager agreement with the defendant. The agreement was in the standard form as prescribed by the British Boxing Board of Control which regulates and controls professional boxing in this country. The contract was for an initial three years, but the defendant had an option to renew the contract for a further three years. The defendant sought to exercise this option. One year into this second period the plaintiff became dissatisfied and claimed to be no longer bound by the contract since it constituted an unreasonable restraint of trade. There was, in the standard form contract, a clause providing for arbitration under the BBBC's rules, should disputes occur. The defendant claimed that arbitration procedure should be exhausted before having recourse to the courts. The plaintiff, however, alleged that the board would not be impartial at any arbitration hearing.

The court, in hearing the preliminary application, considered inter alia, whether the agreement was unenforceable on the ground of being in restraint of trade.

Held

The contract was not a normal commercial contract freely entered into by both parties, but was, by virtue of the BBBC's monopoly, to be subject to more stringent than usual judicial supervision. The contract would only be enforced if it was reasonable. Reasonableness would be tested by the nature of the terms, not how fairly or otherwise the defendant had adhered to conditions laid down by the BBBC. The fact that the manager had negotiated higher than average 'purses' did not alter the fact he was unilaterally able to agree the 'purse' for fights; the plaintiff was unable to negotiate on his own behalf. This was unreasonable, even if the actual sums negotiated were good.

The court decided that the contract contained restrictions on the plaintiff which were restrictive and unreasonable and was therefore unreasonable as a whole.

The defendant could not rely on the arbitration clause; the BBBC was involved in the dispute in the sense that they were defending their policy of dual licensing and therefore would not or might not be 'impartial' as defined under s24(1) of Arbitration Act 1950.

Scott J:

'I have discussed the agreement of 1 April 1987 in terms of restraint of trade. A contract in restraint of trade is prima facie contrary to public policy. It escapes invalidity only if its restrictions are reasonable, or, as Lord Diplock put it, are fair. Lord Diplock said: "For the purpose of this test all the provisions of the contract must be taken into consideration:" *Instone* v *A Schroeder Music Publishing Co Ltd* [1974] 1 WLR 1308, 1316. Taking into consideration all the provisions of the agreement of 1 April 1987, and in particular weighing the restrictions imposed on the boxer under paragraph 4 against the freedom enjoyed by the promoter-manager to fix the terms of the boxer's engagements, I do not think that the terms of this agreement are fair. An agreement containing these restrictions is in the circumstances of conflict of interest that I have described in my opinion contrary to public policy. I do not think that a court of equity should enforce these restrictions.

In summary, the boxer-manager contract of 1 April 1987 was, in my judgment, unreasonable in that it imposed on the plaintiff the paragraph 4(i) restrictions while, at the same time, subjecting him to the contractual obligation of fighting on promotions in which the first defendant was financially interested and on terms unilaterally imposed on him by the first defendant. So long as the plaintiff was prepared to abide by the contract it was capable of having legal effect. As Lord Reid said in the *Esso Petroleum* case [1968] AC 269, 297:

"... an agreement in restraint of trade is not generally unlawful if the parties choose to abide by it: it is only unenforceable if a party chooses not to abide by it."

The plaintiff does not now choose to abide by the contract of 1 April 1987. He is entitled, in my judgment, to take that course.'

Woodstead Finance Ltd* v *Petrou (1986) 136 NLJ 188 Court of Appeal (Sir Nicolas Browne-Wilkinson VC, Mustill and Nourse LJJ)

Undue influence – charge over wife's property

Facts

The husband obtained a loan of £25,000 for six months at an interest rate equivalent to 42% per annum. This loan from the plaintiff company was secured by a charge over the defendant wife's property and by her guarantee. The wife had been told to take independent advice before executing the documents, but did not do so. Did the transaction constitute a manifest and unfair disadvantage to the defendant?

Held

It did not. Following *National Westminster Bank* v *Morgan* [1985] 2 WLR 588, Sir Nicolas Browne-Wilkinson VC said:

> '... unless it can be demonstrated that the grant of the legal charge by the wife to the plaintiff company ... constituted a manifest and unfair disadvantage to her, any defence based on undue influence cannot succeed.'

Whilst the terms of the loan appeared harsh, the uncontradicted evidence was that such terms were normal for short term loans, having regard to the circumstances of the loan and the husband's appalling record of payments. There was, in consequence, no evidence of manifest disadvantage to the wife.

23 Frustration

Blackburn Bobbin Co Ltd* v *T W Allen and Sons Ltd [1918] 2 KB 467 Court of Appeal (Pickford, Bankes and Warrington LJJ)

Frustration – outbreak of war

Facts
In 1914 the defendants agreed to sell to the plaintiffs a quantity of birch timber, which the defendants obtained through import. Delivery was due to commence in July and cease in November. War broke out in August 1914, before any deliveries had been made and imports of timber stopped. The plaintiff claimed damages for breach of contract. The defendant alleged the dissolution of the contract by the war.

Held
The plaintiff was entitled to damages.

Pickford LJ:

> 'Why should a purchaser of goods, not specific goods, be deemed to concern himself with the way in which the seller is going to fulfil his contract by providing the goods he has agreed to sell? The seller in this case agreed to deliver the timber free on rail at Hull and it was no concern of the buyers as to how the sellers intended to get the timber there. I can see no reason for saying – and to free the defendants from liability this would have to be said – that the continuance of the normal mode of shipping the timber from Finland was a matter which both parties contemplated as necessary for the fulfilment of the contract. To dissolve the contract, the matter relied on must be something which both parties had in their minds when they entered into the contract, such as, for instance, the existence of the music hall in *Taylor* v *Caldwell*, or the continuance in readiness of the vessel to perform the contract, as in *Jackson* v *Union Marine Insurance Co*. Here there is nothing to show that the plaintiffs contemplated and there is no reason why they should be deemed to have contemplated that the sellers should continue to have the ordinary facilities for despatching the timber from Finland. As I have said, that was a matter which, to the plaintiffs, was wholly immaterial. It was not a matter forming the basis of the contract they entered into.'

Constantine (Joseph) Steamship Line Ltd* v *Imperial Smelting Corporation Ltd [1942] AC 154 House of Lords (Viscount Simon LC, Viscount Maugham, Lord Russell of Killowen, Lord Wright and Lord Porter)

Frustration – burden of proof

Facts
A ship was damaged by an explosion and thereby rendered unable to perform obligations under a charter party. The defendants pleaded frustration of the charter party when sued by the charterers for damages ensuing out of the failure to perform the charter party. The plaintiffs argued that the owners must prove that the explosion was not due to their negligence.

Held
Frustration was proved and the contract was discharged, despite the fact that the cause of the explosion was never known.

Viscount Simon LC:

> 'Every case in this branch of the law can be stated as turning on the question whether, from the express terms of the particular contract, a further term should be implied which, when its conditions are fulfilled, puts an end to the contract.
>
> If the matter is regarded in this way, the question is as to the construction of a contract, taking into consideration its express and implied terms. The implied term in the present case may well be "this contract is to cease to be binding if the vessel is disabled by an overpowering disaster, provided that disaster is not brought about by the default of either party". This is very similar to an express exception of "perils of the sea" ... If a ship sails and is never heard of again, the shipowner can claim protection for loss of the cargo under the express exception of perils of the sea. To establish that (he must prove) a prima facie case of loss by sea perils and that he is within the exception. If the cargo owner wants to defeat that plea, it is for him, by rejoinder, to allege and prove either negligence or unseaworthiness.'

Commentary
See also *Paal Wilson &Co A/S v Partenreederei Hannah Blumenthal, The Hannah Blumenthal* [1982] 3 WLR 1149.

Davis Contractors Ltd v *Fareham Urban District Council* [1956] AC 696 House of Lords (Viscount Simonds, Lord Morton of Henryton, Lord Reid, Lord Radcliffe and Lord Somervell of Harrow)

Building contract – completion delayed

Facts
The contractors agreed to build houses for the defendant local authority over a period of eight months for a fixed price. Mainly due to labour shortages, the building took almost two years and cost the contractors more than the agreed price. They commenced proceedings, claiming the contract was frustrated and they were entitled to quantum meruit for the work done.

Held
The contract was not frustrated.

Lord Reid:

> 'Frustration has often been said to depend on adding a term to the contract by implication ... I find great difficulty in accepting this as the correct approach ...
>
> It appears to me that frustration depends, at least in most cases, not on adding any implied term, but on the true construction of the terms which are in the contract, read in light of the nature of the contract and of the relevant surrounding circumstances when the contract was made ... The question is whether the contract which they make is, on its true construction, wide enough to apply to the new situation, if it is not, then it is at an end.
>
> In my view, the proper approach to this case is to take ... all facts which throw light on the nature of the contract, or which can properly be held to be intrinsic evidence relevant to assist in its construction and then, as a matter of law, to construe the contract and to determine whether the ultimate situation ... is or is not within the scope of the contract so construed.
>
> The appellant's case must rest on frustration, the termination of the contract by operation of law on the

emergence of a fundamentally different situation. Using the language of Asquith LJ (as he then was), the question is whether the causes of delay or the delays were "fundamental enough to transmute the job the contract had undertaken, and to which it could not apply" (*Parkinson (Sir Lindsay) and Co Ltd* v *Commissioners of Works* [1949] 2 KB 632 at 677). In most cases, the time when the new situation emerges is clear; there has been some particular event which makes all the difference. It may be that frustration can occur as a result of gradual change ... But even so, I think one must see whether there was any time at which the appellants would have said to the respondents that the contract was at an end and that if the work was to proceed, there must be a new contract and I cannot find any time, from first to last, at which they would have been entitled to say that the job had become a job of a different kind which the contract did not contemplate.

In a contract of this kind, the contractor undertakes to do the work for a definite sum and he takes the risk of the cost being greater or less than he expected. If delays occur through no one's fault that may be in the contemplation of the contract, and there may be provision for extra time being given; to that extent, the other party takes the risk of delay. It may be that delay could be of a character so different from anything contemplated that the contract was at an end, but in this case, in my opinion, the most that could be said is that the delay was greater in degree than was to be expected. It was not caused by any new and unforeseeable factor or event. The job proved to be more onerous, but it never became a job of a different kind from that contemplated in the contract.'

Commentary

See also *Pioneer Shipping Ltd* v *BTP Tioxide Ltd. The Nema* [1981] 3 WLR 292.

Ertel Bieber & Co v *Rio Tinto Co Ltd* [1918] AC 260 House of Lords (Lord Dunedin, Lord Atkinson, Lord Parker of Waddington and Lord Sumner)

Frustration – trading with the enemy

Facts

Two contracts made before the outbreak of war (in 1914) provided for the sale by a British company to a German company of cupreous ore, delivery to take place in 1915, 1916, 1917, 1918 and 1919. The contracts contained a suspensory clause (clause 15) suspending their operation if, owing to war, the parties were unable to fulfil their obligations.

Held

The contracts were void and could not be saved by the suspensory clause.

Lord Dunedin:

'I draw the conclusion that upon the ground of public policy the continued existence of contractual relation between subjects and alien enemies or persons voluntarily residing in the enemy country which (i) gives opportunities for the conveyance of information which may hurt the conduct of the war or (ii) may tend to increase the resources of the enemy or cripple the resources of the King's subjects, is obnoxious and prohibited by our law ... Let me now apply this rule to cl 15 on the hypothesis that it does suspend delivery during the war. But for it the contract would immediately end, by it the contract is kept alive, and that not for the purpose of making good rights already accrued, but for the purpose of securing rights in the future by the maintenance of the commercial relation in the present. It hampers the trade of the British subject, and through him the resources of the kingdom. For he cannot in view of the certainly impending liability to deliver (for the war cannot last for ever) have a free hand as he otherwise would. He must either keep a certain large stock undisposed of, and thus unavailable for the needs of the kingdom; or, if he sells the whole of the present stock he cannot sell forward as he would be able to do if he had not the large demand under the contract impending. It increases the resources of the enemy for, if the enemy knows that he is contractually sure of getting the supply as soon as war is over, that not only allows him to denude himself of present stocks, but it represents a present value which may be realised by means of assignation to neutral countries. For these reasons I come to the conclusion that cl 15 is void as against public policy and cannot receive effect. Without cl 15 there is an obvious necessity for intercourse, and the contract is, therefore, avoided as a whole.'

Fibrosa Spolka Akcyjna v *Fairbairn Lawson Combe Barbour Ltd* [1943] AC 32 House of Lords (Viscount Simon LC, Lord Atkin, Lord Russell of Killowen, Lord Macmillan, Lord Wright, Lord Roche and Lord Porter)

Frustration – goods' place of delivery occupied by enemy

Facts
The defendants, a company in Leeds, contracted in July 1939 to sell machinery to the plaintiffs, a Polish company. On 23 September 1939 Gdynia, the port of delivery, was occupied by the Germans. In July 1939 the plaintiffs had made an advance payment of £1,000 and they now sought its return.

Held
They were entitled to succeed.

Lord Macmillan:

'Your Lordships being of one mind that the so-called rule in *Chandler* v *Webster* is unsound, the way lies clear for the decision of the present case. The plaintiffs made a payment to the defendants on account of the price of certain plant which the defendants were to manufacture and deliver to them. Owing to circumstances arising out of the present hostilities the contract has become impossible of fulfilment according to its terms. Neither party is to blame. In return for their money the plaintiffs have received nothing whatever from the defendants by way of fulfilment of any part of the contract. It is thus a typical case of a total failure of consideration. The money paid must be repaid.'

Gamerco SA v *ICM/Fair Warning (Agency) Ltd* [1995] 1 WLR 1226 Queen's Bench Division (Garland J)

Frustration – advance payment made before discharge – recovery

Facts
The plaintiffs, pop concert promoters, agreed to promote a concert to be held by the defendant group at a stadium in Spain. However, the stadium was found by engineers to be unsafe and the authorities banned its use and revoked the plaintiffs' permit to hold the concert. No alternative site was at that time available and the concert was cancelled. Both parties had incurred expenses in preparation for the concert; in particular the plaintiffs had paid the defendants $412,500 on account. The plaintiffs sought to recover the advance payment under s1(2) Law Reform (Frustrated Contracts) Act 1943, and the defendants counterclaimed for breach of contract by the plaintiffs in failing to secure the permit for the concert.

Held
It was an implied term of the contract that the plaintiffs would use all reasonable endeavours to obtain a permit, yet once the permit was granted they could not be required to guarantee that it would not be withdrawn. The contract was frustrated essentially because the stadium was found to be unsafe, a circumstance beyond the control of the plaintiffs. The revocation of the permit, subsequent to its being

obtained by the plaintiffs, was not the frustrating event; the ban on the use of the stadium was. Under s1 of the 1943 Act, the plaintiffs were entitled to recover advance payments made to the defendants. The court did have a discretion to allow the defendants to offset their losses against this, but in all the circumstances of the present case the court felt that no deduction should be made in favour of the defendants and their counterclaim should be dismissed.

Garland J:

'It is convenient to take as a statement of the law passages from the judgment of Bingham LJ in *J Lauritzen AS* v *Wijsmuller BV* [1990] 1 Lloyd's Rep 1, 8:

"The classical statement of the modern law is that of Lord Ratcliffe in *Davis Contractors Ltd* v *Fareham Urban District Council* [1956] AC 696, 729: 'frustration occurs whenever the law recognises that without default of either party a contractual obligation has become incapable of being performed because the circumstances in which performance is called for would render it a thing radically different from that which was undertaken by the contract. Non haec in foedera veni. It was not this that I promised to do.' As Lord Reid observed in the same case, at p721: 'there is no need to consider what the parties thought or how they or reasonable men in their shoes would have dealt with the new situation if they had foreseen it. The question is whether the contract which they did make is, on its true construction, wide enough to apply to the new situation: if it is not, then it is at an end.' Certain propositions, established by the highest authority, are not open to question: 1. The doctrine of frustration was evolved to mitigate the rigour of the common law's insistence on literal performance of absolute promises ... The object of the doctrine was to give effect to the demands of justice, to achieve a just and reasonable result, to do what is reasonable and fair, as is expedient to escape from injustice where such would result from enforcement of a contract in its literal terms after a significant change in circumstances ... 2. Since the effect of frustration is to kill the contract and to discharge the parties from further liability under it the doctrine is not to be lightly invoked, must be kept within very narrow limits and ought not to be extended ... 3. Frustration brings the contract to an end forthwith, without more and automatically. 4. The essence of frustration is that it should not be due to the act or election of the party seeking to rely on it ... 5. A frustrating event must take place without blame or fault on the side of the party seeking to rely on it ..."

There is extensive quotation of authority which it is not necessary to reproduce in this judgment ...'

As to the defendants' right to offset their losses his Lordship continued:

'It is self-evident that any rigid rule is liable to produce injustice. The words, "if it considers it just to do so having regard to all the circumstances of the case", clearly confer a very broad discretion. Obviously the court must not take into account anything which is not "a circumstance of the case" or fail to take into account anything that is and then exercise its discretion rationally. I see no indication in the Act, the authorities or the relevant literature that the court is obliged to incline towards either total retention or equal division. Its task is to do justice in a situation which the parties had neither contemplated nor provided for, and to mitigate the possible harshness of allowing all loss to lie where it has fallen.

I have not found my task easy. As I have made clear, I would have welcomed assistance on the true measure of the defendants' loss and the proper treatment of overhead and non-specific expenditure. Because the defendants have plainly suffered some loss, I have made a robust assumption. In all the circumstances, and having particular regard to the plaintiffs' loss, I consider that justice is done by making no deduction under the proviso ...

... There was no relevant discovery of any material at which I could have looked under the Civil Evidence Act 1968 and from which I might have drawn inferences. The defendants undoubtedly suffered some loss but they have wholly failed to quantify it and, on the evidence available to me, I would decline to pluck a figure from the air.

I therefore allow the plaintiffs' claim for US$412,500 without set-off and dismiss the counterclaim.'

Jackson v *Union Marine Insurance Co Ltd* (1873) LR 10 CP 125 Court of Exchequer Chamber (Blackburn, Mellor and Lush JJ, Bramwell, Cleasby and Amphlett BB)

Charterparty – consequences of delay

Facts
The plaintiff, a shipowner, entered into a charter party in late 1871. The ship was to proceed from Liverpool to Newport and from Newport to San Francisco with a load of iron rails. The plaintiff insured the freight for the voyage. The ship sailed from Liverpool but ran aground. Six weeks later the charterers chartered another ship. The ship was got off three days later, but repairs would take several months. The issue was whether the plaintiff could maintain an action against the charterers for not loading the ship with the cargo once the ship had been repaired.

Held (Cleasby B dissenting)
The delay put an end to the charter party and the charterers were under no obligation to load the vessel.

Bramwell B:
> 'If the charter party were read as a charter for a definite adventure, there was necessarily an implied condition that the vessel should arrive at Newport in time for it ... Not arriving in time put an end to the contract, though as it arose from an expected peril, it gave no cause of action.'

Commentary
See also *Metropolitan Water Board* v *Dick, Kerr & Co Ltd* [1918] AC 119.

Krell v *Henry* [1903] 2 KB 740 Court of Appeal (Vaughan Williams, Romer and Stirling LJJ)

Frustration – cancellation of procession

Facts
In 1902, the defendant hired from the plaintiff a flat in Pall Mall for two days for the purpose of viewing the coronation processions. The King became ill and the coronation cancelled. The plaintiff sued for the agreed hire charge.

Held
The contract was a licence to use the rooms for a particular purpose and, as the foundation of the licence was destroyed, the contract was frustrated.

Vaughan Williams LJ (referring to the principle in *Taylor* v *Caldwell*):
> '... plain that the English Law applies the principle not only to cases where the performance of the contract becomes impossible by the cessation of existence of the thing which is the subject matter of the contract, but also to cases where the event which renders the contract incapable of performance is the cessation or non-existence of an express condition or state of things, going to the root of the contract and essential to its performance. It is said on the one side that the specified thing, state of things, or condition, the continued existence of which is necessary for the fulfilment of the contract, so that the parties entering into the contract must have contemplated the continued existence of that thing, condition or state of things as the foundation of what was to be done under the contract, is limited to things which are either the subject matter of the contract, or a condition or state of things, present or anticipated, which is expressly

mentioned in the contract. But on the other hand, it is said that the condition or state of things need not be expressly specified, but that it is sufficient if that condition or state of things clearly appears by extrinsic evidence to have been assumed by the parties to be the foundation or basis of the contract and the event which causes the impossibility is of such a character that it cannot reasonably be supposed to have been in contemplation of the contracting parties when the contract was made ... I do not think that the principle is limited to cases in which the event causing the impossibility of performance is the destruction or non-existence of some thing which is the subject matter of the contract, or of some condition or state of things expressly specified as a condition of it. I think that you first have to ascertain, not necessarily from the terms of the contract, but, if required, from necessary inference drawn from surrounding circumstances recognised by both contracting parties, what is the substance of the contract and then to ask the question whether that substantive contract needs for its foundation the assumption of the existence of a particular state of things.

Each case must be judged by its own circumstances. In each case one must ask oneself, first, what, having regard to all the circumstances, was the foundation of the contract? Secondly: was the performance of the contract prevented? And thirdly: was the event which prevented the performance of the contract of such a character that it cannot reasonably be said to have been in the contemplation of the parties at the date of the contract? If all these questions are answered in the affirmative (as I think they should be in this case) I think both parties are discharged from further performance of the contract.'

McAlpine, Humberoak Ltd v *McDermott International Inc* (1992) Financial Times 13 March Court of Appeal (Lloyd, Woolf and Russell LJJ)

Frustration – pre-contractual events – revision of contract

Facts
Both parties signed a contract for construction of an oil rig: the defendants were one among a large number of sub-contracting firms. Delays occurred in the plaintiffs' work, largely caused, the plaintiffs argued, by the late submission of large numbers of revised drawings which hindered production. The defendants' counterclaim suggested among other arguments, that the contract was in fact frustrated by the constant revision of plans.

Held
The Court of Appeal stated that the numerous revisions of plan did not transform the contract so as to frustrate it. Indeed, the contract provided for changes of instruction in the form of new construction drawings. Also, since the contract was signed retrospectively, some months after work had begun, the parties were both fully aware of changes necessary at the time of signing the contract.

Maritime National Fish Ltd v *Ocean Trawlers Ltd* [1935] AC 524 Privy Council (Lord Atkin, Lord Tomlin, Lord Macmillan and Lord Wright)

Frustration – act of party setting up

Facts
The defendants operated a fleet of trawlers for fishing. Three were owned and two were chartered. One was chartered from the plaintiffs. A government licence was required to operate the trawlers. The defendants were only able to secure three licences. The defendants allocated two licences to two of their own trawlers and the third to the trawler not chartered from the plaintiffs. The defendants argued that the charter was frustrated.

Held
The charter was not frustrated as it was self–induced by the act and election of the defendants.

Lord Wright:

'The essence of frustration is that it should not be due to the act or election of the party. There does not appear to be any authority which has been directly decided on this point. There is, however, a reference to the question in the speech of Lord Sumner in *Bank Line Ltd* v *Arthur Capel and Co* [1919] AC 435. What he says is:

"One matter I mention only to get rid of it. When the ship-owners were first applied to by the Admiralty for a ship, they named three, of which the Quito was one, and intimated that she was the one they preferred to give up. I think it is now well settled that the principle of frustration of an adventure assumes that the frustration arises without blame or fault on either side. Reliance cannot be placed on a self-induced frustration. Indeed, such conduct might give the other clear party the option to treat the contract as repudiated ..."

However, the point does arise in the facts now before the Board and their Lordships are of the opinion that the loss of the St Cuthbert's licence can correctly be described, quoad the appellants, as a "self-induced frustration".'

Metropolitan Water Board v *Dick, Kerr & Co Ltd* [1918] AC 119 House of Lords (Lord Finlay LC, Lord Dunedin, Lord Atkinson and Lord Parmoor)

Frustration – work forbidden by government

Facts
In July 1914 the parties contracted for the construction of a reservoir and water works. Work commenced on 10 August, but war had been declared six days earlier. The contract allowed six years for completion of the work. In 1916 a government order stopped the work and the greater part of the plant was requisitioned. In the light of the order, it would have been illegal for the work to proceed.

Held
The contract would be treated as having terminated on the date of the government order.

Lord Dunedin:

'The order pronounced under the Defence of the Realm Act not only debarred the respondents from proceeding with the contract, but also compulsorily dispersed and sold the plant. It is admitted that an interruption may be so long as to destroy the identity of the work or service, when resumed, with the work or service when interrupted. But quite apart from mere delay it seems to me that the action as to the plant prevents this contract ever being the same as it was. Express the effect by a clause. If the Water Board had, when the contract was being settled, proposed a clause which allowed them at any time during the contract to take and sell off the whole plant, to interrupt the work for a period no longer than that for which the work has actually been interrupted, and then bound the contractor to furnish himself with new plant and recommence the work, does anyone suppose that Dick, Kerr & Co or any other contractor would have accepted such a clause? And the reason why they would not have accepted it would have been that the contract, when resumed, would be a contract under different conditions from those which existed when the contract was begun. It may be said that it is possible that plant may be cheaper after the war. But no one knows, and the contractor is not bound to submit to an aleatory bargain, to which he has not agreed. It will also be kept in mind that the contract was a measure and value contract. The difference between the new contract and the old is quite as great as the difference between the two voyages in *Jackson* v *Union Marine Insurance Co Ltd* ...

On the whole matter I think that the action of the government, which is forced on the contractor as a vis major, has by its consequences made the contract, if resumed, a work under different conditions from those of the work when interrupted. I have already pointed out the effect as to the plant, and the contract, being a measure and value contract, the whole range of prices might be different. It would, in my judgment, amount, if resumed, to a new contract; and as the respondents are only bound to carry out the old contract and cannot do so owing to supervient legislation, they are entitled to succeed in their defence to this action.'

Commentary

Applied: *Tamplin (F A) Steamship Co Ltd* v *Anglo-Mexican Petroleum Products Co Ltd* [1916] 2 AC 397.

National Carriers Ltd v *Panalpina (Northern) Ltd* [1981] 2 WLR 45 House of Lords (Lord Hailsham of St Marylebone LC, Lord Wilberforce, Lord Simon of Glaisdale, Lord Russell of Killowen and Lord Roskill)

Frustration – closure of access

Facts

In 1974 the appellants leased from the respondent for ten years a warehouse. In 1979 the local authority closed the street giving the only access to the warehouse because of the dangerous condition of the listed building opposite. Permission to demolish the building was given in 1980 and it seemed demolition would be completed and the street reopened in 1981. On closure of the street the appellants had stopped paying rent and the respondents sued for arrears.

Held

The respondents should succeed. Although in exceedingly rare circumstances the doctrine of frustration could apply to an executed lease, the lease had not been frustrated by the closure.

Lord Wilberforce:

'It is said that to admit the possibility of frustration of leases will lead to increased litigation. Be it so, if that is the route to justice. But, even if the principle is admitted, hopeless claims can always be stopped at an early stage, if the facts manifestly cannot support a case of frustration. The present may be an example. In my opinion, therefore, though such cases may be rare, the doctrine of frustration is capable of application to leases of land. It must be so applied with proper regard to the fact that a lease, ie a grant of a legal estate, is involved. The court must consider whether any term is to be implied which would determine the lease in the event which has happened and/or ascertain the foundation of the agreement and decide whether this still exists in the light of the terms of the lease, the surrounding circumstances and any special rules which apply to leases or to the particular lease in question. If the "frustrating event" occurs, during the currency of the lease it will be appropriate to consider the Law Reform (Frustrated Contracts) Act 1943.

I now come to the second question, which is whether on the facts of the case the appellants should be given leave to defend the action: can they establish that there is a triable issue? I have already summarised the terms of the lease. At first sight, it would appear to my mind that the case might be one for possible frustration. But examination of the facts leads to a negative conclusion ...

So the position is that the parties to the lease contemplated, when Kingston Street was first closed, that the closure would probably last for a year or a little longer. In fact it seems likely to have lasted for just over eighteen months. Assuming that the street is reopened in January 1981, the lease will have three more years to run.

My Lords, no doubt, even with this limited interruption the appellants' business will have been severely dislocated. They will have had to move goods from the warehouse before the closure and to acquire alternative accommodation. After reopening the reverse process must take place. But this does not approach the gravity of a frustrating event. Out of ten years they will have lost under two years of use; there will be nearly three years left after the interruption has ceased. This is a case, similar to others, where the likely continuance of the term after the interruption makes it impossible for the lessee to contend that the lease has been brought to an end. The obligation to pay rent under the lease is unconditional, with a sole exception for the case of fire, as to which the lease provides for a suspension of the obligation. No provision is made for suspension in any other case; the obligation remains. I am of opinion therefore that the lessees have no defence to the action for rent.'

Paal Wilson & Co A/S v *Partenreederei Hannah Blumenthal, The Hannah Blumenthal* [1982] 3 WLR 1149 House of Lords (Lord Diplock, Lord Keith of Kinkel, Lord Roskill, Lord Brandon of Oakbrook and Lord Brightman)

Frustration – inordinate and inexcusable delay

Facts
The parties agreed in 1969 to the sale and purchase of a ship: the contract contained an arbitration clause. In 1972 the buyers said that they had some complaints; some months later they commenced arbitration proceedings. Matters proceeded very slowly and in 1980, when the buyers proposed that a date for the hearing be fixed, the sellers issued a writ alleging, inter alia, that the arbitration agreement had been discharged by frustration.

Held
This was not the case.

Lord Brandon of Oakbrook:

'... there are two essential factors which must be present in order to frustrate a contract. The first essential factor is that there must be some outside event or extraneous change of situation, not foreseen or provided for by the parties at the time of contracting, which either makes it impossible for the contract to be performed at all, or at least renders its performance something radically different from what the parties contemplated when they entered into it. The second essential factor is that the outside event or extraneous change of situation concerned, and the consequences of either in relation to the performance of the contract, must have occurred without either the fault or the default of either party to the contract.

It was contended for the sellers that the courts have never defined with precision the meaning of the expression "default" in this context. In this connection reliance was placed on the observations of Viscount Simon LC in *Joseph Constantine Steamship Line Ltd* v *Imperial Smelting Corp Ltd, the Kingswood* where he said:

"... I do not think that the ambit of 'default' as an element disabling the plea of frustration to prevail has as yet been precisely and finally determined. 'Self-induced' frustration, as illustrated by the two decided cases already quoted, involves deliberate choice, and those cases amount to saying that a man cannot ask to be excused by reason of frustration if he has purposely so acted as to bring it about. 'Default' is a much wider term, and in many commercial cases dealing with frustration is treated as equivalent to negligence. Yet in cases of frustration of another class, arising in connection with a contract for personal performance, it has not, I think, been laid down that, if the personal incapacity is due to want of care, the plea fails. Some day it may have to be finally determined whether a prima donna is excused by complete loss of voice from an executory contract to sing if it is proved that her condition was caused by her carelessness in not changing her wet clothes after being out in the rain. The implied term in such a case may turn out to be that the fact of supervening physical incapacity dissolves the contract without inquiring further into its cause, provided, of course, that it has not been deliberately induced in order to get out of the engagement."

I turn now to consider whether what I have described as being, on the authorities, the two factors essential to the frustration of a contract are present in this case. As to that ... neither such factor is present. In the first place there has been in this case no outside event or external change of situation affecting the performance of the agreement to refer at all, and no one, as far as I can see, has been able to put forward an argument that there has. In the second place the state of affairs relied on as causing frustration is delay by one or both of the parties of such a length as to make a fair, or as I prefer to call it satisfactory, trial of the dispute between the parties no longer possible. That delay, however, on the facts as I have stated them earlier, was clearly itself caused by the failure of both parties to comply with what your Lordships' House in *Bremer Vulkan* decided was their mutual contractual obligation owed to one another, namely (after taking the necessary steps to have a third arbitrator appointed) to apply to the full arbitral tribunal as then constituted for directions to prevent the very delay which is now sought to be relied on by the sellers as having frustrated the agreement to refer.

Whatever may be the precise ambit of the expression "default" in this context, and whether it would or would not apply to the case of the prima donna postulated by Viscount Simon LC in the part of his speech in *Joseph Constantine Steamship Line Ltd* v *Imperial Smelting Corp Ltd*, which I quoted above, it is not, in my view, necessary to determine. It is not necessary because I entertain no doubt whatever that the conduct of the parties in the present case, in failing to comply with what this House has held to be their mutual contractual obligation to one another, comes fairly and squarely within such expression.'

Pioneer Shipping Ltd v *BTP Tioxide Ltd, The Nema* [1981] 3 WLR 292 House of Lords (Lord Diplock, Lord Fraser of Tullybelton, Lord Russell of Killowen, Lord Keith of Kinkel and Lord Roskill)

Charterparty – frustration by strikes

Facts
Owners of a vessel chartered her for six or seven consecutive voyages from Sorel in Canada to ports in Europe between April and December. A strike broke out at Sorel while the vessel was away on the first of these voyages and it was still in progress when she arrived back there, thus preventing loading for the second voyage. It was agreed, therefore, that the owners could send the ship on a voyage to Glasgow: the owners sought to extend this voyage, but the charterers refused. The owners nevertheless arranged for the vessel to go to Brazil and Portugal, maintaining that the charterparty had been frustrated, a view which the arbitrator supported.

Held
The arbitrator's decision would not be disturbed.

Lord Roskill:

'In *National Carriers Ltd* v *Panalpina (Northern) Ltd* your Lordships' House recently reviewed the doctrine of frustration and, by a majority, held that it was susceptible of application to leases. It is clear, reading the speeches of your Lordships, that the House approved the now classic statement of the doctrine by Lord Radcliffe in *Davis Contractors Ltd* v *Fareham Urban District Council* ... whatever may have been said in other cases at earlier stages of the evolution of the doctrine of frustration:

"... frustration occurs whenever the law recognises that, without default of either party, a contractual obligation has become incapable of being performed because the circumstances in which performance is called for would render it a thing radically different from that which was undertaken by the contract. Non haec in foedera veni. It was not this that I promised to do."

It should therefore be unnecessary in future cases, where issues of frustration of contracts arise, to search back among the many earlier decisions in this branch of the law when the doctrine was in its comparative infancy. The question in these cases is not whether one case resembles another, but whether, applying Lord Radcliffe's enunciation of the doctrine, the facts of the particular case under consideration do or do not justify the invocation of the doctrine, always remembering that the doctrine is not lightly to be invoked to relieve contracting parties of the normal consequences of imprudent commercial bargains ... Your Lordships' House in *Tsakiroglou & Co Ltd* v *Noblee Thorl GmbH* ... decided that, while in the ultimate analysis whether a contract was frustrated was a question of law, yet as Lord Radcliffe said in relation to that case "that conclusion is almost completely determined by what is ascertained as to mercantile usage and the understanding of mercantile men" ... Another arbitrator might have reached a different conclusion, for clearly there were many points which had to be taken into consideration both ways. But I am quite unable to say that the conclusion which [the arbitrator here] reached was one which he was not, on the facts which he found, fully entitled to reach.

It was not suggested that a strike could never bring about frustration of an adventure. But it was pointed out that most attempts to invoke strikes as a cause of frustration have in the past failed. *The Penelope* is almost the only example of success, and in that case the underlying reasoning of the judgment is far from easy to follow, even though the decision may well be correct.

My Lords, I see no reason in principle why a strike should not be capable of causing frustration of an adventure by delay. It cannot be right to divide causes of delay into classes and then say that one class can and another class cannot bring about frustration of an adventure. It is not the nature of the cause of delay which matters so much as the effect of that cause on the performance of the obligations which the parties have assumed one towards the other.'

Commentary
See also *Shepherd (F C) & Co Ltd* v *Jerrom* [1986] 3 WLR 801.

Shepherd (F C) & Co Ltd v *Jerrom* [1986] 3 WLR 801 Court of Appeal (Lawton, Mustill and Balcombe LJJ)

Frustration – employee's imprisonment

Facts
In September 1979 the applicant entered into a four year contract of apprenticeship with the employers. In June 1981 the applicant was convicted of conspiracy to commit assault and affray and was sentenced to an indeterminate period of Borstal training. Fortunately for the applicant he was released after 39 weeks. However, in September 1981 while the applicant was in Borstal his employers indicated that they considered his contract to be terminated. The applicant complained to an Industrial Tribunal claiming unfair dismissal, and the Tribunal accepted his argument. On appeal the Employment Appeal Tribunal affirmed this decision. However the employers now argued that the applicant had not been dismissed but:

1. the contract of apprenticeship had been frustrated by the custodial Borstal sentence; or
2. the sentence constituted a repudiation of the apprenticeship contract and the applicant had been constructively dismissed.

Held
The Borstal sentence was a frustrating event.

Lawton LJ:

'... The first question is whether what happened was capable in law of frustrating the contract; the second is whether it did frustrate it: this is a question of fact: *Pioneer Shipping Ltd* v *BTP Tioxide Ltd* [1982] AC 724.

'... As to the first of these questions, there was an event, namely, the sentence of Borstal training, which was not foreseen or provided for by the parties at the time of contracting. It was a question of fact whether it rendered performance of the contract radically different from what the parties had contemplated when they entered into it. What has to be decided is whether the outside event and its consequences in relation to the performance of the contract occurred without either the fault or default of either party to it ... There was no fault or default on the part of the employers. They were alleging that because of the unforeseen outside event the contract had been frustrated. If it had been, there had been no dismissal. The oddity of this case is that the apprentice, for his own purposes, is seeking to allege that he was in default so as to keep in being a contract with the employers which the employers would otherwise have been able to say had been terminated by operation of law ... It seems to me that the apprentice is seeking to rely upon his own default, if in law it should be regarded as such, to establish his right to claim for unfair dismissal ...

The apprentice's criminal conduct was deliberate but it did not by itself have any consequences upon the performance of his contract. What affected performance was his sentence of Borstal training which was the act of the Judge and which he would have avoided if he could have done so. It cannot be said, I think, that the concept of "self-induced frustration" can be applied to this case ...

... In *Hare* v *Murphy Bros Ltd* [1974] ICR 603 the court had adjudged that the employee's criminal conduct which had resulted in his being sentenced to 12 months' imprisonment amounted to a breach of his contract of employment of so serious a nature that it constituted a unilateral repudiation of that contract at the date when he was convicted and sentenced ... The court had said that the sentence was not an event frustrating the contract of employment because it had been brought about by employee's own conduct ... I was a member of the court. I agreed that the appeal should be dismissed on what I called the "commensense of the situation" which was not an example of sound legal reasoning. Since it is not clear upon what grounds the court as such decided *Hare*'s case I do not regard it as a binding authority. In my opinion the court can reconsider the problem of the effect of a custodial sentence on a contract of employment. In my judgment such a sentence is capable in law of frustrating the contract ...'

Taylor v *Caldwell* (1863) 3 B & S 826 Court of Queen's Bench (Blackburn J)

Frustration – destruction of hall

Facts
C agreed to hire to T a hall for the purpose of holding a concert therein. Before the day of the concert, the hall was destroyed in a fire. T cancelled the concert and C claimed the letting fee.

Held
The contract of hire was frustrated and C was not liable to pay the rent.

Blackburn J:

'There seems no doubt that where there is a positive contract to do a thing, not in itself unlawful, the contractor must perform it or pay damages for not doing it, although in consequence of unforeseen accidents, the performance of his contract has become unexpectedly burdensome or even impossible ... But this rule is only applicable where the contract is positive and absolute and not subject to any condition either express or implied: and there are authorities which, as we think, establish the principle that where, from the nature of the contract, it appears that the parties must, from the beginning, have known that it could not be fulfilled unless, when the time for the fulfilment of the contract arrived, some particular specified thing continued to exist, so that when entering into the contract, they must have contemplated such continuing existence as the foundation of what was to be done; there, in the absence of any express or implied warranty that the thing shall exist, the contract is not to be construed as a positive contract but as subject to an implied condition that the parties shall be excused in case before breach, performance becomes impossible from the perishing of the thing without default of the contractor.

There seems little doubt that this implication tends to further the great object of making legal construction such as to fulfil the intention of those who entered into the contract ... The principle seems to us to be that in contracts in which the performance depends on the continued existence of a given person or thing, a condition is implied that the impossibility of performance ensuing from the perishing of the person or thing, shall excuse the performance.

In none of these cases is the promise in words other than positive, nor is there any express stipulation that the destruction of the person or thing shall excuse the performance; but that excuse is by law implied, because from the nature of the contract, it is apparent that the parties contracted on the basis of the continued existence of the particular person or chattel. In the present case, looking at the whole contract, we find that the parties contracted on the basis of the continued existence of Music Hall at the time when the concerts were to be given; that being essential to their performance.'

Commentary
Distinguished in *Herne Bay Steam Boat Company* v *Hutton* [1903] 2 KB 683.

Tsakiroglou & Co Ltd v ***Noblee and Thorl GmbH*** [1961] 2 WLR 633 House of Lords (Viscount Simonds, Lord Reid, Lord Radcliffe, Lord Hodson and Lord Guest)

Frustration – alternative route

Facts
In October 1956 the plaintiff agreed to sell to buyers groundnuts for shipment from Port Sudan to Hamburg during November/December 1956. On 7 October 1956, the plaintiff booked cargo space in a vessel scheduled to call at Port Sudan at the relevant time. On 2 November 1956, the Suez Canal was closed. The seller failed to deliver and, when sued, pleaded frustration.

Helds
The contract had not been frustrated as there was the alternative of a reasonable and practicable, though possibly more expensive, route via the Cape of Good Hope.

Lord Reid:

'It appears to me that the only possible way of reaching a conclusion that this contract was frustrated would be to concentrate on the altered nature of the voyage ... What the sellers had to do was simply to find a ship proceeding by what was a practicable and now a reasonable route – if perhaps not yet a usual route – to pay the freight and obtain a proper bill of lading and to furnish the necessary documents to the buyer ... That was their manner of performing their obligations ... I think that such changes in these matters as were made necessary, fell far short of justifying a finding of frustration.'

24 Discharge of the Contract

Afovos Shipping Co SA* v *Pagnan, The Afovos [1983] 1 WLR 195 House of Lords (Lord Hailsham of St Marylebone LC, Lord Diplock, Lord Keith of Kinkel, Lord Roskill and Lord Brightman)

Repudiation – anticipatory breach

Facts
Under the terms of a charterparty, hire was payable semi-monthly in advance. The charterers paid the hire punctually until, due to an error by both parties' banks, one payment was late. The owners claimed that they were entitled to withdraw the vessel, inter alia, under the doctrine of anticipatory breach.

Held
They were not so entitled.

Lord Diplock:

'... The first part of the clause [5] imposes on the respondents as charterers a primary obligation to pay the "said hire" (which by cl 4 had been fixed at a monthly rate and pro rata for any part of a month) punctually and regularly in advance by semi-monthly instalments in the manner specified, which would involve the payment of a minimum of 42 and a maximum of 54 instalments, during the period of the charter. Failure to comply with this primary obligation by delay in payment of one instalment is incapable in law of amounting to a "fundamental breach" of contract by the charterers in the sense to which I suggested in *Photo Production Ltd* v *Securicor Transport Ltd* this expression, if used as a term of legal art, ought to be confined. The reason is that such delay in payment of one half-monthly instalment would not have the effect of depriving the owners of substantially the whole benefit which it was the intention of the parties that the owners should obtain from the unexpired period of the time charter extending over a period of between 21 and 27 months.

The second part of cl 5, however, starting with the word "otherwise" goes on to provide expressly what the rights of the owners are to be in the event of any such breach by the charterers of their primary obligation to make punctual payment of an instalment. The owners are to be at liberty to withdraw the vessel from the service of the charterers; in other words they are entitled to treat the breach when it occurs as a breach of condition and so giving them the right to elect to treat it as putting an end to all their own primary obligations under the charterparty then remaining unperformed. But although failure by the charterers in punctual payment of any instalment, however brief the delay involved may be, is made a breach of condition it is not also thereby converted into a fundamental breach; and it is to fundamental breaches alone that the doctrine of anticipatory breach is applicable.

The general rule is that a primary obligation is converted into a secondary obligation (whether a "general secondary obligation" or an "anticipatory secondary obligation" in the nomenclature of the analysis used in my speech in *Photo Productions Ltd* v *Securicor Transport Ltd*) when and only when the breach of the primary obligation actually occurs. Up until then the primary obligations of both parties which have not yet been performed remain intact. The exception is where one party has manifested to the other party his intention no longer to perform the contract and the result of the non-performance would be to deprive the other party of substantially the whole benefit which it was the intention of the parties that that other party should obtain from the primary obligations of both parties remaining to be performed. In such a case, to which the term "repudiation" is applicable, the party not in default need not wait until the actual breach: he may elect to treat the secondary obligations of the other party as arising forthwith.

The doctrine of anticipatory breach is but a species of the genus repudiation and applies only to fundamental breach. If one party to a contract states expressly or by implication to the other party in advance that he will not be able to perform a particular primary obligation on his part under the contract when the time for performance arrives, the question whether the other party may elect to treat the statement as a repudiation depends on whether the threatened non-performance would have the effect of depriving that other party of substantially the whole benefit which it was the intention of the parties that he should obtain from the primary obligations of the parties under the contract then remaining unperformed. If it would not have that effect there is no repudiation, and the other party cannot elect to put an end to such primary obligations remaining to be performed. The non-performance threatened must itself satisfy the criteria of a fundamental breach.

Similarly, where a party to a contract, whether by failure to take timeous action or by any other default, has put it out of his power to perform a particular primary obligation, the right of the other party to elect to treat this as a repudiation of the contract by conduct depends on whether the resulting non-performance would amount to a fundamental breach. Clearly, in the instant case delay in payment of one semi-monthly instalment of hire would not.'

Ateni Maritime Corporation v *Great Marine* (1991) Financial Times 13 February Court of Appeal (Lloyd, Nourse and Bingham LJJ)

Performance – method and standard of performance

Facts
The buyers agreed to buy a ship under a contract based on a Norwegian Standard Sale form. The contract provided, inter alia, that if on arrival the ship was in any way so defective as to affect its certification, the defects would be made good at the sellers' expense. The work should be to the satisfaction of a named third party, the classification society. The propeller was found to be severely damaged. A damages award against the sellers was appealed by them, on the grounds that in assessing damages the judge had applied too high a standard.

Held
The buyers could not complain if the sellers did no more than was necessary to obtain a clean certificate. They were not able to demand the sellers did work that would restore it to its pre-contractual condition. The buyers were only entitled to such damages as would cover the cost of reasonable repair work.

Avery v *Bowden* (1855) 5 E & B 714 Court of Queen's Bench (Lord Campbell CJ)

Contract – performance becoming illegal

Facts
The plaintiff's ship *Lebanon* was chartered by the defendant and he agreed to load her with a cargo at Odessa within 45 days. At Odessa, the defendant told the captain that he had no cargo for him and advised him to go away. During the 45 days the Crimean War broke out, rendering performance of the contract illegal.

Held
No cause of action has arisen before the outbreak of war.

Lord Campbell CJ:

> 'According to our decision in *Hochster* v *De la Tour*, to which we adhere, if the defendant, within the running days and before the declaration of war, had positively informed the captain of the *Lebanon* that no cargo had been provided or would be provided for him at Odessa, and that there was no use in his remaining there any longer, the captain might have treated this as a breach and renunciation of the contract; and thereupon, sailing away from Odessa, he might have loaded a cargo at a friendly port from another person; whereupon the plaintiff would have had a right to maintain an action on the charterparty to recover damages equal to the loss he had sustained from the breach of contract on the part of the defendant. The language used by the defendant's agent before the declaration of war can hardly be considered as amounting to a renunciation of the contract: but, if it had been much stronger, we conceive that it could not be considered as constituting a cause of action after the captain still continued to insist upon having a cargo in fulfilment of the charterparty.'

Commentary

This decision was affirmed by the Court of Exchequer Chamber (1856) 6 E & B 953.

British and Commonwealth Holdings plc v *Quadrex Holdings Inc* [1989] 3 WLR 723 Court of Appeal (Sir Nicolas Browne-Wilkinson VC, Woolf and Staughton LJJ)

Time 'of the essence'?

Facts

The plaintiff and defendant companies, both wishing to acquire control of a third company, entered into a written agreement whereby the defendant would withdraw its bid, leaving the way clear for the plaintiff to acquire the company and the plaintiff would then sell the company's wholesale broking division to the defendant. The defendant had trouble finding the purchase money for the broking division and on 25 January 1985 the plaintiff served on it a notice fixing 28 February as the final date to complete the contract. The defendant failed to complete and the plaintiff started proceedings claiming damages for the defendant's repudiation of the contract. The defendant denied time was of the essence and further claimed that the plaintiff company was itself in breach and the cause of the delay. At first instance the plaintiff successfully obtained summary judgment with damages to be assessed and an interim order for £75m. The defendant appealed.

Held

1. Although the contract specified completion to take place as soon as reasonably practicable after certain preliminaries had been fulfilled, no date had been fixed or was capable of being fixed at the time of the contract and therefore time was not, originally, 'of the essence'. However the commercial nature of the contract was such that if a date had been specified, it would have been 'of the essence'. If an innocent party, the plaintiff would have been entitled to serve notice making time 'of the essence'; but
2. the plaintiff's status was not that of an innocent party and therefore their ability to issue such a notice was in doubt.

The appeal was therefore allowed, leave given to defend the summary judgment order and the interim order reduced to £5m.

Sir Nicolas Browne-Wilkinson VC:

> 'The phrase "time is of the essence of the contract" is capable of causing confusion since the question in each case is whether time is of the essence of the particular contractual term which has been breached ...

In equity, time is not normally of the essence of a contractual term. The rules of equity now prevail over the old common law rule: see the Law of Property Act 1925 s41. However, in three types of cases time is of the essence in equity: first, where the contract expressly so stipulates; second, where the circumstances of the case or the subject matter of the contract indicate that the time for completion is of the essence; third, where a valid notice to complete has been given. In the present case there was no express stipulation that time was of the essence. The subject matter of the sale (shares in unquoted private companies trading in a very volatile sector) is such that if a date for completion had been specified, in my judgment time would undoubtedly have been of the essence of completion ... For the reasons I have given, time could not be of the essence of completion on a date which was neither specified nor capable of exact determination by the parties. The only question is whether time was made of the essence by the service of a valid notice to complete.

In the ordinary case, three requirements have to be satisfied if time for completion is to be made of the essence by the service of a notice, viz (1) the giver of the notice (the innocent party) has to be ready, willing and able to complete, (2) the other party (the guilty party) has to have been guilty of unreasonable delay before a notice to complete can be served and (3) the notice when served must limit a reasonable period within which completion is to take place.'

Cutter v *Powell* (1795) 6 Term Rep 320 Court of King's Bench (Lord Kenyon CJ, Ashhurst, Grose and Lawrence JJ)

Incomplete performance

Facts
The defendant, master of the Governor Parry, contracted to pay a seaman 30 guineas 'provided he proceeds, continues, and does his duty as second mate in the said ship from hence [Kingston, Jamaica] to the port of Liverpool'. The seaman died in the course of the voyage and his administratrix sued for work and labour done.

Held
Her action could not succeed.

Ashhurst J:

'This is a written contract, and it speaks for itself. As it is entire and, as the defendant's promise depends on a condition precedent to be performed by the other party, the condition must be performed before the other party is entitled to receive anything under it. It has been argued, however, that the plaintiff may now recover on a quantum meruit, but she has no right to desert the agreement for whatever there is an express contract the parties must be guided by it, and one party cannot relinquish or abide by it as it may suit his advantage. Here the intestate was by the terms of his contract to perform a given duty before he could call on the defendant to pay him anything; it was a condition precedent, without performing which the defendant is not liable. That seems to me to conclude the question. The intestate did not perform the contract on his part; he was not indeed to blame for not doing it; but still as this was a condition precedent, and as he did not perform it, his representative is not entitled to recover.'

Dakin (H) & Co Ltd v *Lee* [1916] 1 KB 566 Court of Appeal (Lord Cozens-Hardy MR, Warrington and Pickford LJJ)

Performance – defective work

Facts
The plaintiff builders contracted to execute certain repairs to the defendant's premises. They carried out a substantial part of the work, but failed to perform it exactly in three unimportant respects.

Held
The plaintiffs were entitled to recover the contract price less a reduction for the defective work.

Lord Cozens-Hardy MR:

> 'Take a contract for a lump sum to decorate a house; the contract provides that there shall be three coats of oil paint, but in one of the rooms only two coats of paint are put on. Can anyone seriously say that under these circumstances the building owner could go and occupy the house and take the benefit of all the decorations which had been done in the other rooms without paying a penny for all the work done by the builder, just because only two coats of paint had been put on in one room where there ought to have been three?'

Decro-Wall International SA v *Practitioners in Marketing Ltd* [1971] 1 WLR 361
Court of Appeal (Salmon, Sachs and Buckley LJJ)

Repudiation – breach of term as to time of payment

Facts
The plaintiff French company contracted with the defendants as sole concessionaires for the sale of their goods in the United Kingdom: the defendants undertook to pay within 90 days. However, although the plaintiffs never doubted that payment would be made, the defendants were consistently late payers; this cost the defendants about £20 each time (interest on bank loans), a loss which could have been, but was not, debited to the defendants. The plaintiffs contended that the defendants had repudiated the agreement.

Held
This was not the case.

Salmon LJ:

> 'The first question to be decided on this appeal is whether the defendants, by failing punctually to pay ... repudiated the agreement ... I have come to the conclusion that the learned judge was plainly right in holding that there had been no repudiation by the defendants. Clearly the defendants were in breach of the ... agreement by failing to pay the bills punctually. A breach of contract may be of such a nature as to amount to repudiation and give the innocent party the right (if he desires to exercise it) to be relieved from any further performance of the contract or the breach may entitle the innocent party only to damages. How is the legal consequence of a breach to be ascertained? Primarily from the terms of the contract itself. The contract may state expressly or by necessary implication that the breach of one of its terms will go to the root of the contract and accordingly amount to repudiation. Where it does not do so, the courts must look at the practical results of the breach in order to decide whether or not it does go to the root of the contract: see *Mersey Steel and Iron Co Ltd* v *Naylor, Benzon & Co* ... *Hong Kong Fir Shipping Co Ltd* v *Kawasaki Kisen Kaisha Ltd* ... and *The Mihalis Angelos* ... The same test may be and indeed often has been stated in different language, ie is the term which has been breached of the essence of the contract? Section 10(1) of the Sale of Goods Act 1893 provides:
>
>> "Unless a different intention appears from the terms of the contract, stipulations as to time of payment are not deemed to be of the essence of a contract of sale ..."
>
> The present contract is of course not a simple contract of sale but, in my view, the same principle is to be applied to it. I am confident that the terms of the present contract relating to time of payment of the bills

cannot properly be regarded as of the essence of the contract, or, to put it the other way, there is nothing expressed in or to be implied from the contract to suggest that a failure punctually to pay the bills goes to the root of the contract and thereby amounts to a repudiation.

Counsel for the plaintiffs relied on *Withers v Reynolds* (1831) 2 B & Ad 882 in support of his skilful argument that the failure to pay the bills on time amounted to a repudiation of the contract. In *Withers v Reynolds* there was an instalment contract of sale which called for cash on delivery of each instalment. The time came when the buyer refused to pay cash but insisted on credit for each instalment until the next was delivered. The court held that the seller was not obliged to go on with the contract on the terms which the buyer sought to dictate. This decision is explicable on the basis that the stipulation as to time of payment was intended by the parties to be of the essence of the contract, alternatively that the buyer was seeking to alter the nature of the transaction by turning a cash into a credit transaction. Accordingly, I do not consider that this decision is inimical to the view which I have already expressed.

I now turn to the point to whether the practical consequences of the defendants' late payments in breach of contract were of such a character as to make the breaches go to the root of the contract. The fact that over the years the plaintiffs agreed to 120 and then 180 day bills being substituted for 90 day bills and even then extended payment on a number of occasions does not suggest that they regarded late payment as being of vital importance to them. Nor was it; the plaintiffs obtained a loan from their bank of the full amount of each bill immediately it was accepted by the defendants. So far as the plaintiffs were concerned it is clear from the facts stated earlier in this judgment that the only effect of the late payments was that the plaintiffs may have incurred liability to their bank for a comparatively insignificant sum by way of extra interest which in any event they could have recovered from the defendants. The case would have been quite different if the defendants' breaches had been such as reasonably to shatter the plaintiffs' confidence in the defendants' ability to pay for the goods with which the plaintiffs supplied them. I think that, in such circumstances, the consequences of the breach could properly have been regarded as most serious, indeed fundamental, and going to the root of the contract so that the plaintiffs would have been entitled to refuse to continue doing business with the defendants. As already indicated, however, ... in ... evidence ... the plaintiffs never doubted that, if they went on supplying the defendants with goods, the defendants would meet the bills. They would, however, in all probability, meet them some days late, as they had done throughout the whole course of the dealings between the parties. For these reasons I agree with the learned judge that the defendants' breaches did not amount to a repudiation of the contract; they were not fundamental breaches going to the root of the contract. They certainly gave the plaintiffs no right to treat the contract as at an end.'

Federal Commerce and Navigation Ltd v *Molena Alpha Inc*

See Chapter 19.

Fercometal SARL v *Mediterranean Shipping Co SA, The Simona* [1988] 3 WLR 200 House of Lords (Lord Bridge of Harwich, Lord Templeman, Lord Ackner, Lord Oliver of Aylmerton and Lord Jauncey of Tullichettle)

Wrongful repudiation – effect

Facts
In June 1982 a charterparty provided for the carriage of steel coils from Durban to Bilbao: the charterers were entitled to cancel if the vessel was not ready to load on or before 9 July. On 2 July the shipowners requested an extension as they wished to load other cargo first; if they did this, the charterers' cargo could not be loaded until 13 July. The charterers forthwith cancelled the contract: the owners did not accept this repudiation and on 5 July notified the charterers that the vessel would start loading on 8 July. The vessel arrived in Durban on that day and the owners gave notice of readiness although they were not in fact

ready to load. The charterers rejected the notice and began loading on another vessel which they had engaged after the owners' request for an extension. The owners claimed for deadfreight.

Held
Their claim could not succeed.

Lord Ackner:

> 'When one party wrongly refuses to perform obligations, this will not automatically bring the contract to an end. The innocent party has an option. He may either accept the wrongful repudiation as determining the contract and sue for damages or he may ignore or reject the attempt to determine the contract and affirm its continued existence ...
>
> When A wrongfully repudiates his contractual obligations in anticipation of the time for their performance, he presents the innocent party, B, with two choices. He may either affirm the contract by treating it as still in force or he may treat it as finally and conclusively discharged. There is no third choice, as a sort of via media, to affirm the contract and yet be absolved from tendering further performance unless and until A gives reasonable notice that he is once again able and willing to perform. Such a choice would negate the contract being kept alive for the benefit of *both* parties and would deny the party who unsuccessfully sought to rescind the right to take advantage of any supervening circumstance which would justify him in declining to complete.
>
> Towards the conclusion of his able address, counsel for the owners sought to raise what was essentially a new point ... He submitted that the charterers' conduct had induced or caused the owners to abstain from having the ship ready prior to the cancellation date. Of course, it is always open to A, who has refused to accept B's repudiation of the contract, and thereby kept the contract alive, to contend that, in relation to a particular right or obligation under the contract, B is estopped from contending that he, B, is entitled to exercise that right or that he, A, has remained bound by that obligation. If B represents to A that he no longer intends to exercise that right or requires that obligation to be fulfilled by A and A acts on that representation, then clearly B cannot be heard thereafter to say that he is entitled to exercise that right or that A is in breach of contract by not fulfilling that obligation. If, in relation to this option to cancel, the owners had been able to establish that the charterers had represented that they no longer required the vessel to arrive on time because they had already fixed [another ship] and, in reliance on that representation, the owners had given notice of readiness only after the cancellation date, then the charterers would have been estopped from contending they were entitled to cancel the charterparty. There is, however, no finding of any such representation, let alone that the owners were induced thereby not to make the vessel ready to load by 9 July. On the contrary, the owners on 5 July on two occasions asserted that the vessel would start loading on 8 July and on 8 July purported to tender notice of readiness. Indeed, on the following day they instructed their London solicitors to confirm that the vessel was then open in Durban for the charterers' cargo. There is a total lack of any material to show that the owners, because of the charterers' repudiatory conduct, viewed the cancellation clause as other than fully operative and therefore capable of being triggered by the vessel not being ready on time. The non-readiness of the vessel by the cancelling date was in no way induced by the charterers' conduct. It was the result of the owners' decision to load other cargo first.
>
> In short, in affirming the continued existence of the contract, the owners could only avoid the operation of the cancellation clause by tendering the vessel ready to load on time (which they failed to do), or by establishing (which they could not) that their failure was the result of the charterers' conduct in representing that they had given up their option, which representation the owners had acted on by not presenting the vessel on time.'

Frost v *Knight* (1872) LR 7 Ex 111 Court of Exchequer Chamber (Sir Alexander Cockburn CJ, Byles, Keating and Lush JJ)

Contract – refusal, before contingency, to perform

Facts
The defendant promised the plaintiff that he would marry her on the death of his father. Before father died, he changed his mind and the plaintiff sued for breach of promise.

Held
She was entitled to do so.

Sir Alexander Cockburn CJ:

> 'Considering this to be now settled law ... we should have had no difficulty in applying the principle of the decision in *Hochster* v *De la Tour* to the present case, were it not for the difference which undoubtedly exists between that case and the present, namely, that whereas there the performance of the contract was to take place at a fixed time, here no time is fixed, but the performance is made to depend on a contingency, namely, the death of the defendant's father during the life of both the contracting parties. It is true that in every case of a personal obligation to be fulfilled at a future time, there is involved the possible contingency of the death of the party binding himself before the time of performance arises; but here we have a further contingency, depending on the life of a third person, during which neither party can claim performance of the promise. This being so, we thought it right to take time to consider whether an action would lie before the death of the defendant's father had placed the plaintiff in a position to claim the fulfilment of the defendant's promise. After full consideration, we are of opinion that, notwithstanding the distinguishing circumstances to which I have referred, this case falls within the principle of *Hochster* v *De la Tour* and that consequently the present action is well brought.
>
> The considerations on which the decision in *Hochster* v *De la Tour* is founded are that by the announcement of the contracting party of his intention not to fulfil it, the contract is broken; and that it is to the common benefit of both parties that the contract shall be taken to be broken as to all its incidents, including non-performance at the appointed time, and that an action may be at once brought, and the damages consequent on non-performance be assessed at the earliest moment, as thereby many of the injurious effects of such non-performance may possibly be averted or mitigated.'

Harrods Ltd v *Schwarz-Sackin & Co Ltd* [1991] FSR 209 Court of Appeal (Dillon and Bingham LJJ)

Termination/breach of contract – continued effect of clause

Facts
The plaintiffs terminated their contract with the defendants, who had operated the fine arts department at Harrods. One of the clauses in the contract was a no-advertising clause – that the defendants would not indicate their connection with Harrods, or use Harrods' name in any way. Once the contract had been ended, the defendants began to advertise their previous association with Harrods, who sought an interlocutory injunction to stop this.

Held
Unless a clause is specifically and expressly worded so as to make it clear that its effect is to continue beyond the existence of the contract, no such effect will be implied. All restrictive clauses terminate along with the contract.

Hochster v *De la Tour* (1853) 2 E & B 678 Court of Queen's Bench (Lord Campbell CJ, Coleridge, Erle and Crompton JJ)

Contract – repudiation before date of performance

Facts
The plaintiff agreed on 12 April to enter the service of the defendant as a courier and travel with him on the continent of Europe for three months commencing 1 June. On 11 May the defendant wrote to say that he had changed his mind: on 22 May the plaintiff issued a writ.

Held
The plaintiff was entitled to take this step at that time.

Lord Campbell CJ:

> 'The man who wrongfully renounces a contract into which he has deliberately entered cannot justly complain if he is immediately sued for a compensation in damages by the man whom he has injured: and it seems reasonable to allow an option to the injured party, either to sue immediately or to wait till the time when the act was to be done, still holding it as prospectively binding for the exercise of this option, which may be advantageous to the innocent party, and cannot be prejudicial to the wrongdoer.'

Commentary
See also *Frost* v *Knight* (1872) LR 7 Ex 111 and *Avery* v *Bowden* (1855) 5 E & B 714.

Maple Flock Co Ltd v *Universal Furniture Products (Wembley) Ltd* [1934] 1 KB 148 Court of Appeal (Lord Hewart CJ, Lord Wright and Slesser LJ)

Sale of goods – defect in one instalment

Facts
There was a contract between the parties for the sale of 100 tons of flock, delivery to be made in three loads a week as required. One instalment of one and half tons was defective, but there was no reasonable probability that there would be anything wrong with future deliveries.

Held
The buyers were not entitled to treat the contract as having been repudiated by the sellers.

Lord Hewart CJ:

> 'There may, indeed, be ... cases where the consequences of single breach of contract may be so serious as to involve a frustration of the contract and justify rescission, or, furthermore, the contract might contain an express condition that a breach would justify rescission, in which case effect would be given to such a condition by the court. But none of these circumstances can be predicated of this case. We think the deciding factor here is the extreme improbability of the breach being repeated, and on that ground, and on the isolated and limited character of the breach complained of, there was, in our judgment, no sufficient justification to entitle the respondents to refuse further deliveries as they did.
>
> The appeal must, accordingly, be allowed and judgment entered for the appellants, with costs here and below, for damages for the respondents' breach of contract in refusing further deliveries.'

Millers Wharf Partnership Ltd v *Corinthian Column Ltd* (1990) 61 P & CR 461 Chancery Division (Knox J)

Conditional contracts – performance of conditions after due date – right of rescission

Facts
The plaintiffs agreed to grant the lease of a flat to the defendants, on condition that the plaintiffs should

obtain planning permission for redevelopment by a certain date. Either party should have a right of rescission if planning permission was not obtained by the relevant time. The plaintiffs eventually obtained planning consent, some months after the due date. The defendants eventually exercised their power of rescission. The plaintiffs argued that since the due date had passed and the condition had not been fulfilled yet the defendants had not rescinded, then they had lost the right to rescind. The obtaining of planning consent, the condition on which the contract depended, had been fulfilled by a later date; the defendants had waived their right to rescind by not acting immediately once it became apparent planning permission would not be obtained in the time specified.

Held
The right to rescind still existed, therefore the plaintiffs' action to enforce the contract must fail.

Photo Production Ltd v *Securicor Transport Ltd*
See Chapter 21.

Reardon Smith Line Ltd v *Yngvar Hansen-Tangen*
See Chapter 19.

Southway Group Ltd v *Wolff* (1991) The Independent 30 August Court of Appeal (Parker, Nourse and Bingham LJJ)
Performance of contracts – personal performance

Facts
The question as to whether a contract must be performed in person arose in this contract for services. Before the sale of a warehouse and adjoining land was completed with the plaintiffs, B agreed to carry out certain improvements in accordance with outline specifications. The question asked was whether B could then subcontract the work to an independent contractor. B had entered into a resale agreement with the defendants and then on purchase of the land had delegated all obligations.

Held
The essence of the contract lay in confidence in the expertise of B. B did not have the right to unilaterally delegate the responsibility for the works agreed elsewhere.

Stour Valley Builders v *Stuart* (1993) The Times 9 February Court of Appeal (Lloyd LJ and Connell J)
Accord and satisfaction – effect of keeping and cashing a cheque

Facts
The plaintiff sent the defendant a bill for work done. The defendant, considering the bill too high, sent a cheque to the plaintiff for a lower figure in 'full and final settlement'. The plaintiff, although he kept and cashed the cheque, made it clear that he did not accept it as full payment and wanted the full amount.

Held
In refusing the appeal, the Court of Appeal confirmed the view of the court of first instance that there was

no agreement between the parties to accept the cheque in full and final settlement. To establish accord and satisfaction the burden of proof falls on the debtor to establish that he has offered valuable consideration in return for the creditor accepting a lesser sum in settlement of a larger claim. This the debtor could not do. There was no accord and satisfaction.

Sumpter v *Hedges* [1898] 1 QB 673 Court of Appeal (A L Smith, Chitty and Collins LJJ)

Contract abandoned – payment for work done

Facts
The plaintiff builder contracted to erect certain buildings for the defendant for £565. He did part of the work (to the value of about £333) and received payment of part of the price; he then said he had no money and could not go on. The defendant finished the work, using some of the plaintiff's materials left on site. When the plaintiff sued for work done and materials provided, the judge found that the plaintiff had abandoned the contract, allowed his claim for materials used, but gave him nothing for work done. The plaintiff appealed.

Held
The appeal would be dismissed.

Collins LJ:

> 'I think the case is really concluded by the finding of the learned judge to the effect that the plaintiff had abandoned the contract. If the plaintiff had merely broken his contract in some way so as not to give the defendant the right to treat him as having abandoned the contract, and the defendant had then proceeded to finish the work himself, the plaintiff might perhaps have been entitled to sue on a quantum meruit on the ground that the defendant had taken the benefit of the work done. But that is not the present case. There are cases in which, though the plaintiff has abandoned the performance of a contract, it is possible for him to raise the inference of a new contract to pay for the work done on a quantum meruit from the defendant's having taken the benefit of that work but, in order that that may be done, the circumstances must be such as to give an option to the defendant to take or not to take the benefit of the work done. It is only where the circumstances are such as to give that option that there is any evidence on which to ground the inference of a new contract. Where, as in the case of work done on land, the circumstances are such as to give the defendant no option whether he will take the benefit of the work or not, then one must look to other facts than the mere taking the benefit of the work in order to ground the inference of a new contract. In this case I see no other facts on which such an inference can be founded. The mere fact that a defendant is in possession of what he cannot help keeping, or even has done work upon it, affords no ground for such an inference. He is not bound to keep unfinished a building which in an incomplete state would be a nuisance on his land. I am therefore of opinion that the plaintiff was not entitled to recover for the work which he had done.'

Thornton v *Abbey National plc* (1993) The Times 4 March Court of Appeal (Neill and Beldam LJJ)

Breach of contract – no disadvantage suffered by innocent party

Facts
The defendants were contracted to provide the plaintiff with a replacement car, at intervals of no more than 30 months. They replaced the vehicle outside that period. The plaintiff in an action for breach of

contract argued that the next car to be provided should have been replaced within 30 months of the date on which the last car *should* have been provided, not when it actually was.

Held
The phrase 'at intervals of no more than 30 months' did not mean cars had to be replaced at regular dates. Even though the defendants had breached their contract with the plaintiff they were not debarred from using the 30 month period to calculate when the replacement of the next car was due. Provided the plaintiff suffered no disadvantage, they could, effectively, benefit from their breach of contract. The presumption that a party could not rely on his own wrong to secure an advantage did not apply in the present circumstances.

Toepfer (Alfred C) International GmbH v *Itex Itagrani Export SA* [1993] 1 Lloyd's Rep 360 Queen's Bench Division (Saville J)

Inability to perform contract – intention not to perform – repudiatory breach

Facts
In an fob contract the sellers sold 'one full cargo' of 22,000 tonnes of Argentinian flint maize. The buyers agreed to sell a similar cargo on similar terms to sub-buyers. The sub-buyers nominated a ship (the *Danobar Tanabe*), but they had also nominated the same vessel for another cargo of 6,100 tonnes. Because of draught restrictions this meant that the vessel could only take 15,400 tonnes of maize and not 'one full cargo' as stipulated. The question arose as to whether the nomination of a vessel unable to load the full cargo amounted to evidence of intention to repudiate the contract.

Held
The exchanges did not amount to renunciation by the main buyers. The mere fact that the sub-buyers had contracted to load other goods on the vessel did not in itself establish that the buyers did not wish to or could not perform the contract.

United Dominions Corporation (Jamaica) Ltd v *Shoucair* [1968] 3 WLR 893 Privy Council (Viscount Dilhorne, Lord Guest, Lord Devlin, Lord Pearce and Lord Pearson)

Mortgage – variation of rate of interest

Facts
The appellants lent £55,000 to the respondent on a mortgage, the rate of interest being 9 per cent with no provision for raising it. Following an increase in bank rate, the appellants wrote to the respondent to say that they had increased their interest by a corresponding amount and the respondent confirmed his acceptance of the increase. This increase was not made in accordance with the statutory moneylending law. Did the original mortgage, at 9 per cent, remain unforceable?

Held
It did, as the agreed variation in interest rate did not reveal an intention to rescind the mortgage transaction.

Lord Devlin:

'If the principle in *Morris* v *Baron & Co* applies to this case, the mortgage ... remains in force. The contrary has not been and could not be argued. It would be impossible to contend that a temporary variation in the rate of interest reveals any intention to extinguish the debt and the mortgage. So the question in this appeal is whether the Board should apply to the Moneylending Law the reasoning which *Morris* v *Baron & Co* applied to the Statute of Frauds or whether the Board should apply the reasoning which in *Morris* v *Baron & Co* the House rejected ...

In their Lordships' view the problem – that is, how to handle the consequences of unenforceability – takes the same form under the Moneylending Law as it does under the Statute of Frauds and similar statutes considered in *Morris* v *Baron & Co*. Both the Statute of Frauds and the Moneylending Law are procedural statues enacting that a contract shall not be enforced unless certain matters can be proved. The matters are not in the two cases the same in all respects. Both statutes require the production of a note or memorandum containing all the terms of the contract, but the Moneylending Law requires also that the note must be one that was signed by the borrower before the money was lent and one of which a copy was delivered to the borrower within seven days of the making of the contract. These additional requirements do not in their lordships' view alter the nature of the problem.

The choice before the Board lies between solving the problem by means of what Lord Sumner called formal logic or solving it by giving effect as far as possible to the intention of the parties as was done in *Morris* v *Baron & Co*. The argument for the respondent assumed rightly that their lordships would accept the guidance offered in *Morris* v *Baron & Co*, unless it could be shown that despite the similarity in the operative parts of the statutes there are underlying differences between them that destroy the value of the guidance ...

None of the differences suggested touch that point. The intention of the parties is just as important in moneylending contracts as in any other ... The Board can see no reason for not following *Morris* v *Baron & Co*.'

Vitol SA v *Norelf Ltd* [1995] 3 WLR 549 Court of Appeal (Nourse, Kennedy and Hirst LJJ)

Anticipatory breach – whether mere inaction is capable of constituting acceptance of anticipatory breach.

Facts
The parties entered into a contract for the sale of a cargo of propane for delivery 1–7 March. Loading was not completed until 9 March. The day before (8 March) Vitol sent Norelf a telex, repudiating the contract on the ground that delivery was overdue. On 11 March, Norelf informed Vitol by telex that loading had been completed by 9 March. There was no further contact between the parties for five months. On 15 March, Vitol resold the cargo. On 9 August Norelf claimed the difference between the contract price at which Vitol had agreed to buy and the resale price.

Held
An innocent party could not accept repudiation of a contract merely by failing to perform his obligations under it. Failure to act did not show the clear, unequivocal intention required by law not to affirm the contract.

Nourse LJ:

'The question on this appeal, though it arises in the context of a cif contract for the sale of propane, is one of general importance in the law of contract. Can an innocent party accept a repudiation of the contract merely by failing to perform his own obligations under it?'

Having considered the authorities he continued:

'I express no view as to the need, in general, for the acceptance to be communicated to the party in breach. As the judge said, communication is not in issue in the present case. That is because of the arbitrator's finding that Norelf's failure to take any further step to perform the contract, apparent to Vitol, was both an acceptance and a sufficient communication of it to Vitol. Equally, if there was no acceptance there was no communication. Either way, communication, as a separate requirement, is not in point.

The judge expressed the question he had to decide as being whether, in a matter of law, mere failure to perform contractual obligations can *ever* (my emphasis) constitute acceptance of an anticipatory repudiation by the other party. There was some debate as to whether the judge's formulation of the question in that absolute form was appropriate. While recognising that it is rarely possible to be certain that there may not prove to be circumstances so unusual as to ground an exception to an absolute rule. I am content to answer the question in that form. For the reasons I have given, substantially those advanced by Mr Popplewell in this court, and differing from the judge, I would answer it in the negative.

That makes it necessary to consider the respondent's notice, under which Norelf seeks, alternatively, to rely on its resale of the cargo on 15 March 1991, in the further alternative on its solicitors' letter of 9 August 1991, as an acceptance of Vitol's anticipatory breach of contract. For the reasons to be given in the judgment of Hirst LJ, which I have had the advantage of reading in draft, I agree with him that by virtue of the material provisions of the Arbitration Act 1979, in particular section 1(7), neither of those points can now be taken by Norelf. On a broad view of the case Vitol, having been held to be in repudiatory breach of the contract, may be thought to be fortunate in not having to pay the damages awarded by the arbitrator. But that is no ground for departing from the provisions of the Act.

I would allow this appeal.'

White and Carter (Councils) Ltd v *McGregor* [1962] 2 WLR 17 House of Lords (Lord Reid, Lord Morton of Henryton, Lord Tucker, Lord Keith of Avonholm and Lord Hodson)

Contract – election not to accept repudiation

Facts
The appellants supplied litter bins to local authorities free of charge. They made their profit by fixing advertisements to the bins for which a competitive charge was made. The appellants agreed with the respondents to advertise their business on a fixed number of litter bins for three years. On the same day, the respondents cancelled the contract, but despite their repudiation the appellants went ahead and performed their side of the contract.

Held
Following repudiation by one party, a general right exists to affirm the contract and continue as though no repudiation has taken place.

Lord Reid:

> 'The general rule cannot be in doubt. It was settled in Scotland at least as early as 1848 and it has been authoritatively stated time and time again in both Scotland and England. If one party to a contract repudiates it in the sense of making it clear to the other party that he refused or will refuse to carry out his part of the contract, the other party, the innocent party, has an option. He may accept that repudiation and sue for damages for breach of contract, whether or not the time for performance has come; or he may, if he chooses, disregard or refuse to accept it and then the contract remains in full effect ...
>
> I need not refer to the numerous authorities. They are not disputed by the respondent, but he points out that in all of them, the party who refused to accept the repudiation had no active duties under the contract. The innocent party's option is generally said to be to *wait* until the date of performance and then to claim damages estimated as at that date. There is no case in which it is said that he may, in the face of the repudiation, go on and incur useless expenses in performing the contract and then claim the contract price. The option, it is argued, is merely as to the date at which damages are to be assessed.

'Developing this argument, the respondent points out that in most cases the innocent party cannot complete the contract himself without the other party doing, allowing or accepting something and that it is purely fortuitous that the appellants can do so in this case. In most cases, by refusing co-operation, the party in breach can compel the innocent party to restrict his claim to damages. Then it was said that even where the innocent party can complete the contract without such co-operation, it is against the public interest that he should be allowed to do so. An example was developed in argument. A company might engage an expert to go abroad and prepare an elaborate report and then repudiate the contract before anything was done. To allow such an expert to waste thousands of pounds in preparing the report cannot be right if a much smaller sum of damages would give him full compensation for his loss. It would merely enable the expert to extort a settlement giving him far more than reasonable compensation.

The other ground would be that there is some general equitable principle or element of public policy which requires this limitation of the contractual rights of the innocent party. It may well be that if it can be shown that a person has no legitimate interest, financial or otherwise, in performing the contract rather than claiming damages, he ought not to be allowed to saddle the other party with an additional burden with no benefit to himself. If a party has no interest to enforce a stipulation, he cannot in general enforce it: so it might be said that if a party has no interest to insist on a particular remedy, he ought not to be allowed to insist on it. And just as party is not allowed to enforce a penalty, so he ought not to be allowed to penalise the other party by taking one course when another is equally advantageous to him. If I may revert to the example which I gave of a company engaging an expert to prepare an elaborate report and then repudiating before anything was done, it might be that the company could show that the expert had no substantial or legitimate interest in carrying out the work rather than accepting damages: I would think that the de minimis principle would apply in determining whether his interest was substantial and that he might have a legitimate interest other than an immediate financial interest. But if the expert had no such interest, then that might be regarded as a proper case for the exercise of the general equitable jurisdiction of the court. But that is not this case. Here, the respondent did not set out to prove that the appellants had no legitimate interest in completing the contract and claiming the contract price rather than claiming damages; there is nothing in the findings of fact to support such a case and it seems improbable that any such case could have been proved. It is, in my judgment, impossible to say that the appellants should be deprived of their right to claim the contract price merely because the benefit to them, as against claiming damages and re-letting their advertising space, might be small in comparison with the loss to the respondent: that is the most that could be said in favour of the respondent. Parliament has on many occasions relieved parties from certain kinds of improvident or oppressive contracts, but common law can only do that in very limited circumstances. Accordingly, I am unable to avoid the conclusion that this appeal must be allowed and the case remitted so that decree can be pronounced as craved in the initial writ.'

Lord Hodson (Lord Tucker concurring):

'It may be unfortunate that the appellants have saddled themselves with an unwanted contract, causing an apparent waste of time and money. No doubt this aspect impressed the Court of Session, but there is no equity that can assist the respondent. It is trite that equity will not rewrite an improvident contract where there is no disability on either side. There is no duty laid upon a party to a subsisting contract to vary it at the behest of the other party so as to deprive himself of the benefit given to him by the contract. To hold otherwise would be to introduce a novel equitable doctrine that a party was not to be held to his contract unless the court in the given instance thought it reasonable to do so. In this case it would make an action for debt a claim for a discretionary remedy. This would introduce an uncertainty into the field of contract which appears to be unsupported by authority either in English or Scottish law, save for the one case upon which the Court of Session founded its opinion and which must, in my judgment, be taken to have been wrongly decided.'

Lord Morton of Henryton and Lord Keith of Avonholm delivered dissenting judgments.

25 Remedies for Breach of Contract – Damages

Addis v *Gramophone Co Ltd* [1909] AC 488 House of Lords (Lord Loreburn LC, Lord James of Hereford, Lord Atkinson, Lord Collins, Lord Gorell and Lord Shaw)

Dismissed – measure of damages

Facts
The plaintiff was employed by the defendants as manager of their business in Calcutta, at a weekly salary, plus commission on the trade done. He could be dismissed on six months' notice. In October 1905, the defendants gave him six months' notice but, at the same time, appointed another to act as his successor and took steps to prevent the plaintiff from acting any longer as manager. The plaintiff claimed damages for breach of contract. The jury found for the plaintiff and awarded him £600 for wrongful dismissal and a further £340 in respect of excess commission, over and above what was earned by the plaintiff's successor in the six months between October 1905 and April 1906. The Court of Appeal held, by a majority, that there was no cause of action and entered judgment for the defendants.

Held (Lord Collins dissenting)
This decision would be reversed.

Lord Atkinson:

'The rights of the plaintiff, disembarrassed of the confusing methods by which they were sought to be enforced, are, in my opinion, clear. He had been illegally dismissed from his employment. He could have been legally dismissed by the six months' notice which he in fact received, but the defendants did not wait for the expiry of that period. The damages the plaintiff sustained by this illegal dismissal were (1) the wages for the period of six months during which his formal notice would have been current; (2) the profits or commission which would, in all reasonable probability, have been earned by him during the six months had he continued in the employment; and possibly (3) damages in respect of the time which might reasonably elapse before he could find other employment. He has been awarded a sum possibly of some hundreds of pounds, not in respect of any of these heads of damage, but in respect of the harsh and humiliating way in which he was dismissed, including presumably the pain he experienced by reason, it is alleged, of the imputation upon him conveyed by the manner of his dismissal. This is the only circumstance which makes the case of general importance and this is the only point I think it necessary to deal with.

I have been unable to find any case decided in this country in which any countenance is given to the notion that a dismissed employee can recover in the shape of exemplary damages for illegal dismissal, in effect, damages for defamation, for it amounts to that, except the case of *Maw* v *Jones* (1890) 25 QBD 107 … I have always understood that damages for breach of contract were in the nature of compensation not punishment and that the general rule of law applicable in such cases was that, in effect, stated by Cockburn CJ in *Engell* v *Fitch* (1868) LR 3 QB 314, 330 in these words:

> "By the law of England, as a general rule, a vendor who, from whatever cause, fails to perform his contract, is bound [...] to place the purchaser, so far as money will do it, in the position he would have been in if the contract had been performed [...]"

In *Sikes* v *Wild* (1861) 1 B&S 587, 594, Lord Blackburn says:

> "I do not see how the existence of misconduct can alter the rule of law by which damages for breach of contract are to be assessed. It may render the contract voidable on the ground of fraud, or give a cause of action for deceit, but surely it cannot alter the effect of the contract itself."

> ... in actions of tort motive, if it may be taken into account to aggregate damages as it undoubtedly may be, it may also be taken into account to mitigate them, as may also the conduct of the plaintiff himself who seeks redress. Is this rule to be applied to actions of breach of contract? There are few breaches of contract more common than those which arise where men omit or refuse to pay for what they have bought. Is the creditor or vendor who sues for one of such breaches to have the sum he recovers lessened if he should be shown to be harsh, grasping or pitiless, or even insulting in enforcing his demand, or lessened because the debtor has struggled to pay, has failed because of misfortune and has been suave, gracious and apologetic in his refusal? On the other hand, is that sum to be increased if it should be shown the debtor could have paid readily without any embarrassment, but refused with expressions of contempt and contumely, from a malicious desire to injure his creditor?'

Commentary

Distinguished in *Dunk* v *George Waller & Son Ltd* [1970] 2 WLR 1241. See also *Bliss* v *South East Thames Regional Health Authority* [1985] IRLR 308 and *O'Laoire* v *Jackel International Ltd* (1991) The Times 12 February.

Anglia Television Ltd v *Reed* [1971] 3 WLR 528 Court of Appeal (Lord Denning MR, Phillimore and Megaw LJJ)

Breach of contract – measure of damages

Facts
The plaintiffs, a TV company, incurred considerable expenditure when the main actor withdrew from the project, in breach of contract. The actor did not deny liability but challenged the extent of the plaintiffs' claim, some expenditure having been incurred even before the contract was made.

Held
They were entitled to succeed.

Lord Denning MR:

> 'It seems to me that a plaintiff in such a case as this has an election: he can either claim for loss of profits or for his wasted expenditure. But he must elect between them. He cannot claim both. If he has not suffered any loss of profits – or if he cannot prove what his profits would have been – he can claim in the alternative the expenditure which has been thrown away, that is, wasted by reason of the breach.
>
> If the plaintiff claims the wasted expenditure, he is not limited to the expenditure incurred after the contract was concluded. He can claim also the expenditure incurred before the contract, provided that it was such as would reasonably be in the contemplation of the parties as likely to be wasted if the contract was broken. Applying that principle here, it is plain that when Mr Reed entered into his contract, he must have known perfectly well that much expenditure had already been incurred on director's fee and the like. He must have contemplated – or, at any rate, it is reasonably to be imputed to him – that if he broke his contract, all that expenditure would be wasted, whether or not it was incurred before or after the contract. He must pay damages for all the expenditure so wasted and thrown away.

It is true that if the defendant had never entered into the contract, he would not be liable and the expenditure would have been incurred by the plaintiff without redress: but the defendant, having made his contract and broken it, it does not lie in his mouth to say he is not liable when it was because of his breach that the expenditure has been wasted.'

Commentary
Applied: *Cullinane* v *British 'Rema' Manufacturing Co Ltd* [1953] 3 WLR 923. Applied in *C & P Haulage* v *Middleton* [1983] 1 WLR 1461.

Beoco Ltd v *Alfa Laval Co Ltd* (1994) The Times 12 January Court of Appeal (Balcombe, Stuart-Smith and Gibson LJJ)

Damages – tort principles apply to loss of profit

Facts
The defendant had been responsible for installing a heat exchanger at the plaintiff's factory. A crack appeared in August 1988 and two months later it exploded causing damage to property and economic loss in terms of lost production.

Held
At the time of the botched repair in August 1988 the plaintiff had a claim against the defendant for loss of profits (which were as yet unquantified) and for the cost of the repair. The explosion meant that loss of profits was not sustained as anticipated, but even if the heater had not exploded it was not an efficient one with an 18 year life span, but a defective one with a much shorter life span. There were no authorities in contract, but several in tort and the court felt tortious rules would apply. Assessment of damages would be limited to the cost of replacement of the defective casing of the heater and losses in production occurred up to and including the point of explosion.

Bliss v *South East Thames Regional Health Authority* [1985] IRLR 308 Court of Appeal (Cumming-Bruce and Dillon LJJ and Heilbron J)

Wrongful dismissal – damages for mental distress

Facts
In an action for damages for wrongful dismissal the judge included in the award an amount for the plaintiff's frustration and mental distress.

Held
He should not have done so.

Dillon LJ:

> 'The general rule laid down by the House of Lords in *Addis* v *Gramophone Co Ltd* [1909] AC 488 is that where damages fall to be assessed for breach of contract rather than in tort it is not permissible to award general damages for frustration, mental distress, injured feelings or annoyance occasioned by the breach ... Lord Loreburn regarded the rule ... as too inveterate to be altered ...'

Brace v Calder [1895] 2 QB 253 Court of Appeal (Lord Esher MR, Lopes and Rigby LJJ)

Wrongful dismissal – measure of damages

Facts
The plaintiff was employed by a partnership, consisting of the four defendants, as the manager of their London office. Under his contract with the partners, he was to be employed at a fixed salary for two years subject to clause 5, which gave the partners the right to terminate the agreement on one month's notice, provided they paid him a sum equivalent to the salary he would have received if he had been retained for the full two years. Before the expiry of the two years, two partners retired and the business transferred to the others. Although the continuing partners were willing to retain him in their service on the same terms as before, he declined to serve them. The plaintiff brought an action for wrongful dismissal.

Held (Lord Esher MR dissenting)
The dissolution of the partnership operated as a wrongful dismissal of the plaintiff or a breach of his contract, but he was only entitled to nominal damages.

Lopes LJ:

'There is nothing in this agreement which indicates that in any event, except that mentioned in clause 5, the employment was not to be for the period of two years. On the contrary, the provision contained in clause 5 of the agreement appears to me strong, to show that there was an express agreement to employ the plaintiff for two years. It appears to me, therefore, that the plaintiff was discharged by the defendants and was entitled to damages either on the ground that he was wrongfully discharged, or that there was a breach of a contract to employ him for two years. But in estimating the damages, it must be taken into consideration that the continuing partners were willing to keep him on in their service till the end of the two years at the same salary as before; but he declined to serve them and therefore it was his own fault that he suffered any loss. Consequently, the damages resulting from the breach of contract would be nominal ... In the result, I am of the opinion that there was a breach of the agreement; but the plaintiff is only entitled to nominal damages in respect of it because, in point of fact, he did not suffer any loss through it ...'

Bradburn v Great Western Railway Co (1874) LR 10 Ex 1 Exchequer Division (Bramwell, Piggott and Amphlett BB)

Damages – plaintiff insured

Facts
The plaintiff passenger suffered injury on the defendants' railway as a result of the negligence of the defendants' engine driver. The plaintiff was insured against such accidents: should the amount paid to the plaintiff by his insurance company be deducted from the amount of damages awarded against the defendants?

Held
It should not.

Piggott B:

'I think that the plaintiff is entitled to recover from the railway company the full amount of the damage which they have caused him to suffer by their negligence; and I think that there would be no justice or principle in setting off an amount which the plaintiff has entitled himself to under a contract of insurance,

British Westinghouse Electric and Manufacturing Company Limited v Underground Electric Railways Company of London Limited [1912] AC 673 House of Lords (Viscount Haldane LC, Lord Ashbourne, Lord Macnaghten and Lord Atkinson)

Breach of contract – duty to minimise loss

Facts
By a contract made between the parties in 1902, the appellants agreed to deliver and erect, within a specified period, eight steam turbines and turbo alternators made to certain specifications, at a price of £250,000 payable by the respondents in instalments. The machines supplied were defective in failing to comply with the provisions of the contract in respect to economy and steam consumption. After using the defective machines for some years (and allowing the appellants to attempt repairs) the respondents decided to replace them with eight new Parsons turbines, superior both in efficiency and economy. The respondents claimed damages for breach of contract, either (a) £280,000 or so, being their estimate of the loss caused by the excessive coal consumption of the appellants' machines for a period of 20 years estimated commercial life, or (b) the cost of installing the new Parsons turbines, namely £78,186 plus a further £42,000, being the estimated loss caused by the excess coal consumption during the time the appellants' machines were working and before the Parsons machines were installed.

The arbitrator, to whom the case was initially referred under an arbitration clause in the contract, found as a fact that the purchase of the Parsons turbines by the respondents was a reasonable and prudent course and that it mitigated or prevented the loss and damage which would have been recoverable from the appellants if the respondents had continued to use the appellants' defective machines. He found further that the purchase of the Parsons turbines was to the pecuniary advantage of the respondents and that the superiority of the new machines was such that even if the appellants' machines had complied with the terms of the contract, it would still have been to the respondents' pecuniary advantage at their own cost to have replaced the appellants' machines with the new Parsons machines.

The arbitrator stated a special case for the opinion of the court whether the respondents could recover the cost of replacing the turbines at law. The Divisional Court found for the respondents and the arbitrator awarded a substantial sum to the respondents (though smaller than that claimed). At first instance and in the Court of Appeal, the appellants' motion to set aside the award was dismissed.

Held
The appeal would be allowed. The court had the power to review the arbitrator's award and the principal question was the correct measure of damages.

Lord Haldane LC:

> 'The question thus arising was decided by the Court of Appeal in favour of the respondents. They held that the law as to the measure of damages had been rightly laid down by the Divisional Court. They thought that the purchase of the Parsons machines must be taken to have been merely for the purpose of mitigating

the damages and that the appellants were not entitled to have the pecuniary advantages arising from the subsequent use of these superior machines and the saving of working expenses which would have been incurred even had the appellants' machines been up to the standard of efficiency contracted for, brought into account ...

Upon the question which I have stated, I am unable to agree with the majority of the Court of Appeal.

The arbitrator appears to me to have found clearly that the effect of the superiority of the Parsons machines and of their efficiency in reducing working expenses was, in point of fact such, that all loss was extinguished and actually, the respondents made a profit by the course they took. They were doubtless not bound to purchase machines of a greater kilowatt power than those originally contracted for, but they in fact took the wise course, in the circumstances, of doing so, with the pecuniary advantage to themselves. They had, moreover, used the appellants' machines for several years and had recovered compensation for the loss incurred by reason of these machines not being, during these years, up to the standard required by the contract. After that period, the arbitrator found that it was reasonable and prudent to take the course they actually did in purchasing the more powerful machines and that all remaining loss and damages was thereby wiped out.

In order to come to a conclusion on the question as to damages thus raised, it is essential to bear in mind certain propositions which I think are well established. In some of the cases there are expressions as to the principles governing the measure of general damages which, at first sight, seem difficult to harmonise. The apparent discrepancies are, however, mainly due to the varying nature of the particular questions submitted for decision. The quantum of damage is a question of fact and the only guidance the law can give is to lay down general principles which afford at times but scanty assistance in dealing with particular cases. The judges who give guidance to juries in these cases have necessarily to look at their special character and to mould, for the purpose of different kinds of claim, the expression of the general principles which apply to them and this is apt to give rise to an appearance of ambiguity.

Subject to these observations, I think that there are certain broad principles which are quite well settled. The first is that, as far as possible, he who has proved a breach of the bargain to supply what he contracted to get, is to be placed, as far as money can do it, in as good a situation as if the contract had been performed.

The fundamental basis is thus compensation for pecuniary loss naturally flowing from the breach; but this first principle is qualified by a second which imposes on a plaintiff the duty of taking all reasonable steps to mitigate the loss consequent on the breach and debars him from claiming any part of the damage which is due to his neglect to take such steps. In the words of James LJ in *Dunkirk Colliery Co* v *Lever* (1878) 9 Ch D 20, 25:

> "The person who has broken the contract is not being under any obligation to do anything otherwise than in the ordinary course of business."

As James LJ indicates, this second principle does not impose on the plaintiff an obligation to take any step which a reasonable and prudent man would not ordinarily take in the course of his business. But when, in the course of his business he has taken action arising out of the transaction, which action has diminished his loss, the effect in the actual diminution of the loss he has suffered may be taken into account, even though there was no duty on him to act.'

His Lordship then referred to the decision of the Court of Common Pleas in *Staniforth* v *Lyall* (1830) 7 Bing 169 and continued:

'I think that this decision illustrates a principle which has been recognised in other cases, that provided the course taken to protect himself by the plaintiff in such an action was one which a reasonable and prudent person might, in the ordinary course of business, properly have taken and in fact did take, whether bound to or not, a jury or an arbitrator may properly look at the whole of the facts and ascertain the result in estimating the quantum of damage ...

I think that the principle which applies here is that which makes it right for the jury or arbitrator to look at what actually happened and to balance loss and gain. The transaction was not re inter alios acta, but one in which the person whose contract was broken took a reasonable and prudent course quite naturally arising out of the circumstances in which he was placed by the breach. Apart from the breach of contract, the lapse of time had rendered the appellants' machines obsolete and men of business would be doing the only thing they could properly do in replacing them with new and up to date machines.

The arbitrator does not, in his finding of fact, lay any stress on the increase in kilowatt power of the new machines and I think that the proper inference is that such increase was regarded by him as a natural and prudent course followed by those whose object was to avoid further loss and that it formed part of a continuous dealing with the situation in they found themselves and was not an independent or disconnected transaction.

For the reasons I have given, I think that the questions of law stated by the arbitrator in the special case have been wrongly answered by the courts below. The result is that the award cannot stand and must be sent back to the arbitrator, with a declaration that the contention of the appellants ... was right.'

Commentary
Distinguished in *Hussey* v *Eels* [1990] 2 WLR 234.

C & P Haulage v *Middleton* [1983] 1 WLR 1461 Court of Appeal (Ackner and Fox LJJ)

Contract – damages for breach

Facts
The plaintiffs contracted to allow the defendant use of their premises for a vehicle repair business. This agreement expressly provided for the use to be reviewed every six months and for any fixtures put in by the defendant to be left on the premises. After eleven months, the defendant was summarily ejected from the business. He carried on the business in the garage at his house and claimed damages for the fixtures.

At first instance, the judge found that the defendant would have been entitled to remain in occupation for one further month under the terms of the contract, but as the defendant had not suffered any loss as a result of the breach by the plaintiff, he could recover nominal damages only.

Held
Dismissing the appeal, damages for breach of contract did not include compensating an injured party for entering into a contract or a sum to place him in a better financial position than if the contract had been fully performed. The plaintiffs' failure to give notice terminating the contract was a breach and the defendant was entitled to damages, but he could not be placed in a better position than if the plaintiffs had properly terminated the contract and therefore he could not recover his expenditure on the premises and was entitled only to nominal damages.

Ackner LJ:

'Lord Denning MR in *Anglia TV*, referred to and relied upon the *Cullinane* case [1954] 1 QB 292, where Jenkins LJ said at page 308:

"The general principle applicable to the case is, I apprehend, this; the plant having been supplied in contemplation by both parties that it should be used by the plaintiff in the commercial production of pulverised clay, the case is one in which the plaintiff can claim as damages for the breach of warranty the loss of the profit he can show that he would have made if the plant had been as warranted. Where damages are awarded on that basis, the object in view, as indeed in any other assessment of damages, is to put the plaintiff in the same position, so far as money can put him in the same position, as if the contract had been duly complied with or the subject matter of the contract had conformed to any warranty given."

That is not the approach which the defendant seeks. He is not claiming for the loss of his bargain, which would involve being put in the position that he would have been in if the contract had been performed. He is not asking to be put in that position. He is asking to be put in the position he would have been in if the contract had never been made at all.'

CCC Films (London) Ltd v *Impact Quadrant Films Ltd* [1984] 3 WLR 245 High Court (Hutchison J)

Breach of contract – damages

Facts
The defendants granted to the plaintiff a non-exclusive licence to exploit three films owned by the defendants in various named territories, in consideration for US$12,000. The plaintiff paid in full, but the defendants, in breach of contract, lost the films. The plaintiff claimed $12,000 for total failure of consideration – this was rejected. In the alternative, the plaintiff claimed $12,000 as wasted expenditure. The defendants argued that the plaintiff could only succeed in such a claim if the plaintiff proved he could not assess loss of profits and that the plaintiff must prove that the expenditure would have been recovered if the contract had been fully performed.

Held
The plaintiff had an unfettered right to frame his claim as one for wasted expenditure or loss of profits. He was not confined to framing his claim as one for wasted expenditure only where he established by evidence that he could not prove loss of profits, or that such loss of profits that he could prove was small.

It was established that a claim for wasted expenditure could not succeed in a case where had there been no breach of contract, the returns earned by the plaintiff under the contract would not have been sufficient to recoup the expenditure (*C & P Haulage* v *Middleton* [1983] 1 WLR 1461). In order to defeat a plaintiff's claim for wasted expenditure, the onus was on the defendant to prove that the expenditure would not have recovered had the contract been performed.

Cellulose Acetate Silk Company Limited v *Widnes Foundry (1925) Limited* [1933] AC 20 House of Lords (Lord Atkin, Lord Warrington of Clyffe, Lord Tomlin, Lord Thankerton and Lord Macmillan)

Breach of contract – measure of damages

Facts
The parties contracted for the installation of an acetone recovery plant supplied by the respondents within a period of 18 weeks. Clause 10 of the contract provided that if the work was not completed within the specified period, the respondents were to pay a penalty of £20 per week for every week they were in default. The respondents were 30 weeks late in completing the installation. They claimed the contract price of £19,750 and were given judgment for that sum. The appellants counter claimed for the delay and contended that the £20 per week sum was in the nature of a penalty and they were entitled to recover their actual loss.

Held
The sum of £20 per week was liquidated damages so the respondents were liable for £600 and no more.

Lord Atkin:

'What, then, is the effect of clause 10? If this period of 18 weeks is exceeded, you have to pay, by way of penalty, the sum of £20 per working week for every week you exceed the 18 weeks. I entertain no doubt that what the parties meant was that in the event of delay, the damages, and the only damages, were to be £20 a week – no less and no more. It has to be remembered that the Foundry Company's business in this respect was to supply an accessory to a large business plant for which they had no responsibility. The extent of the purchasers' business might be enormous; their expenses were beyond the sellers' control; and it would be a very ordinary business precaution for the sellers in such a case to say; "We will name a date for delivery, but we will accept no liability to pay damages for not observing the date; for if we were by our default to stop the whole of your business, the damages might be overwhelming in relation to our possible profit out of the transaction. We won't incur any such risk." This precaution the prospective sellers took in their printed condition 10. They definitely negative any liability for delay. The purchasers have ample notice of this in the first quotation form sent to them ... The purchasers pressed for an earlier date; they got it and, getting it without more, they would still only have a business firm's assurance of delivery by that date; they would still be unable to claim damages from them for breach. The sellers ask for an addition to the price in order to enable them to give the earlier delivery; the buyers ask for some compensation if they do not get the delivery they want. It is agreed at £20 per week of delay. It appears to me that such sum is provided as compensation in place of no compensation at all, which would otherwise have been the result. Except that it is called a penalty, which on the cases is far from conclusive, it appears to be an amount of compensation measured by the period of delay. I agree that it is not a pre-estimate of actual damage. I think it must have been obvious to both the parties that the actual damage would be much more than £20 a week; but it was intended to go towards the damage and it was all that the sellers were prepared to pay. I find it impossible to believe that the sellers, who were quoting for delivery at nine months without any liability, undertook delivery at 18 weeks and, in so doing when they engaged to pay £20 a week, in fact made themselves liable to pay full compensation for all loss.

For these reasons, I think the Silk Company are only entitled to recover £20 a week as agreed damages; and that the decision of the Court of Appeal was correct and should be affirmed. In these circumstances, I find it unnecessary to consider what would be the position if this were a penalty. It was argued by appellants that if this were a penalty they would have an option either to sue for the penalty, or to sue for damages for breach of the promise as to time of delivery. I desire to leave open the question whether, where a penalty is plainly less in amount than the prospective damages, there is any legal obligation to suing on it, or, in a suitable case, ignoring it and suing for damages. In the present case the only result of ignoring the penalty might be that the defendants would find themselves confronted with a contract which, by condition 10, deprived them of any compensation at all ...'

Chaplin v *Hicks* [1911] 2 KB 786 Court of Appeal (Vaughan Williams, Fletcher Moulton and Farwell LJJ)

Breach of contract – measure of damages

Facts

In 1908, a letter from the defendant, a well known actor and theatrical manager, was published in a London daily newspaper, in which he said that he was willing that the readers of the newspaper should, by their votes, select twelve young ladies desirous of obtaining engagements as actresses, to whom he would give engagements. Ladies were invited to send their photographs to the newspaper by a given date, together with their name, address and certain personal details. The defendant, with the assistance of a committee, would then select twenty-four photographs to be published in the newspapers and the readers of the newspaper would, out of those, select the twelve winners. So many photographs were sent in that the conditions were altered so that the country could be divided into ten districts, the readers in each district would select the best five ladies and from these fifty, the defendant would himself select the twelve who would receive the promised engagements. The plaintiff agreed to this alteration in the terms of the competition. The defendant was top of her section and became one of the fifty eligible for selection by the defendant. She was invited for an interview, but because she was away at the time the letter was sent, she did not learn of the interview until it was over. The other forty-nine ladies did attend the interview and the defendant made his selection from amongst them. The plaintiff, having failed to secure another appointment, brought this action against the defendant for breach of contract. The jury found that the defendant had not given the plaintiff a reasonable opportunity to present herself for interview and made an award of damages from which the defendant appealed.

Held
The appeal would be dismissed.

Vaughan Williams LJ:

> 'I am of the opinion that this appeal should be dismissed ... The argument for the defendant was based upon two propositions, first that the damages were too remote and secondly that they were unassessable ...
>
> As regards remoteness, the test that is generally applied is to see whether the damages sought to be recovered follow so naturally or by express declaration from the terms of the contract that they can be said to be the result of the breach. This generally resolves itself into the question whether the damages flowing from a breach of contract were such as must have been contemplated by the parties as a possible result of the breach. Now the moment it is admitted that the contract was, in effect, one which gave the plaintiff a right to present herself and to take her chance of getting a prize, and the moment the jury find that she did not have a reasonable opportunity of presenting herself on the particular day, we have a breach attended by neglect of the plaintiff to give her a later opportunity, and when we get a breach of that sort and a claim for loss sustained in consequence of the failure to give the plaintiff an opportunity of taking part in the competition, it is impossible to say that such a result and such damages were not within the contemplation of the parties as the possible direct outcome of the breach of contract ...
>
> ... Then came the point ... that the damages were of such a nature as to be impossible of assessment ... It is said that in a case which involves so many contingencies, it is impossible to say what was the plaintiff's pecuniary loss. I am unable to agree with the contention ... I do not agree with the contention that if certainty is impossible of attainment, the damages for a breach of contract are unassessable ... the fact that damages cannot be assessed with certainty does not relieve the wrongdoer of the necessity of paying damages for his breach of contract ... My view is that under such circumstances as those in this case, the assessment of damages was unquestionably for the jury ... this appeal fails.'

Clayton (Herbert) and Jack Waller Ltd v *Oliver* [1930] AC 209 House of Lords (Lord Buckmaster, Viscount Dunedin, Lord Blanesburgh, Lord Warrington and Lord Tomlin)

Breach of contract – measure of damages

Facts
By a contract contained in two letters, the appellants agreed to engage the respondent to play one of the three leading parts in a music play for six weeks, with an option to the appellant to re-engage the respondent for the run of the play. He was cast in one of the parts and, on reading it, he complained that it was not one of the three leading comedy parts, but the appellants refused to re-cast him and alleged that the part was a good performance of the contract. Thereupon the respondent declined to appear in the production and issued a writ against the appellants. He alleged that in addition to his salary, it was

intended that he should benefit fully from the publicity given to the play and his reputation would have been enhanced by his taking a leading and consequently widely advertised part in an important West End production and that by reason of the breach of contract, he had lost the said publicity and been deprived of the advantages and reputation which would have followed a successful performance. It was found at first instance that the part given to the respondent was a trivial one.

Held
The respondent was entitled to succeed.

Lord Buckmaster:

'... No other part was offered and the result is that the appellants broke their contract. The next question is what was the measure of damages? ... the old and well established rule applied ... the damages are those that may reasonably be supposed to have been in the contemplation of the parties at the time when the contract was made as the probable result of its breach and if any special circumstances were unknown to one of the parties, the damages associated with the flowing from such breach cannot be included. Here both parties knew that as flowing from the contract, the plaintiff would be billed and advertised as appearing at the Hippodrome and in the theatrical profession this is a valuable right.

In assessing the damages, therefore, it was competent for the jury to consider that the plaintiff was entitled to compensation because he did not appear at the Hippodrome ... and in assessing those damages, they may consider the loss he suffered (1) because the Hippodrome is an important place of public entertainment and (2) that in the ordinary course he would have been "billed" and otherwise advertised as appearing at the Hippodrome. The learned judge put the matter as a loss of reputation, which I do not think is the exact expression, but he explained that as the equivalent of loss of publicity and that summarises what I have stated as my view of the true situation.'

Clydebank Engineering v *Don Jose Ramos* see *Clydebank Engineering and Shipbuilding Co* v *Castaneda*

Clydebank Engineering and Shipbuilding Co v *Castaneda* [1905] AC 6 House of Lords (Earl of Halsbury LC, Lord Davey and Lord Robertson)

Breach of contract – liquidated damages

Facts
The appellants contracted to build four torpedo-boat destroyers for the Spanish government within specified periods and the contract stipulated a 'penalty for later delivery ... at the rate of £500 per week'. The purchasers paid for the vessels and claimed for late delivery.

Held
The claim would succeed as the contract had provided for liquidated damages.

Earl of Halsbury LC:

'This is a case in which one party to an agreement has admittedly been guilty of a breach of that agreement. The action was brought by the Spanish government simply for the purpose of enforcing payment of a sum of money which, by agreement between the parties, was fixed as that which the appellants should pay in the events which have happened. Two objections have been made to the enforcement of that payment. The first objection is one which appears on the face of the instrument itself, namely, that it was a penalty, and, therefore, not recoverable without ascertaining the measure of damage resulting from the breach of contract. It was frankly admitted that not much reliance could be placed on the mere use of the words "penalty" on one side, or "damage" on the other. It is clear that neither is conclusive as to the rights of the parties …

Then comes the question whether, under the agreement, the damages are recoverable as an agreed sum, or whether it is simply a penalty to be held over in terrorem, or whether it is a penalty so extravagant that no court ought to enforce it. It is impossible to lay down any abstract rule as to what might or might not be extravagant without reference to the principal facts and circumstances of the particular case. A great deal must depend on the nature of the transaction. On the other hand, it is an established principle in both countries to agree that the damages should be so much in the event of breach of agreement. The very reason why the parties agreed to such a stipulation was that, sometimes, the nature of the damage was such that proof would be extremely difficult, complex and expensive. If I wanted an example of what might be done in this way I need only refer to the argument of counsel as to the measure of damage sustained by Spain through the withholding of these vessels. Suppose there had been no agreement in the contract as to damages, and the Spanish government had to prove damages in the ordinary way, imagine the kind of cross-examination of every person connected with the Spanish administration. It is very obvious that what was intended by inserting these damages in the contract was to avoid a minute, difficult and complex system of examination which would be necessary if they had attempted to prove damage in the ordinary way … If your Lordships look at the nature of the transaction, it is hopeless to contend that the penalty was intended merely to be in terrorem. Both parties recognised that the question was one in which time was the main element of the contract. I have come to the conclusion that the judgment of the court below was perfectly right. There is no ground for the contention that the sum in the contract was not the damages agreed on between the parties for very good and excellent reasons at the time at which the contract was entered into.'

Commentary
See also *Dunlop Pneumatic Tyre Co Ltd* v *New Garage and Motor Co Ltd* [1915] AC 79.

Doyle v *Olby (Ironmongers) Ltd* [1969] 2 WLR 673 Court of Appeal (Lord Denning MR, Winn and Sachs LJJ)

Fraudulent misrepresentation – damages

Facts
After buying an ironmonger's business, things turned out to be very different from what the vendors had led the plaintiff to believe. He was awarded damages for fraudulent misrepresentations and the appeal concerned, inter alia, the measure of damages.

Held
The defendants were bound to make reparation for all the actual damage directly flowing from the fraudulent inducements.

Lord Denning MR:

'On principle the distinction seems to be this: in contract, the defendant has made a promise and broken it. The object of damages is to put the plaintiff in as good a position, as far as money can do it, as if the promise has been performed. In fraud, the defendant has been guilty of a deliberate wrong by inducing the plaintiff to act to his detriment. The object of damages is to compensate the plaintiff for all the loss he has suffered, so far, again, as money can do it. In contract, the damages are limited to what may reasonably be supposed to have been in the contemplation of the parties. In fraud, they are not so limited. The defendant is bound to make reparation for all the actual damage directly flowing from the fraudulent inducement. The person who has been defrauded is entitled to say: "I would not have entered into this bargain at all but for your representation. Owing to your fraud, I have not only lost all the money I paid you, but what is more, I have been put to a large amount of extra expense as well and suffered this or that extra damages." All such damages can be recovered: and it does not lie in the mouth of the fraudulent person to say that they could not reasonably have been foreseen. For instance, in this very case the plaintiff has not only lost money which he paid for the business, which he would never have done if there had been no fraud; he put all that money in and lost it; but also has been put to expense and loss in trying to run a business which has turned out to be a disaster for him. He is entitled to damages for all his loss subject, of course, to giving credit for any benefit that he has received. There is nothing to be taken off in mitigation: for there is nothing more that he could have done to reduce his loss. He did all that he could reasonably be expected to do.'

Dunk v *George Waller & Son Ltd* [1970] 2 WLR 1241 Court of Appeal (Lord Denning MR, Widgery and Karminski LJJ)

Breach of contract – measure of damages

Facts
In breach of an apprenticeship agreement, the employers terminated it while it still had 15 months to run. If the agreement had run its full course, the apprentice would have been entitled to a certificate and this would have given him a better start to his career.

Held
The sum awarded the apprentice should include damages for loss of future prospects.

Lord Denning MR:

'Now, as to the damages. An apprenticeship agreement is of a special character. The apprentice accepted much less wages during the apprenticeship agreement than he would have received if he had gone into the open market as a labourer. At the material time under the apprenticeship agreement he was getting £10 a week. If he had been an unskilled labourer outside in a factory he would have got £20 a week. The difference should have been made up to him by the benefits of apprenticeship, such as the benefit of training, instruction and experience in the various departments of the works. He has been deprived of those benefits for the remaining 65 weeks of the agreement. In order to mitigate the damage, he sought employment elsewhere. He applied for positions as a representative, and so forth, which he did not get. Perhaps he was aiming too high. For 57 weeks he was out of work, receiving unemployment pay. For the last eight weeks he got employment in a slipper factory at £20 per week.

In my opinion he is entitled to damages for his loss of earnings and of training during the remainder of the term of the apprenticeship agreement and also for the diminution of his future prospects. If he had been allowed satisfactorily to complete his apprenticeship he should have got a better post and better wages thereafter. We were referred to some old cases ... which suggest that an apprentice, who has been wrongly dismissed, can only sue for his damage up to the date of his action brought. They are not good law today.

We were also referred to *Addis* v *Gramophone Co Ltd*, when it was said that an employee cannot get compensation –

" ... for the loss he may sustain from the fact that his having been dismissed of itself makes it more difficult for him to obtain fresh employment."

I do not think that that applies in the case of an apprenticeship. The very object of an apprenticeship agreement is to enable the apprentice to fit himself to get better employment. If his apprenticeship is wrongly determined, so that he does not get the benefit of the training for which he stipulated, then it is a head of damage for which he may recover. If the apprentice had continued as an apprentice until the end of his time for the next 15 months, he would have been entitled to a certificate at the end of the apprenticeship agreement certifying that he had served his full period of apprenticeship. That would have given him a better start so that he would earn more than others at any rate for the first year or two.'

Commentary
Distinguished: *Addis* v *Gramophone Co Ltd* [1909] AC 488.

Dunlop Pneumatic Tyre Co Ltd v New Garage and Motor Co Ltd [1915] AC 79
House of Lords (Lord Dunedin, Lord Atkinson, Lord Parker and Lord Parmoor)

Liquidated damages or penalty – question for court

Facts
The appellants manufactured motor tyres and they agreed to supply the respondent retailers on condition that they would not sell at prices below those mentioned in the appellants' price list: if they did, they would pay the appellants £5 for each and every tyre so sold 'as and by way of liquidated damages, and not as a penalty'.

Held
The stipulation was for liquidated damages and the respondents were liable to pay the appellants £5 for each breach of the agreement as to prices.

Lord Dunedin:

'We had the benefit of a full and satisfactory argument, and a citation of the very numerous cases which have been decided on this branch of the law. The matter has been handled, and at a recent date, in the courts of highest resort. I particularly refer to *Clydebank Engineering Co* v *Yzquierdo y Castaneda*, in your Lordships' House, and *Public Works Comr* v *Hills*... in the Privy Council. In ... these cases many of the previous authorities were considered. In view of that fact, and of the number of the authorities available, I do not think it advisable to attempt any detailed review of the various cases, but I shall content myself with stating succinctly the various propositions which I think are deducible from the decisions which rank as authoritative:

(i) Though the parties to a contract who use the words penalty or liquidated damages may prima facie by supposed to mean what they say, yet the expression used is not conclusive. The court must find out whether the payment stipulated is in truth a penalty or liquidated damages. This doctrine may be said to be found passim in nearly every case. (ii) The essence of a penalty is a payment of money stipulated as in terrorem of the offending party; the essence of liquidated damages is a genuine covenanted pre-estimate of damage: *Clydebank Engineering Company* v *Yzquierdo y Castaneda* (1). (iii) The question whether a sum stipulated is penalty or liquidated damages is a question of construction to be decided upon the terms and inherent circumstances of each particular contract, judged of as the time of making of the contract, not as at the time of the breach: *Public Works Comr* v *Hills* ... (iv) To assist this task of construction various tests have been suggested, which, if applicable to the case under consideration, may prove helpful or even conclusive. Such are (a) It will be held to be a penalty if the sum stipulated for is extravagant and unconscionable in amount in comparison with the greatest loss which could conceivably be proved to have followed from the breach – illustration given by Lord Halsbury L C in the *Clydebank Case*. (b) It will be held to be a penalty if the breach consists only in not paying a sum of money, and the sum stipulated is a sum greater than the sum which ought to have been paid: *Kemble* v *Farren*. This, though one of the most ancient instances, is truly a corollary to the last test. Whether it had its historical origin in the doctrine of the common law that, when A promised to pay B a sum of money on a certain day and did not do so, B could only recover the sum with, in certain cases, interest, but could never recover further damages for non-timeous payment, or whether it was a survival of the time when equity reformed unconscionable bargains merely because they were unconscionable – a subject which much exercised Jessel MR, in *Wallis* v *Smith* – probably more interesting than material. (c) There is a presumption (but no more) that it is a penalty when "a single lump sum is made payable by way of compensation, on the occurrence of one or more or all of several events, some of which may occasion serious and others but trifling damages:"

per Lord Watson in *Lord Elphinstone* v *Monkland Iron and Coal Co.* (11 App Cas at p 342). On the other hand: (d) It is no obstacle to the sum stipulated being a genuine pre-estimate of damage that the consequences of the breach are such as to make precise pre-estimation almost an impossibility. On the contrary, that is just the situation when it is probable that pre-estimated damage was the true bargain between the parties: *Clydebank Case* per Lord Halsbury ...

Turning now to the facts of the case, it is evident that the damage apprehended by the appellants owing to the breaking of the agreement was an indirect and not a direct damage. So long as they got their price from the respondents for each article sold, it could not matter to them directly what the respondents did with it. Indirectly it did. Accordingly, the agreement is headed "Price Maintenance Agreement," and the way in which the appellants would be damaged if prices were cut was clearly explained in evidence, and no successful attempt was made to controvert that evidence. But though damages as a whole from such a practice would be certain, yet damages from any one sale would be impossible to forecast. It is just, therefore, one of those cases where it seems quite reasonable for parties to contract that they should estimate the damage at a certain figure, and provided that the figure is not extravagant there would seem no reason to suspect that it is not truly a bargain to assess damages, but rather a penalty to be held in terrorem.'

Commentary
See also *Alder* v *Moore* [1961] 2 WLR 426 and *Bridge* v *Campbell Discount Co Ltd* [1962] 2 WLR 439.

Edwards v *Society of Graphical and Allied Trades* [1970] 3 WLR 713 Court of Appeal (Lord Denning MR, Sachs and Megaw LJJ)

Breach of contract – measure of damages

Facts
The plaintiff joined a trade union, which eventually was incorporated into SOGAT. Under the rules of the union, members were divided into 'full' and 'temporary' categories. If any temporary member was more than six weeks in arrears with his subscription his membership was terminated automatically. The plaintiff was a temporary member and had authorised his employer to deduct his union dues from his wages. Due to an oversight on the part of the employers this deduction was not made and the union declared him no longer a member. Because his employers operated a closed shop system the plaintiff lost his job and various pension rights.

The union admitted that they were at fault in treating the plaintiff's membership as terminated: the only issue therefore was the quantum of damages.

Held
Lord Denning MR:

'... how are the damages to be measured? I think they are to be ascertained by putting the plaintiff in as good a position, so far as money can do it, as if he had never been excluded from the union, taking into account, of course, all contingencies which might have led him to losing his employment anyway and remembering too that it was his duty to do what was reasonable to mitigate the damage ... we must remember that he has now been restored to full membership.'

He awarded him full actual loss to the date of trial and continued:

'Loss from the date of trial – November 1969 – onwards. The judge assessed this loss as if the man had suffered personal injury, incapacitating him from any work except general labouring work. I think that was not the right measure ... I feel that damages in such a case as this are so difficult to assess that I would be inclined to view them somewhat broadly. I would start with the loss of earnings which he might reasonably be expected to have suffered over two years from his expulsion .. I would then work upwards or downwards from that figure, according to the circumstances of the case ...'

Sachs LJ:

'... It is well to record at the outset ... that certain rules laid down in *Addis* v *Gramophone Co Ltd* [1909] AC 488, touching damages for wrongful dismissal, have no application to the present type of case. In other words, whereas in the former class of cases the damages can contain no element for the difficulty the dismissal causes to a plaintiff in getting fresh employment, the essence of the measure in the present case is an assessment of the financial consequences of that very difficulty ... it is necessary first to assess the difference the deprivation of a union card has made to a plaintiff's earnings up to the date of trial and then to add to the resulting figure a quantification of the difference to his future earning capacity likely thereafter to result from the union's wrongful act ... estimated on the chances as to whether and when he may regain work with earnings on the Grade 1 scale current in 100 per cent union shops. That involves considering, among other factors, his chances of remaining a member of the union for any length of time and the chances of their assisting him in obtaining employment in a field over which it has a major influence, as the filling of vacancies ... This is not a case for embarking on detailed calculations or on precise forecasts ... an overall assessment on a broad basis is needed ...'

Megaw LJ:

'... I think that it is convenient to consider the amount of the damage under two heads. First, what is the plaintiff's loss, by reason of the breach of contract, up to the present moment? Second, what is the future loss, if any?

The first head involves consideration of the issue whether the plaintiff acted unreasonably in respect of the termination of his employment (with the second firm) and whether he failed in his duty thereafter to seek to mitigate his loss by pursuing possibilities of employment ... I see no reason to differ from the judge that neither of these matters ought to be treated as constituting a failure by the plaintiff to act reasonably in mitigation of damages. Hence I agree with the judge's figure ... (of) the plaintiff's loss up to the date of judgment ...

The second head, future damage, involves a more difficult question and, for that very reason, it involves looking into the uncertainties of the future. The plaintiff's loss is the difference between what he would have earned if there had been no breach of contract and what he will earn on the assumption that he uses all proper diligence to mitigate his loss ... inevitably it depends upon hypothesis and speculation ... where there are so many incalculables, it would not be right to seek to give an aura of scientific arithmetical or actuarial formulae to the assessment, or to any individual factor on which the assessment partly depends. One must try to assess. One cannot calculate ...'

Export Credits Guarantee Department v *Universal Oil Products Co* [1983] 1 WLR 399 House of Lords (Lord Diplock, Lord Elwyn-Jones, Lord Keith of Kinkel, Lord Roskill and Lord Brightman)

Contract – indemnity clause a penalty?

Facts
In 1970 a number of interlocking multilateral contracts were concluded between three Newfoundland companies, the three defendant companies and a consortium of bankers for the design, construction and

installation of an oil refinery in Newfoundland. The plaintiffs, in consideration of a premium, guaranteed certain payments and the defendants undertook to reimburse them in certain circumstances. These circumstances having arisen, the plaintiffs sought reimbursement, but the defendants contended, inter alia, that their claim should fail as it was a penalty clause.

Held
The plaintiffs' claim would succeed.

Lord Roskill:

'My Lords, one purpose, perhaps the main purpose, of the law relating to penalty clauses is to prevent a plaintiff recovering a sum of money in respect of a breach of contract committed by a defendant which bears little or no relationship to the loss actually suffered by the plaintiff as a result of the breach by the defendant. But it is not and never has been for the courts to relieve a party from the consequences of what may in the event prove to be an onerous or possibly even a commercially imprudent bargain. The defendants could only secure the finance ... if the ECGD were prepared to give ... the guarantee ... required. The ECGD were only prepared to give their guarantee ... on the terms of the premium agreement which included the stringent right of recourse ... The defendants accepted those terms which provided for the right of recourse to arise on the happening of a specified event, and that specified event has now happened. But, as my noble and learned friend Lord Keith observed during the argument, this is not a case where the ECGD are seeking to recover more than their actual loss as compensation by way of damages for breach of a contract to which they were a party. They are seeking, and only seeking, to recover their actual loss, namely the sums which they became legally obliged to pay and have paid ... I am afraid I find it impossible to see how on these facts there can be any room for the invocation of the law relating to penalty clauses.'

Forsikringsaktieselskapet Vesta v *Butcher* [1988] 3 WLR 565 Court of Appeal (O'Connor and Neill LJJ and Sir Roger Ormrod)

Damages for breach of contract – contributory negligence

Facts
A Norwegian insurance company, the plaintiffs, insured a Norwegian fish farm against loss of fish and reinsured 90 per cent of the risk with London underwriters through brokers. It was a condition of both the insurance and the reinsurance that a 24-hour watch be kept on the farm, but the owners told the plaintiffs that they could not accept this clause. The plaintiffs telephoned this information to the brokers and awaited confirmation that the lack of a 24-hour watch was acceptable: the brokers did not pass the information to the reinsurers and the plaintiffs did not follow up the matter: the reinsurance policy contained 'follow settlement' and 'claim control' clauses and also provided that the underwriters were to have sole control of any negotiations and that no payment was to be made to the insured without their consent. Many fish were lost as a result of a severe storm; the plaintiffs settled the owners' claim but, even though a watch would not have saved the fish, the reinsurers repudiated liability, inter alia, on the ground of breach of the 24-hour watch condition. The plaintiffs claimed 90 per cent indemnity from the reinsurers or, alternatively, damages for breach of duty against the brokers for failing to inform the reinsurers that the 24-hour watch condition was unacceptable. The judge held:

1. clauses such as the 24-hour watch condition were to be construed according to Norwegian law which did not provide a valid defence to the plaintiff's claim against the reinsurers;
2. although the brokers had been in breach of contract, no loss had resulted (because the reinsurers were liable) so the plaintiffs were entitled only to nominal damages against them;
3. if the plaintiffs had suffered substantial loss, the damages recoverable from the brokers would have been reduced by 75 per cent because of the plaintiffs' contributory negligence in failing to follow up.

The reinsurers appealed against (1), the brokers cross-appealed against (2) and the plaintiffs cross-appealed against (3).

Held

The appeal and the cross-appeals would be dismissed.

O'Connor LJ:

'The important issue of law is whether on the facts of this case there is power to apportion under the Law Reform (Contributory Negligence) Act 1945 and thus reduce the damages recoverable by Vesta [the plaintiffs].

I start by pointing out that Vesta pleaded its claim against the brokers in contract and tort. This is but a recognition of what I regard as a clearly established principle that where under the general law a person owes a duty to another to exercise reasonable care and skill in some activity, a breach of that duty gives rise to a claim in tort notwithstanding the fact that the activity is the subject matter of a contract between them. In such a case the breach of duty will also be a breach of contract. The classic example of this situation is the relationship between doctor and patient.

Since the decision of the House of Lords in *Hedley Byrne & Co Ltd* v *Heller & Partners Ltd* [1964] AC 465, the relationship between the brokers and Vesta is another example. Counsel for Vesta accepts that this is so but he submits that, if a plaintiff makes his claim in contract, contributory negligence cannot be relied on by the defendant whereas it is available if the claim is made in tort. If this contention is sound then the law has been sadly adrift for a very long time for it would mean that in employers' liability cases an injured employee could debar the employer from relying on any contributory negligence by framing his action in contract.

In support of his submission counsel relied on two decisions at first instance: *AB Marintrans* v *Comet Shipping Co Ltd, The Shinjitsu Maru No 5* [1985] 3 All ER 442 and *Basildon DC* v *J E Lesser (Properties) Ltd* [1985] 1 All ER 20. The judge dealt with this submission as follows ([1986] 2 All ER 488 at 508):

"The question whether the 1945 Act applies to claims brought in contract can arise in a number of classes of case. Three categories can conveniently be identified. (1) Where the defendant's liability arises from some contractual provision which does not depend on negligence on the part of the defendant. (2) Where the defendant's liability arises from a contractual obligation which is expressed in terms of taking care (or its equivalent) but does not correspond to a common law duty to take care which would exist in the given case independently of contract. (3) Where the defendant's liability in contract is the same as his liability in the tort of negligence independently of the existence of any contract" …

In my judgment *Sayers* v *Harlow UDC* [1958] 2 All ER 342 is a category (3) case and the decision of the Court of Appeal that there is power to apportion was not only right but is binding on us just as the judge held it was binding on him.

There are two further possible arguments for saying that there is a power to apportion in a category (3) case even though the claim is made in contract. I will state them but do not find it necessary to analyse or reach a conclusion on them. (i) Contributory negligence was a defence in category (3) cases pleaded in contract before 1945. The argument is supported by railway cases and banking cases. (ii) Just as it has been held that a plaintiff cannot escape the Limitation Act 1980 by pleading a negligence case as trespass to the person so here the court should hold that a plaintiff cannot escape apportionment by pleading the case in contract (see *Letang* v *Cooper* [1964] 2 All ER 929).

I am satisfied that the judge came to the right conclusion on this topic and in respect of it I would dismiss Vesta's appeal.'

Galoo v *Bright Grahame Murray* [1994] 1 WLR 1360 Court of Appeal (Glidewell, Evans and Waite LJJ)

Causation

Facts

The plaintiffs were a series of companies and the defendants were their auditors. The plaintiffs claimed that the defendants had been negligent in failing to discover substantial inaccuracies in the accounts, and that had the defendants performed their duties with reasonable care and skill, the fact that the companies were insolvent would have been shown. In these circumstances the companies would have ceased to trade immediately, and thus losses subsequent to that date would not have occurred. The defendants succeeded at first instance and the plaintiffs appealed.

Held

It was held, dismissing the appeals, that a breach of contract would sound in damages only if it were the dominant or effective cause of the plaintiff's loss, and not if it had merely given the opportunity for the loss to be sustained. In determining whether a breach of contract was the cause of a loss or merely the occasion of it the court would apply common sense to the facts of each case.

Glidewell LJ:

> '... if a breach of contract by the defendant is to be held to entitle the plaintiff to claim damages, it must first be held to have been an "effective" or "dominant" cause of his loss. The test in *Quinn* v *Burch Bros (Builder) Ltd* [1966] 2 QB 370 that it is necessary to distinguish between a breach of contract which causes a loss to the plaintiff and one which merely gives the opportunity for him to sustain the loss, is helpful but still leaves the question to be answered "How does the court decide whether the breach of duty was the cause of the loss or merely the occasion of the loss?" ... The answer in the end is "By the application of the court's common sense".'

Gebrüder Metalmann GmbH & Co KG v *NBR (London) Ltd* [1984] 1 Lloyd's Rep 614 Court of Appeal (Sir John Donaldson MR, Dunn and Browne-Wilkinson LJJ)

Breach of contract – mitigating damage

Facts

Both parties are sugar traders. The plaintiffs sold 2,000 tons of sugar to the defendant buyers who repudiated the contract before the date for delivery of the goods. The plaintiffs accepted the repudiation. The plaintiffs claimed damages and a dispute arose over the basis of assessment and mitigation.

Held

If the plaintiff takes steps to mitigate the loss which actually make the situation worse, provided the action seems reasonable in all the circumstances at the time, then it is unimportant that attempts to mitigate loss did not in fact do so.

Sir John Donaldson MR:

> 'The general rule was that where a contract for the sale of goods was repudiated and the repudiation was accepted before the date for delivery, damages were to be assessed on the difference between the contract price and the market price on the date for delivery.
> That was subject to the exception that, as from the date of breach and the acceptance of the repudiation, the claimant must do what, if anything, was reasonable to decrease the damages.
> The duty of the plaintiff was to act reasonably in all the circumstances, with a view to mitigating his loss.
> In outline, the plaintiffs had a choice – either to sell on the physical market or to make a hedging sale on the terminal market (a market in London and Paris protected from market fluctuations). The plaintiffs sold on the terminal market and received a lower price than the actual market value. On the evidence, it was felt that that was what any reasonable trader would have done, since it involved no delay and they were entitled to the difference between the contract price and terminal market price.'

Browne-Wilkinson LJ stated:

> '... that if there were two methods of mitigating damage, both of which were reasonable in the circumstances, known to the innocent party when the mitigating action was required, it was not possible to say that that party acted unreasonably in selecting one of those methods just because it turned out that the loss would have been less had the other method been adopted.'

Golden Bay Realty Ltd v *Orchard Twelve Investments Ltd* [1991] 1 WLR 981 Privy Council (Lord Templeman, Lord Oliver, Lord Goff, Sir Michael Kerr and Sir Christopher Slade)

Contract in statutory form – relief against penalties applicable?

Facts
A contract made in Singapore for the sale of commercial property was made in accordance with the relevant statutes as applicable locally. This included the Sale of Commercial Properties Act 1979, which provided inter alia that if the vendor failed to complete by the prescribed date he should pay liquidated damages, calculated as according to the SCP Act.

The vendor failed to complete on the appointed day and were thus liable to pay the purchaser liquidated damages until he did finally complete, some two years later.

The vendor appealed against this payment on the basis that it amounted to a penalty clause.

Held
The Privy Council, supporting the Singapore Court of Appeal, refused relief from the provisions of the Act; holding that where the terms and conditions of a contract are prescribed by legislation, the usual rules as to penalty clauses do not apply. The vendor was not entitled to question the validity of the provision relating to liquidated damages by claiming it was penal in nature. Regardless of the purpose of the Act, damages were entitled to be recovered, calculated in accordance with the statutory formula.

Hadley v *Baxendale* (1854) 9 Ex 341 Court of Exchequer (Parke, Alderson, Platt and Martin BB)

Breach of contract – measure of damages

Facts
The plaintiffs, who were the owners of a flour mill, sent a broken mill shaft, by a well known firm of common carriers, to their suppliers at Greenwich, to provide a pattern for a new shaft. The carrier was slow in delivering the shaft and the plaintiffs claimed damages on the footing that the whole of the activities of the mill were held up for want of the shaft.

Held
There should be a new trial.

Alderson B:

> 'Now we think the proper rule in such a case as the present is this: where two parties have made a contract which one of them has broken, the damages which the other party ought to receive in respect of such a breach of contract should be such as may fairly and reasonably be considered either arising naturally, ie according to the usual course of things from such a breach of contract itself, or such as may reasonably be supposed to have been in the contemplation of both parties at the time they made the contract as the

probable result of the breach of it. Now, if the special circumstances under which the contract was actually made were communicated by the plaintiffs to the defendants and thus known to both parties, the damages resulting from the breach of such a contract, which they would reasonably contemplate, would be the amount of injury which would ordinarily follow from a breach of contract under these special circumstances so known and communicated. But on the other hand, if those special circumstances were wholly unknown to the party breaking the contract, he, at the most, could only be supposed to have had in his contemplation the amount of injury which would arise generally and in the great multitude of cases not affected by any special circumstances, from such a breach of contract. For, had the special circumstances been known, the parties might have specially provided for the breach of contract by special terms as to the damages in that case; and of this advantage it would be very unjust to deprive them. Now the above principles are those by which we think the jury ought to be guided in estimating the damages arising out of any breach of contract. It is said that other cases, such as breaches of contract in the non-payment of money, or in the not making a good title to land, are to be treated as exceptions from this and as governed by a conventional rule. But as, in such cases, both parties must be supposed to be cognisant of that well known rule, these cases may, we think, be more properly classed under the rule above enunciated as to cases under known special circumstances, because there both parties may reasonably be presumed to contemplate the estimation of the amount of damages according to the conventional rule. Now in the present case, if we are to apply the principles above laid down, we find that the only circumstances here communicated by the plaintiffs to the defendants at the time the contract was made, were that the article to be carried was the broken shaft of a mill and that the plaintiffs were the millers of that mill. But how do all these circumstances show reasonably that the profits of the mill must be stopped by an unreasonable delay in the delivery of the broken shaft by the carrier to the third person? Suppose the plaintiffs had another shaft in their possession, put up or putting up at the time and that they only wished to send back the broken shaft to the engineer who made it; it is clear that this would be quite consistent with the above circumstances and yet the unreasonable delay in the delivery would have no effect upon the intermediate profits of the mill. Or, again, suppose that at the time of the delivery to the carrier, the machinery of the mill had been in other respects defective, then, also, the same results would follow. Here, it is true that the shaft was actually sent back to serve as a model for a new one and that the want of a new one was the only cause of the stoppage of the mill and that the loss of profits really arose from not sending down the new shaft in proper time and that this arose from the delay in delivering the broken one to serve as a model. But it is obvious that in the great multitude of cases of millers sending off broken shafts to third persons by a carrier, under ordinary circumstances such consequences would not, in all probability, have occurred; and these special circumstances were here never communicated by the plaintiffs to the defendants. It follows, therefore, that the loss of profits here cannot reasonably be considered such a consequence of the breach of contract as could have been fairly and reasonably contemplated by both the parties when they made this contract. For such loss would neither have flowed naturally from the breach of this contract in the great multitude of such cases occurring under ordinary circumstances, nor were the special circumstances, which, perhaps, would have made it a reasonable and natural consequence of such breach of contract, communicated to or known by the defendants ...'

Commentary
Applied in *Wroth* v *Tyler* [1973] 2 WLR 405. Distinguished in *Victoria Laundry (Windsor) Ltd* v *Newman Industries Ltd* [1949] 2 KB 528. See also *Koufos* v *C Czarnikow Ltd* [1967] 3 WLR 1491, *Pilkington* v *Wood* [1953] Ch 770 and *Parsons (H) (Livestock) Ltd* v *Uttley Ingham & Co Ltd* [1977] 3 WLR 990.

Hayes* v *James & Charles Dodd [1990] 2 All ER 815 Court of Appeal (Purchas, Staughton LJJ and Sir George Waller)

Damages – wasted expenditure – anguish and vexation

Facts
Wishing to purchase larger premises for their motor repair business, the plaintiffs began negotiations for a workshop and yard. The availability of a rear access was of vital importance and, relying on the assurance of their solicitors, the defendants, that they would have a right of way over land at the rear of the property, the plaintiffs proceeded with the purchase. Shortly after completion the owner of the adjoining land blocked the rear access and it followed that the plaintiffs could not run their business properly; after 12 months they closed it down and eventually sold the premises at a considerable loss. The trial judge (Hirst J) awarded the plaintiffs damages on the basis of capital expenditure and expenses thrown away and for anguish and vexation. The defendants appealed against this order.

Held
The appeal would be allowed only in relation to the award for anguish and vexation.

Staughton LJ:

> 'The first question in this appeal relates to the basis on which damages should be assessed. Like Hirst J I start with the principle stated by Lord Blackburn in *Livingstone* v *Rawyards Coal Co* (1880) 5 App Cas 25 at 39:
>
>> "… you should as nearly as possible get at that sum of money which will put the party who has been injured, or who has suffered, in the same position as he would have been in if he had not sustained the wrong for which he is now getting his compensation or reparation."
>
> One must therefore ascertain the actual situation of the plaintiffs and compare it with their situation if the breach of contract had not occurred.
>
> What then was the breach of contract? It was not the breach of any warranty that there was a right of way: the defendant solicitors gave no such warranty. This is an important point: see *Petty* v *Sidney Phillips & Son (a firm)* [1982] 3 All ER 705. The breach was of the solicitors' promise to use reasonable skill and care in advising their clients. If they had done that, they would have told the plaintiffs that there was no right of way; and it is clear that, on the receipt of such advice, the plaintiffs would have decided not to enter into the transaction at all. They would have bought no property, spent no money and borrowed none from the bank …
>
> I am quite satisfied that Hirst J was entitled to award damages in this case on the no-transaction basis, and that he was right to do so. Indeed it may well be that the plaintiffs were, as he held, entitled to elect between that method and the successful-transaction method; but I need not express any concluded view on that. So they should recover all the money which they spent, less anything which they subsequently recovered, provided always that they acted reasonably in mitigating their loss. But they were quite properly denied any sum for the profit which they would have made if they had operated their business successfully …
>
> *Mental distress*
>
> Hirst J awarded £1,500 to each of the plaintiffs under this head. There can be no doubt, and it was accepted in this court, that each of them suffered vexation and anguish over the years to a serious extent, for which the sum awarded was but modest compensation. There is, however, an important question of principle involved …
>
> I am not convinced that it is enough to ask whether mental distress was reasonably foreseeable as a consequence, or even whether it should reasonably have been contemplated as not unlikely to result from a breach of contract. It seems to me that damages for mental distress in contract are, as a matter of

policy, limited to certain classes of case. I would broadly follow the classification provided by Dillon LJ in *Bliss* v *South East Thames Regional Health Authority* [1987] ICR 700 at 718:

> "... where the contract which has been broken was itself a contract to provide peace of mind or freedom from distress ..."

It may be that the class is somewhat wider than that. But it should not, in my judgment, include any case whether the object of the contract was not comfort or pleasure, or the relief or discomfort, but simply carrying on a commercial activity with a view to profit. So I would disallow the item of damages for anguish and vexation.'

Heron II, The see *Koufos* v *C Czarnikow Ltd*

Hussey v *Eels* [1990] 2 WLR 234 Court of Appeal (Mustill, Farquharson LJJ and Sir Michael Kerr)

Negligent misrepresentation – damages

Facts
Before contracting to sell their bungalow to the plaintiffs, the defendants untruthfully and negligently stated that the property was not subject to subsidence. After completing the purchase at a price of £53,250, the plaintiffs discovered the subsidence and established that the necessary repairs would cost at least £17,000. After issuing a writ claiming damages for negligent misrepresentation, the plaintiffs sold the property for redevelopment for £78,500. The judge dismissed the plaintiffs' action on the ground that they had not suffered any recoverable loss: the plaintiffs appealed.

Held
The appeal would be allowed and the plaintiffs awarded the difference between the contract price (£53,250) and the property's market value in its unsound condition.

Mustill LJ:

> 'Ultimately, as with so many disputes about damages, the issue is primarily one of fact. Did the negligence which caused the damage also cause the profit, if profit there was? I do not think so. It is true that in one sense there was a casual link between the inducement of the purchase by misrepresentation and the sale two and a half years later, for the sale represented a choice of one of the options with which the plaintiffs had been presented by the defendants' wrongful act. But only in that sense. To my mind the reality of the situation is that the plaintiffs bought the house to live in, and did live in it for a substantial period. It was only after two years that the possibility of selling the land and moving elsewhere was explored, and six months later still that this possibility came to fruition. It seems to me that when the plaintiffs unlocked the development value of their land they did so for their own benefit, and not as part of a continuous transaction of which the purchase of land and bungalow was the inception.'

Commentary
Distinguished: *British Westinghouse Electric and Manufacturing Co Ltd* v *Underground Electric Railways Co of London Ltd* [1912] AC 673.

Iron Trade Mutual Insurance Co Ltd v *JK Buckenham Ltd* [1989] 2 Lloyd's Rep 89 High Court (Kenneth Rokison QC)

Loss suffered on two different occasions – limitation of actions – Latent Damage Act 1986

Facts
This case concerns insurance and re-insurance. The plaintiffs were underwriters and brokers' agents. The defendant firm were insurance and re-insurance brokers. From 1981 the defendants began refusing to pay out on certain contracts, and in 1984 they repudiated the contracts altogether, alleging that the contracts were voidable for non-disclosure of material facts. The plaintiffs sued the brokers for losses occasioned by this framing their action in contract and tort. The defendants' main defence was limitation – the contracts were mainly from 1976 to 1981. Three questions arose:

1. When did the plaintiffs' cause of action accrue?
2. Could the plaintiffs rely on the Latent Damage Act as a means of delaying the limitation period?
3. If the Act applied, what was the relevant starting date for the purposes of the Act?

Held
Based on the three questions listed above, the Act had no application to claims founded on contract, even when the duty concerned is simply a contractual duty to take reasonable care. Therefore the questions as listed need not be considered further.

Commentary
Followed in *Islander Trucking Ltd* v *Hogg Robinson & Gardner Mountain (Marine) Ltd* [1990] 1 All ER 826.

Jackson v *Horizon Holidays Ltd* [1975] 3 WLR 1468 Court of Appeal

Facts
The plaintiff entered into a contract for a holiday for himself, his wife and two children. The holiday failed to comply with the description given by the defendant and the plaintiff sued, claiming damages.

Held
The plaintiff was entitled to damages not only for himself, but also for his wife and children.

Lord Denning MR:

> 'We have had an interesting discussion as to the legal position when one person makes a contract for the benefit of a party. In this case, it was a husband making a contract for the benefit of himself, his wife and children ...
>
> It would equally be a mistake to say that in any of these instances there was a trust. The transaction bears no resemblance to a trust. There was no trust fund and no trust property. No, the real truth is that, in each instance, the father ... was making a contract himself for the benefit of the whole party. In short, a contract by one for the benefit of third persons.
>
> What is the position when such a contract is broken? At present, the law says that the only one who can sue is the one who made the contract. None of the rest of the party can sue, even though the contract was made for their benefit. But when that one does sue, what damages can he recover? Is he limited to his own loss? Or can he recover for the others? ... He can, of course, recover his own damages, but can he not recover for the others? I think he can. The case comes within the principle stated by Lush LJ in *Lloyds* v *Harper*.
>
>> "I consider it to be an established rule of law that where a contract is made with A for the benefit of B, A can sue on the contract for the benefit of B and recover all that B could have recovered if the contract had been made with B himself."
>
> It has been suggested that Lush LJ was thinking of a contract in which A was trustee for B. But I do not think so. He was a common lawyer speaking of the common law. His words were quoted with

considerable approval by Lord Pearce in *Beswick* v *Beswick*. I have myself often quoted them. I think they should be accpeted as correct, at any rate so long as the law forbids the third person themselves to sue for damages. It is the only way a just result can be achieved.'

Commentary

But see *Woodar Investment Developments Ltd* v *Wimpey Construction UK Ltd* [1980] 1 WLR 277.

Jarvis v *Swan Tours Ltd* [1972] 3 WLR 954 Court of Appeal (Lord Denning MR, Edmund Davies and Stephenson LJJ)

Breach of contract – measure of damages

Facts

The plaintiff booked a winter sports holiday. It was advertised in the defendants' brochure as 'a houseparty' with entertainments. The entertainments were not forthcoming and in his second week the plaintiff was the sole guest.

Held

The plaintiff was entitled to recover, not merely the cost of the holiday, but a similar amount as general damages for disappointment and loss of entertainment.

Lord Denning MR:

'What is the legal position? I think that the statements in the brochure were representations or warranties. The breaches of them give Mr Jarvis a right to damages. It is not necessary to decide whether they were representations or warranties: because since the Misrepresentation Act 1967 there is a remedy in damages for misrepresentations as well as for breach of warranty.

The one question in the case is: what is the amount of damages? The judge seems to have taken the difference in value between what he paid for and what he got. He said that he intended to give "the difference between the two values and no other damages" under any other head. He thought that Mr Jarvis had got half of what he paid for. So the judge gave him half the amount which he had paid, namely £31.72. Mr Jarvis appeals to this court. He says that the damages ought to have been much more.

What is the right way of assessing damages? It has often been said that on a breach of contract, damages cannot be given for mental distress. I think that those limitations are out of date. In a proper case, damages for shock can be recovered in tort. One such case is a contract for a holiday, or any other contract to provide entertainment and enjoyment. If the contracting party breaks his contract, damages can be given for the disappointment, the distress, the upset and frustration caused by the breach. I know that it is difficult to assess in terms of money, but it is no more difficult than the assessment which the courts have to make every day in personal injury cases for loss of amenities.

I think the judge was in error in taking the sum paid for the holiday, £63.45, and halving it. The right measure of damages is to compensate him for the loss of entertainment and enjoyment which he was promised and which he did not get.

Looking at the matter quite broadly, I think the damages in this case should be the sum of £125 ... I would allow the appeal accordingly.'

Jobson v *Johnson* [1989] 1 WLR 1026 Court of Appeal (Kerr, Dillon and Nicholls LJJ)

Penalty clause?

Facts
In a sale agreement, in writing, dated 12 August 1982, two brothers agreed to sell 62,666 of their shares in Southend United Football Club Ltd to the defendant's nominee for £40,000. In a side letter written the same day by the defendant and countersigned by the brothers, the defendant agreed to pay a further six half-yearly instalments totalling over £300,000, the payments to begin in February 1984. Paragraph 6 of that side letter made provision for default including the fact that the defendant would, on default, transfer to the brothers shares totalling not less than 44.9 per cent of the issued share capital in the football club, together with variable monetary payments depending on which instalment(s) was/were defaulted. The defendant defaulted at the first instalment. Subsequent arrangements were made for variation of the contract but the defendant, having paid one of the new (varied) instalments again defaulted. The brothers then assigned their rights to the plaintiff who sought to enforce the contract. At first instance Harman J decided that para 6 of the side letter amounted to a penalty clause, but that it was nevertheless enforceable. The defendant appealed.

Held
1. Whether a clause was a penalty clause was a question of construction, to be decided in the light of the circumstances at the time of making the contract and in the present case, since para 6 provided for repurchase of the shares at a fixed price regardless of the extent of the defendant's default, it amounted to a penalty clause.
2. (Kerr LJ dissenting) the penalty clause was unenforceable to the extent that it provided for compensation to the innocent party in excess of his actual loss.

Nicholls LJ:

> 'Although in practice a penalty clause in a contract ... is effectively a dead letter, it is important in the present case to note that, contrary to the submissions of counsel for the defendant, the strict legal position is not that such a clause is simply struck out of the contract, as though with a blue pencil, so that the contract takes effect as if it had never been included therein. Strictly, the legal position is that the clause remains in the contract and can be sued on, but it will not be enforced by the court beyond the sum which represents, in the events which have happened, the actual loss of the party seeking payment. There are many cases which make this clear.'

Commentary
Applied: *Public Works Commissioner* v *Hills* [1906] AC 368, *Wall* v *Rederiaktiebolaget Luggude* [1915] 3 KB 66 and *Bridge* v *Campbell Discount Co Ltd* [1962] 2 WLR 439.

Kaines (UK) Ltd v *Osterreichische Warrenhandelgesellschaft Austrowaren Gesellschaft mbH* [1993] 2 Lloyd's Rep 1 Court of Appeal (Dillon, Stocker and Bingham LJJ)

Anticipatory breach – measure of damages

Facts
On 3 June 1987 the plaintiffs agreed to buy and the defendants to sell 600,000 barrels of crude oil. On receiving notice that the defendants were repudiating the contract, the plaintiffs indicated their acceptance of the repudiation on 18 June. They did not, however, buy in a new cargo until 29 June when prices were much higher.

Held

On dismissing the plaintiffs' appeal and confirming the original award of purely nominal damages, the Court of Appeal said that in the period between 18 June, when the plaintiffs indicated their acceptance of repudiation, and 29 June, when they sought to mitigate their loss by buying in a substitute cargo, prices had dipped sharply, most notably on 25 June, when the price was below the original contract price.

The proper time to buy in was either, immediately, on 18/19 June or else within a reasonable time thereafter. The plaintiffs' decision to wait was effectively a form of speculation and the higher price they had ultimately to pay on 29 June was because of their own failure to assess the market. Had they bought in when the price was low they would have suffered little loss and only minimal inconvenience, and were thus entitled only to nominal damages.

Koufos v *C Czarnikow Ltd (The Heron II)* [1967] 3 WLR 1491 House of Lords (Lord Reid, Lord Morris of Borth-y-Gest, Lord Hodson, Lord Pearce and Lord Upjohn)

Damages – loss of profit

Facts

By a charter party made in London in October 1960 between Nomicos Ltd, as agents for the appellant (the owner of the Heron II) and the respondent charterers, the charterers chartered the Heron II, then in Piraeus expected ready to load 25-27 October all being well to proceed to Constanza and there load a consignment of 3,000 metric tons of sugar and proceed with all convenient speed to Basrah. Lay days were not to commence before 27 October and if the ship was not ready to load by 10 November, the charterers had the option of cancelling the charter party. The charterers also had the option of discharging the cargo at Jeddah. The vessel did load as expected and began the voyage to Basrah, a voyage of approximately 20 days. The vessel deviated from the voyage by calling at Berbera for three days, where she loaded livestock and fodder for Bahrain. The vessel again deviated from the voyage when she called at Bahrain to discharge the livestock and fodder. She stayed there for three days. A third deviation was made, to call at Abadan, for one day. These deviations were made without the knowledge or consent of the charterers. The voyage was prolonged by nine days in all as a result. At all times, the charterers intended to sell the sugar for cash, promptly on arrival. They did so. The shipowners admitted that they were in breach of the charter party and the charterers contended that if the sugar had arrived even five days earlier, it would have commanded a higher price. It was found as a fact that there was, at all material times, a market for sugar in Basrah and the prices fluctuated considerably. The existence of the market was known to the shipowners at all material times, but they did not have any detailed knowledge of it. It was generally known that sugar was a perishable commodity and that there was some urgency in carrying it. However, the fall in the price had been caused by the arrival of a large consignment at Basrah four days earlier. This was nothing unusual or unpredictable. The umpire appointed by the arbitrator held that the charterers were entitled to recover as damages the difference between the price of the sugar when it should have been delivered, and the price when it was in fact delivered. The shipowners appealed and McNair J held that the charterers were only entitled to recover as damages interest on the value of the cargo during the period of delay, plus expenses. The charterers appealed and the Court of Appeal restored the umpire's award. The shipowners then appealed.

Held

Loss of profit was recoverable as damages.

Lord Reid:

'... the question for decision is whether a plaintiff can recover as damages for breach of contract, a loss of a kind which the defendant, when he made the contract, ought to have realised was not unlikely to result from a breach of contract causing delay in delivery. I use the words "not unlikely" as denoting a degree of probability considerably less than an even chance, but nevertheless not very unusual and easily foreseeable.

For over a century, everyone has agreed that remoteness of damage in contract must be determined by applying the rule (or rules) ... in *Hadley* v *Baxendale* ... I am satisfied that the court did not intend that every type of damage which was reasonably foreseeable by the parties when the contract was made, should either be considered as arising naturally, ie in the usual course of things, or be supposed to have been in the contemplation of the parties ... the parties are not supposed to contemplate as grounds for the recovery of damage, any type of loss or damage which, on the knowledge available to the defendant, would appear to him as only likely to occur in a small minority of cases ...

... The crucial question is whether, on the information available to the defendant when the contract is made, he should, or a reasonable man in his position would, have realised that such loss was sufficiently likely to result from the breach of contract to make it proper to hold that the loss flowed naturally from the breach, or that loss of that kind should have been within his contemplation.

The modern rule of tort ... imposes a much wider liability ... And there is good reason for the difference. In contract, if one party wishes to protect himself against a risk which, to the other party, would appear unusual, he can direct the other party's attention to it before the contract is made ... but in tort there is no opportunity for the injured party to protect himself in that way.

For a considerable time there was a tendency to set narrow limits to awards of damages. But later, a more liberal tendency can be seen ... I attach importance to what was said in this regard in *R & H Hall Ltd v W H Pim (Junior) & Co Ltd* (1928) 33 Com Cas 324 HL ...

I think that *Hall*'s case must be taken to have established that damages are not to be regarded as too remote merely because, on the knowledge available to the defendant when the contract was made, the chance of the occurrence of the event which caused the damage would have appeared to him to be rather less than an even chance. I would agree with Lord Shaw that it is generally sufficient that that event would have appeared to the defendant as not unlikely to occur. It is hardly ever possible in this matter to assess probabilities with any degree of mathematical accuracy.

But then it has been said that the liability of defendants has been further extended by *Victoria Laundry (Windsor) Ltd* v *Newman Industries Ltd* [1949] 2 KB 528. I do not think so ...

... what is said to create a "landmark" is the statement of principles by Asquith LJ. This does, to some extent, go beyond the older authorities and in so far as it does so, I do not agree with it. In paragraph (2) it is said, page 539, that the plaintiff is entitled to recover "such part of the loss actually resulting as was, at the time of the contract, reasonably foreseeable as liable to result from the breach". To bring in reasonable foreseeability appears to me to be confusing measure of damages in contract with measure of damages in tort. A great many extremely unlikely results are reasonably foreseeable: it is true that Lord Asquith may have meant foreseeable as a likely result and if that is all he meant, I would not object further than to say that I think that the phrase is liable to be misunderstood. For the same reason, I would take exception to the phrase, page 540, "liable to result" in paragraph (5). Liable is a very vague word, but I think that one would usually say that when a person foresees a very improbable result, he foresees that it is liable to happen, page 390. I agree with the first half of paragraph (6) page 540. For the best part of a century, it has not been required that the defendant could have foreseen that a breach of contract must necessarily result in the loss which has occurred. But I cannot agree with the second half of that paragraph. It has never been held to be sufficient in contract that the loss was foreseeable as "a serious possibility" or "a real danger" or as being "on the cards". It appears to me that in the ordinary use of language, there is a wide gulf between saying that some event is not unlikely or quite likely to happen, and saying merely that it is a serious possibility, a real danger, or on the cards. If the tests of "real danger" or "serious possibility" are in future to be authoritative, then the *Victoria Laundry* case would indeed be a landmark, because it would mean that *Hadley* v *Baxendale* would be differently decided today. I certainly could not understand any court deciding that, on the information available to the carrier in that case, the stoppage of the mill was neither a serious possibility nor a real danger. If those tests are to prevail in the future, then let us cease to pay lip service to the rule in *Hadley* v *Baxendale*. But in my judgment, to adopt these tests would extend liability for breach of contract beyond what is reasonable or desirable. From the limited knowledge which I have of commercial affairs, I would not expect such an extension to be welcomed by the business community and from the legal point of view, I can find little or nothing to recommend it.

It appears to me that without relying in any way on the *Victoria Laundry* case, and taking the principle that had already been established, the loss of profit claimed in this case was not too remote to be recoverable as damages.

For the reasons which I have given, I would dismiss this appeal.'

Lord Morris of Borth-y-Gest:

'... My Lords, in applying the guidance given in *Hadley* v *Baxendale* I would hope that no undue emphasis would be placed upon any one word or phrase. If a party has suffered some special and peculiar loss in reference to some particular arrangements of his which were unknown to the other party and were not communicated to the other party and were not therefore in the contemplation of the parties at the time when they made the contract, then it would be unfair and unreasonable to charge the contract breaker with such special and peculiar loss. If, however, there are not "special and extraordinary circumstances beyond the reasonable prevision of the parties", then it becomes very largely a question of fact as to whether, in any particular case, a loss can "fairly and reasonably" be considered as arising in the normal course of things. The result in any particular case need not depend upon giving pride of place to any one of such phrases as "liable to result" or "likely to result" or "not unlikely to result". Each one of these phrases may be of help, but so may many others.

I regard the illuminating judgment of the Court of Appeal in *Victoria Laundry (Windsor) Ltd* v *Newman Industries Ltd* as a most valuable analysis of the rule. It was there pointed out that in order to make a contract breaker liable under what was called "either rule" in *Hadley* v *Baxendale*, it is not necessary that he should actually have asked himself what loss is liable to result from a breach, but that it suffices that if he had considered the question he would, as a reasonable man, have concluded that the loss in question was liable to result. Nor need it be proved, in order to recover a particular loss, that upon a given state of knowledge he could, as a reasonable man, foresee that a breach must necessarily result in that loss. Certain illustrative phrases are employed in that case. They are valuable by way of exposition but, for my part, I doubt whether the phrase "on the cards" has a sufficiently clear meaning, or possesses such a comparable shade of meanings, as to qualify it to take its place with the various other phrases which line up as expositions of the rule.

If the problem in the present case is that of relating accepted principle to the facts which have been found, I entertain no doubt that if, at the time of their contract, the parties had considered what the consequence would be if the arrival of the ship at Basrah was delayed, they would have contemplated that some loss to the respondents was likely or was liable to result. The appellant, at the time he made his contract, must have known that if, in breach of contract, his ship did not arrive at Basrah when it ought to arrive, he would be liable to pay damages. He would not know that a loss to the respondents was certain or inevitable, but he must, as a reasonable businessman, have contemplated that the respondents would very likely suffer loss and that it would be, or would be likely to be, a loss referable to market price fluctuations at Basrah. I cannot think that he should escape liability by saying that he would only be aware of a possibility of loss but not of a probability or certainty of it. He might have used any one of many phrases. He might have said that a loss would be likely: or that a loss would not be unlikely: or that a loss was liable to result: or that the risk that delay would cause loss to the respondents was a serious possibility: or that there would be a real danger of a loss: or that the risk of his being liable to have to pay for the loss was one that he ought commercially to take into account. As a practical businessman, he would not have paused to reflect on the possible nuances of meaning of any one of these phrases. Nor would he have sent for a dictionary.

Since, in awarding the damages, the aim is to award a sum which as nearly as possible will put the injured party in the position in which he would have been if the breach of contract had not caused him loss and if, in all the circumstances, he had acted reasonably in an effort to mitigate his loss, I think that it must follow that where this delay is in arrival, in many cases the actual loss suffered (above the amount of which there ought to be recovery) can be measured by comparing the market price of the goods at the date when they should have arrived and the market price when they did arrive. That prima facie is the measure of the damages ... I would dismiss the appeal.'

Lord Hodson:

'... The word "probable" in *Hadley* v *Baxendale* covers both parts of the rule and it is of vital importance in applying the rule to consider what the court meant by using this word in its context. The common use of this word is no doubt to imply that something is more likely to happen than not. In conversation, if one says to another, "If you go out in this weather you will probably catch a cold", this is, I think equivalent to saying that one believes there is an odds-on chance that the other will catch a cold.

The word "probable" need not, however, bear this narrow meaning ...

A close study of the rule was made by the Court of Appeal in the case of *Victoria Laundry (Windsor) Ltd* v *Newman Industries Ltd*. The judgment of the court, consisting of Tucker, Asquith and Singleton LJJ, was delivered by Asquith LJ, who suggested the phrase "liable to result" as appropriate to describe the degree of probability required. This may be a colourless expression, but I do not find it possible to improve on it. If the word "likelihood" is used, it may convey the impression that the chances are all in favour of the thing happening, an idea which I would reject.

... I would dismiss the appeal.'

Lord Pearce

'The whole rule in *Hadley* v *Baxendale* limits damages to that which may be regarded as being within the contemplation of the parties ...

I do not think that Alderson B was directing his mind to whether something resulting in the natural course of events was an odds-on chance or not. A thing may be a natural (or even an obvious) result, even though the odds are against it. Suppose a contractor was employed to repair the ceiling of one of the Law Courts and did it so negligently that it collapsed on the heads of those in court. I should be inclined to think that any tribunal (including the learned Baron himself) would have found as a fact that the damage arose "naturally, ie according to the usual course of things". Yet if one takes into account the nights, weekends and vacations, when the ceiling might have collapsed, the odds against it collapsing on top of anybody's head are nearly ten to one. I do not believe that this aspect of the matter was fully considered and worked out in the judgment. He was thinking of causation and type of consequence rather than of odds ...

... The facts of the present case lead to the view that the loss of market arose naturally, ie according to the usual course of things, from the shipowner's deviation. The sugar was being exported to Basrah where, as the respondent knew, there was a sugar market. It was sold on arrival and fetched a lower price than it would have done had it arrived on time. The fall in market price was not due to any unusual or unpredictable factor.

Had this been a case of non-delivery on sale of goods, whether by sea or land, it is uncontested that the defendants would be liable for the loss of market. Had it been a case of delay in sale of goods, the prima facie rule is that the damage is the difference between "the value of the article contracted for at the time when it ought to have been and the time when it actually was delivered" ... I would dismiss the appeal.'

Lord Upjohn:

'... The rule in *Hadley* v *Baxendale* has been followed in a multitude of cases ever since it was decided. I think that apart from some very early criticisms, it would be true to say that it stood without question until the case of *Victoria Laundry (Windsor) Ltd* v *Newman Industries Ltd*, where it received a colourful interpretation from Asquith LJ delivering the judgment of the court.

'My Lords, in my opinion this appeal renders it necessary to determine the following questions:

1. Has the *Victoria Laundry* case purported to alter the law and establish a somewhat different rule from that laid down in *Hadley* v *Baxendale* for the assessment of damages in contract?
2. What, as a practical matter, is the test to be applied in ascertaining whether any particular consequence of a breach of contract should lead to recoverable damages as arising either naturally or such as may have been within the contemplation of the parties in the special circumstances of the case? ...

Upon the first point, it is, I think, clear that on a fair reading of the judgments of the majority of the Court of Appeal, they considered that the *Victoria Laundry* case did alter the law. That case was plainly within the second branch of the rule, but nevertheless, the observations of Asquith LJ were, in general terms, applicable to both branches. I do not myself think that the learned Lord Justice intended to alter the law. He was para-phrasing it and putting it into modern language and I shall refer to this under the next heading. If he was doing more, I would disagree with him. But for my part, I prefer to state the broad rule as follows: What was in the assumed contemplation of both parties, acting as reasonable men, in the light of the general or special facts (as the case may be) known to both parties in regard to damages as the result of a breach of contract; I omit, for the moment, any adjectival qualification of the result, which I deal with in (2) below.

Upon the second point, what, as a practical matter, is to be taken as within the contemplation of both parties as the result of a breach? The words 'probable result' held the field at first; they were used in the enunciation of the rule itself and adopted by Viscount Dunedin in *Hall* v *Pim* who, however, was careful to add that "probable", in his view, did not mean more than an even chance. Lord Shaw of Dunfermline in that case, interpreted the word probable in the sense of the not unlikely result.

Asquith LJ, in *Victoria Laundry*, used the words "likely to result" and he treated that as synonymous with a serious possibility or a real danger. He went on to equate that with the expression "on the cards" but, like all your Lordships, I deprecate the use of that phrase which is far too imprecise and, to my mind, is capable of denoting a most improbable and unlikely event, such as winning a prize on a premium bond on any given drawing.

But in my opinion, Asquith LJ was not attempting to do more than explain the rule ...

It is clear that on the one hand the test of foreseeability, as laid down in the case of tort, is not the test for breach of contract; nor, on the other hand, must the loser establish that the loss was a near certainty or an odds-on probability. I am content to adopt as the test a "real danger" or a "serious possibility". There may be a shade of difference between these two phrases, but the assessment of damages is not an exact science and what to one judge or jury will appear a real danger, will appear to another judge or jury to be a serious possibility. I do not think that the application of that test would have led to a different result in *Hadley* v *Baxendale*. I cannot see why Pickfords, in the absence of express mention, should have contemplated as a real danger or serious possibility that work at the factory would be brought to a halt while the shaft was away.'

Commentary
See also *Parsons (H) (Livestock) Ltd* v *Uttley Ingham & Co Ltd* [1977] 3 WLR 990.

Lavarack v *Woods of Colchester Ltd* [1966] 3 WLR 706 Court of Appeal (Lord Denning MR, Diplock and Russell LJJ)

Breach of contract – measure of damages

Facts
The plaintiff entered into a five-year service agreement with the defendants at £4,000 per annum plus such bonuses as the defendants' directors may at their discretion award. He undertook that he would not, during that time, be engaged or interested in other concerns. After two years or so he was wrongfully dismissed:

immediately afterwards, he accepted employment with M Co at £1,500 per annum and he bought half the shares of that company, hoping that his own work would improve their value. In addition he invested £14,000 in V Co, a rival of the defendants. The following year the defendants discontinued their bonus scheme and, under the new arrangements, the plaintiff would have received an extra £1,000 per annum.

Held (Lord Denning MR dissenting)
The plaintiff was not entitled to £2,000 (2 x £1,000 in lieu of bonuses) and any improvement in the value of the shares in V Co would be disregarded in assessing his damages. However, the estimated increase in the plaintiff's half interest in M Co would be set against the damages awarded as this was part of his mitigation of his loss.

Diplock LJ:

> 'The general rule ... that in an action for breach of contract a defendant is not liable for not doing that which he is not bound to do, has been generally accepted as correct and in my experience at the Bar and on the Bench has been repeatedly applied in subsequent cases. The law is concerned with legal obligations only and the law of contract only with legal obligations created by mutual agreement between contractors – not with the expectations, however reasonable, of one contractor that the other will do something that he has assumed no legal obligation to do ...
>
> In the present case if the defendants had continued their bonus scheme, it may well be that on the true construction of this contract of employment the plaintiff would have been entitled to be recompensed for the loss of the bonus to which he would have been likely to be legally entitled under his service agreement until its expiry. But it is unnecessary to decide this. They were under no contractual obligation to him to continue the scheme and in fact it was discontinued. His legal entitlement under the contract on which he sues would thus have been limited ... to his salary of £4,000 per annum. And there, in my view, is the end of the matter. I know of no principle on which he can claim as damages for breach of one service agreement compensation for remuneration which might have become due under some imaginary future agreement which the plaintiffs did not make with him but might have done if they wished. If this were right, in every action for damages for wrongful dismissal, the plaintiff would be entitled to recover not only the remuneration that he would have received during the currency of his service agreement but also some additional sum for loss of the chance of its being renewed on its expiry.
>
> I would disallow the sum of £2,000 included in the assessment ...'

Lombard North Central plc v *Butterworth* [1987] 2 WLR 7 Court of Appeal (Lawton, Mustill and Nicholls LJJ)

Contract – repudiation – penalty?

Facts
The plaintiffs leased a computer to the defendants for a period of five years. The agreement involved payment of a deposit and 19 subsequent instalments. The contract of lease contained three clauses which are relevant to determination of the dispute:

Clause 2 provided that punctual payment of the instalments was 'of the essence' of the contract; Clause 5 rendered failure to make punctual payments a ground for terminating the contract; and Clause 6 entitled the plaintiffs on termination to all arrears of instalments plus all future instalments.

The defendant defaulted on the sixth instalment. The plaintiffs obtained summary judgment, the master concluding that the defendant had repudiated the contract enabling the plaintiffs to claim future instalments.

The defendant appealed contending that he should not be liable for more than the amount due at the date of termination because:

1. clause 6 was a penalty clause and therefore unenforceable, and
2. the defendant's conduct did not amount to a repudiation of the contract.

Held

Clause 6 was a penalty clause. However clause 2 had the effect of making default in punctual payment a breach going to the root of the contract entitling the plaintiffs to terminate independently of clause 6 and to recover common law damages.

Nicholls LJ:

> '... the criticism of clause 6 advanced on behalf of the defendant was confined to the absence of provision giving credit for the net amount obtained by the plaintiff on any resale of the goods effected by it after retaking possession. Argument in this court took place on the footing that the presence or absence of such a provision, which I shall call a "rescue price allowance" was crucial on the penalty point, counsel for the defendant putting forward that the omission of such allowance was a fundamental objection to the clause ...'

He then went on to consider whether the addition of a 'resale price allowance' would render the clause no longer a penalty.

> '... In my view, in the absence of a repudiatory breach that assumption is misconceived. The ratio of the decision of this court in *Financings Ltd* v *Baldock* [1963] 1 All ER 443 was that when an owner determines a hire-purchase agreement in exercise of a right so to do given him by the agreement, in the absence of repudiation he can recover damages for any breaches up to the date of termination but not thereafter, and a "minimum payment" clause which purports to oblige the hirer to pay larger sums than this is unenforceable as a penalty ... In my view, applying the principle enunciated in *Financings Ltd* v *Baldock* to this case leads inescapably to the conclusion that in the absence of a repudiatory breach clause 6(a) is a penalty insofar as it purports to oblige the defendant, regardless of the seriousness or triviality of the breach which led to the plaintiffs terminating the agreement by retaking possession of the computer. ... From what I have said it will be apparent that I consider that, in the absence of a repudiatory breach, the outcome of this case is not dependent on the inclusion or exclusion of a resale price allowance, and indeed the legal result would have been the same if clause 6 had contained a "resale price allowance" ... I turn to the second issue, which is whether the loss sustained by the plaintiff in this case by reason of the defendant's default in payment of the instalments amounted to the loss of the whole hiring transaction. It would have so amounted if, but only if, the defendant's conduct amounted to a repudiation of the lease agreement and that repudiation was accepted by the plaintiffs ...'

The judge continued by analysing whether in the absence of clause 2, the defendant's conduct amounted to a repudiation and concluded that it did not.

> 'I must now consider that time of payments having been made of the essence by clause 2 it was open to the plaintiffs, once default in payment had occurred, to treat the agreement as repudiated by the defendant, and claim damages for loss of the whole transaction, even though in the absence of this provision such a default would not have had that consequence. ... The provision in clause 2 has to be read and construed in conjunction with the other provisions including clauses 5 and 6. So read, it is to be noted that failure to pay any instalment triggers a right for the plaintiff to terminate the agreement with the expressed consequence that the defendant becomes liable to make payments which assume that the defendant is unable to make good to the plaintiffs the loss by them of the whole transaction. Given that context, the "time of the essence" provision seems to me to be intended to bring about the result that default in punctual payments is to be regarded as a breach going to the root of the contract and, hence, as giving rise to consequences in damages attendant on such a breach.'

Monarch Steamship Co Ltd v *A/B Karlshamns Oljefabriker* [1949] AC 196 House of Lords (Lord Porter, Lord Wright, Lord Uthwatt, Lord du Parcq and Lord Morton of Henryton)

Damages – cost of transshipment following delay

Facts

In April 1939 M chartered S's steamship which sailed to Rashin to load a cargo of soya beans purchased from M by K. The ship left Rashin on 12 May. Contrary to the terms of the charterparty, the ship was unseaworthy: considerable delay resulted from deviations for repairs. On 7 June, in conformity with the charterparty and bills of lading, M nominated Karlshamn as the port of discharge, but S was not told until mid-August that delivery was to be made there. At the outbreak of war (3 September), the voyage (which should have taken 63 days) was still not completed and the ship was ordered by the Admiralty to proceed to Glasgow which she reached on 21 October. There, M took delivery of the cargo and transferred the bills of lading to K who had chartered three neutral ships to carry the cargo to Karlshamn. K sued S for damages for breach of contract in respect of the cost of transshipment.

Held

K was entitled to succeed as the damage was the direct and natural consequence of S's breach of contract in failing to provide a seaworthy ship.

Lord Porter:

'But, it is said, to give such damages ... is to give damages for delay in delivery – a remedy which is not given in the case of carriage of goods by sea. No doubt, expressions of opinion to that effect are to be found, perhaps more frequently in the days of sailing ships when prolonged delay was to be expected, but it never was a rule of law – merely a working practice answering to the circumstances of the time and subject to the consideration that the contract must be reasonably performed. In the present case the result of the delay was to deprive the shipper and his indorsee of the goods at Karlshamn. Of course, if they could replace them by buying other goods there, it was their duty to diminish the damages by doing so, but they could not do so since no soya beans were procurable at Karlshamn and, in default, the only way of placing themselves in the same position as if the contract had been performed was to engage transport to carry the beans to that port. Accepting, then, the view that [S] ought to have foreseen the likelihood of was occuring and of an embargo being imposed, I should find it liable to pay the damages claimed and would dismiss the appeal.'

Lord Wright:

' ... in *Smith, Hogg & Co*'s case the unseaworthiness created in the vessel instability which, combined with negligence of the master, caused the loss. There was no new law laid down in that case. From one point of view unseaworthiness must generally, perhaps always in a sense, be a "remote" cause. To satisfy the definition of unseaworthiness it must exist at the commencement of the voyage. It must, however, still be in effective operation at the time of the casualty if it is to be a cause of the casualty, and from its very nature it must always, or almost always, operate by means of and along with the specific immediate peril. That is because the essence of unseaworthiness as a cause of loss or damage is that the unseaworthy ship is unfit to meet the peril.

In other words, the vessel would not have suffered the loss or injury if she had been seaworthy.'

Naughton v *O'Callaghan* [1990] 3 All ER 191 High Court (Waller J)

Misrepresentation – assessment of damages

Facts
The plaintiffs bought Fondu, a thoroughbred colt, for 26,000 guineas at the 1981 Newmarket sales. On the track, it was unsuccessful, so its value dropped to £1,500. In 1983 the plaintiffs discovered that the colt's pedigree had been incorrectly described in the sales catalogue and a year later they claimed damages for breach of contract and misrepresentation. At the hearing to assess damages there was evidence that, if the colt had been correctly described, it would have sold for about 23,500 guineas at the sales.

Held
The plaintiffs were entitled to the difference between 26,000 guineas and £1,500 (£25,800) and training fees and other expenditure on the horse's keep until it could have been disposed of following discovery of the misrepresentation (£9,820).

Waller J:

> 'What, as it seems to me, makes this case different from the norm is, first, that what the plaintiffs in fact purchased in reliance on the representation in the catalogue was a different animal altogether; second, if they had known of the misrepresentation within a day or so they could, and as I have found would, have sold Fondu for its then value; third, their decision to keep Fondu and race it was precisely what the sellers would have expected; Fondu was not a commodity like, for example, rupee paper, which it would be expected that the defendants would go out and sell; fourth, the fall in Fondu's value if it did not win races was not due to a general fall in the market in racehorses, but was special to Fondu and to be expected if Fondu did not win. It might well not have happened if Fondu had been the different animal as it had been originally described.
>
> Accordingly, in my judgment it would be unjust if the plaintiffs were not entitled to recover the difference between 26,000 guineas and £1,500 ...
>
> It seems to me that there can be no question of the plaintiffs being entitled to recover anything for the training and upkeep of Fondu past the date on which they discovered the true pedigree of Fondu, other than a reasonable figure for the horse's keep until it could have been disposed of. If any sum is recoverable I assess it as £9,820 ...
>
> Is the £9,820 recoverable at all? It seems to me that in relation to this particular horse, applying Winn LJ's test in *Doyle v Olby (Ironmongers) Ltd* [1969] 2 QB 158 at 168, the cost of training and keeping Fondu should be recoverable. But is it right to apply blinkers and consider the purchase of this particular animal and the expenditure on him? The defendant says that expenditure would have been incurred anyway on some yearling purchased at those September sales. To which the plaintiffs retort that that may be so, but if they bought the horse described by the defendant it might have paid for its keep and reaped for them rich rewards.
>
> I have concluded that the plaintiffs are entitled to ask the court to look simply at the contract they made in reliance on the representation which induced them to enter into that bargain. They are entitled to say that there must be no speculation one way or the other about what would have happened if they had not purchased this horse and if no misrepresentation had been made to them. They are entitled to say (putting it in broad terms) we bought one horse and we spent money training it and entering it for races. We discovered two years after the purchase that it was not the horse we thought we had bought; it is not the horse on which we would have spent any money training or keeping, and therefore that is money only spent in reliance on the representation made. The figure I award under this head is thus £9,820.'

Commentary
Doyle v Olby (Ironmongers) Ltd [1969] 2 QB 158: see Chapter 20.

O'Laoire v *Jackel International Ltd* (1991) The Times 12 February Court of Appeal (Sir Nicolas Browne-Wilkinson VC, Stuart-Smith and Leggatt LJJ)

Wrongful dismissal – damages

Facts
The defendants had summarily dismissed the plaintiff and an industrial tribunal had awarded him the statutory maximum (£8,000) by way of compensation for unfair dismissal. In an action for wrongful dismissal, the plaintiff claimed, inter alia, damages for the distress, inconvenience and injury to his feelings and the question also arose as to whether the £8,000 should be deducted from any damages recoverable at common law.

Held
The plaintiff would fail on the first point but succeed on the second. On the question of damages for loss of reputation and injury to feelings, Sir Nicolas Browne-Wilkinson VC had no doubt that the decision of the House of Lords in *Addis* v *Gramophone Co Ltd* [1909] AC 488 excluded those factors from being taken into account. The only exception to that rule arose in the case of contracts of apprenticeship. The plaintiff had said that the circumstances of employment and attitudes had changed since the decision in *Addis*. That was true, but unless and until the House of Lords reconsidered that decision it was binding on the court.

The question of the deduction or otherwise of the £8,000 was a new point which fell to be decided in accordance with principle. In his Lordship's judgment the starting point was to identify the principle upon which the defendants sought to rely. Counsel for the defendants had accepted that the only principle on which he could rely was the rule against double recovery for the same loss. If that rule was to be invoked, the first requirement was to show that the plaintiff would be obtaining compensation under two heads for the same loss. But the defendants were unable to satisfy that requirement. The industrial tribunal had not, and could not, allocate the £8,000 maximum award to any one of the particular elements which together made up the total loss of £100,700 which they had found the plaintiff to have suffered. Therefore, in his Lordship's judgment, since the defendant could not prove a double recovery, there was no basis for setting off the maximum award against the common law damages.

Commentary
Addis v *Gramaphone Co Ltd* [1909] AC 488: see Introduction, above. See also *Bliss* v *South East Thames Regional Health Authority* [1987] ICR 700, above.

Parsons (H) (Livestock) Ltd v *Uttley, Ingham & Co Ltd* [1977] 3 WLR 990 Court of Appeal (Lord Denning MR, Orr and Scarman LJJ)

Breach of contract – damages recoverable

Facts
The plaintiff pig farmers bought from the defendant manufacturers a second bulk food storage hopper 'fitted with ventilated top'. In transporting the hopper to the farm the defendants sealed down the ventilator to stop it rattling. They forgot to unseal it (which the plaintiffs could not have detected as it was 28 feet above the ground); the pig nuts became mouldy, the pigs became ill from a rare type of infection and 254 of them died. The plaintiffs sued for damages.

Held
They were entitled to succeed and to recover by way of damages the losses sustained from the death and sickness of the pigs.

Scarman LJ:

'Two problems are left unsolved by the *Heron II, Koufos* v *C Czarnikow Ltd*: (1) the law's reconciliation of the remoteness principle in contract with that in tort where as, for instance in some product liability cases, there arises the danger of differing awards, the lesser award going to the party who has a contract, even though the contract is silent as to the measure of damages and all parties are, or must be deemed to be, burdened with the same knowledge (or enjoying the same state of ignorance); (2) what is meant by "serious possibility" (or its synonyms): is it a reference to the type of consequence which the parties might be supposed to contemplate as possible though unlikely, or must the chance of it happening appear to be likely? ...

As to the first problem, I agree with Lord Denning MR in thinking that the law must be such that, in a factual situation where all have the same actual or imputed knowledge and the contract contains no terms limiting the damages recoverable for breach, the amount of damages recoverable does not depend on whether, as a matter of legal classification, the plaintiff's cause of action is breach of contract or tort. It may be that the necessary reconciliation is to be found, notwithstanding the strictures of Lord Reid, in holding that the difference between "reasonably foreseeable" (the test in tort) and "reasonably contemplated" (the test in contract) is semantic, not substantial. Certainly Asquith LJ in *Victoria Laundry (Windsor) Ltd* v *Newman Industries Ltd* and Lord Pearce in the *Heron II, Koufos* v *C Czarnikow Ltd* thought so; and I confess I think so too. The second problem, what is meant by a "serious possibility" is, in my judgment, ultimately a question of fact. I shall return to it, therefore, after analysing the facts since I believe it requires of the judge no more, and no less, than the application of common sense in the particular circumstances of the case ...

The court's task, therefore, is to decide what loss to the plaintiffs it is reasonable to suppose would have been in the contemplation of the parties as a serious possibility had they had in mind the breach when they made their contract ...

I would agree with Mr McGregor in his work on Damages that –

"in contract as in tort, it should suffice that, if physical injury or damage is within the contemplation of the parties, recovery is not to be limited because the degree of physical injury or damage could not have been anticipated."

This is so, in my judgment, not because there is, or ought to be, a specific rule of law governing cases of physical injury but because it would be absurd to regulate damages in such cases on the necessity of supposing the parties had a prophetic foresight as to the exact nature of the injury that does in fact arise. It is enough if on the hypothesis predicated physical injury must have been a serious possibility. Though in loss of market or loss of profit cases the factual analysis will be very different from cases of physical injury, the same principles, in my judgement, apply. Given the situation of the parties at the time of contract, was the loss of profit, or market, a serious possibility, something that would have been in their minds had they contemplated breach?

It does not matter, in my judgment, if they thought that the chance of physical injury, loss of profit, loss of market, or other loss as the case may be, was slight or that the odds were against it provided they contemplated as a serious possibility the type of consequence, not necessarily the specific consequence, that ensued on breach ... no more than common sense was needed for them to appreciate that food affected by bad storage conditions might well cause illness in the pigs fed on it.

As I read the judgment under appeal, this was how the judge, whose handling of the issues at trial was such that none save one survives for our consideration, reached this decision. In my judgment, he was right, on the facts as found, to apply the first rule in *Hadley* v *Baxendale*, or, if the case be one of breach of warranty, as I think it is, the rule in s53(2) of the Sale of Goods Act 1893 without enquiring whether, on a juridical analysis, the rule is base on a presumed contemplation. At the end of a long and complex dispute the judge allowed common sense to prevail. I would dismiss the appeal.'

Commentary
Applied: *Hadley* v *Baxendale* (1854) 9 Exch 341 and *Koufos* v *C Czarnikow Ltd* [1967] 3 WLR 1491.

Payzu Ltd v *Saunders* [1919] 2 KB 581 Court of Appeal (Bankes and Scrutton LJJ and Eve J)

Breach of contract – duty to mitigate loss

Facts
The defendant, having agreed to sell the plaintiffs 200 pieces of silk, delivered the final consignment for which the plaintiffs failed to pay punctually. In view of this, the defendant said that she would only deliver further supplies if the plaintiffs paid on delivery. This the plaintiffs would not accept, so they sued for breach of contract, claiming the differences between the contract price and the current market price.

Held
Although the defendant was liable, the plaintiffs' failure to pay promptly for the first consignment not amounting to a repudiation of the contract, the plaintiffs should have mitigated their loss by accepting her cash-on-delivery terms and they were entitled to recover only the amount which they would have lost had they done so.

Scrutton LJ:

> 'Whether it be more correct to say that a plaintiff must minimise his damages, or to say that he can recover no more than he would have suffered if he had acted reasonably, because any further damages do not reasonably follow from the defendant's breach, the result is the same. The plaintiff must take "all reasonable steps to mitigate the loss consequent on the breach" and this simple principle "debars him from claiming any part of the damage which is due to his neglect to take such steps": *British Westinghouse Electric and Manufacturing Co* v *Underground Electric Railways Co of London Ltd* ... per Lord Haldane LC. Counsel for the plaintiffs has contended that in considering what steps should be taken to mitigate the damage all contractual relations with the party in default must be excluded. That is contrary to my experience. In certain cases of personal service it may be unreasonable to expect a plaintiff to consider an offer from the other party who has grossly injured him; but in commercial contracts is is generally reasonable to accept an offer from the party in default. However, it is always a question of fact. About the law there is no difficulty.'

Philips Hong Kong Ltd v *Attorney-General of Hong Kong* (1993) The Times 15 February Privy Council (Lord Templeman, Lord Goff, Lord Browne-Wilkinson and Lord Woolf)

Liquidated damages – penalty clause

Facts
A contract for a highway construction project contained a number of provisions as to liquidated damages. The company appealed on the basis that the rigid application of these provisions could result in the company having to pay more than the cost of the loss sustained and that the provisions were in consequence penal and void.

Held
Unless the parties were on very unequal terms, the desirability of achieving certainty in a commercial contract was paramount. Having regard to the range of losses, the terms that the parties had agreed were perfectly valid liquidated damages clauses. The company's contention that they were penal was dismissed.

Pilkington v *Wood* [1953] Ch 770 High Court (Harman J)

Acquisition of unmarketable title – measure of damages

Facts
The plaintiff had employed the defendant as his solicitor in purchasing a freehold property in Hampshire in 1950. The vendor, Colonel Wilks, purported to convey the property as beneficial owner, but when, in 1951, the plaintiff attempted to sell the property, since he had changed his job from Surrey to Lancashire, it was discovered that Colonel Wilks was a trustee of the property who had himself purchased the property in breach of trust. The defendant solicitor admitted negligence and the only question before the court was the measure of damages. The plaintiff claimed his loss in acquiring an unmarketable title, or alternatively, a property which he could only sell at a substantial loss; special damages in respect of expenses incurred because he was unable to sell the property and buy another in Lancashire (except at a loss), viz hotel expenses in Lancashire, expenses of running a car between Lancashire and Hampshire and nightly telephone calls to his wife; and interest on his overdraft incurred as a result of being unable to sell the property.

Held
Damages connected with the change of employment could not be recovered.

Harman J:

> 'It would appear then, at first sight, that the measure of the defendant's liability is the diminution in the value of the property; that is to say, the difference between the value in 1950, the date of the plaintiff's purchase of the property with a good title, and with the title which it in fact had.
>
> The defendant, however, argues that it is the duty of the plaintiff, before suing him in damages, to seek to recover damages against his vendor, Colonel Wilks, under the covenant for title implied by reason of the conveyance as beneficial owner. It is said that this duty arises because of the obligation which rests on a person injured by a breach of contract to mitigate the damages. The suggestion seems to me to carry the doctrine of mitigation a stage further than it has been carried in any case to which I have been referred ...
>
> Ought then the plaintiff, as a reasonable man, to enter on the litigation suggested? It was agreed that the defendant must offer him a indemnity against the cost and it was suggested on the defendant's behalf that if an adequate indemnity were offered, if, secondly, the proposed defendant appeared to be solvent and if, thirdly, there was a good prima facie right of action against that person, it was the duty of the injured party to embark on litigation in order to mitigate the damage suffered. This is a proposition which, in such general terms, I am not prepared to accept, nor do I think I ought to entertain it here, because I am by no means certain that foundations for it exist ...
>
> I do not propose to attempt to decide whether an action against Colonel Wilks would lie or be fruitful. I can see it would be one attended with no little difficulty. I am of the opinion that the so called duty to mitigate does go so far as to oblige the injured party, even under an indemnity, to embark on a complicated and difficult piece of litigation against a third party. The damage to the plaintiff was done once and for all, directly the voidable conveyance to him was executed. This was the direct result of the negligent advice tendered by his solicitor, the defendant, that a good title had been shown; and in my judgment, it is no part of the plaintiff's duty to embark on the proposed litigation in order to protect his solicitor from the consequences of his own carelessness.

Next, the defendant suggested that the injury might be lightened by a policy of insurance designed to cover the consequences of the defect. As to this, it is enough to say that no satisfactory evidence was adduced that any such policy could be obtained. Policies to cover defects of title are, it appears, common enough when supported by crooked covenants on the part of the author of the defect, here, Colonel Wilks.

It is clear that he would have been entirely unwilling to enter into such a covenant and in the absence of that, there was no evidence that a policy could be obtained nor what its cost would be. In any event, though a policy might mitigate the pecuniary damage, it would not mend the title or make the purchase more attractive to a person buying the property for a home, as this property would be bought.

It remains to consider what is the proper amount of damage. This is necessarily highly speculative. The plaintiff was not bound, in my judgment, to resell in order to quantify it, particularly having regard to the fact that until quite recently, the defendant denied that he was guilty of negligence. It is clear enough with the plaintiff's experience with the purchaser he found, that an ordinary purchaser, finding the title defective in this respect, will merely throw up the purchase and that it would be necessary to explain in advance, by way of condition of sale, the existence of the defect. The result would be, I think, to bring forward a different class of purchaser, namely the speculator willing to chance the future, but only because the property can be had cheap. The several elements to be brought into account are, on the one side, first the sum which would have to be paid before the property was returned to the trust; next the chance that no claim will ever be made and that the title will eventually ripen into security; and thirdly the chance of recovering something against Colonel Wilks on his covenant for title ...

Balancing one factor against the other as best I can after listening to the evidence, I think a fair estimate of the diminution in value of the property from its market price at the date of the breach in 1950 of £6,000 with a good title, ought to be set at £2,000.

Beyond this, which may be styled the general damage, the plaintiff claimed damages under a number of special heads ...

In my judgment, none of these sums is recoverable against the defendant. They do not fall within the second rule in *Hadley* v *Baxendale* (1854) 9 Exch 341 as to remoteness of damage ...

These items were not, in my judgment, within the reasonable contemplation of the parties when the defendant assumed the duty of advising the plaintiff. The change of place of the plaintiff's employment was not one of the chances that could have been known to either of them. It was the voluntary act of the plaintiff, not a result of any contract existing when the bargain was made. The plaintiff chose a new job in Lancashire; he might well have selected one more remote in Kamschatka or less remote in Hampshire. The defendant cannot be responsible for the expense. The plaintiff might have bought or rented accommodation suitable to his new employment and there is no evidence that the defendant knew that his financial position might render this impracticable. Still less can the defendant be called upon to pay for the telephone calls, a luxury no doubt exemplary, yet luxurious.

The fourth head is a sum of 25 guineas paid by the plaintiff to a valuer who, in 1950, was employed by him to to value the property in order to quiet the doubt of the plaintiff's bankers as to his financial position. He complains that he would never have incurred this expense had he known that his title was defective. No doubt this is true; but the defendant cannot be supposed to know that any such step was required by the plaintiff's position or contemplated by him. This claim I reject.

The fifth claim represents the sum paid by the plaintiff to his bank on an overdraft, which he says would not have existed had he been able to sell the property as he contracted to do so as before stated. Here again it is objected that the defendant is being asked to pay for the plaintiff's impecuniosity and it is pointed out that there is no evidence that the defendant knew that the purchase money had been borrowed by the plaintiff and, moreover, that if the plaintiff had been able to sell he would have incurred a new liability similar to the old ... On the whole, I am of the opinion that the plaintiff does not make out his case on this point ...

It appears to me, however, that in order to put the plaintiff as far as possible in the position in which he would have been if there had been no breach, I must treat him as having sold the property at the date when the cause of action arose for what it would then fetch. This price I have assumed to be £4,000. He would then have been £2,000 out of pocket. The plaintiff, therefore, should recoup that sum with interest upon it. Under section 3 of the Law Reform (Miscellaneous Provisions) Act 1934, the court has jurisdiction to award interest on damages from the date when the cause of action arose and, accordingly, the sum of £2,000 will carry interest at 4 per cent per annum from April 22 1950 till the date of this judgment ...'

Public Works Commissioners v *Hills* [1906] AC 368 Privy Council (Lord Loreburn LC, Lord Davey, Lord Dunedin, Lord Atkinson and Sir Arthur Wilson)

Breach of contract – liquidated damages or penalty

Facts
Contracts for the construction of railways for the government of the Cape of Good Hope provided that retention moneys could be forfeited 'as and for liquidated damages sustained by the said government for the non-completion of the said line.' The line was not completed within the specified period.

Held
The government was not entitled to the sums forfeited.

Lord Dunedin:

'In the principal appeal, the government has complained of the judgment in so far as it gives the respondent Hills the sums of £66,146 18s 7d. and £50,000, and claims these ... as being theirs in name of liquidated damages for non-completion of the line within the specified time. Their Lordships have no doubt that the case of the non-completion of a railway would be a natural and proper case in which to make such a stipulation. But the question comes up in each particular case whether such a stipulation has been made, and it is well settled law that the mere form of expression "penalty" or "liquidated damages" does not conclude the matter. Indeed, the form of expression here "forfeited as and for liquidated damages," if literally taken, may be said to be self-contradictory, the word "forfeited" being particularly appropriate to penalty and not to liquidated damages. The House of Lords had occasion to review the law in the matter in *Clydebank Engineering and Shipbuilding Co* v *Castaneda*. It is, perhaps, worthy of remark, in view of certain observations of the learned Chief Justice in the court below, that there was a Scottish case – that is to say, decided according to the rules of a system of law where contract law is based directly on the civil law, and where no complications in the matter of pleading had ever been introduced by the separation of common law and equity. The general principle to be deduced from that judgement seems to be this, that the criterion of whether a sum – be it called penalty or damages – is truly liquidated damages, and as such not to be interfered with by the court, or is truly a penalty which covers the damage if proved, but does not assess it, is to be found in whether the sum stipulated for can or cannot be regarded as a genuine pre-estimate of the creditor's probable or possible interest in the due performance of the principal obligation. The indicia of this question will vary according to circumstances. Enormous disparity of the sum to any conceivable loss will point one way, while the fact of the payment being in terms proportionate to the loss will point the other. But the circumstances must be taken as a whole, and must be viewed as at the time the bargain was made.

Applying this principle to the present case, their Lordships are unable to come to the conclusion that the sum here can be taken as a genuine pre-estimate of loss. The determining factor is that the sum is not a definite sum, but is liable to great fluctuation in amount ... It is obvious that the amount of retained money ... available to be dealt with under ... this contract could not in anyway be estimated as a fixed sum. Their Lordships, therefore hold that the sums are not liquidated damages ...'

Commentary
Applied in *Jobson* v *Johnson* [1989] 1 WLR 1026. See also *Dunlop Pneumatic Tyre Co Ltd* v *New Garage and Motor Co Ltd* [1915] AC 79.

Royscot Trust Ltd v *Rogerson* [1991] 3 WLR 57 Court of Appeal (Balcombe and Ralph Gibson LJJ)

Innocent misrepresentation – measure of damages

Facts
In the course of a hire-purchase transaction, a dealer innocently misrepresented to a finance company the car's value. The question arose, inter alia, as to the measure of damages for innocent misrepresentation under s2(1) of the Misrepresentation Act 1976.

Held
It was the measure of damages for fraudulent misrepresentation and not that for negligence, so that unforeseeable losses were recoverable provided they were not too remote.

Balcombe LJ:

'The finance company's cause of action against the dealer is based on s2(1) of the Misrepresentation Act 1967 ... In view of the wording of the subsection it is difficult to see how the measure of damages under it could be other than the tortious measure and ... that is now generally accepted ...

The first main issue before us was: accepting that the tortious measure is the right measure, is it the measure where the tort is that of fraudulent misrepresentation, or is it the measure where the tort is negligence at common law? The difference is that in cases of fraud a plaintiff is entitled to any loss which flowed from the defendant's fraud, even if the loss could not have been foreseen: see *Doyle* v *Olby (Ironmongers) Ltd* [1969] 2 QB 158. In my judgment the wording of the subsection is clear: the person making the innocent misrepresentation shall be "so liable", ie liable to damages as if the representation had been made fraudulently. This was the conclusion to which Walton J came in *F & B Entertainments Ltd* v *Leisure Enterprises Ltd* (1976) 240 EG 455 at 461 (see also the decision of Sir Douglas Franks QC sitting as a deputy judge of the High Court in *McNally* v *Welltrade International Ltd* [1978] IRLR 497). In each of these cases the judge held that the basis for the assessment of damages under s2(1) of the 1967 Act is that established in *Doyle* v *Olby (Ironmongers) Ltd* ... In my judgment, therefore, the finance company is entitled to recover from the dealer all the losses which it suffered as a result of its entering into the agreements with the dealer and the customer, even if those losses were unforeseeable, provided that they were not otherwise too remote.'

The opinion expressed in the textbooks was that unforeseeable losses were not recoverable in an action under s2(1), but that was inconsistent with certain decided cases and with the clear meaning of the subsection: the words 'so liable' made the representor liable to damages as if the representation had been made fraudulently. It followed that the finance company was entitled to recover from the dealer all the losses which it suffered as a result of entering into the agreements with the dealer and the customer, even if those losses were unforeseeable, provided that they were not otherwise too remote.

Ruxley Electronics and Construction Ltd v *Forsyth; Laddingford Enclosures Ltd* v *Same* [1995] 3 WLR 118 House of Lords (Lords Keith, Bridge, Jauncey, Mustill and Lloyd)

Breach of contract – assessment of damages – damages to include cost of rectifying defect?

Facts
A householder discovered that though he had specified maximum depth, the swimming pool he had ordered to be built was shallower than specified. He sued the builder for damages for breach of contract, arguing that these should include the cost of demolition of the existing pool, and construction of a new

one of the required depth. Despite its shortcomings the pool as built was perfectly serviceable and safe to dive into.

Held

Where the expenditure involved in rectifying the breach was out of all proportion to the benefit of such rectification, the measure of damages was not for the client to be entitled to recover the cost of total reconstruction of the pool, but only a lesser sum by way of compensation for loss of pleasurable amenity.

Lord Bridge:

'My Lords, damages for breach of contract must reflect, as accurately as the circumstances allow, the loss which the claimant has sustained because he did not get what he bargained for. There is no question of punishing the contract breaker. Given this basic principle, the court, in assessing the measure of the claimant's loss, has ultimately to determine a question of fact, although the law has of course developed detailed criteria which are to be applied in ascertaining the appropriate measure of loss in a wide variety of commonly occurring situations. Since the law relating to damages for breach of contract has developed almost exclusively in a commercial context, these criteria normally proceed on the assumption that each contracting party's interest in the bargain was purely commercial and that the loss resulting from a breach of contract is measurable in purely economic terms. But this assumption may not always be appropriate.

The circumstances giving rise to the present appeal exemplify a situation which one might suppose to be of not infrequent occurrence. A landowner contracts for building works to be executed on his land. When the work is complete it serves the practical purpose for which it was required perfectly satisfactorily. But in some minor respect the finished work falls short of the contract specification. The difference in commercial value between the work as built and the work as specified is nil. But the owner can honestly say: "This work does not please me as well as would that for which I expressly stipulated. It does not satisfy my personal preference. In terms of amenity, convenience or aesthetic satisfaction I have lost something." Nevertheless the contractual defect could only be remedied by demolishing the work and starting again from scratch. The cost of doing this would be so great in proportion to any benefit it would confer on the owner that no reasonable owner would think of incurring it. What is the measure of the loss which the owner has sustained in these circumstances? If there is no clear English authority which answers this question, I suspect this may be because parties to this kind of dispute normally have the good sense to settle rather than to litigate.'

Lord Jauncey:

'However I should emphasise that in the normal case the court has no concern with the use to which a plaintiff puts an award of damages for a loss which has been established. Thus irreparable damage to an article as a result of a breach of contract will entitle the owner to recover the value of the article irrespective of whether he intends to replace it with a similar one or to spend the money on something else. Intention, or lack of it, to reinstate can have relevance only to reasonableness and hence to the extent of the loss which has been sustained. Once that loss has been established intention as to the subsequent use of the damages ceases to be relevant.'

Lord Mustill:

'... I add some observations of my own on the award by the trial judge of damages in a sum intermediate between, on the one hand, the full cost of reinstatement, and on the other the amount by which the malperformance has diminished the market value of the property on which the work was done: in this particular case, nil. This is a question of everyday practical importance to householders who have engaged contractors to carry out small building works, and then find (as often happens) that performance has fallen short of what was promised. I think it proper to enter on the question here, although there is no appeal against the award, because the possibility of such a recovery in a suitable case sheds light on the employer's claim that reinstatement is the only proper measure of damage.

The proposition that these two measures of damage represent the only permissible bases of recovery lie at the heart of the employer's case. From this he reasons that there is a presumption in favour of the cost of restitution, since this is the only way in which he can be given what the contractor had promised to provide. Finally, he contends that there is nothing in the facts of the present case to rebut this presumption.

The attraction of this argument is its avoidance of the conclusion that, in a case such as the present, unless the employer can prove that the defects have depreciated the market value of the property the householder can recover nothing at all. This conclusion would be unacceptable to the average householder, and it is unacceptable to me. It is a common feature of small building works performed on residential property that the cost of the work is not fully reflected by an increase in the market value of the house, and that comparatively minor deviations from specification or sound workmanship may have no direct financial effect at all. Yet the householder must surely be entitled to say that he chose to obtain from the builder a promise to produce a particular result because he wanted to make his house more comfortable, more convenient and more conformable to his own particular tastes; not because he had in mind that the work might increase the amount which he would receive if, contrary to expectation, he thought it expedient in the future to exchange his home for cash. To say that in order to escape unscathed the builder has only to show that to the mind of the average onlooker, or the average potential buyer, the results which he has produced seem just as good as those which he had promised would make a part of the promise illusory, and unbalance the bargain. In the valuable analysis contained in *Radford* v *De Froberville* [1977] 1 WLR 1262, Oliver J emphasised, at p1270, that it was for the plaintiff to judge what performance he required in exchange for the price. The court should honour that choice. Pacta sunt servanda. If the appellant's argument leads to the conclusion that in all cases like the present the employer is entitled to no more than nominal damages, the average householder would say that there must be something wrong with the law.

In my opinion there would indeed be something wrong if, on the hypothesis that cost of reinstatement and the depreciation in value were the only available measures of recovery, the rejection of the former necessarily entailed the adoption of the latter; and the court might be driven to opt for the cost of reinstatement, absurd as the consequence might often be, simply to escape from the conclusion that the promisor can please himself whether or not to comply with the wishes of the promise which, as embodied in the contract, formed part of the consideration for the price. Having taken on the job the contractor is morally as well as legally obliged to give the employer what he stipulated to obtain, and this obligation ought not to be devalued. In my opinion however the hypothesis is not correct. There are not two alternative measures of damage, at opposite poles, but only one: namely, the loss truly suffered by the promisee. In some cases the loss cannot be fairly measured except by reference to the full cost of repairing the deficiency in performance. In others, and in particular those where the contract is designed to fulfil a purely commercial purpose, the loss will very often consist only of the monetary detriment brought about by the breach of contract. But these remedies are not exhaustive, for the law must cater for those occasions where the value of the promise to the promisee exceeds the financial enhancement of his position which full performance will secure. This excess, often referred to in the literature as the "consumer surplus" (see for example the valuable discussion by Harris, Ogus and Philips (1979) 95 LQR 581) is usually incapable of precise valuation in terms of money, exactly because it represents a personal, subjective and non-monetary gain. Nevertheless where it exists the law should recognise it and compensate the promisee if the misperformance takes it away.'

Seven Seas Properties Ltd v *Al-Essa* [1993] 3 All ER 577 Chancery Division (G Lightman QC)

Breach of contract – damages – consequences 'in contemplation of' the parties

Facts

The plaintiffs were interested in purchasing the defendants' two properties. They proposed a quick resale at a profit and had in fact already made a resale contract, but they kept their intention of resale to themselves and the defendants only found out about it after the contract had been signed. When they learned of it, they refused to complete, saying that the resale price showed they were selling at too low a price. The plaintiffs sought an action for specific performance in order to complete the resale. Specific performance was granted, but the resale was adversely affected by the delay and the plaintiffs received a lower price than they had paid. They sought damages.

Held

The defaulting party was liable for all loss which might reasonably be supposed to result as a consequence of breach. Since the plaintiffs were careful to keep secret their intention to resell quickly and make a profit from the defendants then they (the defendants) could not be expected to have this in contemplation as a reasonable consequence of breach. It was not enough for the plaintiffs to argue that resale was an option open to any purchaser. The defendants must have been specifically aware of the intention to resell and they were not.

The plaintiffs' claim for damages arising out of the proposed resale would not be permitted.

Sharneyford Supplies Ltd v *Edge*

See Chapter 20.

Staffordshire Area Health Authority v *South Staffordshire Waterworks Co* [1978] 1 WLR 1387 Court of Appeal (Lord Denning MR, Goff and Cumming-Bruce LJJ)

Contract – ability to determine

Facts

Following earlier agreements between the parties, in 1929 they agreed that a hospital was to be supplied with 5,000 gallons of water a day free and additional water at 7d (2.9p) per 1,000 gallons 'at all times hereafter.' In 1975, when the normal rate was 45p per 1,000 gallons, the water company gave six months' notice to terminate the agreement and said that thereafter they would supply 5,000 gallons per day free and charge any excess at normal rates. The hospital authorities contended that the notice was not valid.

Held

It was, as the 1929 agreement could be terminated by reasonable notice.

Lord Denning MR:

'... I think that the rule of strict construction is now quite out of date. It has been supplanted by the rule that written instruments are to be construed in relation the the circumstances as they were known to or contemplated by the parties; and that even the plainest words may fall to be modified if events occur which the parties never had in mind and in which they cannot have intended the agreement to operate.

This modern rule was adumbrated by Cardozo J in 1918 in the New York Court of Appeals in *Utica City National Bank* v *Gunn*:

"To take the primary or strict meaning is to make the whole transaction futile. To take the secondary or loose meaning is to give it efficacy and purpose. In such a situation the genesis and aim of the transaction may rightly guide our choice."

The modern rule has recently been expounded with clarity and authority by Lord Wilberforce in the House of Lords in the case of *Reardon Smith Line Ltd* v *Hansen-Tangen* when he said:

"When one speaks of the intention of the parties to the contract, one is speaking objectively – the parties cannot themselves give direct evidence of what their intention was – and what must be ascertained is what is to be taken as the intention which reasonable people would have had if placed in the situation of the parties. Similarly, when one is speaking of the aim, or object, or commercial purpose, one is speaking objectively of what reasonable persons would have had in mind in the situation of the parties ... what the court must do must be to place itself in thought in the same factual matrix as that in which the parties were."

As I understand this modern rule, we are no longer to go by the strict construction of the words as judges did in the 19th century. We are to put ourselves in the same situation as the parties were at the time they drew up the instrument, to sit in their chairs with our minds endowed with the same facts as theirs were, and envisage the future with the same degree of foresight as they did. So placed we have to ask ourselves: what were the circumstances in which the contract was made? Does it apply in the least to the new situation which has developed? If events occur for which they have made no provision, and which were outside the realm of their speculations altogether, or of any reasonable persons sitting in their chairs, then the court itself must take a hand and hold that the contract ceases to bind ...

I do not think that the water company could have determined the agreement immediately after it was made. That cannot have been intended by the parties. No rule of construction could sensibly permit such a result. But, in the past 50 years, the whole situation has changed so radically that one can say with confidence: "The parties never intended that the supply should be continued in these days at that price." Rather than force such unequal terms on the parties, the court should hold that the agreement could be and was properly determined in 1975 by the reasonable notice of six months. This does not mean of course, that on the expiry of the notice the water company can cut off the supply to the hospital. It will be bound to continue it. All that will happen is that the parties will have to negotiate fresh terms of payment. These should take into account the history ... In the light of that history, it seems to me plain that the 1929 agreement should be up-dated so as to have regard to the effect of inflation ...'

Surrey CC v Bredero Homes Ltd [1992] 3 All ER 302 Chancery Division (Ferris J)

Contract – damages for breach – measurement of compensation

Facts
The plaintiff council having originally acquired land for road widening purposes, found it to be surplus to requirements and decided to offer the whole site with a view to its being used for a housing estate. The council agreed to sell the land to the defendant company for £1.52m, subject to Bredero Homes obtaining the necessary planning consent. The defendant duly obtained consent and the land was transferred to it. In the transfer documents was, inter alia, a clause containing a covenant that the housing estate would be constructed according to the terms and conditions of the planning consent. In fact, Bredero Homes subsequently obtained fresh planning consent, which allowed them to build at a greater density than originally planned. Of course, since they built more houses, the scheme was more profitable. The council was aware of the breach of covenant, but took no steps until, after the last house was sold, they sued for breach of covenant.

Held
In assessing the correct remedy it should be remembered that it was no longer possible to restrain the breach of covenant. The council had its chance at the time to secure an injunction but failed to do so. There was no justification for assessing damages as a substitute for an injunction, since there were no grounds on which such relief could now be awarded. Nor could damages be assessed on the basis of what the plaintiffs might have demanded in return for relaxing the covenant; they had lost any control over enforcement of the covenant by their conscious decision not to seek an injunction. If one considered what the council's position would have been had the covenant been enforced, with its position now, it was clear that the council had suffered no real loss. The loss of such value as the covenant had was because of the plaintiffs' decision not to enforce it. Nominal damages only would be awarded.

The Texaco Melbourne (1991) Financial Times 7 August Queen's Bench Division (Webster J)

Currency of damages

Facts
Following a breach of contract it fell to be decided whether damages should be paid in US dollars, or in Ghanaian cedis.

Held
That in deciding, regard should be had to the currency in which the loss was felt, but also to what was fair and equitable. Although the ship owners had felt the loss in cedis, because the value of the cedi had fallen drastically since the time of the contract, and because of stringent Ghanaian currency controls, it would be more reasonable to quantify the award in dollars.

Victoria Laundry (Windsor) Ltd v *Newman Industries Ltd* [1949] 2 KB 528 Court of Appeal (Tucker, Asquith and Singleton LJJ)

Damages – loss of profits

Facts
The defendant engineers agreed to sell a boiler to the plaintiff launderers and dyers, knowing the nature of the plaintiffs' business, that the boiler was needed for that business and that it was wanted for immediate use: they did not know, however, that it was required to extend the business. As a result of the fault of a third party, the boiler was damaged while it was being loaded on to the plaintiffs' vehicle: delivery was therefore delayed and the plaintiffs claimed damages for breach of contract.

Held
They were entitled to succeed and the damages awarded could take account of any loss of profits resulting from the enforced delay in extending their business.

Asquith LJ:

> 'The defendants were an engineering company supplying a boiler to a laundry. We reject the submission for the defendants that an engineering company knows no more than the plain man about boilers or the purposes to which they are commonly put by different classes of purchasers, including laundries. The defendant company were not, it is true, manufacturers of this boiler or dealers in boilers, but they gave a highly technical and comprehensive description of this boiler to the plaintiffs ... Of the uses or purposes to which boilers are put, they would clearly know more than the uninstructed layman. Again, they know they were supplying the boiler to a company carrying on the business of laundrymen and dyers, for use in that business. The obvious use of a boiler, in such a business, is surely to boil water for the purpose of washing or dyeing. A laundry might conceivably buy a boiler for some other purpose, for instance, to work radiators or warm bath water water for the comfort of its employees or directors, or to use for research, or to exhibit in a museum. All these purposes are possible, but the first is the obvious purpose which, in the case of a laundry, leaps to the average eye. If the purpose then be to wash or dye, why does the company want to wash or dye, unless for purposes of business advantage, in which term we, for the purposes of the rest of this judgment, include maintenance or increase of profit or reduction of loss? We shall speak henceforward not of loss of profit, but of "loss of business". No commercial concern commonly purchases for the purposes of its business a very large and expensive structure like this ... with any other motive, and no supplier, let alone an engineering company, which has promised delivery of

such an article by a particular date with knowledge that it was to be put into use immediately on delivery, can reasonably contend that it could not foresee that loss of business (in the sense indicated above) would be liable to result to the purchaser from a long delay in the delivery thereof. The suggestion that, for all the supplier knew, the boiler might have been needed simply as a "stand-by" to be used in a possibly distant future, is gratuitous and was plainly negatived ...'

Commentary

Distinguished: *Hadley* v *Baxendale* (1854) 9 Exch 341. See also *Koufos* v *C Czarnikow Ltd* [1967] 3 WLR 1491.

Watts v *Morrow* [1991] 1 WLR 1421 Court of Appeal (Brown, Ralph Gibson and Bingham LJJ)

Measure of damages – surveyor's report negligent – damages for distress and inconvenience

Facts

Mr and Mrs Watts purchased a house for £177,500 relying on a surveyor's report prepared by the defendant. They bought the house as a second home and did not take up possession for some time, when they found that defects existed beyond those mentioned in the report. Repairs cost £34,000. At first instance the court awarded this sum, plus general damages of £4,000 for 'distress and inconvenience'. The surveyor appealed on the quantum of damages.

Held

The proper measure of damages was the sum needed to put the plaintiffs in as good a position as if the contract had been properly performed, that is: the difference between the value of the property as it was represented to be and its value in its true condition. Damages for distress and inconvenience were set too high and should be reduced to £1,500.

Bingham LJ:

'A contract-broker is not in general liable for any distress, frustration, anxiety, displeasure, vexation, tension or aggravation which his breach of contract may cause to the innocent party. This rule is not, I think, founded on the assumption that such reactions are not foreseeable, which they surely are or may be, but on considerations of policy.

But the rule is not absolute. Where the very object of a contract is to provide pleasure, relaxation, peace of mind or freedom from molestation, damages will be awarded if the fruit of the contract is not provided or if the contrary result is procured instead. If the law did not cater for this exceptional category of case it would be defective. A contract to survey the condition of a house for a prospective purchaser does not, however, fall within this exceptional category.

In cases not falling within this exceptional category, damages are ion my view recoverable for physical inconvenience and discomfort caused by the breach and mental suffering directly related to that inconvenience and discomfort. If those effects are foreseeably suffered during a period when defects are repaired I am prepared to accept that they sound in damages even though the cost of the repairs is not recoverable as such.'

Weld-Blundell v *Stephens* [1920] AC 956 House of Lords (Viscount Finlay, Lord Dunedin, Lord Sumner, Lord Parmoor and Lord Wrenbury)

Special damages?

Facts
The appellant employed the respondent chartered accountant to investigate the financial position of a company in which he was financially interested. In his letter of instructions, the appellant referred to a former manager and an auditor in defamatory terms. The respondent handed the letter to his partner who was to carry out the investigation and the partner negligently left it at the company's office. There is was found and damages for libel were awarded against the appellant who now sued the respondent for breach of duty, claiming as special damages the damages and cost which he had been ordered to pay in the libel actions.

Held (Viscount Finlay and Lord Parmoor dissenting)
His claim would fail.

Lord Sumner:
'This special application to contracts of the rule as to remoteness depends, like other matters, of contract, on mutuality and agreement on some communication between the parties at or before the time when the contract is made, some knowledge and acceptance by the one party of the purpose or intention of the other in entering into the contract. There is no evidence of anything of the kind here. It is true that the respondent said that he realised the letter was dangerous when he got it, but that answer did not purport to refer to actions brought upon it. There are plenty of other ways in which it might make mischief, and, indeed, when Mr Stephens asked the counsel who was cross-examining him. "Do you mean dangerous in the sense that it was libellous?" – all the answer he got was: "A highly dangerous letter to the interest of Mr Weld-Blundell unless it was kept from the knowledge of those whose names are referred to in it." To that it was that he replied that he realised it was dangerous. As a matter of fact, nothing passed between the parties on the subject and so far was any such special contemplation from the appellant's mind that, when Messrs Comins & Co's solicitors asked him to apologise for his letter his answer was: "I suppose you will not venture to deny my right, even in this land of fools and rogues, to say or write what I please to my own servants, such as Comins, Hurst, Stephens, & Co more especially when, as in this case, I limit my remarks to what is and has been a subject of common knowledge to and among all of them or, as you put it, among the entire gang in my employment." Clearly, Mr Weld-Blundell thought he could write to Mr Stephens what he liked without being under any legal liability, whether the letter became known or not. There is no evidence that any such thing was in the contemplation of either party; certainly it was not in that of both. There is, therefore, no ground for applying to the defendant's breach of contract in this case any other measure of damages than such as would have applied, if it had been a breach of a non-contractual duty.'

White Arrow Express Ltd v *Lamey's Distribution Ltd* [1995] TLR 430 Court of Appeal (Sir Thomas Bingham MR, Rose and Morritt LJJ)

Breach of contract – quantification of damage

Facts
The plaintiffs, who carried on a mail order business, contracted with the defendants, who operated a road transport company, to collect and deliver goods sold to customers. Terms were agreed for an 'enhanced' level of performance by the defendants. It was accepted that the defendants performed a routine service but not the 'enhanced' service specifically agreed and for which the plaintiffs had paid. At first instance the court held that the plaintiffs were only entitled to recover nominal damages.

Held
In principle an innocent party who did not receive the 'enhanced' service negotiated for, could receive

more than just nominal damages. Quantification of the loss was, however, for the plaintiffs to provide, or at least to prove evidence from which the courts could draw inferences. The plaintiffs had undoubtedly paid for a superior service and had not received it, but they had not established specific loss or damage to goods, loss or damage to goodwill or any similar aspect. No more than nominal damages could be paid.

Sir Thomas Bingham MR:

'... the plaintiffs' claim was not based on any damage to or loss of goods, nor on any complaints or claims by customers agents or suppliers, nor on any damage to or loss of goodwill, nor on any quasi-contractual or restitutionary principle. I have no doubt that the broad principles asserted by both sides were correct. It is elementary that a breach of contract, without more, did not entitle the innocent party to recover more than nominal loss. Such a party had to demonstrate specific heads of loss or persuade the court to draw an inference of loss.'

Wroth v *Tyler* [1973] 2 WLR 405 High Court (Megarry J)

Contract of sale – wife's objection

Facts

The defendant entered into an agreement to sell his bungalow, with vacant possession, to the plaintiffs for £6,050. Completion was fixed for 31 October 1971. The day after the defendant entered into the agreement, his wife, who had not shown any opposition to the sale, but who was not enthusiastic about it, entered in the Land Charges Register a notice under s1 of the Matrimonial Homes Act 1967, without informing the defendant. The entry was revealed by a notice sent by the Land Registry to the defendant's building society, which notified the defendant's solicitors who, in turn, informed the defendant. The defendant tried to persuade his wife to remove the notice, but was unsuccessful. Consequently, he was unable to complete, but he offered to pay damages. The plaintiffs issued a writ in early 1972, seeking specific performance and damages in lieu or in addition. Judgment was given in December 1972.

Held

The plaintiffs were not entitled to an order for specific performance, with vacant possession or subject to the rights of occupation of the defendant's wife. However, they were entitled to damages for loss of bargain and here they would not be simply nominal. In the event, they were quantified as at the date of the judgment and they were assessed at £5,500.

Megarry J:

'The rule of common law is, that where a party sustains a loss by reason of a breach of contract, he is, so far as money can do it, to be placed in the same situation, with respect to damages, as if the contract had been performed.

... on principle, I would say that damages "in substitution" for specific performance, must be a substitute, giving as nearly as may be what specific performance would have given ... the court has jurisdiction to award such damages as will put the plaintiff into as good a position as if the contract had been performed, even if to do so means awarding damages assessed by reference to a period subsequent to the date of the breach. This seems to me to be consonant with the nature of specific performance, which is a continuing remedy ... The conclusion that I have reached therefore, is that as matters stand, I ought to award damages to the plaintiffs of the order of £5,000 in substitution for decreeing specific performance ... This is a dismal prospect for the defendant but ... it is the plaintiffs who are wholly blameless.'

Commentary

Applied: *Hadley* v *Baxendale* (1854) 9 Exch 341 and *Bain* v *Fothergill* (1874) LR 7 HL 158. Applied in *Sharneyford Supplies Ltd* v *Edge* [1987] 2 WLR 363.

26 Remedies for Breach of Contract – Equitable Remedies

Alghussein Establishment* v *Eton College [1988] 1 WLR 587 House of Lords (Lord Bridge of Harwich, Lord Elwyn-Jones, Lord Ackner, Lord Goff of Chieveley and Lord Jauncey of Tullichettle)

Party able to rely on own default?

Facts
In 1978 the respondents entered into an agreement with the appellants' predecessors in title as tenants for a 99 year lease for development. Although no time limit was fixed, the tenants undertook to use their best endeavours to proceed with and complete the development. The agreement also provided for this immediate grant of the lease on completion of the development 'provided that if for any reason due to the wilful default of the tenant the development shall remain uncompleted on the 29th day of September 1983 the lease shall forthwith be granted ...' By October 1984 the appellants had still not started the work: the respondents purported to treat the agreement as being repudiated and the appellants sought specific performance of the agreement and the grant of the lease.

Held
The appellants could not succeed.

Lord Jauncey of Tullichettle:

> 'Even if it were appropriate to imply the provision [for the completion of the development] into any lease to be granted under the proviso ... and I make this assumption without deciding the matter one way or the other, there remains the question whether ... the agreement contains clear express provisions to contradict the presumption that it was not the intention of parties that either should be entitled to rely on his own breach in order to obtain a benefit. I find no such clear express provision. Although the proviso refers specifically to the wilful default of the tenant, it does not state that the tenant should be entitled to take advantage thereof. It is one thing for wilful default of a party to be made the occasion on which a provision comes into operation but is quite another thing for that party to be given the right to rely on that default.'

Commentary
See also *Micklefield* v *SAC Technology Ltd* [1990] 1 WLR 1002 in Chapter 21.

American Cyanamid Co* v *Ethicon Ltd [1975] 2 WLR 316 House of Lords (Lord Diplock, Viscount Dilhorne, Lord Cross of Chelsea, Lord Salmon and Lord Edmund Davies)

Interlocutory injunctions – principle governing grant

Facts
The plaintiffs believed that the defendants were about to infringe their patent relating to surgical sutures and they sought an interlocutory injunction.

Held
The injunction would be granted.

Lord Diplock:

'... The use of such expressions as "a probability", "a prima facie case", or "a strong prima facie case" in the context of the exercise of a discretionary power to grant an interlocutory injunction leads to confusion as to the object sought to be achieved by this form of temporary relief. The court no doubt must be satisfied that the claim is not frivolous or vexatious; in other words, that there is a serious question to be tried.

It is no part of the court's function at this stage of the litigation to try to resolve conflicts of evidence on affidavit as to facts on which the claims of either party may ultimately depend nor to decide difficult questions of law which call for detailed argument and mature considerations. These are matters to be dealt with at the trial ... So unless the material available to the court at the hearing of the application for an interlocutory injunction fails to disclose that the plaintiff has any real prospect of succeeding in his claim for a permanent injunction at the trial, the court should go on to consider whether the balance of convenience lies in favour of granting or refusing the interlocutory relief that is sought.

As to that, the governing principle is that the court should first consider whether if the plaintiff were to succeed at the trial in establishing his right to a permanent injunction he would be adequately compensated by an award of damages for the loss he would have sustained as a result of the defendant's continuing to do what was sought to be enjoined between the time of the application and the time of the trial. If damages in the measure recoverable at common law would be adequate remedy and the defendant would be in a financial position to pay them, no interlocutory injunction should normally be granted, however strong the plaintiff's claim appeared to be at that stage. If, on the other hand, damages would not provide an adequate remedy for the plaintiff in the event of his succeeding at the trial, the court should then consider whether, on the contrary hypothesis that the defendant were to succeed at the trial in establishing his right to do that which was sought to be enjoined, he would be adequately compensated under the plaintiff's undertaking as to damages for the loss he would have sustained by being prevented from doing so between the time of the application and the time of the trial. If damages in the measure recoverable under such and undertaking would be an adequate remedy and the plaintiff would be in a financial position to pay them, there would be no reason on this ground to refuse an interlocutory injunction.

It is where there is doubt as to the adequacy of the respective remedies in damages available to either party or to both, that the question of balance of convenience arises. It would be unwise to attempt even to list all the various matters which may need to be taken into consideration in deciding where the balance lies, let alone to suggest the relative weight to be attached to them. These will vary from case to case.

Where other factors appear to be evenly balanced it is a counsel of prudence to take such measures as are calculated to preserve the status quo. If the defendant is enjoined temporarily from doing something that he has not done before, the only effect of the interlocutory injunction in the event of his succeeding at the trial is to postpone the date at which he is able to embark on a course of action which he has not previously found it necessary to undertake; whereas to interrupt him in the conduct of an established enterprise would cause much greater inconvenience to him since he would have to start again to establish it in the event of his succeeding at the trial.

Save in the simplest cases, the decision to grant or to refuse an interlocutory injunction will cause to whichever party is unsuccessful on the application some disadvantages which his ultimate success at the trial may show he ought to have been spared and the disadvantages may be such that the recovery of damages to which he would then be entitled either in the action or under the plaintiff's undertaking would not be sufficient to compensate him fully for all of them. The extent to which the disadvantages to each party would be incapable of being compensated in damages in the event of his succeeding at the trail is always a significant factor in assessing where the balance of convenience lies; and if the extent of the uncompensatable disadvantage to each party would not differ widely, it may not be improper to take into account in tipping the balance the relative strength of each party's case as revealed by the affidavit evidence adduced on the hearing of the application. This, however, should be done only where it is apparent on the facts disclosed by evidence as to which there is no credible dispute that the strength of one party's case is disproportionate to that of the other party. The court is not justified in embarking on anything resembling a trial of the action on conflicting affidavits in order to evaluate the strength of either party's case.

I would reiterate that, in addition to those to which I have referred, there may be many other special factors to be taken into consideration in the particular circumstances of individual cases. The instant appeal affords one example of this.

Returning, therefore, to the instant appeal, it cannot be doubted that the affidavit evidence shows that there are serious questions to be tried.'

Decro-Wall International SA v *Practitioners in Marketing Ltd*

See Chapter 24.

Evening Standard Co Ltd v *Henderson* [1987] IRLR 64 Court of Appeal (Lawton and Balcombe LJJ)

Injunction – contract of service

Facts
Mr Henderson was employed on the London *Evening Standard* for 17 years. His contract of employment provided that during the time of his employment he could not work for the employer's competitors and that to terminate his contract he must give 12 months' notice. In breach of contract Mr Henderson gave two months' notice to terminate as he wished to begin working for a rival newspaper. The plaintiffs sought an injunction to prevent Mr Henderson working for a rival for the ten months of the unexpired contractual notice period.

Held
The injunction should be granted.

Lawton LJ:

'... By the time this case got to this court it was accepted by the plaintiffs that they could not get an injunction against the defendant on the grounds they first thought they could because ... you cannot get an injunction against an employee under a contract of service to enforce a negative covenant if the consequence of that injunction would be to put the employee in the position that he would either have to go on working for his former employers or starve or be idle ... the plaintiffs had to consider carefully what they should do. They decided that one way out of the problem was to offer to pay the defendant his salary and other contractual benefits until such time as his notice, if it had been in proper form ...

What we have to ask ourselves is: what, in the circumstances of this case, is the balance of convenience? If the defendant leaves the employment of the plaintiffs today, as he says he intends to do, and takes himself off straight away or very shortly to the rival newspaper, the plaintiffs, in my judgment, will undoubtedly suffer damage but it will be difficult to quantify those damages ... the injunction must not force the defendant to work for the plaintiffs and it must not reduce him, certainly to a condition of starvation or to a condition of idleness, whatever that may mean. But all that, in my judgment, is overcome by the fact that the plaintiffs have made the offer they have ...'

Hill v C A Parsons & Co Ltd [1971] 3 WLR 995 Court of Appeal (Lord Denning MR, Sachs and Stamp LJJ)

Wrongful dismissal – injunction

Facts
The plaintiff, a chartered engineer aged 63, had been employed by the defendants for 35 years. He was due to retire at 65 and his pension depended on the average salary during the last three years' service. Following a strike, the defendants said that persons of the plaintiff's grade had to join a certain union; he refused and the defendants purported to dismiss him. In his action for wrongful dismissal, he sought an interim injunction.

Held
The injunction would be granted.

Lord Denning MR:

'In these circumstance, it is of the utmost importance to Mr Hill … that the notice … should not be held to terminate [his] employment. Damages would not be at all an adequate remedy. If ever there was a case where an injunction should be granted against the employers, this is the case. It is quite plain that the employers have done wrong. I know that the employers have been under pressure from a powerful trade union. That may explain their conduct, but it does not excuse it. They have purported to terminate Mr Hill's employment by a notice which is too short by far. They seek to take advantage of their own wrong by asserting that his services were terminated by their own "say so" at the date selected by them – to the grave prejudice of Mr Hill. They cannot be allowed to break the law in this way. It is, to my mind, a clear case for an injunction.

The judge said that he felt constrained by the law to refuse an injunction. But that is too narrow a view of the principles of law. He has overlooked the fundamental principle that, whenever a man has a right, the law should give a remedy. The Latin maxim is ubi jus ibi remedium. This principle enables us to step over the trip-wires of previous cases and to bring the law into accord with the needs of today. I would allow the appeal, accordingly and grant an injunction restraining the company from treating the notice … as having determined Mr Hill's employment.'

Johnson v Agnew [1979] 2 WLR 487 House of Lords (Lord Wilberforce, Lord Salmon, Lord Fraser of Tullybelton, Lord Keith of Kinkel and Lord Scarman)

Damages – date of assessment

Facts
In November 1973 the parties contracted for the sale and purchase of a house and land, the properties being mortgaged separately. The purchaser paid part of the deposit and accepted the vendor's title but did not complete by 6 December, the contract date. On 21 December the vendors gave notice that 21 January 1974 was the final date for completion, but the purchaser failed to complete and on 8 March the vendors commenced proceedings. An order for specific performance was made on 27 June, although it was not entered until 26 November, by which time the mortgagees of the house had obtained an order for possession. In March 1975 the land mortgagees obtained such an order and on 3 April and 20 June respectively the land and house mortgagees contracted sales, completions taking place in July.

Held
The vendors were entitled not only to an order discharging the specific performance order but also to damages for breach of contract assessed at 3 April 1975.

Lord Wilberforce:

'The general principle for the assessment of damages is compensatory, ie that the innocent party is to be placed, so far as money can do so, in the same position as if the contract had been performed. Where the contract is one of sale, this principle normally leads to assessment of damages as at the date of the breach ... But this is not an absolute rule; if to follow it would give rise to injustice, the court has power to fix such other date as may be appropriate in the circumstances.

In cases where a breach of a contract for sale has occurred, and the innocent party reasonably continues to try to have the contract completed, it would to me appear more logical and just rather than tie him to the date of the original breach, to assess damages as at the date when (otherwise than by his default) the contract is lost. Support for this approach is to be found in the cases ... In the present case if it is accepted, as I would accept, that the vendors acted reasonably in pursuing the remedy of specific performance, the date on which that remedy became aborted (not by the vendors' fault) should logically be fixed as the date on which damages should be assessed. Choice of this date would be in accordance both with common law principle ... and with the wording of [Lord Cairns'] Act "in substitution for ... specific performance." The date which emerges from this is 3 April 1975, the first date on which mortgagees contracted to sell a portion of the property. I would vary the order of the Court of Appeal by substituting this date for that fixed by them, viz 26 November 1974. The same date (3 April 1975) should be used for the purpose of limiting the respondents' right to interest on damages.'

Leeds Industrial Co-operative Society v *Slack* [1924] AC 851 House of Lords (Earl of Birkenhead, Viscount Finlay, Lord Dunedin, Lord Sumner and Lord Carson)

Injunction – award of damages in lieu

Facts

The parties owned premises on opposite sides of a narrow passage. The defendants demolished theirs and commenced rebuilding: the plaintiffs maintained that the new building already had, and when completed would even more, infringe their right to light and they sought an injunction. At the date of the trial, it was found that the new building had not yet interfered unlawfully with the plaintiffs' ancient lights.

Held (Lord Sumner and Lord Carson dissenting)

An award of damages could be made in lieu of an injunction and the measure of damages would be the damage to be sustained following completion of the building.

Viscount Finlay:

'Does [Lord Cairns' Act] empower the court to award damages in lieu of an injunction when injury is threatened, but has not yet been done?

In my opinion, this question must be answered in the affirmative. The power given is to award damages to the party injured, either in addition to or in substitution for an injunction. If the damages are given in addition to the injunction, they are to compensate for the injury which has been done, and the injunction will prevent its continuance, or repetition. But if damages are given in substitution for an injunction, they must necessarily cover not only injury already sustained, but also injury that would be inflicted in the future by the commission of the act threatened. If no injury has yet been sustained, the damages will be solely in respect of the damage to be sustained in the future by injuries which the injunction, if granted, would have prevented. The power conferred on a Court of Chancery by Lord Cairns' act included power to give damages in respect of a past injury. This in itself was a useful extension of jurisdiction, as it would prevent the hardship involved by the necessity of going to another court to get such relief. But the enactment did not stop there. In terms it gave power to substitute damages for an injunction. Such a substitution in the very nature of things involves that the damages are to deal with what would have been prevented by the injunction, if granted. In the present case the building has not proceeded far enough to constitute an actionable wrong in respect of the plaintiff's lights, and an injunction would prevent the commission of that wrong in the future. On what principle can it be said that, until there has been some interference with the plaintiff's windows, the court cannot give damages in lieu of an injunction against obstruction? Such a construction would impose a purely arbitrary and meaningless restriction on the relief to be given under the Act.'

Lumley v *Wagner* (1852) 1 De GM & G 604 Lord Chancellor's Court (Lord St Leonards LC)

Injunction – contract for personal services

Facts
The defendant cantatrice bound herself to sing for three months at the plaintiff's London theatre and 'not to use her talents' at any other place during that time.

Held
An injunction could be granted to restrain her from appearing at another theatre.

Lord St Leonards LC:

'It was objected that the operation of the injunction in the present case was mischievous, excluding the defendant Johanna Wagner from performing at any other theatre while this court had no power to compel her to perform at Her Majesty's Theatre. It is true that I have not the means of compelling her to sing, but she has no cause of complaint if I compel her to abstain from the commission of an act which she has bound herself not to do, and thus possibly cause her to fulfil her engagement. The jurisdiction which I now exercise is wholly within the power of the court, and, being of opinion that it is a proper case for interfering, I shall leave nothing unsatisfied by the judgment I pronounce. The effect, too, of the injunction, in restraining Johanna Wagner from singing elsewhere may, in the event of an action being brought against her by the plaintiff, prevent any such amount of vindictive damages being given against her as a jury might probably be inclined to give if she had carried her talents and exercised them at the rival theatre. The injunction may also, as I have said, tend to the fulfilment of her engagement, though, in continuing the injunction, I disclaim doing indirectly what I cannot do directly.'

Commentary
See also *Warner Brothers Pictures Inc* v *Nelson* [1937] 1 KB 209 and *Page One Records Ltd* v *Britton* [1968] 1 WLR 157.

Mareva Compania Naviera SA v *International Bulk Carriers SA, The Mareva* [1980] 1 All ER 213 Court of Appeal (Lord Denning MR, Roskill and Ormrod LJJ)

Injunction – danger of transfer of assets out of jurisdiction

Facts
The plaintiffs sought, inter alia, damages for alleged repudiation of a charterparty and, on an ex parte application, a judge had granted an injunction restraining the defendants from removing or disposing out of the jurisdiction monies in their London bank account.

Held
The injunction would be extended.

Lord Denning MR:

'... Section 45 of the Supreme Court of Judicature (Consolidation) Act 1925 says:

"A mandamus or an injunction may be granted or a receiver appointed by an interlocutory Order of the Court in all cases in which it shall appear to the Court to be just or convenient ..."

In *Beddow* v *Beddow* Jessel MR Gave a very wide interpretation to that section. He said: "I have unlimited power to grant an injunction in any case where it would be right or just to do so ..."

There is only one qualification to be made. The court will not grant an injunction to protect a person who has no legal or equitable right whatever ... But, subject to that qualification, the statute gives a wide general power to the courts. It is well summarised in *Halsbury's Laws of England:*

" ... now, therefore, whenever a right, which can be asserted either at law or in equity, does not exist, then whatever the previous practice may have been, the Court is enabled by virtue of this provision, in a proper case, to grant an injunction to protect that right."

In my opinion that principle applies to a creditor who has a right to be paid the debt owing to him, even before he has established his right by getting judgement for it. If it appears that the debt is due and owing, and there is a danger that the debtor may dispose of his assets so as to defeat it before judgment, the court has jurisdiction in a proper case to grant an interlocutory judgment so as to prevent him disposing of those assets. It seems to me that this is a proper case for the exercise of this jurisdiction. There is money in a bank in London which stands in the name of these charterers. The charterers have control of it. They may at any time dispose of it or remove it out of this country. If they do so, the shipowners may never get their charter hire. The ship is now on the high seas. It has passed Cape Town on its way to India. It will complete the voyage and the cargo will be discharged. And the shipowners may not get their charter hire at all. In the face of this danger, I think this court ought to grand an injunction to restrain the charterers from disposing of these moneys now in the bank in London until the trial or judgment in this action. If the charterers have any grievance about it when they hear of it, they can apply to discharge it. But meanwhile the shipowners should be protected. It is only just and right that this court should grant an injunction. I would therefore continue the injunction.'

Page One Records Ltd v *Britton* [1968] 1 WLR 157 High Court (Stamp J)

Injunction – contract for personal services

Facts

The defendant musicians ('The Troggs') appointed the plaintiffs their manager for five years. During that time, they sought an interlocutory injunction to restrain them from engaging any other manager.

Held

The injunction would be refused.

Stamp J:

' ... It was said in this case, that if an injunction is granted The Troggs could, without employing any other manager or agent, continue as a group on their own or seek other employment of a different nature. So far as the former suggestion is concerned, in the first place, I doubt whether consistently with the terms of the agreements which I have read, The Troggs could act as their own managers; and, in the second place, I think that I can and should take judicial notice of the fact that these groups, if they are to have any great success, must have managers. Indeed, it is the plaintiffs' own case that The Troggs are simple persons, of no business experience, and could not survive without the services of a manager. As a practical matter on the evidence before me, I entertain no doubt that they would be compelled, if the injunction were granted on the terms that the plaintiffs seek, to continue to employ the first plaintiff as their manager and agent and it is, I think, on this point that this case diverges from the *Lumley* v *Wagner* case ... and the cases which have followed it, including the *Warner Brothers* case: for it would be a bad thing to put pressure on The Troggs to continue to employ as a manager and agent in a fiduciary capacity one, who, unlike the plaintiff in those cases who had merely to pay the defendant money, has duties of a personal and fiduciary nature to perform and in whom The Troggs, for reasons good, bad or indifferent, have lost confidence and who may, for all I know, fail in its duty to them.

On the facts before me on this interlocutory motion, I should, if I granted the injunction, be enforcing a contract for personal services in which personal services are to be performed by the first plaintiff. In *Lumley* v *Wagner*, Lord St Leonards LC in his judgment, disclaimed doing directly what he could not do directly; and in the present case, by granting an injunction I would, in my judgment, be doing precisely that. I must, therefore, refuse the injunction.'

Patel v *Ali* [1984] 2 WLR 960 High Court (Goulding J)

Specific performance – hardship

Facts

Two couples (defendants) live in a house which they contract to sell to the plaintiffs. One defendant is adjudicated bankrupt, another defendant becomes very ill, has a child and undergoes amputation of one leg. Her husband is sent to prison for two years. She later has another child. The plaintiffs apply for specific performance.

Held

The court could and would refuse specific performance on the ground of hardship consequent to the contract, even where it was not caused by the plaintiff; that in view of the change of circumstances and that provided the plaintiffs had an effective remedy in damages, it would be just not to allow specific performance.

Goulding J:

'Another limitation suggested by counsel for the plaintiffs was that, in the reported cases, as he said, hardship successfully relied on has always related to the subject matter of the contract and has not been just a personal hardship of the defendant. Certainly, mere pecuniary difficulties, whether of purchaser or of vendor, afford no excuse from performance of a contract. In a wider sense than that, I do not think the suggested universal proposition can be sustained ...

The important and true principle, in my view, is that only in extraordinary and persuasive circumstances can hardship supply an excuse for resisting performance of a contract for the sale of immovable property. A person of full capacity who sells or buys a house takes the risk of hardship to himself and his dependants, whether arising from existing facts or unexpectedly supervening in the interval before completion. This is where, to my mind, great importance attaches to the immense delay in the present case, not attributable to the defendant's conduct. Even after issue of the writ, she could not complete, if she had wanted to, without the concurrence of the absent Mr Ahmed. Thus, in a sense, she can say she is being asked to do what she never bargained for, namely to complete the sale after more than four years, after all the unforeseeable changes that such a period entails. I think that in this way she can fairly assert that specific performance would inflict on her "a hardship amounting to injustice" to use the phrase employed by James LJ, in a different but comparable context, in *Tamplin* v *James* (1880) 15 Ch D 215 at 221. Equitable relief may, in my view, be refused because of an unforeseen change of circumstances not amounting to legal frustration, just as it may on the ground of mistake insufficient to avoid a contract at law.

In the end, I am satisfied that it is within the court's discretion to accede to the defendant's prayer if satisfied that it is just to do so. An, on the whole, looking at the position of both sides after the long unpredictable delay for which neither seeks to make the other responsible, I am of opinion that it *is* just to leave the plaintiffs to their remedy in damages if that can indeed be effective.'

Posner v *Scott-Lewis* [1986] 3 WLR 531 High Court (Mervyn Davies J)
Specific performance – personal services

Facts
Under the terms of the leases of the plaintiff tenants at Danes Court, the defendant landlord was obliged to employ a resident porter to keep the communal area clean, to be responsible for the boilers and to collect rubbish from the flats. The resident porter left, but continued to do the work on a part-time basis. If the defendant was thereby in breach of the covenant, could the covenant be specifically enforced?

Held
The defendant was in breach and the court could and would make an order for specific performance.

Mervyn Davies J:

> 'Drawing attention to ... differences between [*Ryan* v *Mutual Tontine Westminster Chambers Association* [1893] 1 Ch 116] and the present case, counsel for the plaintiffs submitted that *Ryan's* case should be distinguished. in short, he said that since the resident porter's functions at Danes Court were already obligations of the lessor to the lessees, there were no duties on the part of the porter towards the tenants that the tenants were seeking to enforce. All that was required was the appointment of a resident porter, whereas in *Ryan's* case the plaintiff was in effect seeking to enforce performance of duties said to be owed by the porter to the plaintiff. I do not accept or reject counsel for the plaintiffs able argument. I suspect that it is difficult to distinguish *Ryan's* case. However that may be, *Ryan's* case has been remarked on in many later authorities.
>
> In *C H Giles & Co Ltd* v *Morris* [1972] 1 WLR 307 at 318-319 Megarry J, after referring to *Ryan's* case said:
>
> > "One day, perhaps, the courts will look again at the so-called rule that contracts for personal services or involving the continuous performance of services will not be specifically enforced. Such a rule is plainly not absolute and without exception, nor do I think it can be based on any narrow consideration such as difficulties of constant superintendence by the court. Mandatory injunctions are by no means unknown, and there is normally no question of the court having to send its officers to supervise the performance of the order of the court. Prohibitory injunctions are common, and again there is no direct supervision by the court. Performance of each type of injunction is normally secured by the realisation of the person enjoined that he is liable to be punished for contempt if evidence of his disobedience to the order is put before the court; and if the injunction is prohibitory, actual committal will usually, so long as it continues, make disobedience impossible. If instead the order is for specific performance of a contract for personal services, a similar machinery of enforcement could be employed, again without there being any question of supervision by any officer of the court. The reasons why the court is reluctant to decree specific performance of a contract for personal services (and I would regard it as a strong reluctance rather than a rule) are, I think, more complex and more firmly bottomed on human nature ... The present case, of course is a fortiori, since the contract of which specific performance has been decreed requires not the performance of personal services or any continuous series of acts, but merely procuring the execution of an agreement which contains a provision for such services or acts."
>
> Those observations do not of themselves enable me to disregard *Ryan's* case. But then one comes to *Shiloh Spinners Ltd* v *Harding* [1973] 2WLR 28. Lord Wilberforce seems to say that "the impossibility for the courts to supervise the doing of work" may be rejected as a reason against granting relief (see [1973] AC 691 at 724). Finally there is *Tito* v *Waddell* No 2, *Tito* v *A-G* [1977] 2 WLR 496 ...
>
> In the light of those authorities it is, I think, open to me to consider the making of an order for specific

performance in this case, particularly since the order contemplated is in the fortiori class referred to by Megarry J in the last sentence of the extract from the *Giles'* case [1972] 1 WLR 307 at 318 quoted above. Damages here could hardly regarded as an adequate remedy.

Whether or not an order for specific performance should be made seems to me to depend on the following considerations: (a) is there a sufficient definition of what has to be done in order to comply with the order of the court; (b) will enforcing compliance involve superintendence by the court to an unacceptable degree; and (c) what are the respective prejudices or hardships that will be suffered by the parties if the order is made or not made?

As to (a) one may in this case sufficiently define what has to be done by the defendants by ordering the defendants, within say two months to employ a porter to be resident at Danes Court for the purpose of carrying out the ... duties. It is to be borne in mind that there is still a vacant flat available for a resident porter. As to (b), I do not see that such an order will occasion any protracted superintendence by the court. If the defendants without good cause fail to comply with the order in due time, then the plaintiffs can take appropriate enforcement proceedings against the defendants. As to (c), I see no hardship or prejudice resulting to the defendants from the order. They will simply be performing what they have promised to do and what has been carried out by the lessors over the past 20 years. On the other hand I see considerable inconvenience, if not exactly hardship, for the plaintiffs if, having bargained for a resident porter and paid a premium and having enjoyed his presence for 20 years, they are to be expected for the future to be content with a porter who simply walks up and down the stairs for two hours only during the day doing his cleaning and refuse collection. It follows that there should be an order for specific performance.'

Price v *Strange* [1977] 3 WLR 943 Court of Appeal (Buckley, Scarman and Goff LJJ)

Specific performance – mutual availability of remedy

Facts
In 1966 the defendant sublet her flat to the plaintiff: the sub-tenancy expired in 1971 but he held over, continuing to pay rent. In February 1974 the defendant orally agreed to grant the plaintiff an underlease at an increased rent, the plaintiff agreeing (also orally) to execute certain repairs to the interior and exterior. He paid, and the defendant accepted, rent at the increased rate and completed the interior repairs, but before he could execute the exterior repairs the defendant repudiated the agreement and had the work carried out at her own expense. Nevertheless, she continued to accept rent for a further five months. The plaintiff sought specific performance, but the judge dismissed the action on the ground that the parties were not mutual at the date of the contract since the plaintiff's obligation to execute repairs could not be specifically enforced.

Held
A decree of specific performance would be granted.

Goff LJ:

'Surely the defence of want of mutuality should be governed by the state of affairs as seen at the hearing, since one is dealing not with a question affecting the initial validity of the contract, but with whether or not the discretionary remedy of specific performance should be granted ...

In my judgement ... the true principle is that one judges the defence of want of mutuality on the facts and circumstances as they exist at the hearing, albeit in the light of the whole conduct of the parties in relation to the subject-matter, and in the absence of any other disqualifying circumstances, the court will grant specific performance if it can be done without injustice or unfairness to the defendant ...

If, therefore, the plaintiff had been allowed to finish the work and had done so, I am clearly of opinion that it would have been right to order specific performance, but we have to consider what is the proper order, having regard to the fact that he was allowed to do an appreciable part and then not allowed to finish. Even so, in my judgment the result is still the same for the following reasons.

First, the defendant by standing by and allowing the plaintiff to spend time and money in carrying out an appreciable part of the work, created an equity against herself ...

Secondly, the work has in fact been finished. The court will not be deterred from granting specific performance in a proper case, even though there remain obligations still to be performed by the plaintiff, if the defendant can be properly protected: see ... also *C H Giles & Co Ltd* v *Morris,* where Megarry J said:

"... the court may refuse to let the disadvantages and difficulties of specifically enforcing the obligation to perform personal services outweigh the suitability of the rest of the contract for specific performance, and the desirability of the contract as a whole being enforced. After all, pacta sunt servanda."

Still more readily should it act where the work has been done so that the defendant is not at risk of being ordered to grant the underlease and having no remedy except in damages for subsequent non-performance of the plaintiff's agreement to put the premises in repair.

Thirdly the defendant can be fully recompensed by a proper financial adjustment for the work she has had carried out.

I am fully satisfied that the law is as I have stated it to be, but even if I were wrong and the defence of mutuality ought to be considered according to the position at the date of the contract, still it is conceded, and in my judgment unquestionably correctly, that such a defence may be waived ... Then on the facts of this case the defence clearly was waived. Not only did the defendant permit the plaintiff to start on the work which would of itself be sufficient in my view, but she also accepted the increased rent payable under the contemplated underlease and went on doing so after her purported repudiation.

For these reasons I would allow this appeal and order specific performance but on terms that the plaintiff do pay to the defendant proper compensation for the work done by her. As a matter of strict right that must take the form of an enquiry what amount it would have cost the plaintiff to complete the works himself, with an order that he do pay or allow the defendant the amount certified with a set-off against any costs payable by the defendant, the costs of the enquiry being reserved. The plaintiff has however offered, subject to any question whether the expense incurred by the defendant was unnecessary or extravagant, to compensate her more handsomely by paying or allowing the actual cost to her, and it may well be possible, and certainly in the best interests of the parties, for them to agree a figure and so obviate proceeding with the enquiry, which could well involve them in further considerable litigation and expense.'

Commentary
See also *Sutton* v *Sutton* [1984] 2 WLR 146.

Quadrant Visual Communications Ltd v *Hutchinson Telephone (UK) Ltd* (1991) The Times 4 December Court of Appeal (Stocker, Butler-Sloss and Waller LJJ)

Equitable remedies – terms of the contract purporting to exclude – courts' discretion cannot be fettered

Facts
In a contract made between the two parties one particular clause appeared to exclude equitable remedies. There was some doubt about the construction of the clause.

Held
Once there was a request for an equitable remedy (in this case specific performance) its discretion could not be fettered. Whatever the construction of the clause it was the decision of the court alone as to whether to grant or refuse any equitable remedy.

Ryan v *Mutual Tontine Westminster Chambers Association* [1893] 1 Ch 116 (Court of Appeal)

Specific performance – supervision required

Facts
The defendant landlords covenanted to maintain in constant attendance a resident porter for the benefit of the plaintiff and the other tenants in the block. They appointed one Benton to this port, but he spent much of his time working as a chef, leaving his wife, charwomen and others to discharge his portering responsibilities. The plaintiff sought, inter alia, specific performance of this covenant.

Held
His claim would fail as the contract would require supervision of an order that the court was not prepared to undertake.

Commentary
But see *Posner* v *Scott-Lewis* [1986] 3 WLR 531.

Shell UK Ltd v *Lostock Garage Ltd*

See Chapter 19.

Sky Petroleum Ltd v *VIP Petroleum Ltd* [1974] 1 WLR 576 High Court (Goulding J)

Specific performance – when may be ordered

Facts
In 1970 the plaintiffs agreed that they would, for a minimum period of ten years, buy all the petrol needed for their filling stations from the defendants. Three years later the defendants purported to terminate the contract and the plaintiffs sought an interlocutory injunction to restrain the defendants from withholding supplies. At the time, the plaintiffs had little prospect of obtaining petrol from another supplier.

Held
The injunction would be granted.

Goulding J:

> 'Now I come to the most serious hurdle in the way of the plaintiff company which is the well-known doctrine that the court refuses specific performance of a contract to sell and purchase chattels not specific or ascertained. That is a well-established and salutary rule and I am entirely unconvinced by counsel for the plaintiff company when he tells me that an injunction in the form sought by him would not be specific enforcement at all. The matter is one of substance and not of form and it is, in my judgment, quite plain that I am for the time being specifically enforcing the contract if I grant an injunction. However the ratio behind the rule is, as I believe, that under the ordinary contract for the sale of non-specific goods, damages are a sufficient remedy. That, to my mind, is lacking in the circumstances of the present case. The evidence suggests, and indeed it is common knowledge, that the petroleum market is in an unusual state in which a would-be buyer cannot go out into the market and contract with another, seller, possibly at some sacrifice as to price. Here, the defendant company appears for practical purposes to be the plaintiff company's sole means of keeping its business going, and I am

prepared so far to depart from the general rule as to try to preserve the position under the contract until a later date. I therefore propose to grant an injunction.'

Sutton v *Sutton* [1984] 2 WLR 146 High Court (John Mowbray QC)
Specific performance – agreement to transfer property on divorce

Facts
Seven years after their marriage, the parties bought the matrimonial home, the husband alone being responsible for the mortgage and, although the wife contributed to the purchase, the house was conveyed into the husband's name. Some years later they separated and the husband sought a divorce. They orally agreed that the wife would consent to a divorce, take over the mortgage and not apply for maintenance; the husband would let her keep her savings and transfer the house to her. After decree absolute, the husband refused to transfer the house, although the wife had paid off the mortgage. She sought specific performance and the husband contended that the agreement was not legally enforceable.

Held
The wife could not succeed as the agreement, which had not be made subject to the court's approval, purported to oust the court's jurisdiction.

John Mowbray QC:

> *Part performance*
> In my view, Mrs Sutton's consenting to the divorce as agreed was an act of part performance. It is true that she was quite content to be divorced and that in the abstract consenting to a divorce does not indicate any contract, let alone a contract about land. But here the term about the house was in the petition which must have been posted to her when her formal consent was sought under the postal procedure which was followed. That means that her consent to the petition was itself, in the circumstances, tied to the contract about the house. *Steadman* v *Steadman* [1974] 3 WLR 56 is authority for that ...
>
> *Mutuality*
> Counsel for Mr Sutton argued that there was no mutuality, so specific performance should not be granted. He pointed out that Mrs Sutton's promise not to ask for maintenance was not enforceable. That is common ground. I shall come to the reasons later. Mrs Sutton herself said, in cross-examination, that her offer not to ask for maintenance was a big thing to offer. I find that it was an important part of the bargain. If this point had been taken early enough it might well have afforded a defence, but Mrs Sutton's consent to the divorce was at any rate an appreciable part of the agreement. Mr Sutton stood by and let her perform that part of her bargain irretrievably, and that raised an equity which prevents him from asserting this defence: see *Price* v *Strange* [1977] 3 WLR 943 ... For similar reasons, it is no defence to specific performance that Mr Sutton could not have compelled Mrs Sutton to consent to the divorce. Now she has consented and the divorce has been granted, that point comes too late.
>
> *Ousting the jurisdiction*
> The agreement between Mr and Mrs Sutton was that she would consent to the divorce, take over the mortgage and not ask for maintenance, and he would let her keep her savings and car and make over the house to her. They obviously intended by that agreement to dispose of the whole financial consequences of the divorce. There is a plain implication that he was not to transfer any other property to her and that she was not to make any payment or transfer to him. The agreement was not made subject to the court's approval. If it is enforceable as a contract, it leaves nothing for the court to do under ss23 and 24 of the Matrimonial Causes Act 1973 which empower the court to order maintenance and make property adjustments ...
>
> The agreement between Mr and Mrs Sutton purported to dispose of the whole financial consequences of

the divorce, both maintenance and property questions. If it was enforceable as a contract there was nothing left for the court to do under ss23 or 24 of the 1973 Act because the agreement prejudged and foreclosed all financial questions.

The House of Lords decided in *Hyman* v *Hyman* [1929] AC 601 that a wife could not validly contract with her husband not to apply for maintenance on a divorce and that a contract of that kind did not prevent her from applying. Lord Hailsham LC stated the principle like this:

" ... I am prepared to hold that the parties cannot validly make an agreement either (1) not to invoke the jurisdiction of the Court, or (2) to control the powers of the Court when its jurisdiction is invoked."

That is the rule of public policy which survived the disappearance of the rule against collusion. In my judgment, it applies to the contract here and prevents the financial settlement it contained, including Mr Sutton's promise to transfer the bungalow, from being enforced as a contract.'

Warner Brothers Pictures Inc v *Nelson* [1937] 1 KB 209 High Court (Branson J)

Injunction – contract of service

Facts

Bette Davis (Mrs Nelson) contracted to appear in the plaintiffs' films and the plaintiffs alleged that, in breach of her contract, she intended to appear in another company's film. The plaintiffs sought an injunction.

Held

The injunction would be granted.

Branson J:

'The case before me is therefore one in which it would be proper to grant an injunction unless to do so would in the circumstances be tantamount to ordering the defendant to perform her contract or remain idle or unless damages would be the more appropriate remedy.

With regard to the first of these considerations, it would, of course, be impossible to grant an injunction covering all the negative covenants in the contract. That would, indeed, force the defendant to perform her contract or remain idle; but this objection is removed by the restricted form in which the injunction is sought. It is confined to forbidding the defendant, without the consent of the plaintiffs, to render any services for or in any motion picture or stage production for anyone other than the plaintiffs.

It was also urged that the difference between what the defendant can earn as a film artiste and what she might expect to earn by any other form of activity is so great that she will in effect be driven to perform her contract. That is not the criterion adopted in any of the decided cases. The defendant is stated to be a person of intelligence, capacity and means, and no evidence was adduced to show that, if enjoined form doing the specified acts otherwise than for the plaintiffs, she will not be able to employ herself both usefully and remuneratively in other spheres of activity, though not as remuneratively as in her special line. She will not be driven, although she may be tempted, to perform the contract, and the fact that she may be so tempted is no objection to the grant of an injunction. This appears from the judgment of Lord St Leonards LC in *Lumley* v *Wagner* ...

With regard to the question whether damages is not the more appropriate remedy, I have the uncontradicted evidence of the plaintiffs as to the difficulty of estimating the damages which they may suffer from the breach by the defendant of her contract. I think it is not inappropriate to refer to the fact that, in the contract between the parties ... there is a formal admission by the defendant that her services, being "of a special, unique, extraordinary and intellectual character" gives them a particular value, "the loss of which cannot be reasonably or adequately compensated in damages" and that a breach may "cost the producer great and irreparable injury and damage," and the artiste expressly agrees that the producer shall be entitled to the remedy of injunction. Of course, parties cannot contract themselves out of the law; but it assists, at all events, on the question of evidence as to the applicability of an injunction in the present case, to find the parties formally recognising that which is now before the court as a matter of evidence, that in cases of this kind injunction is a more appropriate remedy than damages.'

Commentary
See also *Page One Records Ltd* v *Britton* [1968] 1 WLR 157.